Timothy Taylor's

Macroeconomics
Economics and the Economy
Second Edition

Timothy Taylor

Journal of Economic Perspectives
Macalester College

For Instructors:
- PowerPoint® slides
- Computerized test bank

For Students:
- Textbook available in three e-formats and in print
- e-Study Guide
- e-Lecture Guide

TEXTBOOK\MEDIA
- Select Textbooks
- Unique student options
- Uniquely affordable prices

When ordering this title, use ISBN 1-930789-25-5

To order the Micro version, use ISBN 1-930789-21-1
To order the complete version, use ISBN 1-930789-13-0

Cover photos by:
Carsten Reisinger © Fotolia
Pavel Losevsky © Fotolia
Wimbledon © Fotolia
Vova Pomortzeff © Fotolia
Timothy Taylor photo courtesy of Annie Dunnigan Design LLC.

Timothy Taylor's Macroeconomics: Economics and the Economy, Edition 2

Copyright © 2011, 2008 Timothy Taylor. Published by Textbook Media

ISBN 1-930789-25-5

Printed in the United States of America by Textbook Media.

10 9 8 7 6 5 4 3

Brief Contents

Contents

Preface

When authors describe their reasons for writing an economics textbook, it seems customary to proclaim lofty goals, like teaching students "to think like economists" so that they can become more informed voters and citizens. Paul Samuelson, the author of the most famous introductory economics textbook for the second half of the twentieth century, famously said: "I don't care who writes a nation's laws—or crafts its advanced treaties—if I can write its economics textbooks." On my best days, I have sufficient time and energy to lift my eyes to the horizon, strike a statuesque pose, and proclaim exalted goals. But most of the time, I'm just a workaday teacher and my goals are more limited and concrete.

The pedagogical approach of this textbook is rooted in helping students master the tools that they need to solve problems for a course in introductory economics. Indeed, one of the great pleasures of writing the book is having the opportunity to open up and to share my teaching tool-kit of step-by-step explanations, practical examples, and metaphors that stick in the mind. On quizzes and exams, I do not ask broad or open-ended questions about informed citizenship and thinking like an economist. At the most basic level, my goal for an economics class is that students should feel well-prepared for quizzes and exams.

The preparation that students need to perform well in an introductory economics class can be divided into three parts. First, an introductory economics class involves mastering a specialized vocabulary. I sometimes tell students that learning economics is akin to learning a foreign language—with the added difficulty that terms in economics like "demand" or "supply" or "money" sound like standard English, and thus learning economics often requires that students to drop their preconceptions about what certain words mean.

Second, students need to acquire some basic analytical tools. There are four central analytical models in an introductory economics course: budget constraints, supply and demand, cost curves, and aggregate demand/aggregate supply. These four models are used for a very wide variety of applications; still, there are only four of them. There are also a few key formulas and equations to learn with regard to topics like growth rates over time and elasticity.

Third, students must learn to recognize when these terms and tools apply and to practice using them. I often tell students not to bother memorizing particular questions and answers from the textbook or homework, because my quiz and exam questions will ask them to apply what they have learned in contexts they have not seen before. To provide a variety of contexts, this book describes many economic issues and events, drawn from recent times and past history, and also drawn both from U.S. and international experiences. When students see a concept or analytical skill applied in a number of ways, they learn to focus on the underlying and unifying idea. I've also found that students do take away knowledge of many economic events and episodes—although different students seem to focus on an unpredictable (to me) array of examples, which is perhaps as it should be in an introductory course.

As a workaday teacher, the goal of helping students master the material so that they can perform well on my quizzes and exams is lofty enough—and tough enough—for me. There's an old joke that economics is the science of taking what is obvious about human behavior and making it incomprehensible. Actually, in my experience, the process works in the other direction. Many students spend the opening weeks of an introductory economics course feeling as if the material is difficult, even impossible, but by the middle and the end of the class, what seemed so difficult early in the term has become obvious and straightforward. As a course in introductory economics focuses on one lesson after another and one chapter after another, it's easy to get tunnel vision. But when raise your eyes at the end of class, it can be quite astonishing to look back and see how far you have come. As students apply the terms and models they have learned to a series of real and hypothetical examples, they often find to their surprise that they have also imbibed a considerable amount about economic thinking and the real-world economy. Learning always has an aspect of the miraculous.

As always, my family makes a significant contribution to the existence of this book. In the three years since the first edition, the U.S. and world economy has been convulsed by a Great Recession. The task of updating figures and examples for this second edition is inevitably large, but thinking about how to building connections from the concepts in the text to the economic events of the last few years made it larger. During the process of preparing this second edition, my wife has dealt lovingly with a distracted husband; my children, with a father who was sleep-deprived or "at the office." In a very real sense, then, this book is from my dear ones to the students and instructors who use it. I hope that it serves you well.

Timothy Taylor
St. Paul, Minnesota
October 6, 2010

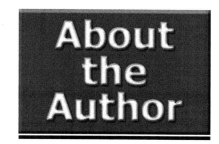

Timothy T. Taylor

Journal of Economic Perspectives
Macalester College   St. Paul, MN 55105

For 20 years the Managing Editor, *Journal of Economic Perspectives*, Saint Paul, MN.

Published quarterly by the American Economic Association. Circulation: 22,000.

Education

September 1982-May 1984   M.A. Stanford University, Stanford, CA.
Studied economics, focusing on public finance,
industrial organization, and economic history.

September 1978-May 1982   B.A. Haverford College, Haverford, PA.
Majored in economics and political science. Graduated
magna cum laude and Phi Beta Kappa.

Selected Papers

"Recommendations for Further Reading," *Journal of Economic Perspectives*. A regular column, eight pages in length and containing 25-30 recommended articles, reports, or interviews that Tim Taylor has been writing for this quarterly journal since the Spring 2005 issue.

"Medicare: Apocalypse ... Later," *Milken Institute Review,* Third Quarter 2005, pp. 42-47. Available at *http://www.milken-inst.org.*

"In Defense of Outsourcing," *Cato Journal,* Spring/Summer 2005, 25:2, pp. 367-377. Available at *http://www.cato.org/pubs/journal/index.html.*

"Shortfalls in the Long Run: Predictions about the Social Security Trust Fund," co-authored with James R. Hines Jr., *Journal of Economic Perspectives,* Spring 2005, 19:2, pp. 3-9.

"The Economy in Perspective," *The Public Interest,* Fall 2004, pp. 85-99.

"Dumping the Lump: A Century of Misunderstanding," *Milken Institute Review,* Third Quarter 2004, pp. 82-87. Available at *http://www.milken-inst.org.*

"The Truth about Globalization," *The Public Interest,* Spring 2002, pp. 24-44. Available at *http://www.thepublicinterest.com.* Reprinted in Harf, James E. and Mark Owen Lombardi. 2005. *Taking Sides: Clashing Views on Controversial Global Issues.* McGraw-Hill/Dushkin, Dubuque, Iowa. pp. 208-216.

Teaching Awards

Lecturer for Economics 5010, "Economic Immersion," at the Hubert H. Humphrey Institute of Public Affairs at the University of Minnesota during Fall 1996. In 1997, voted by students as Teacher of the Year for the Humphrey Institute.

Lecturer for Economics 1101 and 1102, courses in principles of micro- and macroeconomics, at the University of Minnesota during Fall 1995 and Winter 1996, respectively. Based on student and departmental evaluations, named a Distinguished Instructor by the Department of Economics.

Lecturer for Economics 1 at Stanford University, at least one quarter each year from 1989 to 1993. Enrollment ranged from 300-500 students. In 1992, winner of the award for excellent teaching in a large class (more than 30 students) from Associated Students of Stanford University.

The Interconnected Economy

People don't produce most of what they consume. They don't grow most of their own food, make their own clothes, build their own houses, or provide their own health care and education. Instead, people mainly consume goods and services that others have produced, and in turn, what people produce is mainly consumed by others. This basic fact about the human condition raises questions. What goods will be produced? What quantities of each good will be produced? How will the goods that are produced be allocated across the population? What role will be played by the decisions of individuals about consuming, working and saving? What role will be played by organizations like business firms? What role will be played by government?

Since a modern economy contains thousands upon thousands of different products that are produced, bought and consumed, the study of economics must address an extraordinary array of topics. Are gasoline prices likely to rise? Should a new restaurant open or an existing restaurant close? Will it pay off for a high school graduate to go on to college? Can environmental protection go hand in hand with a rising level of consumption of goods and services? Why did the U.S. and world economy suffer such a sharp slowdown starting in 2008? What determines the number of people who want to work but cannot find jobs? When should the government cut taxes and when should it raise them? Why do people in some countries have high incomes while those in other countries have low incomes? An introductory course in economics will help you develop the analytical tools and vocabulary for thinking and communicating about these issues.

This first chapter introduces some ways in which economies are interconnected. It discusses the range of alternatives from a market-oriented economy to a command economy. It describes how an economy divides up the tasks that are involved in production of goods and services, and how the total production of goods and services is increased as a result. This chapter will also explain the difference between "microeconomics" and "macroeconomics" and present an overview of how the chapters of this book are organized.

What Is an Economy?

An **economy** is the set of social arrangements that answers three fundamental questions: 1) What is produced? 2) How is it produced? 3) For whom is it produced? Thus, **economics** is the study of the production, distribution and consumption of goods and services. In an economics textbook published in 1890, the famous English economist Alfred Marshall (1842–1924) wrote more poetically that economics involved the study of people "as they live and move and think in the ordinary business of life."

economy: The social arrangements that determine what is produced, how it is produced, and for whom it is produced.

economics: The study of the production, distribution and consumption of goods and services.

Market-Oriented vs. Command Economies

Countries display a wide range of economic institutions. At one end of the spectrum is a market-oriented economy. A **market** is an institution that brings together buyers and sellers of goods or services, who may be either individuals or business firms. In a **market-oriented economy**, most economic decisions about what to produce, how to produce it, and for whom to produce it are made by these buyers and sellers. In a **command economy**, at the other extreme, the government either makes most economic decisions itself or at least strongly influences how the decisions are made.

The U.S. economy is positioned toward the market-oriented end of the spectrum. Many countries in Europe and Latin America, while primarily market-oriented, have a greater degree of government involvement in economic decisions than does the U.S. economy. Countries like China and Russia, while they are closer to having a market-oriented system now than several decades ago, remain closer to the command economy end of the spectrum. In countries like Cuba, Libya, and North Korea, the command economy predominates.

Markets and government rules are always entangled. Even economies that are primarily market-oriented have government laws and rules to support market operations. At a minimum, these laws govern matters like safeguarding private property against theft, protecting people from violence, enforcing legal contracts, preventing fraud, and collecting taxes. Conversely, even the most command-oriented economies operate with substantial **black markets**, which are markets where the buyers and sellers make transactions without the government's approval. The question of how to organize economic institutions is typically not a black-or-white choice between all market or all government, but instead involves a balancing act over the appropriate combination of market freedom and government rules.

market: An institution that brings together buyers and sellers of goods or services.

market-oriented economy: An economy in which most economic decisions are made by buyers and sellers, who may be individuals or firms.

command economy: An economy in which the government either makes or strongly influences how most economic decisions are made.

black markets: An illegal market that breaks government rules on prices or sales.

The Interconnectedness of an Economy

In a modern economy, the economic life of every individual is interrelated, at least to a small extent, with the economic lives of thousands or even millions of other individuals. Imagine that when an economic transaction occurs, it leaves behind a line that is visible for people who wear special economist glasses.

The Index of Economic Freedom

Who's in control of economic decisions? Are people free to do what they want and to work where they want? Are businesses free to produce when they want and what they choose, and to hire and fire as they wish? Are banks free to choose who will receive loans? Or does the government control these kinds of choices? Each year, researchers at the Heritage Foundation and the *Wall Street Journal* look at 50 different categories of economic freedom for countries around the world. In each category, they give each nation a score based on extent of economic freedom in that category.

The 2009 Index of Economic Freedom report ranked 179 countries around the world: some examples of the most free and the least free countries are listed here. Several countries were not ranked because of extreme instability that made judgments about economic freedom impossible. These countries include Afghanistan, Iraq, and Sudan.

The assigned rankings are inevitably based on estimates, yet even these rough measures can be useful for discerning trends. In 2009, 84 of the 179 countries ranked shifted toward greater economic freedom, although 95 of the countries shifted toward less economic freedom. In recent decades, the overall trend has been a *higher level of economic freedom around the world.*

Countries with the Most Economic Freedom	*Countries with the Least Economic Freedom*
1. Hong Kong	170. Sao Tomé and Principe
2. Singapore	171. Libya
3. Australia	172. Comoros
4. Ireland	173. Democratic Republic of Congo
5. New Zealand	174. Venezuela
6. United States	175. Eritrea
7. Canada	176. Burma
8. Denmark	177. Cuba
9. Switzerland	178. Zimbabwe
10. United Kingdom	179. North Korea

For example, if you buy a loaf of bread at the grocery store, a blue line stretches from the store to your kitchen. When you pump gas into your car, a red line runs from the gas station to your car. A green line connect you to your employer, a purple line to the bank where you keep your checking and savings accounts, and a yellow line to the shop where you get your hair cut. This network of lines would also capture the transactions through which goods are produced. A loaf of bread would have colorful lines running to the bakery, to the company that manufactured the plastic bag for packaging, to the farm where the wheat was grown, and to the mill where the wheat was ground into flour. In turn, because the wheat farm used tractors, and trucks transported the bread to the store, lines would also extend from the loaf of bread to tractor and truck manufacturers and to trucking companies. These lines representing economic transactions also extend to those concerned with the financial side of these businesses: the bankers who provide loans and checking and savings accounts to firms, the accountants who deal with payroll and taxes, and the managers who authorize sending out the checks.

If you could put on special economist glasses to see all the economic lines of connection, a single loaf of bread would appear with a network of lines that eventually reached all over town, across the state and the country, and even around the world. In a modern economy, every person, every business firm, and every product is at the center of a starburst of economic interconnections.

The Division of Labor

The formal study of economics began when Adam Smith (1723–1790) published his famous book *The Wealth of Nations* in 1776. Many authors had written on economic subjects in the centuries before Smith, but he was the first to address the subject in a comprehensive way. In the first chapter of *The Wealth of Nations*, Smith introduces the idea of the **division of labor**, which means the way in which the work required to produce a good or service is divided into a number of tasks that are performed by different workers.

division of labor: The way in which the work required to produce a good or service is divided into tasks performed by different workers.

To illustrate the division of labor, Adam Smith used the example of how the tasks of making a pin were divided in a pin factory. He counted the multiple tasks involved with making a pin, including the steps involved in drawing out a piece of wire, cutting it to the right length, straightening it, putting a head on one end and a point on the other, and packaging pins for sale. In observing pin factories, Smith counted 18 distinct tasks that were often done by different people. Modern businesses divide tasks as well. Even a relatively simple business like a restaurant divides up the task of serving meals into a range of jobs like top chefs, less-skilled kitchen help, servers to wait on the tables, a greeter at the door, janitors to clean up, and a business manager to handle paychecks and bills—not to mention the economic connections a restaurant has with suppliers of food, furniture, kitchen equipment, and the building where it is located. A complex business like a large manufacturing factory or a hospital can have hundreds of job classifications.

Adam Smith was once walking with a friend, talking enthusiastically about the division of labor, and he got so excited with the subject that he tumbled into a pit where workers were tanning hides, a foul-smelling process. Smith was the prototypical never-married, absent-minded professor. He frequently went walking, started talking to himself, and would completely lose track of time and distance. But being one of the first to put on economist glasses and perceive the division of labor must have been a highly distracting experience.

Why the Division of Labor Increases Production

When the tasks involved with producing a good or service are divided and subdivided, workers and businesses can produce a greater quantity of output. In his observations of pin factories, Smith observed that one worker alone might make 20 pins in a day, but that a small business of 10 workers (some of whom would need to do two or three of the 18 tasks involved with pin-making), could make 48,000 pins in a day. How can a group of workers, each specializing in certain tasks, produce so much more than the same number of workers who try to produce the entire good or service by themselves? Smith offered three reasons.

First, **specialization** in a particular small job allows workers to focus on the types of production where they have an advantage. People have different skills, talents, and interests, so they will be better at some jobs than others. The particular advantages workers may be based on educational choices, which are in turn shaped by interests and talents: for example, only those with medical degrees qualify to become doctors. For some goods, specialization will be affected by geography: for example, it's easier to be a wheat farmer in North Dakota than in Florida, but easier to run a tourist hotel in Florida than in North Dakota. If you live in or near a big city, it's easier to attract enough customers to operate a successful dry cleaning business or movie theater than if you live in a sparsely populated rural area.

specialization: When workers or firms focus on particular tasks in the overall production process for which they are well-suited.

Second, workers who specialize in certain tasks often learn to produce more quickly and with higher quality. This pattern holds true for many workers, including assembly line laborers who build cars, stylists who cut hair, and doctors who perform heart surgery. In fact, specialized workers often know their jobs well enough to suggest innovative ways to do their work faster and better. A similar pattern often operates within businesses. In many cases, a business that focuses on one or a few products (sometimes called its "core competency") is more successful than firms that try to make a wide range of products.

Third, specialization allows economic agents, or actors, to take advantage of **economies of scale**, a term referring to the fact that for many goods, as the level of production increases, the average cost of producing each individual unit declines. For example, if a factory produces only 100 cars per year, each car will be quite expensive to make on average. However, if a factory produces 10,000 or 50,000 cars each year, then it can set up an assembly line with huge machines and workers performing specialized tasks, and the average cost of production per car will be lower. The ultimate result of workers who can focus on their preferences and talents, learn to do their specialized jobs better, and work in larger organizations is that society as a whole can produce and consume far more than if each person tried to produce individually all of the goods and services that the individual wishes to consume.

economies of scale: When the average cost of producing each individual unit declines as total output increases.

Trade and Markets

The division of labor works together with markets to buy and sell goods and services. In an economy, workers use the pay that they receive for doing their jobs to purchase the other goods and services that they desire.

As a result, you don't have to know anything about electronics or sound systems to play a DVD—you just buy a DVD player and insert the disk. You don't have to know anything about artificial fibers or the construction of sewing machines if you need a jacket—you just buy the jacket and wear it. You don't need to know anything about internal combustion engines to operate a car—you just sit down and drive. Instead of trying to acquire all the knowledge and skills involved in producing all of the goods and services that you wish to consume, the market allows you to learn a specialized set of skills and then use the pay you receive to buy goods and services. The economy is a social mechanism that coordinates this division of labor, specialization and markets.

The Rise of Globalization

Recent decades have seen a trend toward **globalization**, which means that buying and selling in markets have crossed national borders to an increasing extent. As a result, firms and workers from different countries are increasingly interconnected. Globalization has occurred for a number of reasons. Improvements in shipping and air cargo have driven down transportation costs. Innovations in computing and telecommunications have made it easier and cheaper to manage long-distance economic connections of production and sales. Many valuable products and services in the modern economy can take the form of information—for example, computer software; financial advice; travel planning; music, books and movies; and blueprints for designing a building. These products and many others can be transported over telephones and computer networks at ever-lower costs. Finally, international agreements and treaties between countries have encouraged greater trade.

globalization: The trend in which buying and selling in markets have increasingly crossed national borders.

Exhibit 1–1   The Extent of Globalization (exports/GDP)

One way to measure globalization is to look at the export/GDP ratio. For the world economy and for most individual countries, the ratio of exports/GDP has risen in recent decades.

Country	1970	1980	1990	2000	2007
Some High Income Countries					
United States	6%	10%	10%	11%	12%
Belgium	52%	58%	71%	86%	89%
Canada	23%	28%	26%	46%	40%
France	16%	21%	21%	29%	27%
Italy	16%	22%	20%	29%	29%
Japan	11%	14%	10%	11%	16%
Sweden	24%	29%	30%	46%	52%
Some Middle Income Countries					
Brazil	7%	9%	8%	11%	14%
Mexico	8%	11%	19%	31%	28%
South Korea	14%	32%	28%	41%	42%
Some Low Income Countries					
Chad	16%	17%	13%	17%	50%
China	3%	11%	19%	23%	43%
India	4%	6%	7%	6%	21%
Nigeria	8%	29%	43%	53%	40%

Exhibit 1-1 presents one measure of globalization. It shows the percentage of domestic economic production that was exported for a selection of countries from 1970 to 2007. **Exports** are the goods and services that are produced domestically and sold in another country; conversely, **imports** are the goods and services that are produced abroad and then sold domestically. The size of total production in an economy is measured by the gross domestic product, often abbreviated as GDP. (The details of how GDP is calculated are presented in Chapter 7.) Thus, the ratio of exports divided by GDP measures what share of a country's total economic production is sold in other countries.

In recent decades, the export/GDP ratio has generally risen, both worldwide and for the U.S. economy. Interestingly, the share of U.S. exports in proportion to the U.S. economy is well below the global average, in part because large economies like the United States can contain more of the division of labor inside their national borders. However, smaller economies like Belgium, Korea, and Canada need to trade across their borders with other countries to take full advantage of division of labor, specialization, and economies of scale. In this sense, the enormous U.S. economy is less affected by globalization than most other countries. Exhibit 1-1 also shows that many medium- and low-income countries around the world, like Mexico and China, have also experienced a surge of globalization in recent decades. If an astronaut in orbit could put on special economist glasses that make all economic transactions visible as brightly colored lines, and look down at planet Earth, globalization means that the astronaut would see more connections stretching around the world.

exports: Goods and services that are produced domestically and sold in another country.

imports: Goods and services produced abroad and then sold domestically.

Microeconomics and Macroeconomics

Microeconomics focuses on the actions of particular actors within the economy, like households, workers, and business firms. In contrast, **macroeconomics** looks at the economy as a whole, focusing on issues like the rate of growth of production of goods and services, the number of unemployed people, the inflationary increase in prices, and levels of exports and imports. Microeconomics and macroeconomics are not separate subjects, but rather complementary perspectives on the overall subject of the economy.

To understand why microeconomic and macroeconomic perspectives are both useful, consider the problem of studying a biological ecosystem like a lake. One person who sets out to study the lake might focus on specific topics: certain kinds of algae or plant life; the characteristics of particular fish or snails; or the trees surrounding the lake. Another person might take an overall view and instead consider the entire ecosystem of the lake from top to bottom; what eats what, how the system stays in a rough balance, and what environmental stresses affect this balance. Both approaches are useful, and both examine the same lake, but the viewpoints are different. In a similar way, both microeconomics and macroeconomics study the same economy, but each has a different viewpoint.

Whether you are looking at lakes or economics, the micro and the macro insights should blend with each other. In studying a lake, the micro insights about particular plants and animals help to understand the overall food chain, while the macro insights about the overall food chain help to explain the environment in which individual plants and animals live. In economics, the micro decisions of individual businesses are influenced by whether the macroeconomy is healthy; for example, firms will be more likely to hire workers if the overall economy is growing. In turn, the performance of the macroeconomy ultimately depends on the microeconomic decisions made by households and businesses.

In this book, Chapters 1–6 introduce some basic tools of economics. This first chapter lays out the basic meaning of the economy and economics. Chapter 2 introduces how economic decision-making works. Chapter 3 shows how trade and exchange can be mutually beneficial, using the example of trade between nations in the global economy. Chapters 4 and 5 discuss how forces of supply and demand determine prices—and what happens when a government attempts to set prices directly. Chapter 6 discusses the debate over globalization and protectionism. With this foundation established, Chapters 7–20 focus on macroeconomics. Regardless of whether you are looking through the microeconomics microscope or the macroeconomics telescope, the fundamental subject material of the interconnected economy doesn't change.

Microeconomics: The Circular Flow Diagram

The **circular flow diagram** in Exhibit 1-2 pictures the economy as consisting of two groups—households and firms—that interact in three markets: a *goods and services market*, a *labor market*, and a *financial capital market*.

In the **goods and services market**, firms are sellers and households are buyers, so the arrow for goods and services leads from firms to households. Payments for these goods and services flow back in the other direction, from households to firms, so the arrow for payments flows back in the opposite direction.

microeconomics: The branch of economics that focuses on actions of particular actors within the economy, like households, workers, and business firms.

macroeconomics: The branch of economics that focuses on the economy as a whole, including issues like growth, unemployment, inflation, and the balance of trade.

circular flow diagram: A diagram that views the economy as consisting of households and firms interacting in a goods and services market, a labor market, and a financial capital market.

goods and services market: A market in which firms are sellers of what they produce and households are buyers.

What's the difference between a "business," a "firm," a "company," and a "corporation"? The short answer for practical purposes is "not much." A *business* is an organization that produces and sells, regardless of whether the customers are individuals or other businesses. A *company* is one term for the group of people who form a business. One definition of a *firm* is a "business company." A *corporation* refers to a specific legal status, where the business is treated as a separate legal entity that can sign contracts, own property, and borrow money, apart from those who manage or own the business. In this book, "firm" will typically be used to refer to all kinds of businesses and companies, whether they are officially corporations or not, but "business" and "company" will sometimes be used as well.

Clearing It Up

Firm, Business, Company, Corporation

Exhibit 1-2 The Circular Flow Diagram

The circular flow diagram shows how households and firms interact in the goods and services market, the labor market and the financial capital market. The direction of the arrows shows that in the goods and services market, households receive goods and services and pay firms for them. In the labor market, households work and receive payment from firms. In the financial capital market, households provide financial capital—that is, savings and financial investment—while firms pay them for that capital by providing a rate of return—for example, an interest payment.

In the **labor market**, households sell their labor as workers to business firms. Conversely, firms buy labor when they hire workers. Thus, the flow of labor runs from households to firms, but the flow of payments for labor—in the form of wages, salaries, bonuses, and benefits—flows from firms to households.

In the **financial capital market**, individuals or firms who save money and make financial investments are suppliers of financial capital. Those who borrow money or receive financial investments are the recipients of financial capital. For example, someone who deposits money in a savings account at a bank is supplying financial capital, and someone who receives a loan from the bank is demanding financial capital. Individual households and firms can be either suppliers or demanders of capital, depending on whether they are saving or whether they are borrowing. However, in the circular flow diagram, the convention is to draw the most common direction of the financial capital flow as running from households to firms—that is, households taken as a group are saving and making financial investments.

Payment for financial capital is called the **rate of return**. Suppliers of financial capital expect that they will eventually receive back both the amount of their original

labor market: The market in which households sell their labor as workers to business firms or other employers.

financial capital market: The market in which those who save money provide financial capital and receive a rate of return from those who wish to raise money and pay a rate of return.

rate of return: The payment from those who have received financial capital to those who provided it.

The concept of a financial capital market can be confusing, because the words "capital" and "investment" can take on two different meanings. Financial capital or financial investment refers to flows of money from those people or firms who save and make a financial investment to those who borrow or receive the financial investment. Real capital or real investment usually refers to physical items like buildings or equipment, although the terms are sometimes also applied to intangible business investments, like the spending on research and development that seeks to produce new inventions. In short, you can stub your toe on real capital investment, but not on financial capital investment. Financial capital and real capital are often interrelated. Those who receive financial capital often invest those funds in real physical capital. Discussions of capital and investment throughout the book will specify whether the discussion is about real or financial capital and investment. But be warned: outside the pages of this book, and in casual conversation, the terms "capital" and "investment" can take on either meaning.

Clearing It Up

Real and Financial
Capital and Investment

financial investment, called the **principal**, plus an additional amount called the rate of return. Conversely, demanders of financial capital expect to pay back the original principal they received, plus a rate of return, in exchange for receiving the financial investment. One common example of a rate of return is an **interest rate** charged for borrowing financial capital. If one person loans $10,000 to another person for one year at an 8% annual interest rate, then the lender—the supplier of financial capital—expects to be repaid $10,000 of principal plus $800 of interest as a rate of return. Meanwhile the borrower—the demander of financial capital—expects to pay back the $10,000 of principal plus $800 in interest. However, the rate of return is not always an interest rate. For example, a person might pay $10,000 for a half-ownership of a small business, with an agreement that the rate of return will be half of any future profits earned by the business. In this case, the rate of return could be high or low, depending on the profits that are eventually earned, if any.

principal: The amount of an original financial investment, before any rate of return is paid.

interest rate: A payment calculated as a percentage of the original amount saved or borrowed, and paid by the borrower to the saver.

The circular flow diagram is an example of a **model**, which is a simplified representation of an object or situation that includes enough of the key features to be useful. For example, an architect who is planning a major office building will often build a physical model that sits on a tabletop to show how the entire city block will look after the new building is constructed. Companies often build models of their new products, which are often more rough and unfinished than the final product will be, but can still demonstrate how the new product will work. Economic models like the circular flow diagram are not physical models, but instead are diagrams or graphs or even mathematical equations that represent economic patterns or theories.

model: A simplified representation of an object or situation that includes enough of the key features to be useful.

The circular flow diagram shown in Exhibit 1-2 is a deliberately simple model. A more complex circular flow model could add a box for "government," and then show arrows for taxes paid flowing to the government and government spending programs going to households and firms. Boxes could also be added for the "rest of the world," with arrows showing the exports flowing to those countries and imports flowing back from those countries. But models should be only as complex as needed to illustrate the issue at hand—and not more so. Although issues of government and international economic connections will arise throughout the book, the structure and order of the microeconomics chapters is based on how households and firms interact in these three main markets.

Macroeconomics: Goals, Frameworks, and Tools

When nations desire a healthy macroeconomy, they typically focus on four goals: growth in the standard of living, a low level of unemployment, low inflation, and a sustainable balance of trade between countries. After an overview of macroeconomics and how to measure the size of the economy using gross domestic product in Chapter 7, these four goals are the subject of Chapters 8–11.

Macroeconomics involves thinking about how these four goals relate to each other, and in particular how pursuing any one of these goals might necessitate trade-offs with other goals. Such analysis requires an understanding of how the macroeconomy works, both in the short-run (ranging from months to a couple of years) and in the long-run (ranging from several years to a decade and more). Chapters 12–14 present theoretical frameworks for short-run and long-run macroeconomic analysis, with names like the *aggregate supply/aggregate demand model*, the *Keynesian model*, and the *neoclassical model*.

monetary policy: Policy that involves altering the quantity of money and thus affecting the level of interest rates and the extent of borrowing.

With macroeconomic goals in mind and the frameworks for analyzing how these goals relate to each other in place, the final step is to think about how macroeconomic policy pursues these goals. The two main tools of macroeconomic policy include **monetary policy**, which involves policies that affect bank lending, interest rates and financial capital markets, and **fiscal policy**, which involves government spending and taxes. Chapters 15–20 will discuss how these policy tools can be used to pursue the four main macroeconomic goals.

fiscal policy: Economic policies that involve government spending and taxes.

Studying Economics Doesn't Mean Worshiping the Economy

Many newcomers to the study of economics either fear or hope that the subject will mainly discuss why business firms and markets are always right. Such expectations are inaccurate. Economics overlaps with the study of business decisions, but it reaches much farther to encompass all aspects of production, distribution and consumption. Economics is concerned with the well-being of *all* people, including those with jobs and those without jobs, and those with high incomes and those with low incomes. Economics acknowledges that production of useful goods and services can create problems of environmental pollution. It explores the question of how investing in education helps to develop workers' skills. It probes questions like how to tell when big businesses or big labor unions are operating in a way that benefits society as a whole, and when they are operating in a way that benefits their owners or members at the expense of others. It discusses how government spending, taxes, and regulations affect decisions about production and consumption. Economics is a structured methodology for investigating these kinds of issues and many others. John Maynard Keynes (1883–1946), one of the greatest economists of the twentieth century, addressed this theme when he wrote: "[Economics] is a method rather than a doctrine, an apparatus of the mind, a technique of thinking, which helps its possessor to draw correct conclusions."

While the study of economics requires paying attention to the problems that can be generated in society's process of production, distribution and consumption, economics is based on the belief that a higher standard of living is a goal worth pursuing. In 1900, the population of the United States had the highest average income level of any country in the world. However, from a modern perspective, people had a very low standard of living. In the United States of 1900, only one-third of all homes had running water; in rural areas, almost nobody did. Just 3 percent of homes were lit by electricity; most used coal, oil or kerosene. About 10 percent of those aged 14–17 attended high school; about 6 percent of students graduated from high school; and about 2 percent graduated from college. Life expectancy at birth was just 47 years, and out of every 1,000 babies born, 140 died before they were a year old. (Now life expectancy is above 75 years, and out of every 1,000 babies born, fewer than 10 die in the first year.) The typical workweek for a man was 60 hours, spread over six days. While relatively few women worked in the paid labor force, the typical woman spent about 40 hours a week on meals and meal clean-up, another seven hours per week on laundry, another seven hours on cleaning the home, and an untold number of hours on child care, gardening, making and repairing clothes, fetching water, and filling the stove with wood or coal. The average woman had 10 pregnancies, so even with a high level of infant mortality, she spent about 15 years of her life either pregnant or looking after an infant. Child labor was widespread; the 1900 U.S. Census reports that one-fourth of boys aged 10–15 held a job.

Today, we look back at the people who lived 100 years ago and wonder how they managed. But remember that in 1900, the United States had the highest average income of any country in the world. It had an average standard of living slightly above the United Kingdom; almost double that of France or Germany; almost triple that of the richer nations of Latin America at that time, including Argentina and Chile; and quadruple the standard of living of Japan or Mexico (which had about the same standard of living at that time).

Few of us today would wish to return to the standard of living in 1900, because most of us believe that it is better to be educated than illiterate, to live longer and to have fewer babies die, to work fewer hours at less physically demanding tasks, and to have all the life-saving, labor-saving inventions developed since that time. This pattern of dramatic advances in the standard of living continues today. Look at the extraordinary advances in recent years in computers and the Internet, in telecommunications, in medicine and health, in biological sciences and genetics, and in new materials.

The economic challenge for society is to chart a course that encourages the beneficial aspects of economic growth while finding ways to curb any undesirable or unwanted side effects like pollution, unemployment and poverty. The introductory course in economics should make you more informed about these issues. When you read newspaper or magazine articles about economic issues, you will begin to recognize terminology and arguments. When you hear classmates, co-workers, or political candidates talking about economics, you will improve your ability to distinguish common sense from nonsense. You will find new ways of thinking about current events and about personal and business decisions, as well as current events and politics. The study of economics does not dictate the answers, but it can illuminate the different choices.

Key Concepts and Summary

1. The **economy** is the way in which a society organizes the production, distribution, and consumption of goods and services. It is the set of social institutions that answers three questions: what is produced; how is it produced; and for whom is it produced.

2. In a **market-oriented economy**, individuals and businesses make most economic decisions, with government playing a background role. In a **command economy**, the government makes most economic decisions; individual and business decisions play only a background role. Most economies lie somewhere between these two extremes and have a substantial role for both the market and the government, although the emphasis varies in different countries.

3. A modern economy is amazingly interconnected. Every person and every good is linked by economic transactions—sometimes directly, often indirectly—to a vast array of other goods, people, and businesses.

4. A modern economy displays a **division of labor**, in which people earn income by specializing in what they produce and then use that income to purchase the products they wish.

5. The division of labor allows individuals and firms to specialize and to produce more for several reasons: a) It allows the agents to focus on areas of advantage due to natural factors and skill levels; b) It encourages the agents to learn and invent; c) It allows agents to take advantage of **economies of scale**.

6. The last few decades have seen **globalization** evolve as a result of growth in commercial and financial networks that cross national borders, making businesses and workers from different economies increasingly interdependent.

7. **Microeconomics** and **macroeconomics** are two different perspectives on the economy. The microeconomic perspective focuses on parts of the economy: individuals, firms, and industries. The macroeconomic perspective looks at the economy as a whole, focusing on overall issues like growth in the standard of living, unemployment, inflation, and levels of foreign trade.

8. The **circular flow diagram** shows how households and firms interact in the **goods and services market**, the **labor market**, and the **financial capital market**.

9. Macroeconomics has four main goals: growth in the standard of living, low unemployment, low inflation, and a sustainable balance of trade. It has two types of policies for pursuing these goals: **monetary policy** and **fiscal policy.**

Review Questions

1. What are the three basic questions that every economy must address?

2. What is the key difference between a market-oriented economy and a command economy?

3. What does the phrase "division of labor" mean?

4. Give the three reasons that explain why the division of labor increases an economy's level of production?

5. What is globalization? How do you think it might have affected the economy over the past decade?

6. What is the difference between microeconomics and macroeconomics?

7. Are households primarily buyers or sellers in the goods and services market? The labor market? The financial capital market? Are firms primarily buyers or sellers in each of these three markets?

8. What are the four primary goals of macroeconomics

Choice in a World of Scarcity

In November 1968, the Rolling Stones recorded a song called: "You Can't Always Get What You Want." But economists had already been singing a similar tune for many years. For example, an English economist named Lionel Robbins (1898–1984) wrote *An Essay on the Nature and Significance of Economic Science* in 1932, in which he described the problem of not always getting what you want in this way:

> The time at our disposal is limited. There are only twenty-four hours in the day. We have to choose between the different uses to which they may be put. The services which others put at our disposal are limited. The material means of achieving ends are limited. We have been turned out of Paradise. We have neither eternal life nor unlimited means of gratification. Everywhere we turn, if we choose one thing we must relinquish others which, in different circumstances, we would wish not to have relinquished. Scarcity of means to satisfy given ends is an almost ubiquitous condition of human nature. Here then, is the unity of subject of Economic Science, the forms assumed by human behavior in disposing of scarce means.

Economics studies how every person, every firm, and every society must make choices, because none of them can have everything that they desire.

This chapter begins with a discussion of three broad categories of choices made by individuals and households: choices about which goods to consume, how many hours to work, and how much to borrow or save. Not coincidentally, these three categories of choices match the three main markets of microeconomics discussed in the circular flow diagram in Chapter 1: the markets for goods, labor, and financial capital. The discussion then introduces a framework for thinking

15

about society's choices. Finally, the chapter discusses some concerns over whether the economic approach to facing scarcity and making choices describes accurately either how choices *are* actually made or how choices *should* be made.

Choosing What to Consume

People live in a world of scarcity: that is, they can't have all the time, money, possessions, and experiences they wish. Since people must choose, they inevitably face trade-offs, in which they have to give up things that they desire to get other things that they desire more. When economists analyze how individuals make these choices, they divide the decision process into two steps. The first step is to consider what choices are possible for individuals. The second step is to think about which choices individuals actually make, based on their individual preferences. The model that economists use for illustrating the process of individual choice in a situation of scarcity is the **budget constraint,** sometimes also called the **opportunity set,** a diagram which shows what choices are possible.

budget constraint:
A diagram which shows what choices are possible, given the prices.

opportunity set: Another name for the budget constraint.

A Consumption Choice Budget Constraint

To illustrate how the budget constraint model applies to choices about how much of each good to consume, consider the case of Alphonso, illustrated in Exhibit 2-1. Each graph in Exhibit 2-1 shows a different combination of Alphonso's income and the prices for two goods, burgers and bus tickets. In Exhibit 2-1a, Alphonso has $10 in spending money each week that he can allocate between bus tickets for getting to work and the burgers that he eats for lunch. Burgers cost $2 each, and bus tickets in Alphonso's town are 50 cents. Different combinations of choices that are possible for Alphonso are shown in the table and also depicted graphically in the accompanying budget constraint. Each combination of burgers and bus tickets shown in the table and the budget constraint adds up to exactly $10. Thus, the points along the budget constraint represent what consumption opportunities are possible for Alphonso.

How Changes in Income and Prices Affect the Budget Constraint

Changes in income will alter the budget constraint. For example, say that Alphonso's spending money increases to $12 per week. Exhibit 2-1b shows both his original budget constraint and his new budget constraint. In the new budget constraint, each combination of burgers and bus tickets at the given prices now adds up to $12. A higher income level means that the budget constraint will be to the right of the original budget constraint; conversely, a lower income level means that the budget constraint will lie to the left of the original budget constraint.

Now suppose Alphonso's income remains the same, but the price of one of the goods increases. Changes in the price of goods will affect Alphonso's budget constraint. In other words, his income level stays at $10 per week, but the price of bus tickets rises to $1 each, while the price of burgers remains at $2. Exhibit 2-1c shows how this change in price alters the budget constraint. A higher price for one good causes the budget constraint to shift inward; more specifically, the budget constraint swings inward as if on a hinge attached to the vertical axis or the horizontal axis—depending on which good's price has risen. Conversely, a lower price for one good would lead to an outward shift of the budget constraint.

Exhibit 2-1   Alphonso's Consumption Choice Opportunity Set

(a) Each point on the opportunity set represents a combination of burgers and bus tickets whose total cost adds up to Alphonso's income of $10. The slope of the budget line is determined by the relative price of burgers and bus tickets. All along the budget set, giving up a burger means gaining four bus tickets.

(b) If Alphonso's income increases from $10 to $12, his opportunity set shifts to the right of the original budget set. The lower line is the original budget set, and the upper line is the new budget set. On the new budget set, each combination of burgers and bus tickets now adds up to a total cost of $12. However, because the trade-off of burgers for bus tickets is unchanged—still one burger for every four bus tickets—the slope of the budget line is unchanged.

(c) Alphonso's income remains at $10, as in (a), but the cost of bus tickets rises from 50 cents to $1. This change causes the budget set to swing inward, as if on a hinge at the upper left. If Alphonso wishes to purchase only burgers, the change in price of bus tickets doesn't alter how many he can buy. However, giving up a burger now adds only two bus tickets, not four. The budget line slopes more steeply as a result.

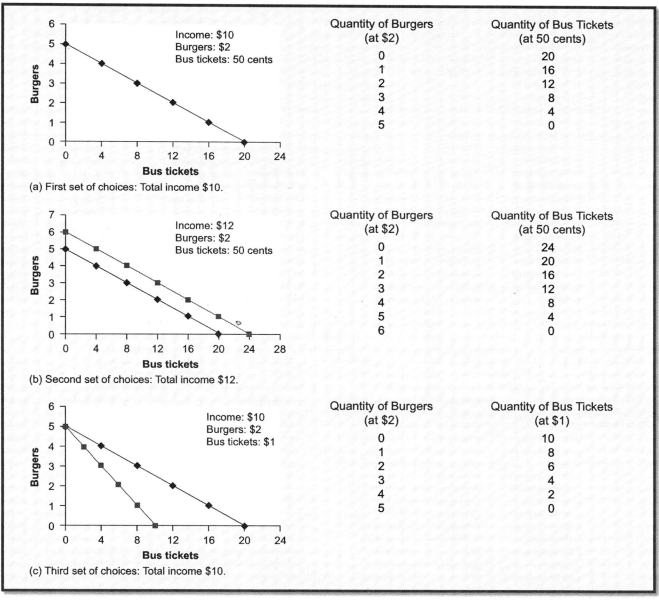

(a) First set of choices: Total income $10.

Income: $10
Burgers: $2
Bus tickets: 50 cents

Quantity of Burgers (at $2)	Quantity of Bus Tickets (at 50 cents)
0	20
1	16
2	12
3	8
4	4
5	0

(b) Second set of choices: Total income $12.

Income: $12
Burgers: $2
Bus tickets: 50 cents

Quantity of Burgers (at $2)	Quantity of Bus Tickets (at 50 cents)
0	24
1	20
2	16
3	12
4	8
5	4
6	0

(c) Third set of choices: Total income $10.

Income: $10
Burgers: $2
Bus tickets: $1

Quantity of Burgers (at $2)	Quantity of Bus Tickets (at $1)
0	10
1	8
2	6
3	4
4	2
5	0

As an economics student, you will need to know how to sketch budget constraints quickly and accurately. Here's a suggestion: Start by calculating, based on income and the prices of the two goods, how much of each good each person could buy if that person were not buying any of the other good. These calculations will determine the points on the two axes of the budget constraint. Then the other points form a straight line between these endpoints.

Clearing It Up

Sketching Budget
Constraints

A change in income causes the budget constraint to shift so that the new budget constraint is parallel to the original. However, a change in prices causes the slope of the budget constraint to change so that the budget constraint is steeper or flatter. Why are the effects different? The slope of the budget constraint is determined by the relative price of the two goods, which is calculated by taking the price of one good and dividing it by the price of the other good. The *relative* price conveys the trade-off between the two goods, in this case burgers and bus rides. In Alphonso's first budget constraint in Exhibit 2-1*a*, if he gives up one burger, he can take four additional bus trips because the price of a burger is four times the price of a bus trip (that is, $2 versus 50 cents). The slope of this budget constraint shows that a loss of 1 burger equals a gain of 4 bus tickets. In Exhibit 2-1*b*, income changes but the relative prices of the two goods don't change, and so the slope of the budget constraint doesn't change either. In Exhibit 2-1*c*, however, giving up one burger means gaining only two bus trips (that is, $2 versus $1), and so the slope of the budget constraint changes to a loss of 1 burger means a gain of only 2 bus tickets.

Personal Preferences Determine Specific Choices

What choice will Alphonso make along his budget constraint? The answer is simple: Alphonso will choose what he personally prefers. In economics, **utility** refers to the level of satisfaction or pleasure that people receive from their choices. Thus, when people make the choices that provide the highest level of satisfaction, economists say that they are "maximizing utility." In Alphonso's case, if he prefers to sit at home and eat, he buys a lot of burgers and chooses some point like *A* or *B* on the budget constraint in Exhibit 2-2. If he prefers to travel around town, he buys lots of bus tickets and chooses some point like *D* or *E* on the budget constraint. It's Alphonso's choice.

utility: The level of satisfaction or pleasure that people receive from their choices.

However, the logic of the budget constraint dictates that Alphonso's choice will be a point on the actual budget constraint itself: choice *B* with four burgers and four bus tickets—not a choice that is above the budget set or below it. Alphonso might desire a point like *H* in Exhibit 2-2 with five burgers and 16 bus tickets, offering more of both goods than choice *B*. However, choice *H* is outside the budget constraint, which means that Alphonso can't afford it. Conversely, Alphonso won't choose a point like *J* with two burger and four bus tickets, which is inside the boundary of the budget constraint, because he could instead select a choice on the budget set itself like *B* that would have at least as much of one good and more of the other—or a choice that would offer even more of both goods. In this simple model, Alphonso doesn't have any other goods on which to spend his money, and so if he doesn't spend his money, it is wasted.

The budget constraint diagram shows what choices are possible, but it does not specify which choice is made. If two people have the same income and face the same prices, then they have identical budget constraints; but if those two people have different personal preferences, they will make different choices.

The Origins of Economic Utility

In the late eighteenth century, a philosopher and occasional economist named Jeremy Bentham (1748–1832) constructed a philosophy called "utilitarianism," which was based on the "happiness principle" that all of society's decisions ought to be made according to the amount of pleasure and pain that they cause individuals. Bentham wrote: "The greatest happiness of the greatest number is the foundation of morals and legislation."

Utilitarianism may not sound very radical, but consider some of its implications for the world of the late eighteenth and early nineteenth century. The utilitarian philosophy did not say that the happiness of a king, queen, or member of the nobility was more important than the happiness of an average person. It did not place the happiness of

men above the happiness of women. It did not say that the happiness of the unemployed, criminals, children, or the poor was any less important than the happiness of anyone else.

Bentham was the unofficial leader of a group called the Philosophical Radicals, who favored voting rights for all with a secret ballot, government programs to provide jobs for the unemployed, government-run banks to help the poor save money, better conditions in prisons, limits on child labor, and—important to economists—market competition and free trade among countries. The Philosophical Radicals weren't always right, but at least by modern standards, they were on the side of the angels more often than not.

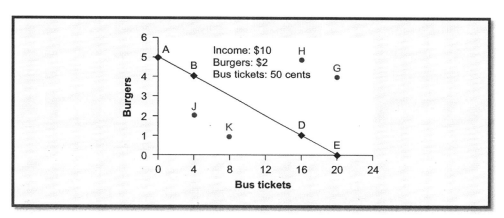

Exhibit 2-2   Personal Preferences Determine the Actual Choice

If Alphonso likes burgers a lot, he will probably choose points *A* or *B*. If he likes bus tickets a lot, he will probably choose points *D* or *E*. Points *H* and *G* beyond the opportunity set are unattainable, given his level of income, no matter how much Alphonso might like them. Points *J* and *K* would be wasteful. For example, rather than choosing point *J*, he could have both more burgers and the same number of bus tickets at point *B*. Similarly, instead of choosing point *K*, he could have the same number of burgers but many more bus tickets at point *D*.

From a Model with Two Goods to the Real World of Many Goods

The budget constraint diagram containing just two goods may seem so simple as to be simple-minded. In a modern economy, people choose from thousands of goods, not just two.

However, thinking about a model with many goods is straightforward. Instead of drawing just one budget constraint, showing the trade-off between two goods, you can draw multiple budget constraints, showing the possible trade-offs between many different pairs of goods. Or in more advanced classes in economics, you would use mathematical equations that include many possible goods and services that can be purchased, together with their quantities and prices, and show how the total spending adds up to the overall amount of money available. However, the graph with two goods clearly illustrates three basic concepts: (1) how the budget constraint is determined by income and prices; (2) how changes in income or relative prices cause a budget constraint to shift; and (3) how the personal preferences of an individual are represented by the point that is chosen on the budget constraint.

Choosing Between Labor and Leisure

The budget constraint applies to the labor-leisure choice just as it does to the decision of what quantity of goods to consume. But in the labor-leisure budget constraint, the decision isn't about what quantities of goods to buy, given their prices a limited amount of income; instead, it's about what number of hours to work, given the wage that can be earned and the limited number of hours in a day. Again, the first step is to use the budget constraint to show what is possible, while the second step is for each individual to make their personally preferred choice that maximizes utility.

An Example of a Labor-Leisure Budget Constraint

Beulah has a job as an assistant manager of a fast-food restaurant. She can work as many as 60 hours per week if she chooses. Of course, most people don't have jobs that let them choose exactly how many hours to work each week; but most people have at least some flexibility about whether to look for a part-time or a full-time job or whether to work overtime or take on a second job. Thus, it isn't unreasonable to imagine people making choices about the number of hours they work. Exhibit 2-3 shows two of Beulah's labor-leisure budget constraints.

In Exhibit 2-3a, Beulah's wage is $9 per hour. The table and the budget constraint show the trade-off that she faces between income and leisure. Because Beulah receives an hourly wage, the more hours she works, the more her income rises and her leisure diminishes. The horizontal axis of the exhibit measures both labor hours and leisure hours *at the same time,* but in opposite directions. The quantity of hours of leisure is measured from left to right, while the quantity of hours of labor is measured from right to left. Since Beulah has a total of 60 hours available that she could work, the horizontal axis shows how she divides up this time between leisure and work.

How a Change in Wages Affects the Labor-Leisure Budget Constraint

A change in the wage will shift Beulah's budget constraint. If her wage rises to $11 per hour, perhaps because she has gained more experience or training, then the trade-offs that she faces change as well. Both her original budget constraint and her new set of trade-offs are shown in Exhibit 2-3b. A new wage changes the slope of the budget constraint because a new wage means a different trade-off between hours of leisure and income.

Making a Choice Along the Labor-Leisure Budget Constraint

Living in a world of scarcity—no one has more than 24 hours in a day—requires that people must make choices about how to spend their time, but the fact of scarcity doesn't dictate what choices they make. In deciding how many hours to work, Beulah will make a choice that maximizes her utility; that is, she will choose according to her preferences for leisure time and income. If she chooses to work 60 hours per week, she will have more income to spend on food, rent, clothing, cars, vacations, or other material goods. However, if she prefers leisure time over material satisfactions, she may choose to work fewer hours so that she has more time for family, friends, and low-cost hobbies such as reading or yoga. Exhibit 2-4 illustrates both possibilities. If Beulah prefers a relatively high level of income, then she will choose a point close to A, with $540 of income, 60 hours of work and no leisure. If she prefers instead a relatively high level of leisure, she might choose a point like C with 50 hours of leisure, 10 hours of work, and $90 in income.

The labor-leisure budget constraint involves illustrating three factors—hours of labor, hours of leisure, and dollars of income—on only two axes. This illustration only works because the hours of both labor and leisure appear on the horizontal axis. After all, all leisure means no labor, and all labor means no leisure. On the horizontal axis, hours of leisure are measured from left to right, but hours of labor are measured from right to left. The trade-off here is between the two goods of leisure and income because labor is not a "good" in itself, but instead a mechanism for earning income.

Exhibit 2-3   Beulah's Labor-Leisure Opportunity Set

Hours worked	Leisure time	Income
0	60	$0
10	50	$90
20	40	$180
30	30	$270
40	20	$360
50	10	$450
60	0	$540

Wage: $9
60 hours

(a) First set of choices: Wage $9 per hour. The points on the opportunity set show what combinations of leisure and income that Beulah can have with her 60 hours of time, given that she can earn a wage of $9 per hour. The trade-off between leisure and income, which is the wage $9 per hour, determines the slope of the line.

Hours worked	Leisure time	Income
0	60	$0
10	50	$110
20	40	$220
30	30	$330
40	20	$440
50	10	$550
60	*0*	*$660*

Wage: $11
60 hours

(b) Second set of choices: Wage $11 per hour. If Beulah's wage increases from $9 per hour to $11 per hour, her 60 hours of time has not changed, but the trade-off that she faces between leisure and income has changed. With the higher wage, giving up a certain number of hours of leisure brings a higher income, so the budget set rotates upward.

Beulah might desire a combination of income and leisure that is outside her budget constraint; for example, she would probably like to have both 60 hours of leisure and $540 of income, which is the choice shown at point *S*. However, the budget constraint shows the limits of what choices are possible, given the wage and hours available, and choices beyond the budget constraint are not possible. Moreover, Beulah will not choose a point inside the budget constraint like *T*, which is 50 hours of labor, 10 hours of leisure, and $200 of income. In effect, a choice like *T* would mean that Beulah was working for only $4 per hour (that is, $200 of income divided by 50 hours of work), when she can

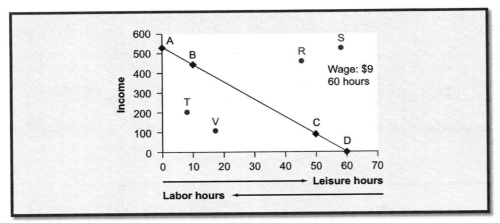

If Beulah strongly prefers income, she will work a lot of hours and choose a point like *A* or *B*. If she strongly prefers leisure, she will work few hours and make a choice like *C* or *D*. Given that she has 60 hours of time and a wage of $9 per hour, she cannot choose points like *R* or *S* that are outside her budget set. Points like *T* or *V* inside her budget set would be wasteful; they would be like giving up hours of leisure but not being paid.

actually earn a wage of $9 per hour. Thus, the labor-leisure budget constraint illustrates: (1) how the budget set of possible choices for leisure and income are determined by the wage rate and the total quantity of hours that can be worked; (2) how changes in the wage rate cause the budget constraint to shift; and (3) how the personal preferences of an individual for choosing between leisure and income are represented by the point that is chosen on the budget constraint.

Choosing Between Present and Future Consumption

An intertemporal choice reaches across time. Borrowing money is an intertemporal choice, because it involves borrowing money to spend in the present but promising to repay in the future. Saving money is also an intertemporal choice, because it involves less consumption in the present, but the ability to consume more in the future. The intertemporal choice budget constraint shows the trade-off between present and future consumption.

Interest Rates: The Price of Intertemporal Choice

In the consumption choice budget constraint presented earlier, the trade-off between goods is determined by the relative prices of the two goods. In the labor-leisure budget constraint, the trade-off between leisure and income is based on the wage. In the intertemporal choice budget constraint, the trade-off between present consumption and future consumption is based on the interest rate or the rate of return. The price of borrowing money is the interest that you pay on the loan. The reward for saving money is the interest that you receive. Interest rates are worth more discussion, because they may seem less familiar than other prices.

The key to understanding the economic function of interest rates is to recognize that $100 you will receive in the future has less economic value than $100 you receive today. Imagine that a friend owes you $100, and when the time comes to pay, the friend says: "Hey, no problem, I'll have the money for you in five years." You protest, and your supposed friend says, "Hey, you are still getting repaid your full $100, so what are you complaining about?" You probably aren't going to persuade this loser, your former friend, to repay you sooner, but you can offer three arguments as to why $100 in the future doesn't have the same value as $100 today:

1. *Risk of not being repaid.* The future is uncertain. Your friend could get hit by a bus. You could get hit by a bus. (The way this friendship is going, you could run over your former friend with a bus.) Having $100 in your pocket is a sure thing. Having a promise of $100 is uncertain. Anytime someone borrows money, whether the lender is a friend or a bank, the lender must be concerned about the risk of not being repaid. Part of the interest rate is a **risk premium,** that is, a payment to make up for the risk of not being repaid in full.

risk premium: A payment to make up for the risk of not being repaid in full.

2. *Inflation.* In most years, there is a rise in the price level called **inflation.** In recent U.S. history, this increase has typically been 1-3% per year, but in some other countries the rate of inflation has been much higher. If the overall level of prices rises by 3% then on average a dollar will buy 3% less in terms of goods and services at the end of the year. If that 3% is being subtracted each year from the buying power of the currency, then being repaid $100 in the future will provide less buying power than receiving the money immediately. A lender demands an interest rate in part to compensate for any expected inflation, so that the money that is repaid in the future will have at least as much buying power as the money that was originally loaned. (The concept of inflation, along with its underlying causes and policy solutions, is discussed at length in the macroeconomics section of the book.)

inflation: Rise in the overall level of prices.

3. *Time value of money.* Even if you knew with complete certainty that the $100 will be repaid in the future, and even if the rate of inflation is zero, it is still annoying to wait several years for repayment. If you have the money now, you can spend it on something now if you wish to do so and receive benefits from that spending. Being forced to wait is an intangible cost, but still a cost. This cost of having to wait is referred to as the **time value of money.**

time value of money: The cost of having to wait for repayment.

Thus, when explaining to your friend why you should receive interest payments if you need to wait five years for your money, you can point out that an interest rate has three components:

Interest rate = Risk premium + Expected rate of inflation + Time value of money.

In effect, interest payments are a compensation for the risk of not being repaid, the fact that inflation tends to reduce the buying power of money over time, and the unpleasantness of having to wait to have money available.

Thinking about these three components of interest rates helps to explain why interest rates differ across times and places. At times and places when inflation is high, interest rates will also be high. Differences in interest rates at a point in time can usually be traced to the different risk premiums involved. For example, when the U.S. government borrows money the interest rate is quite low, perhaps an annual rate of 3–4%, because the chance that the federal government will not repay what it has borrowed is quite low. A large corporation might pay an annual interest rate of 6–7% because, although the firm is still unlikely not to pay back the loan, the risk is greater than with a federal government. A medium-size or small firm would pay a still higher interest rate because it has a greater risk of not repaying the loan. Individuals pay a relatively low interest rate when they borrow money from a bank to purchase a home because the bank (the lender) does a credit check before lending any money in the first place. The credit check is supposed to ensure that a home buyer has the financial means to cover the cost; if the buyer is unable to meet the payments, the bank can take the house and sell it. However, individuals pay a higher interest rate on credit card borrowing because there is a greater risk that such loans will not be repaid.

The Power of Compound Interest

Interest rates are usually expressed in annual terms. For example, an annual interest rate of 7% means that if you borrow $100 you will need to repay $107 a year from now, or if you save $100 you will receive $7 in interest payments a year from now. But what if you are planning to save money for a period of many years, allowing the interest to accumulate over time? The formula for starting with a certain amount of money in the present, and a certain interest rate or rate of return, and figuring how much it would be worth at a date in the future is:

$$(\text{Amount at present}) \times (1 + \text{interest rate})^{\text{number of years}} = \text{Amount at future time}$$

For example, Christopher is planning to make a financial investment of $500. He will put this money in a savings account that pays an interest rate of 6% annually and leave it in the account for some years as the interest accumulates.

Exhibit 2-5 applies this formula for Christopher and shows what his financial investment would be worth at various dates in the future. Notice that if he leaves the financial investment alone for 20 years, the original $500 will more than triple in value to $1,603; if he leaves the financial investment alone for 40 years, it will increase more than 10-fold to $5,143. How can a seemingly moderate interest rate like 6% per year produce such large increases? The answer lies in the power of **compound interest**, which refers to the situation when interest payments are allowed to accumulate, so that in later time periods, the interest rate is paid not only on the original amount, but also on the interest that has accumulated in previous years. In the equation for how a financial investment increases in value over time, the number of years is an exponent. When quantities are raised to high exponential powers, they will eventually expand very quickly. The exponent represents the power of compound interest—as time goes by, Christopher is not just earning interest on his original $500, but also on the earlier interest he earned. If interest rates are relatively low, compound interest doesn't make much of a practical difference over a short time period of a few years. But over several decades, even a relatively low interest rate will compound in a way that yields significant returns on the initial financial investment.

compound interest: When interest payments accumulate, so that in later time periods, the interest rate is paid on the interest that has been earned and reinvested in previous years.

An Example of Intertemporal Choice

Consider the case of Desdemona, who is lucky enough to receive a gift of $10,000 from a wealthy aunt. She faces a choice: how much money should she consume now, and how much should she save for future consumption? Again, the first step is to use the budget constraint to show the range of possible choices, while the second step is to illustrate the individually preferred choice that maximizes her utility.

Starting with $500, interest rate of 6%			
After 1 year	$500 (1 + .06)^1 = $530	After 10 years	$500 (1 + .06)^{10} = $895
After 2 years	$500 (1 + .06)^2 = $562	After 20 years	$500 (1 + .06)^{20} = $1,603
After 5 years	$500 (1 + .06)^5 = $669	After 40 years	$500 (1 + .06)^{40} = $5,143

Exhibit 2-5
Christopher's Potential Savings

Exhibit 2-6   Desdemona's Intertemporal Budget Constraint

The points along the budget set represent the combinations of present and future consumption that are available to Desdemona, based on her inheritance of $10,000 and an interest rate of 9% per year. The trade-off between present consumption and future consumption—and thus the slope of the budget line—is determined by the interest rate. Choices like Q or P are unavailable to Desdemona, even if she would like them. She will not make choices like R or S because they give up present consumption without taking future consumption, which would be wasteful. Thus, she will choose among points like A through F, based on her personal preferences.

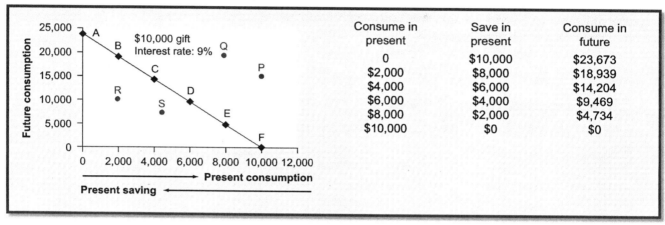

Consume in present	Save in present	Consume in future
0	$10,000	$23,673
$2,000	$8,000	$18,939
$4,000	$6,000	$14,204
$6,000	$4,000	$9,469
$8,000	$2,000	$4,734
$10,000	$0	$0

In the intertemporal choice budget constraint, the two axes represent consumption in the present and consumption in the future. Let's assume that if Desdemona saves some of the money, she can earn an annual interest rate of 9% for the next 10 years. Exhibit 2-6 shows Desdemona's choices in both a table and a budget constraint. The levels of future consumption that are available to her 10 years from now are calculated by using the formula for compound interest. At one extreme, she can consume all of the $10,000 in the present and have nothing left in the future. At the other extreme, she can save the entire $10,000, consume none of it in the present, and have $23,673 to spend 10 years from now.

In Exhibit 2-6, both present consumption and present savings are shown on the horizontal axis. Consumption is measured from left to right; saving is measured from right to left. In effect, the horizontal axis shows how the income that is available in the present is divided into either consumption or savings. (This approach applies the same logic as the way in which hours of labor and leisure were both shown on the horizontal axis in the labor-leisure budget constraint.) If the interest rate rises, then the budget constraint has a steeper slope; a lower interest rate causes the budget constraint to shift downward to a flatter slope.

Desdemona will seek to maximize her utility and choose the option that brings her the greatest degree of satisfaction. Inevitably, this choice will be one of the points on the budget constraint such as A, B, C, D, E, or F. Even if Desdemona wants to choose a point like Q, with $8,000 of consumption in the present, $2,000 of savings, and $20,000 of future consumption, she can't have it because choice Q is outside her budget constraint. Moreover, Desdemona will not choose a point inside the budget constraint like R, with $2,000 in present consumption and $10,000 in future consumption because such a choice would be like throwing away money. Instead of choosing R, Desdemona would certainly prefer a choice like C with more consumption in both the present and the future.

In the real world, the trade-off between present and future consumption is considerably more complex than the basic intertemporal budget constraint shown here. Instead of making one decision in the present about whether to consume now or save for 10 years from now, people receive income in many different years and make decisions about how much to save over different periods of time. Moreover, financial investments usually don't pay a guaranteed rate of return, so people need take into account the risk and uncertainty of investments. Later chapters will take up the details of financial investing in greater detail. But the basic intertemporal budget constraint here illustrates three themes: (1) how the budget constraint of possible choices for present and future consumption are determined by the quantity of income in the present and the interest rate; (2) how changes in the interest rate will cause the intertemporal budget constraint to shift; and (3) how the personal preferences of an individual for present and future consumption are represented by the point that is chosen on the intertemporal budget constraint.

Three Implications of Budget Constraints: Opportunity Cost, Marginal Decision-Making, and Sunk Costs

The budget constraint framework has some possibly unexpected implications for how a sensible utility-maximizing individual will make decisions. Let's now draw out three of those implications, involving *opportunity cost, marginal decision making,* and *sunk costs.*

Opportunity Cost

When most people want to know the cost of an item or a service, they look for a price tag. When economists want to determine cost, they go one step further. They use the idea of **opportunity cost**, which is whatever must be given up to obtain something that is desired. In the examples discussed earlier, if Alphonso wants more burgers, the opportunity cost is measured in bus tickets; if he wants more bus tickets, the opportunity cost is measured in burgers. In Beulah's labor-leisure choice, if she wants more income, the opportunity cost is hours of leisure; if she wants more leisure time, the opportunity cost is dollars of income. In Desdemona's intertemporal choice, the opportunity cost of greater consumption in the present is less consumption in the future and vice versa. The idea of opportunity cost, as its name implies, is that the cost of one item is the lost opportunity to do or consume something else.

opportunity cost:
Whatever must be given up to obtain something that is desired.

  In many cases, it is reasonable to refer to the opportunity cost as the price. If your cousin buys a new bicycle for $300, then $300 measures the amount of "other consumption" that he has given up. For practical purposes, there may be no special need to identify the specific alternative product or products that could have been bought with that $300, but sometimes the price as measured in dollars may not accurately capture the true opportunity cost. This problem can loom especially large when costs of time are involved. For example, consider a boss who decides that all employees will attend a two-day retreat to "build team spirit." The out-of-pocket monetary cost of the event may involve hiring an outside consulting firm to run the retreat. But an opportunity cost exists as well: during the two days of the retreat, none of the employees are doing any other work. Attending college is another case where the opportunity cost exceeds the monetary cost. The out-of-pocket costs of attending college include tuition, books, room and board, and other expenses. But in addition, during the hours that you are attending class and studying, it is impossible to work at a paying job. Thus, college imposes both an out-of-pocket cost and an opportunity cost of lost earnings—and both costs should be taken into account.

Opportunity Cost in the Airport

After the terrorist plane hijackings on September 11, 2001, many steps were proposed to improve air travel safety. For example, the federal government could provide armed "sky marshals" who would travel inconspicuously with the rest of the passengers. The cost of having a sky marshal on every flight would be roughly $3 billion per year. Retrofitting all U.S. planes with reinforced cockpit doors to make it harder for terrorists to take over the plane would have a price tag of $450 million. Buying more sophisticated security equipment for airports, like three-dimensional baggage scanners and cameras linked to face recognition software, could cost another $2 billion.

But the single biggest cost of greater airline security doesn't involve spending money. It's the opportunity cost of additional waiting time at the airport. About 750 million passengers took plane trips in the United States in 2008. Since the 9/11 hijackings, security screening has become more intensive, and consequently, the procedure takes longer than in the past. Say that, on average, each air passenger spends one extra hour in the airport per trip. Economists commonly place a value on time to convert an opportunity cost in time into a monetary figure. Because many air travelers are relatively high-paid business people, conservative estimates set the average price of time for air travelers at $20 per hour. By these estimates, the opportunity cost of delay in airports is 750 million hours × 20 dollars/hour, or $15 billion per year. Clearly, the opportunity costs of waiting time can be just as important as costs that involve direct spending.

In some cases, making the opportunity cost explicit can alter behavior. Imagine, for example, that you are an employee who goes out to lunch every day and spends $8 at a local restaurant. You may know perfectly well that bringing a lunch from home would only cost $3 a day, but somehow referring to the opportunity cost of buying lunch at the restaurant as $5 each day (that is, the $8 it costs minus the $3 your lunch from home would cost) doesn't seem to matter much. However, if you work 250 days a year, that $5 per day adds up to $1,250 for a year—which is the cost of a decent vacation. If the opportunity cost is described as "a nice vacation" instead of "$5 a day," you might make different choices.

Marginal Decision-Making and Diminishing Marginal Utility

The budget constraint framework helps to emphasize that most choices in the real world aren't about getting all of one thing or all of another; that is, they aren't about choosing either the point at one end of the budget constraint or else the point all the way at the other end. Instead, most choices involve **marginal analysis**, which involves comparing the benefits and costs of choosing a little more or a little less of a good.

The utility that a person receives from consuming the first unit of a good is typically more than the utility received from consuming the fifth or the tenth unit of that same good. When Alphonso makes his choice between burgers and bus tickets, for example, the first few bus rides that he chooses might provide him with a great deal of utility—perhaps they help him get to a job interview or a doctor's appointment. But later bus rides might provide much less utility—they may only serve to kill time on a rainy day. Similarly, the first burger that Alphonso chooses to buy may be on a day when he missed breakfast and is ravenously hungry. However, if Alphonso has a burger every single day, the last few burgers may taste pretty boring. Similarly, if Beulah is working 60 hours per week and thinking about whether to take a few hours of leisure, that break may provide her with a great deal of utility. But if she is working only 10 hours a week, with 50 hours of leisure already, then taking a few more hours of leisure seems likely to provide much less utility.

marginal analysis:
Comparing the benefits and costs of choosing a little more or a little less of a good.

Can Economics Take Pride in Being the "Dismal Science"?

Economics is often called the dismal science. Yet few people would toss that phrase around so easily if they knew its origin. The "dismal science" phrase originated with British essayist Thomas Carlyle (1795-1881). In an 1849 article, Carlyle described the study of "political economy," as economics was then called, as a "dreary, desolate and indeed quite abject and distressing one; what we might call, by way of eminence, the *dismal science.*"

This put-down has echoed through time. But not many people know *why* Carlyle disliked economics. The "dismal science" comment appeared in his essay "Occasional Discourse on the Negro Question." In that essay, Carlyle made the racist argument that white

landowners should compel black people in the West Indies to give up their natural laziness and instead to work hard and have some purpose in their otherwise meaningless lives. Carlyle didn't just believe that black people should be ordered around by whites; he believed that all the "weak" people, black and white alike, should be compelled by the strong to do "the work they were appointed for," as he put it.

Carlyle thought economics was the "dismal science" because it rested on the assumption that people, regardless of race and social status, were best suited to make their own decisions about their own lives. Carlyle's insult is one that economists can wear with pride.

The general pattern that consumption of the first few units of any good tends to bring a higher level of utility to a person than consumption of later units is a common pattern. Economists refer to this pattern the **law of diminishing marginal utility**, which means that as a person receives more of a good, the additional or marginal utility from each additional unit of the good declines.

The law of diminishing marginal utility explains why people and societies rarely make all-or-nothing choices. You wouldn't say, "My favorite food is (say) ice cream, so I will eat nothing but ice cream from now on." Instead, even if you get a very high level of utility from your favorite food, if you ate it exclusively, the additional or marginal utility from those last few servings would not be very high. Similarly, most workers don't say: "I enjoy leisure, so I'll never work." Instead, workers recognize that even though some leisure is very nice, a combination of all leisure and no income isn't so attractive. Thus, the budget constraint framework suggests that when people make choices in a world of scarcity, they will use marginal analysis and think about whether they would prefer a little more or a little less.

law of diminishing marginal utility: As a person receives more of a good, the marginal utility from each additional unit of the good is smaller than from the previous unit.

Sunk Costs

In the budget constraint framework, all decisions involve what will happen next: that is, what quantities of goods will be consumed, how many hours will be worked, or how much will be saved. These decisions do not look back to past choices. Thus, the budget constraint framework assumes that **sunk costs**, which are costs that were incurred in the past and cannot be recovered, should not affect the current decision.

Consider the case of Edgar who pays $8 to see a movie, but after watching the film for 30 minutes he knows that it's truly terrible. Should he stay and watch the rest of the movie because he paid $8, or should he leave? The money he spent is a sunk cost and unless the theater manager is feeling kindly, Edgar won't get a refund. But staying in the movie still means paying an opportunity cost in time. Thus, Edgar's choice is whether to spend the next 90 minutes suffering through a cinematic disaster or to do something—anything—else. The lesson of sunk costs is to forget about the money that's irretrievably gone and instead to focus on the marginal costs and benefits of future options.

For people and firms alike, dealing with sunk costs can be frustrating. It often means admitting an earlier error in judgment. Many firms, for example, find it hard to give up on a new product that is doing poorly because they spent so much money in

sunk cost: Costs that were incurred in the past and cannot be recovered, and thus should not affect current decisions.

creating and launching the product. But the lesson of sunk costs is to ignore them and make decisions based on what will happen in the future.

The budget constraint or opportunity set framework provides a framework for thinking about how individuals make economic decisions like what to consume, how much to work, and how much to save. The purpose of this model is not to tell utility-maximizing individuals what they *should* do, but only to convey the range of available choices for what individuals *could* do, and to provide a way of showing what choices people actually make.

The Production Possibilities Frontier and Social Choices

In a world of scarcity, individuals cannot have everything they want and must instead make a choice along a budget constraint. Firms cannot have all the profits they want and must struggle to come up with new ways of pleasing customers. Society as a whole cannot have everything it might want, either. A production possibilities frontier is a graph that shows the combinations of output that are possible for an economy to produce. In effect, a **production possibilities frontier** is a budget constraint for the economy as a whole.

An example of a production possibilities frontier faced by every economy is the macroeconomic choice between consumption and real investment. Consumption refers to goods and services that are used up this year. Real investment (as opposed to financial investment) refers to expenditures on equipment (like machinery) that can be used to produce goods or services for some years into the future. Thus, expenditures on consumption often serve a more immediate need or desire, but expenditures on investment typically help to increase the economy's level of output in the future.

A production possibilities frontier for the choice between consumption and investment is shown in Exhibit 2-7 by the line labeled PPF_1. At point A, the economy is devoting all of its resources to producing goods for current consumption and nothing to investment. At points B, C, and D, the economy is gradually shifting toward lower levels of consumption and higher levels of investment. At point E, at the other end of the production possibilities frontier, the economy is devoting all of its resources to producing goods for real investment and no resources to current consumption. In a market-oriented economy, the choice between consumption and real investment is not made by the government or by any single organization, but rather is the result of many decisions made by households and firms. However, government policies can use taxes, regulations and other policies to influence the choices of individuals as to how much they should consume or save, and also to influence the eagerness with which firms will make real investments. Just as different people will make different choices along a budget constraint, according to their personal preferences, different societies will make choices about how much to consume and to invest.

Over time, societies that invest a greater share of GDP will tend to expand their ability to produce output. Therefore, a society that chooses a high level of consumption and low level of investment, like point B, will find that in the future its production possibilities frontier shifts outward only a bit, perhaps from PPF_1 to PPF_2. However, a society that consumes relatively less in the present and invests more, like point D, will find that in the future its production possibilities frontier has shifted outward more dramatically, from PPF_1 to PPF_3. Thus, a consumption-investment production

production possibilities frontier: A diagram that shows the combinations of output that are possible for an economy to produce.

Exhibit 2-7 The Consumption and Investment Trade-Off

A production possibilities frontier shows the possible combinations of output that a society can produce. Points A, B, C, and D illustrate some possible choices along PPF₁, moving from all consumption at A to greater investment at B, C, and D. PPF₂ and PPF₃ show an outward shift of the frontier, which would happen as an economy grows and can afford more of both consumption and investment.

possibilities frontier shows the range of choices available to society, illustrates which choice will happen, and even has implications for how the PPF will shift in the future.

The Shape of the Production Possibilities Frontier and Diminishing Marginal Returns

The budget constraints presented earlier in this chapter, showing individual choices about what quantities of goods to consume, how much to work and how much to save, were all straight lines. The reason for these straight lines was that the slope of the budget constraint was determined by relative prices of the two goods in the consumption budget constraint, by the wage in the labor-leisure budget constraint, and by the interest rate in the intertemporal budget constraint. However, the production possibilities frontier for consumption and investment was drawn as a curved line. Why does the PPF have a different shape?

Consider another example of a production possibilities frontier that arises when government decision makers must decide how much money to spend on competing government priorities, like education and improving health. Exhibit 2-8 shows a production possibilities frontier for this trade-off. In this diagram there are no specific numbers on the axes because there is no single way to measure levels of education and health. However, when you think of improvements in education, you can think of accomplishments like more years of school completed, fewer high-school dropouts, and higher scores on standardized tests. When you think of improvements in health, you can think of longer life expectancies, lower levels of infant mortality, and fewer outbreaks of disease. At choice A, the government is committing all of its resources to producing health and none to education; at choice D, the government is committing all resources to education and none to health. As the economy grows over time this production possibilities frontier will shift to the right, making it possible for society to have more of both education and health. But in the immediate present, choosing more of one means choosing less of the other.

To understand why the PPF is curved, start by considering point A at the top left-hand side of the PPF. At point A, literally all of the available resources are being devoted to health and literally none to education. This situation would be extreme and even ridiculous. For example, children are seeing a doctor every day, whether they are sick or not, but not attending school. People are having cosmetic surgery on every

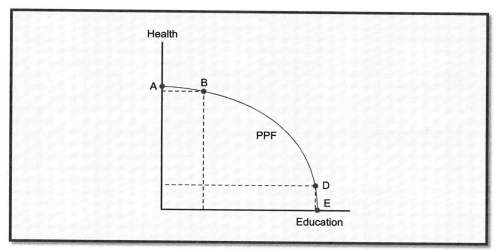

Health

A   B

PPF

D
E

Education

Exhibit 2-8   A Health
vs. Education Production
Possibilities Frontier
This production possibilities
frontier shows a trade-off
between devoting social
resources to health and
devoting them to education.
At choices like *A* and *B*,
most social resources go to
health. At choices like *D* and
E, most go to education. The
curvature of the PPF shows
that when a large share of
resources is already devoted
to health (as at point *B*),
devoting still more resources
to health and moving to point
A produces only a small gain
in health but a substantial
loss in education. Thus,
the curvature of the PPF
demonstrates the law of
diminishing marginal returns.

part of their bodies, but no high school or college education exists. Now imagine that some of these resources are diverted from health to education, so that the economy is at point *B* instead of point *A*. Diverting some marginal resources away from *A* to *B* causes relatively little reduction in health because the last few marginal dollars going into health care services aren't producing much additional gain in health. However, putting those marginal dollars into education, which is completely without resources at point *A*, can produce relatively large gains. For this reason, the shape of the PPF from *A* to *B* is relatively flat, representing a relatively small drop-off in health and a relatively large gain in education.

Now consider the other end, at the lower right, of the production possibilities frontier. Imagine that society starts at choice *D*, which is devoting nearly all resources to education and very few on health, and moves to point *E*, which is devoting *all* spending to education and none to health. For the sake of concreteness, you can imagine in the movement from *D* to *E*, the last few doctors must become high school science teachers, the last few nurses must become school librarians rather than dispensers of vaccinations, and the last few emergency rooms are turned into kindergartens. The gains to education from adding these last few resources to education are very small. However, the opportunity cost loss to health will be fairly large, and thus the slope of the PPF between *D* and *E* is steep, showing a small gain in education and a large drop in health.

The lesson here is not that society is likely to make an extreme choice like devoting no resources to education at point *A* or no resources to health at point *E*. Instead, the lesson is that the gains from committing additional marginal resources to education depend on how much is already being spent. If very few resources are currently committed to education, then an increase of a certain amount can bring relatively large gains; on the other side, if a large number of resources are already being committed to education, then an increase of a certain amount will bring relatively smaller gains. This pattern is common enough that it has been given a name: **the law of diminishing returns**, which holds that as additional increments of resources are added to a certain purpose, the marginal benefit from those additional increments will decline. This pattern is common. When government spends a certain amount more on reducing crime, for example, the original gains in reducing crime could be relatively large. But additional increases typically cause relatively smaller reductions in crime, and paying for enough police and security to reduce crime to nothing at all would be tremendously expensive.

**the law of diminishing
returns:** As additional
increments of resources are
added to producing a good
or service, the marginal
benefit from those additional
increments will decline.

The curvature of the production possibilities frontier shows that as additional resources are added to education, moving from left to right along the horizontal axis, the original gains are fairly large, but gradually diminish. Similarly, as additional resources are added to health, moving from bottom to top on the vertical axis, the original gains are fairly large, but again gradually diminish. In this way, the law of diminishing returns produces the outward-bending shape of the production possibilities frontier.

Productive Efficiency and Allocative Efficiency

The study of economics does not presume to tell a society what choice it should make along its production possibilities frontier. In a market-oriented economy with a democratic government, the choice will involve a mixture of decisions by individuals, firms, and government. However, economics can point out that some choices are unambiguously better than others. In everyday usage, the concept of efficiency refers to lack of waste. An inefficient machine operates at high cost, while an efficient machine produces without wasting energy or materials. An inefficient organization operates with long delays and high costs, while an efficient organization meets schedules, is focused, and performs within budget.

To an economist, **efficiency** refers to the situation in which it is impossible to get more of one thing without experiencing a trade-off of less of something else. The production possibilities frontier can illustrate two kinds of efficiency: *productive efficiency* and *allocative efficiency*. Exhibit 2-9 illustrates these ideas using a production possibilities frontier between consumption and investment.

Productive efficiency means that, given the available inputs and technology, it is impossible to produce more of one good without decreasing the quantity that is produced of another good. Thus, all choices on the PPF in Exhibit 2-9, including *A, B, C, D,* and *E,* display productive efficiency. As a firm moves from any one of these choices to any other, either consumption increases and investment declines or vice versa. However, any choice inside the production possibilities frontier is productively inefficient and wasteful because it is possible to produce more of one good, the other good, or some combination of both goods. For example, point *R* is productively inefficient because it is possible at choice *C* to have more of both goods: investment on the horizontal axis

efficiency: When it is impossible to get more of something without experiencing a trade-off of less of something else.

productive efficiency: When it is impossible to produce more of one good without decreasing the quantity produced of another good.

Consumption

Exhibit 2-9 Productive and Allocative Efficiency

Productive efficiency means it is impossible to produce more of one good without decreasing the quantity that is produced of another good. Thus, all choices along a given PPF like *B, C,* and *D* display productive efficiency, but *R* does not. Allocative efficiency means that the particular mix of goods being produced—that is, the specific choice along the production possibilities frontier—represents the allocation that society most desires.

is higher at point C than point R (E_2 is greater than E_1) and consumption on the vertical axis is also higher at point C than point R (H_2 is great than H_1).

Allocative efficiency means that the particular mix of goods being produced— that is, the specific choice along the production possibilities frontier—represents the allocation that society most desires. How to determine what a society desires can be a controversial question, and it will be addressed in political science, sociology and philosophy classes as well as in economics. Only one of the productively efficient choices will be the allocatively efficient choice for society as a whole.

allocative efficiency:
When the mix of goods being produced represents the allocation that society most desires.

Why Society Must Choose

Every economy faces two situations in which it may be able to expand consumption of all goods. In the first case, a society may discover that it has been using its resources inefficiently, in which case by improving efficiency and moving to the production possibilities frontier it can have more of some or all goods. In the second case, as an economy grows over a period of years, the production possibilities frontier for a society will tend to shift outward and society will be able to afford more of all goods. But improvements in productive efficiency take time to discover and implement, and economic growth happens only gradually. Thus, a society must face scarcity and choose between tradeoffs in the present. For government, this process often involves trying to identify where additional spending could do the most good and where reductions in spending would do the least harm. At the individual and firm level, the market economy coordinates a process in which firms seek to produce goods and services in the quantity, quality, and price that people want. But for both the government and the market economy in the short term, increases in production of one good typically mean offsetting decreases somewhere else in the economy.

Confronting Objections to the Economic Approach

It's one thing to understand the economic approach to decision-making and another thing to feel comfortable applying it. The sources of discomfort typically fall into two categories: that people don't act in the way that fits the economics model, and that even if people did act that way, they should try not to. Let's consider these arguments in turn.

A First Objection: People, Firms, and Society Don't Act Like This

The economic approach to decision-making seems to require more information than most individuals possess and more careful decision-making than most individuals actually display. After all, do you or any of your friends draw a budget constraint and mutter to yourself about maximizing utility before you head to the shopping mall? Do members of the U.S. Congress contemplate production possibilities frontiers before they vote on the annual budget? The messy ways in which people and societies operate somehow doesn't look much like neat budget constraints or smoothly curving production possibilities frontiers.

However, the economics approach can be a useful way to analyze and understand the trade-offs of economic decisions even if it doesn't describe how those decisions are actually made. To appreciate this point, imagine for a moment that you are playing basketball, dribbling to the right, and throwing a bounce-pass to the left to a teammate who is running toward the basket. A physicist or engineer could work out the correct speed and trajectory for the pass, given the different movements involved and the weight and bounciness of the ball. But when you're playing basketball, you don't perform any of these calculations. You just pass the ball, and if you're a good player, you will do so with high accuracy. Someone might argue: "The scientist's formula of the bounce-pass requires a far greater knowledge of physics and far more specific information about speeds of movement and weights than the basketball player actually has, so it must be an unrealistic description of how basketball passes are actually made." This reaction would be wrongheaded. The fact that a good player can throw the ball accurately because of practice and skill, without making a physics calculation, doesn't mean that the physics calculation is wrong.

Similarly, from an economic point of view, someone who goes shopping for groceries every week has a great deal of practice with how to purchase the combination of goods that will provide that person with utility, even if the shopper doesn't phrase decisions in terms of a budget constraint. Government institutions may work imperfectly and slowly, but in general, a democratic form of government feels pressure from voters and social institutions to make the choices that are most widely preferred by people in that society. Thus, when thinking about the economic actions of groups of people, firms, and society, it is reasonable as a first approximation to analyze them with the tools of economic analysis.

A Second Objection: People, Firms, and Society Shouldn't Do This

The economics approach portrays people as self-interested. For some critics of this approach, even if self-interest is an accurate description of how people behave, these behaviors are not moral. Instead, the critics argue that people should be taught to care more deeply about others. Economists offer several answers to this concerns.

First, economics is not a form of moral instruction. Rather, it seeks to describe economic behavior as it actually exists. Philosophers draw a distinction between **positive statements,** which describe the world as it is, and **normative statements**, which describe how the world should be. In the study of economics, positive and normative arguments often blend into each other: for example, if an economist analyzes a proposal for building a subway system in a certain city and finds that the benefits are higher than the costs, then is this study a positive analysis that merely states what *will* happen or a normative analysis which describes what *should* happen? But even if the line between positive and normative statements isn't always crystal clear, economic analysis does try to remain rooted in the study of the actual people who inhabit the actual economy. Yes, if the world were populated by saints, the economy would look different. But it isn't.

positive statements: Statements which describe the world as it is.

normative statements: Statements which describe how the world should be.

Second, self-interested behavior and profit-seeking can be labeled with other names, such as personal choice and freedom. The ability to make personal choices about buying, working, and saving is an important personal freedom. Some people may choose high-pressure, high-paying jobs so that they can earn and spend a lot of money. Others may earn a lot of money and give it to charity or spend it on their friends and family. Others may devote themselves to a career that can require a great deal of time, energy and expertise but does not offer high financial rewards, like being an elementary school teacher or a social worker. Still others may choose a job that does not take lots of their time or provide a high level of income, but still leaves time for family, friends, and contemplation. Some people may prefer to work for a large company; others might

The Budget Constraint and the Production Possibilities Frontier

When you study economics, you may feel buried under an avalanche of diagrams: diagrams in the text, diagrams in the lectures, diagrams in the problems, diagrams on exams. Your goal should be to recognize the common underlying logic and pattern of the diagrams, not to memorize each of the individual diagrams.

This chapter uses only one basic diagram, although it is presented with different sets of labels. The consumption choice budget constraint, the labor-leisure budget constraint, and the intertemporal choice budget constraint for individuals, along with the production possibilities frontier for society as a whole, are all the same basic diagram. The exhibit shows an individual budget constraint and a production possibilities frontier for two goods, Good 1 and Good 2. The trade-off diagram always illustrates three basic themes: scarcity, trade-offs, and economic efficiency.

The first theme is scarcity. It is not feasible to have unlimited amounts of both goods. Budget constraints can shift, either as a result of movements of income or of prices. Production possibilities frontiers can shift, too, either as a national economy expands or as the trade-offs between the two goods shift. But even if the budget constraint or a PPF shifts, scarcity remains—just at a different level.

The second theme is trade-offs. As depicted in the budget constraint or the production possibilities frontier, it is necessary to give up some of one good to gain more of the other good. The details of this trade-off vary. In a budget constraint, the trade-off is determined by the relative prices of the goods: that is, the relative price of two goods in the consumption choice budget constraint; the relative price of labor and leisure (the wage) in the labor-leisure budget constraint; and the relative price of present and future consumption (the principal saved plus the interest rate or rate of return) in the intertemporal choice budget constraint. These trade-offs appear as a straight line. However, the trade-offs in many production possibilities frontiers are represented by a curved line because the law of diminishing returns holds that as resources are added to an area, the marginal gains tend to diminish. But regardless of the specific shape, trade-offs remain.

The third theme is economic efficiency or getting the most benefit from scarce resources. All choices on the production possibilities frontier show productive efficiency because in such cases, there is no way to increase the quantity of one good without decreasing the quantity of the other. Similarly, when an individual makes a choice along a budget constraint, there is no way to increase the quantity of one good without decreasing the quantity of the other. The choice on a production possibilities set that is socially preferred, or the choice on an individual's budget constraint that is personally preferred, will display allocative efficiency.

The basic budget constraint/production possibilities frontier diagram will recur throughout this book. Some examples include using these trade-off diagrams to analyze one source of the gains from international trade and to examine the trade-offs between environmental protection and economic output, between equality of incomes and economic output, and the macroeconomic trade-off between consumption and investment. Don't be confused by the different labels. The budget constraint/production possibilities frontier diagram is always just a tool for thinking carefully about scarcity, trade-offs, and efficiency in a particular situation.

The Trade-Off Diagram

(a) An individual opportunity set.

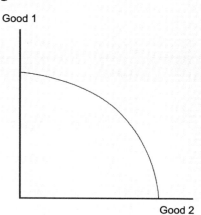

(b) A social production possibilities frontier.

want to start their own business. People's freedom to make their own economic choices has a moral value worth respecting.

Third, self-interested behavior can lead to positive social results. For example, when people work hard to make a living, they create economic output. Consumers who are looking for the best deals will encourage businesses to offer goods and services that meet their needs. Adam Smith, writing in the *Wealth of Nations*, christened this property the "invisible hand." In describing how consumers and producers interact in a market economy, Smith wrote:

> Every individual … generally neither intends to promote the public interest, nor knows how much he is promoting it. He intends only his own security, only his own gain. And he is in this led by an invisible hand to promote an end which was no part of his intention. By pursuing his own interest he frequently promotes that of society more effectually than when he really intends to promote it.

The metaphor of the invisible hand suggests the remarkable possibility that broader social good can emerge from selfish individual actions.

Fourth, even people who focus on their own self-interest in the economic part of their life often set aside their own narrow self-interest in other parts of life. For example, you might focus on your own self-interest when asking your employer for a raise or negotiating to buy a car. But then you might turn around and focus on other people when you volunteer to read stories at the local library, help a friend move to a new apartment, or donate money to a charity. Thus, self-interest is a reasonable starting point for analyzing many economic decisions, without needing to imply that people never do anything that is not in their own immediate self-interest.

Facing Scarcity and Making Trade-offs

The study of economics is rooted in a fundamental insight about the human condition. The world we live in is a place of scarcity, whether measured in terms of time, money, natural resources, or material goods. As a result, people must face trade-offs and make choices. The main economic trade-offs for individuals are their decisions about what to consume, how much to work, and how much to save. For society as a whole and for government decision-makers, the task is to use scarce resources as efficiently as possible to meet people's needs. Economics delves into the questions of how individuals, firms and government will interact, and thus into the decisions that society will make about what to produce, how to produce, and for whom to produce.

Key Concepts and Summary

1. The real world is one of scarcity: that is, a world in which people's desires exceed what is possible. As a result, economic behavior involves trade-offs in which individuals, firms, government and society must give up one thing that they desire to obtain things that they desire more.

2. Individuals face three main categories of trade-offs: the consumption choice of what quantities of goods to consume, the labor-leisure choice of what quantity of hours to work, and the intertemporal choices that involve costs in the present and benefits in the future, or benefits in the present and costs in the future.

3. The **budget constraint,** sometimes called the **opportunity set,** illustrates the range of choices available. The slope of the budget constraint is determined by the relative price of the choices. Choices beyond the budget constraint are impossible. Choices inside the budget constraint are wasteful.

4. People will choose along their budget constraints in a way that maximizes their satisfaction or **utility,** which is based on their own distinctive personal preferences.

5. An interest rate has three components: the **risk premium** to cover the risk of not being repaid, the rate of expected **inflation,** and the **time value of money.** The formula for how **compound interest** accumulates over time is:

$$(\text{Amount at present}) * (1 + \text{Interest rate})^{\text{number of years}} = \text{Amount at future time}$$

6. **Opportunity cost** measures cost by what is given up in exchange. Sometimes opportunity cost can be measured in money, but it is often useful to consider whether time should be included as well, or to measure it in terms of the actual resources that must be given up.

7. Most economic decisions and trade-offs are not all-or-nothing. Instead, they involve **marginal analysis,** which means they are about decisions on the margin, involving a little more or a little less.

8. The **law of diminishing marginal utility** points out that as a person receives more of something—whether it is a specific good or another resource—the additional marginal gains tend to become smaller.

9. Because **sunk costs** occurred in the past and cannot be recovered, they should be disregarded in making current decisions.

10. A **production possibilities frontier** defines a set of choices faced by society as a whole. The shape of the PPF is typically curved outward, rather than straight. Choices outside the PPF are unattainable and choices inside the PPF are wasteful. Over time, a growing economy will tend to shift the PPF outwards.

11. The **law of diminishing returns** holds that as increments of additional resources are devoted to producing something, the marginal increase in output will become smaller and smaller.

12. All choices along a production possibilities frontier display **productive efficiency;** that is, it is impossible to use society's resources to produce more of one good without decreasing production of the other good. The specific choice along a production possibilities frontier that reflects the mix of goods that society prefers is the choice with **allocative efficiency.**

13. **Positive statements** describe the world as it is, while **normative statements** describe how the world should be. Even when economics analyzes the gains and losses from various events or policies, and thus draws normative conclusions about how the world should be, the analysis of economics is rooted in a positive analysis of how people, firms and government actually behave, not how they should behave.

Review Questions

1. Explain why scarcity leads to trade-offs.

2. Name the three main categories of economic trade-offs that individuals face.

3. What determines the slope of the consumption choice budget constraint? The labor-leisure budget constraint? The intertemporal budget constraint?

4. Explain why individuals make choices that are directly on the budget constraint, rather than inside the budget constraint or outside it.

5. Does the economic approach specify what choices people should make? Why or why not?

6. What does it mean to "maximize utility"?

7. What are the three components of the interest rate?

8. What is the formula for how compound interest accumulates over time?

9. What is opportunity cost?

10. What is the law of diminishing marginal utility?

11. What are sunk costs?

12. What does a production possibilities frontier illustrate?

13. Why is a production possibilities frontier typically drawn as a curve, rather than a straight line?

14. Explain why societies cannot make a choice above their production possibilities frontier and should not make a choice below it.

15. What are diminishing marginal returns?

16. What is productive efficiency? Allocative efficiency?

17. What's the difference between a positive and a normative statement?

18. Is the economic model of decision-making intended as a literal description of how individuals, firms, and the government actually make decisions?

3

International Trade

Nationaleconomies are becoming more intimately interconnected in the process known as globalization. From 1950 to 2000, the size of the world economy as measured by production of goods and services increased about six-fold, while world exports—that is, goods produced in one country but sold in another country—rose by a factor of 15. Similarly, the size of the U.S. economy increased fivefold from 1950 to 2000, while U.S. exports rose more than twentyfold. When trade is growing faster than the economy as a whole, national economies are being affected to a greater extent by international economic forces. Although globalization took a half-step backward during the global economic slowdown that started around 2008, the overall trend is expected to continue in the 21st century.

Reminders of international trade are all around. As a consumer, the food on your table might include fresh fruit from Chile, cheese from France, bottled water from Scotland. Your wireless phone might have been made in Sweden or Finland. The clothes you wear might be designed in Italy and manufactured in China. The toys you give to a child might have come from India. The car you drive might be from Japan, Germany, or Korea. The gasoline in the tank might be from Saudi Arabia, Mexico, or Nigeria. As a worker, if your job is involved with farming, machinery, airplanes, cars, scientific instruments, or many other technology-related industries, the odds are good that a hearty proportion of the sales of your employer—and hence the money that pays your salary—comes from export sales.

Exhibit 3-1 shows the volume of international merchandise trade (that is, trade in goods) between countries in different regions of the world. The columns of the table show the region of the country where trade started; the rows show the region of the country where the exports ended up. Thus, the first entry in the top column shows that $2,014 billion in exports was traded from one country in North America

39

Exhibit 3-1 The Network of World Trade in Merchandise, 2008 (in billions of U.S. dollars)

The rows of the table show where trade is going to; the columns show where trade is coming from. For example, the second entry in the first row shows that $164 billion in merchandise was produced in Latin America and sold in North America.

From To	North America	Latin America	European Union	Commonwealth of Independent States	Africa	Middle East	Asia
North America	$ 1,014	$ 164	$323	$ 16	$33	$60	$375
Latin America	169	158	109	8	16	11	100
European Union	434	88	3,973	218	171	156	440
Commonwealth of Independent States	36	10	405	134	10	24	76
Africa	121	18	202	1	53	14	113
Middle East	116	6	106	7	36	122	568
Asia	775	127	748	108	121	196	2,181

to another country in North America. The first entry in the second column shows that $164 billion in exports traveled from countries in Latin America to countries in North America. Most of the region names should be self-explanatory, but one that may be unclear is the Commonwealth of Independent States, which includes Russia, Ukraine, and other countries that before 1991 were republics of the Soviet Union.

Several patterns from this table are worth noting. First, the bulk of world trade involves high-income areas of the world, either as exporters, importers, or both. For example, the single biggest number in Exhibit 3-1 is the $3,973 billion that countries in the European Union sell to each other. The level of trade between North American countries appears low compared to Europe, but this is because the region of European Union includes 25 nations while the trade in the North American region is mainly between the United States and Canada. Remember, exports from Germany to Sweden count as international trade, but sales from California to New York would not be counted in this table, since they occur within the U.S. economy.

Second, trade between high-income regions and low-income regions is fairly extensive. Perhaps the most vivid example of this point is trade of $2,181 billion between the nations of Asia, which is the second-highest number in Exhibit 3-1. The region of Asia includes the high-income economy of Japan, the low-income economy of China, and medium-income countries like South Korea, Thailand, and Indonesia. More generally, high-income regions are important as markets to the other regions. The countries of Africa, for example, export more than three times as much to the European Union as they do to other countries of Africa. Countries of Latin America sell more to North America than they do to each other.

Finally, trade between some regions is very low; for example, between Africa and Latin America, or between the Middle East and the Commonwealth of Independent States. Indeed, some of these regions appear to have relatively few connections to other regions of the global economy.

The American statesman Benjamin Franklin (1706–1790) once wrote: "No nation was ever ruined by trade." Many economists would phrase their attitudes toward international trade in an even more positive manner. The circumstantial evidence that international trade confers overall benefits on the economy is strong. Trade has accompanied economic growth in the United States and around the world. Many of the national economies that have shown the most rapid growth in the last few decades—for example, Japan, South Korea, China and India —have also dramatically expanded their international trade. There is no modern example of a country that has shut itself off from world trade and still become prosperous.

This chapter will explore the reasons that international trade provides economic gains. The discussion will draw on themes and analytic tools developed in earlier chapters. For example, Chapter 1 suggested three reasons why the division of labor and specialization, followed by trade, can increase output among individuals: specialization allows the parties to produce according to their advantages; it encourages learning and innovation; and it allows taking advantage of economies of scale. This chapter will spell out in detail how these three reasons create benefits in international trade. The production possibility frontier, introduced in Chapter 2, will be used to analyze how all countries can benefit from trade.

But although international trade provides economic gains, it is also a powerful and disruptive force. World exports of goods and services totaled roughly $20 trillion dollars in 2008. Domestic producers of goods often feel threatened by competition from those trillions of dollars of imports flowing into their country. Workers fear that when foreign producers sell within their country, their jobs may be at risk. These fears create an awkward situation for politicians, who both want to embrace the benefits of international trade and also to block international trade from causing disruption for the firms and workers in their country. Chapter 6 will discuss public policy with regard to international trade, which often consists of a self-contradictory mix of international treaties to encourage trade and national actions to limit trade.

Absolute Advantage

Perhaps the most obvious case where international trade can benefit the countries who participate is the situation where each country has a particular product that it can produce relatively cheaply compared to other countries. For example, finding oil in Saudi Arabia is pretty much just a matter of drilling a hole, but producing oil in other countries can require considerable exploration and costly technologies for drilling and extraction—if indeed other countries have any oil at all. The United States has some of the richest farmland in the world, which makes it relatively easier to grow corn and wheat here than in many other countries—like the deserts of Saudi Arabia, for example. Brazil and Colombia have climates especially suited for growing coffee. Chile and Zambia have some of the world's richest copper mines. When each country has a product which it can produce relatively cheaply, then all countries can benefit from producing that product and trading with each other.

A Numerical Example of Absolute Advantage and Trade

To illustrate the benefits of trade between two countries who each have a product that they produce relatively cheaply, consider a hypothetical world with two countries, named Saudi Arabia and the United States, and two products, oil and corn. Saudi Arabia can produce oil more cheaply, while the United States can produce corn more cheaply. Exhibit 3-2 illustrates the advantages of the two countries, expressed in terms of how much a worker can produce in each country. A worker in Saudi Arabia can produce six

	Saudi Arabia	United States
One worker can produce	6 barrels of oil	2 barrels of oil
One worker can produce	1 bushel of corn	8 bushels of corn

Exhibit 3-2 Absolute Advantage: How Much Can One Worker Produce?
A worker in Saudi Arabia can produce more oil, by a margin of 6 barrels to 2 barrels. However, a worker in the United States can produce more corn, by a margin of 8 bushels to 1 bushel.

absolute advantage:
When one nation can produce a product at lower cost relative to another nation.

barrels of oil, while a worker in the United States could produce only two barrels of oil. However, a worker in the United States can produce eight bushels of corn, while a worker in Saudi Arabia can produce only one bushel of corn.

When one nation can produce a product at lower cost relative to another nation, it is said to have an **absolute advantage** in producing that product. In this example, Saudi Arabia has an absolute advantage in the production of oil and the United States has an absolute advantage in the production of corn. Two nations that each have an absolute advantage in certain products can both benefit if each nation specializes (at least to some extent) in the area of its absolute advantage and then the nations trade with each other.

The production possibilities frontier provides an analytical tool for illustrating this point. Exhibit 3-3 presents two production possibility frontiers for the possible levels of production in a world without trade, one for Saudi Arabia and one for the United States, based on the assumption that the economy of Saudi Arabia has 40 workers and the United States economy has 80 workers. If all 40 workers in the Saudi economy produced oil, that country could produce 240 barrels (that is, $40 \times 6 = 240$); if all the Saudi workers focused on corn, that economy could produce 40 bushels ($40 \times 1 = 40$). The table under the figure shows some of the in-between choices, and the points from the table are graphed on the figure. Meanwhile, if the U.S. economy devoted all 80 workers to oil it could produce 160 barrels (that is, $80 \times 2 = 160$), but if it devoted all 80 workers to corn it could produce 640 bushels ($80 \times 8 = 640$).

The slope of the production possibility frontier is determined by the opportunity cost of expanding production of one good, measured by how much of the other good would be lost. The information in Exhibit 3-2 can be interpreted in terms of opportunity costs. For example, in the U.S. economy the opportunity cost of producing 2 barrels of oil, which requires one worker, is the loss of the 8 bushels of corn that the worker could have produced otherwise. Thus, in the U.S. production possibility frontier in Exhibit 3-3, every increase in oil production of 1 barrel reflects a decrease of 4 bushels of corn. In the economy of Saudi Arabia, the opportunity cost of producing 1 bushel of corn, which requires one more worker, is the loss of the 6 barrels of oil that workers could otherwise have produced. The slope of the Saudi production possibility frontier shows that every rise of 1 bushel of corn leads to a fall of 6 barrels of oil.

For the sake of the argument, let's say that before trade occurs, the most desired point for each nation—as determined by the preferences of its citizens—was the point halfway down each production possibility frontier, shown as point A on each production possibility frontier. Thus, in the world before trade, the Saudi Arabian economy will devote 20 workers to each product, and produces 120 barrels of oil and 20 bushels of corn, while the U.S. economy devotes 40 workers to each product and produces 80 barrels of oil and 320 bushels of corn. Of course, each nation would prefer a choice like point B, which offers more of both goods, but since choice B is above the production possibility frontier, that choice isn't possible for either country.

However, if each of the two nations specializes in its area of absolute advantage and then trades, it becomes possible to expand global production of both goods. Exhibit 3-4 provides the calculations. The table on the left shows output of oil and corn in

When the possibility frontier was introduced in Chapter 2, it was drawn with an outward-bending shape, which illustrated that as inputs were transferred from one area to another—like from producing education to producing health—there were diminishing marginal returns. In the examples in this chapter, the *PPFs* are drawn as straight lines, which means that returns are not diminishing. When a marginal unit of labor is transferred away from growing corn and toward producing oil, the decline in the quantity of corn and the increase in the quantity of oil is always the same. The linear production possibilities frontier is a less realistic model. But a straight line is easier for purposes of calculation than a curve, and it illustrates the economic themes like absolute advantage just as clearly.

CLEARING IT UP

Yes, A Production Possibility Frontier Can Be Straight

Exhibit 3-3   Production Possibilities Frontiers and Absolute Advantage

The tables show several points along the production possibilities frontiers for each country, based on the numbers for what workers produce in Exhibit 3-2 and assuming 40 Saudi workers and 80 U.S. workers. Point *A* in the two figures is the point that each country would most prefer, given its production possibilities in the absence of trade. Each country would prefer a point like *B* in the two figures, with more of both goods, but in a world without trade, a choice like *B* is impossible. Through specialization and trade, however, a point like *B* becomes possible for both countries.

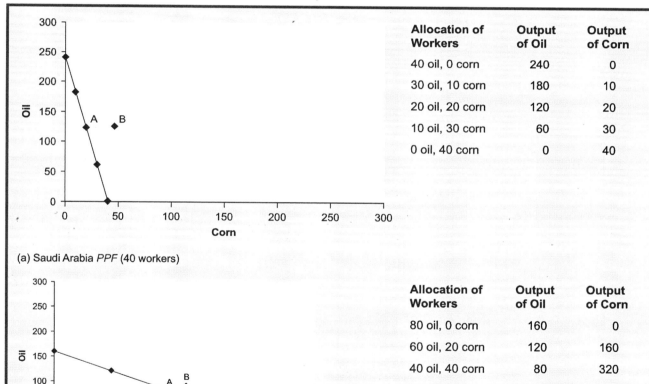

Allocation of Workers	Output of Oil	Output of Corn
40 oil, 0 corn	240	0
30 oil, 10 corn	180	10
20 oil, 20 corn	120	20
10 oil, 30 corn	60	30
0 oil, 40 corn	0	40

(a) Saudi Arabia *PPF* (40 workers)

Allocation of Workers	Output of Oil	Output of Corn
80 oil, 0 corn	160	0
60 oil, 20 corn	120	160
40 oil, 40 corn	80	320
20 oil, 60 corn	40	480
0 oil, 80 corn	0	640

(b) U.S. *PPF* (80 workers)

	Quantity produced before trade		Quantity produced after specialization	
	Oil	Corn	Oil	Corn
Saudi Arabia	120	20	240	0
United States	80	320	0	640
TOTAL	200	340	240	640

Exhibit 3-4 How Specialization by Absolute Advantage Expands Output

The first two columns show the quantity of oil and corn that would be produced in each country, at its preferred point A as shown in Exhibit 3-3 before trade occurs. The last two columns show output after specialization has occurred, so that each country is producing only one good. The bottom "TOTAL" row shows the combined production of each good. The total quantity produced of each good is greater than in the situation before specialization, which is what allows both countries, after trade, to consume more of both goods. As a result, both countries can be better off.

the two countries before trade, and by adding up the output in the countries, it shows global output of the two goods. Now assume that Saudi Arabia decides to specialize on its absolute advantage and produce only oil, thus producing 240 barrels of oil, and the United States specializes on its absolute advantage in farming, producing 640 bushels of corn. When each nation specializes in this way, Exhibit 3-4 shows that the total output of both products rises. It becomes possible, with trade, to consume at higher levels that would have been impossible without trade.

Consider the trading positions of the United States and Saudi Arabia after they have specialized in their areas of absolute advantage. If the United States can trade an amount of corn *less than* 320 bushels and receives in exchange an amount of oil *greater than* 80 barrels, it will have more of both goods than it did before trade. Similarly, if Saudi Arabia can trade an amount of oil less than 120 barrels and receive in exchange an amount of corn greater than 20 bushels, it will have more of both goods than it did before specialization and trade. Exhibit 3-5 illustrates the range of trades that would benefit both sides. Any trade where the United States exports more than 20 bushels of corn but less than 320 bushels of corn, and receives in exchange imports from Saudi Arabia at least 80 barrels of oil but no more than 120 barrels of oil, will benefit both sides. As a specific example, a trade where the United States exports 200 bushels of corn to Saudi Arabia and Saudi Arabia exports 100 barrels of oil to the United States would allow both countries to consume more of both goods than they could before specialized production and trade occurred.

Trade and Opportunity Cost

The underlying reason why trade benefits both sides is rooted in the concept of opportunity cost. If the United States wants to expand domestic production of oil in a world without trade, its opportunity cost (based on the numbers in Exhibit 3-2) is that it must give up 4 bushels of corn for every 1 additional barrel of oil. If the United States could find a way to give up *less than* 4 bushels of corn to receive 1 barrel of oil, it would be better off. Thus, any trade where the United States gives up less than 320 bushels of

The U.S. Economy, after Specialization, Will Benefit If It:	The Saudi Arabian Economy, after Specialization, Will Benefit If It:
Exports no more than 320 bushels of corn in exchange for	Imports at least 20 bushels of corn in exchange for
Imports of at least 80 barrels of oil	Exports of less than 120 barrels of oil

Exhibit 3-5 The Range of Trades That Benefit Both the United States and Saudi Arabia

corn to receive at least 80 barrels of oil—notice the 4:1 ratio—makes the United States better off. By specializing in corn production and then trading with Saudi Arabia for oil, the U.S. economy can possess more corn and oil at a cheaper opportunity cost than its own domestic production allows.

The same insight holds for Saudi Arabia. If Saudi Arabia wishes to expand domestic production of corn in a world without trade, then based on its opportunity costs (as shown in Exhibit 3-2) it must give up 6 barrels of oil for every 1 additional bushel of corn. If Saudi Arabia could find a way to give up less than 6 barrels of oil for an additional bushel of corn (or equivalently, to receive more than 1 bushel of corn for 6 units of oil), it would be better off. Thus, any trade where Saudi Arabia can export no more than 120 barrels of oil in exchange for at least 20 units of corn—notice again that the ratio of 120:20 is the country's domestic opportunity cost of 6:1—will make the country better off.

Cost is measured as opportunity cost. In this example, the opportunity cost of 1 bushel of corn is only ¼ barrel of oil in the United States, but the opportunity cost of 1 bushel of corn is 6 barrels of oil in Saudi Arabia. Similarly, the opportunity cost of 1 barrel of oil in the United States is 4 bushels of corn, but the opportunity cost of 1 barrel of oil in Saudi Arabia is 1/6 bushel of corn. In effect, trade lets each country take advantage of the lower opportunity cost of production in the other country. This example would reach the same general conclusion showing benefits from specialization and trade if the number of workers in the two economies was altered, or if the original starting point involved dividing up the labor in some way other than having half the workers producing each good.

Limitations of the Numerical Example

This demonstration of how both nations can benefit from specializing in their absolute advantage and trading has some limitations.

First, the example does not explain how the extra output of oil and corn will be divided up. It describes a range of trades that can benefit both sides, but it doesn't say who will receive what share of the total benefit. Perhaps the two countries will split the extra output equally. Perhaps the U.S. economy will get most of the extra output, and the Saudi economy only a little bit. Perhaps the reverse will be true. In the real economy, the price at which corn exchanges for oil will be determined by demand and supply (discussed in Chapter 4), which will lead to a specific price and quantity for each good. This example shows only that both countries *can* be better off with specialization and trade, not *how much* each country is better off.

Second, this example has only two hypothetical countries and two goods, while the real world has over 200 countries and tens of thousands of goods. However, the example remains useful as a model that illustrates a key underlying principle: Differences in opportunity costs can allow trade to benefit all participants.

Third, this example assumes that the opportunity costs of trading oil for corn production, or vice versa, are always the same and unvarying in both countries. This premise simplifies the calculations. But in the real world, countries will typically find that they have certain resources that are better-suited or worse-suited to producing oil or corn. Saudi Arabia has some relatively fertile land and some land where drilling for oil is more costly. Conversely, the United States has some areas of poor farmland, as well as areas where oil is accessible and close to the surface. In numerical examples with constant opportunity costs, it often makes sense to specialize in the production of just one product. But in the real world, it will make sense to give up only on the more

The First Wave of Globalization

A second wave of globalization began in the second half of the twentieth century. But the first wave of globalization started in the nineteenth century and lasted up to the beginning of World War I. Over that time, global exports as a share of global GDP rose from less than 1% of GDP in 1820 to 9% of GDP in 1913. As the Nobel Prize-winning economist Paul Krugman of Princeton University wrote in 1995:

> It is a late-twentieth-century conceit that we invented the global economy just yesterday. In fact, world markets achieved an impressive degree of integration during the second half of the nineteenth century. Indeed, if one wants a specific date for the beginning of a truly global economy, one might well choose 1869, the year in which both the Suez Canal and the Union Pacific railroad were completed. By the eve of the First World War steamships and railroads had created markets for standardized commodities, like wheat and wool, that were fully global in their reach. Even the global flow of information was better than modern observers, focused on electronic technology, tend to realize: the first submarine telegraph cable was laid under the Atlantic in 1858, and by 1900 all of the world's major economic regions could effectively communicate instantaneously.

This first wave of globalization crashed to a halt in the first half of the twentieth century. World War I severed many economic connections. During the Great Depression of the 1930s, many nations misguidedly tried to fix their own economies by reducing foreign trade with others. World War II further hindered international trade. Global flows of goods and financial capital rebuilt themselves only slowly after World War II. It was not until the early 1980s that global economic forces again became as important, relative to the size of the world economy, as they were before World War I.

costly ways of producing certain products, and the specialization in one product won't be so extreme.

A skeptic about the gains from international trade might start asking other questions at this point. What if one nation becomes dependent on the other for oil or food, and then the exporter cuts off the supply? What if oil workers in the United States lose jobs when oil is imported from Saudi Arabia and farmers in Saudi Arabia lose jobs when corn is imported from the United States? These questions are good ones and they will be taken up, along with many others questions, in the discussion of public policies about international trade in Chapter 6. But first, let's first continue painting the picture of how international trade can provide economic benefits.

Comparative Advantage

The concept of absolute advantage is based on the assumption that each nation has a cost advantage in producing a certain product. But what happens to the possibilities for trade if one country, typically a high-income country with well-educated workers, technologically advanced equipment, and the most up-to-date production processes, can produce all products more cheaply than a low-income country? If the high-income country has a cost advantage in all products, then it may seem as if the low-income country would have nothing to trade. However, one of the most powerful insights in economic analysis, developed by the famous English economist David Ricardo (1772–1823) early in the nineteenth century, points out that even when one country has an absolute advantage in all products, trade can still benefit both sides.

There are several different ways of presenting information that shows absolute advantage in producing at lower costs. Exhibit 3-2 showed the different quantities that a single worker could produce. Exhibit 3-5 shows the different number of workers needed to produce a single unit of quantity. Other alternatives would be to measure work with hours, instead of workers, and to say how many hours it takes to produce a unit of a good or how many units could be produced in an hour. Don't be confused by the different labels in these kinds of tables. Focus on the underlying economic meaning: which nation can produce a certain good more cheaply, which means with a lower level of inputs. If in a certain nation a single worker produces more of a product, relative to the other country, or if it takes fewer workers to produce a fixed amount of a product, relative to the other country, then that nation has an absolute advantage in producing that product.

CLEARING IT UP

Different Ways of Presenting Absolute Advantage

	United States	Mexico
Production	Amount of Labor	Amount of Labor
1,000 pairs of shoes	4 workers	5 workers
1,000 refrigerators	1 worker	4 workers

Exhibit 3-6   Identifying Comparative Advantage

It takes fewer workers in the United States (4) to produce 1,000 pairs of shoes than it does in Mexico (5). It also takes fewer workers in the United States (1) to produce 1,000 refrigerators than it does in Mexico (4). Thus, the United States has an absolute advantage in the production of both goods. However, the comparative advantage of the United States—where its absolute advantage is relatively greatest—lies in refrigerators. The comparative advantage of Mexico—where its absolute disadvantage is relatively least—lies in shoes.

Identifying Comparative Advantage

Consider the situation described in Exhibit 3-6 of trade between the United States and Mexico. In this example, it takes 4 U.S. workers to produce 1,000 pairs of shoes, but it takes 5 Mexican workers to do so. It takes 1 U.S. worker to produce 1,000 refrigerators, but it takes 4 Mexican workers to do so. In this example, the United States has an absolute advantage in productivity with regard to both shoes and refrigerators; that is, it takes fewer workers in the United States than in Mexico to produce both a given number of shoes and a given number of refrigerators. However, even in this case, Ricardo showed that both sides could benefit from trade.

Ricardo's clever insight was that even though the United States has an absolute advantage at producing both products with less labor, the United States does not produce both products more cheaply from an opportunity cost point of view. In Mexico, the opportunity cost of producing 1,000 extra pairs of shoes, and using the labor of 5 workers, means taking those 5 workers away from the production of refrigerators, where they would have produced 1,250 refrigerators. (Exhibit 3-6 shows that in Mexico it takes 4 workers to produce 1,000 refrigerators, so 5 workers would produce 1,250 refrigerators; that is, 5/4 × 1,000.) In the United States, the opportunity cost of producing an extra 1,000 pairs of shows involves the labor of four workers, and moving those four workers away from refrigerator production has an opportunity cost of 4,000 refrigerators (that is, one worker can produce 1,000 refrigerators in the United States, so 4 workers could produce 4,000). Measured in opportunity cost terms, it is cheaper to produce shoes in Mexico, where the opportunity cost is 1,250 refrigerators for every 1,000 shoes, and more expensive to produce shoes in the United States, where the opportunity cost of 1,000 pairs of shoes is 4,000 refrigerators.

Next consider the opportunity cost of producing refrigerators. Producing an extra 1,000 refrigerators in Mexico requires 4 workers. If those four workers are moved out of shoe production, the opportunity cost is 800 pairs of shoes (if it takes 5 Mexican workers to produce 1,000 pairs of shoes, than 4 workers can produce 800 shoes—4/5 × 1,000). Producing an extra 1,000 refrigerators in the United States, using one worker, would have an opportunity cost of only 250 pairs of shoes (if it takes 4 U.S. workers to make 1,000 pairs of shoes, then one worker can make 250 pairs). Measured in opportunity cost terms, producing 1,000 refrigerators is more expensive in Mexico, where it costs 800 pairs of shoes, and less expensive in the United States, where the opportunity cost is only 250 pairs of shoes.

A nation which has can produce at a lower cost *when measured in terms of opportunity cost* is said to have a **comparative advantage.** Even though the United States has an absolute advantage in needing fewer workers to produce a given quantity of either shoes or refrigerators, Mexico has a comparative advantage in production of shoes and the United States has a comparative advantage in the production of refrigerators. Comparative advantage identifies the area where a producer's absolute advantage is relatively greatest, or *where the producer's absolute disadvantage in productivity is relatively least.* The United States can produce 1,000 shoes with four-fifths as many workers as Mexico (4 versus 5), but can produce 1,000 refrigerators with only one-quarter as many workers (1 versus 4). Thus, the comparative advantage of the United States, where its absolute productivity advantage is relatively greatest, lies with refrigerators, and Mexico's comparative advantage, where its absolute productivity disadvantage is least, is in the production of shoes.

comparative advantage: The goods in which a nation has its greatest productivity advantage or its smallest productivity disadvantage; also, the goods that a nation can produce at a lower cost when measured in terms of opportunity cost.

Mutually Beneficial Trade with Comparative Advantage

When nations increase production in their area of comparative advantage and trade with each other, both sides can benefit. Again, the production possibility frontier offers a useful tool. Consider a situation where the United States and Mexico each has 40 workers. The tables under the figures in Exhibit 3-7 show the level of output for different divisions of labor, using the figures for the productivity of labor given in Exhibit 3-6. For example, if the United States divides its labor so that 40 workers are making shoes, then since it takes 4 workers in the United States to make 1,000 shoes, a total of 10,000 shoes will be produced (if 4 workers can make 1,000 shoes, then 40 workers will make 10,000 shoes). If the 40 workers in the United States are making refrigerators, and each worker can produce 1,000 refrigerators, then a total of 40,000 refrigerators will be produced. The choices from the tables are graphed on the production possibility frontiers in Exhibit 3-7. As always, the slope of the production possibility frontier for each country is determined by the opportunity costs as labor is transferred from production of shoes to production of refrigerators, or vice versa.

Let's say that in the situation before trade, each nation prefers to allocate half of its labor to production of each good, as shown at point A. Exhibit 3-8 shows the output of each good for each country and the total output for the two countries. Of course, both countries would prefer a choice like point B with more of both goods, but a choice like B that is above the production possibility frontier is impossible in a world without trade. (Choosing the halfway point is only to make a convenient example. The argument for how trade according to comparative advantage can benefit both parties works just the same if the nation's original choice is a point one-third of the way, or one-quarter of the way, or any choice between the endpoints of the production possibility frontier.)

Now, have each country transfer some amount of labor toward its area of comparative advantage. For example, the United States transfers 6 workers away from shoes and toward producing refrigerators. As a result, U.S. production of shoes decreases by 1,500 units (6/4 × 1,000), while its production of refrigerators increases by 6,000 (that is, 6/1 × 1,000). Mexico also moves production toward its area of comparative advantage, transferring 10 workers away from refrigerators and toward production of

Exhibit 3-7   Comparative Advantage with Production Possibility Frontiers

The tables show several points along the production possibilities frontiers for each country, based on the numbers for what workers produce in Exhibit 3-6 and assuming 40 workers for each country. In the absence of trade, each country would most prefer point A, given its production possibilities. While a point like B provides more of both goods, in a world without trade, a choice like B is impossible. Through specialization and trade, a point like B becomes possible for both countries, showing that both countries can benefit from trade.

(a) U.S. *PPF* (40 workers)

How many workers producing each good?	Output of shoes	Output of Refrigerators
40 to shoes, 0 to refrigerators	10,000 pairs	0 refrigerators
30 to shoes, 10 to refrigerators	7,500 pairs	10,000 refrigerators
20 to shoes, 20 to refrigerators	5,000 pairs	20,000 refrigerators
10 to shoes, 30 to refrigerators	2,500 pairs	30,000 refrigerators
0 to shoes, 40 to refrigerators	0 pairs	40,000 refrigerators

(b) Mexico *PPF* (40 workers)

How many workers producing each good?	Output of shoes	Output of Refrigerators
40 to shoes, 0 to refrigerators	8,000 pairs	0 refrigerators
30 to shoes, 10 to refrigerators	6,000 pairs	2,500 refrigerators
20 to shoes, 20 to refrigerators	4,000 pairs	5,000 refrigerators
10 to shoes, 30 to refrigerators	2,000 pairs	7,500 refrigerators
0 to shoes, 40 to refrigerators	0 pairs	10,000 refrigerators

Exhibit 3-8   Calculating Gains from Trade with Comparative Advantage

This table shows the total production of shoes and refrigerators before trade. It also shows total production after the United States transfers 6 workers from shoes to refrigerators and Mexico transfers 10 workers from refrigerators to shoes through specialization.

	Production before trade		Production after specialization	
	Shoes	Refrigerators	Shoes	Refrigerators
United States	5,000	20,000	5,000 − 1,500	20,000 + 6,000
Mexico	4,000	5,000	4,000 + 2,000	5,000 − 2,500
Total	9,000	25,000	9,500	28,500

In the example in the text, why have the United States move 6 workers from shoes to refrigerators, and why have Mexico move 10 workers from refrigerators and shoes? Why 6? Why 10?

CLEARING IT UP

Choosing Numbers So Comparative Advantage Examples Work

To show that specializing according to comparative advantage can benefit all parties, the shift in production must allow total combined production of both goods to increase. But here's a potential problem: If the United States shifts an equal amount of labor away from shoes that Mexico shifts toward shoes, then overall combined production of shoes will decline—because the U.S. economy has an absolute advantage in shoe production. Thus, Mexico must shift more labor toward shoes than the United States shifts away from shoes to make up for its absolute productivity advantage in shoes, so that overall combined production of shoes will increase. Having Mexico shift 10 workers toward shoes when the United States shifts 6 workers away from shoes will work for this purpose. So will any combination of numbers where the ratio of Mexican labor toward shoes to U.S. labor away from shoes is at least 5/4 to make up for the fact that it takes 5 workers in Mexico to produce the same number of shoes that takes 4 U.S. workers.

shoes. As a result, production of refrigerators in Mexico falls by 2,500 (10/4 × 1,000), but production of shoes increases by 2,000 pairs (10/5 × 1,000). Notice that when both countries shift toward their comparative advantage, their combined production of both goods rises, as shown in Exhibit 3-8. The reduction of shoe production by 1,500 pairs in the United States is more than offset by the gain of 2,000 pairs of shoes in Mexico, while the reduction of 2,500 refrigerators in Mexico is more than offset by the additional 6,000 refrigerators produced in the United States.

This numerical example illustrates the remarkable insight of comparative advantage: Even when one country has an absolute advantage in all goods and another country has an absolute disadvantage in all goods, both countries can still benefit from trade. Even though the United States has an absolute advantage in producing both refrigerators and shoes, it makes economic sense for the United States to specialize more in refrigerators, where it has a comparative advantage, and to import some shoes instead. Conversely, even though Mexico has an absolute disadvantage in both refrigerators and shoes, it can still play an active and productive role in world trade by focusing on its comparative advantage in shoes.

How Opportunity Cost Sets the Boundaries of Trade

This example shows that both parties can benefit from specializing in their comparative advantage and trading. By using the opportunity costs in this example it is possible to identify the range of possible trades that would benefit each side.

Mexico started out before specialization and trade by producing 4,000 pairs of shoes and 5,000 refrigerators. Then in the numerical example given, Mexico shifted production toward its comparative advantage and produced 6,000 shoes but only 2,500 refrigerators. Thus, if Mexico can export no more than 2,000 pairs of shoes in exchange for imports of at least 2,500 refrigerators, then it will be able to consume more of both goods than before trade and it will be unambiguously better off. Conversely, the United States started off before specialization and trade producing 5,000 pairs of shoes and 20,000 refrigerators. In the numerical example given, it then shifted toward comparative advantage, producing only 3,500 shoes but 26,000 refrigerators. If the United States can export no more than 6,000 refrigerators in exchange for imports of at least 1,500 pairs of shoes, then it will be able to consume more of both goods and will be unambiguously better off. The range of trades that can benefit both nations is shown in Exhibit 3-9. For

The U.S. Economy, after Specialization, Will Benefit If It:	The Mexican Economy, after Specialization, Will Benefit If It:
Exports Fewer than 6,000 refrigerators in exchange for	*Imports* at least 2,500 refrigerators in exchange for
Imports of at least 1,500 pairs of shoes	*Exports* of no more than 2,000 pairs of shoes

Exhibit 3-9 The Range of Trades That Benefit Both the United States and Mexico

example, a trade where the U.S. exports 4,000 refrigerators to Mexico in exchange for 1,800 pairs of shoes would benefit both sides, in the sense that both countries would be able to consume more of both goods than in a world without trade.

Trade allows each country to take advantage of lower opportunity costs in the other country. If Mexico wants to produce more refrigerators without trade, it must face its domestic opportunity costs and reduce shoe production. But if Mexico instead produces more shoes and then trades for refrigerators produced in the United States, where the opportunity cost of producing refrigerators is lower, Mexico can in effect take advantage of the lower opportunity cost in the United States for producing refrigerators. Conversely, when the United States specializes in its comparative advantage of refrigerator production and trades for shoes produced in Mexico, international trade allows the United States to take advantage of the lower opportunity cost of shoe production in Mexico.

The theory of comparative advantage shows that the gains from international trade do not just result from the absolute advantage of producing at lower cost, but also from pursuing comparative advantage and producing at a lower opportunity cost.

Comparative Advantage Goes Camping

To build a greater intuitive understanding of how comparative advantage can benefit all parties, set aside examples that involve national economies for a moment and consider the situation of a group of friends who decide to go camping together. The friends have a wide range of skills and experiences, but one person in particular, Jethro, has done lots of camping before and is a great athlete besides. Jethro has an absolute advantage in all aspects of camping: he is faster at carrying a backpack, gathering firewood, paddling a canoe, setting up tents, making a meal, and washing up. So here's the question: Because Jethro has an absolute productivity advantage in everything, should he do all the work?

Of course not. Even if Jethro is willing to work like a mule while everyone else sits around, he still has only 24 hours in a day. If everyone sits around and waits for Jethro to do everything, not only will Jethro be an unhappy camper, but there won't be much output for his group of six friends to consume. The theory of comparative advantage suggests that everyone will benefit if they figure out their areas of comparative advantage; that is, the area of camping where their productivity disadvantage is least, compared to Jethro. For example, it may be that Jethro is 80% faster at building fires and cooking meals than anyone else, but only 20% faster at gathering firewood and 10% faster at setting up tents. In that case, Jethro should focus on building fires and making meals, and others should attend to the other tasks, each according to where their productivity disadvantage is smallest. If the campers coordinate their efforts according to comparative advantage, they can all gain.

The Power of the Comparative Advantage Example

The two-country, two-good numerical illustration of comparative advantage, like the example of absolute advantage, has its limitations. While the example shows that both sides can benefit from specialization according to comparative advantage and trade, it doesn't explain exactly how much extra production will occur, or how the gains from trade will be divided up. It is (again) an example with two goods and two countries. It assumes production possibility frontiers that are straight lines representing constant trade-offs, rather than outward-bending curves with varying trade-offs.

But these limitations are all contained in one basic point: this example is a model, not a literal description of the U.S. or the Mexican economy. The power of a model is to reveal the key features of how something works. The model of comparative advantage shows why even the most productive country in the world and the least productive country can both gain from trading with each other, if they each focus on the products where they possess a comparative advantage. Even the most productive country will have some product where its absolute advantage is greatest. Even the country with an absolute productivity disadvantage in every single product will have an area where its absolute disadvantage is smallest.

Comparative advantage ranks among the most sophisticated insights in all of economics; indeed, an understanding of comparative advantage is one way of distinguishing economists from non-economists.

Intra-industry Trade between Similar Economies

Absolute and comparative advantage explain a great deal about patterns of global trade. For example, they help to explain the patterns noted at the start of this chapter, like why you may be eating fresh fruit from Chile or Mexico, or why lower productivity regions like Africa and Latin America are able to sell a substantial proportion of their exports to higher productivity regions like the European Union and North America. But absolute and comparative advantage, at least at first glance, do not seem especially well-suited to explain other common patterns of international trade.

The Prevalence of Intra-industry Trade between Similar Economies

The theory of comparative advantage suggests that trade should happen between economies with large differences in their opportunity costs of production. But roughly half of all world trade involves shipping goods between the fairly similar high-income economies of the United States, Canada, the European Union, Japan, Australia and New Zealand. About half of U.S. trade is with the other high-income economies of the world, like Canada, Europe, and Japan, as shown in Exhibit 3-10, rather than with the much more different economies of Latin America or Africa.

Moreover, the theories of absolute and comparative advantage suggest that each economy should specialize to a degree in certain products, and then exchange those products. But a high proportion of trade is **intra-industry trade**—that is, trade of goods within the same industry. Exhibit 3-11 shows some of the largest categories of U.S. exports and imports. In all of these categories, the United States is both a substantial exporter and a substantial importer of goods from the same industry. For example, in 2008 the United States exported $277 billion of transportation equipment, but imported

intra-industry trade:
International trade of goods within the same industry.

	U.S. Exports Go to . . .	U.S. Imports Come from . . .
European Union	21.1%	17.4%
Canada	20.3%	16.4%
Japan	5.1%	6.6%
Mexico	11.7%	15.6%
China	5.4%	10.1%

Exhibit 3-10 Where U.S. Exports Go and U.S. Imports Originate (2008) About half of U.S. trade is with similar high-income nations of the world, like Canada, the countries of the European Union, and Japan.

Exhibit 3-11 Some Intra-Industry U.S. Exports and Imports in 2008

Many of the leading U.S. exports, as measured by these broad categories, are also leading U.S. imports. This pattern illustrates the importance of intra-industry trade for the U.S. economy.

Some U.S. Exports	Quantity of Exports (billions of dollars)	Quantity of Imports (billions of dollars)
Agricultural commodities	$37	$53
Food	$34	$38
Manufacturing	$1,585	$911
Minerals and ores	$8	$11
Chemicals	$160	$147
Transportation equipment	$277	$202
Machinery (except electrical)	$121	$122
Electrical equipment	$67	$33
Computers and electronic products	$312	$136

$202 billion of transportation equipment. About 60% of U.S. trade and 60% of European trade is intra-industry trade.

Why do similar economies engage in intra-industry trade? What can be the economic benefit of having workers of fairly similar skills making cars, computers, machinery and other products which are then shipped in directions across the oceans to and from the United States, the European Union, and Japan? There are two reasons: how the division of labor leads to learning, innovation, and unique skills; and economies of scale.

Gains from Specialization and Learning

Consider the category of "machinery," where the U.S. economy has considerable intra-industry trade. Machinery comes in many varieties, so the U.S. may be exporting machinery for manufacturing with wood, but importing machinery for photographic processing. The underlying reason why a country like the United States, Japan, or Germany produces one kind of machinery rather than another is usually not related to U.S., German, or Japanese firms and workers having generally higher or lower skills—but just that in working on very specific and particular products, firms in certain countries have developed unique and different skills.

Specialization in the world economy can be very finely split. In fact, recent years have seen a trend in international trade called **splitting up the value chain.**

splitting up the value chain: When many of the different stages of producing a good happen in different geographic locations.

Exhibit 3-12
Economies of Scale

Production Plant S, which produces a small level of output 30, has an average cost of production of $30 per toaster oven. Production Plant M, which produces at a medium level of output 50, has an average cost of production of $20 per toaster oven. Production Plant L, which produces at a large level of output 150, has an average cost of production of only $10 per toaster oven. Production Plant V, which produces at the very high level of output of 200, would still have an average cost of production of $10 per toaster oven. Thus, production plant M can produce toaster ovens more cheaply than plant S because of economies of scale, and plants L or V can produce more cheaply than S or M because of economies of scale. However, the economies of scale end at an output level of 150. Plant V, despite being larger, cannot produce more cheaply on average than plant L.

The "value chain" describes how a good is produced in stages; for example, the value chain for making a toaster oven would include making metal, plastic, elements that provide the heat, electrical cords, designing how the parts will fit together, assembly of the toaster ovens, packaging, shipping, and selling in a retail store. Thanks in large part to improvements in technology for communication, sharing of information, and transportation, it has become easier to split up the value chain so that instead of being done in a single large factory, all of these steps can be split up among different firms operating in different places and even different countries. Because of splitting up the value chain, international trade often doesn't involve whole finished products like automobiles or refrigerators being traded between nations. Instead, it involves shipping more specialized goods like, say, automobile dashboards or the shelving that fits inside refrigerators. Intra-industry trade between similar countries produces economic gains because it allows workers and firms to learn and innovate on particular products—and often to focus on very particular parts of the value chain.

Economies of Scale, Competition, Variety

A second broad reason that intra-industry trade between similar nations produces economic gains involves economies of scale. The concept of economies of scale, as introduced in Chapter 1, means that as the scale of output goes up, average costs of production decline—at least up to a point. Exhibit 3-12 illustrates economies of scale for a plant producing toaster ovens. The horizontal axis of the figure shows the quantity of production by a certain firm or at a certain manufacturing plant. The vertical axis measures the average cost of production. Thus, Production Plant S, which produces a small level of output 30, has an average cost of production of $30 per toaster oven. Production Plant M, which produces at a medium level of output 50, has an average cost of production of $20 per toaster oven. Production Plant L, which produces at a large level of output 150, has an average cost of production of only $10 per toaster oven. However, Production Plant V, which produces at the very high level of output of 200, would still have an average cost of production of $10 per toaster oven. In this example, a small or medium plant, like S or M, will not be able to compete in the market with a large or a very large plant like L or V, because the firm that operates L or V will be able to produce and sell at a lower cost. In this example, economies of scale operate up to point L, but beyond point L to V, additional scale of production does not continue to reduce average costs of production. Economies of scale are a common feature in many industries.

The concept of economies of scale becomes especially relevant to international trade when one or two large producers could supply the entire country because of economies of scale. For example, a single large automobile factory could probably supply all the cars purchased in a smaller economy like the United Kingdom or Belgium in a given year. However, if a country has only one or two large factories producing cars, and no international trade, then consumers in that country would have relatively little choice between kinds of cars (other than the color of the paint and other nonessential options), and little or no competition will exist between different car manufacturers.

International trade provides a way to combine the lower average production costs of economies of scale and still have competition and variety for consumers. Large automobile factories in different countries can make and sell their products around the world. If the U.S. automobile market was made up of only General Motors, Ford, and Chrysler, the level of competition and consumer choice would be quite a lot lower than when the U.S. carmakers must face competition from Toyota, Honda, Suzuki, Fiat, Mazda, Mitsubishi, Nissan, Volkswagen, Kia, Hyundai, BMW, Subaru and others. Greater competition brings with it innovation and responsiveness to what consumers want. America's car producers make far better cars now than they did several decades ago and much of the reason is competitive pressure, especially from East Asian and European carmakers.

Dynamic Comparative Advantage

The sources of gains from intra-industry trade between similar economies—namely, the learning that comes from a high degree of specialization and splitting up the value chain and from economies of scale—do not contradict the earlier theory of comparative advantage. Instead, they help to broaden the concept of comparative advantage.

In intra-industry trade, the level of worker productivity isn't determined by climate or mineral deposits. It isn't even determined by the general level of education or skill. Instead, the level of worker productivity is determined by how firms engage in specific learning about specialized products, including taking advantage of economies of scale to the extent possible. In this vision, comparative advantage can be dynamic—that is, it can evolve and change over time as new specific skills are developed and as the value chain is split up in new ways. This line of thinking also suggests that countries are not destined to have the same comparative advantage forever, but must instead be flexible in response to ongoing changes in comparative advantage.

Intra-industry trade between similar trading partners allows the gains from learning and innovation that arise when firms and workers specializing in the production of a certain product (and with the trend toward splitting up the value chain, this learning can become very specialized, indeed). It also allows the gains from using economies of scale for large-scale production, while avoiding the problem of having only one large supplier in a market, and instead allowing fierce competition between different producers to offer the combination of variety, price and quantity that will satisfy their customers.

The Size of Benefits from International Trade

It's hard to measure the economic gains from international trade with precision. After all, measuring the gains from trade would require comparing the world economy with international trade with a world economy that did not have international trade—which means figuring out what the world economy would look like if international trade did not exist. Such calculations are bound to be controversial.

However, estimating the gains from expanding trade is more practical. For example, the nations of the world meet together through the World Trade Organization (WTO) to negotiate ways in which they can reduce government taxes or regulations that have the effect of limiting trade. Negotiations in the WTO happen in "rounds," where all countries negotiate one agreement to encourage trade, then take a year or two off, and then start negotiating a new agreement. It often takes 7–10 years from beginning to end of a round of WTO negotiations. The current round of negotiations is called the "Doha round" because it was officially launched in Doha, the capital city in the country of Qatar, in November 2001. In 2009, economists from the World Bank summarized recent research and found that the Doha round of negotiations would increase the size of the world economy by $160 billion to $385 billion per year, depending on the precise deal that ended up being negotiated. In the context of a global economy which currently produces more than $30 trillion of goods and services each year, this amount is not huge: it's an increase of 1% or less in the global economy. But before dismissing the gains from trade too quickly, it's worth remembering four points.

First, a gain of a few hundred billion dollars is enough money to deserve attention! Moreover, remember that this increase is not a one-time event; it would persist each year into the future.

Second, this estimate of $160 billion to $385 billion measures only the expected gains from the most recent round of trade negotiations. In other words, it measures only the economic gains from expanding international trade somewhat from the levels it had already reached in the mid-2000s, before the Doha round of trade negotiations was finalized. Measuring the gains from all international trade would be a multiple of this number.

Third, this estimate of gains may be on the low side because some of the gains from trade are not measured especially well in economic statistics. For example, while it is possible to estimate the economic gains from taking advantage of comparative advantage or economies of scale, it is difficult to measure the potential advantages to consumers of having a variety of products available and a greater degree of competition among producers. Perhaps the most important unmeasured factor is that trade between countries, especially when firms are splitting up the value chain of production, often involves a transfer of knowledge that can involve skills in production, technology, management, finance, and law. These transfers of knowledge may be especially important in helping low-income countries of the world improve their standard of living.

Fourth, the gains from expanding trade are probably most important for the low-income economies in the world. In some ways, the giant U.S. economy has less need for international trade, because it can already take advantage of internal trade within its economy. The United States has a variety of different climates, natural resources, and geographic areas where workers are more skilled or less skilled. It is a large enough economy that firms can become extremely specialized and focused on producing small slices of the value chain. In the huge U.S. economy, large firms can take advantage of economies of scale and still compete against each other within the U.S. economy.

However, many smaller national economies around the world, in regions like Latin America, Africa, the Middle East, and Asia, have much more limited possibilities for trade inside their countries or their immediate regions. Their possibilities for gains from purely internal trade will be smaller. Without international trade, they may have little ability to benefit from comparative advantage, slicing up the value chain, or economies of scale. Moreover, smaller economies often have fewer competitive firms making goods within their economy and thus firms have less pressure from other firms to provide the goods and prices that consumers want.

The economic gains from expanding international trade are measured in hundreds of billions of dollars and the gains from international trade as a whole probably reach well into the trillions of dollars. The potential for gains from trade may be especially high among the smaller and lower-income countries of the world.

From Interpersonal to International Trade

Most people find it easy to believe that they personally would not be better off if they tried to grow and process all of their own food, to make all of their own clothes, to build their own car and house from scratch, and so on. Instead, we all benefit from living in economies where people and firms can specialize and trade with each other.

This same argument applies at the level of the community. Most of us, whether we live in small towns or suburbs or large cities, would find it rather difficult if our town or city tried to be self-sufficient—for example, to produce all of its own food within the city limits, along with clothing, health care, housing, and all inputs and machinery that are used in producing these goods. There are clear economic gains when people and firms from one community trade with people and firms from other communities.

This same argument continues to apply at the level of states or provinces. The people of Vermont or New Mexico, for example, would find that their standard of living suffered considerably if they attempted to consume only what was produced inside the boundaries of their state, without trading with California, Texas, New York, and all the other states.

The benefits of trade do not stop at national boundaries, either. Chapter 1 explained that the division of labor could increase output for three reasons: workers with different characteristics can specialize in the types of production where they have an advantage (which this chapter has spelled out as comparative and absolute advantage); firms and workers who specialize in a certain product become more productive with learning and practice; and economies of scale. These three reasons apply from the individual and community level right up to the international level. If it makes sense to you that interpersonal, inter-community trade and inter-state trade offer economic gains, it should make sense that international trade offers gains, too.

International trade currently involves about $20 trillion worth of goods and services thundering around the globe. Any economic force of that size, even if it confers overall benefits, is certain to cause disruption and controversy. This chapter has only made the case that trade brings economic benefits. Later chapters, especially Chapter 6, will discuss in detail the public policy arguments over whether to restrict international trade.

Key Concepts and Summary

1. A country has an **absolute advantage** in those products in which it has a productivity edge over other countries.

2. Two countries that each have an absolute advantage in different products can gain from specializing (at least to some extent) in the product where they have an absolute advantage and then trading.

3. A country has a **comparative advantage** where its cost of production, measured in opportunity cost terms, is lowest. Equivalently, a country has a comparative advantage in whatever product where either its absolute advantage is relatively greatest or where its absolute disadvantage is relatively least.

4. Two countries can benefit from specializing (at least to some extent) in the product where each has a comparative advantage and then trading with each other. This statement holds true even if one of the countries has an absolute advantage in both products.

5. A large share of global trade happens between high-income economies that are quite similar in having well-educated workers and advanced technology. These countries practice **intra-industry trade,** in which they import and export the same products at the same time, like cars, machinery, and computers.

6. In the case of intra-industry trade between similar economies, the gains from trade come from specialized learning in very particular tasks and from economies of scale.

7. The gains of international trade are very large, especially for smaller countries, but can be difficult to measure with precision.

Review Questions

1. What is absolute advantage?

2. In what situations does absolute advantage provide a reason for gains from trade?

3. What is comparative advantage? Explain in two ways, first using the idea of opportunity cost and second using the idea of relatively large or small absolute advantages and absolute disadvantages.

4. Is it possible to have an absolute advantage in the production of a certain good but not to have a comparative advantage in the production of that good? Explain.

5. Is it possible to have a comparative advantage in the production of a good but not to have an absolute advantage? Explain.

6. In what situations does comparative advantage provide a reason for gains from trade?

7. What is intra-industry trade?

8. What are the two main sources of economic gains from intra-industry trade?

9. What is splitting up the value chain?

10. Why might intra-industry trade seem surprising from the point of view of comparative advantage? How does intra-industry trade fit with the idea of comparative advantage?

11. Are the gains from international trade more likely to be relatively more important to larger or smaller countries?

Demand and Supply

W hen people talk about prices, the discussion often takes a judgmental tone. A bidder in an auction pays thousands of dollars for a dress once worn by Diana, Princess of Wales. A collector spends thousands of dollars for some drawings by John Lennon of the Beatles. Mouths gape. Surely such purchases are a waste of money? But when economists talk about prices, they are less interested in making judgments than in gaining a practical understanding of what determines prices and why prices change. In 1933, the great British economist Joan Robinson (1903–1983) explained how economists perceive price:

> The point may be put like this: You see two men, one of whom is giving a banana to the other, and is taking a penny from him. You ask, How is it that a banana costs a penny rather than any other sum? The most obvious line of attack on this question is to break it up into two fresh questions: How does it happen that the one man will take a penny for a banana? and: How does it happen that the other man will give a penny for a banana? In short, the natural thing is to divide up the problem under two heads: Supply and Demand.

As a contemporary example, consider a price often listed on large signs beside well-traveled roads: the price of a gallon of gasoline. Why was the average price of gasoline in the United States $1.77 per gallon in January 2009? Why did the price for gasoline rise to $2.60 per gallon six months later by June 2009? To explain why prices are at a certain level and why that level changes over time, economic analysis focuses on the determinants of what gasoline buyers are willing to pay and what gasoline sellers are willing to accept. For example, the price of a gallon of gasoline in June of a given year is nearly always higher than the price in January of that year; over recent decades, gasoline prices in midsummer have averaged about 10 cents per gallon more than their midwinter low. The likely reason is that people want to drive more in the summer, and thus they are willing to pay more for gas at that time. However, in 2009, gasoline prices rose by much more than the average winter-to-summer rise, which suggests that other factors related to those who buy gasoline and firms that sell it changed during those six months, too.

This chapter introduces the economic model of demand and supply. The discussion begins by examining how demand and supply determine the price and the quantity sold in markets for goods and services, and how changes in demand and supply lead to changes in prices and quantities. Then in Chapter 5, the very same demand and supply model is applied to markets for labor and financial capital. In Chapter 6, the same supply and demand model is applied to international trade. In situation after situation, in different places around the world, across different cultures, even reaching back into history, the demand and supply model offers a useful framework for thinking about what determines the prices and quantities of what is bought and sold.

Demand, Supply, and Equilibrium in Markets for Goods and Services

Markets for goods and services include everything from accounting services, air travel, and apples to zinc, zinfandel wine, and zucchini. Let's first focus on what economists mean by demand, what they mean by supply, and then how demand and supply interact in an economic model of the market.

Demand for Goods and Services

Economists use the term **demand** to refer to a relationship between price and the quantity demanded. Price is what a buyer pays (or the seller receives) for a unit of the specific good or service. **Quantity demanded** refers to the total number of units that are purchased at that price. A rise in price of a good or service almost always decreases the quantity demanded of that good or service; conversely, a fall in price will increase the quantity demanded. When the price of a gallon of gasoline goes up, for example, people look for ways to reduce their purchases of gasoline by combining several errands, commuting by carpool or mass transit, or taking weekend or vacation trips by car close to home. Economists refer to the relationship that a higher price leads to a lower quantity demanded as the **law of demand.**

Exhibit 4-1 gives an example in the market for gasoline. The table which shows the quantity demanded at each price is called a **demand schedule.** Price in this case is measured per gallon of gasoline. The quantity demanded is measured in millions of gallons over some time period (for example, per day or per year) and over some geographic area (like a state or a country). A **demand curve** shows the relationship between price and quantity demanded on a graph, with quantity on the horizontal axis and the price per gallon on the vertical axis. The demand schedule shown by the table and the demand curve shown on the graph are two ways of describing the same relationship between price and quantity demanded.

Each individual good or service needs to be graphed on its own demand curve, because it wouldn't make sense to graph the quantity of apples and the quantity of oranges on the same diagram. Demand curves will appear somewhat different for each product; for example, they may appear relatively steep or flat, or they may be straight or curved. But nearly all demand curves share the fundamental similarity that they

demand: A relationship between price and the quantity demanded of a certain good or service.

quantity demanded: The total number of units of a good or service purchased at a certain price.

law of demand: The common relationship that a higher price leads to a lower quantity demanded of a certain good or service.

demand schedule: A table that shows a range of prices for a certain good or service and the quantity demanded at each price.

demand curve: A line that shows the relationship between price and quantity demanded of a certain good or service on a graph, with quantity on the horizontal axis and the price on the vertical axis.

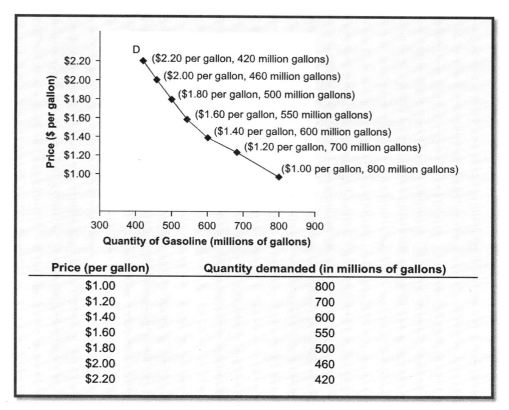

Price (per gallon)	Quantity demanded (in millions of gallons)
$1.00	800
$1.20	700
$1.40	600
$1.60	550
$1.80	500
$2.00	460
$2.20	420

Exhibit 4-1   A Demand Curve for Gasoline

The table that shows quantity demanded of gasoline at each price is called a demand schedule. The demand schedule shows that as price rises, quantity demanded decreases. These points are then graphed on the figure, and the line connecting them is the demand curve D. The downward slope of the demand curve again illustrates the pattern that as price rises, quantity demanded decreases. This pattern is called the law of demand.

slope down from left to right. In this way, demand curves embody the law of demand; as the price increases, the quantity demanded decreases, and conversely, as the price decreases, the quantity demanded increases.

Supply of Goods and Services

When economists talk about **supply,** they are referring to a relationship between price received for each unit sold and the **quantity supplied,** which is the total number of units sold in the market at a certain price. A rise in price of a good or service almost always leads to an increase in the quantity supplied of that good or service, while a fall in price will decrease the quantity supplied. When the price of gasoline rises, for example, profit-seeking firms are encouraged to expand exploration for oil reserves; to carry out additional drilling for oil; to make new investments in pipelines and oil tankers to bring the oil to plants where it can be refined into gasoline; to build new oil refineries; to purchase additional pipelines and trucks to ship the gasoline to gas stations; and to open more gas stations or to keep existing gas stations open longer hours. The

supply: A relationship between price and the quantity supplied of a certain good or service.

quantity supplied: The total number of units of a good or service sold at a certain price.

In economic terminology, supply is not the same as quantity supplied. When economists refer to supply, they mean the relationship between a range of prices and the quantities supplied at those prices, a relationship that can be illustrated with a supply curve or a supply schedule. When economists refer to quantity supplied, they often mean only a certain point on the supply curve, or sometimes, they are referring to the horizontal axis of the supply curve or one column of the supply schedule.

Clearing It Up

Supply Is Not the Same as Quantity Supplied

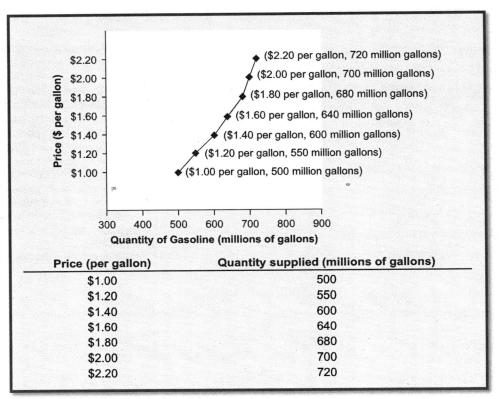

Price (per gallon)	Quantity supplied (millions of gallons)
$1.00	500
$1.20	550
$1.40	600
$1.60	640
$1.80	680
$2.00	700
$2.20	720

Exhibit 4-2   A Supply Curve for Gasoline

The supply schedule is the table that shows quantity supplied of gasoline at each price. As price rises, quantity supplied also increases. The supply curve S is created by graphing the points from the supply schedule and then connecting them. The upward slope of the supply curve illustrates the pattern that a higher price leads to a higher quantity supplied—a pattern that is common enough to be called the law of supply.

pattern that a higher price is associated with a greater quantity supplied is so common that economists have named it the **law of supply.**

Exhibit 4-2 illustrates the law of supply, again using the market for gasoline as an example. A **supply schedule** is a table that shows the quantity supplied at a range of different prices. Again, price is measured per gallon of gasoline and quantity demanded is measured in millions of gallons. A **supply curve** is a graphical illustration of the relationship between price, shown on the vertical axis, and quantity, shown on the horizontal axis. The supply schedule and the supply curve are just two different ways of showing the same information. Notice that the horizontal and vertical axes on the graph for the supply curve are the same as for the demand curve.

Just as each product has its own demand curve, each product has its own supply curve. The shape of supply curves will vary somewhat according to the product: steeper, flatter, straighter, or curved. But nearly all supply curves share a basic similarity: they slope up from left to right. In that way, the supply curve illustrates the law of supply: as the price rises, the quantity supplied increases, and conversely, as the price falls, the quantity supplied decreases.

law of supply: The common relationship that a higher price is associated with a greater quantity supplied.

supply schedule: A table that shows a range of prices for a good or service and the quantity supplied at each price.

supply curve: A line that shows the relationship between price and quantity supplied on a graph, with quantity supplied on the horizontal axis and price on the vertical axis.

Equilibrium—Where Demand and Supply Cross

Because the graphs for demand and supply curves both have price on the vertical axis and quantity on the horizontal axis, the demand curve and supply curve for a particular good or service can appear on the same graph. Together, demand and supply determine the price and the quantity that will be bought and sold in a market.

Exhibit 4-3 illustrates the interaction of demand and supply in the market for gasoline. The demand curve D is identical to Exhibit 4-1. The supply curve S is identical to Exhibit 4-2. When one curve slopes down, like demand, and another curve slopes up, like supply, the curves intersect at some point.

In every economics course you will ever take, when two lines on a diagram cross, this intersection means something! The point where the supply curve S and the demand curve D cross, designated by point E in Exhibit 4-3, is called the equilibrium. The **equilibrium price** is defined as the price where quantity demanded is equal to quantity supplied. The **equilibrium quantity** is the quantity where quantity demanded and quantity supplied are equal at a certain price. In Exhibit 4-3, the equilibrium price is $1.40 per gallon of gasoline and the equilibrium quantity is 600 million gallons. If you had only the demand and supply schedules, and not the graph, it would be easy to find the equilibrium by looking for the price level on the tables where the quantity demanded and the quantity supplied are equal.

The word equilibrium means "balance." If a market is balanced at its **equilibrium** price and quantity, then it has no reason to move away from that point. However, if a market is not balanced at equilibrium, then economic pressures arise to move toward the equilibrium price and the equilibrium quantity.

equilibrium price: The price where quantity demanded is equal to quantity supplied.

equilibrium quantity: The quantity at which quantity demanded and quantity supplied are equal at a certain price.

equilibrium: The combination of price and quantity where there is no economic pressure from surpluses or shortages that would cause price or quantity to shift.

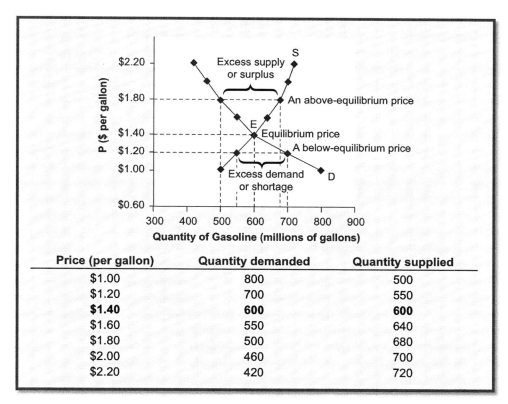

Price (per gallon)	Quantity demanded	Quantity supplied
$1.00	800	500
$1.20	700	550
$1.40	**600**	**600**
$1.60	550	640
$1.80	500	680
$2.00	460	700
$2.20	420	720

Exhibit 4-3 Demand and Supply for Gasoline

The demand curve D and the supply curve S intersect at the equilibrium point E, with a price of $1.40 and a quantity of 600. The equilibrium is the only price where quantity demanded is equal to quantity supplied. At a price above equilibrium like $1.80, quantity supplied of 680 exceeds the quantity demanded of 500, so there is excess supply or a surplus. At a price below equilibrium such as $1.20, quantity demanded of 700 exceeds quantity supplied of 550, so there is excess demand or a shortage.

Imagine, for example, that the price of a gallon of gasoline was above the equilibrium price; that is, instead of $1.40 per gallon, the price is $1.80 per gallon. This above-equilibrium price is illustrated by the dashed horizontal line at the price of $1.80 in Exhibit 4-3. At this higher price of $1.80, the quantity demanded drops from the equilibrium quantity of 600 to 500. This decline in quantity reflects how people and businesses react to the higher price by seeking out ways to use less gasoline, like sharing rides to work, taking mass transit, and avoiding faraway vacation destinations. Moreover, at this higher price of $1.80, the quantity supplied of gasoline rises from the 600 to 680, as the higher price provides incentives for gasoline producers to expand their output. At this above-equilibrium price, there is **excess supply**, or a **surplus**; that is, the quantity supplied exceeds the quantity demanded at the given price. With a surplus, gasoline accumulates at gas stations, in tanker trucks, in pipelines, and at oil refineries. This accumulation puts pressure on gasoline sellers. If a surplus of gasoline remains unsold, those firms involved in making and selling gasoline are not receiving enough cash to pay their workers and to cover their expenses. In this situation, at least some gasoline producers and sellers will be tempted to cut prices, because it's better to sell at a lower price than not to sell at all. Once some sellers start cutting gasoline prices, others will follow so that they won't lose sales to the earlier price-cutters. These price reductions in turn will stimulate a higher quantity demanded. Thus, if the price is above the equilibrium level, incentives built into the structure of demand and supply will create pressures for the price to fall toward the equilibrium.

excess supply: When at the existing price, quantity supplied exceeds the quantity demanded; also called a "surplus."

surplus: When at the existing price, quantity supplied exceeds the quantity demanded; also called "excess supply."

Now suppose that the price is below its equilibrium level at $1.20 per gallon, as shown by the dashed horizontal line at this price in Exhibit 4-3. At this lower price, the quantity demanded increases from 600 to 700 as drivers take longer trips, spend more minutes warming up their car in the driveway in wintertime, stop sharing rides to work, and buy larger cars that get fewer miles to the gallon. However, the below-equilibrium price reduces gasoline producers' incentives to produce and sell gasoline, and the quantity supplied of gasoline falls from 600 to 550. When the price is below equilibrium, there is **excess demand**, or a **shortage**; that is, at the given price the quantity demanded, which has been stimulated by the lower price, now exceeds the quantity supplied, which had been depressed by the lower price. In this situation, eager gasoline buyers mob the gas stations, only to find many stations running short of fuel. Oil companies and gas stations recognize that they have an opportunity to make higher profits by selling what gasoline they have at a higher price. As a result, the price increases toward the equilibrium level.

excess demand: At the existing price, the quantity demanded exceeds the quantity supplied, also called "shortage."

shortage: At the existing price, the quantity demanded exceeds the quantity supplied, also called "excess demand."

Shifts in Demand and Supply for Goods and Services

A demand curve shows how quantity demanded changes as the price rises or falls. A supply curve shows how quantity supplied changes as the price rises or falls. But what happens when factors other than price influence quantity demanded and quantity supplied? For example, what if demand for, say, vegetarian food becomes popular with more consumers? Or what if the supply of, say, diamonds rises not because of any change in price, but because companies discover several new diamond mines? A change in price leads to a different point on a specific demand curve or a supply curve, but a shift in some economic factor other than price can cause the entire demand curve or supply curve to shift.

The *Ceteris Paribus* Assumption

A demand curve or a supply curve is a relationship between two and only two variables: quantity on the horizontal axis and price on the vertical axis. Thus, the implicit assumption behind a demand curve or a supply curve is that no other relevant economic factors are changing. Economists refer to this assumption as *ceteris paribus,* a Latin phrase meaning "other things being equal." Any given demand or supply curve is based on the *ceteris paribus* assumption that all else is held equal. If all else is not held equal, then the demand or supply curve itself can shift.

ceteris paribus: Other things being equal.

An Example of a Shifting Demand Curve

The original demand curve D_0 in Exhibit 4-4 shows at point Q that at a price of $20,000 per car, the quantity of cars demanded would be 18 million. The original demand curve D_0 also shows how the quantity of cars demanded would change as a result of a higher or lower price; for example, if the price of a car rose to $22,000, the quantity demanded would decrease to 17 million, as at point R.

The original demand curve D_0, like every demand curve, is based on the *ceteris paribus* assumption that no other economically relevant factors change. But now imagine that the economy expands in a way that raises the incomes of many people. As a result of the higher income levels, a **shift in demand** occurs, which means that compared to the original demand curve D_0, a different quantity of cars will now be demanded at every

shift in demand: When a change in some economic factor related to demand causes a different quantity to be demanded at every price.

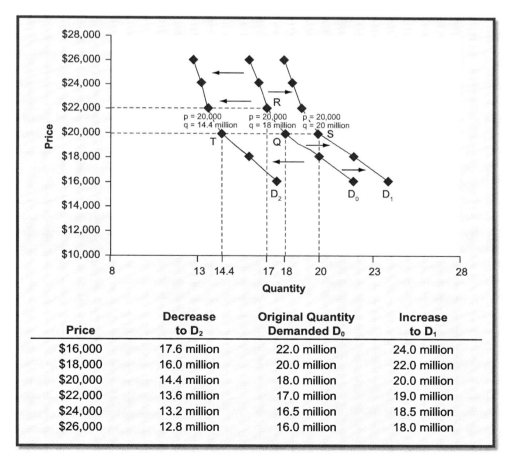

Exhibit 4-4   Shifts in Demand: A Car Example

Increased demand means that at every given price, the quantity demanded is higher, so that the demand curve shifts to the right from D_0 to D_1. Decreased demand means that at every given price, the quantity demand is lower, so that the demand curve shifts to the left from D_0 to D_2.

Price	Decrease to D_2	Original Quantity Demanded D_0	Increase to D_1
$16,000	17.6 million	22.0 million	24.0 million
$18,000	16.0 million	20.0 million	22.0 million
$20,000	14.4 million	18.0 million	20.0 million
$22,000	13.6 million	17.0 million	19.0 million
$24,000	13.2 million	16.5 million	18.5 million
$26,000	12.8 million	16.0 million	18.0 million

price. On the original demand curve, a price of $20,000 means a quantity demanded of 18 million, but after higher incomes cause an increase in demand, a price of $20,000 leads to a quantity demanded of 20 million, at point S. Exhibit 4-4 illustrates the shift in demand as a result of higher income levels with the shift of the original demand curve D_0 to the right to the new demand curve D_1.

This logic works in reverse, too. Imagine that the economy slows down so that many people lose their jobs or work fewer hours and thus suffer reductions in income. In this case, the shift in demand would lead to a lower quantity of cars demanded at every given price, and the original demand curve D_0 would shift left to D_2. The shift from D_0 to D_2 represents a decrease in demand; that is, at any given price level, the quantity demanded is now lower. In this example, a price of $20,000 means 18 million cars sold along the original demand curve, but only 14.4 million cars sold after demand has decreased.

When a demand curve shifts, it does not mean that the quantity demanded by every individual buyer changes by the same amount. In this example, not everyone would have higher or lower income and not everyone would buy or not buy an additional car. Instead, a shift in a demand captures an overall pattern for the market as a whole.

Factors That Shift Demand Curves

A change in any one of the underlying factors that determine what quantity people are willing to buy at a given price will cause a shift in demand. Graphically, the new demand curve lies either to the right or to the left of the original demand curve. Various factors may cause a demand curve to shift: changes in income, change in population, changes in taste, changes in expectations, and changes in the prices of closely related goods. Let's consider these factors in turn.

A *change in income* will often move demand curves. A household with a higher income level will tend to demand a greater quantity of goods at every price than a household with a lower income level. For some luxury goods and services, such as expensive cars, exotic spa vacations, and fine jewelry, the effect of a rise in income can be especially pronounced. However, a few exceptions to this pattern do exist. As incomes rise, many people will buy fewer popsicles and more ice cream, less chicken and more steak, they will be less likely to rent an apartment and more likely to own a home, and so on. **Normal goods** are defined as those where the quantity demanded rises as income rises, which is the most common case; **inferior goods** are defined as those where the quantity demanded falls as income rises.

Changes in the composition of the population can also shift demand curves for certain goods and services. The proportion of elderly citizens in the U.S. population is rising from 9.8% in 1970, to 12.6% in 2000, and to a projected (by the U.S. Census Bureau) 20% of the population by 2030. A society with relatively more children, like the United States in the 1960s, will have greater demand for goods and services like tricycles and day care facilities. A society with relatively more elderly persons, as the United States is projected to have by 2030, has a higher demand for nursing homes and hearing aids.

Changing tastes can also shift demand curves. In demand for music, for example, 50% of sound recordings sold in 1990 were in the rock or pop music categories. By 2007, rock and pop had fallen to 43% of the total, while sales of rap/ hip-hop, religious, and country categories had increased. Tastes in food and drink have changed, too. From 1980 to 2007, the per person consumption of chicken by Americans rose from 33 pounds per year to 61 pounds per year, and consumption of cheese rose from 17 pounds per year to 32 pounds per year. Changes like these are largely due to movements in taste,

normal goods: Goods where the quantity demanded rises as income rises.

inferior goods: Goods where the quantity demanded falls as income rises.

which change the quantity of a good demanded at every price: that is, they shift the demand curve for that good.

Changes in expectations about future conditions and prices can also shift the demand curve for a good or service. For example, if people hear that a hurricane is coming, they may rush to the store to buy flashlight batteries and bottled water. If people learn that the price of a good like coffee is likely to rise in the future, they may head for the store to stock up on coffee now.

The demand curve for one good or service can be affected by *changes in the prices of related goods*. Some goods and services are **substitutes** for others, which means that they can replace the other good to some extent. For example, if the price of cotton rises, driving up the price of clothing, sheets, and other items made from cotton, then some people will shift to comparable goods made from other fabrics like wool, silk, linen, and polyester. A higher price for a substitute good shifts the demand curve to the right; for example, a higher price for tea encourages buying more coffee. Conversely, a lower price for a substitute good has the reverse effect.

Other goods are **complements** for each other, meaning that the goods are often used together, so that consumption of one good tends to increase consumption of the other. Examples include breakfast cereal and milk; golf balls and golf clubs; gasoline and sports utility vehicles; and the five-way combination of bacon, lettuce, tomato, mayonnaise, and bread. If the price of golf clubs rises, demand for a complement good like golf balls decreases. A higher price for skis would shift the demand curve for a complement good like ski resort trips to the left, while a lower price for a complement has the reverse effect.

substitutes: Goods that can replace each other to some extent, so that greater consumption of one good can mean less of the other.

complements: Goods that are often used together, so that consumption of one good tends to increase consumption of the other.

Summing Up Factors That Change Demand

Six factors that can shift demand curves are summarized in Exhibit 4-5. The direction of the arrows indicates whether the demand curve shifts represent an increase in demand or a decrease in demand based on the six factors we just considered. Notice that a change in the price of the good or service itself is *not* listed among the factors that can shift a demand curve. A change in the price of a good or service causes a movement along a specific demand curve, and it typically leads to some change in the quantity demanded, but it doesn't shift the demand curve. Notice also that in these diagrams, the demand curves are drawn without numerical quantities and prices on the horizontal and vertical axes. The demand and supply model can often be a useful conceptual tool even without attaching specific numbers.

When a demand curve shifts, it will then intersect with a given supply curve at a different equilibrium price and quantity. But we are getting ahead of our story. Before discussing how changes in demand can affect equilibrium price and quantity, we first need to discuss shifts in supply curves.

An Example of a Shift in a Supply Curve

A supply curve shows how quantity supplied will change as the price rises and falls, based on the *ceteris paribus* assumption that no other economically relevant factors are changing. But if other factors relevant to supply do change, then the entire supply curve can shift. Just as a shift in demand is represented by a change in the quantity demanded at every price, a **shift in supply** means a change in the quantity supplied at every price. In thinking about the factors that affect supply, remember the basic motivation of firms: to earn profits. If a firm faces lower costs of production, while the prices for the output the firm produces remain unchanged, a firm's profits will increase. Thus, when costs of

shift in supply: When a change in some economic factor related to supply causes a quantity to be supplied at every price.

Exhibit 4-5   Some Factors That Shift Demand Curves

The left-hand panel *(a)* offers a list of factors that can cause an increase in demand from D_0 to D_1. The right-hand panel *(b)* shows how the same factors, if their direction is reversed, can cause a decrease in demand from D_0 to D_1. For example, greater popularity of a good or service increases demand, causing a shift in the demand curve to the right, while lesser popularity of a good or service reduces demand, causing a shift of the demand curve to the left.

(a) Factors that increase demand

(b) Factors that decrease demand

production fall, a firm will supply a higher quantity at any given price for its output, and the supply curve will shift to the right. Conversely, if a firm faces an increased cost of production, then it will earn lower profits at any given selling price for its products. As a result, a higher cost of production typically causes a firm to supply a smaller quantity at any given price. In this case, the supply curve shifts to the left.

As an example, imagine that supply in the market for cars is represented by S_0 in Exhibit 4-6. The original supply curve, S_0, includes a point with a price of $20,000 and a quantity supplied of 18 million cars, labeled as point J, which represents the current market equilibrium price and quantity. If the price rises to $22,000 per car, *ceteris paribus,* the quantity supplied will rise to 20 million cars, as shown by point K on the S_0 curve.

Now imagine that the price of steel, an important ingredient in manufacturing cars, rises, so that producing a car has now become more expensive. At any given price for selling cars, car manufacturers will react by supplying a lower quantity. The shift of supply from S_0 to S_1 shows that at any given price, the quantity supplied decreases. In this example, at a price of $20,000, the quantity supplied decreases from 18 million on the original supply curve S_0 to 16.5 million on the supply curve S_1, which is labeled as point L.

Conversely, imagine that the price of steel decreases, so that producing a car becomes less expensive. At any given price for selling cars, car manufacturers can now expect to earn higher profits and so will supply a higher quantity. The shift of supply to the right from S_0 to S_2 means that at all prices, the quantity supplied has increased. In this example, at a price of $20,000, the quantity supplied increases from 18 million on the original supply curve S_0 to 19.8 million on the supply curve S_2, which is labeled M.

Factors That Shift Supply Curves

A change in any factor that determines what quantity firms are willing to sell at a given price will cause a change in supply. Some factors that can cause a supply curve to shift include: changes in natural conditions, altered prices for inputs to production, new technologies for production, and government policies that affect production costs.

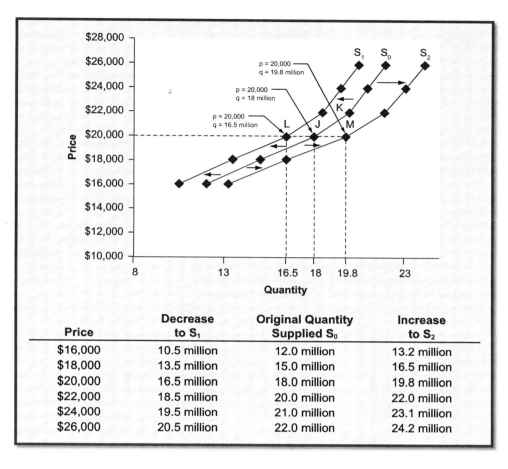

Exhibit 4-6 Shifts in Supply: A Car Example
Increased supply means that at every given price, the quantity supplied is higher, so that the supply curve shifts to the right from S_0 to S_2. Decreased supply means that at every given price, quantity supplied of cars is lower, so that the supply curve shifts to the left from S_0 to S_1.

Price	Decrease to S_1	Original Quantity Supplied S_0	Increase to S_2
$16,000	10.5 million	12.0 million	13.2 million
$18,000	13.5 million	15.0 million	16.5 million
$20,000	16.5 million	18.0 million	19.8 million
$22,000	18.5 million	20.0 million	22.0 million
$24,000	19.5 million	21.0 million	23.1 million
$26,000	20.5 million	22.0 million	24.2 million

The cost of production for many agricultural products will be affected by *changes in natural conditions.* For example, the area of northern China which typically grows about 60% of the country's wheat output experienced its worst drought in at least 50 years in the second half of 2009. A drought decreases the supply of agricultural products, which means that at any given price a lower quantity will be supplied; conversely, especially good weather would shift the supply curve to the right.

Goods and services are produced using combinations of labor, materials, and machinery. When *the price of a key input to production changes,* the supply curve is affected. For example, a messenger company that delivers packages around a city may find that buying gasoline is one of its main costs. If the price of gasoline falls, then in the market for messenger services, a higher quantity will be supplied at any given price per delivery. Conversely, a higher price for key inputs will cause supply to shift to the left.

When a firm discovers a *new technology,* so that it can produce at a lower cost, the supply curve will shift as well. For example, in the 1960s a major scientific effort nicknamed the Green Revolution focused on breeding improved seeds for basic crops like wheat and rice. By the early 1990s, more than two-thirds of the wheat and rice in low income countries around the world was grown with these Green Revolution seeds—and the harvest was twice as high per acre. A technological improvement that reduces costs of production will shift supply to the right, so that a greater quantity will be produced at any given price.

Government policies can affect the cost of production and the supply curve through taxes, regulations, and subsidies. For example, the U.S. government imposes a tax on alcoholic beverages that collects about $8 billion per year from producers. There is a wide array of government regulations that require firms to spend money to provide a cleaner environment or a safer workplace. A government subsidy, on the other hand, occurs when the government sends money to a firm directly or when the government reduces the firm's taxes if the firm carries out certain actions. For example, the U.S. government pays more than $20 billion per year directly to firms to support research and development. From the perspective of a firm, taxes or regulations are an additional cost of production that shifts supply to the left, leading the firm to produce a lower quantity at every given price. However, government subsidies reduce the cost of production and increase supply.

Summing Up Factors That Change Supply

Natural disasters, changes in the cost of inputs, new technologies, and the impact of government decisions all affect the cost of production for firms. In turn, these factors affect firms' willingness to supply at a given price. Exhibit 4-7 summarizes factors that change the supply of goods and services. Notice that a change in the price of the product itself is *not* among the factors that shift the supply curve. Although a change in price of a good or service typically causes a change in quantity supplied along the supply curve for that specific good or service, it does not cause the supply curve itself to shift.

Because demand and supply curves appear on a two-dimensional diagram with only price and quantity on the axes, an unwary visitor to the land of economics might be fooled into believing that economics is only about four topics: demand, supply, price, and quantity. However, demand and supply are really "umbrella" concepts: demand covers all of the factors that affect demand, and supply covers all of the factors that affect supply. The factors other than price that affect demand and supply are included by using shifts in the demand or the supply curve. In this way, the two-dimensional demand and supply model becomes a powerful tool for analyzing a wide range of economic circumstances.

Exhibit 4-7   Some Factors That Shift Supply Curves

The right-hand panel *(a)* offers list of factors that can cause an increase in supply from S_0 to S_1. The left-hand panel *(b)* shows that the same factors, if their direction is reversed, can cause a decrease in supply from S_0 to S_1.

Shifts in Equilibrium Price and Quantity: The Four-Step Process

Let's begin with a single economic event. It might be an event that affects demand, like a change in income, population, tastes, prices of substitutes or complements, or expectations about future prices. It might be an event that affects supply, like a change in natural conditions, input prices, or technology, or government policies that affect production. How does this economic event affect equilibrium price and quantity? We can analyze this question using a four-step process.

Step 1: Think about what the demand and supply curves in this market looked like before the economic change occurred. Sketch the curves.

Step 2: Decide whether the economic change being analyzed affects demand or supply.

Step 3: Decide whether the effect on demand or supply causes the curve to shift to the right or to the left, and sketch the new demand or supply curve on the diagram.

Step 4: Compare the original equilibrium price and quantity to the new equilibrium price and quantity.

To make this process concrete, let's consider one example that involves a shift in supply and one that involves a shift in demand.

Good Weather for Salmon Fishing

In summer 2000, weather conditions were excellent for commercial salmon fishing off the California coast. Heavy rains meant higher than normal levels of water in the rivers, which helps the salmon to breed. Slightly cooler ocean temperatures stimulated growth of plankton, the microscopic organisms at the bottom of the ocean food chain, thus providing everything in the ocean with a hearty food supply. The ocean stayed calm during fishing season, so commercial fishing operations didn't lose many days to bad weather. How did these weather conditions affect the quantity and price of salmon? Exhibit 4-8 uses the four-step approach to work through this problem.

1. Draw a demand and supply diagram to show what the market for salmon looked like before the good weather arrived. The original equilibrium E_0 was $3.25 per pound and the original equilibrium quantity was 250,000 fish. (This price per pound is what commercial buyers pay at the fishing docks; what consumers pay at the grocery is higher.)

2. Did the economic event affect supply or demand? Good weather is a natural condition that affects supply.

3. Was the effect on supply an increase or a decrease? Good weather increases the quantity that will be supplied at any given price. The supply curve shifts to the right from the S_0 to S_1.

4. Compare the new equilibrium price and quantity to the original equilibrium. At the new equilibrium, E_1, the equilibrium price fell from $3.25 to $2.50, but the equilibrium quantity increased from 250,000 salmon to 550,000 fish. Notice that the equilibrium quantity demanded increased, even though the demand curve did not move.

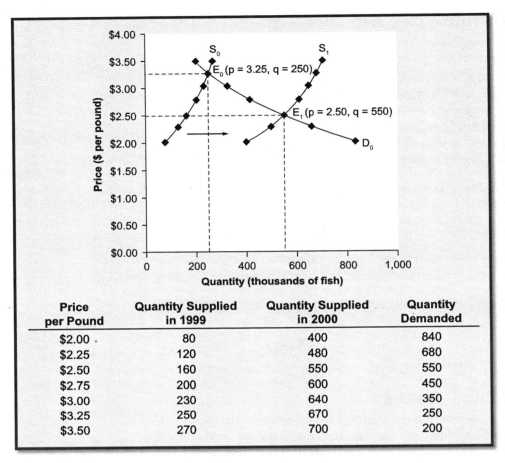

Price per Pound	Quantity Supplied in 1999	Quantity Supplied in 2000	Quantity Demanded
$2.00	80	400	840
$2.25	120	480	680
$2.50	160	550	550
$2.75	200	600	450
$3.00	230	640	350
$3.25	250	670	250
$3.50	270	700	200

Exhibit 4-8 Good Weather for Salmon Fishing: The Four-Step Process

Step 1: Draw a demand and supply diagram to illustrate what the market for salmon looked like in the year before the good weather arrived. The demand curve D_0 and the supply curve S_0 show that the original equilibrium price is $3.25 per pound and the original equilibrium quantity is 250,000 fish.

Step 2: Will the change described affect supply or demand? Good weather is an example of a natural condition that affects supply.

Step 3: Will the effect on supply be an increase or decrease? Good weather is a change in natural conditions that increases the quantity supplied at any given price. The supply curve shifts to the right, moving from the original supply curve S_0 to the new supply curve S_1, which is shown in both the schedule and the figure.

Step 4: Compare the new equilibrium price and quantity to the original equilibrium. At the new equilibrium E_1, the equilibrium price falls from $3.25 to $2.50, but the equilibrium quantity increases from 250,000 to 550,000 salmon.

In short, good weather conditions increased supply for the California commercial salmon fishing industry. The result was a higher equilibrium quantity of salmon bought and sold in the market at a lower price.

Seal Hunting and New Drugs

As the catch of whales dwindled, Canada's seal industry had become the only remaining large-scale hunt for marine mammals. In the late 1990s, about 280,000 Canadian seals were killed each year. In 2000, the number dropped to 90,000 seals. What happened? One major use of seals was that some of their body parts were used as ingredients in traditional medications in China and other Asian nations that promised to treat male impotence. However, pharmaceutical companies—led by Pfizer Inc., which invented the drug Viagra—developed some alternative and medically proven treatments for male impotence. How would the invention of Viagra, and other drugs to treat mail impotence, affect the harvest of seals? Exhibit 4-9 illustrates the four-step analysis.

1. Draw a demand and supply diagram to illustrate what the market for seals looked like in the year before the invention of Viagra. In Exhibit 4-9, the demand curve D_0 and the supply curve S_0 show the original relationships. In this case, the analysis is performed without specific numbers on the price and quantity axes. (Not surprisingly, detailed annual data on quantities and prices of seals body parts are not readily available.)

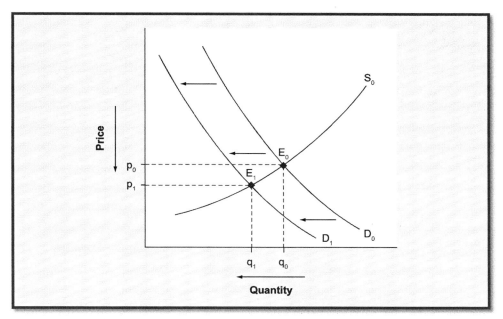

Exhibit 4-9   The Seal Market: A Four-Step Analysis

Step 1: Draw a demand and supply diagram to illustrate what the market for seals looked like in the year before the invention of Viagra. The demand curve D_0 and the supply curve S_0 show the original relationships.

Step 2: Will the change described affect supply or demand? A newly available substitute good, like Viagra, will affect demand for the original product, seals.

Step 3: Will the effect on demand be positive or negative? A less expensive substitute product will tend to mean a lower quantity demanded of the original product, seal, at every given price, causing the demand curve for seal to shift to the left from D_0 to D_1.

Step 4: Compare the new equilibrium price and quantity to the original equilibrium price. The new equilibrium E_1 occurs at a lower quantity and a lower price than the original equilibrium E_0.

2. Did the change described affect supply or demand? A newly available substitute good, like Viagra, will affect demand for the original product, seal body parts.

3. Was the effect on demand an increase or a decrease? An effective substitute product for male impotence, means a lower quantity demanded of the original product at every given price, causing the demand curve for seals to shift left to the new demand curve D_1.

4. Compare the new equilibrium price and quantity at E_1 to the original equilibrium price and quantity at E_0. The new equilibrium E_1 occurs at a lower quantity and a lower price than the original equilibrium E_0.

The extremely sharp decline in the number of Canadian seals killed in the late 1990s, together with anecdotal evidence that the price of seal body parts dropped sharply at this time, suggests that the invention of drugs to treat male impotence helped reduce the number of seals killed. In fact, some environmentalists are hoping that such drugs may reduce demand for other common ingredients for traditional male potency medicines, including tiger bones and monkey heads.

The Interconnections and Speed of Adjustment in Real Markets

In the real world, many factors that affect demand and supply can change all at once. For example, the demand for cars might increase because of rising incomes and population, and it might decrease because of rising gasoline prices (a complementary good). Likewise, the supply of cars might increase because of innovative new technologies that reduce the cost of car production, and it might decrease as a result of new government regulations requiring the installation of costly pollution-control technology. Moreover, rising incomes and population or changes in gasoline prices will affect many markets, not just cars. How can an economist sort out all of these interconnected events? The answer lies in the *ceteris paribus* assumption. Look at how each economic event affects each market, one event at a time, holding all else constant.

One common mistake in applying the demand and supply framework is to confuse the shift of a demand or a supply curve with the movement along a demand or supply curve. As an example, consider a problem that asks whether a drought will increase or decrease the equilibrium quantity and equilibrium price of wheat. Lee, a student in an introductory economics class, might reason:

"Well, it's clear that a drought reduces supply, so I'll shift back the supply curve, as in the shift from the original supply curve S_0 to S_1 shown on the diagram (call this Shift 1). So the equilibrium moves from E_0 to E_1, the equilibrium quantity is lower and the equilibrium price is higher. Then, a higher price makes farmers more likely to supply the good, so the supply curve shifts right, as shown by the shift from S_1 to S_2 on the diagram (shown as Shift 2), so that the equilibrium now moves from E_1 to E_2. But the higher price also reduces demand and so causes demand to shift back, like the shift from the original demand curve D_0 to D_1 on the diagram (labeled Shift 3), and the equilibrium moves from E_2 to E_3."

At about this point, Lee suspects that this answer is headed down the wrong path. Think about what might be wrong with Lee's logic, and then read the answer that follows.

Answer: Lee's first step is correct: that is, a drought shifts back the supply curve of wheat and leads to a prediction of a lower equilibrium quantity and a higher equilibrium price. The rest of Lee's argument is wrong, because it mixes up shifts in supply with quantity supplied, and shifts in demand with quantity demanded. A higher or lower price never shifts the supply curve, as suggested by the shift in supply from S_1 to S_2. Instead, a price change leads to a movement along a given supply curve. Similarly, a higher or lower price never shifts a demand curve, as suggested in the shift from D_0 to D_1. Instead, a price change leads to a movement along a given demand curve. Remember, a change in the price of a good never causes the demand or supply curve for that good to shift.

Clearing It Up

Shifts of Demand or Supply versus Movements along a Demand or Supply Curve

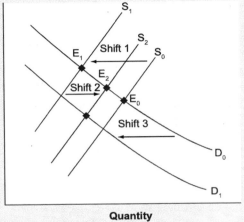

In the four-step analysis of how economic events affect equilibrium price and quantity, the movement from the old to the new equilibrium seems immediate. But as a practical matter, prices and quantities often do not zoom straight to equilibrium. More realistically, when an economic event causes demand or supply to shift, prices and quantities set off in the general direction of equilibrium. Indeed, even as they are moving toward one new equilibrium, prices are often then pushed by another change in demand or supply toward another equilibrium.

Price Ceilings and Price Floors in Markets for Goods and Services

Controversy often surrounds the prices and quantities that are established by demand and supply. After all, every time you buy a gallon of gasoline, pay the rent for your apartment, or pay the interest charges on your credit card, it's natural to wish that the price had been at least a little lower. Every time a restaurant sells a meal, a department store sells a sweater, or a farmer sells a bushel of wheat, it's natural for the profit-seeking seller to wish that the price had been higher. In some cases, discontent over prices turns into public pressure on politicians, who may then pass legislation to prevent a certain price from climbing "too high" or falling "too low." The demand and supply model

What's a Price Bubble? A Story of Housing Prices

According to data from the Federal Housing Finance Agency, the average price of a U.S. single-family home rose about 1–3% per year in the first half of the 1990s; 3–5% per year in the second half of the 1990s; 7–8% per year in the early 2000s; and more than 10% per year from late 2004 to early 2006.

Although no one seriously expected price increases of 10% per year to continue for long, what happened next was still a shock. Although certain metropolitan areas or states had seen declines in housing prices from time to time, there had not been a nationwide decline in housing prices since the Great Depression of the 1930s. But housing prices started falling in 2006, and through much of 2008 and 2009, housing prices were falling at a rate of 4–5% per year. Of course, these national averages understate the experience of certain parts of the country where both the boom and the bust were much larger.

Economists refer to this chain of events as a price "bubble." Remember that one possible reason for demand to shift is expectations about the future. If many people expect that housing prices are going to rise in the future, demand for housing will shift to the right—thus helping

the prediction of higher prices come true. For a time, a cycle of expecting higher prices, increases in demand, and resulting higher prices can be self-reinforcing. But this process cannot last forever. At some unpredictable time, many people recognize that the expectations of ever-higher future prices are unrealistic, at which point demand shifts back in the other direction and the price bubble deflates. Price bubbles are not just observed in housing: they are also seen from time in markets for collectible items, and in stock markets.

The bursting of the price bubble in housing—which happened in many countries around the world, not just the United States—has caused great economic difficulties. Those who owned homes watched the value of this asset decline. Some of those who borrowed money to buy a house near the peak of the bubble found a few years later, after the bubble had burst, that what they owed to the bank was much more than the house was worth. When many people began to default on their mortgage loans, banks and other financial institutions then faced huge losses. The bursting of the price bubble in housing helped to trigger the global economic slowdown that started in 2008.

shows how people and firms will react to the incentives provided by these laws to control prices, in ways that will often lead to undesirable costs and consequences. Alternative policy tools can often achieve the desired goals of price control laws, while avoiding at least some of the costs and trade-offs of such laws.

Price Ceilings

Price controls are laws that the government enacts to regulate prices. Price controls come in two flavors. A **price ceiling** keeps a price from rising above a certain level, while a **price floor** keeps a price from falling below a certain level. This section uses the demand and supply framework to analyze price ceilings; the next section turns to price floors.

In many markets for goods and services, demanders outnumber suppliers. There are more people who buy bread than companies that make bread; more people who rent apartments than landlords; more people who purchase prescription drugs than companies that manufacture such drugs; more people who buy gasoline than companies that refine and sell gasoline. Consumers, who are also potential voters, sometimes unite behind a political proposal to hold down a certain price. In some cities, for example, renters have pressed political leaders to pass rent control laws, a form of price ceiling that usually works by stating that rents can only be raised by a certain maximum percentage each year.

Rent control can become a politically hot topic when rents begin to rise rapidly. Rents might rise for many reasons. Perhaps a change in tastes makes a certain suburb or town a more popular place to live. Perhaps locally based businesses expand, bringing higher incomes and more people into the area. Changes of this sort can cause a change in the demand for rental housing, as illustrated in Exhibit 4-10. The original equilibrium E_0 lies at the intersection of supply curve S_0 and demand curve D_0, corresponding to an

price controls: Government laws to regulate prices.

price ceiling: A law that prevents a price from rising above a certain level.

price floor: A law that prevents a price from falling below a certain level.

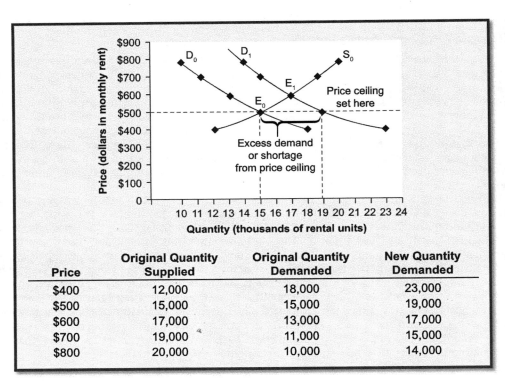

Exhibit 4-10   A Price Ceiling Example—Rent Control

The original intersection of demand and supply occurs at E_0. Demand shifts from D_0 to D_1. The new equilibrium would be at E_1—except that a price ceiling prevents the price from rising. Because the price doesn't change, the quantity supplied remains at 15,000. However, after the change in demand, the quantity demanded rises to 19,000. There is excess demand, also called a shortage.

Price	Original Quantity Supplied	Original Quantity Demanded	New Quantity Demanded
$400	12,000	18,000	23,000
$500	15,000	15,000	19,000
$600	17,000	13,000	17,000
$700	19,000	11,000	15,000
$800	20,000	10,000	14,000

equilibrium price of $500 and an equilibrium quantity of 15,000 units of rental housing. The effect of greater income or a change in tastes is to shift the demand curve for rental housing to the right, as shown by the data in the table and the shift from D_0 to D_1 on the graph. In this market, at the new equilibrium E_1, the price of a rental unit would rise to $600 and the equilibrium quantity would increase to 17,000 units.

Long-time apartment dwellers will dislike these price increases. They may argue, "Why should *our* rents rise because a lot of newcomers want to move in?" The current apartment-dwellers are also voters, and they may elect local politicians who pass a price ceiling law that limits how much rents can rise.

For simplicity, let's assume that a rent control law is passed to keep the price at the original equilibrium of $500 for a typical apartment. In Exhibit 4-10, the horizontal line at the price of $500 shows the legally fixed maximum price set by the rent control law. However, the underlying forces that shifted the demand curve to the right have not vanished. At that price ceiling, the quantity demanded exceeds the quantity supplied: that is, at a price of $500 the quantity supplied remains at the same 15,000 rental units, but the quantity demanded is 19,000 rental units. Thus, people who would like to rent in this area are knocking on the doors of landlords, searching for apartments. A situation of excess demand, also called a shortage, results when people are willing to pay the market price but cannot purchase (or in this case rent) what they desire.

Rent control has been especially popular in wartime and during times of high inflation. New York City, the most prominent U.S. city that has imposed rent control laws for a long period, put rent control in place as a "temporary" measure during World War II. Rent control was also especially popular during the 1970s, when all prices in the U.S. economy were rising rapidly as part of an overall process of inflation. By the mid-1980s, more than 200 American cities, with about 20% of the nation's population, had rent control laws. But in the last two decades, the political pendulum began swinging against rent control. Thirty-one states adopted laws or constitutional amendments banning rent control outright. In many cities that kept some form of rent control, the focus of the law shifted from trying to hold rents below the equilibrium price to offering ways for resolving disputes between tenants and landlords, like disagreements about maintenance, pets, and noise. But in New York City, relatively strict rent controls have persisted into the 2000s.

Although the effect of rent control laws in the United States has faded in recent years, price ceilings are often proposed for other products. For example, price ceilings to limit what producers can charge have been proposed in recent years for prescription drugs, on doctor and hospital fees, the charges made by some automatic teller bank machines, and auto insurance rates. Many low-income countries around the world, including nations in Africa and Asia, have also imposed price ceilings on basic items like bread. In the early 2000s, the government of the African country of Zimbabwe tried to help its ordinary citizens by placing ceilings on the prices of ordinary household items like bread, wheat, and cooking oil. But many producers of these items, faced with the low prices, went out of business. The goal of the price ceiling had been to keep necessities affordable to all, but the result was that the quantity of the products declined and shortages occurred.

Price ceilings are enacted in an attempt to keep prices low for those who demand the product. But when the market price is not allowed to rise to the equilibrium level, quantity demanded exceeds quantity supplied, and thus a shortage occurs. Those who manage to purchase the product at the lower price given by the price ceiling will benefit, but sellers of the product will suffer, along with those who are not able to purchase the product at all.

Price Floors

Price floors are enacted when discontented sellers, feeling that prices are too low, appeal to legislators to keep prices from falling. A price floor is the lowest legal price that can be paid in markets for goods and services, labor, and financial capital. Price floors are sometimes called "price supports," because they support a price by preventing it from falling below a certain level.

Around the world, many countries have passed laws to keep farm prices higher than they otherwise would be. In the annual budget of the European Union, roughly half of all spending late in the first decade of the 2000s—about $65 billion per year—is used to keep prices high for Europe's farmers. Thanks to this policy, the prices received by European farmers for such agricultural staples as wheat, barley, rice, milk, and beef have held substantially above the price prevailing in the world market for several decades.

Exhibit 4-11 illustrates the effects of a government program that assures a price above the equilibrium by focusing on the market for wheat in Europe. In the absence of government intervention, the price would adjust so that the quantity supplied would equal the quantity demanded at the equilibrium point E_0, with price p_0 and quantity Q_0. However, policies to keep prices high for farmers keeps the price above what would have been the market equilibrium level—the price p_f shown by the dashed horizontal line in the diagram. The result is a quantity supplied of Q_s in excess of the quantity demanded Q_d. When quantity supply exceeds quantity demanded, then a situation of excess supply exists, also called a surplus. The high-income countries of the world, including the United States, Europe and Japan, spend a total of about $1 billion *per day* in supporting their farmers. If the government is willing to purchase the excess supply (or to provide payments for others to purchase it), then farmers will benefit from the price floor but taxpayers and consumers of food will pay the costs. Numerous proposals have been offered for reducing farm subsidies. But in many countries, political support

Exhibit 4-11   The European Wheat Prices: A Price Floor Example

The intersection of demand D and supply S would be at the equilibrium point E_0. However, a price floor set at p_f holds the price above E_0 and prevents it from falling. The result of the price floor is that the quantity supplied Q_s exceeds the quantity demanded Q_d. There is excess supply, also called a surplus.

for subsidies for farmers—and indirectly, for what is viewed as the traditional rural way of life—remains strong.

Responses to Price Controls: Many Margins for Action

Although a government can set price floors or price ceilings, it cannot control how households and firms react to these price controls. Attempts to control prices often have unintended consequences. The focus of the discussion so far has been on reactions that take the form of changes in quantity demanded or quantity supplied, and thus on understanding why price ceilings commonly lead to shortages and price floors lead to surpluses. However, buyers and sellers in real-world markets have many other ways in which they can react to price controls. The ability of households and firms to react in a variety of ways to government rules is called the problem of "many margins for action."

One alternative reaction occurs when buyers and seller decide to break the government rules on prices or sales, which is referred to as **black market.** Consider a landlord who

black market: An illegal market that breaks government rules on prices or sales.

Price Controls of 1776

During the American Revolution, a number of states imposed price ceilings on many goods. After Rhode Island passed price control laws in 1776, the city of Providence reported on the effects to the state legislature in 1777:

> [The effect] is so intricate, variable, and complicated, that it cannot remain any time equitable . . . It was made to cheapen the articles of life, but it has It was made to cheapen the articles of life, but it has in fact raised their prices, by producing an artificial and in some respects a real scarcity. It was made to unite us in good agreement respecting prices; but hath produced animosity, and ill will between town and country, and between buyers and sellers in general. It was made to bring us up to some equitable standard of honesty . . . but hath produced a sharping set of mushroom peddlars, who adulterate their commodities, and take every advantage to evade the . . . act, by quibbles and lies.

Price control laws are often popular in the short run, because they look like an easy fix, but they become less popular over time as shortages occur, social tensions arise, and efforts to evade the laws gain force. The problems noted by the citizens of Providence, Rhode Island, in 1775 apply today as they did more than 200 years ago.

owns rent-controlled property. Suppose that although the law dictates the cap on the rent that the landlord can charge, a potential tenant is willing to pay more than the rent control law allows to live in the apartment. If this "extra rent" is paid in cash, then who will know?

A second margin for action is "side payments," which are additional payments that are made along with the actual price paid. In New York City, with its long history of rent control, landlords have devised innovative charges like a "nonrefundable cleaning deposit" and a "nonrefundable key deposit," or they may require several months' rent in advance. These charges can have the effect of making the tenant pay more than the actual rent.

A third margin for action involves quality adjustment. In the case of rent control, a landlord may keep the rent low but put off needed maintenance or installing new appliances. The result is a lower-priced apartment—but also a lower-quality apartment.

A fourth margin for action involves shifting who is involved in the transaction. In cities with rent control, it isn't unusual for a tenant living in a rent-controlled apartment not to move out officially; instead, the tenant sublets the apartment to someone else. In this case, the original tenant pays the rent-controlled rate but charges the market rate to the new renter and pockets the difference.

Those who favor price floors and price ceilings are often quite aware of the actions that can circumvent the underlying purpose of price controls. Thus, supporters of price controls also favor rules that will include penalties for black markets, make side payments illegal, require certain quality levels, and prohibit shifts in who is involved in the transaction. However, establishing rules or laws that will limit all of the alternative margins for action is like trying to block a flowing stream with your fingers. Shutting down the many margins for action by which citizens and firms respond to price controls is much easier said than done.

Policy Alternatives to Price Ceilings and Price Floors

The economic analysis of how price ceilings can create shortages and price floors create surpluses can be disheartening. If you want to pursue a policy goal of assuring that people have a sufficient quantity of affordable housing, but rent controls are just price ceilings that cause housing shortages, what alternative policy can you advocate? If you want to pursue a policy goal of supporting farmers, but farm price supports lead to storehouses of surplus grain rotting at high cost to taxpayers and consumers, then what alternative policy can you advocate? The same demand and supply model that shows

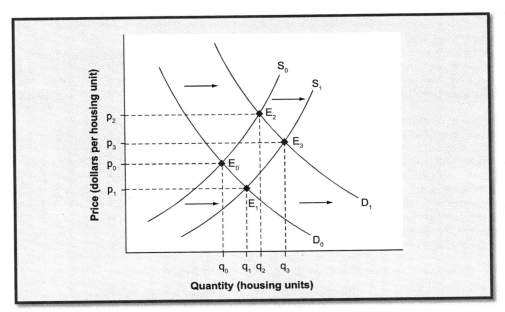

Exhibit 4-12   Policies for Affordable Housing: Alternatives to Rent Control

The original equilibrium is the intersection of demand D_0 and supply S_0 at the equilibrium E_0. Providing subsidies to low-income buyers of housing will shift the demand curve from D_0 to D_1, leading to a new equilibrium at E_2. Alternatively, a policy of providing subsidies to builders of affordable housing would shift the supply curve from S_0 to S_1, leading to a new equilibrium at E_1. Undertaking both demand-side and supply-side policies would move the market to equilibrium E_3, at the intersection of the new demand curve D_1 and the new supply curve S_1. As drawn here, both of these policies will increase the equilibrium quantity of affordable housing. An increase in demand will also raise the price of affordable housing, but as long as the subsidy received by buyers is larger than the higher price, buyers will not be adversely affected by the higher price that occurs from an increase in demand.

that price ceilings and price floors often have unintended, undesirable consequences of creating surpluses and shortages, can also suggest alternate public policies that do not have these same trade-offs.

Let's return to the issue of rent control. If the goal is to have an expanded supply of affordable housing, then a rightward shift in a demand curve, a supply curve, or both as shown in Exhibit 4-12, can accomplish this goal. A shift to the right in the supply of affordable housing from S_0 to S_1, for example, might be achieved if a government grants subsidies to builders who construct apartment buildings that include have relatively smaller rental units, which will have a more affordable price in the market. This step taken alone would cause a shift to the right from the original equilibrium, E_0, to the new equilibrium, E_1, and would increase the quantity of housing from q_0 to q_1. A shift to the right in the demand curve from D_0 to D_1 might be achieved by giving a subsidy to low-income renters, perhaps in the form of cash or of a voucher that the renters could use to pay some of the rent, so that low-income renters could then have more to spend on housing. This step taken alone would cause a shift to the right from the original equilibrium, E_0, to the new equilibrium, E_2, and would increase the quantity of affordable housing from q_0 to q_2. Instituting *both* sets of policies would shift supply from S_0 to S_1, demand from D_0 to D_1, the equilibrium from the original E_0 to E_3, and the quantity of affordable housing from q_0 to q_3.

Any combination of these policies is likely to be more useful in expanding affordable housing than rent control, because these policies tend to increase the quantity of affordable housing, whereas rent control tends to decrease it. Moreover, these alternative policies sidestep many of the problems that arise when suppliers and demanders react to price controls.

Similarly, there are a number of alternative policies to support farmers or rural areas that do not involve setting price floors for crops. For example, the government could provide income directly to farmers, especially to those with lower incomes. The government might also assist rural economies in many other ways: establishing new branches of state colleges and universities in agricultural areas, creating parks or nature preserves that might attract tourists, supporting research into new methods of producing and using local crops to help the local farmers stay ahead, helping to build transportation links to rural areas, and subsidizing high-speed Internet cable connections across rural areas or wireless phone service. All of these alternative policies would help rural communities while avoiding the problem of price floors, because these alternative policies don't encourage farmers to produce an excess supply of surplus food.

With alternative policies like these readily available, why do governments enact price floors and price ceilings? One reason is that in public policy debates over price controls, people often don't take into account the unintended but predictable tradeoffs. Another reason is that government sometimes views laws about price floors and ceilings as having zero cost, while giving subsidies to demanders or suppliers requires a government to collect taxes and spend money. The point here is not to endorse every proposal for using targeted subsidies or tax breaks to change demand and supply. Each policy proposal must be evaluated according to its own costs and benefits. But before reaching for the seemingly easy policy tool of price controls, with all of their undesired if predictable consequences and trade-offs, it is wise to consider alternative policies to shift demand and supply so as to achieve the desired new market equilibrium.

Supply, Demand, and Efficiency

In the market equilibrium, where the quantity demanded equals quantity supplied, nothing is wasted. No excess supply sits unsold, gathering dust in warehouses. No shortages exist that cause people to stand in long lines or rely on political connections to acquire goods—alternatives that involve wastes of time and energy. All those who wish to purchase or sell goods at the equilibrium market price are able to purchase or sell the quantity that they desire, as movements of the equilibrium price bring quantity demanded and supplied into balance.

The familiar demand and supply diagram holds within it the concept of economic efficiency, which was introduced in Chapter 2. To economists, an efficient outcome is one where it is impossible to improve the situation of one party without imposing a cost on someone else. Conversely, if a situation is inefficient, it becomes possible to benefit at least one party without imposing costs on others. Thus, the definition of productive efficiency in Chapter 2 was that economy was producing without waste, and getting all it could out of its scarce resources, in the sense that it was impossible to get more of good A without a reduction in good B. Efficiency in the demand and supply model has the same basic meaning: the economy is getting as much benefit as possible from its scarce resources and all the possible gains from trade have been achieved.

Consumer Surplus, Producer Surplus, Social Surplus

Consider the example of a market for portable devices that can store and play digital music and other audio files shown in Exhibit 4-13. The equilibrium price is $80 and the equilibrium quantity is 28 million. To see the benefits received by consumers, look at the segment of the demand curve above the equilibrium point and to the left. This portion of the demand curve shows that at least some demanders would have been willing to pay more than $80 for a portable music player. For example, point J shows that if the price was $90, the quantity demanded of the portable music player would have been 20 million. Those consumers who would have been willing to pay $100 for a portable music

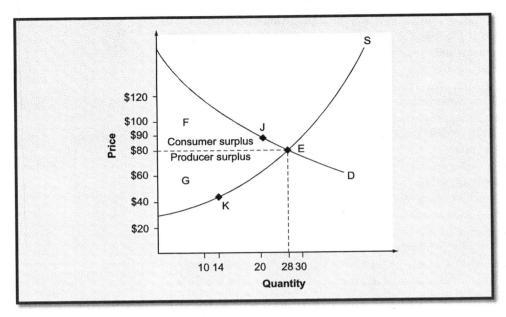

Figure 4-13   Consumer and Producer Surplus

The triangular area labeled by F shows the area of consumer surplus, which shows that the equilibrium price in the market was less than what many of the consumers were willing to pay. For example, point J on the demand curve shows that even at the price of $90, consumers would have been willing to purchase a quantity of 20. But those consumers only needed to pay the equilibrium price of $80. The triangular area labeled by G shows the area of producer surplus, which shows that the equilibrium price received in the market was more than what many of the producers were willing to accept for their products. For example, point K on the supply curve shows that at a price of $40, firms would have been willing to supply a quantity of 14. However, in this market those firms could receive a price of $80 for their production. The sum of consumer surplus and producer surplus—that is, F + G—is called social surplus.

player based on the utility they expect to receive from it, but who were able to pay the equilibrium price of $80, clearly received a benefit. Remember, the demand curve traces out the willingness to pay for different quantities. The amount that individuals would have been willing to pay minus the amount that they actually paid is called **consumer surplus.** Consumer surplus is the area labeled F—that is, the area between the market price and the segment of the demand curve above equilibrium.

The equilibrium price also benefits producers. The supply curve shows the quantity that firms are willing to supply at each price. For example, point K on Exhibit 4-13 illustrates that at a price of $40, firms would still have been willing to supply a quantity of 14 million. Those producers who would have been willing to supply the portable music players at a price of $40, but who were instead able to charge the equilibrium price of $80, clearly received a benefit. **Producer surplus** is the amount that a seller is paid for a good minus the seller's actual cost. In Exhibit 4-13, producer surplus is the area labeled G—that is, the area between the market price and the segment of the supply curve below the equilibrium.

Social surplus is the sum of consumer surplus and producer surplus. In Exhibit 4-13, social surplus would thus be shown as the area F + G. Social surplus is larger at equilibrium quantity and price than it would be at any other quantity. At the efficient level of output, it is impossible to produce greater consumer surplus without reducing producer surplus, and it is impossible to produce greater producer surplus without reducing consumer surplus.

Inefficiency of Price Floors and Price Ceilings

The imposition of a price floor or a price ceiling will prevent a market from adjusting to its equilibrium price and quantity, and thus will create an inefficient outcome. But there is an additional twist here. Along with creating inefficiency, price floors and ceilings will also transfer some consumer surplus to producers, or some producer surplus to consumers. Let's consider a price ceiling and a price floor in turn.

consumer surplus: The benefit consumers receive from buying a good or service, measured by what the individuals would have been willing to pay minus the amount that they actually paid.

producer surplus: The benefit producers receive from selling a good or service, measured by the price the producer actually received minus the price the producer would have been willing to accept.

social surplus: The sum of consumer surplus and producer surplus.

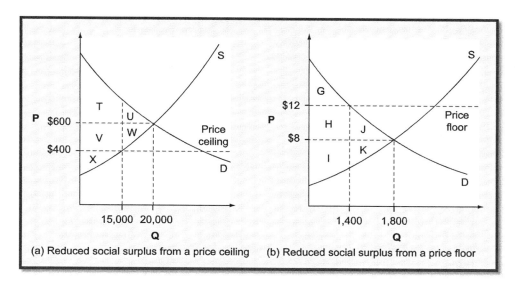

Figure 4-14   Efficiency and Price Floors and Ceilings

(a) The original equilibrium price is $600 with a quantity of 20,000. Consumer surplus is T + U, and producer surplus is V + W + X. A price ceiling is imposed at $400, so firms in the market now produce only a quantity of 15,000. As a result, the new consumer surplus is T + V, while the new producer surplus is X. In effect, the price ceiling transfers the surplus V from producers to consumers, but also causes deadweight loss in social surplus of U + W.

(b) The original equilibrium is $8 at a quantity of 1,800. Consumer surplus is G + H + J, and producer surplus is I + K. A price floor is imposed at $12, which means that quantity demanded falls to 1,400. As a result, the new consumer surplus is G, and the new producer surplus is H + I. In effect, the price floor causes the area H to be transferred from consumer to producer surplus, but also causes a deadweight loss in social surplus of J + K.

deadweight loss: The loss in social surplus that occurs when a market produces an inefficient quantity.

Imagine that several firms develop a promising but expensive new drug for treating back pain. If this therapy is left to the market, the equilibrium price will be $600 per month and 200,000 people will use the drug, as shown in Exhibit 4-14a. The original level of consumer surplus is the T + U and producer surplus is V + W + X. However, the government decides to impose a price ceiling of $400 to make the drug more affordable. At this price ceiling, firms in the market now produce only a quantity of 150,000. As a result, two changes occur. First, an inefficient outcome occurs and the total surplus of society is reduced. **Deadweight loss** is the name for the loss in social surplus that occurs when the economy produces at an inefficient quantity. In Exhibit 4-14a, the deadweight loss is the area U + W. When deadweight loss exists, it is possible for both consumer and producer surplus to increase, in this case because the price control is blocking some suppliers and demanders from transactions that they would both be willing to make. A second change from the price ceiling is that some of the producer surplus is transferred to consumers. After the price ceiling is imposed, the new consumer surplus is T + V, while the new producer surplus is X. In other words, the price ceiling transfers the area of surplus V from producers to consumers.

For the case of a price floor shown in Exhibit 4-14b, envision a situation where a city with several movie theaters that are all losing money. The current equilibrium is a price of $8 per movie, with 1,800 people attending movies. The original consumer surplus is G + H + J, and producer surplus is I + K. The city government is worried that movie theaters will go out of business, thus reducing the entertainment options available to citizens, so it decides to impose a price floor of $12 per ticket. As a result, the quantity demanded of movie tickets falls to 1,400. The new consumer surplus is G, and the new producer surplus is H + I. In effect, the price floor causes the area H to be transferred from consumer to producer surplus, but also causes a deadweight loss of J + K.

This analysis shows that a price ceiling, like a law establishing rent controls, will transfer some producer surplus to consumers—which helps to explain why consumers often favor them. Conversely, a price floor like a guarantee that farmers will receive a certain price for their crops will transfer some consumer surplus to producers, which explains why producers often favor them. However, both price floors and price ceilings block some transactions that buyers and sellers would have been willing to make, and create deadweight loss. Removing such barriers so that prices and quantities can adjust to their equilibrium level will increase the economy's social surplus.

Demand and Supply as a Social Adjustment Mechanism

The demand and supply model emphasizes that prices are not set only by demand or only by supply, but by the interaction between the two. In 1890, the famous economist Alfred Marshall wrote that asking whether supply or demand determined a price was like arguing "whether it is the upper or the under blade of a pair of scissors that cuts a piece of paper." The answer is that both blades of the demand and supply scissors are always involved.

The adjustments of equilibrium price and quantity in a market-oriented economy often occur without much government direction or oversight. If the coffee crop in Brazil suffers a terrible frost, then the supply curve of coffee shifts to the left and the price of coffee rises. Some people—call them the coffee addicts—continue to drink coffee and pay the higher price. Others switch to tea or soft drinks. No government commission is needed to figure out how to adjust coffee prices; or which companies will be allowed to process the remaining supply; or which supermarkets in which cities will get how much coffee to sell; or which consumers will ultimately be allowed to drink the brew. Such adjustments in response to price changes happen all the time in a market economy, often so smoothly and rapidly that we barely notice them. Think for a moment of all the seasonal foods that are available and inexpensive at certain times of the year, like fresh corn in midsummer, but more expensive at other times of the year. People alter their diets and restaurants alter their menus in response to these fluctuations in prices without fuss or fanfare. For both the U.S. economy and the world economy as a whole, demand and supply is the primary social mechanism for answering the basic questions about what is produced, how it is produced, and for whom it is produced.

Key Concepts and Summary

1. A **demand schedule** is a table that shows the **quantity demanded** at different prices in the market. A **demand curve** shows the relationship between quantity demanded and price in a given market on a graph. The **law of demand** points out that a higher price typically leads to a lower quantity demanded.

2. A **supply schedule** is a table that shows the **quantity supplied** at different prices in the market. A **supply curve** shows the relationship between quantity supplied and price on a graph. The **law of supply** points out that a higher price typically leads to a higher quantity supplied.

3. The **equilibrium price** and **equilibrium quantity** occur where the supply and demand curves cross. The **equilibrium** occurs where the quantity demanded is equal to the quantity supplied.

4. If the price is below the equilibrium level, then the quantity demanded will exceed the quantity supplied. **Excess demand** or a **shortage** will exist. If the

price is above the equilibrium level, then the quantity supplied will exceed the quantity demanded. **Excess supply** or a **surplus** will exist. In either case, economic pressures will push the price toward the equilibrium level.

5. Economists often use the *ceteris paribus* or "other things equal" assumption, that while examining the economic impact of one event, all other factors remain unchanged for the purpose of the analysis.

6. Factors that can shift the demand curve for goods and services, causing a different quantity to be demanded at any given price, include changes in tastes, population, income, prices of **substitute** or **complement** goods, and expectations about future conditions and prices.

7. Factors that can shift the supply curve for goods and services, causing a different quantity to be supplied at any given price, include natural conditions, input prices, changes in technology, and government taxes, regulations, or subsidies.

8. When using the supply and demand framework to think about how an event will affect the equilibrium price and quantity, proceed through four steps: (a) Sketch a supply and demand diagram to think about what the market looked like before the event; (b) decide whether the event will affect supply or demand; (c) decide whether the effect on supply or demand is negative or positive, and draw the appropriate shifted supply or demand curve; (d) compare the new equilibrium price and quantity to the original ones.

9. **Price ceilings** prevent a price from rising above a certain level. When a price ceiling is set below the equilibrium price, quantity demanded will exceed quantity supplied, and excess demand or shortages will result. **Price floors** prevent a price from falling below as certain level. When a price floor is set above the equilibrium price, quantity supplied will exceed quantity demanded, and excess supply or surpluses will result.

10. Price floors and price ceilings often lead to unintended consequences, because buyers and sellers have many margins for action. These margins include **black markets,** side payments, quality adjustments, and shifts in who is involved in the transaction.

11. Policies that shift supply and demand explicitly, through targeted subsidies or taxes, are often preferable to policies that attempt to set prices, because they avoid the shortages, surpluses, and other unintended consequences that price ceilings and floors typically produce.

12. **Consumer surplus** is the gap between the price that consumers are willing to pay, based on their preferences, and the market equilibrium price. **Producer surplus** is the gap between the price for which producers are willing to sell a product, based on their costs, and the market equilibrium price. **Social surplus** is the sum of consumer surplus and producer surplus. Total surplus is larger at the equilibrium quantity and price than it will be at any other quantity and price. **Deadweight loss** is loss in total surplus that occurs when the economy produces at an inefficient quantity.

Review Questions

1. In the economic view, what determines the level of prices?

2. What does a downward-sloping demand curve mean about how buyers in a market will react to a higher price?

3. Will demand curves have the same exact shape in all markets?

4. What does an upward-sloping supply curve mean about how sellers in a market will react to a higher price?

5. Will supply curves have the same shape in all markets?

6. What is the relationship between quantity demanded and quantity supplied at equilibrium?

7. How can you locate the equilibrium point on a demand and supply graph?

8. When analyzing a market, how do economists deal with the problem that many factors that affect the market are changing at the same time?

9. If the price is above the equilibrium level, would you predict excess supply or excess demand? If the price is below the equilibrium level, would you predict a shortage or a surplus?

10. Explain why a price that is above the equilibrium level will tend to fall toward equilibrium. Explain why a price that is below the equilibrium level will tend to rise toward the equilibrium.

11. Name some factors that can cause a shift in the demand curve in markets for goods and services.

12. Does a price ceiling attempt to make a price higher or lower?

13. How does a price ceiling set below the equilibrium level affect quantity demanded and quantity supplied?

14. Does a price floor attempt to make a price higher or lower?

15. How does a price floor set above the equilibrium level affect quantity demanded and quantity supplied?

16. Make a list of ways that buyers and sellers may respond to price ceilings and price floors, other than changes in quantity.

17. Why might economists commonly prefer public policies that shift demand and/or supply rather than imposing price ceilings or price floors?

18. What's the difference between demand and quantity demanded?

19. Name some factors that can cause a shift in the supply curve in markets for goods and services.

20. Is supply the same thing as quantity supplied? Explain.

21. What is consumer surplus? How is it illustrated on a demand and supply diagram?

22. What is producer surplus? How is it illustrated on a demand and supply diagram?

23. What is total surplus? How is it illustrated on a demand and supply diagram?

24. What is the relationship between total surplus and economic efficiency?

25. What is deadweight loss?

5

Labor and Financial Capital Markets

Thinking about demand and supply curves in markets for labor and markets for financial capital requires a shift in perspective about the identity of demanders and suppliers. In markets for goods and services, individuals act as consumers on the demand side of the market, while firms appear on the supply side. But in labor markets, individuals are the suppliers of labor, while firms and other employers who hire labor are on the demand side. In markets for financial capital, both individuals and firms can play roles as savers who supply financial capital and also as borrowers who demand it.

Most college students play an active role in both labor and financial capital markets. Employment is a fact of life for most college students: 46% of all college students ages 16–24—and 81% of part-time students—were employed in 2007. Most college students are also heavily involved in financial markets, primarily as borrowers. Among full-time college students, about half take out a loan to help finance their education each year, and those loans average about $6,000 per year. Many college students also borrow using credit cards and car loans. As this chapter will illustrate, labor markets and financial capital markets can be analyzed with the same tools of demand and supply as markets for goods and services.

Demand and Supply at Work in Labor Markets

Markets for labor have demand and supply curves, just like markets for goods and services. The law of demand applies in labor markets just as it does in goods and services markets. Specifically, a higher salary or wage—that is, a higher price in the labor market—leads to a decrease in quantity of labor demanded by employers, while a lower salary or wage leads to an increase in the quantity of labor demanded. The law of supply functions in labor markets, too; that is, a higher price for labor leads to a higher quantity of labor supplied.

Equilibrium in the Labor Market

In 2008, about 35,000 nurses worked in the Minneapolis–St. Paul, Minnesota, metropolitan area. They work for a variety of employers: hospitals, doctors' offices, schools, health clinics, and nursing homes. Exhibit 5-1 illustrates how demand and supply determine equilibrium in this labor market. Let's walk through the elements of the figure one step at a time.

The horizontal axis shows the quantity of nurses hired. In this example, labor is measured by number of workers, but another common way to measure the quantity of labor is by the number of hours worked. The vertical axis shows the price for nurses' labor—that is, how much they are paid. In this example, the price of labor is measured by salary on an annual basis, although in other cases the price of labor could be measured by monthly or weekly pay, or even the wage paid per hour. The demand and supply schedules accompanying the exhibit list the quantity supplied and quantity demanded of nurses at different salaries.

As the salary for nurses rises, the quantity demanded will fall. Some hospitals and nursing homes may cut back on the number of nurses they hire, or they may lay off some of their existing nurses. Employers who face higher nurses' salaries may also try to look after patients by investing in physical equipment, like computer monitoring and

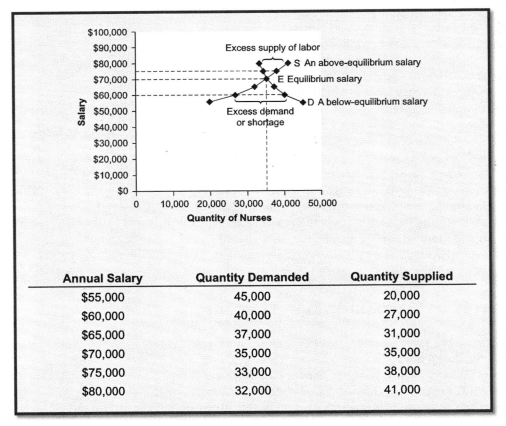

Annual Salary	Quantity Demanded	Quantity Supplied
$55,000	45,000	20,000
$60,000	40,000	27,000
$65,000	37,000	31,000
$70,000	35,000	35,000
$75,000	33,000	38,000
$80,000	32,000	41,000

Exhibit 5-1   A Labor Market Example: Demand and Supply for Nurses in Minneapolis–St. Paul

The demand curve D of those employers who want to hire nurses intersects with the supply curve S of those who are qualified and willing to work as nurses at the equilibrium point E. The equilibrium salary is $70,000 and the equilibrium quantity is 35,000 nurses. At an above-equilibrium salary of $75,000, quantity supplied increases to 38,000, but the quantity of nurses demanded at the higher pay declines to 33,000. At this above-equilibrium salary, an excess supply or surplus of nurses would exist. At a below-equilibrium salary of $60,000, quantity supplied declines to 27,000, while the quantity demanded at the lower wage increases to 40,000 nurses. At this below-equilibrium salary, excess demand or a surplus exists.

diagnostic systems, or by using lower-paid health care aides to reduce the number of nurses they need to hire.

As salaries for nurses rise, the quantity supplied will rise. If nurses' salaries in Minneapolis–St. Paul are higher than in other cities, more people will be willing to train as nurses; more nurses will move to Minneapolis–St. Paul to find jobs; and those currently trained as nurses will be more likely to pursue nursing as a full-time job, rather than trying other jobs.

At equilibrium, the quantity supplied and the quantity demanded are equal. Thus, every employer who wants to hire a nurse at this equilibrium wage can find a willing worker, and every nurse who wants to work at this equilibrium salary can find a job. In Exhibit 5-1, the supply curve S and demand curve D intersect at the equilibrium point E. The equilibrium quantity of nurses in the Minneapolis–St. Paul area is 35,000, and the average annual salary is $70,000. This example simplifies the nursing market by focusing on the "average" nurse. In reality, or course, the market for nurses is actually made up of many smaller markets, like markets for nurses with varying degrees of experience and credentials. But many markets contain closely related products that differ in quality, for instance, even a simple product like gasoline comes in regular, premium, and super-premium, each with a different price. Even in such cases, discussing the average price of gasoline or the average salary for nurses can still be useful.

When the price of labor is not at the equilibrium, economic incentives tend to move salaries toward the equilibrium. For example, if salaries for nurses in Minneapolis–St. Paul were above the equilibrium at $75,000 per year, then 38,000 people want to work as nurses, but employers want to hire only 33,000 nurses. At that above-equilibrium salary, excess supply or a surplus results. In a situation of excess supply in the labor market, with many applicants for every job opening, employers who hire nurses will have an incentive to offer lower wages than they otherwise would have. The salary will move down toward equilibrium.

In contrast, if the salary is below the equilibrium at, say, $60,000 per year, then a situation of excess demand or a shortage arises. In this case, employers encouraged by the relatively lower wage want to hire 40,000 nurses, but only 27,000 individuals want to work as nurses in Minneapolis–St. Paul. In response to shortage, some employers in this metropolitan area will offer higher pay in order to attract the nurses. Other employers will have to match the higher pay to keep their own employees. The higher salaries will encourage more nurses to train or work in Minneapolis–St. Paul. Again, price and quantity in the labor market will move toward equilibrium.

Shifts in Labor Demand

The demand curve for labor shows what quantity of labor employers wish to hire at any salary or wage, under the *ceteris paribus* assumption that all other relevant economic factor are held constant. At least three types of economic events can cause a shift in the demand for labor, so that a higher or lower quantity of labor is hired at every salary or wage: changes in the quantity of the product being produced with that labor; changes in how that output is produced; and government regulations affecting firms that demand labor.

A change in the quantity of the product being produced with a certain kind of that labor will alter the demand for that kind of labor. Expenditures on health care increased from about 9% of the U.S. economy in 1980 to 17% of the economy by 2009. When people spend more dollars on health care services, the demand for nurses increases at every given wage level, too. Demand for nurses may expand even more rapidly in the future, because the proportion of Americans over the age of 65 will increase in the opening decades of the twenty-first century and the elderly tend to consume more health care. Conversely, when the quantity produced of a certain product decreases, then demand for workers who make that product decreases, too.

Demand for labor may also shift because of changes in how output is produced. Firms that want to earn high profits look for a combination of inputs—workers, materials, and equipment—to keep costs low. Hospitals have sometimes tried to hold down costs by hiring health care aides rather than better-trained and higher wage nurses.

Government regulations can also affect the quantity of workers that firms wish to hire at any given wage. For example, government rules may require nurses, rather than less-trained health care workers, to carry out certain medical procedures, while prohibiting nurses from carrying out other procedures. Changes in government rules can increase or decrease the quantity demanded of nurses at any given price.

Shifts in Labor Supply

On the supply side of the labor market, two main factors will affect how many people want to work at a certain job at a given salary level. One issue is how the job is perceived by workers relative to other choices. For example, there seems to have been a shift in the tastes of workers such that nursing looks relatively less attractive compared to other alternative jobs. One reason for that shift is that the job options open to women in health care, law, and business have expanded in recent decades.

Government policies can also affect the supply of labor for jobs. On one side, the government may support rules that set high qualifications for certain jobs: academic training, certificates or licenses, or experience. When these qualifications are made tougher, the supply of workers in that job will decrease at any given wage. On the other hand, the government may also reduce the required level of qualifications or else subsidize training; for example, government might offer subsidies for nursing schools or nursing students. Such provisions would shift the supply curve of nurses to the right.

A change in salary will lead to a movement along labor demand or labor supply curves, but it will not shift those curves. However, other events like those sketched here will cause either the demand or the supply of labor to shift, and thus will move the labor market to a new equilibrium salary and quantity.

Technology and Wage Inequality: The Four-Step Process

Economic events can change equilibrium salary (or wage) and quantity of labor. Consider how the wave of new information technologies like computer and telecommunications networks have affected low-skill and high-skill workers in the U.S. economy. From the perspective of employers who demand labor, these new technologies are often a substitute for low-skill laborers like file clerks who used to keep file cabinets full of paper records of transactions. However, these new technologies are a complement to high-skill managers, who benefit from the technological advances by being able to monitor more information, communicate more easily, and juggle a wider array of responsibilities. Thus, how will the new technologies affect the wages of high-skill and low-skill workers? For this question, the four-step process for analyzing how shifts in supply or demand affect a market (introduced in Chapter 4) works in this way.

1. What did the markets for low-skill labor and high-skill labor look like before the arrival of the new technologies? In Exhibits 5-2a and 5-2b, S_0 is the original supply

Quantity of Low-skill Labor
(a) Technological change and low-skill labor

Quantity of High-skill Labor
(b) Technological change and high-skill labor

Exhibit 5-2
Technology and Wages: Applying Demand and Supply

Step 1: What did the market look like before the change? In this case there are two markets: low-skill labor and high-skill labor. In each market, the original demand curve for labor is D_0, the original supply curve for labor is S_0, and the original equilibrium is E_0, where the equilibrium wage is w_0 and the equilibrium quantity is q_0.

Step 2: Does the new technology affect the supply of labor or the demand for labor? The new technology affects demand for labor.

Step 3: How will the new technology alter demand for the two types of labor? As the technology substitute for low-skill labor becomes cheaper, demand for low-skill labor will shift to the left, as shown by the shift from D_0 to D_1 in the market for low-skill labor. As the technology complement for high-skill labor becomes cheaper, demand for high-skill labor will shift to the right, as shown by the shift from D_0 to D_1 in the market for high-skilled labor.

Step 4: Compare the new equilibrium to the original equilibrium. The new equilibrium for low-skill labor at E_1 has a lower wage and quantity than the original equilibrium E_0 in the market for low-skill labor. The new equilibrium for high-skilled labor at E_1 has a higher wage and quantity than the original equilibrium.

curve for labor and D_0 is the original demand curve for labor. In each graph, the original point of equilibrium, E_0, occurs at the price w_0 and the quantity q_0. The equilibrium pay for high-skill labor in Exhibit 5-2b exceeds the equilibrium pay for low-skill labor.

2. Does the new technology affect the supply of labor from households or the demand for labor from firms? The technology change described here affects demand for labor by firms that hire workers.

3. Will the new technology increase or decrease demand? Based on the description earlier, as the technology substitute for low-skill labor becomes available, demand for low-skill labor will shift to the left from D_0 to D_1. As the technology complement for high-skill labor becomes cheaper, demand for high-skill labor will shift to the right from D_0 to D_1.

4. The new equilibrium for low-skill labor, shown as point E_1 with price w_1 and quantity q_1, has a lower wage and quantity hired than the original equilibrium, E_0. The new

equilibrium for high-skill labor, shown as point E_1 with price w_1 and quantity q_1, has a higher wage and quantity hired than the original equilibrium E_0.

Thus, the demand and supply model predicts that the new computer and communications technologies will raise the pay of high-skill workers but reduce the pay of low-skill workers. Indeed, from the 1970s to the mid-2000s, the wage gap widened between high-skill and low-skill labor. In 1980, for example, a college graduate earned about 30% more than a high school graduate with comparable job experience, but by 2008, a college graduate earned about 70% more than an otherwise comparable high school graduate. Many economists believe that the trend toward greater wage inequality across the U.S. economy was primarily caused by the new technologies.

Price Floors in the Labor Market: Living Wages and Minimum Wages

In contrast to goods and services markets, price ceilings are rare in labor markets, because rules that prevent people from earning income are not politically popular. There is one exception: sometimes limits are proposed on the high incomes of top business executives.

The labor market, however, presents some prominent examples of price floors, which are often used as an attempt to increase the wages of low-paid workers. The U.S. government sets a **minimum wage,** a price floor that makes it illegal for an employer to pay employees less than a certain hourly rate. In mid-2009, the U.S. minimum wage was raised to $7.25 per hour. Local political movements in a number of U.S. cities have pushed for a higher minimum wage, which they call a *living wage*. Promoters of living wage laws maintain that the minimum wage is too low to ensure a reasonable standard of living. They base this conclusion on the calculation that, if you work 40 hours a week at a minimum wage of $7.25 per hour for 50 weeks a year, your annual income is $14,500, which is less than the official U.S. government definition of what it means for a family with one parent and children to be in poverty.

minimum wage: A price floor that makes it illegal for an employer to pay employees less than a certain hourly rate.

Supporters of the living wage argue that full-time workers should be assured a high enough wage so that they can afford the essentials of life: shelter, food, clothing, and health care. Since Baltimore passed the first living wage law in 1994, several dozen cities enacted similar laws in the late 1990s and into the 2000s. The living wage ordinances do not apply to all employers, but they have specified that all employees of the city or employees of firms that are hired by the city be paid at least a certain wage that is usually a few dollars per hour above the U.S. minimum wage.

Exhibit 5-3 illustrates the situation of a city considering a living wage law. The wage appears on the vertical axis, because the wage is the price in the labor market. Before the passage of the living wage law, the equilibrium wage is $10 per hour and the city hires 1,200 workers at this wage. However, a group of concerned citizens persuades the city council to enact a living wage law requiring employers to pay no less than $12 per hour. In response to the higher wage, the horizontal dashed line in the graph, 1,600 workers look for jobs with the city. At this higher wage, the city, as an employer, is willing to hire only 700 workers. At the price floor, the quantity supplied exceeds the quantity demanded, and a surplus of labor exists in this market.

The Minimum Wage as an Example of a Price Floor

The U.S. minimum wage is a price floor that is set either very close to the equilibrium wage or even slightly below it. About 1% of American workers are actually paid the minimum wage. In other words, the vast majority of the U.S. labor force had its wages

Exhibit 5-3   A Living Wage: Example of a Price Floor

The original equilibrium in this labor market is a wage of $10/hour and a quantity of 1,200 workers, shown at point E. Imposing a wage floor at $12/hour leads to an excess supply of labor. At that wage, the quantity of labor supplied is 1,600 and the quantity of labor demanded is only 700.

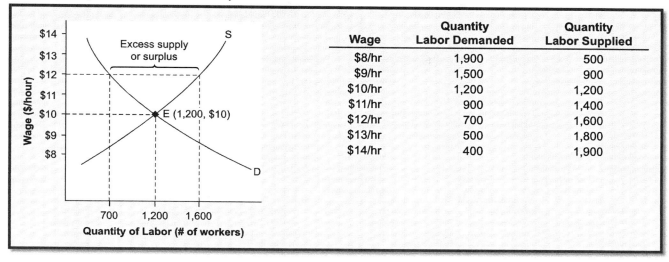

Wage	Quantity Labor Demanded	Quantity Labor Supplied
$8/hr	1,900	500
$9/hr	1,500	900
$10/hr	1,200	1,200
$11/hr	900	1,400
$12/hr	700	1,600
$13/hr	500	1,800
$14/hr	400	1,900

determined in the labor market, not as a result of the government price floor. In many cities, the federal minimum wage is apparently below the market price for unskilled labor, because employers offer more than the minimum wage to checkout clerks and other low-skill workers without any government prodding.

Economists have attempted to estimate how much the minimum wage reduces the quantity demanded of low-skill labor. A typical result of such studies is that a 10% increase in the minimum wage would decrease the hiring of unskilled workers by 1–2%, which seems a relatively small reduction. In fact, some studies have even found no effect of a higher minimum wage on employment at certain times and places—although these studies are controversial.

Let's suppose that the minimum wage set lies just slightly *below* the equilibrium wage level. Wages could fluctuate according to market forces above this price floor, but they would not be allowed to move beneath the floor. In this situation, the price floor minimum wage is said to be *nonbinding*—that is, the price floor isn't determining the market outcome. Even if the minimum wage moves just a little higher, it will still have no effect on the quantity of employment in the economy, as long as it remains below the equilibrium wage. Even if the minimum wage is increased by enough so that it rises slightly above the equilibrium wage and becomes binding, only a small excess supply gap between the quantity demanded and quantity supplied of low-skill labor.

These insights help to explain why U.S. minimum wage laws have historically had only a small impact on employment. Since the minimum wage has typically been set close to the equilibrium wage for low-skilled and sometimes even below it, it hasn't had a large effect in creating an excess supply of labor. However, if the minimum wage were increased dramatically—say, if it were doubled to match some of the living wages that some U.S. cities have considered—then its impact on reducing the quantity demanded of employment would be far more powerful. Minimum wages in other countries are often higher relative to wages across the economy than in the United States. For example, in the United States, a full-time minimum wage worker would earn about one-third of the

The Maze of Minimum Wage Arguments

Although there is controversy over just how much raising the minimum wage will affect the quantity demanded of low-skill labor, let's say for the sake of the argument that a 10% rise in the minimum wage will reduce the employment of low-skill workers by 2%. Does this outcome prove that raising the minimum wage by 10% is bad public policy? Not necessarily.

If 98% of those receiving the minimum wage have a pay increase of 10%, but 2% of those receiving the minimum wage lose their jobs, do the gains for society as a whole greater than the losses? The answer is not clear, because job losses even for a small group may outweigh modest income gains for others. To complicate the issue further, we need to consider who exactly are the minimum wage workers losing their jobs. If the 2% of minimum wage workers who lose their jobs are struggling to support families, that's one thing. If those who lose their job are high school students picking up spending money over summer vacation, that's something else. Another complexity arises from the fact that many minimum wage workers don't work full-time for an entire year. Imagine a minimum wage worker who holds different part-time jobs for a few months at a time, with some weeks in between without any work. The worker in this situation receives the 10% raise in the minimum wage when working, but also ends up working 2% fewer hours during the year. Overall, this worker's income would rise because the 10% pay raise would more than offset the 2% fewer hours worked.

Of course, the preceding arguments do not prove that raising the minimum wage is necessarily a good idea either. There may well be other, better public policy options for helping low-wage workers. The lesson from this maze of minimum wage arguments is that even those who agree on the basic analysis of how a proposed economic policy affects quantity demanded and quantity supplied may still disagree on whether the policy is a good idea.

total annual income of an average worker in the U.S. economy. In Australia, France, and Ireland, a full-time worker at the minimum wage in those countries would earn about half of what an average worker makes in those economies. In these countries, an increase in the minimum wage would thus be likely to have a greater effect in reducing employment among low-wage workers than a similar percentage increase in the minimum wage would have in the United States.

Demand and Supply in Financial Capital Markets

In the U.S. economy, $1.5 trillion was saved in 2009. Some of the savings ended up in banks, which in turn loaned the money to individuals or businesses that wanted to borrow money. Some was invested in private companies or loaned to government agencies that wanted to borrow money to raise funds for purposes like building roads or mass transit. Some firms took their savings and reinvested the money in their own business.

At this point, we'll avoid getting tangled in all the different kinds of financial investments—like bank accounts, stocks, and bonds. The task at hand is to determine how the demand and supply model links those who wish to supply financial capital with those who demand financial investments. Those who save money and make financial investments, whether individuals or businesses, are on the supply side of the financial capital market. Those who borrow money or firms who receive financial investments are on the demand side of the financial capital market.

Who Demands and Who Supplies in Financial Capital Markets

In any market, the price is what suppliers receive and what demanders pay. In financial capital markets, those who supply financial capital through saving expect to receive a rate of return, while those who demand financial capital by receiving funds expect to pay a rate of return. This rate of return can come in a variety of forms, depending on the type of financial investment. A straightforward example of a rate of return, often used for simplicity, is the interest rate. For example, when you supply money into a savings account at a bank, you receive a certain interest rate. If you demand a loan to buy a car or a computer, you will need to pay interest on the money you borrow.

Let's consider the market for borrowing money with credit cards. The United States has 180 million credit card holders, who hold a total of 1.4 billion cards (an average of about eight cards per person). If you use a credit card to make a purchase, but do not pay the bill by the deadline, you have borrowed money from the credit card company and will need to pay interest. A typical credit card interest rate ranges from 12% to 18% per year. In 2010, Americans had about $900 billion outstanding in credit card debts not paid on time. About half of U.S. families with credit cards report that they almost always pay the full balance on time, but one-quarter of U.S. families with credit cards say that they "hardly ever" pay off the card in full. While credit card companies have different annual payments, different penalties for late payment, and different interest rates, let's say that on average the annual interest rate for credit card borrowing is 15% per year. Thus, Americans pay tens of billions of dollars every year in interest on their credit cards—a total that doesn't include fees, like basic fees for the credit card or fees for late payments.

Exhibit 5-4 illustrates demand and supply in the financial capital market for credit cards. The horizontal axis of the financial capital market shows the quantity that is loaned or borrowed in this market. The vertical or price axis of the financial capital market shows the rate of return, which in the case of credit card borrowing can be measured with an interest rate. The demand and supply schedule accompanying the figure shows the quantity of financial capital that consumers demand at various interest rates and the quantity that credit card firms (often banks) are willing to supply.

The laws of demand and supply continue to apply in the financial capital markets. According to the law of demand, a higher rate of return (that is, a higher price) will decrease the quantity demanded. As the interest rate rises, consumers will reduce the quantity that they borrow. According to the law of supply, a higher price increases the quantity supplied. Consequently, as the interest rate paid on credit card borrowing rises, more firms will be eager to issue credit cards and to encourage customers to use them. Conversely, if the interest rate on credit cards falls, the quantity of financial capital supplied in the credit card market will decrease.

Equilibrium in Financial Capital Markets

In the financial capital market for credit cards shown in Exhibit 5-4, the supply curve S and the demand curve D cross at the equilibrium point E. The equilibrium occurs at an interest rate of 15%, where the quantity of financial capital demanded and the quantity supplied are equal at an equilibrium quantity of $600 billion.

If the interest rate (remember, this measures the "price" in the financial capital market) is above the equilibrium level, then an excess supply, or a surplus, of financial capital will arise in this market. For example, at an interest rate of 21%, the quantity of financial capital supplied increases to $750 billion, while the quantity demanded decreases to $480 billion. At this above-equilibrium interest rate, firms are eager to supply loans to credit card borrowers, but relatively few people or businesses wish to borrow. As a result, some credit card firms will lower the interest rates (or other fees) they charge to attract more business. This strategy will push the interest rate down toward the equilibrium level.

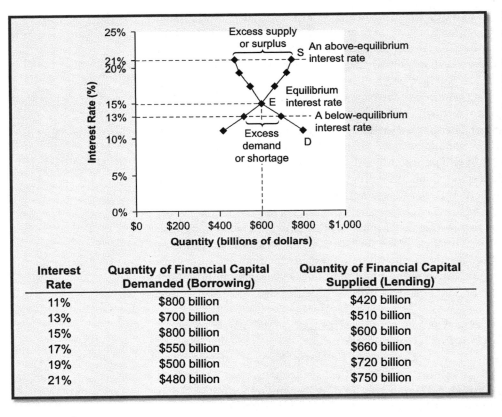

Exhibit 5-4   Demand and Supply for Borrowing Money with Credit Cards

In this market for credit card borrowing, the demand curve D for borrowing financial capital intersects the supply curve S for lending financial capital at equilibrium E. At the equilibrium, the interest rate (the "price" in this market) is 15% and the quantity of financial capital being loaned and borrowed is $600 billion. The equilibrium is the price where the quantity demanded and the quantity supplied are equal. At an above-equilibrium interest rate like 21%, the quantity of financial capital supplied would increase to $750 billion, but the quantity demanded would decrease to $480 billion. A situation of excess supply or surplus would exist. At a below-equilibrium interest rate like 13%, the quantity of financial capital demanded would increase to $700 billion, but the quantity of financial capital supplied would decrease to $510 billion. A situation of excess demand or shortage would exist.

Interest Rate	Quantity of Financial Capital Demanded (Borrowing)	Quantity of Financial Capital Supplied (Lending)
11%	$800 billion	$420 billion
13%	$700 billion	$510 billion
15%	$800 billion	$600 billion
17%	$550 billion	$660 billion
19%	$500 billion	$720 billion
21%	$480 billion	$750 billion

If the interest rate is below the equilibrium, then excess demand or a shortage of financial capital occurs in this market. At an interest rate of 13%, the quantity of financial capital that credit card borrowers demand increases to $700 billion; but the quantity that credit card firms are willing to supply is only $510 billion. In this situation, credit card firms will perceive that they are overloaded with eager borrowers and conclude that they have an opportunity to raise interest rates or fees. Thus, the interest rate will face economic pressures to creep up toward the equilibrium level.

Shifts in Demand and Supply in Financial Capital Markets

The demand and supply of financial capital involves an intertemporal trade-off—that is, making a decision in the present with an eye on the future. Thus, an economic factor can shift demand or supply of financial capital if it alters the balance that people have struck between past and present.

Those who supply financial capital face two broad decisions: how much to save, and how to divide up their savings among different forms of financial investments. In thinking about how much to save, people must decide what they will need in the future to address expected or unexpected events. For example, the Social Security program in which the government sends checks to workers and their families after retirement tended to reduce the quantity of financial capital that workers saved. In deciding between different forms of financial investments, suppliers of financial capital will have to consider the rates of return and the risks involved with different choices. If Investment A becomes more risky, or the return diminishes, then savers will shift their funds to Investment B—and the supply curve of financial capital for Investment A will shift back to the left while the supply curve of capital for Investment B shifts to the right.

Those who demand financial capital want the money now and are willing to repay in the future. For example, individuals might borrow money to purchase a long-term possession such as a condominium, a house or a car. A business might seek financial investment so that it has the funds to build a factory or invest in a research and development project that won't pay off for five years, ten years or even more. Thus, when consumers and businesses have greater confidence that they will be able to repay in the future, the quantity demanded of financial capital at any given interest rate will shift to the right. For example, in the late 1990s many businesses became extremely confident that investments in new technology would have a high rate of return, and their demand for financial capital shifted to the right. Conversely, during the economic doldrums of 2008 and 2009, their demand for financial capital at any given interest rate shifted to the left.

The United States as a Global Borrower: The Four-Step Process

In the global economy, trillions of dollars of financial investment cross national borders every year. Each year in the opening decade of the 2000s, financial investors from foreign countries were investing several hundred billion dollars per year more in the U.S. economy than U.S. financial investors were investing abroad. Imagine that the U.S. economy, for one reason or another, became viewed as a less desirable place for foreign investors to put their money. Using the four-step process for analyzing how changes in supply and demand affect equilibrium outcomes, how would this change affect the equilibrium price and quantity in the U.S. financial capital markets?

1. Draw a diagram showing demand and supply for financial capital that represents the original scenario in which foreign investors are pouring money into the U.S. economy. Exhibit 5-5 shows a demand curve, D, and a supply curve, S, where the supply of capital includes the funds arriving from foreign investors. The original equilibrium E_0 occurs at interest rate r_0 and quantity of financial investment q_0.

2. Will the diminished confidence in the U.S. economy as a place to invest affect demand or supply? The inflow of capital from foreign investors affects the supply of financial capital into the U.S. economy.

3. Will supply increase or decrease? When the enthusiasm of foreign investors' diminishes for investing their money in the U.S. economy, the supply of financial capital shifts to the left. Exhibit 5-5 shows the supply curve shift from S_0 to S_1.

4. Thus, foreign investors' diminished enthusiasm leads to a new equilibrium, E_1, which occurs at the higher interest rate, r_1, and the lower quantity of financial investment, q_1.

This example describes one of the macroeconomic concerns for the U.S. economy in recent years. The U.S. economy has experienced an enormous inflow of foreign capital. By 2008, U.S. investors had accumulated $20 trillion of foreign assets, but foreign investors owned a total $23 trillion of U.S. assets. If foreign investors were to pull their money out of the U.S. economy and invest elsewhere in the world, the result could be a lower quantity of financial investment capital in the United States, available only at a higher interest rate. This reduced inflow of foreign financial investment could impose hardship on U.S. consumers and firms interested in borrowing.

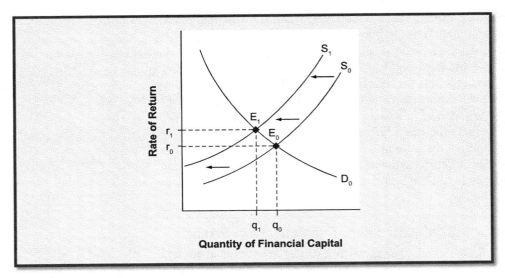

In a modern economy, financial capital often moves invisibly through electronic transfers between one bank account and another. Yet these flows of funds can be analyzed with the same tools of demand and supply as markets for goods or labor.

Price Ceilings in Financial Capital Markets: Usury Laws

As discussed earlier, about 180 million Americans own credit cards, and their interest payments and fees total tens of billions of dollars each year. It's little wonder that political pressures sometimes arise for setting limits on the interest rates or fees that credit cards companies can charge. The firms that issue credit cards, including banks, oil companies, phone companies, and retail stores, respond that the higher interest rates are necessary to cover the losses created by those who borrow on their credit cards and who do not repay on time or at all. These companies also point out that credit card holders can avoid paying interest if they pay their bills on time.

Consider the credit card market as illustrated in Exhibit 5-6. In this financial capital market, the vertical axis shows the interest rate (which is the price in the financial capital market). Demanders in the credit card market are households; suppliers are the companies that issue credit cards. This exhibit does not use specific numbers, which would be hypothetical in any case, but instead focuses on the underlying economic relationships. Imagine that a law imposes a price ceiling that holds the interest rate charged on credit cards at the interest rate r_c, which lies below the interest rate r_0 that would otherwise have prevailed in the market. The price ceiling is shown by the horizontal dashed line in Exhibit 5-6. The demand and supply model predicts that at the lower price ceiling interest rate, the quantity demanded of credit card debt will increase from its original level of Q_0 to Q_D; however, the quantity supplied of credit card debt will decrease from the original Q_0 to Q_S. At the price ceiling r_c, quantity demanded will exceed quantity supplied. Consequently, a number of people who want to have credit cards and are willing to pay the prevailing interest rate will find that companies are unwilling to issue cards to them. The result will be a credit card shortage.

Many states do have **usury laws,** which impose an upper limit on the interest rate that lenders can charge. However, in many cases these upper limits are so high that they

Exhibit 5-5   The United States as a Global Borrower: The Four-Step Process

Step 1: Draw a diagram showing demand and supply for financial capital that represents the original scenario. The demand curve D intersects the supply curve S of financial capital, which includes the funds arriving from foreign investors, at the equilibrium E_0.

Step 2: Will diminished confidence in the U.S. economy as a place to invest affect demand or supply? The inflow of financial capital from foreign investors into the U.S. economy affects supply.

Step 3: Which way will supply shift? The diminished enthusiasm of foreign investors for sending their money to the U.S. economy will shift the supply curve of capital to the left from S_0 to S_1.

Step 4: Compare the new equilibrium to the original. The new equilibrium E_1 occurs at the higher interest rate r_1, compared to r_0, and the lower quantity of financial investment q_1, compared to q_0.

Payday Advances: Valuable Service or Predatory Lending?

A "payday advance" works this way. When you receive a payday advance, you then write a personal check to the business that is providing the advance. For example, say that the check you write is for $200. The payday advance firm gives you $180 cash on the spot. It then agrees not to cash your check for a certain period of time—usually ranging from a week to a month—until you receive your next paycheck. In this example, when the payday advance firm cashes the check, it effectively collects a charge of $20 for lending $180 for a few weeks or a month.

Consumer protection groups have asserted that this charge, which is not officially an "interest rate" but a "fee," is outrageously high, and want a price ceiling to limit what they view as excessive interest rates. After all, a 10% interest charge per month, if compounded over 12 months, works out to an interest rate of $(1 + .10)^{12} = 314\%$ per year.

Companies that offer the payday advances point out that they provide cash on the spot, without credit checks or other fees. They point out that the cash advance may offer the recipient a way to pay for unexpected expenses like an emergency car repair. They argue that many of their customers have no other options for ready cash. They admit that some customers may borrow unwisely, but observe that customers can borrow unwisely in many ways, including with credit cards.

About 6% of the U.S. population—call it 19 million people—has taken out a payday loan. Roughly $50 billion in payday loans are made each year. Is a price ceiling law needed in the area of payday advances, to protect consumers who may be unsophisticated, low-income, or lacking access to regular banks? Or is a payday advance just another service that people should be free to buy or not buy, as they choose, without government rules?

Exhibit 5-6   Credit Card Interest Rates: Another Price Ceiling Example

The original intersection of demand D and supply S occurs at equilibrium E_0. However, a price ceiling is set at the interest rate r_c, below the equilibrium interest rate r_0 and so the interest rate cannot adjust upward to the equilibrium. At the price ceiling, the quantity demanded, Q_D exceeds the quantity supplied, Q_S. There is excess demand, also called a shortage.

are well above the market interest rate. For example, if the interest rate is not allowed to rise above 30% per year, it can still fluctuate below that level according to market forces. A price ceiling that is set at a relatively high level is non-binding, and it will have no practical effect unless the equilibrium price zooms high enough to exceed the price ceiling.

usury laws: Laws that impose an upper limit on the interest rate that lenders can charge.

Don't Kill the Price Messengers

Prices exist in markets for goods and services, for labor, and for financial capital. In all of these markets, prices serve as a remarkable social mechanism for collecting,

Demand and Supply Curves

Just as it would be foolish to try to learn the arithmetic of long division by memorizing every possible combination of numbers that can be divided by each other, it would be foolish to try to memorize every specific example of demand and supply in this chapter, this textbook, or this course. Demand and supply is not primarily a list of examples; it's a model to analyze prices and quantities. Even though demand and supply diagrams have many labels, they are fundamentally the same in their logic. Your goal should be to understand the underlying model. The demand and supply analysis is the second fundamental diagram for this course. (The opportunity set model introduced in Chapter 2 was the first.)

The exhibit displays a general demand and supply curve. The horizontal axis shows the different measures of quantity: a quantity of a good or service, or a quantity of labor for a given job, or a quantity of financial capital. The vertical axis shows a measure of price: the price of a good or service, the wage in the labor market, or the rate of return (like the interest rate) in the financial capital market.

The demand and supply model can explain the existing levels of prices, wages, and rates of return. To carry out such an analysis, think about the quantity that will be demanded at each price and the quantity that will be supplied at each price—that is, think about the shape of the demand and supply curves—and how these forces will combine to produce equilibrium. Demand and supply can

also be used to explain how economic events will cause changes in prices, wages, and rates of return. There are only four possibilities: the economic event may cause the demand curve to shift right or to shift left; or it may cause the supply curve to shift right or to shift left. The key to analyzing the effect of an economic event on equilibrium prices and quantities is to determine which of these four possibilities occurred.

Demand and Supply Curves

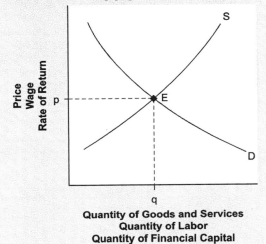

Quantity of Goods and Services
Quantity of Labor
Quantity of Financial Capital

combining, and transmitting information that is relevant to the market—namely, the relationship between demand and supply—and then serving as messengers to convey that information to buyers and sellers. In a market-oriented economy, no government agency or guiding intelligence oversees the set of responses and interconnections that result from a change in price. Instead, each consumer reacts according that person's preferences and budget set, and each profit-seeking producer reacts to the impact on its expected profits.

For example, if you are thinking about taking a plane trip to Hawaii, but the ticket turns out to be expensive during the week you intend to go, you merely look at the price and decide, based on the price, whether or not to fly. The price could be high because the cost of an input like jet fuel increased or because demand surged during that week. Or maybe the airline has raised the price temporarily to see how many people are willing to pay it. Perhaps all of these factors are present at the same time. But you don't need to analyze the market and break down the price change into its underlying factors. You just have to look at the price of a ticket and decide whether to fly.

Producers also commonly react to price changes without much caring why they occur. Imagine the situation of a farmer who grows oats and learns that the price of oats has risen. The higher price could be due to an increase in demand caused by a new scientific study proclaiming that eating oats is especially healthful. Or perhaps the price of a substitute grain, like corn, has risen, and people have responded by buying more oats. But the oat farmer does not need to know the details. The farmer only needs to know that the price of oats has increased and that it will be profitable to expand production as a result.

The actions of individual consumers and producers as they react to prices overlap and interlock in markets for goods, labor and financial capital. A change in any single market is transmitted through these multiple interconnections to other markets. The vision of the role of flexible prices helping markets to reach equilibrium and linking different markets together helps to explain why price controls can be so counterproductive. There is an old proverb: "Don't kill the messenger." This saying dates back to ancient times, when messengers carried information between distant cities and kingdoms. When a messenger arrived bearing bad news, there was an emotional impulse to kill the messenger. But killing the messenger didn't eliminate the bad news. Moreover, killing the messenger had an undesirable side effect: Other messengers would refuse to bring news to that city or kingdom, depriving the citizens of future information. A custom developed that messengers should not be held personally responsible for the news that they brought.

Those who seek price controls are trying to kill the messenger—or at least to stifle an unwelcome message that prices are bringing about the equilibrium level of price and quantity. But price controls do nothing to affect the underlying forces of demand and supply. Changes in demand and supply will continue to reveal themselves through consumers' and producers' reactions with respect to quantity demanded and quantity supplied. Moreover, immobilizing the price messenger through price controls will deprive everyone in the economy of critical information. Without this information, it becomes difficult for everyone—buyers and sellers alike—to react in a flexible and appropriate manner as changes occur throughout the economy.

Key Concepts and Summary

1. In the labor market, households are on the supply side of the market and firms are on the demand side. In the market for financial capital, households and firms can be on either side of the market: they are suppliers of financial capital when they save or make financial investments, and demanders of financial capital when they borrow or receive financial investments.

2. In the demand and supply analysis of labor markets, the price can be measured by the annual salary or hourly wage received. The quantity of labor can be measured in various ways, like number of workers or the number of hours worked.

3. Three factors can shift the demand curve for labor: a change in the quantity of the product that the labor produces; a change in the production process that uses more or less labor; and a change in government policy that affects the quantity of labor that firms with to hire at a given wage. Two factors can shift the supply curve for labor: how desirable a job appears to workers relative to the alternatives for reasons other than pay; and how government policy either restricts or encourages the quantity of workers trained for the job.

4. In the demand and supply analysis of financial capital markets, the "price" is the rate of return or the interest rate received. The quantity is measured by the money that flows from those who supply financial capital to those who demand it.

5. Two factors can shift the supply of financial capital to a certain investment: anything which makes people want to alter their existing levels of present and future consumption; and when the riskiness or return on one investment changes relative to other investments. Factors that can shift demand for capital include business confidence and consumer confidence in the future—since financial investments received in the present are typically repaid in the future.

Review Questions

1. What is the "price" commonly called in the labor market? What is the "price" commonly called in the financial capital market?

2. Are households demanders or suppliers in the goods market? Are firms demanders or supplies in the goods market? What about the labor market and the financial capital market?

3. Name some factors that can cause a shift in the demand curve in labor markets.

4. Name some factors that can cause a shift in the supply curve in labor markets.

5. Name some factors that can cause a shift in the demand curve in financial capital markets.

6. Name some factors that can cause a shift in the supply curve in financial capital markets.

Globalization and Protectionism

Imports of goods and services stir up worries everywhere. Some firms and workers in high-income countries like the United States, Japan, or the nations of the European Union fear that they will suffer if they must compete against firms in low-income countries of Latin America, Asia, or Africa that can pay lower wages. Conversely, some firms and workers in lower-wage countries like Mexico, India or South Africa fear that they will suffer if they must compete against the very productive workers and advanced technology in high-income countries. Some environmentalists worry that multinational firms may evade environmental protection laws by moving their production to countries with loose or nonexistent pollution standards. Some politicians worry that their nation may become overly dependent on key imported products, like oil. All of these fears tend to reach the same basic policy recommendation: Imports of foreign products should be reduced or even cut off. Government policies to reduce or block international trade are called **protectionism**, because they have the effect of protecting domestic producers from foreign competition.

Protectionism takes three main forms. **Tariffs** are taxes imposed on imported products, and by making imported products more expensive to consumers, they discourage imports. **Import quotas** are numerical limitations on the quantity of products that can be imported. Finally, **nontariff barriers** are all the other ways that a nation can draw up rules, regulations, inspections, and paperwork to make it more costly or difficult to import products. A rule that every imported product must be opened by hand and inspected with a magnifying glass, by one of just three government inspectors available at any given time, can limit imports just as effectively as high tariffs or low import quotas.

As one example, the United States has imposed to barriers to imports of textiles for decades. From the mid-1970s up to 2004, for example, the

protectionism: Government policies to reduce or block imports.

tariffs: Taxes imposed on imported products.

import quotas: Numerical limitations on the quantity of products that can be imported.

nontariff barriers: All the other ways a nation can draw up rules, regulations, inspections, and paperwork to make it more costly or difficult to import products.

international Multi-Fibre Arrangement specified exactly the quota of textile imports that each high-income country would accept from each low-income country. By 2009, the United States had phased out its import quotas on textiles. However, U.S. tariffs on textile and apparel imports were among the highest for any industry, averaging 10% overall, but ranging as high as 32% on man-made fiber sweaters and 28% on certain women's and girls' woven man-made fiber pants. There are also nontariff barriers in the form of "rules-of-origin" regulations, in which certain textiles are made in the United States, shipped to other countries, combined in making apparel with textiles made in those other countries—and then re-exported back to the United States at a lower tariff rate.

Despite these interlocking import quotas, tariffs, and nontariff barriers, the share of apparel sold in the United States that is imported rose from about half in 1999 to about three-quarters today. A federal agency, the U.S. International Trade Commission (ITC), estimated in 2009 that the continuation of present trends will lead the number of U.S. jobs in textiles and apparel to fall from 541,000 in 2007 to 361,000 by 2013. The ITC further estimated that removing the remaining tariff and nontariff barriers would cause the number of jobs in this industry to fall by 50,000 more. However, the U.S. textile industry jobs that are saved by import quotas come at a cost. Because textile and apparel protectionism adds to the costs of imports, consumers end up paying billions of dollars more for clothing each year. The ITC also points out that when the United States eliminates trade barriers in one area, then consumers spend the money they save on that product elsewhere in the economy—so that there is no overall loss of jobs for the economy as a whole. Of course, workers in some of the poorest countries of the world who would otherwise have jobs producing textiles, but find their opportunities blocked by tariff and nontariff barriers, would gain considerably if the United States reduced its barrier to trade in textiles.

This chapter begins with an economic analysis of who benefits from protectionism and who pays the costs of protectionism, using demand and supply analysis. The chapter then considers a list of concerns raised about global trade and in particular about imports. For example, how do imports affect the number of jobs, the level of wages, and work conditions? How might imports affect promising but immature domestic industries? What about the trade and environmental issues? The primary international agreement through which nations negotiate over their trade rules—including rules about tariffs, quotas, and nontariff barriers—is the World Trade Organization. The membership of the WTO includes about 150 nations, which includes most of the major (and minor) economies of the world. The chapter closes with a discussion of the history and direction of the WTO, as well as various regional trade treaties.

Protectionism: An Indirect Subsidy from Consumers to Producers

To the noneconomist, restricting imports may appear to be nothing more than taking sales from foreign producers and allowing domestic producers to achieve greater sales. But this analysis is incomplete, because firms do not operate in a vacuum. Instead, firms sell their products either to consumers or to other firms (if they are business suppliers). A demand and supply analysis of protectionism shows that protectionism is just not a matter of domestic gains and foreign losses, but a policy that imposes substantial domestic costs as well.

Demand and Supply Analysis of Protectionism

Consider international trade in sugar between two countries called Tartar and Plaque, illustrated in Exhibit 6-1. In the original supply and demand equilibrium without trade, the equilibrium price of sugar in Tartar is 12 cents per pound, with an equilibrium output of 30 tons. In Plaque, the equilibrium price of sugar in a world without trade is 24 cents per pound, with an equilibrium quantity of 80 tons. These equilibrium points are labeled with the point E.

If international trade between Tartar and Plaque now becomes possible, profit-seeking firms will spot an opportunity: buy sugar cheaply in Tartar, and sell it at a higher price in Plaque. As sugar is shipped from Tartar to Plaque, the quantity of sugar produced in Tartar will be greater than the quantity consumed in that country (with the extra production being exported) and the amount produced in Plaque is less than the amount consumed in that country (with the extra consumption being imported). The quantity of trade will be determined when price of sugar is the same in two countries—and thus there is no incentive to trade further. As shown in Exhibit 6-1, the equilibrium with trade occurs at a price of 16 cents per pound. At that price, the sugar

Exhibit 6-1   The Sugar Trade between Tartar and Plaque

Before trade, sugar sells in Tartar for 12 cents a pound and in Plaque for 24 cents per pound. When trade is allowed, businesses will buy sugar cheaply in Tartar and sell it in Plaque. The result with free trade will be that Tartar exports 15 pounds of sugar, Plaque imports 15 pounds of sugar, and the price is the same in the two countries at 20 cents per pound. If trade is only partly open between the countries, it will lead to an outcome between the free-trade and no-trade possibilities.

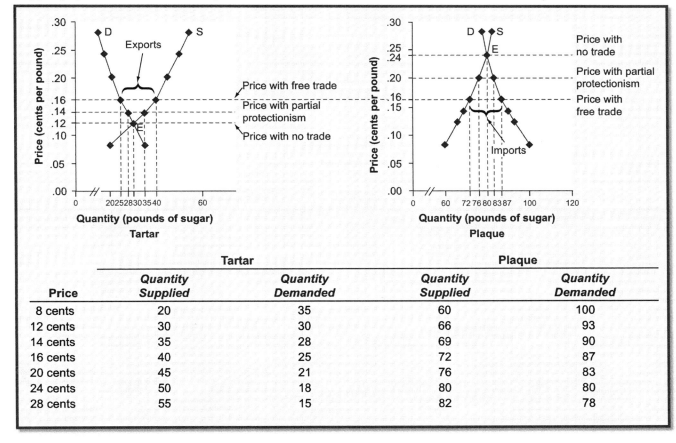

	Tartar		Plaque	
Price	Quantity Supplied	Quantity Demanded	Quantity Supplied	Quantity Demanded
8 cents	20	35	60	100
12 cents	30	30	66	93
14 cents	35	28	69	90
16 cents	40	25	72	87
20 cents	45	21	76	83
24 cents	50	18	80	80
28 cents	55	15	82	78

Low-Income Countries and Agricultural Trade

Here is a stark comparison about social priorities, which has been widely publicized by the international aid organization Oxfam.

High-income countries of the world—meaning primarily the United States, Canada, countries of the European Union, and Japan—subsidize their domestic farmers by roughly $1 billion per day, including the value both of direct subsidies to farmers and indirect subsidies that come in the form of limiting imports of farm products. However, the total amount of foreign aid from these same high-income countries to the poor countries of the world is about $70 billion per year.

The support of farmers in high income countries is devastating to the chances of farmers in low-income countries. Even when their climate and land are well-suited to products like cotton, rice, sugar or milk, the high income countries block their exports. In some cases, the situation gets even worse when the governments of high-income countries, having bought and paid for an excess supply of farm products, gives away those products in poor countries and drives local farmers out of business altogether. In the past, shipments of excess milk from the European Union to Jamaica have caused great hardship for Jamaican dairy farmers. Shipments of excess rice from the United States to Haiti drove thousands of low-income rice farmers in Haiti out of business. The opportunity costs of protectionism aren't paid just by domestic consumers, but also by foreign producers—and for many agricultural products, those foreign producers are the world's poor.

farmers of Tartar supply a quantity of 40 tons, while the consumers of Tartar buy only 25 tons. The extra 15 tons of sugar production, shown by the horizontal gap between the demand curve and the supply curve in Tartar, is exported to Plaque. In Plaque, at a price of 16 cents, the farmers produce a quantity of 72 tons and consumers demand a quantity of 87 tons. The excess demand of 15 tons by the consumers of Plaque, shown by the horizontal gap between demand and domestic supply at the price of 16 cents, is supplied by imported sugar.

The sugar farmers of Plaque are likely to argue that, if only they could be protected from sugar imported from Tartar, the country of Plaque would have higher domestic sugar production, more jobs in the sugar production industry, and Plaque's sugar farmers would receive a higher price. If the country of Plaque sets a high tariff on imported sugar, or sets an import quota at zero, then the result will be that the quantity of sugar traded between countries level could be reduced to zero, and the prices in each country will return to their levels before trade was allowed.

Blocking only some trade is also possible. For example, say that Plaque passed a sugar import quota of 7 tons; that is, Plaque will import no more than 7 tons of sugar, which means that Tartar can export no more than 7 tons of sugar. As a result, the price of sugar in Plaque will be 20 cents, which is the price where the quantity demanded is 7 tons greater than the domestic quantity supplied. Conversely, if Tartar can only export 7 tons of sugar, then the price of sugar in Tartar will be 14 cents per pound, which is the price where the domestic quantity supplied in Tartar is 7 tons greater than domestic demand. In general, when a country sets a low or medium tariff or import quota, then the equilibrium price and quantity will end up in between the cases of no trade at all and completely free trade.

Who Benefits and Who Pays?

Using the demand and supply model, consider the impact of protectionism on producers and consumers in each of the two countries. For producers of the protected good, the sugar farmers of Plaque, restricting imports is clearly positive. Without a need to face imported products, these producers are able to sell more, at a higher price. For consumers in the country with the protected good, the sugar consumers of Plaque,

Life Savers, Eh?

Life Savers, the hard candy with the hole in the middle, were invented in 1912 by Clarence Crane in Cleveland, Ohio. Starting in the late 1960s and for 35 years afterward 46 billion Life Savers a year, in 200 million rolls, were produced by a plant in Holland, Michigan. But in 2002, the Kraft Company announced that Michigan plant would be closed and Life Saver production moved across the border to Montreal, Canada.

One reason is that Canadian workers are paid slightly less, especially since the Canadian government takes care of health care costs. But a main reason is that the U.S. government keeps the price of sugar high for the benefits of sugar farmers, with a combination of a government price floor program and strict quotas on imported sugar. In 2008, the U.S. price for sugar was 21 cents a pound; the price in the rest of the world was 14 cents a pound. Life Saver production uses over 100 tons of sugar each day, because the candies are 95% sugar.

A number of other candy companies have reduced U.S. production and expanding foreign production, as well. But while the candy industry is especially affected by the cost of sugar, the costs are spread more broadly. U.S. consumers pay roughly $1 billion per year in higher food prices because of elevated sugar costs. Meanwhile, sugar producers in low-income countries are driven out of business, because they cannot sell their output in the U.S. market.

restricting imports is clearly negative. They end up buying a lower quantity of the good and paying a higher price for what they do buy, compared to the equilibrium quantity and price without trade.

The fact that protectionism pushes up prices for consumers in the country enacting such protectionism is not always acknowledged openly, but it's not controversial. After all, if protectionism didn't benefit domestic producers, there wouldn't be much point in enacting such policies in the first place. Protectionism is simply a method of requiring consumers to subsidize producers. The subsidy is indirect, since it is paid by consumers through higher prices, rather than a direct subsidy paid by the government with money collected from taxpayers. But protectionism works like a subsidy, nonetheless. The American humorist Ambrose Bierce defined "tariff" this way in his satirical 1911 book, *The Devil's Dictionary:* "Tariff, n. A scale of taxes on imports, designed to protect the domestic producer against the greed of his consumer."

The effect of protectionism on producers and consumers in the foreign country is complex. When an import quota is used to impose partial protectionism, the sugar producers of Tartar receive a lower price for the sugar they sell in Tartar—but a higher price for the sugar they are allowed to export to Plaque. Indeed, notice that some of the price of protectionism, paid by domestic consumers, ends up in the hands of foreign producers in this case. Foreign consumers of sugar in Tartar would seem to benefit from protectionism in Plaque, because it reduced the price of sugar that they pay. On the other hand, at least some of these consumers of sugar in Tartar also work as sugar farmers, so their incomes and jobs are reduced by protectionism. Moreover, if trade between the countries is shut down, consumers of Tartar would miss out on better prices for the goods that Tartar is importing—which do not appear in our single-market example of sugar protectionism.

But the central focus here is not on how protectionism affects other countries, but how it affects one's own country. Protectionism is a policy where the domestic consumers of a product (consumers may include either households or other firms) are required to pay higher prices to benefit domestic producers of that product. In addition, when a country enacts protectionism, it loses the economic gains it would have been able to achieve through a combination of comparative advantage, learning, and economies of scale that were discussed Chapter 3. With these overall costs and benefits in mind, let us now consider, one by one, a number of arguments that have been made for restricting imports.

International Trade and Its Effects on Jobs, Wages, and Working Conditions

In theory, at least, imports might injure workers in several different ways: fewer jobs, lower wages, or poor working conditions. Let's consider these in turn.

Fewer Jobs?

In the early 1990s, the United States was negotiating the North American Free Trade Agreement with Mexico, an agreement that would reduce tariffs, import quotas, and nontariff barriers to trade between the United States, Mexico, and Canada. H. Ross Perot ran for U.S. President in 1992 as a third-party candidate, and one of his prominent campaign arguments was to claim that if the United States expanded trade with Mexico, there would be a "giant sucking sound" as U.S. employers relocated to Mexico so that they could pay lower wages. After all, average wages in Mexico were at that time about one-eighth the U.S. level. Well, NAFTA passed Congress, President Bill Clinton signed it into law, and it took effect in 1995. For the next six years, the U.S. economy had some of the most rapid job growth and low unemployment in the history of the country. Those who feared that open trade with Mexico would lead to a dramatic decrease in jobs were proven 100% wrong.

This result was no surprise to economists. After all, the trend toward globalization has been going on for decades, not just since NAFTA took effect in 1995. U.S. imports were equal to 5.4% of the U.S. economy in 1970, but to about 14% in 2005. If trade did reduce the number of available jobs, then the United States should have been seeing a steady loss of jobs for decades. While the U.S. economy does experience rises and falls in unemployment rates—like the rising unemployment rate that started in spring 2008 and reached 10% by late 2009—the number of jobs is not falling over extended periods of time. The number of U.S. jobs rose from 78 million in 1970 to 140 million in 2009, and the share of U.S. adults with jobs rose from 57% in 1970 to 63% in 2007, before sinking back to 59% during the stagnant economy of 2009.

Protectionism certainly saves jobs *in the specific industry being protected*, but for two reasons, it costs jobs in other unprotected industries. First, if consumers are paying higher prices to the protected industry, they inevitably have less money to spend on goods from other industries, and so jobs are lost in those other industries. Second, if the protected product is sold to other firms, like sugar or steel, so that other firms must now pay a higher price for a key input, then those firms will have a hard time competing against foreign producers who don't need to pay the higher price. The hidden opportunity cost of using protectionism to save jobs in one industry sacrifices the jobs that are not created in other industries. This is why the U.S. International Trade Commission, in its study of barriers to trade mentioned at the start of this chapter, predicts that reducing trade barriers would not lead to an overall loss of jobs. Protectionism reshuffles jobs from industries that are not protected from imports to industries that are protected, but it doesn't create more jobs.

Moreover, the costs of saving jobs through protectionism can be very high. Exhibit 6-2 shows some estimates of the consumer costs in higher prices of "saving jobs" through protectionism. Saving a job through protectionism typically costs much more than the actual worker's salary. For example, a study published in 2002 compiled evidence that using protectionism to save an average job in the textile and apparel industry would cost $199,000 per job saved.

Industry Protected with Import Tariffs or Quotas	Annual Cost per Job Saved
Sugar	$826,000
Polyethylene resins	$812,000
Dairy products	$685,000
Frozen concentrated orange juice	$635,000
Ball bearings	$603,000
Machine tools	$479,000
Women's handbags	$263,000
Glassware	$247,000
Apparel and textiles	$199,000
Rubber footwear	$168,000
Women's nonathletic footwear	$139,000

Exhibit 6-2   Cost to U.S. Consumers of Saving a Job through Protectionism

A number of different studies have attempted to estimate the cost to consumers in higher prices per job saved through protectionism. Here is a sample of results, compiled by economists at the Federal Reserve Bank of Dallas.

Why does it cost so much to save jobs through protectionism? The basic reason is that not all of the extra money paid by consumers because of protectionism goes to save the jobs of workers. For example, if tariffs are imposed on steel imports so that buyers of steel pay a higher price, U.S. steel companies earn greater profits, buy more equipment, pay bigger bonuses to managers, give pay raises to existing employee—and also avoid firing some additional workers. Only part of the higher price of protected steel goes toward saving jobs. Also, when an industry is protected, the economy as a whole loses the benefits of playing to its comparative advantage. Thus, part of the higher price that consumers pay for protected goods is wasted by this lost economic efficiency.

There's a bumper sticker that speaks to the threat some U.S. workers feel over imported products: "Buy American—Save U.S. Jobs." A more accurate, if less catchy, bumper sticker might say: "Block Imports—Save Jobs for Some Americans, Lose a Roughly Equal Number of Jobs for Other Americans, and Also Pay High Prices."

Trade and Wages

Even if trade does not reduce the number of jobs, it could affect the wages of workers. Here, it is important to separate issues about the average level of wages from issues about whether the wages of certain workers may be helped or hurt by trade.

Because trade raises the amount that an economy can produce by letting firms and workers play to their comparative advantage, trade will also cause the average level of wages in an economy to increase. Workers who can produce more will be more desirable to employers, which will shift the demand for their labor out to the right, and increase wages in the labor market.

However, even if trade increases the overall wage level, it will still benefit some workers and hurt others. Workers in industries that are confronted by competition from imported products may find that demand for their labor decreases and shifts back to the left, so that their wages decline with a rise in international trade. Conversely, workers in industries that benefit from selling in global markets may find that demand for their labor shifts out to the right, so that trade raises their wages.

One concern is that while globalization may be benefiting high-skilled, high-wage workers, it may also impose costs on low-skilled, low-wage workers. After all, high-skilled

U.S. workers presumably benefit from increased sales of sophisticated products like computers, machinery, and pharmaceuticals on world markets. Meanwhile, low-skilled U.S. workers must now compete against extremely low-wage workers worldwide for making simpler products like toys and clothing. Chapter 16 will discuss the inequality of wages in the U.S. economy in detail. But there are a number of reasons to believe that while globalization has helped some U.S. industries and hurt others, it has not focused its negative impacts on the wages of low-skilled Americans.

First, it seems unlikely that intra-industry trade, where the U.S. trades similar goods like machinery, computers and cars with other high-wage economies like Canada, Japan, Germany, and the United Kingdom, has a heavier impact on the wages of low-skill, low-wage Americans. After all, most U.S. workers in these industries have above-average skills and wages—and many of them are doing quite well in the world of globalization. Remember, intra-industry trade makes up about half of all U.S. trade.

Second, many low-skilled U.S. workers hold service jobs that cannot be replaced by imports from low-wage countries. For example, lawn care services or moving and hauling services or hotel maids cannot be imported from countries of long distances like China or Bangladesh. Competition from imported products is not the primary determinant of their wages.

Finally, while the focus of the discussion here is on wages, it's worth pointing out that low-wage U.S. workers suffer from protectionism *in all the industries that they don't work in,* because protectionism forces them to pay higher prices for basic necessities like clothing and food.

The benefits and costs of increased trade in terms of its effect on wages are not distributed evenly across the economy. However, the growth of international trade has helped to raise the productivity of U.S. workers as a whole—and thus helped to raise the average level of wages.

Labor Standards

Workers in many low-income countries around the world labor under conditions that would be illegal for a worker in the United States. Workers in countries like China, Thailand, Brazil, South Africa and Poland are often paid less than the U.S. minimum wage. For example, in the United States the minimum wage is $7.25 per hour; a typical wage in many low-income countries might be more like $7.25 *per day*, or often much less. Moreover, working conditions in low-income countries may be highly unpleasant, or even unsafe. In the worst cases, production may involve the labor of small children or even workers who are treated nearly like slaves. These concerns over standards of foreign labor don't affect the majority of U.S. trade, which is intra-industry and carried out with other high-income countries that have labor standards similar to the United States, but it is nonetheless morally and economically important.

In thinking about labor standards in other countries, it's important to draw some distinctions between what is truly unacceptable and what is merely painful to think about. Most people, economists included, have little difficulty with the idea that production by six-year-olds confined in factories or by slave labor is morally unacceptable, and they would support aggressive efforts to eliminate such practices—including shutting out imported products made with such labor. But many cases are less clear-cut. An article in the *New York Times* several years ago described the case of Ahmed Zia, a 14-year-old boy from Pakistan. He earned $2 per day working in a carpet factory. He dropped out of school in second grade. Should the United States and other countries refuse to purchase rugs made by Ahmed and his co-workers? If the carpet factories were to close, the likely

The International Labor Organization

The International Labor Organization (ILO), founded in 1919, is the international body for establishing and monitoring labor standards. The ILO has passed rules, or "conventions," affecting more than 180 areas of employment, but member nations have a choice of which to ratify. For example, the first convention, passed in 1919, calls for an eight-hour workday and a 48-hour work week. An example of a more recent convention, adopted in 2007, calls for improved working conditions for those who work in the fishing industry.

If a nation has ratified a convention, the ILO has the power to investigate complaints about violations; complaints can come from workers, employers, or other countries. The ILO does not have power to impose financial penalties or limitations on trade. Instead, it depends on building consensus and publicity to encourage nations to sign conventions and to comply with conventions they have signed. The ILO might be given greater enforcement power—say, by carrying out its own investigations of labor conditions or by imposing fines—that do not involve limitations on trade.

As of 2009, the United States has ratified just 14 of the 188 ILO conventions. This isn't necessarily unreasonable. Many countries sign off on ILO conventions, but then do little to comply. For example, 169 countries have ratified a convention against discrimination in employment and occupation that was passed in 1958. The United States has not ratified this convention. But it seems clear from a glance around the world that employment discrimination by race, gender, and religion is lower in the United States than in many of the countries that have ratified the convention. The United States is quite cautious about ratifying ILO conventions because it views workplace issues as fundamentally a domestic issue, and no one else's business. Of course, this makes it hard for the United States to preach to other nations about their own workplace issues, too.

Country	Number of ILO Conventions Ratified, 2009
High-Income Economies	
United States	14
Canada	28
France	102
Japan	41
Germany	72
United Kingdom	68
Middle-Income Economies	
Brazil	81
Mexico	70
Saudi Arabia	15
Korea, Republic of	24
Indonesia	18
Poland	81
Russian Federation	53
Low-Income Economies	
China	22
India	40
Ghana	47
Nigeria	34

alternative job for Ahmed is farm work, and as Ahmed says of his carpet-weaving job: "This makes much more money and is more comfortable." Other workers may have even less attractive alternative jobs, perhaps scavenging garbage or prostitution. The real problem for Ahmed and many others in low-income countries isn't that globalization has made their lives worse, but rather that they have so few good life alternatives.

Similar issues apply to adult workers in low-income counties that produce goods for export to the United States and other high-income economies like the European Union and Japan. Many of these workers receive wages that would be illegally low in the United States and other high-income countries. They are unprotected by U.S. rules that seek to assure holidays, safe workplaces, and prohibitions against discrimination and sexual harassment. Nonetheless, the jobs they have making carpets or toys or shoes pay much better than their alternative jobs. Low wages and poor working conditions are not a clever ploy by people in low-income countries to sell more in world markets. For them, jobs with wages and working conditions that Americans wouldn't touch with a 10-foot pole can still look like a great step forward.

There is some irony when the U.S. government or U.S. citizens take issue with labor standards in low-income countries, because the United States is not a world leader in government laws to protect employees. In western European countries and Canada, all citizens are guaranteed health insurance by the government; the United States has not offered such a guarantee. Many European workers receive six weeks or more of vacation per year; in the United States, vacations are often two or three weeks per year. If European countries accused the United States of using unfair labor standards to make U.S. products cheaply, and announced that they would shut out all U.S. imports until the United States adopted guaranteed national health insurance, added more national holidays, and doubled vacation time, Americans would be outraged. Yet when U.S. protectionists start talking about restricting imports from poor countries because of low wage levels and poor working conditions, they are making a very similar argument.

The Infant Industry Argument

Imagine a country that wants to start its own computer industry, but at present, the country has no computer firms that can produce at a low enough price and high enough quality to compete in world markets. However, the politicians, business leaders, and workers of this country hope that if the local industry only had a chance to get established, before it needed to face international competition, then a domestic company or group of companies could develop the skills, management, technology, and economies of scale that it needs to become a successful profit-earning domestic industry. Thus, the **infant industry argument** for protectionism is to block imports for a limited time, to give the infant industry time to mature, before eventually it starts competing on equal terms in the global economy.

infant industry argument: An argument to block imports for a short time, to give the infant industry time to mature, before eventually it starts competing on equal terms in the global economy.

The infant industry argument is theoretically possible, even sensible: give an industry a short-term indirect subsidy through protection, and then reap the long-term economic benefits of having a vibrant healthy industry. But practical implementation is tricky. In many countries, infant industries have gone from babyhood to senility and obsolescence without ever maturing. Meanwhile, the infant industry protectionism that was supposed to be short-term often took a very long time to be repealed. As one example, Brazil treated its computer industry as an infant industry from the late 1970s until about 1990. Thus, in an attempt to establish its computer industry in the global economy, Brazil largely barred imports of computer products for several decades. This policy guaranteed increased sales for the Brazilian computer industry. But by the mid-1980s, Brazil had a backward and out-of-date computer industry, typically lagging the world standards for price and performance by 3–5 years—a long time in this fast-moving industry. After more than a decade, during which Brazilian consumers and industries that would have benefited from up-to-date computers paid the costs and Brazil's computer industry never competed effectively on world markets, Brazil phased out its infant industry policy for computers.

Protectionism for infant industries always imposes costs on domestic users of the product, and typically has provided little benefit in the form of stronger competitive industries.

Several countries in East Asia offer an exception where infant industry protection has been used with some success. Japan, Korea, Thailand and other countries in this region have sometimes provided a package of indirect and direct subsidies targeted at certain industries, including protection from foreign competition and government loans at interest rates below the market equilibrium. In Japan and Korea, for example, subsidies helped get their domestic steel and auto industries up and running.

Why did the infant industry policy of protectionism and other subsidies work fairly well in East Asia? A study by the World Bank in the early 1990s offered some guidelines to countries thinking about infant industry protection: (1) Don't hand out protectionism and other subsidies to all industries, but focus on a few industries where your country has a realistic chance to be a world-class producer. (2) Be very hesitant about using protectionism in areas like computers, where many other industries rely on having the best products available, because it's not useful to help one industry by imposing high costs on many other industries. (3) Have clear guidelines for when the infant industry policy will end. In Korea in the 1970s and 1980s, a common practice was to link protectionism and subsidies to export sales in global markets. If export sales rose, then the infant industry had succeeded and the protectionism could be phased out. If export sales didn't rise, then the infant industry policy had failed and the protectionism could be phased out. Either way, the infant industry protectionism would be temporary.

Following these rules is easier said than done. Politics often intrudes, both in choosing which industries will receive the benefits of being treated as "infants" and in choosing when to phase out import restrictions and other subsidies.

Also, if the government of a country wishes to impose costs on its citizens so that it can provide subsidies to a few key industries, it has many tools for doing so: direct government payments, loans, targeted tax reductions, government support of research and development to develop new technologies, and so on. The point here is not necessarily to advocate such subsidies, but merely to point out that when industrial subsidies are desired, it is not necessary to provide them through protectionism.

The Dumping Argument

Dumping means selling goods below their cost of production. **Anti-dumping laws** seek to block imports that are sold below the cost of production and to impose tariffs that would increase the price of these imports to reflect their cost of production.

dumping: Selling internationally traded goods below their cost of production.

anti-dumping laws: Laws that block imports sold below the cost of production and impose tariffs that would increase the price of these imports to reflect their cost of production.

The Growth of Anti-Dumping Cases

Since dumping is not allowed under the rules of the World Trade Organization, nations that believe they are on the receiving end of dumped goods can file a complaint with the WTO. Anti-dumping complaints have risen in recent years, from about 100 cases per year in the late 1980s to about 200 new cases each year in the mid and late 2000s. Individual countries also frequently started their own anti-dumping investigations. The U.S. government has dozens of anti-dumping orders in place from past investigations. In 2009, for example, some U.S. imports that were under anti-dumping orders included pasta from Turkey, steel pipe fittings from Thailand, pressure-sensitive plastic tape from Italy, preserved mushrooms and lined paper products from India, and cut-to-length carbon steel and nonfrozen apple juice concentrate from China.

Why Might Dumping Occur?

Why would foreign firms export a product at less than its cost of production—which presumably means making a loss? This question has two possible answers, one innocent and one more sinister.

The innocent explanation is that market prices are set by demand and supply, not by the cost of production. Perhaps demand for a product shifts back to the left or supply shifts out to the right, which drives the market price to low levels—even below the cost of production. When a local store has a going-out-of-business sale, for example, it may sell goods at below the cost of production. If international companies find that there is excess supply of steel or computer chips or machine tools that is driving the market price down below their cost of production—well, this may be the market in action.

The sinister explanation is that dumping is part of a long-term strategy in which foreign firms would sell at below the cost of production in the short-term for a time, and when they have driven out the domestic U.S. competition, they would then raise prices. This scenario is sometimes called "predatory pricing."

Should Anti-Dumping Cases Be Limited?

Anti-dumping cases pose two questions. How much sense do they make in economic theory? How much sense do they make as practical policy?

In terms of economic theory, the case for anti-dumping laws is weak. In a market governed by demand and supply, the government doesn't guarantee that firms will be able to make a profit. After all, low prices are difficult for producers, but benefit consumers. Moreover, although there are plenty of cases in which foreign producers have driven out domestic firms, there are zero documented cases in which the foreign producers then jacked up prices. Instead, the foreign producers typically continue competing hard against each other and providing low prices to consumers.

But even if one could make a case that the government should sometimes enact antidumping rules in the short term, and then allow free trade to resume shortly thereafter, there is a growing concern that anti-dumping investigations often involve more politics than careful analysis. Calculating the appropriate "cost of production" under law can be as much an art as a science; for example, if a company built a new factory two years ago, should part of the cost of factory be counted in this year's cost of production? When a domestic industry complains loudly enough, government regulators seem very likely to find that unfair dumping has occurred. Indeed, a common pattern has arisen where a domestic industry files an anti-dumping complaint, the governments meet and negotiate a reduction in imports, and then the domestic producers drop the anti-dumping suit. In such cases, anti-dumping cases often appear to be little more than a cover story for imposing tariffs or import quotas.

In the 1980s, almost all of the anti-dumping cases were initiated by the United States, Canada, the European Union, Australia and New Zealand. But by the 2000s, countries like Argentina, Brazil, South Korea, South Africa Mexico, and India have been filing the majority of the anti-dumping cases before the WTO. As the number of anti-dumping cases has increased, and as countries like the United States and the European Union feel targeted by anti-dumping actions of others, the WTO may well propose some additional guidelines to limit the reach of anti-dumping laws.

The Environmental Protection Argument

The potential for global trade to affect the environment has become controversial. A president of the Sierra Club, an environmental lobbying organization, once wrote: "The consequences of globalization for the environment are not good. . . . Globalization, if we are lucky, will raise average incomes enough to pay for cleaning up some of the mess that we have made. But before we get there, globalization could also destroy enough of the planet's basic biological and physical systems that prospects for life itself will be radically compromised." If free trade means the destruction of life itself, then even economists would convert to protectionism! But while globalization—and economic activity of all kinds—can pose environmental dangers, it seems quite possible that with the appropriate safeguards in place, the environmental impacts of trade can be minimal. In some cases, trade may even bring environmental benefits.

In general, high-income countries like the United States, Canada, Japan, and the nations of the European Union have relatively strict environmental standards. In contrast, middle- and low-income countries of the world like Brazil, Nigeria, India, and China have lower environmental standards. The general view of the governments of such countries is that as soon as their people have enough to eat, decent health care, and longer life expectancies, then they will spend more money on sewage treatment plants, scrubbers to reduce air pollution from factory smokestacks, national parks to protect wildlife, and so on. This gap in environmental standards between high-income and low-income countries raises two worrisome possibilities in a world of increasing global trade: the "race to the bottom" scenario and the question of how quickly environmental standards will improve in low-income countries. Let us consider these two issues in turn.

The Race to the Bottom Scenario

The **race to the bottom** scenario of global environmental degradation runs like this. Profit-seeking multinational companies shift their production from countries with strong environmental standards to countries with weak standards, thus reducing their costs and increasing their profits. Faced with such behavior, countries reduce their environmental standards to attract multinational firms, which after all provide jobs and economic clout. As a result, global production becomes concentrated in countries where it can pollute the most and environmental laws everywhere race to the bottom.

race to the bottom:
When production locates in countries with the lowest environmental (or other) standards, putting pressure on all countries to reduce their environmental standards.

Although the race-to-the-bottom scenario sounds plausible, it does not appear to describe reality. In fact, the financial incentive for firms to shift production to poor countries to take advantage of their weaker environmental rules does not seem especially powerful. When firms decide where to locate a new factory, they look at many different factors: the costs of labor and financial capital; whether the location is close to a reliable suppliers of the inputs that they need; whether the location is close to customers; the quality of transportation, communications and electrical power networks; the level of taxes; and the competence and honesty of the local government. The cost of environmental regulations is a factor, too, but typically environmental costs are no more than 1–2% of the costs faced by a large industrial plant. The other factors that determine choice of location are much more important than trying to skimp on environmental protection costs.

When an international company does choose to build a plant in a low-income country with lax environmental laws, it typically builds a plant similar to those that it operates in high-income countries with stricter environmental standards. Part of the reason for this decision is that designing an industrial plant is a complex and costly task, and so if a plant works well in a high-income country, companies prefer to use the same design everywhere. Also, companies realize that if they create an environmental disaster in a low-income country, it is likely to cost them a substantial amount of money in paying for damages, lost trust, and reduced sales—and by building up-to-date plants everywhere they minimize such risks. As a result of these factors, foreign-owned plants in low-income countries often have a better record of compliance with environmental laws than do locally-owned plants.

Perhaps the hardest task for those who predict a race to the bottom scenario is explaining why it hasn't already happened. After all, globalization has been expanding for decades—and at the same time, environmental standards have been growing stronger both in high-income and in low-income countries of the world. For low-income countries, globalization has often meant importing some of the environmental values of high-income countries—and also having higher income levels to afford greater environmental protection. Apparently, the competitive pressures from mobile multinational firms that might encourage governments to reduce their environmental standards are not nearly as strong as the counterbalancing pressures to increase environmental standards.

Pressuring Low-Income Countries for Higher Environmental Standards

In some cases, the issue is not so much whether globalization will pressure low-income countries to reduce their environmental standards, but instead whether the threat of blocking international trade can be used to pressure these countries into adopting stronger environmental standards. For example, restrictions on ivory imports in high-income countries, along with stronger government efforts to catch elephant poachers, have been credited with helping to reduce the illegal poaching of elephants in certain African countries.

However, it would be highly undemocratic for the well-fed citizens of high-income countries to attempt to dictate to the ill-fed citizens of low-income countries what domestic policies and priorities they must adopt, and how they should balance environmental goals against other priorities for their citizens. Also, if high-income countries want stronger environmental standards in low-income countries, they have many other options than the threat of protectionism. For example, high-income countries could pay for anti-pollution equipment in low-income countries, or could help to pay for national parks. High-income countries could help pay for and carry out the scientific and economic studies that would help environmentalists in low-income countries to make a more persuasive case for the economic benefits of protecting the environment: after all, environmental protection is very important to two industries of key importance in many low-income countries—agriculture and tourism. Environmental advocates can set up standards for labeling products, like "this tuna caught in a net that kept dolphins safe" or "this product made only with wood not taken from rain forests," so that consumer pressure can reinforce environmentalist values. The United Nations sponsors treaties to address issues such as climate change and global warming, the preservation of biodiversity, the spread of deserts, and the environmental health of the seabed, as well as other issues. Countries that share a national border or are within a region often sign environmental agreements about air and water rights, too. The World Trade Organization is also becoming more aware of environmental issues and more careful about assuring that increases in trade don't inflict environmental damage. Along with these other policy tools, high-income countries could refuse to import a limited number of specific products where the product is very closely linked to the environmental danger—like not importing the ivory from elephant tusks.

These concerns about the race to the bottom or pressuring low-income countries for more strict environmental standards do not apply very well to the roughly half of all U.S. trade that occurs with other high-income countries of the world. Indeed, many European countries have stricter environmental standards in certain industries than the United States.

The Unsafe Consumer Products Argument

One argument for shutting out certain imported products is that they are unsafe for consumers; indeed, consumer rights groups have sometimes warned that the World Trade Organization would require nations to reduce their health and safety standards for imported products. This fear seems exaggerated. The WTO explains its current agreement on this subject in this way: "It allows countries to set their own standards. But it also says regulations must be based on science. . . . And they should not arbitrarily or unjustifiably discriminate between countries where identical or similar conditions prevail." Thus, under WTO rules, it is perfectly legitimate for the United States to pass laws requiring that all, say, food products or cars sold in the United States meet certain safety standards approved by the U.S. government, whether or not other countries choose to pass similar standards. However, such standards must have some scientific basis, and it would be unfair to impose, say, one set of health and safety standards for domestically produced goods but a different set of standards for imports, or one set of standards for imports from Europe and a different set of standards for imports from Latin America.

The National Interest Argument

It is sometimes argued that nation should not depend too heavily on other countries for supplies of certain key products. This argument has been made for commodities that are important to the U.S. economy as a whole, like oil, and for special materials or technologies that might have weapons applications. But upon closer consideration, this argument for protectionism proves rather weak.

The issue is not whether certain products, like oil, are highly important to the U.S. economy both for personal use in transportation and heating and for a wide array of industrial uses. Oil provides about 40% of all the energy in the United States and more than half of the oil used in the U.S. economy is imported. Several times in the last few decades, when disruptions in the Middle East have shifted the supply curve of oil back to the left and sharply raised the price of oil, the effects have been felt across the U.S. economy.

But none of this makes a very convincing argument for restricting imports of oil. If the United States needs to be protected from a possible cutoff of foreign oil, then a more reasonable strategy would be to import 100% of the United States' petroleum supply now, and save the U.S. domestic oil resources for when or if the foreign supply is cut off. It might also be useful to import extra oil and put it into a stockpile for use in an emergency, as the U.S. government did by starting a Strategic Petroleum Reserve in 1977. Moreover, it may be necessary to discourage people from using oil, and to start a high-powered program to seek out alternatives to oil. A straightforward way to do this would be to raise taxes on oil. (Such a tax increase on oil could be offset with cuts in other taxes, so that the total tax burden need not rise.) But it makes no sense to argue that because oil is highly important to the U.S. economy, then the United States should shut out oil imports and use up its domestic supplies of oil more quickly.

Whether or not to limit certain kinds of imports of key technologies or materials that might be important to weapons systems is a slightly different issue. If weapons builders are not confident that they can continue to obtain a key product in wartime,

Public Attitudes about Global Trade

How do people around the world feel about expanding trade between nations? In summer 2007, the Pew Foundation surveyed 45,000 people in 47 countries. One of the questions asked about opinions on growing trade ties between countries. The table below shows the percentages who answered either "very good" or "somewhat good" for a selection of countries.

For those who think of the United States as the world's leading supporter of expanding trade, the survey results may be perplexing. When adding up the shares of those who say that growing trade ties between countries are "very good" or "somewhat good," Americans are the least favorable country toward increasing globalization, while the Chinese and South Africans rank highest. In fact, among the 47 countries surveyed the United States ranked by far the lowest on this measure, followed by Egypt, Italy, and Argentina.

	Growing Trade Ties between Countries Are . . .		
	Very Good	Somewhat Good	Total
China	38%	53%	91%
South Africa	42%	43%	87%
South Korea	24%	62%	86%
Germany	30%	55%	85%
Canada	29%	53%	82%
United Kingdom	28%	50%	78%
Mexico	22%	55%	77%
Brazil	13%	59%	72%
Japan	17%	55%	72%
United States	14%	45%	59%

they might decide to avoid designing weapons that use this key product, or they can go ahead and design the weapons and stockpile enough of the key high-tech components or materials to last through an armed conflict. Indeed, there is a U.S. Defense National Stockpile Center that has built up reserves of many materials from aluminum oxides, antimony, and bauxite to tungsten, vegetable tannin extracts and zinc (although many of these stockpiles have been reduced and sold in recent years). But why shut out a high technology product, like a specialized type of computer chip or screen, for all the potential civilian-sector users—including businesses that may need the technology so that their products can be competitive in world markets—just because makers of weapons are hesitant to rely on it? If the concern is to build up top-level technological capabilities for domestic producers, it is usually better to have domestic firms competing hard in world markets—perhaps with some direct government subsidies for research and development in key areas—rather than sheltering domestic producers from foreign competition.

One final reason why economists often treat the national security argument skeptically is that almost any product can be touted by lobbyists and politicians as vital to national security. In 1954 the United States became worried that it was importing half of the wool required for military uniforms, so it declared wool and mohair to be "strategic materials" and began to give subsidies to wool and mohair farmers. Although wool was removed from the official list of "strategic" materials in 1960, the subsidies for mohair continued for almost 40 years until they were repealed in 1993, and then reinstated in 2002. All too often, the national interest argument has become an excuse for handing out the indirect subsidy of protectionism to certain industries or companies. After all, decisions about what constitutes a key strategic material are made by politicians, not nonpartisan analysts.

National Security and Scissors and Shears

What follows is actual testimony before Congress in the early 1960s from a lobbyist arguing that the national interest demands a higher tariff on imported scissors and shears.

[M]y name is B.C. Dueschle. I am vice president of the Acme Shear Co., located in Bridgeport, Conn. I appear before this committee as president of the Shears, Scissors & Manicure Implement Manufacturers Association, the only national trade association of domestic manufacturers of scissors and shears. The scissors and shears industry is a distinct industry and should not be confused with the larger industry and the flatware industries. . . .

We have never requested or suggested that a complete embargo be placed on the import of scissors and shears. All that we have asked for and desire is a fair competitive opportunity, not an advantage. . . .

We realize that the domestic scissor and shear industry with its 1,000-plus employees accounts for only a fraction of 1% of the gross national product, but we see this as no justification for letting the industry be completely destroyed by imports produced with low-cost labor.

The workers in the domestic scissor and shear industry do not want to become wards of the State; they want to use their skills, which have taken many years to develop. These workers are not interested in retraining; over many years they have developed a skill they are proud of and want to continue the work they are happy doing. . . .

Under the provisions of this bill, scissors and shears would be buried in a category with many other items and the duty cut 50%. This would mean a reduction of at least 20 cents per pair at the retail level for scissors and shears now being retailed at $1 to 1.29 per pair. . . .

These few remaining manufacturers would be forced to close their doors and discharge their employees. The United States would then become wholly dependent on imported scissors and shears.

We cannot understand how it would be in the national interest to permit such a loss. We would lose the skills of the employees and management of the industry as well as the capital investment in production equipment. In the event of a national emergency and imports cutoff, the United States would be without a source of scissors and shears, basic tools for many industries and trades essential to our defense.

The scissors and shear industry is one of the oldest in the world. The skill was brought to the United States from Germany at a time when the United States needed new industry and a scissors and shear industry in particular.

Scissors and shears of all sizes and types are used in every school, retail establishment, office, factory, hospital, and home in the United States. Scissors cannot be classified as a luxury, gimmick, or novelty.

Scissors are used to separate us from our mothers at birth; to cut our toenails; to trim the leather in our shoes; to cut and trim the materials used in every piece of clothing that we wear.

They are used to cut our fingernails, to trim our mustaches, the hair in our ears and nose, and to cut the hair on our heads—even down to the end of the road when our best suit or dress is cut down the back so that the undertaker can dress us for the last ride. Scissors are truly used from birth to death. They are essential to our health, education, and general welfare.

I ask you gentlemen, is this industry one that should be permitted to become extinct in this country?

How Trade Policy Is Enacted: Global, Regional, and National

These public policy arguments about how nations should react to globalization and trade are fought out at several levels: at the global level through the World Trade Organization and through regional trade agreements between pairs or groups of countries.

The World Trade Organization

The World Trade Organization was officially born in 1995, but its history is somewhat longer. In the years after the Great Depression and World War II, there was a worldwide push to build institutions that would tie the nations of the world together. For example, the United Nations officially came into existence in 1945. The World Bank, with a focus on assisting the poorest people in the world, and the International Monetary Fund, with a focus on addressing issues raised by international financial transactions, were both created in 1946. The General Agreement on Tariffs and Trade (GATT), which provided a forum in which nations could come together to negotiate over reductions in tariffs and other barriers to trade started in 1947. In 1995, the GATT transformed itself into the World Trade Organization.

The GATT process was to negotiate an agreement to reduce barriers to trade, sign that agreement, pause for breath, and then start negotiating the next agreement. The rounds of talks in the GATT, and now the WTO, are shown in Exhibit 6-3. Notice that the early rounds of GATT talks took a relatively short time, included a relatively small number of countries, and focused almost entirely on reducing tariffs. Since the 1970s, however, rounds of trade talks have taken years, included a large number of countries, and included an ever-broadening range of issues.

The sluggish pace of GATT negotiations led to an old joke that GATT really stood for Gentleman's Agreement to Talk and Talk. But the slow pace of international trade talks is understandable, even sensible. Having dozens of nations agree to any treaty is a lengthy process. GATT often set up separate trading rules for certain industries, like agriculture, and separate trading rules for certain countries, like the low-income countries in the world. There were rules, exceptions to rules, opportunities to opt out of rules, and precise wording to be fought over in every case. Like the GATT before it, WTO is not a world government, with power to impose its decisions on others. The total staff of the WTO in 2008 is about 625 people and its annual budget is $180 million, which makes it smaller in size than many large universities.

Regional Trading Agreements

Many nations belong both to the World Trade Organization and to regional trading agreements. The best-known of these regional trading agreements is the European Union. In the years after World War II, leaders of the nations of Europe reasoned that if they could tie their economies together more closely, they might be more likely to avoid another devastating war. Their efforts evolved into what is now known as the European Union. The EU, as it is often called, has a number of goals. For example, in

Exhibit 6-3   The Negotiating Rounds of GATT and the World Trade Organization

Year	Place or Name of Round	Main Subjects	Number of Countries Involved
1947	Geneva	Tariff reduction	23
1949	Annecy	Tariff reduction	13
1951	Torquay	Tariff reduction	38
1956	Geneva	Tariff reduction	26
1960–61	Dillon round	Tariff reduction	26
1964–67	Kennedy round	Tariffs and anti-dumping measures	62
1973–79	Tokyo round	Tariffs, nontariff barriers	102
1986–94	Uruguay round	Tariffs, nontariff barriers, services, intellectual property, dispute settlement, textiles, agriculture, creation of WTO	123
2001–	Doha round	Agriculture, services, intellectual property, competition, investment, environment, dispute settlement	147

the early 2000s it introduced a common currency for Europe, the euro, and phased out the old national forms of money like the German mark and the French franc. Another key element of the union is to eliminate barriers to the mobility of goods, labor and capital across Europe.

For the United States, perhaps the best-known regional trading agreement is the North American Free Trade Agreement (NAFTA), which reduced barriers to trade between the United States, Mexico, and Canada. NAFTA was signed into law by President Bill Clinton in November 1993 and took effect in 1995. However, the U.S. also participates in some less-known regional trading agreements, like the Caribbean Basin Initiative that offers reduced tariffs for imports from these countries, and a free trade agreement with Israel.

The world has seen a flood of regional trading agreements in recent years. About 100 such agreements are now in place; a few of the more prominent ones are listed in Exhibit 6-4. Some are just agreements to talk and talk; others set specific goals for reducing tariffs, import quotas, and nontariff barriers. One economist described the current trade treaties as a "spaghetti bowl," which is what a map with lines connecting all the countries with trade treaties looks like. There is some concern among economists who favor free trade that some of these regional agreements may promise free trade, but actually act as a way for the countries within the regional agreement to try to limit trade from anywhere else. In some cases, the regional trade agreements may even conflict with the broader agreements of the World Trade Organization.

Trade Policy at the National Level

Yet another dimension of trade policy, along with international and regional trade agreements, happens at the national level. The United States, for example, imposes import quotas on sugar, because of a fear that such imports would drive down the price of sugar and thus injure domestic sugar producers. One of the jobs of the U.S. Department of Commerce is to determine if imports from other countries are being dumped at less than a governmentally-determined "fair" price. If so, the U.S. International Trade Commission—a government agency—determines whether domestic industries have been substantially injured by the dumping, and if so, the president can impose tariffs that are intended to offset the unfairly low price.

In the arena of trade policy, the battle often seems to be between national laws that increase protectionism and international agreements that try to reduce protectionism, like the WTO. Why would a country pass laws or negotiate agreements to shut out certain foreign products, like sugar or textiles, while simultaneously negotiating to reduce trade barriers in general?

One plausible answer is that international trade agreements offer a method for countries to restrain their own special interests. A member of Congress can say to an industry lobbying for tariffs or quotas on imports: "Sure would like to help you, but that pesky WTO agreement just won't let me." In this way, international trade agreements are like hiring a personal trainer; they pressure you to follow through on the healthy behavior that you should be doing, anyway.

Long-Term Trends in Barriers to Trade

In the newspaper headlines, trade policy appears rife with disputes and acrimony. Countries are almost constantly threatening to challenge "unfair" trading practices of other nations. Cases are brought before the dispute settlement procedures of the WTO, the European Union, NAFTA, and other regional trading agreements. Politicians in national

Trade Agreements	Participating Countries
Asia Pacific Economic Cooperation (APEC)	Australia, Brunei, Canada, Chile, People's Republic of China, Hong Kong, China, Indonesia, Japan, Republic of Korea, Malaysia, Mexico, New Zealand, Papua New Guinea, Peru, Philippines, Russia, Singapore, Chinese Taipei, Thailand, United States, Vietnam
European Union (EU)	Austria, Belgium, Bulgaria, Cyprus, Czech Republic, Denmark, Estonia, Finland, France, Germany, Greece, Hungary, Ireland, Italy, Latvia, Lithuania, Luxembourg, Malta, Netherlands, Poland, Portugal, Romania, Slovakia, Slovenia, Spain, Sweden, United Kingdom
North America Free Trade Agreement (NAFTA)	Canada, Mexico, United States
Latin American Integration Association (LAIA)	Argentina, Bolivia, Brazil, Chile, Columbia, Ecuador, Mexico, Paraguay, Peru, Uruguay, Venezuela
Association of Southeast Asian Nations (ASEAN)	Brunei, Cambodia, Indonesia, Laos, Malaysia, Myanmar, Philippines, Singapore, Thailand, Vietnam
Southern African Development Community (SADC)	Angola, Botswana, Congo, Lesotho, Malawi, Mauritius, Mozambique, Namibia, Seychelles, South Africa, Swaziland, Tanzania, Zambia, Zimbabwe
Asia-Pacific Trade Agreement (Bangkok Agreement)	Bangladesh, China, India, Republic of Korea, Laos, Sri Lanka

Exhibit 6-4   Some Regional Trade Agreements

legislatures, goaded on by lobbyists, often threaten to pass bills that will "establish a fair playing field" or "prevent unfair trade"—although most such bills seek to accomplish these high-sounding goals by placing more restrictions on trade. Protesters in the streets may object to specific trade rules or to the entire practice of international trade.

But through all the controversy, the general trend in the last 60 years is clearly toward lower barriers to trade. The average level of tariffs on imported products charged by industrialized countries was 40% in 1946. By 1990, after decades of GATT negotiations, it was down to less than 5%. Indeed, one of the reasons that GATT negotiations shifted from focusing on tariff reduction in the early rounds to a broader agenda was that tariffs had been reduced so dramatically that there wasn't much more to do in that area. U.S. tariffs have followed this general pattern; after rising sharply during the Great Depression, they have dropped off to less than 2% by the end of the century. Although measures of import quotas and nontariff barriers are less exact than those for tariffs, they generally appear to be at lower levels, too.

Thus, the last half-century has seen both a dramatic reduction in government-created barriers to trade, like tariffs, import quotas, and nontariff barriers, and also a number of technological developments that have made international trade easier, like advances in transportation, communication, and information management. The result has been the powerful surge of international trade called globalization.

People often think of international trade agreements as similar to arms control treaties. In arms control treaties, the two sides negotiate to reduce their weapons; in a trade agreement, they negotiate to reduce their trade barriers. From this point of view, nations enact trade barriers they way they build missiles, to show their toughness and resolve, and they are willing to give up those trade barriers, like their missiles, only if other nations are also willing to disarm.

But this analogy, while it may appear reasonable on the surface, is terribly off the mark. Trade is not a form of warfare. War is fundamentally a lose-lose situation; both sides suffer losses until one side gives up. Trade is fundamentally a win-win situation, where both sides make voluntary exchanges and make mutual gains. One writer said: "As to trade as war, it is hard to think of two things more antithetical. When free to do so, buyers and sellers make deals to their mutual advantage, each walking away happy. This is some form of war? If it is, let's substitute it for all the other forms."

Clearing It Up

Trade Is Not War

The Trade-offs of Trade Policy

Economists readily acknowledge that international trade is not all sunshine and roses and happy endings. On average and over time, the average person gains from international trade, both as a worker who has greater productivity and higher wages because of the benefits of specialization and comparative advantage, and as a consumer who can benefit from shopping all over the world for a greater variety of quality products at attractive prices. But the average person is hypothetical, not real, representing a mix of those who have done very well, those who have done all right, and those who have done poorly. It is a legitimate concern of public policy not just to focus on the average or on the success stories, but also on those have not been so blessed. Workers in other countries, the environment, and prospects for new industries and materials that might be of key importance to the national economy are also all legitimate issues. The common belief among economists is that it is better to embrace the gains from trade, and then to deal with the costs and trade-offs with other policy tools, rather than cutting off trade to avoid the costs and trade-offs—but also losing the benefits of international trade.

To gain a better intuitive understanding for this argument, consider a hypothetical American company called Technotron. Technotron invents a new scientific technology that allows the firm to increase the output and quality of its goods with a smaller number of workers at a lower cost. As a result of this technology, other U.S. firms in this industry will lose money and will also have to lay off workers—and some of the competing firms will even go bankrupt. Should the U.S. government protect the existing firms and their employees by making it illegal for Technotron to use its new technology?

Most people who live in market-oriented economies would oppose trying to block new technology. Certainly, there is a case that society should provide temporary support and assistance for those who find themselves without work. Many would argue for government support of programs that encourage retraining and acquiring additional skills. Government might also support research and development efforts, so that other firms may find ways of outdoing Technotron. But blocking the new technology altogether seems like a mistake. After all, few people would advocate giving up electricity because it caused so much disruption to the kerosene and candle business. Few would suggest holding back on improvements in medical technology because they might cause companies selling older and less effective medical care to lose money. In short, most people view disruptions due to technological change as a necessary cost that is worth bearing.

Now, imagine that Technotron's new "technology" is as simple as this: the company imports what it sells from another country. In other words, think of foreign trade as a type of innovative technology. The objective situation is now exactly the same as before. Because of Technotron's new technology—which in this case is importing goods from another county—other firms in this industry will lose money and lay off workers. But just as it would have been inappropriate and ultimately foolish to respond to the disruptions of new scientific technology by trying to shut it down, it would be inappropriate and ultimately foolish to respond to the disruptions of international trade by trying to restrict trade.

Some workers and firms will suffer because of international trade. But in a living, breathing market-oriented economy, some workers and firms will always be experiencing disruptions, for a wide variety of reasons. Corporate management can be better or worse. Workers for a certain firm can be more productive or less. Tough domestic competitors can create just as much disruption as tough foreign competitors. Sometimes a new product is a hit with consumers; sometimes it's a flop. Sometimes a company is blessed by a run of good luck or stricken with a run of bad luck. For some firms, international trade will offer great opportunities for expanding productivity and jobs; for other firms, trade will impose stress and pain. The disruption caused by international trade is not fundamentally different from all the other disruptions caused by the other workings of a market economy. Trying to prevent all the disruptions of a market-oriented economy from happening has an opportunity cost: it means blocking the economic gains from trade.

In other words, the economic analysis of free trade doesn't rely on a belief that foreign trade is not disruptive or does not pose trade-offs; indeed, the story of Technotron begins with a particular disruptive market change—a new technology—that causes real trade-offs. But in thinking about the disruptiveness of foreign trade, or any of the other possible costs and trade-offs of foreign trade discussed in this chapter, the best public policy solutions typically don't involve protectionism, but instead involve finding ways for public policy to address the particular issues while still allowing the benefits of international trade to occur.

Key Concepts and Summary

1. There are three tools for restricting the flow of trade: **tariffs, import quotas,** and **nontariff barriers.** When a country places limitations on imports from abroad, regardless of whether it uses tariffs, quotas, or nontariff barriers, it is said to be practicing **protectionism.**

2. Protectionism will raise the price of the protected good in the domestic market, which causes domestic consumers to pay more but benefits producers.

3. As international trade increases, it contributes to a shift in jobs away from industries where that economy does not have a comparative advantage and toward industries where it does have a comparative advantage. Overall, however, the increase in trade does not have much affect on the number of jobs.

4. Global trade should raise the average level of wages by increasing productivity. However, this increase in average wages may include both gains to workers in certain jobs and industries and losses to others.

5. In thinking about labor practices in low-income countries, it's useful to draw a line between what is unpleasant to think about and what is morally objectionable. For example, low wages and long working hours in poor countries are unpleasant to think about, but for people in low-income parts of the world, it may well be the best option open to them. Practices like child labor and forced labor are morally objectionable and the rules of the WTO allow any country to refuse to import products made using these practices.

6. The **infant industry argument** for protectionism is that small domestic industries need to be temporarily nurtured and protected from foreign competition for a time so that they can grow into strong competitors. In some cases, notably in East Asia, this approach has worked. But often, the infant industries never grow up.

7. **Dumping** occurs when prices are set at below the cost of production. The strategy is to set prices at a level below production costs, absorb losses until competitors are driven out of the market, and then, when competition has been eliminated or greatly reduced, to raise prices substantially and earn high profits. While there are some historical examples where this strategy has worked, it does not appear to arise very often, if at all, in global trade. More often, anti-dumping complaints seem to be a convenient excuse for imposing protectionism.

8. Low-income countries typically have lower environmental standards than high-income countries because they are more worried about immediate basics such as food, education and health care. There are a variety of ways for high-income countries to encourage stronger environmental standards in low-income countries, including some movement to make sure that new opportunities opened up by free trade don't injure the environment. Except for a small number of extreme cases, shutting off trade seems unlikely to be an effective method of pursuing a cleaner environment.

9. Under the rules of the World Trade Organization, countries are allowed to set whatever standards for product safety they wish, but the standards must be the same for domestic products as for imported products. If there is a dispute over whether a health and safety standard is being imposed without a scientific basis, it can be appealed to the WTO.

10. The national interest argument for protectionism holds that it is unwise to import certain key products because if the nation becomes dependent on key imported supplies, it could be vulnerable to a cutoff. However, it is often wiser to stockpile resources and to use foreign supplies when available, rather than preemptively restricting foreign supplies so as not to become dependent on them.

11. Trade policy is determined at many different levels: administrative agencies within government; laws passed by the legislature; regional negotiations between a small group of nations (sometimes just two); and global negotiations through the World Trade Organization.

12. During the second half of the twentieth century, trade barriers have in general declined quite substantially both in the U.S. economy and in the global economy.

13. One reason why countries sign international trade agreements to commit themselves to free trade is to give themselves protection against their own special interests. When an industry lobbies for protection from foreign producers, politicians can point out that because of the trade treaty, their hands are tied.

14. International trade certainly disrupts what would otherwise have been the pattern of an economy. This is hardly surprising, since all sorts of competitive market forces are disruptive, whether domestic or international, often causing companies and industries to rise and fall. Government has a role to play in cushioning workers against the disruptions of the market. But just as it would be unwise in the long term to clamp down on new technology and other causes of disruption in domestic markets, it would be unwise to clamp down on foreign trade. In both cases, the disruption brings with it economic benefits.

Review Questions

1. Who does protectionism protect? What does it protect them from?

2. Name and define three policy tools for enacting protectionism.

3. How does protectionism affect the price of the protected good in the domestic market?

4. Does international trade, taken as a whole, increase the total number of jobs, decrease the total number of jobs, or leave the total number of jobs about the same?

5. Is international trade likely to have roughly the same effect on the number of jobs in each individual industry?

6. How is international trade, taken as a whole, likely to affect the average level of wages?

7. Is international trade likely to have about the same effect on everyone's wages?

8. Do the jobs for workers in low-income countries that involve making products for export to high-income countries typically pay these workers more or less than their next-best alternative?

9. What's an infant industry? Why does protecting it often work better in theory than in practice?

10. What is dumping? Why does prohibiting it often work better in theory than in practice?

11. What is the race to the bottom scenario?

12. Which group of countries typically has more strict environmental standards: countries with higher incomes or lower incomes?

13. Do the rules of international trade require that all nations impose the same consumer safety standards?

14. What is the national interest argument for protectionism with regard to certain products?

15. Name several of the international treaties where countries negotiate with each other over trade policy.

16. What is the general trend of trade barriers over recent decades: higher, lower, or about the same?

17. If opening up to free trade would benefit a nation, then why don't nations just eliminate their trade barriers, and not bother with international trade negotiations?

7

The Macroeconomic Perspective

Macroeconomics and microeconomics are two different perspectives on the subject of economics. What seems sensible from a microeconomic point of view can have unexpected or counterproductive results at the macroeconomic level. For example, imagine that you are sitting at an event with a large audience, like a live concert or a basketball game. A few people decide that they want a better view, and so they stand up. However, when these people stand up, they block the view for some other people, and the others need to stand up as well if they wish to see. Eventually, nearly everyone is standing up, and as a result, no one can see much better than before. The individually rational decision of some individuals at the micro level—stand up to see better—ended up being self-defeating at the macro level.

Or consider the case of a farmer who finds out that the long-range weather forecast is for an especially fine growing season. The farmer decides to plant extra acreage to take advantage of the fine weather. However, if all farmers see the same forecast, and all decide to plant extra, then the result will be a shift out to the right of the supply curve that depresses the equilibrium market price for all farmers. In this case, the microeconomic rational behavior of individual farmers who are seeking higher profits ends up with an outcome—low prices—that none of them desired.

Finally, consider the case of a country in which many foreign individuals and firms are making financial investments. A rumor circulates that the economy of this country may be weakening, and that some of its leading companies may go bankrupt. The foreign investors become worried. They start selling their assets in the country and declining to make any new investments. But when many foreign investors react in this way, the country's economy actually does become much weaker from a lack of loans and financial investment capital, and many leading companies go bankrupt as a result. Again, individually rational, cautious decisions by investors—in this case, reducing the amount invested in the country—leads to a self-fulfilling prophecy that their investments turn out poorly.

These stories have a common theme: Individually rational motivations help economic agents coordinate their behavior in some ways, but in some cases they can also lead to undesired outcomes. In such cases, society may wish to create other coordinating mechanisms. In the case of people in a crowd trying to see better, for example, the coordinating mechanism is often social pressure: that is, the group accepts that people will stand up in moments of excitement, but if someone stands at other times, then others in the audience yell at them to sit down. In macroeconomic settings, government may in certain situations be able to play a coordinating role to avoid unwanted outcomes.

This chapter begins the discussion of macroeconomics by focusing on the single most common measure of the size of the macro economy: gross domestic product or GDP. Since the macro economy involves all the buying and selling transactions that occur, GDP can be measured in two ways: by looking at the overall demand for goods and services, or by looking at what is produced. The chapter will discuss comparing GDP across countries, patterns of GDP in the long run and the short run, and the extent to which GDP captures or does not capture the broader concept of a society's standard of living.

The chapters that follow will first discuss macroeconomic goals, then frameworks for analysis, and finally policy tools. Exhibit 7-1 illustrates the structure. In thinking about the overall health of a macro economy, it is useful to consider four goals. *Economic growth*, which can be approximated by the growth of gross domestic product, ultimately determines the prevailing standard of living in a country. *Unemployment*, the situation in which people want to work but can't find a job, is not only potentially devastating for individuals and families—but society as a whole loses the value of the output that could have been produced. *Inflation* refers to a rise in the overall level of prices. The difficulty arises because not all prices rise at the same time. For example, if many people face a situation where the prices that they pay for food, shelter, and health care are rising much faster than the wages they receive for their labor, there will be widespread unhappiness. Finally, a sustainable *balance of trade* refers to the flows of goods and financial capital back and forth between countries. Although the gains from trade in the global economy can produce economic gains for all nations, trade imbalances can also be a source of macroeconomic disruption and instability. One or more of these statistics are in the news almost every day. The next four chapters—from Chapters 8–11—will explore and explain these four goals.

None of these macroeconomic goals is straightforward to analyze from a microeconomic perspective. For example, microeconomic analysis of supply and demand can explain why equilibrium quantity might increase in a single market for a good or a service, but it does not offer a simple method for explaining overall growth in the entire macroeconomy. Microeconomic analysis can explain why a firm or an industry might hire more or fewer workers, but it does not offer a simple method for explaining why many or most firms might become unwilling to hire at the same time, thus creating the macroeconomic problem of unemployment. Microeconomic analysis can explain why the price might rise or fall for a particular product, but it doesn't offer any simple way of discussing why most prices might all rise by about the same amount at the same time in a process of inflation. Finally, microeconomic analysis can explain why a firm might have success selling its goods abroad and why consumers might want to buy goods from abroad, but it offers no easy framework for discussing the implications of the overall balance of exports and imports—that is, the balance of trade.

Exhibit 7-1
Macroeconomic Goals,
Framework, and Policies
The discussion of
macroeconomics in the
chapters that follow will
discuss four goals of
macroeconomics, present
several analytical frameworks
for thinking about how
these goals may interact
and conflict, and finally,
discuss two broad sets of
macroeconomic policies.

Several different analytical frameworks exist for thinking about how these four macroeconomic goals relate to each other, and how pursuing one goal may in some cases or over the short run or the long run involve trade-offs with other goals. These frameworks have names like "aggregate supply and aggregate demand models," "sticky price Keynesian models," and "flexible price neoclassical models." At this point, these names are just empty words, but they will be explained from Chapters 12–14.

With the goals and frameworks in mind, the stage is set to discuss how the macroeconomic policy tools available to government, working through the analytical frameworks, will affect the ultimate policy goals. *Monetary policy* includes policies that affect money, banking, interest rates, and exchange rates, and these policies are discussed in Chapters 15–17.

Fiscal policy means policies that involve government taxes or spending, and applications of fiscal policy are discussed in Chapters 18–19. Chapter 20, the final chapter of the macroeconomic section, offers overall lessons of macroeconomics in a global context.

Measuring the Size of the Economy: Gross Domestic Product

The size of a nation's overall economy is typically measured by its **gross domestic product** or **GDP,** which is the value of the output of all goods and services produced within a country. The measurement of GDP thus involves counting up millions of different goods and services—cars, haircuts, computers, steel, bananas, college educations, and everything else—and summing them into a total value. As a conceptual matter, this task is straightforward: take the quantity of everything produced, multiply it by the price that everything for which everything sold, and add up the total. In 2009, the U.S. GDP totaled $14.2 trillion.

Each of the market transactions that enter into GDP must involve both a buyer and a seller. Thus, the GDP of an economy can be measured either by the total of what is demanded in the economy, or by the total of what is produced in the economy.

**gross domestic product
(GDP):** The value of the
output of all goods and
services produced within a
country.

GDP Measured by Components of Demand

GDP as measured by demand is commonly divided into five parts: consumption, investment, government, exports, and imports. Exhibit 7-2 shows how these five factors add up to the GDP in 2009. Exhibit 7-3*a* shows the levels of consumption, investment and government consumption over time, expressed as a percentage of GDP, while Exhibit 7-3*b* shows the levels of exports and imports as a percentage of GDP over time. A few patterns about each of these components are worth noticing.

Exhibit 7-2
Components of GDP in
2009: From the Demand
Side

Components of GDP on the Demand Side (in trillions of dollars)		Percentage of Total
Consumption	$9.9	70.2%
Investment	$1.6	11.3%
Government	$2.9	20.6%
Exports	$1.6	11.4%
Imports	−$1.9	−13.5%
Total	*$14.2*	*100%*

Exhibit 7-3   Components of GDP on the Demand Side

(a) Consumption is about two-thirds of GDP, but it moves relatively little over time. Investment hovers around 15% of GDP, but it increases and declines more than consumption. Government spending on goods and services is around 20% of GDP.

(b) Exports are added to total demand for goods and services, while imports are subtracted from total demand. Thus, if exports are equal to imports, international trade as a whole has no impact on the size of GDP. If exports exceed imports, as in most of the 1960s and 1970s in the U.S. economy, a trade surplus exists. If imports exceed exports, as in recent years, than a trade deficit exists.

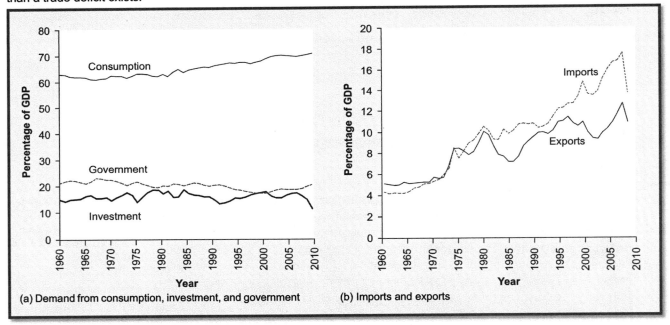

(a) Demand from consumption, investment, and government   (b) Imports and exports

Consumption (C) by households is the largest component of GDP, accounting for about two-thirds of the GDP in any year. However, consumption is a gentle elephant: when viewed over time, it doesn't jump around too much.

Investment (I) by businesses refers to real purchases of physical plant and equipment by businesses. Investment demand is far smaller than consumption demand, typically accounting for only about 15–20% of GDP. However, it moves up and down more noticeably than consumption. Investment is a cat in a bag: it jumps around unexpectedly.

Government (G) demand in the United States appears relatively small, at about 20% of GDP. This proportion may seem too low. Indeed, government in the United States (including the federal, state and local levels) collects about one-third of GDP in taxes.

How Statisticians Measure GDP

Economists have an old, sad joke that there are two things you never want to watch being made: sausages and economic statistics. The joke comes to mind in considering the task of the government economists at the Bureau of Economic Analysis, within the U.S. Department of Commerce, who piece together estimates of GDP from a variety of sources.

Once every five years, in the second and seventh year of each decade, the Bureau of the Census carries out a detailed census of businesses throughout the United States. In between, the Census bureau carries out a monthly survey of retail sales. These figures are adjusted with foreign trade data, to account for exports that are produced in the United States and sold abroad and for imports that are produced abroad and sold here. Once every 10 years, the Census Bureau does a comprehensive survey of housing and residential finance. Together, these sources provide the main basis for figuring what is produced for consumers.

For investment, the Census Bureau does a monthly survey of construction and an annual survey of expenditures on physical capital equipment.

For what is purchased by the federal government, the statisticians rely on the U.S. Department of the Treasury. An annual Census of Governments gathers information on state and local governments. Because a lot of government spending at all levels is involves hiring people to provide services, a large portion of government spending can also be tracked through payroll records collected by state governments and by the Social Security Administration.

With regard to foreign trade, the Census Bureau compiles a monthly record of all import and export documents. Additional surveys cover transportation and travel, and adjustment needs to be made for financial services that are produced in the United States for foreign customers.

Many other sources contribute to the estimates of GDP. Information on energy comes from the U.S. Department of Transportation and Department of Energy. Information on health care is collected by the Health Care Financing Administration. Surveys of landlords find out about rent. The Department of Agriculture collects statistics on farming.

All of these bits and pieces of information arrive in different forms, at different time intervals. The Bureau of Economic Analysis melds them together to produce estimates of GDP on a quarterly basis (that is, every three months). These estimates are then updated and revised. The "advance" estimate of GDP for a certain quarter is released one month after a quarter. The "preliminary" estimate comes out one month after that. The "final" estimate is published one month later, but it isn't actually final. In July, roughly, updated estimates for the previous calendar year are released. Then, once every five years, after the results of the latest detailed five-year business census have been processed, the BEA revises all of the past estimates of GDP according to the newest methods and data, going all the way back to 1929.

When you read newspaper reports of recent GDP announcements, be aware that the "advance," "preliminary" and "final" announcements of quarterly GDP during a year usually don't change much. However, the annual revisions released each summer can be substantial; enough to make GDP growth appear quite different than the quarterly reports released earlier that year.

However, much of that money is passed directly to citizens, through programs like Social Security, welfare payments to the poor, or interest payments on past government borrowing. In these cases, the money that passes through government hands is counted as part of consumption. The only part of government spending counted in demand is—returning to the basic definition of GDP—government purchases of goods or services produced in the economy. Examples would include when the government buys a new fighter jet for the Air Force or when it pays workers who deliver government services.

When thinking about the demand for domestically produced goods in a global economy, it is important to count demand for *exports* (X)—that is, domestically made goods that are sold abroad. However, if one is going to add in the extra demand generated by foreign buyers, one must also subtract out *imports* (M)—that is, goods produced in other countries that are purchased in this country. The gap between exports and imports is called the **trade balance.** If a country's exports are larger than its imports, then a country is said to have a **trade surplus.** In the United States, exports typically exceeded imports in the 1960s and 1970s, as shown in Exhibit 7-3b. But since the early 1980s, imports have typically exceeded exports, and so the United States has experienced a **trade deficit** in most years. Indeed, the trade deficit grew quite large in the late 1990s and in the mid-2000s. Exhibit 7-3 also shows that imports and exports have both risen

trade balance: Gap between exports and imports.

trade surplus: When exports exceed imports.

trade deficit: When imports exceed exports.

substantially in recent decades, even after the declines during the recessionary period in 2008 and 2009, illustrating the process of globalization. If exports and imports are equal, then foreign trade has no effect on the total GDP of the economy. However, even if exports and imports are balanced overall, foreign trade might still have powerful effects on particular industries and workers by causing nations to shift workers and physical capital investment toward specializing in one industry rather than another.

Based on these five components of demand, GDP can be measured as:

$$GDP = Consumption + Investment + Government + Trade\ balance$$

$$GDP = C + I + G + (X - M).$$

Remember this definition. It will prove important for analyzing connections in the macro economy and for thinking about macroeconomic policy tools.

GDP Measured by What Is Produced

Everything that is purchased with components of demand must also be produced. Exhibit 7-4 breaks down what is produced into five categories: **durable goods, nondurable goods,** services, structures, and the change in **inventories.** Before going into detail about these categories, notice that total GDP measured according to what is produced is exactly the same as the GDP measured by looking at the five components of demand. Since every market transaction must have both a buyer and a seller, GDP must be the same whether measured by what is demanded or what is produced. Exhibit 7-5 shows these components of what is produced, expressed as a percentage of GDP, since 1960. Again, a few patterns stand out.

durable goods: Long-lasting goods like cars and refrigerators.

nondurable goods: Short-lived goods like food and clothing.

inventories: Goods that have been produced, but not yet been sold.

In thinking about what is produced in the economy, many non-economists immediately focus on solid, long-lasting goods, like cars and computers. But by far the largest part of GDP is services, rather than goods. Moreover, services have been a growing share of GDP over time. A detailed breakdown of the leading service industries would include health care, education, law, and financial services. It has been decades since most of the U.S. economy involved making solid objects. Instead, the most common jobs in a modern economy involves a worker looking at pieces of paper; meeting with co-workers, customers or suppliers; making phone calls; or looking at a computer screen.

Even within the overall category of goods, long-lasting durable goods like cars and refrigerators are about the same share of the economy as short-lived nondurable goods like food and clothing. The category of structures includes everything from homes, to office buildings, shopping malls, and factories. Inventories is a small category that

	Components of GDP on the Supply Side (in trillions of dollars)	Percentage of Total
Goods		
Durable goods	$1.9	13.4%
Nondurable goods	$1.9	13.4%
Services	$9.4	66.2%
Structures	$1.1	7.7%
Change in inventories	−$0.2	−1.1%
Total	$14.2	100%

Exhibit 7-4
Components of GDP on the Supply Side in 2009

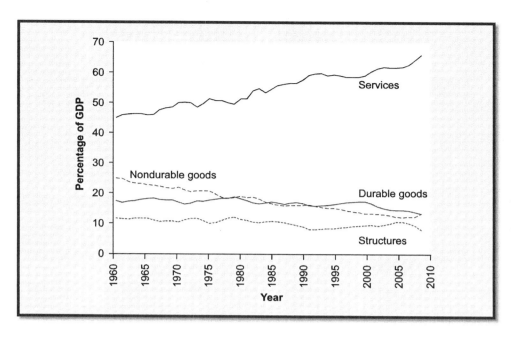

Exhibit 7-5
Components of Supply

Services are the largest single component of aggregate supply, representing over half of GDP. Nondurable goods used to be larger than durable goods, but in recent years, both categories are about 20% of GDP. Structures hover around 10% of GDP. The change in inventories, the final component of aggregate supply, is not shown here; it is typically less than 1% of GDP.

refers to the goods that have been produced by one business but have not yet been sold to consumers, and are still sitting in warehouses and on shelves. The amount of inventories sitting on shelves will tend to decline if business is better than expected, or to rise if business is worse than expected.

The Problem of Double Counting

One danger for the statisticians who calculate GDP is to avoid the mistake of **double counting,** in which output is counted two or more times as it travels through the stages of production. This problem arises because in an economy with a division of labor, most products must work through an interconnected network of producers. For example, imagine what would happen if the government statisticians who calculate GDP first counted the value of mining iron ore, and then counted the value of the steel that used that iron ore, and then counted the value of the car that used that steel. In this example, the value of the original iron ore would have been counted three times—once at each stage of production.

To avoid this problem, which could overstate the size of the economy considerably, government statisticians count just the **final goods and services** in the chain of production that are sold for consumption, investment, government, and trade purposes. This need to avoid double counting (or triple counting, or worse) explains why neither the method of measuring GDP—what is demanded or what is produced—includes the many **intermediate goods and services** that businesses provide to other businesses. The value of what businesses provide to other businesses is captured in the final products at the end of the production chain. Similarly, the value of people's work is included in the price of the goods and services that are eventually produced.

The concept of GDP is fairly straightforward: it's just the value of all final goods and services bought and sold in the economy everything. But in a decentralized, market-oriented economy, actually calculating the more-than $14 trillion dollar U.S.

double counting:
A potential mistake to be avoided in measuring GDP, in which output is counted two or more times as it travels through the stages of production.

final goods and services:
Output used directly for consumption, investment, government, and trade purposes; contrast with "intermediate goods."

intermediate goods and services: Output provided to other businesses at an intermediate stage of production, not for final users; contrast with "final goods and services."

Cousins of GDP

In the world of economic statistics, too much is never enough. There are several different but closely related ways of measuring the size of the economy other than GDP.

One of the closest cousins of GDP is GNP, or gross national product. GDP includes only what is produced by labor and capital located within a country's borders. However, GNP adds what is produced by a nation's labor and capital that are located in the rest of the world, and subtracts out any payments sent home to other countries by foreign labor and capital located in the United States. In other words, GNP is based more on production of citizens and firms from a country, wherever they are located, and GDP is based on what happens within the geographic boundaries of a certain country. For the United States, the gap between GDP and GNP is relatively small; in recent years, only about 0.2%. But for small nations, which may have a substantial share of their population working abroad and sending money back home, the difference can be substantial.

Net national product, or NNP, is calculated by taking GNP and then subtracting the value of how much physical capital is worn out, or reduced in value because of aging, over the course of a year. The process by which capital ages and loses value is called "depreciation." The NNP can be further subdivided into national income, which includes all income to businesses and individuals, and personal income, which includes only income to people.

For practical purposes, it isn't vital to memorize these definitions. However, it is important be aware that these differences exist and to know what statistic you are looking at, so that you don't accidentally compare, say, GDP in one year or for one country with GNP or NNP in another year or another country.

GDP—along with how it is changing every few months—is a full-time job for a brigade of government statisticians.

Comparing GDP among Countries

When comparing the GDP of different countries, two issues immediately arise. First, the GDP of a country is measured in its own currency: the United States uses the U.S. dollar; Canada, the Canadian dollar; most countries of western Europe, the euro; Japan, the yen; Mexico, the peso; and so on. Thus, comparing GDP between two countries requires converting from one currency to another. A second problem is that countries have very different numbers of people. For instance, the United States has a much larger economy than Mexico or Canada, but it also has roughly three times as many people as Mexico and nine times as many people as Canada. Thus, comparing GDP across countries requires a way of adjusting for different currencies and for different population levels.

Converting Currencies with Exchange Rates

To compare the GDP of two different countries with different currencies, it is necessary to use an **exchange rate,** which is the rate at which one currency exchanges for another. Exchange rates can always be expressed either as the units of country A currency that need to be traded for a single unit of country B currency, or units of country B currency that need to traded for a single unit of country A currency. For example, the exchange rate between the Mexican peso and the U.S. dollar can be expressed either as approximately 11 Mexican pesos per 1 U.S. dollar; or to put it the other way, it takes 1/13 of a U.S. dollar (about 8 cents) to buy a peso. It is equally accurate to express the exchange rate in either way, so you can choose whichever measure is more convenient.

exchange rate: The rate at which one currency exchanges for another.

Exchange rates are published each day in the "Business" section of major newspapers and are available at banks and many websites. An illustrative list of exchange rates from early 2010 appears in Exhibit 7-6. Each exchange rate is expressed in two ways: the foreign currency per one U.S. dollar, and the amount in U.S. dollars to buy a unit of foreign currency. These two measures are the reciprocals of each other; in mathematical

The most common mistake that students make when using exchange rates to convert between currencies is to put the exchange rate upside down: for example, they might use the U.S. dollars per euro exchange rate when they meant to use the euros per U.S. dollar exchange rate. To avoid this error, write out the currency units when doing these calculations. Then, you will notice that that the currency units that you are converting away from cancel out in the numerator and denominator of the multiplication calculation, as shown in the conversion of U.S. and Japanese GDP in the text, leaving behind the currency units into which you are converting.

Clearing It Up

Write Out the Exchange
Rate Units

Country (currency)	Currency per U.S. Dollar	U.S. Dollar Equivalent
Brazil (real)	1.792	0.558
Britain (pound)	0.668	1.497
Canada (dollar)	1.027	0.974
China (yuan)	6.826	0.146
Egypt (pound)	5.477	0.183
Euro	0.736	1.359
India (rupee)	45.520	0.022
Indonesia (rupiah)	9195.000	0.000
Japan (yen)	90.025	0.011
Mexico (peso)	12.632	0.079
Nigeria (naira)	150.600	0.007
Russia (ruble)	29.766	0.034
South Africa (rand)	7.403	0.135
United States (dollar)	1.000	1.000

Exhibit 7-6
Examples of Exchange
Rates in Early 2010

terms, multiplying the currency per U.S. dollar exchange rate times the U.S. dollars per foreign currency exchange rate will always equal 1.

Using the exchange rate to convert GDP from one currency to another is straightforward. Say that the task is to compare Japan's GDP of 500 trillion yen with the U.S. GDP of $14 trillion. The exchange rate is 90 yen = $1. (These numbers are realistic for early 2010, but rounded off to simplify the calculations.) To convert Japan's GDP into U.S. dollars, multiply:

$$\text{Japan's GDP in yen} \times \frac{\$}{\text{yen}} = \text{exchange rate}$$

$$500 \text{ trillion yen} \times \frac{\$1}{90 \text{ yen}} = \$5.55 \text{ billion dollars}$$

Of course, it is equally possible to convert the U.S. GDP into yen:

$$\text{U.S. GDP in \$} \times \frac{\text{yen}}{\$} = \text{U.S. GDP in yen}$$

$$\$14 \text{ trillion} \times \frac{90 \text{ yen}}{\$1} = 1{,}260 \text{ trillion yen}$$

Exhibit 7-7   Exchange Rates and Gross Domestic Product (GDP), 2008

The second column shows the size of each country's GDP, measured in billions of units of its own currency in 2008. The third column shows the exchange rate, measured in terms of how many units of domestic currency to each U.S. dollar. The fourth column takes the GDP in the nation's own currency, multiplies by 1/exchange rate in the third column, and thus calculates the country's GDP in U.S. dollars.

Country	GDP in Domestic Currency	Domestic Currency/ U.S. Dollars	GDP (in billions of U.S. dollars)
Brazil	2,080 billion reals	1.792	$1,161
Canada	1,437 billion dollars	1.027	1,400
China	29,556 billion yuan	6.826	4,330
Egypt	892 billion pounds	5.477	163
Germany	2,686 billion euros	0.736	3,650
India	55,534 billion rupees	45.520	1,220
Indonesia	4,726,230 billion rupiah	9195.000	514
Japan	442,022 billion yen	90.025	4,910
Mexico	13,768 billion pesos	12.632	1,090
Nigeria	31,927 billion nairas	150.600	212
Russia	47,922 billion rubles	29.766	1,610
South Africa	2,050 billion rand	7.403	277
United Kingdom	1,770 billion pounds	0.668	2,650
United States	14,258 billion dollars	1.000	14,258

In either case, GDP in the United States is more than double that of GDP in Japan.

To compare the size of several economies, you must convert all of the different measures of GDP into a common currency. The second column of Exhibit 7-7 shows the size of each country's GDP, measured in billions of units of its own currency. The third column shows the exchange rate, measured in U.S. dollars per unit of foreign currency. The fourth column takes the GDP in each country's own currency, multiplies by 1/exchange rate in the third column, and thus expresses the GDP for each country in U.S. dollars.

Converting to Per Capita GDP

The U.S. economy has the largest GDP in the world, by a considerable amount. But the United States is also a populous country; in fact, it is the third-largest country by population in the world, although well behind China and India. So is the U.S. economy larger than other countries just because the United States has more people than most other countries, or because the U.S. economy is actually larger on a per-person basis? This question can be answered by calculating a country's **per capita GDP**; that is, the GDP divided by the population.

per capita GDP: GDP divided by the population.

The second column of Exhibit 7-8 lists the GDP of the same selection of countries that appeared in the previous two exhibits, showing their GDP as converted into U.S. dollars. The third column gives the population for each country. The fourth column lists the per capita GDP, which is calculated by dividing the second column by the third.

Exhibit 7-8 illustrates that a country with a small population can have a smaller GDP, but a larger per capita GDP, than a country with a larger population. For example, the GDP of China is much larger than that of Mexico, but the per capita GDP of Mexico is much larger than China. Looking ahead several decades, it is quite possible that

Country	GDP (in billions of U.S. dollars)	Population (in millions)	Per Capita GDP (U.S. dollars)
Brazil	1,161	192	6,048
Canada	1,400	33	42,028
China	4,330	1,326	3,266
Egypt	163	82	1,999
Germany	3,650	82	44,436
India	1,220	1,140	1,070
Indonesia	514	228	2,252
Japan	4,910	128	38,448
Mexico	1,090	106	10,249
Nigeria	212	151	1,401
Russia	1,610	142	11,354
South Africa	277	49	5,689
United Kingdom	2,650	61	43,160
United States	14,258	307	46,442

Exhibit 7-8   Per Capita GDP in 2008

economic growth in China will cause China to have the largest overall economy in the world—while still having a much lower per capita GDP than the United States. After all, because China has more than four times as many people as the United States, its per capita GDP needs only to be more than one-fourth as large as the U.S. per capita GDP for China's total GDP to exceed that of the United States.

The high-income nations of the world—including the United States and Canada, the western European countries and Japan—typically have per capita GDP in the range of $20,000 to $50,000. Middle-income countries, which include much of Latin America, Eastern Europe, and some countries in East Asia, have per capita GDP in the range of $6,000 to $12,000. The low-income countries in the world, many of them located in Africa and Asia, often have per capita GDP of less than $2,000 per year, and in some cases even less than $1,000 per year.

The Pattern of GDP over Time

For most high-income countries of the world, the long-term pattern of GDP looks generally similar. GDP rises gradually over time, but the road can be bumpy.

Exhibit 7-9 illustrates this general pattern with data on U.S. GDP and per capita GDP. These GDP data are presented after adjusting for inflation. As the discussion of inflation in Chapter 10 will explore in detail, GDP can rise either because a greater quantity of goods and services are being produced, or because the prices of goods and services are higher as a result of inflation. By stripping out the effects of inflation, the remaining rise in GDP shown in the exhibits represents only an increase in the quantity of goods and services produced. Chapter 10 will also discuss just how this adjustment for inflation is performed.

Exhibit 7-9a shows the pattern of total U.S. GDP since 1900. The generally upward long-term path of GDP has been regularly interrupted by short-term declines in GDP. A significant decline in national output is called a **recession.** An especially lengthy and deep recession is called a **depression.** The severe drop in GDP that occurred

recession: A significant decline in national output.

depression: An especially lengthy and deep decline in output.

Exhibit 7-9   U.S. GDP, 1900–2009

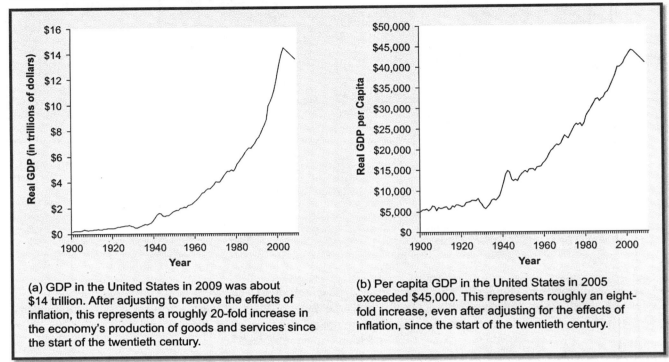

(a) GDP in the United States in 2009 was about $14 trillion. After adjusting to remove the effects of inflation, this represents a roughly 20-fold increase in the economy's production of goods and services since the start of the twentieth century.

(b) Per capita GDP in the United States in 2005 exceeded $45,000. This represents roughly an eight-fold increase, even after adjusting for the effects of inflation, since the start of the twentieth century.

during the Great Depression of the 1930s is clearly visible, as is the Great Recession of 2007–2009. The most significant human problem associated with recessions (and their larger, uglier cousins, depressions) is that a slowdown in production means that many firms will need to hire fewer people, or even to lay off or fire some of the workers that they have. Losing a job imposes painful financial and personal costs on the worker, and often on their extended family as well. In addition, even those who keep their jobs are likely to find that wage raises are scanty at best—or they may even be asked to take pay cuts. Exhibit 7-9b shows the corresponding rise in per capita GDP (again adjusted for inflation). Even though the U.S. population nearly quadrupled over the twentieth century, GDP on a per capita basis has multiplied eight-fold since 1900. The per capita growth rate of GDP over the twentieth century averaged about 2% per year.

Exhibit 7-10 lists the pattern of recessions and expansions in the U.S. economy since 1900. The highest point of the economy, before the recession begins, is called the **peak;** conversely, the lowest point of a recession, before a recovery begins, is called the **trough.** Thus, a recession lasts from peak to trough, and an economic upswing runs from trough to peak. The movement of the economy from peak to trough and trough to peak is called the **business cycle.** It is intriguing to notice that the three longest trough-to-peak expansions of the twentieth century have happened since 1960. The most recent recession started in December 2007 and seems to have ended in summer 2009.

These patterns of GDP growth suggest that the health of the macroeconomy, as measured by GDP, poses two main issues: economic growth and recessions. The time frame for worrying about economic growth is over the long term; the time frame for worrying about recessions is the short term. This long-term/short-term approach to thinking about GDP will play a central role in macroeconomic analysis.

peak: During the business cycle, the highest point of output before a recession begins.

trough: During the business cycle, the lowest point of output in a recession, before a recovery begins.

business cycle: The relatively short-term movement of the economy in and out of recession.

Trough	Peak	Months of Contraction	Months of Expansion
December 1900	September 1902	18	21
August 1904	May 1907	23	33
June 1908	January 1910	13	19
January 1912	January 1913	24	12
December 1914	August 1918	23	44
March 1919	January 1920	7	10
July 1921	May 1923	18	22
July 1924	October 1926	14	27
November 1927	August 1929	23	21
March 1933	May 1937	43	50
June 1938	February 1945	13	80
October 1945	November 1948	8	37
October 1949	July 1953	11	45
May 1954	August 1957	10	39
April 1958	April 1960	8	24
February 1961	December 1969	10	106
November 1970	November 1973	11	36
March 1975	January 1980	16	58
July 1980	July 1981	6	12
November 1982	July 1990	16	92
March 1991	March 2001	8	120
November 2001	December 2007	8	73
June 2009	—	18	—

Exhibit 7-10 Dates of U.S. Business Cycles since 1900

How Well Does GDP Measure the Well-Being of Society?

The level of per capita GDP clearly captures some element of what is meant by the phrase "standard of living." Most of the migration in the world, for example, involves people who are moving from countries with relatively low per capita GDP to countries with relatively high per capita GDP. Similarly, it is not common to find many people in a high-income country who choose to deny themselves the benefits of electricity, plumbing, modern medicine, automobile and plane travel, and choose instead to live only with the income levels and technologies that were available 50 or 100 years ago in high-income countries—or with the technologies that are still in common use in low-income countries.

However, "standard of living" is a broader term than GDP. GDP focuses on production that is bought and sold in markets. Standard of living includes all elements that affect people's happiness, whether they are bought and sold in the market or not. To illuminate the gap between GDP and standard of living, it's useful to spell out some things that GDP does not cover that are clearly relevant to standard of living.

Some Differences between GDP and Standard of Living

GDP includes spending on recreation and travel, but it does not cover leisure time. Clearly, however, there is a substantial difference between an economy that is large because people work long hours, and an economy that grows because people work the same number of hours but are more productive with their time. For example, the per capita GDP of the U.S. economy is larger than the per capita GDP of Germany, as was shown in Exhibit 7-8, but it's also true that the average U.S. worker works several hundred hours more per year more than the average German worker. The calculation of GDP doesn't take the German worker's extra weeks of vacation into account.

GDP includes what is spent on environmental protection, health care, and education, but it does not include actual levels of environmental cleanliness, health, and learning. Thus, GDP includes the cost of buying pollution-control equipment, but it does not address whether the air and water are actually cleaner or dirtier. GDP includes spending on medical care, but does not address whether life expectancy or infant mortality have risen or fallen. Similarly, it counts spending on education, but doesn't address directly how much of the population can read, write, or do basic mathematics.

GDP includes production that is exchanged in the market, but it does not cover production that is not exchanged in the market. For example, hiring someone to mow your lawn or clean your house is part of GDP, but doing these tasks yourself is not part of GDP. One remarkable change in the U.S. economy in recent decades is that as of 1970, only about 42% of women participated in the paid labor force. By the first decade of the 2000s, about 60% of women participated in the paid labor force. As women have entered the labor force, many of the services that they used to produce in the non-market economy like food preparation and child care have shifted to some extent into the market economy, which makes the GDP appear larger even if more services are not actually being consumed.

GDP includes newly produced goods and services, but does not count the buying and selling of previously existing assets. For example, a house built this year is counted in GDP, but a house built in the past that is sold this year is not part of GDP—because nothing new was produced this year. Although the price of the old house is not part of GDP, the amount paid to a realtor for the service of assisting with the transaction is counted in this year's GDP.

GDP has nothing to say about the level of inequality in society. Per capita GDP is only an average. When per capita GDP rises by 5%, it could mean that everyone in the society has risen by 5%, or that some groups have risen by more while others have risen by less—or even declined. GDP has nothing in particular to say about the amount of variety available. If a family buys 100 loaves of bread in a year, GDP doesn't care whether they are all white bread, or whether the family can choose from wheat, rye, pumpernickel and many others—it just looks at whether the total amount spent on bread is the same.

GDP has nothing much to say about what technology and products are available. The standard of living in, say 1950 or 1900 wasn't affected only by how much money people had—it was also affected by what they could buy. No matter how much money you had in 1950, you could not buy a CD player or a portable phone.

In certain cases, it isn't clear that a rise in GDP is even a good thing. If a city is wrecked by a hurricane, and then experiences a surge of rebuilding construction activity, it would be peculiar to claim that the destruction of the hurricane was therefore economically beneficial. If people are led by a rising fear of crime to pay for installation of bars and burglar alarms on all their windows, it is hard to believe that this increase in GDP has made them better off. Some people would argue that sales of certain goods, like pornography or extremely violent movies, do not represent a gain to society's standard of living.

The Human Development Index

Economists have long recognized that GDP is not a complete measure of social well-being. In 1990, an economist named Mahbud ul Haq at the United Nations Development Programme decided to do something about it. The UNDP began publishing an annual Human Development Report. Each year, along with a discussion of economic and social issues affecting low-income countries, the Report includes a Human Development Index, which ranks countries in three broad areas: health, as measured by life expectancy; education, as measured by school enrollment and adult literacy; and material standard of living, as measured by per capita GDP.

By blending per capita GDP with measures of health and education, countries with good levels of health and education may rank higher in the Human Development Index than other countries that have greater per capita GDP. For example, in the rankings published in 2009, the U.S. per capita GDP was 30% higher than that of Australia. However, life expectancy in Australia was three years greater than in the United States and a higher proportion of Australians are enrolled in school (including college) than in the United States. Thus, in the HDI rankings, Australia ranked above the United States.

To choose another example, the per capita GDP of Russia is about one-third above that of Costa Rica. In addition, the average education level is higher in Russia. However, live expectancy in Costa Rica is 79 years while in Russia it is only 66 years, and given the formula used for computing the HDI rankings, Costa Rica ends up well ahead of Russia.

The HDI rankings are controversial. Are these factors, measured in these specific ways, the right ones to include? What about making additional adjustments for gender or racial equality, the level of poverty, or environmental quality? Are the three factors weighted properly, or is, say, adult literacy getting too much weight and per capita GDP too little weight? The UNDP readily acknowledges: "The concept of human development is much deeper and richer than what can be captured in any composite index or even by a detailed set of statistical indicators."

Does a Rise in GDP Overstate or Understate the Rise in the Standard of Living?

The fact that per capita GDP does not fully capture the broader idea of standard of living has led to a concern that the increases in GDP over time are illusory. It is at least theoretically possible that while the measured GDP is rising, the standard of living could be falling if human health, environmental cleanliness, and other factors that aren't included in GDP are worsening. Fortunately, this fear appears to be overstated.

In some ways, the rise in GDP *understates* the actual rise in the standard of living. For example, the typical workweek for a U.S. worker has fallen over the last century from about 60 hours per week to less than 40 hours per week. Life expectancy and health have risen dramatically, and so has the average level of education. Since 1970, the air and water in the United States have generally (with some exceptions) been getting cleaner. New technologies have been developed for many functions, including entertainment, travel, information, and health. A much wider variety of basic products like food and clothing is available today than several decades ago. Because GDP does not capture leisure, health, a cleaner environment, the possibilities created by new technology, or an increase in variety, the actual rise in the standard of living for Americans in recent decades has exceeded the rise in GDP.

On the other side, rates of crime, levels of traffic congestion, and inequality of incomes are higher in the United States now than they were in the 1960s. Moreover, a substantial number of services that used to be provided, primarily by women, in the non-market economy are now part of the market economy that is counted by GDP. By ignoring these factors, GDP would tend to overstate the true rise in the standard of living.

The positive factors ignored by GDP are probably larger than the negative factors ignored by GDP, in which case GDP over time would understate the true rise in the standard of living. But that judgment is a controversial one.

GDP Is Rough, but Useful

It would be foolish and blinkered to believe that a high level of GDP should be the only goal of macroeconomic policy or government policy more broadly. But even though GDP does not measure broader standard of living with any precision, it still reveals something important about the standard of living. In most countries, a significantly higher per capita GDP occurs hand in hand with other improvements in everyday life along many dimensions like education, health, environmental protection.

No single number can capture all the elements of a term as broad as "standard of living." Per capita GDP has real limitations, which must always be kept in mind. Nonetheless, per capita GDP is a reasonable, rough-and-ready measure of the standard of living.

Conclusion

There is sometimes a tendency to speak as if certain parts of the economy deserve more emphasis than others: for example, that high-technology industries are more important to the economy than established industries, like making paper, or service jobs in areas, like tourism. Even within the high-tech industries, certain hot new firms—perhaps those involved in the Internet or in biotechnology—are sometimes claimed to be more important than older established firms.

This desire to treat certain industries like favorite children is often misguided, because an economy is not like a country's Olympic team. In the Olympics, a country can celebrate if a few of its top athletes perform well. In the Olympics, it doesn't matter if the rest of the people in the country, watching on television, are fat and lazy and out of shape. But in an economy, every business counts. For an economy as a whole, it doesn't work especially well to have a few wonderful, world-class companies, while the rest of the economy is flabby and inefficient. After all, people work everywhere in the economy and buy goods from everywhere in the economy. Everyone throughout the economy needs good products, good jobs, good pay, and a generally rising standard of living.

Key Concepts and Summary

1. In a number of cases, behavior that seems rational at the microeconomic level for individuals and firms can end up leading to unexpected or even counterproductive outcomes at the macroeconomic level.

2. The size of a nation's economy is commonly measured by its **gross domestic product** or **GDP,** which measures the value of the output of all goods and services produced within the country. GDP is measured by taking the quantities of all goods and services produced, multiplying them by their prices, and summing the total.

3. Since GDP measures what is bought and sold in the economy, it can be measured either by the sum of what is demanded in the economy or what is produced. Demand can be divided into consumption, investment, government, exports, and imports. What is produced in the economy can be divided into **durable goods, nondurable goods,** services, structures, and **inventories.**

4. To avoid **double-counting**, GDP counts only final output of goods and services, not the production of intermediate goods or the value of labor in the chain of production.

5. In comparing GDP figures between countries, it is necessary to useful to convert to a common currency using **exchange rates** and to divide by population to calculate **per capita GDP.**

6. In the long term, the key issue concerning GDP is real per capita growth. In the short run, the key issue concerning GDP is shortening or reducing the size of **recessions** and **depressions**—or avoiding them completely.

7. GDP is an indicator of a society's standard of living, but it is only a rough indicator. GDP does not directly take account of leisure, environmental quality, levels of health and education, activities conducted outside the market, changes in inequality of income, increases in variety, increases in technology, or the (positive or negative) value that society may place on certain types of output.

Review Questions

1. What are the main components of measuring GDP with what is demanded?

2. What are the main components of measuring GDP with what is produced?

3. Would you usually expect GDP as measured by what is demanded to be greater than GDP measured by what is supplied, or the reverse?

4. Why is double counting a danger when measuring GDP?

5. What are the two main difficulties that arise in comparing the GDP of different countries?

6. What are the typical patterns of GDP for a high-income economy like the United State's in the long-run and the short-run?

7. List some of the reasons why GDP should not be considered a precise measure of the standard of living in a country.

8

Economic Growth

Every country worries about economic growth. In the United States and other high-income countries, will economic growth continue to provide the same remarkable gains in standard of living that it has in the last century? Can middle-income countries like South Korea, Brazil, Egypt, or Poland catch up to the higher-income countries, or must they remain in the second tier of per-capita income? Of the world's population of 6.7 billion people, 2.6 billion are scraping by on incomes that average less than $2 per day. Can the world's poor be lifted from their fearful poverty? As economist Robert E. Lucas Jr., the 1995 Nobel laureate in economics, once noted: "The consequences for human welfare involved in questions like these are simply staggering: Once one starts to think about them, it is hard to think about anything else."

Dramatic movements in a nation's standard of living are possible. After the Korean War in the late 1950s, the Republic of Korea, often referred to as South Korea, was one of the poorest economies in the world, along with low-income countries of Africa and south Asia. Most South Koreans worked in peasant agriculture. Per capita GDP was perhaps $200 per year. But from the 1960s to the early twenty-first century, a time period well within the lifetime and memory of a single adult, the economy of South Korea has blossomed. Over these four decades, per capita GDP increased by more than 6% per year. Per capita GDP for the Republic of Korea now exceeds $27,000, which places South Korea firmly among the middle-income countries of the world, near nations like Italy, New Zealand and Israel. Measured by total GDP, South Korea ranked as the world's 13th-largest economy overall in 2008—just slightly larger than the economy of Canada. This transformation for a nation of 48 million people is extraordinary.

South Korea is a standout example, but it is not the only case of rapid and sustained economic growth. Other nations of East Asia, like Thailand and

Indonesia, have seen very rapid growth as well. The economy of China has grown enormously since market-oriented economic reforms were enacted around 1980. In a longer historical perspective, per capita GDP in high-income economies like the United States has grown dramatically as well, as the U.S. economy has been transformed from primarily rural and agricultural economies to a modern economy based on services, manufacturing and technology.

This chapter begins with a brief overview of patterns of economic growth around the world in the last two centuries. It then discusses the power of even seemingly low levels of economic growth to transform living standards over time; the key macroeconomic ingredients for growth; and the link from worker productivity to economic growth. The discussion concludes by examining the prospects for countries with lower levels of per capita GDP to catch up to the high-income countries.

The Relatively Recent Arrival of Economic Growth

Economic growth is a relatively recent experience for the human race: it didn't really start until about 1800. Before then, while kings and conquerors could afford some extravagances, the standard of living of average people hadn't changed much for centuries. The famous economist John Maynard Keynes wrote in 1930:

> From the earliest times of which we have record—back, say, to two thousand years before Christ—down to the beginning of the eighteenth century, there was no very great change in the life of the average man living in the civilized centers of the earth. Ups and downs certainly. Visitations of plague, famine, and war. Golden intervals. But no progressive, violent change.

But progressive, powerful economic change started in the late eighteenth and early nineteenth centuries, first in Great Britain, and soon spreading to the United States, Germany, and other countries. The **Industrial Revolution** arrived—a term which refers to the widespread use of power-driven machinery and the economic and social changes that resulted in the first half of the 1800s. Ingenious machines—the steam engine, the power loom, and the locomotive—performed tasks that would have taken vast numbers of workers. The jobs for ordinary people working with these machines were often dirty and dangerous by modern standards, but their alternative jobs for that time in peasant agriculture and small-village industry were often dirty and dangerous, too. The new jobs of the Industrial Revolution typically offered higher pay and chance for social mobility. A self-reinforcing cycle began: new inventions and investments created profits, profits provided funds for new investment and invention, and the investments and inventions provided opportunities for further profits. Slowly, a group of national economies in Europe and North America emerged from centuries of economic stagnation and lifted off. During the last two centuries, the average rate of growth of per capita GDP in the leading industrialized countries has averaged about 2% per year.

A growth rate of just 2% per year might seem too slow to explain the phenomenal changes in the standard of living over the last two centuries. But never forget that seemingly low rates of growth, compounded over time, can have mighty results. Thus, if a country's per capita GDP starts at a level of 100, and then grows for 200 years at 2%, its per capita GDP at the end of that period will be:

$$100 (1 + .02)^{200} = 5,248$$

Industrial Revolution: The widespread use of power-driven machinery and the economic and social changes that occurred in the first half of the 1800s.

In other words, a 2% annual growth rate continued over 200 years means that per capita GDP will rise by a multiple of more than 52!

The Industrial Revolution led to a widening of the inequality between nations as some economies took flight, while others, like many of those in Africa or Asia, remained close to a subsistence standard of living. By one calculation, the 17 countries of the world with most developed economies had, on average, 2.4 times the per capita GDP of the world poorest economies in 1870; by 1960, the most developed economies had 4.2 times the per capita GDP of the poorest economies.

However, by the middle of the twentieth century, some countries had shown that catching up was possible. Japan's economic growth took off in the 1960s and 1970s, with a growth rate of real per capita GDP averaging 11% per year during those decades. Certain countries in Latin America experienced a boom in economic growth in the 1960s as well: in Brazil, for example, per capita GDP expanded by an average annual rate of 9% from 1968 to 1973. In the 1970s, some economies in east Asia zoomed as well, including South Korea, Thailand, and Taiwan. In these countries, growth rates of 11–12% per year in per capita GDP were not uncommon. More recently, the economy of China, with its population of 1.3 billion people, grew at a per capita rate 9% per year from 1984 into the 2000s. India, with a population of 1.1 billion, has shown promising signs of economic growth in the 1990s, with growth in per capita GDP of about 4% per year during the 1990s and climbing toward more like 7–8% per year in the 2000s.

These waves of catch-up economic growth have not touched all shores. In certain African countries like Niger, Tanzania, Nigeria, and Sudan, for example, per capita GDP at the start of the 2000s was still less than $300, not much higher than it was in the nineteenth century and for centuries before that. But in thinking about the overall situation of low-income people around the world, the good economic news from China (population: 1.3 billion) and India (population: 1.1 billion) is nonetheless astounding and heartening.

Economic growth in the last two centuries has made a striking change in the human condition. Richard Easterlin, an economist at the University of Southern California, wrote in 2000:

> By many measures, a revolution in the human condition is sweeping the world. Most people today are better fed, clothed, and housed than their predecessors two centuries ago. They are healthier, live longer, and are better educated. Women's lives are less centered on reproduction and political democracy has gained a foothold. Although western Europe and its offshoots have been the leaders of this advance, most of the less developed nations have joined in during the 20th century, with the newly emerging nations of sub-Saharan Africa the latest to participate. Although the picture is not one of universal progress, it is the greatest advance in the human condition of the world's population ever achieved in such a brief span of time.

Worker Productivity and Economic Growth

Per capita GDP offers one measure of economic prosperity; that is, taking the total output of goods and services in an economy—the GDP—and dividing by the population. A useful alternative measure is to start with GDP and divide by the number of workers in an economy, or the number of hours that are worked. The value of what is produced per worker, or per hour worked, is called **productivity**.

productivity: What is produced per worker, or per hour worked.

An economy's rate of productivity growth is closely linked to the growth rate of its per capita GDP, although the two aren't identical. For example, if the percentage of the population who hold jobs in an economy increases, per capita GDP will increase but the productivity of individual workers need not be affected. But over the long term, the only way that per capita GDP can grow continually is if the productivity of the average worker rises.

A common measure of U.S. productivity is output per hour in the business sector. This measure excludes government workers, because their output is not sold in the market and so their productivity is hard to measure, and farming, which accounts for only a relatively small share of the U.S. economy. Exhibit 8-1 shows that the average amount produced by a U.S. worker in an hour averaged about $53 in 2009, about twice as much as an average worker produced per hour in 1966. Exhibit 8-2 shows average annual rates of productivity growth averaged over five-year periods since 1960. U.S. productivity growth was fairly strong in the 1960s but then dropped lower in the 1970s and 1980s, before rising again in the second half of the 1990s and especially the first half of the 2000s. In fact, the rate of productivity increase measured by the change in output per hour worked averaged 3% per year from 1960–1973; 1% per year from 1973 to 1982; 1.7% per year from 1982 to 1995; 2.1% from 1995 to 1999; 3.5% from 2000 to 2004; and then back to 2.1% from 2005–2009.

A hot controversy has been boiling among economists in recent years about the resurgence of U.S. productivity in the second half of the 1990s. One school of thought argued that the United States had developed a "new economy," based on the extraordinary advances in communications and information technology of the 1990s. The most optimistic proponents of the new economy argued that it would generate higher average productivity growth for decades to come. The pessimists, on the other hand, argued that even five or ten years of stronger productivity growth doesn't prove that higher productivity will last for the long term. It's hard to infer anything about long-term productivity trends during the later part of the 2000s, because the steep recession of 2007–2009, with its sharp but not completely synchronized declines in output and

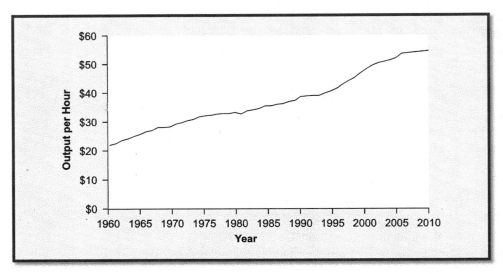

Exhibit 8-1 Output per Hour Worked in the U.S. Economy, 1960–2009

Output per hour worked is a measure of worker productivity. In the U.S. economy, worker productivity rose more quickly in the 1960s and since the mid-1990s than during the 1970s and 1980s. However, these growth rate differences are only a few percentage points per year, so you have to look carefully to see them in the upward slope of the figure. The average U.S. worker produced nearly $53 per hour in 2009. The output-per-hour numbers have been adjusted to remove the effects of price inflation.

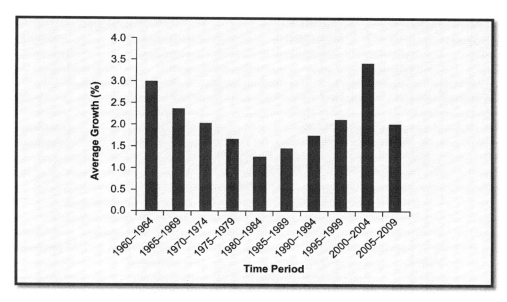

Exhibit 8-2   Annual Rate of Productivity Growth in Output per Hour Worked: Five-Year Averages

U.S. growth in worker productivity was very high in the early 1960s, then declined to lower levels in the 1970s and the 1980s. The late 1990s and early 2000s saw a productivity rebound, but then productivity sagged in the late 2000s. Some think the productivity rebound of the late 1990s and early 2000s marks the start of a "new economy" built on higher productivity growth, but this cannot be determined until more time has passed.

employment, complicates any interpretation. Of course, the controversy over the path of productivity rates will gradually be resolved by the passage of time and additional data.

Productivity growth is also closely linked to the average level of wages received by workers. Over time, the amount that firms are willing to pay workers will depend on the value of the output that those workers produce. If a few employers tried to pay their workers less than what those workers produced, then those workers will receive job offers with higher wages from other profit-seeking employers. If a few employers mistakenly paid their workers more than what those workers produced, the employers would soon end up making losses, and would either have to reduce wages or go out of business. Over the long run, productivity per hour is the most important determinant of the average wage level in any economy.

The Power of Sustained Economic Growth

Nothing is more important for people's standard of living than sustained economic growth. Even small changes in the rate of growth, when compounded over long periods of time, make an enormous difference in the standard of living. Consider Exhibit 8-3, in which the rows of the table show several different rates of growth in per capita GDP and the columns show different periods of time. Assume for simplicity that an economy starts with a per capita GDP of 100. The table then applies the formula

GDP at starting date × (1 + growth rate of GDP)^{years} = GDP at end date

to calculate what GDP will be at the given growth rate at the future time. For example, an economy that starts with a GDP of 100 and grows at 3% per year will reach a GDP of 209 after 25 years; that is, $100\,(1.03)^{25} = 209$.

The slowest rate of per capita GDP growth in the table, just 1% per year, is similar to what the United States experienced during its weakest years of productivity growth. The second highest rate, 3% per year, is close to what the U.S. economy experienced during the strong economy of the late 1990s and into the 2000s. The higher rates of per capita growth, 5% or 8% per year, represent the experience of rapid growth in economies like Japan, Korea, and China.

Exhibit 8-3 teaches that even a few percentage points of difference in economic growth rates will have a profound effect if sustained and compounded over time. For example, an economy growing at a 1% annual rate over 50 years will see its per capita GDP rise by a total of 64%, from 100 to 164 in this example. However, a country growing at a 5% annual rate will see (almost) this same amount of growth—from 100 to 163—over just 10 years. Rapid rates of economic growth can be transforming. At an 8% rate of growth, young adults starting at age 20 would see the average standard of living in their country more than double by the time they had reached age 30, and grow nearly seven-fold by the time they had reached age 45.

The Aggregate Production Function

To analyze the sources of economic growth, whether measured by per capita GDP or by worker productivity, it is useful to think about a **production function,** which is a process of turning economic inputs like labor, machinery, and raw materials into outputs like goods and services used by consumers. A microeconomic production function would describe the inputs and outputs of a firm, or perhaps an industry. In macroeconomics, the connection from inputs to outputs for the entire economy is called an **aggregate production function.**

production function:
The process of a firm turning economic inputs like labor, machinery, and raw materials into outputs like goods and services used by consumers.

aggregate production function: The process of an economy as a whole turning economic inputs like labor, machinery, and raw materials into outputs like goods and services used by consumers.

At time zero, GDP =100. Apply the formula:

GDP at starting date × (1 + growth rate of GDP)^{years} = GDP at end date

	10 Years	25 Years	50 Years
1%	110	128	164
3%	134	209	438
5%	163	338	1,147
8%	216	685	4,690

Exhibit 8-3   Growth of GDP over Different Time Horizons

Components of the Aggregate Production Function

Exhibit 8-4 presents two aggregate production functions. In the first production function (Exhibit 8-4*a*), the output is GDP. The inputs are population, human capital, physical capital, and technology.

The category of population is reasonably self-explanatory: more population usually means more workers, who can then produce additional output. The category of **physical capital** includes the plant and equipment used by firms. **Human capital** is the name that economists give the skills and education of workers. As the phrase "human capital" implies, economists make a useful analogy between the intangible skills of workers and the physical capital of the economy. In both cases, investments are made that pay off in longer-term productivity in the future.

The category of **technology** is the joker in the deck. When most people think of new technology, inventions like the laser, the transistor, or some new wonder drug come to mind. Such prominent inventions are included in the category of technology, but much more is included as well. The economy is full of small new technologies: the bleach that cleans clothes a little whiter, the portable phone that shrinks a little smaller; the improved design of a car tire that grabs the road better; the computer monitor that tilts at a slightly more comfortable angle. Added together, the vast number of ongoing small changes like

physical capital: The plant and equipment used by firms in production.

human capital: The skills and education of workers.

technology: All the ways in which existing machines produce more or higher quality, as well as producing different and altogether new products.

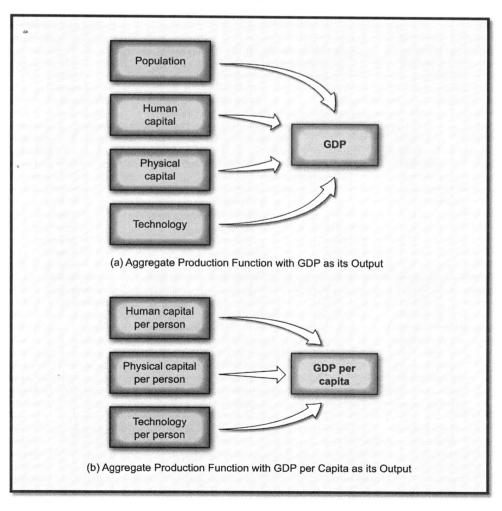

(a) Aggregate Production Function with GDP as its Output

(b) Aggregate Production Function with GDP per Capita as its Output

Exhibit 8-4
Aggregate Production Functions

An aggregate production function shows what goes into producing the output for an overall economy.

(a) This aggregate production function has GDP as its output.

(b) This aggregate production function uses GDP per capita, which because it is calculated on a per-person basis means that the "population" input is already figured into the other factors and doesn't need to be listed separately.

these may be every bit as important as the relatively few major technological inventions. But technology, as economists use the term, includes still more. It includes new ways of organizing work, like the invention of the assembly line, as well as new methods for assuring better quality of output in factories. In short, technology comprises all the advances by which people figure out how to make the existing machines produce more or higher quality, as well as including different and altogether new products.

When discussing economic growth, it is often useful to focus on per capita GDP, to avoid studying changes in the size of GDP that represent only having more people in the economy, and focus on those increases in GDP which represent an actual rise in the standard of living on a per person basis. Using per capita GDP also makes it easier to compare countries with smaller numbers of people, like Belgium or Uruguay or Zimbabwe with countries that have larger populations like the United States or the Russian Federation or Nigeria.

For this purpose, divide everything in the first aggregate production function in Exhibit 8-4*a* by the population. This creates a revised aggregate production function where the output is per capita GDP (that is, GDP divided by population) and the inputs are the average level of human capital per person, the average level of physical capital per person, and the level of technology per person—see Exhibit 8-4*b*. In effect, any growth that occurs because of a rise in population is divided out.

When society has a higher level of capital per person, it is called **capital deepening.** The idea of capital deepening can apply both to additional human capital per worker and to additional physical capital per worker.

capital deepening: When an economy has a higher average level of physical and/or human capital per person.

Exhibit 8-5 illustrates the human capital deepening for U.S. workers by showing that the proportion of the U.S. population with a high school and a college degree is rising. As recently as 1970, for example, only about half of U.S. adults had at least a high school degree; by the start of the twenty-first century, more than 80% of adults had a high school degree. The idea of human capital deepening also applies to the years of experience that workers have, but the average experience level of U.S. workers hasn't changed much in recent decades. Thus, the key dimension for deepening human capital in the U.S. economy focuses more on additional education and training than on a higher average level of work experience.

Physical capital deepening in the U.S. economy is shown in Exhibit 8-6, which shows that the rise in the average amount of physical capital per worker has risen substantially over time. The average U.S. worker in the late 2000s was working with physical capital worth three times as much as the average worker of the early 1950s.

Not only does the current U.S. economy have better-educated workers with more physical capital than it did several decades ago, but these workers can use more advanced technologies. Growth in technology is impossible to measure with a simple line on a graph, but evidence that we live in an age of technological marvels is all around us: discoveries in genetics; in the structure of particles; the wireless Internet; and other inventions almost too numerous to count. The U.S. Patent and Trademark Office has typically been issuing more than 150,000 patents annually in recent years.

This recipe for economic growth and worker productivity—a mix of human capital, physical capital, and technology—applies beyond the border of the U.S. economy. In South Korea's economy, for example, universal enrollment in primary school (the equivalent of kindergarten through sixth grade in the United States) had already been achieved back in 1965, when Korea's per capita GDP was still near its rock bottom low. By the late 1980s, Korea had achieved almost universal secondary school education (the equivalent of a high school education in the United States). With regard to physical

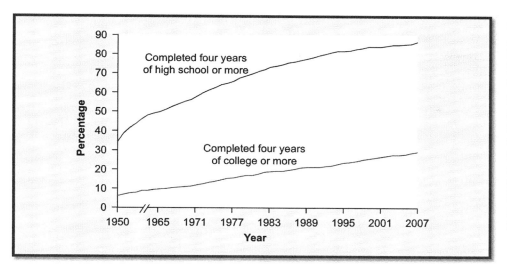

Exhibit 8-5
A Human Capital Deepening in the U.S. Economy: Education Level of Those Age 25 and Older

Rising levels of education show the deepening of human capital in the U.S. economy. Notice that even today, relatively few American adults have completed a four-year college degree. There is clearly room for additional deepening of human capital to occur.

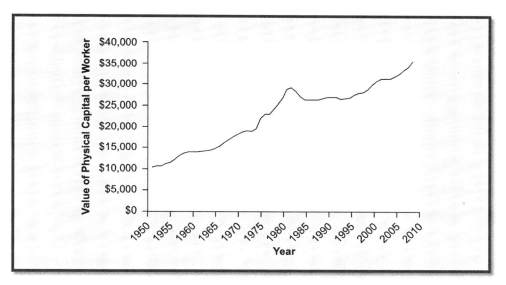

Exhibit 8-6   Physical Capital per Worker in the United States, 1950–2008

The value of the physical capital, measured by plant and equipment, used by the average worker in the U.S. economy has risen over the decades. The increase may have leveled off a bit in the 1970s and 1980s, which were not, coincidentally, times of slower-than-usual growth in worker productivity. There is a renewed increase in physical capital per worker in the late 1990s, followed by a flattening in the early 2000s. (The numbers in the graph are adjusted to remove the effect of price inflation.)

capital, Korea's rates of investment had been about 15% of GDP at the start of the 1960s, but doubled to 30–35% of GDP by the late 1960s and early 1970s. With regard to technology, South Korean students went to universities and colleges around the world to get scientific and technical training, and South Korean firms reached out to study and form partnerships with firms that could offer them technological insights. These factors combined to foster South Korea's high rate of economic growth.

Growth Accounting Studies

Since the late 1950s, economists have performed "growth accounting" studies to calculate what specific portion of economic growth is accounted for by deepening of physical capital, deepening of human capital, and technology. The usual approach of these studies is to estimate how much of per capita economic growth can be attributed to growth in physical capital and human capital, which can be measured at least roughly, and then to attribute whatever residual increase in output that can't be explained by these factors to growth in technology. The exact numerical estimates differ from study

Girl's Education and Economic Growth in Low-Income Countries

In the low-income countries of the world, in the early 2000s, about 110 million children between the ages of 6–11 are not in school—and about two-thirds of them are girls. In Bangladesh, for example, the illiteracy rate for those aged 15–24 was 61% for females, compared to 40% for males. In Egypt, for this age group, illiteracy was 38% for females and 24% for males. Cambodia had 59% illiteracy for females and 25% for males. Nigeria had 18% illiteracy for females in the 15–24 age bracket and 11% for males.

Whenever any child does not receive a basic education, it is both a human and an economic loss. In low-income countries, wages typically increase by an average of 10 to 20 percent with each additional year of education. But there is some intriguing evidence that helping girls in low-income countries to close the education gap with boys may be especially important, because of the social role that many of the girls will play as mothers and homemakers.

Girls in low-income countries who receive more education tend to grow up to have fewer, healthier, better educated children. Their children are more likely to be better-nourished and to receive basic health care like immunizations.

Economic research on women in low-income economies backs up these findings. When 20 women get one additional year of schooling, as a group they will on average have one less child. When 1,000 women get one additional year of schooling, on average 1–2 fewer women from that group will die in childbirth. When a woman stays in school an additional year, that factor alone means that on average, each of her children will spend an additional half-year in school.

Of course, these benefits should be combined with the benefits of education that apply to both genders, like more productive workers, broader personal horizons, and greater control over one's life.

to study and from country to country, depending on how researcher measured these three main factors being considered over what time horizons. But for studies of the U.S. economy, three lessons commonly emerge from these growth accounting studies.

First, technology is typically the most important contributor to U.S. economic growth. Growth in human capital and physical capital often explain only half or less than half of the economic growth that occurs. New ways of doing things are tremendously important to economic growth.

Second, while investment in physical capital is essential to growth in worker productivity and per capita GDP, building human capital is at least as important as physical capital. Economic growth is not just a matter of more machines and buildings. One vivid example of the power of human capital and technological knowledge occurred in Europe in the years after World War II. During the war, a large share of Europe's physical capital—factories, roads, vehicles—was destroyed. However, the powerful combination of skilled workers and technological knowledge, working within a market-oriented economic framework, rebuilt Europe's productive capacity to an even higher level within less than two decades.

A third lesson is that these three factors of human capital, physical capital, and technology work together. Workers with a higher level of education and skills are often better at coming up with new technological innovations. These technological innovations are often ideas that cannot increase production until they become a part of new investment in physical capital. New machines that embody technological innovations often require additional training, which builds skills of workers further. If the recipe for economic growth is to succeed, an economy needs all the ingredients of the aggregate production function.

A Healthy Climate for Economic Growth

The sources of economic growth—technology, human capital, and physical capital—need to combine within a healthy overall economic climate. At the microeconomic level, a healthy economic climate will have a market orientation, because the rewards that are available in a market provide incentives to encourage economic growth. Workers have an incentive to acquire additional human capital because in a market-oriented economy, the additional education and skills will pay off in higher wages. Firms have an incentive to make investment in physical capital and in training their workers, because they expect to earn higher profits as a result. Both individuals and firms look for new technologies, because small inventions can make your work easier or improve your products, and major inventions can be worth a fortune. This market orientation of healthy economies typically reaches beyond national borders and includes openness to international trade.

A general orientation toward markets doesn't rule out some important roles for government. Government often plays a role in setting up and funding the education system, especially at the primary and secondary level. Government regulations and taxes can favor savings and investment, or discourage it. Governments can administer laws in a fair and impartial way, or they can offer favoritism and patronage that encourages business to try to make money by lobbying government ministers, rather than by providing goods and services that consumers desire. Governments can encourage international trade, or surrender to protectionism. Governments can play a key role in overseeing the safety of banks and the financial system, in enforcing contracts, and in supporting infrastructure projects like roads and electricity generators. Governments can support scientific research and technical training that helps to create and spread new technologies, or not. Governments can protect the ability of inventors to profit from their inventions, or not. Governments also have a role to play in preventing the economy from sinking deep into recession or inflation, either of which can create a situation where individuals and firms are under such great stress from dismal macroeconomic conditions that they have little chance to plan the investments and discoveries that lead to economic growth.

Thus, the full recipe for growth in per capita GDP and worker productivity would include human capital deepening, physical capital deepening, and technological gains, operating in a market-oriented economy with supportive government policies.

Future Economic Convergence?

Some low-income and middle-income economies around the world have shown a pattern of **convergence,** in which their economies grows faster than those of high-income countries. GDP increased by an average rate of 2.7% per year in the 1990s and 2.3% per year from 2000–2008 in the high-income countries of the world, which includes the United States, Canada, the countries of the European Union, Japan, Australia and New Zealand.

convergence: When economies with low per capita incomes are growing faster than economies with high per capita incomes.

Exhibit 8-7 lists 10 countries of the world which belong to an informal "fast growth club:" specifically, these countries averaged GDP growth (after adjusting for inflation) of at least 5% per year in both the time periods from 1990–2000 and from 2000–2008. Since economic growth in these countries has been exceeding the average of the world's high-income economies, the economies of these countries have been converging with the high-income countries. The second part of Exhibit 8-7 lists the "slow growth club," which consists of countries that averaged GDP growth of 2% per year or less (after adjusting for inflation) during both time periods. The final portion of the exhibit shows GDP growth rates for the countries of the world divided by income.

Exhibit 8-7
Economic Growth Around
the World

Country	Average Growth Rate of GDP	
	1990–2000	2000–2008
Fast-Growth Club (5% or more per year in both time periods)		
Cambodia	7.1%	9.1%
China	10.6%	9.9%
India	6.0%	7.1%
Ireland	7.5%	5.1%
Jordan	5.0%	6.3%
Lao	6.5%	6.8%
Mozambique	6.4%	7.3%
Sudan	5.4%	7.3%
Uganda	7.1%	7.3%
Vietnam	7.9%	7.3%
Slow-Growth Club (2% or less per year in both time periods)		
Central African Republic	2.0%	0.8%
France	2.0%	1.8%
Germany	1.8%	1.3%
Guinea-Bissau	1.2%	0.2%
Haiti	−1.5%	0.3%
Italy	1.6%	1.2%
Jamaica	0.9%	1.4%
Japan	1.3%	1.3%
Switzerland	1.0%	2.0%
World Overview		
High income	2.7%	2.3%
Low income	3.8%	5.6%
Middle income	4.7%	6.1%

Each of the countries in Exhibit 8-7 has its own unique story of investments in human and physical capital, technological gains, market forces, government policies, and even lucky events. But an overall pattern of convergence over the last two decades is clear. The low-income countries have GDP growth faster than the middle-income countries, which in turn have GDP growth faster than the high-income countries. More specifically, two prominent members of the fast-growth club are China and India, which between them have nearly 40% of the world's population. Some prominent members of the slow-growth club are high-income countries like France, Germany, Italy and Japan. Will this pattern on economic convergence persist into future decades? This question is controversial among economists. Here are some of the main arguments on both sides.

Arguments Favoring Convergence

Several arguments suggest that low-income countries might have an advantage achieving greater worker productivity and economic growth in the future.

A first argument is based on diminishing marginal returns. Even though deepening human and physical capital will tend to increase per capita GDP, the law of diminishing returns suggests that as an economy continues to increase its human and physical capital, the marginal gains to economic growth will diminish. For example, raising the average education level of the population by two years from a tenth grade level to a

The Challenges of Africa's Geography and Climate for Economic Growth

Many of the poorest countries of the world are in Africa, where the per capita GDP early in the twenty-first century was still only about $500. There are many reasons for poor economic performance, but some recent economic research has suggested that Africa's economic growth may have been limited by its geography and climate.

In many parts of the world, water transportation by river and ocean has helped to link together economies, but this doesn't work well for Africa. Other continents have major river systems that can be navigated by ocean-going vessels: like the Mississippi in North America, the Amazon in South America, the Rhine in Europe, or the Yangtze in Asia. But major rivers in Africa like the Nile, the Niger, the Congo, and the Zambezi have a number of steep waterfalls. Small boats might be transported around such waterfalls, but not large vessels. Moreover, Africa has a relatively straight coastline and thus relatively few natural ports with access to the ocean. Western Europe has one-eighth the land area of Africa, but its winding coastline is actually 50 percent longer.

As a result, in low-income countries in the world outside of Africa, more than half of the population lives within 60 miles of a sea or river. But in Africa, only one-fifth of the population lives within 60 miles of a sea or river.

Much of Africa has poor soil quality and little rain, which makes the challenges of agriculture different and more difficult than in other regions.

Africa is more tropical than any other region of the world; specifically, 93% of the land area of Africa is between the tropic of Cancer (an imaginary line drawn around the world at a latitude of 23.5 degrees north of the equator) and the tropic of Capricorn (an imaginary line drawn around the world at a latitude of 23.5 degrees south of the equator).

A tropical climate poses many challenges for economic growth. Many technologies that are developed for climates like the United States or Europe, like those for agriculture and construction, don't transfer well to tropical climates. Certain plant, animal, and human diseases that would be killed off or weakened by winter, like the malaria carried by mosquitoes, seem to thrive in a tropical climate. Moreover, Africa's tropical location means that it is a long way from the world's major markets in North America and Europe.

None of these arguments prove that Africa's economies cannot grow; indeed, a number of African countries have shown encouraging progress toward faster growth in the 2000s. Nor do these arguments disprove the general recipe for economic growth of investments in human capital, physical capital, and technology, operating in a market-oriented environment. But they do suggest that the nations of Africa face some distinctive economic challenges and will have to discover their own unique path to economic growth.

high school degree (while holding all other inputs constant) would produce a certain increase in output. An additional two-year increase, so that the average person had a two-year college degree, would increase output further, but the marginal gain would be smaller. Yet another additional two-year increase in the level of education, so that the average person would have a four-year college bachelor's degree, would increase output still further, but the marginal increase would again be smaller. A similar lesson holds for physical capital. If the quantity of physical capital available to the average worker increases, by, say, $5,000 to $10,000 (again, while holding all other inputs constant), it will increase the level of output. An additional increase from $10,000 to $15,000 will increase output further, but the marginal increase will be smaller.

Low-income countries like China and India tend to have lower levels of human capital and physical capital; as a result, an investment in capital deepening should have a larger marginal effect in low-income countries than in high-income countries, where levels of human and physical capital are already relatively high. This factor should give low-income economies a chance for converging economic growth.

A second argument is that low-income countries may find it easier to improve their technologies than high-income countries. The reason is high-income countries must continually invent new technologies, whereas low-income countries can often find ways of applying technology that had already been invented and is well-understood. An economist named Alexander Gerschenkron (1904–1978) gave this phenomenon a memorable name—"the advantages of backwardness." Of course, he didn't literally mean that it was an advantage to have a lower standard of living. But he was pointing out that a country that is behind has some extra potential for catching up.

Finally, optimists argue that many countries have observed the experience of those countries that have grown more quickly and have learned from it. Moreover, once the people of a country begin to enjoy the benefits of an increased standard of living, they may be more likely to build and support the market-friendly institutions that will help provide this standard of living.

Arguments That Convergence Is Neither Inevitable Nor Likely

If the growth of an economy depended only on the deepening of human capital and physical capital, then the growth rate of that economy would be expected to slow down over the long run as these inputs run into diminishing marginal returns. However, there is another crucial factor in the aggregate production function: technology.

The development of new technology can provide a way for an economy to sidestep the diminishing marginal returns of capital deepening. Exhibit 8-8 shows how. The horizontal axis of the figure measures the amount of capital deepening, which on this figure is an overall measure that includes deepening of both physical and human capital. The amount of human and physical capital per worker increases as you move from left to right from C_1 to C_2 to C_3. The vertical axis of the diagram measures per capita output. Start by considering the lowest line in this diagram, labeled Technology 1. Along this aggregate production function, the level of technology is being held constant, so the line shows only the relationship between capital deepening and output. As capital deepens from C_1 to C_2 to C_3 and the economy moves from R to U to W, per capita output does increase—but the way in which the line starts out steeper on the left but then flattens as it moves to the right shows the diminishing marginal returns, as additional marginal amounts of capital deepening increase output by ever-smaller amounts. The shape of the aggregate production line Technology 1 shows how the ability of capital deepening by itself to generate sustained economic growth is limited, since diminishing returns will eventually set in.

Now bring improvements in technology into the picture. Improved technology means that with a given set of inputs, more output is possible. The production function labeled Technology 1 is based on one level of technology, but Technology 2 is based on an improved level of technology, so for every level of capital deepening on the horizontal axis, it produces a higher level of output on the vertical axis. In turn, production function Technology 3 represents a still higher level of technology, so that for every level of inputs on the horizontal axis, it produces a higher level of output on the vertical axis than either of the other two aggregate production functions.

Most healthy, growing economies are both deepening their human and physical capital and increasing technology at the same time. As a result, the economy can move from a choice like point R on the Technology 1 aggregate production function to a point like S on Technology 2 and on a point like T on the still higher aggregate production function Technology 3. With the combination of technology and capital deepening, the rise in per capita GDP in high-income countries does not need to fade away because of diminishing returns. The gains from technology can offset the diminishing returns involved with capital-deepening.

Will technological improvements themselves run into diminishing returns over time; that is, will it become continually harder and more costly to discover new technological improvements? Perhaps someday. But at least over the last two centuries since the Industrial Revolution, improvements in technology haven't run into diminishing marginal

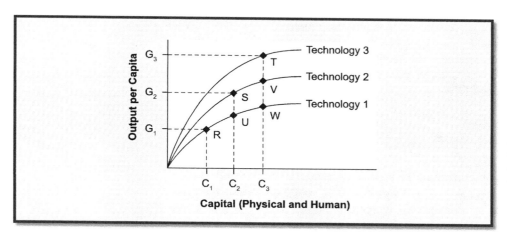

Exhibit 8-8   Capital Deepening and New Technology

Imagine the economy starts at point *R,* with the level of physical and human capital C_1 and the GDP per capita at G_1. If the economy relies only on capital deepening, while remaining at the technology level shown by the Technology 1 line, then it would face diminishing marginal returns as it moved from point *R* to point *U* to point *W.* However, now imagine that capital deepening is combined with improvements in technology. Then, as capital deepens from C_1 to C_2, technology improves from Technology 1 to Technology 2, and the economy moves from *R* to *S.* Similarly, as capital deepens from C_2 to C_3, technology increases from Technology 2 to Technology 3, and the economy moves from *S* to *T.* With improvements in technology, there is no longer any reason that economic growth must necessarily slow down.

returns. Modern inventions, like the Internet or discoveries in genetics or materials science, don't seem to provide smaller gains to output than earlier inventions like the steam engine or the railroad. One reason that technological ideas don't seem to run into diminishing returns is that the ideas of new technology can often be widely applied at a marginal cost that is very low or even zero. A specific additional machine, or an additional year of education, must be used by a specific worker or group of workers. But a new technology or invention can be used by many workers across the economy at very little marginal cost.

The argument that it is easier for a low-income country to copy and to adapt existing technology than it is for a high-income country to invent new technology isn't necessarily true, either. A society's performance when it comes to adapting and using new technology isn't automatic, but is the result of whether the economic, educational, and public policy institutions of the country are supportive. In theory, perhaps, low-income countries have many opportunities to copy and adapt technology, but if they lack the appropriate supportive economic institutions, the theoretical possibility that backwardness might have certain advantages is of little practical relevance.

The Slowness of Convergence

Although economic convergence between the high-income countries and the rest of the world seems possible and even likely, it will proceed only slowly. Consider, for example, one country that starts off with a per capita GDP of $40,000, which would roughly represent a typical high-income country today, and another country that starts out at $4,000, which is roughly the level in low-income but not impoverished countries like Indonesia, Guatemala, or Egypt. Say that the rich country chugs along at a 2% annual growth rate of per capita GDP, while the poorer country grows at the aggressive rate of 7% per year. After 30 years, per capita GDP in the rich country will be $72,450 (that is, $40,000 $(1 + .02)^{30}$), while in the poor country it will be $30,450 (that is, $3,000 $(1 + .07)^{30}$). Convergence has occurred; the rich country used to be 10 times as wealthy as the poor one, and now it is only about 2.4 times as wealthy. But even after 30 consecutive years of very rapid growth, people in the low-income country are still likely to feel quite poor compared to people in the rich country. Moreover, as the poor country catches up, its opportunities for catch-up growth are reduced, and its growth rate may slow down somewhat.

The slowness of convergence illustrates again that small differences in annual rates of economic growth accumulate to huge differences over time. The high-income countries have been building up their advantage in standard of living over decades—more than a century in some cases. Even in an optimistic scenario, it will take decades for the low-income countries of the world to catch up significantly.

Key Concepts and Summary

1. Since the **Industrial Revolution** of the nineteenth century, a process of economic growth began in which the world's leading economies—mostly those in Western Europe and North America—expanded per capita GDP at an average rate of about 2% per year. In the last half century, countries like Japan, Korea, and China, have shown potential for catch-up growth at higher rates, which has helped them to converge with the leading economies.

2. **Productivity** can be measured as the level of GDP per worker or GDP per hour. The rate of productivity growth is the primary determinant of its rate of long-term economic growth.

3. Over decades and generations, seemingly small differences of a few percentage points in the annual rate of economic growth make an enormous difference in per capita GDP.

4. An **aggregate production function** specifies how certain inputs in the economy, like human capital, physical capital, and technology, lead to the output measured as per capita GDP.

5. **Capital deepening** refers to a greater amount of capital per worker. It can apply to a greater amount of **human capital** per worker, in the form of higher education or skills, or to a greater amount of **physical capital** per worker.

6. **Technology,** in its economic meaning, refers broadly to all new methods of production, which include major scientific inventions but also small inventions and even better forms of management or company organization.

7. The recipe for growth in per capita GDP is to improve human capital, physical capital, and technology, in a market-oriented environment with supportive public policies and institutions.

8. **Convergence** refers to the issue of when, or if, countries with lower levels of per capita GDP will catch up to countries with higher levels of per capita GDP.

9. Because high-income economies will run into diminishing marginal returns to their investments in human capital and physical capital, and because high-income economies must continually invent new technologies, lower-income economies have a chance for convergent growth. However, many high-income economies have developed economic and political institutions that provide a healthy economic climate for an ongoing stream of technological innovations. The ongoing stream of technological innovations can counterbalance diminishing returns to investments in human and physical capital.

Review Questions

1. What was the Industrial Revolution?

2. How is per capita GDP calculated differently from worker productivity?

3. How do gains in worker productivity lead to gains in per capita GDP?

4. How much should a nation be concerned if its rate of economic growth is just 2% slower than other nations?

5. What is an aggregate production function? Describe one.

6. What is capital deepening?

7. What do economists mean when they refer to improvements in technology?

8. What is the overall recipe for growth in per capita GDP or worker productivity?

9. For a high-income economy like the United States, what elements of the aggregate production function are most important in bringing about growth in per capita GDP?

10. What do economists mean by convergence?

11. List some arguments for and against the likelihood of convergence.

9

Unemployment

Unemployment is typically described in newspaper or television reports as a percentage; for example, from August 2009 to November 2009, the U.S. unemployment rate rose from 9.7% to 10.0%, but by June 2010, it had fallen to 9.5%. At a glance, the changes between the percentages may seem small. But remember that the U.S. economy has about 150 million adults who either have jobs or are looking for them. A rise or fall of just 0.1% in the unemployment rate of 150 million potential workers translates into 150,000 people, which is roughly the total population of a city like Syracuse, New York, Brownsville, Texas, or Pasadena, California. Large movements in the unemployment rate, like the increase from 5% in April 2008 to 10% by November 2009, mean an additional 7.5 million people who are looking for jobs and can't find them.

Unemployment can be a terrible and wrenching life experience—like a bone-breaking automobile accident or a messy divorce—whose consequences can be fully understood only by someone who has experienced it personally. For unemployed individuals and their families, there is the day-to-day financial stress of not knowing where the next paycheck is coming from. There are painful adjustments, like watching your savings account dwindle, selling a car and buying a cheaper one, or moving to a less expensive place to live. Even when the unemployed person finds a new job, it may pay less than the previous one. For many people, their job is one important part of their sense of self. When unemployment separates people from the workforce, it can affect family relationships and mental and physical health.

The human costs of unemployment alone would justify making a low level of unemployment an important priority for public policy. But the costs of unemployment also include economic costs to the broader society. When millions of unemployed but willing workers cannot find jobs, an economic resource is going unused. An economy with high unemployment is like a company operating with a functional but unused factory. The opportunity cost of unemployment is the output that could have been produced by the unemployed workers. One way in which this opportunity cost becomes apparent is through its effect on government budgets. Employed workers pay their share of taxes; unemployed workers collect government support checks.

This chapter will discuss how to define and calculate unemployment rates. It will consider the patterns of unemployment over time, for the U.S. economy as a whole, for some different groups in the U.S. economy, and for other countries. We'll then consider an economic explanation for unemployment, and how it explains the patterns of unemployment and suggests public policies for reducing unemployment.

Unemployment and the Labor Force

Unemployment may seem an obvious concept. President Calvin Coolidge, who was known in his time as Silent Cal for the brevity of his comments, once reportedly said: "When people are out of work, unemployment results." But when a concept runs into reality, it can get complicated.

In or Out of the Labor Force?

Should everyone without a job should be counted as unemployed? Of course not. Children, for example, should not be counted as unemployed. Surely, the elderly who voluntarily left employment some years ago and are enjoying a happy retirement shouldn't be counted as unemployed. Many full-time college students have only a part-time job, or no job at all, but it seems inappropriate to count them as suffering the pains of unemployment. Some people are not working because they are ill, or on vacation, or on parental leave. Some people line up a new job and then take a month or two of vacation after leaving the previous job and before starting the new job; surely, they aren't suffering from unemployment in any meaningful sense of the word. In some marriages, one parent stays home with the children and the other holds a paying job: if the stay-at-home spouse is happy with that role and not looking for work, it would seem perverse to refer to this person as "unemployed."

These questions raise a common underlying theme. The adult population isn't just divided into employed and unemployed. A third group exists: people who don't have a job, and for some reason—retirement, looking after children, taking a voluntary break before a new job—aren't interested in having a job, either. Economists refer to this third group of those who are not working and not looking for work as **out of the labor force.**

out of the labor force:
Those who are not working and not looking for work.

The U.S. unemployment rate, which is based on a monthly survey carried out by the U.S. Bureau of the Census, asks a series of questions to divide up the adult population into employed, unemployed, or not in the labor force. To be classified as unemployed, a person must be without a job, currently available to work, and actively looking for work in the previous four weeks. Thus, a person who doesn't have a job but who is not currently available to work or has not actively looked for work in the last four weeks is counted as out of the labor force.

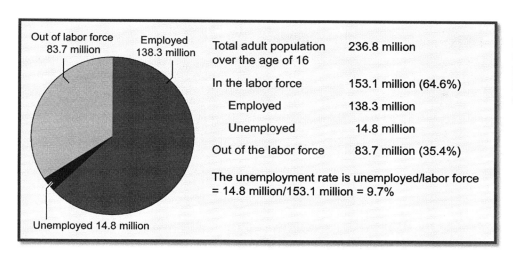

Exhibit 9-1
Employed, Unemployed, Out of the Labor Force Distribution of Adult Population (age 16 and older), 2009

Calculating the Unemployment Rate

Exhibit 9-1 shows the three-way division of the over-16 adult population. In 2009, 64.6% of the adult population was "in the labor force"; that is, either employed or without a job but looking for work. Those in the labor force can be divided into the employed and the unemployed. The **unemployment rate** is not the percentage of the total adult population without jobs, but rather the percentage of adults who are in the labor force but who do not have jobs:

$$\text{Unemployment rate} = \frac{\text{Unemployed people}}{\text{Total labor force}}.$$

unemployment rate: The percentage of adults who are in the labor force and thus seeking jobs, but who do not have jobs.

In this example, the unemployment rate can be calculated as 14.8 million unemployed people divided by 153.1 million people in the labor force, which works out to a 9.7% rate of unemployment.

Controversies over Measuring Unemployment

There is always controversy, gently simmering, over whether the lines between unemployment and being out of the labor force are drawn in the best ways. For example, what about people who don't have jobs and would be available to work, but have gotten discouraged at the lack of available jobs in their area and stopped looking? Such people, and their families, may be suffering the pains of unemployment. But the survey counts them as out of the labor force, because they aren't actively looking for work. Other people may tell the Census Bureau that they are ready to work and looking for a job, but really, truly, they aren't that eager to work and aren't looking very hard at all. They are counted as unemployed, although they might more accurately be classified as out of the labor force. Still other people may have a job, perhaps doing something like yard work, child care, or cleaning houses, but aren't reporting the income earned to the tax authorities. They may report being unemployed, when they actually working.

Although the unemployment rate gets most of the public and media attention, economic researchers at the Bureau of Labor Statistics publish a wide array of surveys and reports that try to measure these kinds of issues and to develop a more nuanced

U.S. Unemployment Statistics

The unemployment rate announced by the U.S. Bureau of Labor Statistics each month is based on the Current Population Survey (CPS), which has been carried out every month since 1940. Great care is taken to make this survey representative of the country as a whole. The country is first divided into 3,137 counties or cities, and then these divisions are grouped into 1,973 geographic areas. The U.S. Bureau of the Census then selects 729 of these areas to survey. The 729 areas are then divided into "enumeration districts" of about 300 households each, and each "enumeration district" is divided into clusters of about four dwelling units. Every month, 1,500 Census Bureau employees call about 15,000 of the four-household clusters, for a total of 60,000 households. Households are interviewed for four consecutive months, then rotated out of the survey for eight months, and then interviewed again for the same four months the following year, before leaving the sample permanently.

Based on this survey, unemployment rates are calculated by state, industry, urban and rural areas, gender, age, race or ethnicity, and level of education. A wide variety of other data is available, too. For example, how long have people been unemployed? Did they become unemployed because they quit, or were laid off, or their employer went out of business? Is the unemployed person the only wage earner in the family? The Current Population Survey is a treasure trove of information about employment and unemployment.

and complete view of the labor market. It's not exactly a hot news flash that economic statistics are imperfect. But imperfect measures like the unemployment rate can still be quite informative, when interpreted knowledgeably and sensibly.

Patterns of Unemployment

The unemployment rate can be viewed from different angles: as a measure of the labor market situation in the overall U.S. economy, as a perspective on the labor market experiences of different groups, and in an international context.

The Historical U.S. Unemployment Rate

Exhibit 9-2 shows the historical pattern of U.S. unemployment since 1948. Several patterns stand out.

1. Unemployment rates do fluctuate over time. During the deep recessions of the early 1980s and of 2007–2009, unemployment reached roughly 10%. For comparison, during the Great Depression of the 1930s, the unemployment rate reached more than 25% of the labor force.

2. Unemployment rates in the late 1990s and into the mid 2000s were rather low by historical standards. The unemployment rate was below 5% from 1997 to 2000 and during almost all of near 5% 2006 to 2007. The previous time unemployment had been less than 5% for three consecutive years was three decades earlier, from 1968 to 1970.

3. The unemployment rate never falls all the way to zero. Indeed, it never seems to get below 3%—and it stays that low only for very short periods.

4. The timing of rises and falls in unemployment matches fairly well with the timing of upswings and downswings in the overall economy. During periods of recession and depression, unemployment is high. During periods of economic growth, unemployment tends to be lower.

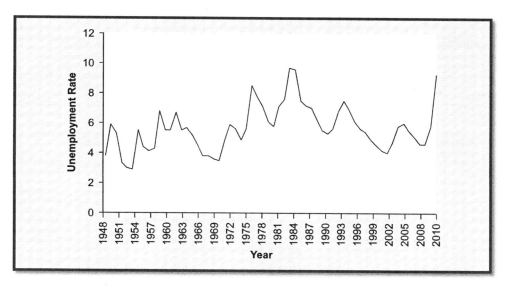

Exhibit 9-2   The U.S. Unemployment Rate, 1948–2009

The U.S. unemployment rate moves up and down as the economy moves in and out of recessions. But over time, the unemployment rate seems to return to a range of 4% to 6%. There does not seem to be a long-term trend toward the U.S. unemployment rate moving generally higher or generally lower.

5. No significant upward or downward trend in unemployment rates is apparent. This point is especially worth noting because the U.S. population nearly quadrupled from 76 million in 1900 to over 300 million by 2010. Moreover, a higher proportion of U.S. adults are now in the paid workforce, because women have entered the paid labor force in significant numbers in recent decades. Women composed 18% of the paid workforce in 1900 and half of the paid workforce in 2010. But despite the increased number of workers, as well as other economic events like globalization and the continuous invention of new technologies, the economy has provided jobs without causing any long-term upward or downward trend in unemployment rates.

Unemployment Rates by Group

Unemployment is not distributed evenly across the U.S. population. Exhibit 9-3 shows unemployment rates broken down in various ways: by gender, age, and race/ethnicity.

The unemployment rate for women had historically tended to be higher than the unemployment rate for men, perhaps reflecting the historical pattern than many women were seen as "secondary" earners. By about 1980, however, the unemployment rate for women was essentially the same as that for men, as shown in Exhibit 9-3a. During the recession of 2007–2009, the unemployment rate climbed higher for men than for women.

Younger workers tend to have higher unemployment, while middle-aged workers tend to have lower unemployment, probably because the middle-aged workers feel the responsibility of needing to have a job more heavily. Elderly workers have extremely low rates of unemployment, because those who do not have jobs often exit the labor force by retiring, and thus are not counted in the unemployment statistics. Exhibit 9-3b shows unemployment rates for women divided by age; the pattern for men is similar.

The unemployment rate for African-Americans is substantially higher than the rate for other racial or ethnic groups, a fact that surely reflects to some extent a pattern of discrimination that has constrained blacks' labor market opportunities. However, the gaps between unemployment rates for white and for blacks and Hispanics diminished in the 1990s, as shown in Exhibit 9-3c. In fact, unemployment rates for blacks and Hispanics were at the lowest levels for several decades in the mid-2000s.

Exhibit 9-3   Unemployment Rate

(a) By gender, 1970–2009. Unemployment rates for men used to be lower than unemployment rates for women, but in recent decades, the two rates have been very close, often with the unemployment rate for men somewhat higher.

(b) For women by age, 1970–2009. Unemployment rates are highest for the very young and become lower with age. This pattern occurs because adult workers in the 25–54 age bracket typically feel more pressure to find or to keep a job, while younger workers move in and out of jobs (and in and out of the labor force) more easily. Meanwhile, if older workers cannot find a job, they often retire and leave the labor force—which means that they are not counted in the unemployment statistics.

(c) By race and ethnicity, 1980–2009. Although unemployment rates for all groups tend to rise and fall together, the unemployment rate for whites has been lower than the unemployment rate for blacks and Hispanics in recent decades.

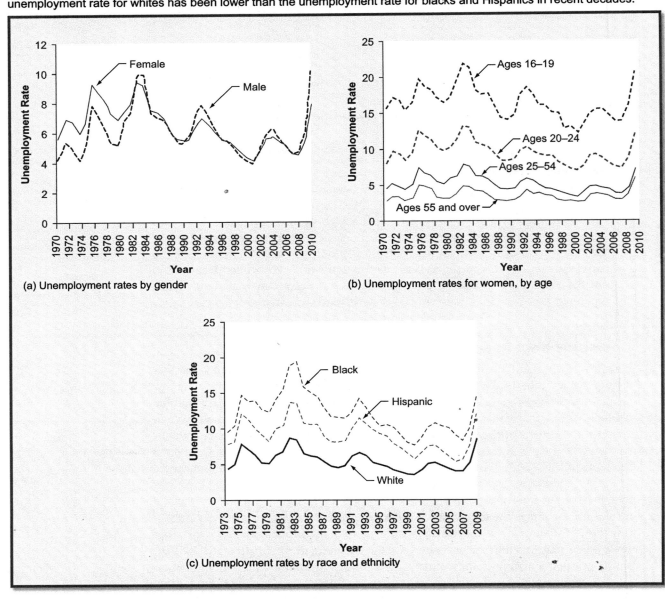

(a) Unemployment rates by gender

(b) Unemployment rates for women, by age

(c) Unemployment rates by race and ethnicity

Country	1991	1996	2001	2006	2008
United States	6.8%	5.4%	4.8%	4.4%	5.8%
Canada	9.8%	8.8%	6.4%	6.2%	5.4%
Japan	2.1%	3.4%	5.1%	4.5%	4.1%
France	9.5%	12.5%	8.7%	10.1%	7.5%
Germany	5.6%	9.0%	8.9%	9.8%	7.6%
Italy	6.9%	11.7%	9.6%	7.8%	6.9%
Sweden	3.1%	9.9%	5.0%	5.2%	6.0%
United Kingdom	8.8%	8.1%	5.1%	5.5%	5.7%

Exhibit 9-4
International Comparisons
of Unemployment Rates

Finally, those with less education typically suffer higher unemployment. In early 2010, for example, the unemployment rate for those with a college degree was 4.9%; for those with some college but not a four-year degree, the unemployment rate was 8.2%; for high school graduates with no additional degree the unemployment rate was 10.8%; and for those without a high school diploma, the unemployment rate was 14.5%. This pattern may arise because additional education offers better connections to the labor market, or it may occur because the labor market opportunities for low-skilled workers are less attractive than the opportunities for the more highly skilled, because of lower pay, and so low-skilled workers are less motivated to find jobs.

International Unemployment Comparisons

From an international perspective, the U.S. unemployment rate typically has looked a little better than average. Exhibit 9-4 compares unemployment rates for 1991, 1996, 2001, and 2008 (that is, before the unemployment effects of the recession were fully felt) from several other high-income countries.

However, cross-country comparisons of unemployment rates need to be treated with care, because each country has slightly different survey tools for measuring unemployment and also different labor markets. For example, Japan's unemployment rates appear quite low, but Japan's economy has been mired in slow growth and recession since the late 1980s, and Japan's unemployment rate probably paints too rosy a picture of its labor market. In Japan, workers who lose their jobs are often quick to exit the labor force and not look for a new job, in which case they are not counted as unemployed. In addition, Japanese firms are often quite reluctant to fire workers, and so Japanese firms have substantial numbers of workers who are on reduced hours or officially employed, but doing very little. This Japanese pattern is perhaps best viewed as an unusual method for society to provide support for the unemployed, rather than a sign of a healthy economy.

Comparing unemployment rates in the United States and other high-income economies with unemployment rates in Latin America, Africa, Eastern Europe, and Asia is very difficult. One reason is that the statistical agencies in many poorer countries lack resources and technical capabilities of the U.S. Bureau of the Census. But a more difficult problem with international comparisons is that in many low-income countries, most workers aren't involved in the labor market through an employer who pays them regularly. Instead, workers in these poor countries are engaged in short-term work, subsistence activities, and barter. Moreover, the effect of unemployment is very different in high-income and low-income countries.

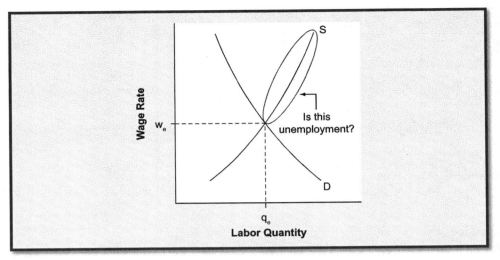

In a labor market with flexible wages, the equilibrium will occur at the intersection of the supply curve S and the demand curve D, at wage w_e and quantity q_e. So how does unemployment enter the picture? One possible answer is that the unemployed are people who want to supply labor but are not willing to do so at the equilibrium wage. These people are represented by the circled part of the supply curve. While there are probably some people in this category, this doesn't seem to convey what is meant by unemployment. For most unemployed people, the problem is not that they are demanding higher wages than others of their skill level are receiving. Instead, the problem is that they can't find someone who is hiring and willing to pay the wage that others of their skill level are receiving.

Unemployed workers in the developed economies have access to various government programs like unemployment insurance, welfare, and food stamps, while such programs may barely exist in poorer countries. Although unemployment is a serious problem in many low-income countries, it manifests itself in a different way than in high-income countries.

Why Unemployment Is a Puzzle for Economists

From the standpoint of the supply-and-demand model, unemployment presents a puzzle. In a supply-and-demand model of a labor market, as illustrated in Exhibit 9-5, the labor market should move toward and equilibrium wage and quantity. At the equilibrium wage w_e, the equilibrium quantity q_e of labor supplied by workers should be equal to the quantity of labor demanded by employers. So where does unemployment occur in this model?

Looking for Unemployment with Flexible Wages

One possibility is that some of the people being counted as unemployed are actually on the upper-right portion of the supply curve of labor, above the equilibrium, in the circled area in Exhibit 9-5. That is, they would be willing to work if the wage were higher, but at the equilibrium wage, they aren't willing to work. The U.S. government economic statisticians count these people as unemployed, because they say that they are ready and looking for work, but in fact these people aren't willing to take the wages that they are being offered in the labor market.

Probably a few people are unemployed because of unrealistic expectations about wages, but they don't represent the majority of the unemployed. Instead, unemployed people often have friends or acquaintances of similar skill levels who are employed, and the unemployed would be willing to work at the jobs and wages similar to what is being received by those people. But the employers of their friends and acquaintances don't seem to be hiring.

To economists, this kind of unemployment is something of a riddle. The definition of market equilibrium is that at the equilibrium wage, the quantity of labor demanded by employers will equal the quantity supplied. The supply and demand model can explain why wages will adjust up and down, and why the quantity of labor employed will rise and fall. But unemployment typically represents a situation in which people are willing to work at the market wage appropriate to their skills and experience, but still have trouble finding an employer to hire them. How can this situation occur?

Why Wages Might Be Sticky Downward

If a model with flexible wages does not describe unemployment very well—because it predicts that anyone willing to work at the going wage can always find a job—then it may prove useful to consider economic models in which wages are not flexible or adjust only very slowly. In particular, even though wage increases may occur with relative ease, wage decreases are few and far between.

One set of reasons why wages may be "sticky downward," as economists put it, involves economic laws and institutions. For low-skilled workers being paid the minimum wage, it is illegal to reduce their wages. For union workers operating under a multiyear contract with a company, wage cuts might violate the contract and create a labor dispute or a strike. However, minimum wages and union contracts aren't a sufficient reason why wages would be sticky downward for the U.S. economy as a whole. After all, out of the 150 million or so workers in the U.S. economy, only about 1.4 million—less than 2% of the total—are paid the minimum wage. Similarly, only about 12% of American wage and salary workers are represented by a labor union. In other high-income countries, more workers may have their wages determined by unions or the minimum wage may be set at a level that applies to a larger share of workers. But for the United States, these two factors combined affect only about one-fifth or less of the labor force.

Thus, economists looking for reasons why wages might be sticky downwards have focused on factors that may characterize most labor relationships in the economy, not just a few. A number of different theories have been proposed, but they share a common tone.

One argument is that even employees who are not union members often work under an **implicit contract,** which is that the employer will try to keep wages from falling when the economy is weak or the business is having trouble, and the employee will not expect huge salary increases when the economy or the business is strong. This wage-setting behavior acts like a form of insurance: the employee has some protection against wage declines in bad times, but pays for that protection with lower wages in good times. Clearly, this sort of implicit contract means that firms will be hesitant to cut wages, lest workers feel betrayed and work less hard or even leave the firm.

Efficiency wage theory argues that the productivity of workers will increase if they are paid more, and so employers will often find it worthwhile to pay their employees somewhat more than market conditions might dictate. One reason is that employees who are paid better than their other alternatives will be more productive is that they recognize that if they were to lose their current jobs, they would suffer a decline in salary. As a result, they will be motivated to work harder and to stay with the current employer. In addition, employers know that it is costly and time-consuming to hire and train new employees, so they would prefer to pay workers a little extra now rather than to lose them and have to hire and train new workers. Thus, by avoiding wage cuts, the employer minimizes costs of training and hiring new workers, and reaps the benefits of well-motivated employees.

implicit contract: An unwritten agreement in the labor market that the employer will try to keep wages from falling when the economy is weak or the business is having trouble, and the employee will not expect huge salary increases when the economy or the business is strong.

efficiency wage theory: The theory that the productivity of workers, either individually or as a group, will increase if they are paid more.

The *adverse selection of wage cuts* argument points out that if an employer reacts to poor business conditions by reducing wages for all workers, then best workers, with the best employment alternatives at other firms, are the most likely to leave and the least-attractive workers, with fewer employment alternatives, are more likely to stay. Consequently, firms are more likely to choose which workers should depart, through layoffs and firings, rather than trimming wages across the board. Sometimes companies that are going through tough times can persuade workers to take a pay cut for the short term, and still retain most of the firm's workers. But these stories are notable because they are so uncommon. It is far more typical for companies to lay off some workers, rather than to cut wages for everyone.

The **insider-outsider model** of the labor force argues that those already working for firms are "insiders," while new employees, at least for a time, are "outsiders." A firm depends on its insiders to grease the wheels of the organization, to be familiar with routine procedures, to train new employees, and so on. However, cutting wages will alienate the insiders and damage the firm's productivity and prospects.

insider-outsider model: A model which divides workers into "insiders" already working for the firm who know the procedures and "outsiders" who are recent or prospective hires.

Finally, the *relative wage coordination argument* points out that even if most workers were hypothetically willing to see a decline in their own wages in bad economic times *as long as everyone else also experiences such a decline,* there is no obvious way for a decentralized economy to implement such a plan. Instead, workers confronted with the possibility of a wage cut will worry that other workers will not have such a wage cut, and so a wage cut means being worse off both in absolute terms and relative to others. As a result, workers fight hard against wage cuts.

These theories of why wages tend not to move downward differ in their logic and their implications, and figuring out the strengths and weaknesses of each theory is an ongoing subject of research and controversy among economists. But for present purposes, their common element is what matters. The value of labor is determined, at least in part, by the motivation and morale of employees, and employers must pay attention to these factors. Employees are different—some are more productive than others—and employers want to hang on to the better workers. In addition, employers know that there are costs of hiring and training, and so they want to avoid excessive turnover of their labor force. All of these reasons tend to imply that wages will decline only very slowly, if at all, even when the economy or a business is having tough times. When wages are inflexible and unlikely to fall, then either short-run or long-run unemployment can result.

The Short Run: Cyclical Unemployment

Let's make the plausible assumption that wages have an element of stickiness to them—in particular, that wages are sticky about moving downward. Let's also make the plausible assumption that in the short run from a few months to a few years, the quantity of hours that that the average person is willing to work for a given wage doesn't change much, so the labor supply curve doesn't shift much. In addition, make the standard *ceteris paribus* assumption that there is no substantial short-term change in the age structure of the labor force, institutions and laws affecting the labor market, or other possibly relevant factors.

One primary determinant of the demand for labor from firms is how they perceive the state of the macroeconomy. If firms believe that business is expanding, then at any given wage they will desire to hire a greater quantity of labor, and the labor demand curve shifts to the right. Conversely, if firms perceive that the economy is slowing down

(a) Rising demand for labor, wages rise

(b) Falling demand for labor, sticky wages, and unemployment

Exhibit 9-6   Rising Wage and Low Unemployment/Where Is the Unemployment in Supply and Demand?

(a) In a labor market where wages are able to rise, an increase in the demand for labor from D_0 to D_1 leads to an increase in equilibrium quantity of labor hired from q_0 to q_1 and a rise in the equilibrium wage from w_0 to w_1.

(b) In a labor market where wages do not decline, a fall in the demand for labor from D_0 to D_1 leads to a decline in the quantity of labor demanded at the original wage w_0 from q_0 to q_2. These workers will want to work at the prevailing wage w_0, but won't be able to find jobs.

or entering a recession, then they will wish to hire a lower quantity of labor at any given wage, and the labor demand curve will shift to the left.

The interaction between shifts in labor demand and wages that are sticky downward are illustrated in Exhibit 9-6. Exhibit 9-6a illustrates the situation in which the demand for labor shifts to the right from D_0 to D_1. In this case, the equilibrium wage rises from w_0 to w_1 and the equilibrium quantity of labor hired increases from q_0 to q_1. It doesn't hurt employee morale at all for wages to rise! However, Exhibit 9-6b shows the situation in which the demand for labor shifts to the left, from D_0 to D_1, as it would tend to do in a recession. Because wages are sticky downward, they do not adjust toward what would have been the new equilibrium wage q_1, at least not in the short run. Instead, after the shift in the labor demand curve, the same quantity of workers is willing to work at that wage as before; however, the quantity of workers demanded at that wage has declined from the original equilibrium q_0 to q_2. The gap between the original equilibrium quantity q_0 and the new quantity demanded of labor q_2 represents workers who would be willing to work at the going wage but can't find jobs. The gap represents the economic meaning of unemployment.

This analysis helps to explain the connection noted earlier, that unemployment tends to rise in recessions and to decline during expansions. The overall state of the economy shifts the labor demand curve, and combined with wages that are sticky downwards, unemployment changes. The rise in unemployment that occurs because of a recession is known as **cyclical unemployment,** because it is closely tied to the business cycle.

cyclical unemployment: Unemployment closely tied to the business cycle, like higher unemployment during a recession.

The Long Run: The Natural Rate of Unemployment

Cyclical unemployment explains why unemployment rises during a recession and falls during an economic expansion. But what explains the remaining level of unemployment even in good economic times? Even when the U.S. economy is growing strongly, the unemployment rate only rarely dips as low as 4%. Moreover, the discussion earlier in this chapter pointed out that unemployment rates in many European countries like Italy, France, and Germany have often been remarkably high at various times in the last few decades. Why does some level of unemployment persist even when economies are growing strongly? Why are unemployment rates continually higher in certain economies, through good economic years and bad? Economists have a term to describe the remaining level of unemployment that occurs even when the economy is healthy: it is called the **natural rate of unemployment.**

The natural rate of unemployment is not "natural" in the sense that water freezes at 32 degrees Fahrenheit or boils at 212 degrees Fahrenheit. It is not a physical and unchanging law of nature. Instead, it is only the "natural" rate because it is the unemployment rate that would result from the combination of economic, social and political factors that exist at a time—not including recession. These forces include the usual pattern of companies expanding and contracting their workforces in a dynamic economy, social and economic forces that affect the labor market, or public policies that affect either the eagerness of people to work or the willingness of businesses to hire. Let's discuss these factors in more detail.

natural rate of unemployment: The unemployment rate that would exist in a growing and healthy economy from the combination of economic, social and political factors that exist at a time.

Frictional Unemployment

In a market economy, some companies are always going broke for a variety of reasons: old technology; poor management; good management that happened to make bad decisions; shifts in tastes of consumers so that less of the firm's product is desired; a large customer who went broke; or tough domestic or foreign competitors. Conversely, other companies will be doing very well for just the opposite reasons and looking to hire more employees. In a perfect world, all of those who lost jobs would immediately find new ones. But in the real world, it takes time to find out about new jobs, to interview and figure out if the new job is a good match, perhaps to sell a house and buy another. The unemployment that occurs in the meantime, as workers move between jobs, is called **frictional unemployment.**

In the mid-2000s, before the recession of 2007–2009 hit, it was nevertheless true that about 7% of U.S. workers saw their jobs disappear in any three-month period. But in periods of economic growth, these destroyed jobs are counterbalanced for the economy as a whole by a larger number of jobs created. In 2005, for example, there were typically about 7.5 million unemployed people at any given time in the U.S. economy. Even though about two-thirds of those unemployed people found a job in 14 weeks or less, the unemployment rate didn't change much during the year, because those who found new jobs were largely offset by others who lost jobs.

frictional unemployment: Unemployment that occurs as workers move between jobs.

Of course, it would be preferable if people who were losing jobs could immediately and easily move into the new jobs being created, but in the real world, that isn't possible. Someone who is laid off by a textile mill in South Carolina can't turn around and immediately become a computer programmer in California. Instead, the adjustment process happens in ripples. Some people find new jobs near their old ones, while others find that they must move to new locations. Some people can do a very similar job with a different company, while others must start new career paths. Some people may be near retirement and decide to look only for part-time work, while others want an employer that offers a fruitful long-term career path. The frictional unemployment that results from people moving between jobs in a dynamic economy may account for 1–2 percentage points of total unemployment.

The level of frictional unemployment will depend to some extent on how willing people are to move to new areas to find jobs—which in turn may depend on history and culture. The extent of frictional unemployment will also depend on how easy it is for workers to learn about alternative jobs, which may reflect the ease of communications about job prospects in the economy.

Frictional unemployment and the natural rate of unemployment also seem to depend on the age distribution of the population. Exhibit 9-3*b* showed that unemployment rates are typically lower for people between about 25–54 years of age than they are for those who are either younger or older. "Prime-age workers," as those in the 25–54 age bracket are sometimes called, are typically at a place in their lives when they want very much to have a job and income arriving at all times. But some proportion of those who are under 30 may still be trying out jobs and life options and some proportion of those over 55 are eying retirement. In both cases, the relatively young or old tend to worry less about unemployment than those in-between, and their periods of frictional unemployment may be longer as a result. Thus, a society with a relatively high proportion of relatively young or old workers will tend to have a higher unemployment rate than a society with a higher proportion of its workers in middle age.

Productivity Shifts and the Natural Rate of Unemployment

Unexpected shifts in productivity can have a powerful effect on the natural rate of unemployment. Over time, the level of wages in an economy will be determined by the productivity of workers. After all, if a business paid workers more than could be justified by their productivity, the business will ultimately lose money and go bankrupt. Conversely, if a business tries to pay workers less than their productivity, then in a competitive market economy other businesses will find it worthwhile to hire away those workers and pay them more.

However, adjustments of wages to productivity levels will not happen quickly or smoothly. Wages are typically reviewed only once or twice a year. In many modern jobs, it's difficult to measure productivity at the individual level. For example, how precisely would one measure the quantity produced by an accountant who is one of many people working in the tax department of a large corporation? Because productivity is difficult to observe, wages increases are often set determined based on recent experience with productivity; if productivity has been rising at, say, 2% per year, then wages rise at that level as well. However, when productivity changes unexpectedly, it can affect the natural rate of unemployment for a time.

The U.S. economy in the 1970s and 1990s provides two vivid examples of this process. In the 1970s, productivity growth slowed down unexpectedly (as discussed in the previous chapter). For example, output per hour of U.S. workers in the business sector increased at an annual rate of 3.3% per year from 1960 to 1973, but only 0.8% from 1973 to 1982. Exhibit 9-7*a* illustrates the situation where the demand for labor—that is, the quantity of labor that business is willing to hire at any given wage—has been shifting out a little each year because of rising productivity, from D_0 to D_1 to D_2. As a result, equilibrium wages have been rising each year from w_0 to w_1 to w_2. But when productivity unexpectedly slows down, the pattern of wage increases does not adjust right away. Wages keep rising each year from w_2 to w_3 to w_4. But the demand for labor is no longer shifting up. As a result, a gap opens up where the quantity of labor supplied at wage level w_4 is greater than the quantity demanded. The natural rate of unemployment rises; indeed, in the aftermath of this unexpectedly low productivity in the 1970s, the national unemployment rate did not fall below 7% from 1980 until 1987. Over time, the rise in wages will adjust to match the slower gains in productivity, and the unemployment rate will ease back down. But this process may take years.

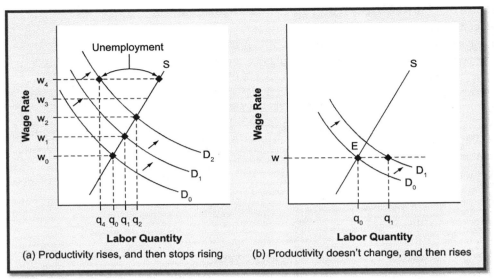

Exhibit 9-7
Unexpected Productivity Changes and Unemployment

(a) Productivity rises, and then stops rising

(b) Productivity doesn't change, and then rises

(a) Productivity is rising for a time, increasing the demand for labor from D_0 to D_1, and then from D_1 to D_2. Employers and workers become used to the pattern of wage increases, from w_0 to w_1, and from w_1 to w_2. Then productivity suddenly stops increasing. However, the expectations of employers and workers for wage increases don't shift immediately, so wages keep rising as before, from w_2 to w_3, and from w_3 to w_4. But the demand for labor has not increased, and so at wage w_4, unemployment exists where the quantity supplied of labor exceeds the quantity demanded.

(b) Now imagine that the rate of productivity increase has been zero for a time, so employers and workers have come to accept the equilibrium wage level w. But then productivity increases unexpectedly, shifting demand for labor from D_0 to D_1. At the wage w, this means that the quantity demanded of labor exceeds the quantity supplied, and with job offers extremely plentiful, the unemployment rate in this situation will be very low.

The late 1990s provide an opposite example: instead of the surprise decline in productivity in the 1970s, productivity unexpectedly rose in the mid-1990s. The annual growth rate of real output per hour of labor increased from 1.7% from 1980 to 1995, to an annual rate of 2.6% from 1995–2001. Let's simplify the situation a bit, so that the economic lesson of the story is easier to see graphically, and say that productivity had not been increasing at all in earlier years, so the intersection of the labor market was at point E in Exhibit 9-7b, where the demand curve for labor D_0 intersects the supply curve for labor. As a result, real wages were not increasing. Now productivity jumps upward, which shifts the demand for labor out to the right, from D_0 to D_1, but at least for a time, wages are still being set according to the earlier expectations of no productivity growth, so wages do not rise. The result is that at the prevailing wage level w, the quantity of labor demanded q_D will for a time exceed the quantity of labor supplied q_S, and unemployment will be very low—actually below the natural level of unemployment for a time. This pattern of unexpectedly high productivity helps to explain why the unemployment rate stayed below 4.5%—quite a low level by historical standards—from 1998 until after the U.S. economy had entered a recession in 2001.

Average levels of unemployment will tend to be somewhat higher on average when productivity is unexpectedly low and conversely, will tend to be somewhat lower on average when productivity is unexpectedly high. But over time, wages do eventually adjust to reflect productivity levels.

Public Policy and the Natural Rate of Unemployment

Public policy can also have a powerful effect on the natural rate of unemployment. On the supply side of the labor market, public policies to assist the unemployed can affect how eager people are to find work. For example, if a worker who loses a job is guaranteed a hearty package of unemployment insurance, welfare benefits, food stamps, and government medical benefits, then the opportunity cost of being unemployed is lower and that worker will be less eager to seek a new job. What seems to matter most is not just the generosity of these benefits, but how long such benefits last. A society that provides generous help for the unemployed that cuts off after,

How U.S. Unemployment Insurance Works

Unemployment insurance is a joint federal–state program, established by federal law in 1935. The federal government sets minimum standards for the program, but most of the administration is done by state governments.

The funding for the program is a federal tax collected from employers. The federal government requires that the tax be collected on the first $7,000 in wages paid to each worker; however, states can choose to collect the tax on a higher amount if they wish, and 41 states have set a higher

limit. States can choose the length of time that benefits will be paid, although most states limit unemployment benefits to 26 weeks—with extensions possible in times of especially high unemployment. The fund is then used to pay benefits to those who become unemployed. Average unemployment benefits are equal to about one-third of the wage earned by the person in their previous job, but the level of unemployment benefits varies considerably across states.

States That Pay, on Average, Less Than $300/Week		States That Pay, on Average, More Than $520/Week	
Alabama	$235	Connecticut	$576
Arizona	$240	Hawaii	$523
Florida	$275	Massachusetts	$628
Louisiana	$258	Minnesota	$538
Mississippi	$210	New Jersey	$560
Nebraska	$298	Pennsylvania	$547
South Dakota	$285	Rhode Island	$641
Tennessee	$275		

Average Weekly Unemployment Benefits by State in 2009

say, six months, may provide less of an incentive for unemployment than a society that provides less generous help that lasts for several years. Conversely, government assistance for job search or retraining can in some cases encourage people back to work sooner.

On the demand side of the labor market, government rules and social institutions can affect the willingness of firms to hire. For example, if government makes it hard for businesses to start up or to expand, by wrapping new businesses in bureaucratic red tape, then businesses will become more discouraged about hiring. Government regulations can make it harder to start a business by requiring that a new business obtain many permits and pay many fees, or by restricting the types and quality of products that can be sold. Other government regulations like zoning laws may limit where business can be done, or whether businesses are allowed to be open during evenings or on Sunday. Whatever defenses may be offered for such laws in terms of social value—like the value some Christians place on not working on Sunday—these kinds of restrictions impose a barrier between some willing workers and other willing employers, and thus contribute to a higher natural rate of unemployment. Similarly, if government makes it difficult to fire or lay off workers, businesses may react by trying not to hire more workers than strictly necessary—since laying these workers off would be costly and difficult. High minimum wages may discourage businesses from hiring low-skill workers. Government rules may encourage and support powerful unions, which can then push up wages for union workers, but at a cost of discouraging businesses from hiring union workers.

The Natural Rate of Unemployment in Recent Years

The natural rate of unemployment includes all the factors influencing demand for labor and supply of labor, whether these factors are determined by the characteristics of the population, or of employers, or of public policy—all the relevant factors except recession, which is covered by the idea of cyclical unemployment. The underlying economic, social and political factors that determine the natural rate of unemployment can change over time, which means that the natural rate of unemployment can change over time, too.

Estimates by economists of the natural rate of unemployment in the U.S. economy in the early 2000s run at about 4.5 to 5.5%. Back in the 1980s, estimates of the natural rate of unemployment were commonly in the range of 6.0 to 6.5%. For a number of reasons, economists believe that the natural rate of unemployment in the U.S. economy declined from the 1980s to the 1990s and early 2000s.

1. The Internet has provided a remarkable new tool through which job-seekers can find out about jobs at different companies and can make contact with resumes and cover letters with relative ease. An Internet search is far easier than trying to find a list of local employers and then hunting up phone numbers for all of their human resources departments, requesting a list of jobs and application forms, and so on.

2. The growth of the temporary worker industry has probably helped to reduce the natural rate of unemployment. In the early 1980s, only about 0.5% of all workers held jobs through temp agencies; by the early 2000s, the figure had risen above 2%. Temp agencies can provide jobs for workers while they are looking for permanent work. They can also serve as a clearinghouse, helping workers find out about jobs with certain employers and getting a tryout with the employer. For many workers, a temp job is a stepping-stone to a permanent job that they might not have heard about or gotten any other way, so the growth of temp jobs will tend to reduce frictional unemployment, too.

3. The aging of the "baby boom generation"—that especially large generation of Americans born between 1946 and 1963—meant that the proportion of young workers in the economy was relatively high in the 1970s, as the boomers entered the labor market, but is relatively low today. As noted earlier, middle-aged workers are far more likely to keep steady jobs than younger workers, a factor which tends to reduce the natural rate of unemployment.

The combined result of these factors is that the natural rate of unemployment was on average lower in the 1990s and the early 2000s than in the 1980s. For example, from 1980 to 1986 the unemployment rate did not fall below 7%—despite rapid economic growth from 1983 to 1986. From 1990 up to 2007, the unemployment rate exceeded 7% in only one year—the recession year of 1992 when cyclical unemployment pushed the unemployment rate to 7.5%. The Great Recession of 2007 to 2009 pushed monthly unemployment rates above 10% in late 2009. But even at that time, the Congressional Budget Office was forecasting that by 2015, unemployment rates would fall back to about 5%.

The Natural Rate of Unemployment in Europe

By the standards of other high-income economies, the natural rate of unemployment in the U.S. economy appears relatively low. Through good economic years and bad, many European economies had unemployment rates hovering near 10%, or even higher, since the 1970s. European rates of unemployment have been higher not because recessions in Europe have been deeper, but rather because the conditions underlying supply and demand for labor have been different in Europe, in a way that has created a created a much higher natural rate of unemployment.

Many European countries have a combination of generous welfare and unemployment benefits, together with nests of rules that impose additional costs on businesses when they hire. In addition, many European countries have laws that require firms to give workers months of notice before laying them off and to provide substantial severance or retraining packages after laying them off. The legally required notice before laying off a worker can be more than three months in Spain, Germany, Denmark, and Belgium, and the legally required severance package can be as high as a year's salary or more in Austria, Spain, Portugal, Italy, and Greece. Such laws will surely discourage laying off or firing current workers. But when companies know that it will be difficult to fire or lay off workers, they also become hesitant about hiring in the first place.

The typically higher levels of unemployment in many European countries in recent years, which have prevailed even when Europe's economies are growing at a solid pace, are attributable to the fact that the sorts of laws and regulations that lead to a high natural rate of unemployment are much more prevalent in Europe than in the United States.

A Preview of Policies to Fight Unemployment

Later chapters will provide a detailed discussion of how to fight unemployment, when these policies can be discussed in the context of the full array of macroeconomic goals and frameworks for analysis. But even at this preliminary stage, it is useful to preview the main themes concerning policies to fight unemployment.

The remedy for unemployment will depend on the diagnosis. Cyclical unemployment is a short-term problem, caused because the economy is in a recession. Thus, the preferred solution will be to avoid or minimize recessions. As later chapters will discuss, this policy can be enacted by stimulating the overall buying power in the economy, so that firms perceive that sales and profits are possible, which makes them eager to hire.

Dealing with the natural rate of unemployment is trickier. There isn't much to be done about the fact that in a market-oriented economy, firms will hire and fire workers. Nor is there much to be done about how the evolving age structure of the economy, or unexpected shifts in productivity, will affect the natural rate of unemployment for a time. However, as the example of high ongoing unemployment rates for many European countries illustrates, government policy clearly can affect the natural rate of unemployment that will persist in an economy even when GDP is growing. When a government enacts policies that will affect workers or employers, it must examine how these policies will affect the information and incentives that employees and employers have to seek each other out. For example, the government may also have a role to play in helping some of the unemployed with job searches. The design of government programs that offer assistance to unemployed workers and protections to employed workers may need to be rethought so that they will not unduly discourage the supply of labor. Similarly, rules that make it difficult for businesses to begin or to expand may need to be redesigned so that they will not unduly discourage the demand for labor. The message is not that all laws affecting labor markets should be repealed, but only that when such laws are enacted, a society that cares about unemployment will need to consider the trade-offs involved.

Key Concepts and Summary

1. Unemployment imposes high costs. Unemployed individuals suffer from loss of income and from stress. An economy with high unemployment suffers an opportunity cost of unused resources.

2. The adult population can be divided into those in the labor force and those **out of the labor force.** In turn, those in the labor force are divided into employed and unemployed. A person without a job must be willing and able to work and actively looking for work to be counted as unemployed; otherwise, a person without a job is counted as being out of the labor force.

3. The **unemployment rate** is defined as the number of unemployed persons divided by the number of persons in the labor force (not the overall adult population).

4. The U.S. unemployment rate rises during recessions and depressions, but falls back to the range of 4–6% when the economy is strong. The unemployment rate never falls to zero.

5. Despite enormous growth in the size of the U.S. population and labor force in the twentieth century, along with other major trends like globalization and new technology, the unemployment rate shows no long-term rising trend.

6. Unemployment rates differ by group: higher for African-Americans and Hispanics than for whites; higher for less educated than more educated; higher for the young than the middle-aged. Women's unemployment rates used to be higher than men's, but in recent years men's and women's unemployment rates have been very similar.

7. In recent years, unemployment rates in the United States have compared favorably with unemployment rates in most other high-income economies.

8. In a labor market with flexible wages, unemployment is a puzzle, since wages will adjust in such a market so that quantity demanded of labor always equals the quantity supplied of labor at the equilibrium wage.

9. Many theories have been proposed for why wages might not be flexible, but instead may adjust only in a "sticky" way, especially when it comes to downward adjustments: **implicit contracts, efficiency wage theory,** adverse selection of wage cuts, **insider-outsider model,** and relative wage coordination.

10. **Cyclical unemployment** rises and falls with the business cycle.

11. The **natural rate of unemployment** is the rate of unemployment that would be caused by the economic, social and political forces in the economy *even when the economy is not in a recession.* These factors include the **frictional unemployment** that occurs when people are put out of work for a time by the shifts of a dynamic and changing economy and any laws concerning conditions of hiring and firing that have the undesired side effect of discouraging job formation.

Review Questions

1. What does it mean to be in or out of the labor force?

2. How is the unemployment rate calculated?

3. Are all adults who do not hold jobs counted as unemployed?

4. Over the long term of decades, has the U.S. unemployment rate generally trended up, trended down, or remained at basically the same level?

5. Whose unemployment rates are commonly higher in the U.S. economy: Whites or nonwhites? The young or the middle-aged? College graduates or high school graduates?

6. Are U.S. unemployment rates typically higher, lower, or about the same as unemployment rates in other high-income countries?

7. Why is unemployment considered a puzzle in a labor market with flexible wages?

8. Name and explain some of the reasons why wages are likely to be sticky, especially in downward adjustments.

9. When would you expect cyclical unemployment to be rising? Falling?

10. What forces create the natural rate of unemployment for an economy?

11. Would you expect the natural rate of unemployment to be roughly the same in different countries?

12. Would you expect the natural rate of unemployment to remain the same within one country over the long run of several decades?

13. What is frictional unemployment?

Inflation

Inflation refers to a general and ongoing rise in the level of prices in an economy. This definition includes two ways in which inflation differs from the rises and falls in prices that happen in microeconomic markets. The first difference is that price changes in the microeconomic supply-and-demand model referred to a price in a particular market, like cars or oranges or phone service. While inflation does not mean that every single price in the economy rises by the same amount, it does imply that pressure for price increases reaches across most markets, not just one. The second difference is that price increases in the supply-and-demand model were one-time events, representing a shift from a previous equilibrium to a new one. While one occasionally sees references to inflation over short time periods, the term typically implies an ongoing rise in prices. If inflation happened for one year and then stopped—well, then it wouldn't be inflation any more.

The most obvious result for inflation is that people remember back a few decades to when everything seemed to cost so much less and reminisce about how you could buy three gallons of gasoline for a dollar and then go see a discounted afternoon movie for another dollar. Exhibit 10-1 compares some prices of common goods in 1970 and 2009. Of course, the average prices shown in this table may not reflect the prices where you live. For example, housing is much more expensive in certain states or cities. In addition, certain products have evolved over recent decades. A new car in 2009, all loaded up with antipollution equipment, safety gear, computerized engine controls, and many other technological advances was a more advanced machine than a car in 1970. But put detailed issues like these to one side for the moment, and look at the overall pattern. The primary reason behind these price rises in Exhibit 10-1—and all the price rises for all of the other products in the economy—isn't specific to the market for housing or cars or gasoline or movie tickets. Instead, it's part of a general inflationary rise in the level of all prices. In

inflation: A general and ongoing rise in the level of prices in an economy.

	1970	2009
Pound of ground beef	66 cents	$2.41
Pound of butter	87 cents	$3.13
Movie ticket	$1.55	$7.18
Sales price of existing home	$23,000	$198,100
New car	$3,000	$23,000
Gallon of gasoline	36 cents	$3.27
Average hourly wage for a manufacturing worker	$3.23	$18.08
Per capita GDP	$5,069	$47,375

Exhibit 10-1   Price Comparisons: 1970 and circa 2009

the year 2009, $1 had about the same purchasing power in overall terms of goods and services as 18 cents did back in 1972, because of the amount of inflation over that time.

Moreover, the power of inflation doesn't just affect goods and services, but wages and income levels, too. The second to last row of Exhibit 10-1 shows that the average hourly wage for a manufacturing worker increased more than five-fold for 1970 to 2009. Sure, the average worker in 2009 is better educated and more productive than the average worker in 1970—but not five times more productive! Sure, per capita GDP increased substantially from 1970 to 2009, but is the average person in the U.S. economy really nine times better off in just 39 years? It doesn't seem plausible.

This chapter begins by showing how to combine prices of specific goods and services to create a measure of overall inflation. It discusses the historical and recent experience of inflation both in the United States and in other countries around the world. Earlier chapters have sometimes included a note under an exhibit or a parenthetical reminder in the text saying that the numbers had been adjusted for inflation. In this chapter, it's time to show how to use inflation statistics to adjust other economic variables, so that you can tell how much of, say, the rise in GDP over different periods of time can be attributed to an actual increase in the production of goods and services and how much should be attributed to the fact that prices for everything have risen. Inflation has consequences for many people and firms throughout the economy, in their roles as lenders and borrowers, wage-earners, taxpayers, and consumers. The chapter concludes with a discussion of some imperfections and biases in the inflation statistics, and a preview of policies that will be discussed in later chapters for fighting inflation.

Combining Prices to Measure the Inflation Rate

A modern economy has millions of goods and services whose prices are continually quivering in the breezes of supply and demand. How can all of these shifts in price be boiled down to a single inflation rate? As with many problems in economic measurement, the conceptual answer is reasonably straightforward, but practical difficulties arise in applying the concept.

The Changing Price of a Basket of Goods

To calculate the rate of inflation, economists begin with the concept of a **basket of goods and services,** consisting of specified quantities of different items. Then inflation can be calculated in terms of how the overall cost of buying the basket of goods changes over time.

basket of goods and services: A hypothetical group of different items, with specified quantities of each one, used as a basis for calculating how the price level changes over time.

Exhibit 10-2   A College Student's Price Index

Items	Quantity	(Time 1) Price	(Time 1) Amount Spent	(Time 2) Price	(Time 2) Amount Spent	(Time 3) Price	(Time 3) Amount Spent	(Time 4) Price	(Time 4) Amount Spent
Hamburgers	20	$3.00	$60.00	$3.20	$64.00	$3.10	$62.00	$3.50	$70.00
Aspirin	1	$10.00	$10.00	$10.00	$10.00	$10.00	$10.00	$10.00	$10.00
Movies	5	$6.00	$30.00	$6.50	$32.50	$7.00	$35.00	$7.50	$37.50
Total			$100.00		$106.50		$107.00		$117.50

In thinking about how to combine individual price changes into an overall inflation rate, many people find that their first impulse is to calculate the average of the price changes of many goods. But such a calculation could easily be misleading, because some price increases matter more than others. Changes in the prices of goods for which people spend a larger share of their incomes will matter more than changes in the prices of goods for which people spend a smaller share of their incomes. An increase of 10% in the rental rate on apartments matters more to most people than whether the price of carrots rises by 10%. To construct an overall measure that captures inflation in the prices of many different items and also gives greater weight to the items on which people spend more money, economists consider the total cost of purchasing a basket of goods and services, where the basket will include quantities of the goods and services being purchased that reflect what people actually buy.

Consider the simple basket of goods with only three items, represented in Exhibit 10-2. Say that in any given month, a college student spends money on 20 hamburgers, 1 bottle of aspirin, and 5 movies. Prices for these items over four years are given in the table. Prices of some goods in the basket may rise while others fall. In this example, the price of aspirin doesn't change over the four years, while movies increase in price and hamburgers bounce up and down. Each year, the cost of buying the given basket of goods at the prices prevailing at that time is shown.

To calculate the annual rate of inflation in this example, find the percentage change in the cost of purchasing the overall basket of goods between the time periods. The general equation for percentage changes between two years, whether in the context of inflation or in any other calculation, is:

$$\frac{\text{(Level in new year – level in original year)}}{\text{(level in original year)}} \times 100 = \text{percentage change}$$

From period 1 to period 2, the total cost of purchasing the basket of goods in Exhibit 10-2 rises from $100 to $106.50. Therefore, the percentage change over this time—the inflation rate—is:

$$\frac{(106.50 - 100)}{100} \times 100 = 6.5\%$$

From period 1 to period 2, the overall change in the cost of purchasing the basket rises from $106.50 to $107. Thus, the inflation rate over this time, again calculated by the percentage change, is approximately:

$$\frac{(107 - 106.50)}{106.50} \times 100 = 0.5\%$$

This calculation of the change in the total cost of purchasing a basket of goods takes into account how much is spent on each good. Hamburgers are the lowest-priced good in this example, and aspirin is the highest-priced. But if an individual buys a greater quantity of a low-price good, then it makes sense that changes in the price of that good should have a larger impact on the buying power of that person's money. The larger impact of hamburgers shows up in the "amount spent" column, where in all time periods hamburgers are the largest item within total spending.

Index Numbers

The numerical results of a calculation based on a basket of goods can get a little messy. The simplified example in Exhibit 10-2 has only three goods and the prices are in even dollars, not numbers like 79 cents or $124.99. If the list of products was much longer, and more realistic prices were used, the total quantity spent over a year might be some messy-looking number like $17,147.51 or $27,654.92.

To simplify the task of interpreting the price levels for more realistic and complex baskets of goods, the price level in each period is typically not reported as a dollar amount for buying the basket of goods but rather as an **index number.** Index numbers work in this way. Arbitrarily choose one year to be the base year, and in the base year, set the index equal to 100. In the example above, say that time period 3 is chosen as the base year, and so the total amount of spending in that year—$107—is set equal to 100. Then, the total amount of spending for all other years is expressed in proportion to the level in the base year. The formula for the calculation is:

index number: When one arbitrary year is chosen to equal 100, and then values in all other years are set proportionately equal to that base year.

$$\frac{\text{Total amount spent in base year}}{\text{Index number in base year, always 100}} = \frac{\text{Total amount spent in other year}}{\text{Index number in other year}}$$

Thus, if period 3 is the base period, then the index number for period 1 would be:

$$\frac{107}{100} = \frac{100}{x} \quad x = 93.4$$

Calculations for the other index numbers, based on the example presented in Exhibit 10-2 are shown in Exhibit 10-3. Because the index numbers are calculated so that they are in exactly the same proportion as the total dollar cost of purchasing the basket of goods, the inflation rate can be calculated based on the index numbers, using the percentage change formula. Thus, the inflation rate from period 1 to period 2 would be

$$\frac{(99.5 - 93.4)}{93.4} \times 100 = 6.5\%$$

which is the same answer that was derived when measuring inflation based on the dollar cost of the basket of goods at different times.

The two graphs in Exhibit 10-4 illustrate the change in the price level over time. In Exhibit 10-4a, two lines are plotted: one is based on the dollar values taken from Exhibit 10-1; the other is based on the index numbers just calculated. Notice that the shape of the line is exactly the same in either case, because the index numbers are constructed to reflect exactly the same pattern as the dollar figures. One line lies above the other only because the index was set up so that $107 in spending during period 3 is equal to an index number of 100.

	Total Spending	Index Number	Inflation Rate Since Previous Period
Time 1	$100	$\dfrac{107}{100} = \dfrac{100}{x}$ $x = 93.4$	—
Time 2	$106.50	$\dfrac{107}{100} = \dfrac{106.50}{x}$ $x = 99.5$	$\dfrac{(99.5 - 93.4)}{93.4}$ $100 = 6.5\%$
Time 3	$107	100 (chosen arbitrarily)	$\dfrac{(100 - 99.5)}{99.5}$ $100 = 0.5\%$
Time 4	$117.50	$\dfrac{107}{100} = \dfrac{117.50}{x}$ $x = 109.8$	$\dfrac{(109.8 - 100)}{100}$ $100 = 9.8\%$

Exhibit 10-3
Calculating Index Numbers

Exhibit 10-4   Using Price Levels and Index Numbers to Calculate Inflation Rates

The left-hand axis shows the cost of purchasing the college student's basket of goods as measured in dollars. The right-hand axis shows the cost of purchasing the basket of goods after converting to an index number. The two lines move in exactly the same way, since after all, the index numbers were calculated in such a way as to mirror exactly the dollar numbers. The percentage change in the price level from one time period to the next, whether the price level is measured in terms of money or as a price index, will be the inflation rate.

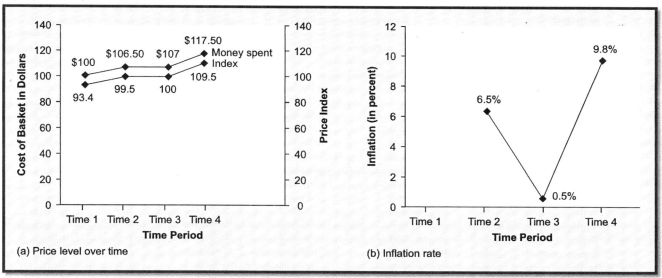

(a) Price level over time

(b) Inflation rate

Exhibit 10-4*b* shows the rate of inflation in periods 2, 3, and 4. It's not possible to calculate an inflation rate for period 1, because the price level in the previous time period isn't provided, so it's impossible to say how much the price level changed in period 1 compared to the previous time period. The inflation rate will be exactly the same whether it is calculated based on the dollar spending totals in Exhibit 10-2 or on the index numbers in Exhibit 10-3.

If the inflation rate is the same whether it is based on dollar values or index numbers, then why bother with the index numbers? The advantage is that indexing allows easier

Inflation in Massachusetts in 1780

In 1780, the state of Massachusetts wanted to encourage soldiers to sign up to fight in the Revolutionary War. However, the value of the new U.S. currency was unstable and inflation was high, so prospective soldiers worried that even if they survived the fighting, their pay could end up being worth almost nothing. How could the government address their worries?

In one of the first known examples of using a basket of goods to calculate inflation for public policy purposes, Massachusetts legislators devised their own way of calculating the inflation rate. They decreed that soldiers would be paid "in the then current Money of the State, in a greater or lesser Sum, according as Five Bushels of Corn, Sixty-eight Pounds and four-seventh Parts of a Pound of Beef, Ten Pounds of Sheep Wool, and Sixteen Pounds of Sole Leather shall then cost, more or less than One Hundred and Thirty Pounds of Current Money." In other words, soldiers would be paid 130 pounds in real value, adjusted for inflation in the price of the four goods.

The uneven and strange-sounding units—five bushels, 68 4/7 pounds, ten pounds, and 16 pounds—were chosen so that the overall amount spent on each good would be the same at the start of the calculation.

The Massachusetts legislature appointed county agents to collect price data every month. However, many of the Massachusetts agents had trouble doing the calculations, and others didn't collect data at all. Then, the central administrators seem to have taken what price data did exist and understated the actual level of price increases reported by the agents. After all, the state administrators knew that finding a high rate of inflation would have cost Massachusetts more money when the time came to pay the soldiers.

eyeballing of the inflation numbers. If you glance at two index numbers like 107 and 110, you know automatically that the rate of inflation between the two years is about 3%. By contrast, imagine that the price levels were expressed in absolute dollars of a large basket of goods, so that when you looked at the data, the numbers were $19,493.62 and $20,009.32. Most people find it difficult to eyeball those kinds of numbers and say that it's a change of about 3%. However, the two numbers expressed in absolute dollars are exactly in the same proportion of 107 to 110 as the previous example.

Two final points about index numbers are worth remembering. First, index numbers have no dollar signs or other units attached to them. Although index numbers can be used to calculate a percentage inflation rate, the index numbers themselves do not have percentage signs on them. Index numbers just mirror the proportions found in other data. They transform the other data so that the data are easier to work with.

Second, the choice of a base year for the index number—that is, the year that is automatically set equal to 100—is arbitrary. In the official inflation statistics, it is common to use one base year for a few years, and then to update it, so that the base year of 100 is relatively close to the present and eyeballing the recent data is easier. But any base year that is chosen for the index numbers will result in exactly the same inflation rate. To see this in the previous example, imagine that year 1, when total spending was $100 was also chosen as the base year, and given an index number of 100. At a glance, you can see that the index numbers would now exactly match the dollar figures, the inflation rate in the first period would be 6.5%, and so on.

Measuring Changes in the Cost of Living

The most commonly cited measure of inflation in the United States is the **Consumer Price Index (CPI)**. The CPI is calculated by government statisticians at the U.S. Bureau of Labor Statistics based on the price level based on a basket of goods and services that represents the purchases of the average consumer. However, in recent years, the statisticians at the Bureau of Labor Statistics have paid considerable attention to a subtle problem: measuring how the total cost of buying a fixed basket of goods has evolved over time is conceptually not quite the same as measuring a change in the cost of living,

Consumer Price Index (CPI): A measure of inflation calculated by U.S. government statisticians based on the price level from a basket of goods and services that represents the purchases of the average consumer.

which represents how much it costs for a person to feel that their consumption provides an equal level of satisfaction or utility.

To understand the distinction, imagine that over the past 10 years, the cost of purchasing a fixed basket of goods increased by 25% and your salary also increased by 25%. Has your personal standard of living held constant? If you don't necessarily purchase the same identical fixed basket of goods every year, then an inflation calculation based on the cost of a fixed basket of goods may be a misleading measure of how your cost of living has changed. Two problems arise here: substitution bias and quality/new goods bias.

When the price of a good rises, consumers tend to purchase less of it and to seek out substitutes instead. Conversely, as the price of a good falls, people will tend to purchase more of it. This pattern implies that goods with generally rising prices should tend over time to become less important in the overall basket of goods used to calculate inflation, while goods with falling prices should tend to become more important. However, a fixed and unchanging basket of goods assumes that consumers are locked into buying exactly the same goods, regardless of price changes—not a very appealing assumption. Thus, **substitution bias** is that the rise in the price of a fixed basket of goods over time tends to overstate the rise in a consumer's true cost of living, because it doesn't take into account that the person can substitute between goods according to changes in their relative prices.

The other major problem in using a fixed basket of goods as the basis for calculating inflation is how to deal with the arrival of improved versions of older goods or altogether new goods. Consider the problem that arises if a cereal is improved by adding 12 essential vitamins and minerals—and also if a box of the cereal costs 5% more. It would clearly be misleading to count the entire resulting higher price as inflation, because the new price is being charged for a product of higher (or at least different) quality. Ideally, one would like to know how much of the higher price is due to the quality change, and how much of it is just a higher price, but even the producer may not know. This problem occurs all the time, as quality changes and price changes happen together.

A new product can be thought of as an extreme improvement in quality—from something that didn't exist to something that does. However, the basket of goods that was fixed in the past obviously doesn't include new goods created since then. The bundle of goods used in the Consumer Price Index is revised and updated over time, and so new products are gradually included. But the process takes some time. For example, room air conditioners were widely sold in the early 1950s, but were not introduced into the basket of goods behind the Consumer Price Index until 1964. The VCR and personal computer were available in the late 1970s and widely sold by the early 1980s, but didn't enter the CPI basket of goods until 1987. By 1996, there were more than 40 million cellular phone subscribers in the United States—but cell phones weren't yet part of the CPI basket of goods. The parade of inventions has continued, with the CPI inevitably lagging a few years behind.

substitution bias:
An inflation rate calculated using a fixed basket of goods over time tends to overstate the true rise in the cost of living, because it doesn't take into account that the person can substitute away from goods whose prices rise by a lot.

How U.S. Government Statisticians Measure the Consumer Price Index

When the U.S. Bureau of Labor Statistics (BLS) calculates the Consumer Price Index, a first task is to decide upon a basket of goods that is representative for the purchases of the average household. This is done by using the Consumer Expenditure Survey, a national survey of about 7,000 households, which provides detailed information on spending habits. Consumer expenditures are broken up into eight major groups, shown below, which in turn are broken up into more than 200 individual item categories, some of which also appear in the table.

For each of the 200 individual expenditure items, the BLS chooses several hundred very specific examples of that item and looks at the prices of those examples. Thus, in figuring out the "breakfast cereal" item under the overall category of "Foods and beverages," the BLS picks several hundred examples of breakfast cereal: one example might be the price of a 24-oz. box of a particular brand of cereal sold at a particular store. The specific products and sizes and stores chosen are statistically selected to reflect what

people buy and where they shop. The basket of goods in the Consumer Price Index thus consists of about 80,000 products; that is, several hundred specific products in over 200 broad-item categories. About one-quarter of these 80,000 specific products are rotated out of the sample each year, and replaced with a different set of products.

The next step is to collect data on prices. Data collectors visit or call about 23,000 stores in 87 urban areas all over the United States every month to collect prices on these 80,000 specific products. A survey of 50,000 landlords or tenants is also carried out to collect information about rents.

The Consumer Price Index is then calculated by taking the 80,000 prices of individual products and combining them, using weights determined by the quantities of these products that people buy and allowing for factors like substitution between goods and quality improvements, into price indexes for the 200 or so overall items. Then, the price indexes for the 200 items are combined into an overall Consumer Price Index.

The Eight Major Categories in the Consumer Price Index

1. Food and beverages (breakfast cereal, milk, coffee, chicken, wine, full-service meals and snacks)
2. Housing (renter's cost of housing, homeowner's cost of housing, fuel oil, bedroom furniture)
3. Apparel (men's shirts and sweaters, women's dresses, jewelry)
4. Transportation (new vehicles, airline fares, gasoline, motor vehicle insurance)
5. Medical care (prescription drugs and medical supplies, physicians' services, eyeglasses and eye care, hospital services)
6. Recreation (televisions, cable television, pets and pet products, sports equipment, admissions)
7. Education and communication (college tuition, postage, telephone services, computer software and accessories)
8. Other goods and services (tobacco and smoking products, haircuts and other personal services, funeral expenses)

The arrival of new goods creates problems with respect to the accuracy of measuring inflation. The reason that people buy new goods, presumably, is that the new goods offer better value for money than existing goods. Thus, if the price index leaves out new goods, it overlooks one of the ways in which the cost of living is improving. In addition, the price of a new good is often higher when it is first introduced and then declines over time. If the new good isn't included in the CPI for some years, until its price is already lower, the CPI may miss counting this price decline altogether. Taking these arguments together, the **quality/new goods bias** is that the rise in the price of a fixed basket of goods over time tends to overstate the rise in a consumer's true cost of living, because it doesn't take into account how improvements in the quality of existing goods or the invention of new goods improves the standard of living.

quality/new goods bias: Inflation calculated using a fixed basket of goods over time tends to overstate the true rise in cost of living, because it doesn't take into account improvements in the quality of existing goods or the invention of new goods.

Practical Solutions for the Substitution and the Quality/New Goods Biases

By the early 2000s, the Bureau of Labor Statistics was using alternative mathematical methods for calculating the Consumer Price Index, more complicated than just adding up the cost of a fixed basket of goods, to allow for some substitution between goods.

It was also updating the basket of goods behind the CPI more frequently, so that new and improved goods will be included more rapidly. For certain products, the BLS was carrying out studies to try to measure the quality improvement; for example, with computers an economic study can try to adjust for changes in speed, memory, screen size, and other characteristics of the product, and then calculate the change in price after these changes in the product are taken into account. But these adjustments are inevitably imperfect, and exactly how to make such these adjustments is often the source of controversy between professional economists.

By the early 2000s, the substitution bias and quality/new goods bias had been somewhat reduced, so that since then the rise in the CPI probably overstates the true rise in inflation by only about 0.5% per year. Over one or a few years, this isn't much, but over a period of decade or two, even half of a percent per year compounds to a more significant amount.

When measuring inflation (and other economic statistics, too), a trade-off arises between simplicity and interpretation. If the inflation rate is calculated with a basket of goods that is fixed and unchanging, then the calculation of an inflation rate is straightforward, but the problems of substitution bias and quality/new goods bias will arise. However, when the basket of goods is allowed to shift and evolve to reflect substitution toward lower relative prices, quality improvements, and new goods, the technical details of calculating the inflation rate grow more complex.

Alternative Price Indexes: PPI, GDP Deflator, and More

The basket of goods behind the Consumer Price Index represents an average hypothetical U.S. consumer, which is to say that it doesn't exactly capture anyone's personal experience. When the task is to calculate an average level of inflation, this approach works fine. But what if one is concerned about inflation experienced by a certain group, like the elderly, or the poor, or single-parent families with children, or Hispanic-Americans? In specific situations, a price index based on the buying power of the average consumer may not feel quite right.

This problem has a straightforward solution. If the Consumer Price Index doesn't serve the desired purpose, then invent another index, based on a basket of goods appropriate for the group of interest. Indeed, the Bureau of Labor Statistics publishes a number of experimental price indexes: some for particular groups like the elderly or the poor, some for different geographic areas, some for certain broad categories of goods like food or housing.

The BLS also calculates several price indexes that are not based on baskets of consumer goods. For example, the **Producer Price Index** is based on prices paid for supplies and inputs by producers of goods and services. It can be broken down into price indexes for different industries, commodities, and stages of processing (like finished goods, intermediate goods, crude materials for further processing, and so on). There is an **International Price Index** based on the prices of merchandise that is exported or imported. An **Employment Cost Index** measures wage inflation in the labor market. The **GDP deflator** is a price index that includes all the components of GDP (that is, consumption plus investment plus government plus exports minus imports).

What's the best measure of inflation? As the Bureau of Labor Statistics says: "The 'best' measure of inflation for a given application depends on the intended use of the data."

Producer Price Index: A measure of inflation based on prices paid for supplies and inputs by producers of goods and services.

International Price Index: A measure of inflation based on the prices of merchandise that is exported or imported.

Employment Cost Index: A measure of inflation based on wage paid in the labor market.

GDP deflator: A measure of inflation based on all the components of GDP.

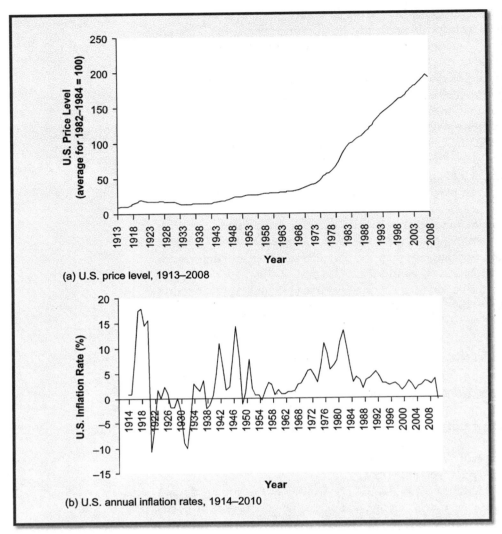

(a) U.S. price level, 1913–2008

(b) U.S. annual inflation rates, 1914–2010

Exhibit 10-5
U.S. Price Level and
Inflation Rates since 1913

(a) The U.S. price level
rose relatively little over the
first half of the twentieth
century but has increased
more substantially in recent
decades. The upward
slope of the price level was
especially steep in the 1970s,
which reflects the high rate of
inflation in that decade.

(b) Inflation during the
twentieth century was highest
just after World Wars I and
II, and during the 1970s.
Deflation—that is, negative
inflation—occurred several
times in the first half of the
century, and in 2009 as well.
Inflation rates since the 1990s
have been in the low single
digits.

Inflation Experiences

In the last two decades, inflation has been relatively low in the U.S. economy, with
the Consumer Price Index typically rising 2–4% per year. But looking back over the
twentieth century, waves of inflation have sometimes occurred at double-digit rates.

Historical Inflation in the U.S. Economy

Exhibit 10-5*a* shows the level of prices in the Consumer Price Index stretching
back to 1913. In this case, the base year when the CPI is set to equal 100 is set for
the average level of prices that existed from 1982 to 1984. Exhibit 10-5*b* shows the
annual percentage changes in the CPI over time, which is the inflation rate. These
two graphs, showing the price level as expressed by the CPI and the annual inflation
rate derived from those price levels, are analogous to the two graphs of Exhibit 10-4
showing the price level for the college student's price index and the inflation rate
derived from that calculation.

The first two waves of inflation are easy to characterize in historical terms: they are right after World War I and World War II. However, there are also two periods of severe negative inflation—called **deflation**—in the early decades of the twentieth century: one following the deep recession of 1920–21 and the other during the Great Depression of the 1930s. (Since inflation is a time when the buying power of money in terms of goods and services is reduced, deflation will be a time when the buying power of money in terms of goods and services increases.) For the period from 1900 to about 1960, the major inflations and deflations nearly balanced each other out, so the average annual rate of inflation over these years was only about 1% per year. A third wave of more severe inflation arrived in the 1970s and departed in the early 1980s.

deflation: Negative inflation.

Times of recession or depression often seem to be times when inflation is decreasing, as in the recession of 1920–1921, the Great Depression, the recession of 1980–1982, and the Great Recession in 2009. Conversely, the rate of inflation often but not always seems to start moving up when the economy is growing very strongly, like right after wartime or the 1960s. The previous chapter noted that recessions are typically accompanied by higher levels of unemployment. The frameworks for macroeconomic analysis that will be developed in later chapters will need to explain why recession often accompanies higher unemployment and lower inflation, while rapid economic growth often brings lower unemployment but higher inflation.

Inflation around the World

Around the rest of the world, the pattern of inflation has been very mixed. Many industrialized countries, not just the United States, had relatively high inflation rates in the 1970s; for example, in 1975, Japan's inflation rate was 11% and the inflation rate for the United Kingdom was 24%. In the 1980s, inflation rates came down in the United States and in Europe and have largely stayed down.

Countries with controlled economies in the 1970s, like the Soviet Union and China, historically had very low rates of measured inflation—because prices were forbidden to rise by law! However, these countries also had perpetual shortages of goods, since forbidding prices to rise acts like a price ceiling and creates a situation where quantity demanded often exceeds quantity supplied. As Russia and China made a transition toward more market-oriented economies, they also experienced outbursts of inflation, although the statistics for these economies should be regarded as somewhat shakier. Inflation in China averaged about 10% for much of the 1980s and early 1990s, although it has dropped off since then. Russia experienced **hyperinflation**—that is, extremely high rates of inflation—of 2500% per year back in the early 1990s, although by 2006 Russia's consumer price inflation had dipped below 10% per year.

hyperinflation: Extremely high rates of inflation.

Many countries in Latin America experienced raging hyperinflation during the 1980s and early 1990s, with inflation rates often well above 100% per year. In 1990, for example, both Brazil and Argentina saw inflation climb above 2000%. Certain countries in Africa experienced extremely high rates of inflation, sometimes bordering on hyperinflation, in the 1990s. Nigeria, the most populous country in Africa, had an inflation rate of 75% in 1995.

In the early 2000s, the problem of inflation appears to have diminished for most countries, at least in comparison to the worst times of recent decades. In recent years, the world's worst example of hyperinflation was in Zimbabwe, where at one point the government was issuing bills with a face value of $100 trillion (in Zimbabwean dollars)—that is, the bills had $100,000,000,000,000 written on the front, but were almost worthless. But in many countries, the memory of double-digit, triple-digit, and even quadruple-digit inflation is not very far in the past.

Year	Nominal GDP (billions of dollars)	GDP Deflator (2005 = 100)
1960	$527	19
1965	$720	20
1970	$1,040	24
1975	$1,635	34
1980	$2,795	48
1985	$4,213	62
1990	$5,803	72
1995	$7,400	82
2000	$9,873	89
2005	$12,455	100
2009	$14,259	110

Exhibit 10-6   Nominal Values and Price Indexes

Adjusting Nominal Values to Real Values

Looking at economic statistics without considering inflation is like looking through a pair of binoculars and trying to guess how close something is: unless you know how strong the lenses are, you can't guess the distance very accurately. Similarly, if you don't know the rate of inflation, it is difficult to figure out if a rise in GDP is due mainly to a rise in the overall level of prices or to a change in quantities of goods produced. The **nominal value** of any economic statistic refers to the number that is actually announced at that time, while the **real value** refers to the statistic after it has been adjusted for inflation.

nominal value: The economic statistic actually announced at that time, not adjusted for inflation; contrast with real value.

real value: An economic statistic after it has been adjusted for inflation; contrast with nominal value.

Nominal to Real GDP

The first column in Exhibit 10-6 gives the U.S. GDP at five-year intervals since 1960 in nominal dollars; that is, in the dollars prevailing in each stated year. The second column gives the price level over that time measured by the GDP deflator, which is the measure of inflation based on a basket of goods that includes everything in GDP (using a base year of 2005 for when the index number is set equal to 100).

If an unwary analyst compared nominal GDP in 1960 to nominal GDP in 1990, it might appear that GDP had risen by a factor of eleven over this time (that is, GDP of $5,803 billion in 1990 divided by GDP of $527 billion in 1960). But this calculation would be highly misleading. As the GDP deflator shows, the price level in 1990 was almost four times higher than in 1960 (the deflator for 1990 was 72 vs. a level of 19 in 1960). Clearly, much of the apparent growth in nominal GDP was due to inflation, not an actual change in real economic activity.

To adjust nominal GDP into real terms, you need to factor out the inflation that has occurred. After all, the dollars used to measure nominal GDP in 1960 are worth more than the inflated dollars of 1990—and the price index tells exactly how much more. To calculate the real gain in GDP from 1960 to 1990, we can measure the nominal 1960 GDP in 1990 dollars, using the price index for the two different years:

When converting nominal annual values into real values, here are three tips.

1. Make sure that you convert all nominal figures into a single common year.
2. Be sure that you don't get the numerator and the denominator in the price index expression turned upside down.
3. When you have calculated an answer, apply your common sense. If you are working forward in time during a period of inflation, then the nominal number should grow when converted to real dollars. If you are working backward in time during a period of inflation, the nominal number should shrink. If your answer offends common sense, look back to the first two tips to see what you might have done wrong.

$$\text{1960 GDP in 1960 dollars} \times \frac{\text{price level in 1990}}{\text{price level in 1960}} = \text{1960 GDP in 1990 dollars}$$

$$\$527 \text{ billion} \times \frac{72}{19} = \$1,997 \text{ billion}$$

To find the percentage change from the 1960 GDP in 1990 dollars to the 1990 GDP, also measured in 1990 dollars, calculate:

$$\frac{(\text{1990 GDP in 1990 dollars} - \text{1960 GDP in 1990 dollars})}{\text{1960 GDP in 1990 \$}} \times 100 = \% \text{ change}$$

$$\frac{(5,803 - 1,997)}{1,997} \times 100 = 190\% \text{ growth in real GDP from 1960 to 1990}$$

The calculation also works in reverse. Convert the nominal 1990 GDP into 1960 dollars.

$$\text{1990 GDP in 1990 dollars} \times \frac{\text{price level in 1960}}{\text{price level in 1990}} = \text{1990 GDP in 1960 dollars}$$

$$\$5,803 \text{ billion} \times \frac{19}{72} = \$1,531 \text{ billion}$$

Then calculate the percentage change, and the answer is exactly the same 190%.

Any change in nominal dollar amounts over time—the price of a gallon of gasoline, wages, the price of a house, the buying power of a pension—can be adjusted for inflation in this way. Exhibit 10-7 shows the nominal GDP since 1960 and the real GDP over that time. Because 2005 is the base year, the nominal and real values are exactly the same in that year. However, over time, the rise in nominal GDP looks much larger than the rise in real GDP (that is, the nominal GDP line rises more steeply than the real GDP line), because the rise in nominal GDP is exaggerated by the presence of inflation, especially in the 1970s.

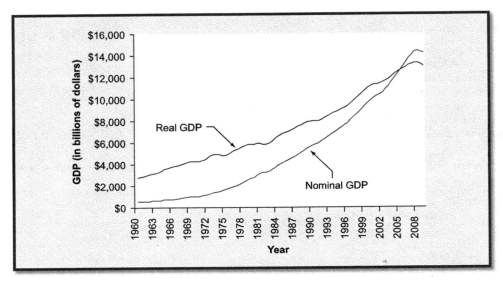

Exhibit 10-7   Nominal and Real GDP, 1960–2009

The lighter line measures U.S. GDP in nominal dollars. The darker line measures U.S. GDP in real dollars, where all dollar values have been converted to 2005 dollars. Since real GDP is expressed in 2005 dollars, the two lines cross in 2005. However, real GDP will appear higher than nominal GDP in the years before in 2005, because dollars were worth less in 2005 than in previous years. Conversely, real GDP will appear lower in the years after 2005, because dollars were worth more in 2005 than in later years.

Nominal to Real Interest Rates

Adjusting from nominal to real terms affects interest rates, too. Any interest rate can be divided into three components (as discussed in Chapter 2): the time value of money, the inflation rate, and the risk that a particular loan will not be repaid in full. No lender would be willing to lend without believing that the amount repaid will offer compensation for all three elements. The **real interest rate** is defined as the nominal rate of interest with inflation subtracted out. That is:

real interest rate: The rate of interest with inflation subtracted.

$$\text{Real interest rate} = \text{Nominal interest rate} - \text{Inflation rate}$$

The real interest rate represents how much in additional buying power a lender or investor receives, or alternatively, how much a borrower or supplier of capital has to pay. Consider a person who takes out a home mortgage, borrowing money to buy a house, at a nominal rate of 8%. From the lender's point of view, say that out of the 8% nominal interest that is paid, 3 percentage points is accounted for by the expected lower value of inflated dollars in the future. Thus, the borrower and the lender enter into the loan expecting that the real rate of interest paid will be 5%. However, if inflation is lower than both parties expected, the actual real rate of interest will be higher than expected; conversely, if inflation is consistently higher than expected, the real rate of interest will be lower than expected.

Looking only at nominal interest rates can be very misleading, as Exhibit 10-8 illustrates. The top line of the figure shows the nominal interest rate that banks were charging for home mortgages for a loan made during a given year over the last several decades. The lower line is the real interest rate in that year; the gap between the two lines results from subtracting the rate of inflation as measured by the Consumer Price Index for that year. By this measure, the real interest rate clearly bounces around. When inflation suddenly jumps up, as in the mid-1970s, the real interest rate became very low for a time, before nominal interest rates adjusted upward. Conversely, when inflation diminishes substantially, as in the mid-1980s, real interest rates can be quite high for a couple of years before they edge back down. During the Great Recession in 2009, inflation was near-zero, so the nominal and real interest rates were about the same.

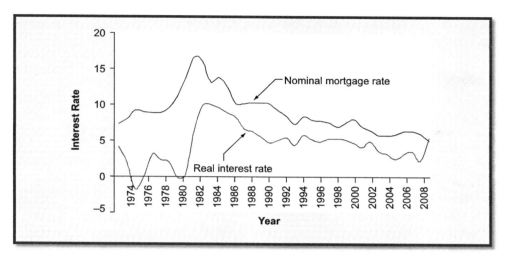

Exhibit 10-8   Nominal versus Real Home Mortgage Rates, 1970–2009

The top line shows the nominal interest rate charged for home mortgages. The bottom line shows the real interest rate, calculated by subtracting the inflation rate for that year. The sharp rise in inflation in the mid-1970s caused the real interest rate to plummet for a few years. Then lenders, recognizing the higher inflation rate, pushed up their nominal interest rates in the early 1980s. The reduction in inflation in the early 1980s led to quite high real interest rates for a few years, although both nominal and real interest rates declined somewhat in the 1990s.

The real rate of interest is what ultimately matters. Receiving 200% nominal interest every year can be a bad deal—if the inflation rate is 250% per year. Better to get a 4% nominal return in a country with only 2% inflation!

The Dislocations of Inflation

Economists usually oppose inflation, but they oppose it in a milder way than many non-economists. Robert Shiller, an economist at Yale University, carried out several surveys during the 1990s about attitudes toward inflation. One of his questions asked, "Do you agree that preventing high inflation is an important national priority, as important as preventing drug abuse or preventing deterioration in the quality of our schools?" Answers were on a scale of 1–5, where 1 meant "Fully agree" and 5 meant "Completely disagree." For the U.S. population as a whole, 52% answered "Fully agree" that preventing high inflation was a highly important and just 4% said "Completely disagree." However, among professional economists, only 18% answered "Fully agree," while the same percentage of 18% answered "Completely disagree."

The Land of Funny Money

What are the economic dislocations and problems caused by inflation, and why do economists often regard them with less concern than the general public? Consider a very short story: "The Land of Funny Money."

> One morning, everyone in the Land of Funny Money awakened to find that everything denominated in money was 20% larger. The change was completely unexpected. Every price in every store was 20% higher. Paychecks were 20% higher. Interest rates were 20 percentage points higher. The amount of money, everywhere from wallets to savings accounts, was 20% larger. This overnight inflation of prices made newspaper headlines everywhere in the Land of Funny Money. But the headlines quickly disappeared, as people realized that in terms of what they could actually buy with their incomes, this inflation had no economic impact. Everyone's pay could still buy exactly the same set of goods as it did before. Everyone's savings were still sufficient

to buy exactly the same car or vacation or retirement that they could have bought before. Equal levels of inflation in all wages and prices ended up not mattering much at all.

When the people in Robert Shiller's surveys explained their concern about inflation, one typical reason was that they feared that as prices rose, they wouldn't be able to afford to buy as much. In other words, people were worried because they did not live in a place like the Land of Funny Money, where all prices and wages rose simultaneously. Instead, people live here on Planet Earth, where prices might rise while wages did not rise at all, or where wages rose more slowly than prices.

Economists note that over most periods, the inflation level in prices is roughly similar to the inflation level in wages, and so they reason that on average, over time, people's economic status is not greatly changed by inflation. If all prices, wages, and interest rates adjusted automatically and immediately with inflation, as in the Land of Funny Money, then no one's purchasing power or profits or real loan payments would change. However, if other economic variables do not move exactly in synch with inflation, or if they adjust for inflation only after a time lag, then inflation can cause three types of problems: unintended redistributions of purchasing power, blurred price signals, and difficulties in long-term planning.

Unintended Redistributions of Purchasing Power

Inflation can cause redistributions of purchasing power that hurt some and help others.

People who are hurt by inflation include those who are holding a lot of cash, whether it is in a safe deposit box or in a cardboard box under the bed. When inflation happens, the buying power of cash is diminished. But cash is only an example of a more general problem: anyone who has financial assets invested in a way that the nominal return doesn't keep up with inflation will tend to suffer from inflation. For example, if a person has money in a bank account that pays 4% interest, but inflation rises to 5%, then the real rate of return for the money invested in that bank account is negative 1%.

The problem of a good-looking nominal interest rate being transformed into an ugly-looking real interest rate can be worsened by taxes. The U.S. income tax is charged on the nominal interest received in dollar terms, without an adjustment for inflation. Thus, a person who invests $10,000 and receives a 5% nominal rate of interest is taxed on the $500 received—no matter whether the inflation rate is 0% or 5% or 10%. If inflation is 0%, then the real interest rate is 5% and all $500 is a gain in buying power. But if inflation is 5%, then the real interest rate is zero and the person had no real gain—but owes income tax on the nominal gain anyway. If inflation is 10%, then the real interest rate is *negative* 5% and person is actually falling behind in buying, but would still owe taxes on the $500 in nominal gains.

Inflation can cause unintended redistributions for wage earners, too. Wages do typically creep up with inflation over time, eventually. The last row of Exhibit 10-1 at the start of this chapter showed that average hourly wage in the U.S. economy increased from $3.23 in 1970 to $18.08 in 2009, which is increase by a factor of more than five. Over that time period, the Consumer Price Index increased by an almost identical amount. However, increases in wages may lag behind inflation for a year or two, since wage adjustments are often somewhat sticky and occur only once or twice a year. Moreover, the extent to which wages keep up with inflation creates insecurity for workers and may involve painful, prolonged conflicts between employers and employees.

The mathematical formula for the effect of how a certain percentage rate of inflation will cause the price level to increase over time is exactly the same formula in mathematical terms as two formulas you have already seen in earlier chapters: the formula for how a certain percentage interest rate will cause an amount of savings to increase over time from Chapter 2, and the formula for how a certain percentage rate of economic growth causes GDP to rise over time as discussed in Chapter 8. In all three cases, seemingly low rates of growth can have large effects when compounded over long periods of time.

Clearing It Up

Yet Again, Compound Growth Rates

One sizeable group of people has often received a large share of their income in a form that doesn't increase over time: retirees who receive a private company pension. Most pensions have traditionally been set as a fixed nominal dollar amount per year at retirement. Even if inflation is low, the combination of inflation and a fixed income can create a substantial problem over time. A person who retires on a fixed income at age 65 will find that losing just 1–2% of buying power per year to inflation compounds to a considerable loss of buying power after a decade or two. If the price index for the consumption of a retiree is set at 100 at age 65 but rises 2% per year, then in 20 years that price level will reach:

$$100 \, (1 + .02)^{20} = 149$$

It will now take $149 to purchase the same basket of goods that sold for $100 dollars at the beginning of the time period, and retirees living on a fixed dollar income will find that their standard of living has substantially eroded. Of course, if inflation is higher than the moderate level of 2%, the problem will be that much worse.

However, ordinary people can sometimes benefit from the unintended redistributions of inflation, too. Consider someone who borrows $10,000 to buy a car at a fixed interest rate of 9%. If inflation is 3% at the time the loan is made, then loan must be repaid at a real interest rate of 6%. But if inflation rises to, say 9%, then the real interest rate on the loan is zero! In this case, the borrower's benefit from inflation is the lender's loss. A borrower paying a fixed interest rate, who benefits from inflation, is just the flip side of an investor receiving a fixed interest rate, who suffers from inflation. The lesson is that when interest rates are fixed, rises in the rate of inflation tend to penalize suppliers of financial capital, who end up being repaid in dollars that are worth less because of inflation, while demanders of financial capital end up better off, because they can repay their loans in dollars that are worth less than originally expected.

The unintended redistributions of buying power caused by inflation may have a broader effect on society. America's widespread acceptance of market forces rests on a perception that people's actions have a reasonable connection to market outcomes. But when inflation causes a retiree who built up a pension or invested at a fixed interest rate to suffer, while someone who borrowed at a fixed interest rate benefits from inflation, it's hard to believe that this outcome was deserved in any way. Similarly, when homeowners benefit from inflation because the price of their homes rises, while renters suffer because they are paying higher rent, it's hard to see any useful incentive effects. One of the reasons that inflation is so disliked by the general public is a sense that it makes economic rewards and penalties more arbitrary—and therefore likely to be perceived as unfair.

German Hyperinflation and Hitler's Rise to Power

Germany suffered an intense hyperinflation of its currency, the Mark, in the years after World War I, which helped create the climate of social turmoil that Adolf Hitler could take advantage of in his rise to power. Robert Shiller of Yale University describes the connection:

> A fact that is probably little known to young people today, even in Germany, is that the final collapse of the Mark in 1923, the time when the Mark's inflation reaches astronomical levels (inflation of 35,974.9% in November 1923 alone, for an annual rate that month of 4.69 × 1028%), came in the same month as did Hitler's Beer Hall Putsch, his Nazi Party's armed attempt to overthrow the German government. This failed putsch resulted

in Hitler's imprisonment, at which time he wrote his book *Mein Kampf*, setting forth an inspirational plan for Germany's future, suggesting plans for world domination. . . .

Most people in Germany today probably do not clearly remember these events; this lack of attention to it may be because its memory is blurred by the more dramatic events that succeeded it (the Nazi seizure of power and World War II). However, to someone living through these historical events in sequence . . . [the putsch] may have been remembered as vivid evidence of the potential effects of inflation.

Blurred Price Signals

Prices are the messengers in a market economy, conveying information about conditions of demand and supply. Inflation blurs those price messages. Inflation means that price signals are perceived more vaguely, like a radio program received with a lot of static. If the static becomes severe, it's hard to tell what's happening.

In Israel, when inflation accelerated to an annual rate of 500% in 1985, some stores stopped posting prices directly on items, since they would have had to put new labels on the items or shelves every few days to reflect inflation. Instead, a shopper just took items from a shelf and went up to the checkout register, to find out the price for that day. Obviously, this situation makes comparing prices and shopping for the best deal rather difficult. When the levels and changes of prices become uncertain, businesses and individuals find it harder to react to economic signals. In a world where inflation is at a high rate, but bouncing up and down to some extent, does a higher price of a good mean that inflation has risen, or that supply of that good has decreased, or that demand for that good has increased? Should a buyer of the good take the higher prices as an economic hint to start substituting other products—or have the prices of the substitutes risen by an equal amount? Should a seller of the good take a higher price as a reason to increase production—or is the higher price only a sign of a general inflation in which the prices of all inputs to production are rising as well? The true story will presumably become clear over time, but at a given moment, who can say? High and variable inflation means that the incentives in the economy to adjust in response to changes in prices are weaker. Markets will adjust toward their equilibrium prices and quantities more erratically, slowly and many individual markets will experience a greater chance of surpluses and shortages.

Problems of Long-Term Planning

Inflation can make long-term planning difficult. In discussing unintended redistributions, we considered the case of someone trying to plan for retirement with a pension that is fixed in nominal terms and a high rate of inflation. But similar problems arise for all people trying to save for retirement, who must consider what their money will really buy several decades in the future when the rate of future inflation cannot be known with certainty.

Inflation, especially at moderate or high levels, will pose substantial planning problems for businesses, too. A firm can make money from inflation—for example, by paying bills and wages as late as possible so that it can pay in inflated dollars, while collecting revenues as soon as possible. A firm can also suffer losses from inflation, as in the case of a retail business that gets stuck holding too much cash, only to see the value of that cash eroded by inflation. But when a business spends its time focusing on how to profit by inflation, or at least how to avoid suffering from it, an inevitable trade-off strikes: less time is spent on improving products and services or on figuring out how to make existing products and services more cheaply. An economy with high inflation rewards businesses that have found clever ways of profiting from inflation, which are not necessarily the businesses that excel at productivity, innovation, or quality of service.

In the short term, low or moderate levels of inflation may not pose an overwhelming difficulty for business planning, because costs of doing business and sales revenues may rise at similar rates. But if inflation varies substantially over the short or medium term, then it may make sense for businesses to stick to shorter-term strategies. The evidence as to whether relatively low rates of inflation reduce productivity is controversial among economists. There is some evidence that if inflation can be held to moderate levels of less than, say, 30% per year, it need not prevent a nation's real economy from growing at a healthy pace. For some countries that have experienced hyperinflation of several thousand percent per year, an annual inflation rate of 20–30% may feel as if it is basically the same as zero! However, several economists have pointed to the suggestive fact that when U.S. inflation heated up in the early 1970s, U.S. growth in productivity slowed down, and when inflation slowed down in the 1980s, productivity edged up again not long thereafter.

Some Benefits of Inflation?

Although the economic effects of inflation are primarily negative, two countervailing points are worth noting. First, the impact of inflation will differ considerably according to whether it is creeping up slowly at 0–2% per year, galloping along at 10–20% per year, or racing to the point of hyperinflation at, say, 40% per *month*. Hyperinflation can rip an economy and a society apart. But an annual inflation rate of 2% or 3% or 4% is a long way from a national crisis.

Second, an argument is sometimes made that moderate inflation may help the economy by making wages in labor markets more flexible. The discussion of unemployment in the previous chapter pointed out that wages tend to be sticky in their downward movements and that unemployment can result. A little inflation could nibble away at real wages, and thus help real wages to decline if necessary. In this way, even if a moderate or high rate of inflation may act as sand in the gears of the economy, perhaps a low rate of inflation serves as oil for the gears of the labor market. This argument is controversial. A full analysis would have to take all the effects of inflation into account. But it does offer another reason to believe that, all things considered, very low rates of inflation may not be especially harmful.

Indexing and Its Limitations

When a price, wage, or interest rate is adjusted automatically with inflation, it is said to be **indexed.** An indexed payment rises according to the index number that measures inflation. A wide array of indexing arrangements is observed in private markets and

indexed: When a price, wage, or interest rate is adjusted automatically for inflation.

government programs. Since the negative effects of inflation depend in large part on having inflation unexpectedly affect one part of the economy but not another—say, increasing the prices that people pay but not the wages that workers receive—indexing will take some of the sting out of inflation.

Indexing in Private Markets

In the 1970s and 1980s, labor unions commonly negotiated wage contracts that had **cost-of-living adjustments**—known as **COLAs**—which guaranteed that their wages would keep up with inflation. These contracts were sometimes written as, say, COLA plus 3%. Thus, if inflation was 5%, the wage increase would automatically be 8%, but if inflation rose to 9%, the wage increase would automatically be 12%. COLAs are a form of indexing applied to wages.

> **cost-of-living adjustments (COLAs):** A contractual provision that wage increases will keep up with inflation.

Loans often have built-in inflation adjustments, too, so that if the inflation rate rises by 2%, then the interest rate charged on the loan rises 2% as well. An **adjustable rate mortgage,** a kind of loan used to purchase a home in which the interest rate varies with the rate of inflation, is referred to as an **ARM.** Often, a borrower will be able receive a lower interest rate if borrowing with an ARM, compared to a fixed rate loan. The reason is that with an ARM, the lender is protected against the risk that higher inflation will reduce the real loan payments, and so the risk premium part of the interest rate can be correspondingly lower.

> **adjustable rate mortgage (ARM):** A loan used to purchase a home in which the interest rate varies with the rate of inflation.

A number of ongoing or long-term business contracts also have provisions that prices will be adjusted automatically according to inflation. Sellers like such contracts because they are not locked into a low nominal selling price if inflation turns out higher than expected; buyers like such contracts because they are not locked into a high buying price if inflation turns out to be lower than expected. A contract with automatic adjustments for inflation in effect agrees on a real price to be paid, rather than a nominal price.

Indexing in Government Programs

Many government programs are indexed to inflation. The U.S. income tax code is designed so that as a person's income rises above certain levels, the tax rate on the marginal income earned rises as well; this is what is meant by the expression "move into a higher tax bracket." For example, according to the basic tax tables from the Internal Revenue Service, in 2009 a single person owed 10% of all income from $0 to $8,350: 15% of all income from $8,350 to $33,950: 25% of all income from $33,950 to $82,250; 28% of all income from $82,250 to $171,550: 33% of all income from $171,550 to $372,950; and 35% of income from $372,950 and above. Because of the many complex provisions in the rest of the tax code, the taxes owed by any individual cannot be exactly determined based on these numbers, but these numbers illustrate the basic theme that tax rates as the marginal dollar of income rises. Until the late 1970s, if nominal wages increased along with inflation, people were moved into higher tax brackets and owed a higher proportion of their income in taxes, even though their real income had not risen! This "bracket creep," as it was called, was eliminated by law in 1981. Now, the income levels where higher tax rates kick in are indexed to rise automatically with inflation.

The Social Security program offers two examples of indexing. Since the passage of the Social Security Indexing Act of 1972, the level of Social Security benefits increases each year along with the Consumer Price Index. Also, Social Security is funded by payroll taxes, which are imposed on the income earned up to a certain amount—$106,800 in 2010. This level of income is adjusted upwards each year according to the rate of inflation, so that the indexed rise in the benefit level is accompanied by an indexed increase in the Social Security tax base.

As yet another example of a government program affected by indexing, in 1996 the U.S. government began offering indexed bonds. Bonds are means by which the U.S. government (and many private-sector companies as well) borrows money; that is, investors buy the bonds, and then the government repays the money with interest. Traditionally, government bonds have paid a fixed rate of interest. This policy gave a government that had borrowed an incentive to encourage inflation, because it could then repay its past borrowing in inflated dollars at a lower real interest rate. But indexed bonds promise to pay a certain real rate of interest above whatever inflation rate occurs. In the case of, say, a retiree trying to plan for the long term and worried about the risk of inflation, indexed bonds which guarantee a rate of return higher than inflation—no matter the level of inflation—can be a very comforting investment.

Might Indexing Reduce Concern Over Inflation?

Indexing may seem like an obviously useful step. After all, when individuals, firms, and government programs are indexed against inflation, then people can worry less about the arbitrary redistributions and other effects of inflation.

However, some of the fiercest opponents of inflation express grave concern about indexing. They point out that indexing is always partial. Not every employer will provide COLAs for workers. Not all companies can assume that costs and revenues will rise in lockstep with the general rates of inflation. Not all interest rates for borrowers and savers will change to match inflation exactly. But as partial inflation indexing spreads, the political opposition to inflation may diminish. After all, older people whose Social Security benefits are protected against inflation, or banks that have loaned their money with adjustable rate loans, no longer have as much reason to care whether inflation heats up. In a world where some people are indexed against inflation and some are not, financially savvy businesses and investors may seek out ways to be protected against inflation, while the financially unsophisticated and small businesses may suffer from it most heavily.

A Preview of Policy Discussions of Inflation

This chapter has focused on how inflation is measured, historical experience with inflation, how to adjust nominal variables into real ones, how inflation affects the economy, and how indexing works. The causes of inflation have barely been hinted at, and government policies to deal with inflation have not been addressed at all. These issues will be taken up in depth in later chapters. However, it is useful to offer a preview here.

The cause of inflation can be summed up in one sentence: too many dollars chasing too few goods. The great surges of inflation early in the twentieth century came after wars, which are a time when government spending is very high, but consumers have little to buy, because production is going to the war effort. Governments also commonly impose price controls during wartime. But after the war, the price controls end and pent-up buying power surges forth, driving up inflation. On the other hand, if too few dollars are chasing too many goods, then inflation will decline or even turn into deflation. Therefore, slowdowns in economic activity, as in major recessions and the Great Depression, are typically associated with a reduction in inflation or even outright deflation. The policy implications are clear. If inflation is to be avoided, the amount of purchasing power in the economy must grow at roughly the same rate as the production of goods. Macroeconomic policies that the government can make to affect the amount of purchasing power—through taxes, spending, and regulation of interest rates and credit—can thus cause inflation to rise or can reduce inflation to lower levels.

Key Concepts and Summary

1. The price level is measured by using a **basket of goods and services** and calculating how the total cost of buying that basket of goods will increase over time. The price level is often expressed in terms of **index numbers,** which transform the cost of buying the basket of goods and services into a series of numbers in the same proportion to each other, but with an arbitrary base year of 100.

2. The rate of **inflation** is measured as the percentage change between price levels over time.

3. Measuring price levels with a fixed basket of goods will always have two problems: the **substitution bias,** by which a fixed basket of goods does not allow for buying more of what is relatively less expensive and less of what is relatively more expensive; and the **quality/new goods bias,** by which a fixed basket cannot take into account improvements in quality and the advent of new goods. These problems can be reduced in degree—for example, by allowing the basket of goods to evolve over time—but they cannot be totally eliminated.

4. The most commonly cited measure of inflation is the **Consumer Price Index (CPI),** which is based on a basket of goods representing what the typical consumer buys.

5. Different measures of inflation are based on different baskets of goods. The **GDP deflator** is based on a basket of goods representing everything in GDP. The **Producer Price Index** is based on a basket of goods representing supplies and inputs bought by producers of goods and services.

6. In the U.S. economy, the annual inflation rate in the last two decades has typically been around 2–4%. The periods of highest inflation in the United States in the twentieth century occurred during the years after World Wars I and II, and in the 1970s. The period of lowest inflation—actually, with **deflation**—was the Great Depression of the 1930s.

7. The **nominal value** of an economic statistic is the commonly announced value. The **real value** is the value after adjusting for changes in inflation.

8. To convert nominal economic data from several different years into real, inflation-adjusted data, the starting point is to choose arbitrarily a base year and then use a price index to convert the measurements so that they are measured in the money prevailing in the base year. The formula is:

$$\text{Nominal economic variable measured in currency from the original year} \times \frac{\text{Price index in base year}}{\text{Price index in original year}} = \text{Economic variable measured in currency from the base year}$$

9. The **real interest rate** is the nominal interest rate minus the rate of inflation.

10. Unexpected inflation will tend to hurt those whose money received, in terms of wages and interest payments, does not rise with inflation. In contrast, inflation can help those who owe money that can be paid in less valuable, inflated dollars.

11. Low rates of inflation have relatively little economic impact over the short term. But over the medium and the long term, even low rates of inflation can complicate future planning. High rates of inflation can muddle price signals in the short term and prevent market forces from operating efficiently, and can vastly complicate long-term savings and investment decisions.

12. A payment is said to be **indexed** if it is automatically adjusted for inflation. Examples of indexing in the private sector include wage contracts with **cost-of-living adjustments (COLAs)** and loan agreements like **adjustable rate mortgages (ARMs).** Examples of indexing in the public sector include tax brackets and Social Security payments.

Review Questions

1. How is a basket of goods used to measure the price level?

2. Why are index numbers used to measure the price level?

3. What's the difference between the price level and the rate of inflation?

4. Why does "substitution bias" arise if the inflation rate is calculated based on a fixed basket of goods?

5. Why does the "quality/new goods bias" arise if the inflation rate is calculated based on a fixed basket of goods?

6. What's the difference between the following measures of inflation: the Consumer Price Index, the Producer Price Index, and the GDP deflator?

7. What has been a typical range of inflation in the U.S. economy in the last decade or so?

8. Over the last century, during what periods was the U.S. inflation rate highest and lowest?

9. What is deflation?

10. What's the difference between a series of economic data over time measured in nominal terms versus the same data series over time measured in real terms?

11. How do you convert a series of nominal economic data over time to real terms?

12. How do you convert a nominal interest rate to a real interest rate?

13. Identify several parties likely to be helped and hurt by inflation.

14. What is indexing?

15. Name several forms of indexing in the private and public sector.

The Balance of Trade

The **balance of trade** refers to the gap, if any, between a nation's **exports**, or what its producers sell abroad, and a nation's **imports**, or the foreign-made products and services purchased by households and businesses. If exports exceed imports, the economy is said to have a **trade surplus**. If imports exceed exports, the economy is said to have a **trade deficit**. If exports and imports are equal, then trade is balanced. But what happens when trade is out of balance and large trade surpluses or deficits exist?

Germany, for example, has experienced substantial trade surpluses in recent decades, in which exports have greatly exceeded imports. In 2007, Germany exported $1,559 billion of goods and services and imported $1,326 billion, for a trade surplus of $233 billion. In contrast, the U.S. economy in recent decades has experienced large trade deficits, in which imports have considerably exceeded exports. In 2009, U.S. imports were $2,535 billion while exports were $2,116 billion, so that for the U.S. economy, imports exceeded exports by a sizeable $419 billion.

A series of macroeconomic events triggered by unbalanced trade has led some economies into deep recessions. The typical sequence of events begins with large trade deficits. At some point, foreign investors became pessimistic about the economy and moved their money to other countries and the economy dropped into deep recession, with GDP often falling 10% or more in a single year. Mexico suffered through this sequence of events in 1995. A number of countries in East Asia—like Thailand, South Korea, Malaysia and Indonesia—came down with the same economic illness in 1997–98. In the late 1990s and into the early 2000s, Russia and Argentina had the same experience. What are the connections between imbalances of trade in goods and services and the flows of international financial capital that have set off these economic avalanches?

balance of trade: The gap, if any, between a nation's exports and imports.

exports: Goods and services that are produced domestically and sold in another country.

imports: Goods and services produced abroad and then sold domestically.

trade surplus: When exports exceed imports.

trade deficit: When imports exceed exports.

The starting point is to define the balance of trade in more detail and to sketch some patterns of trade balances both in the United States and around the world. The discussion then turns to examining the intimate connection between international flows of goods and services and international flows of financial capital, which to economists are really just two sides of the same coin. Some perhaps surprising conclusions emerge from this discussion. It is often assumed that trade surpluses like those in Germany must be a positive sign for an economy while trade deficits like those in the United States must be harmful. But as it turns out, both trade surpluses and deficit can be either beneficial or harmful for an economy in certain circumstances. Moreover, it is often presumed that an economy with a larger involvement in foreign trade is more likely to suffer a larger trade imbalance. However, it turns out that the extent to which a national economy is involved in global trade—as measured, say, by exports as a share of GDP—is not very strongly related to the issue of whether the economy has a substantial trade imbalance, nor to the underlying economic meaning of trade imbalances. As in the previous chapters on the macroeconomic goals of growth, unemployment and inflation, the focus of this chapter is to lay a firm foundation for understanding what trade imbalances are, and then later chapters will discuss the underlying causes and macroeconomic policy responses in greater detail.

Measuring Trade Balances

A few decades ago, it was common to measure flows of trade by amounts of goods; that is, the solid, physical items that were transported by ships or trucks or airplanes between countries. The balance of trade measured by comparing exports and imports of goods is called the **merchandise trade balance.** But in most high-income economies, including the United States, goods make up less than half of GDP, while services compose more than half. The last two decades have seen a surge in international trade in services, powered by technological advances in telecommunications and computers that have made it possible for work in customer service, finance, law, advertising, management consulting, software, product design, and other areas to be performed in one country and sold in another. Most global trade still takes the form of goods, rather than services, and the merchandise trade balance is still announced by the government and reported prominently in the newspapers. Old habits are hard to break. But economists typically rely on a broader measure of international trade that includes goods, services, and other factors like international flows of income and foreign aid. This broad measure of the trade is called the **current account balance.**

merchandise trade balance: The balance of trade looking only at goods.

current account balance: A broad measure of the balance of trade that includes trade in goods and services, as well as international flows of income and foreign aid.

Components of the U.S. Current Account Balance

Exhibit 11-1 breaks down the four main components of the U.S. current account balance for 2009. The first line shows the merchandise trade balance; that is, exports and imports

	Exports	Imports	Balance
Goods	$1,046	$1,562	−$516
Services	$509	$371	$138
Income payments	$561	$472	$89
Unilateral transfers	—	$130	−$130
Current account balance	*$2,116*	*$2,535*	*−$419*

Exhibit 11-1
Components of the U.S. Current Account Balance for 2009 (measured in billions of dollars)

How the U.S. Government Collects Trade Statistics

Statistics on the balance of trade are compiled by the Bureau of Economic Analysis within the U.S. Department of Commerce, using a variety of different sources.

Importers and exporters of merchandise must file monthly documents with the Census Bureau, which provides the basic data for merchandise trade. To measure international trade in services—which can happen over a telephone line or computer network without any physical goods being shipped—the BEA carries out a set of surveys. Another set of BEA surveys track investment flows, and there are even specific surveys to collect travel information from U.S. residents visiting Canada and Mexico. For measuring unilateral transfers, the BEA has access to official U.S. government spending on aid, and then also carries out a survey of charitable organizations that make foreign donations.

This information on international flows of goods and capital is then cross-checked against other available data. For example, the Census Bureau also collects data from the shipping industry, which can be used to check the data on trade in goods. All companies involved in international flows of capital—including banks and financial investments like stocks—must file reports, which are ultimately compiled by the U.S. Department of the Treasury. Information on foreign trade can also be cross-checked by looking at data collected by other countries on their foreign trade with the United States, and also at the data collected by various international organizations. Take these data sources, stir carefully, and you have the U.S. balance of trade statistics.

of goods. Because imports exceed exports, the balance in the final column is negative, showing a merchandise trade deficit.

The second row provides data on trade in services. In services, the U.S. economy is running a surplus. Although the level of trade in services is still relatively small compared to trade in goods, the importance of services in trade has expanded substantially over the last few decades. For example, U.S. exports of services were equal to about one-half of U.S. exports of goods in 2009, compared to one-fifth back in 1980.

The third component of the current account balance, labeled "Income payments," refers to returns received by U.S. financial investors on their foreign investments, and payments made by parties in the U.S. economy to foreign investors who had invested their funds here. The reason for including these returns on foreign investment in the overall measure of trade, along with goods and services, is that from an economic perspective, financial investment is just as much an economic transaction as shipments of cars or wheat or oil: it's just trade that is happening in the financial capital market. A return on investment is a payment for letting someone else use your financial capital. A payment made from a U.S. company to a foreign investor, in which money flows from the U.S. economy to another country, is fundamentally the same thing as a payment made for a service provided from another country, except that in this case, the "service" consists of providing financial capital. Conversely, a payment made by a foreign firm to a U.S. investor, in which money flows from the foreign country to the U.S. economy, looks in economic terms just like an export of a service. The U.S. economy was running a modest surplus in "Income payments" in 2009.

The final category of the current account balance is "unilateral transfers," which can be thought of as payments made by government, private charities, or individuals in which money is sent abroad without any direct good or service being received. For example, economic or military assistance from the U.S. government to other countries fits into this category, as does spending by charities to address poverty or social inequalities abroad. When an individual in the U.S. sends money overseas, as in the case of a worker from another country who sends money back home, it is also counted in this category. The current account balance treats these unilateral payments like imports, because they also involve a stream of payments leaving the country. For the U.S. economy, unilateral transfers are almost always negative—that is, transfer payments for economic and military assistance flow out from the United States to other countries, rather than the reverse. But this pattern doesn't always hold. In 1991, for example, when the United States led an international coalition against Saddam Hussein's Iraq in the Gulf War, many other nations agreed that they would make payments to the United States to offset the U.S. war expenses. These payments were large enough that in 1991, the overall U.S. balance on unilateral transfers was a positive $10 billion.

Merchandise trade remains the biggest single factor in the overall balance of trade. But trade in services is growing rapidly, and for a complete picture, the other two elements in the current account balance of payments shouldn't be neglected.

Trade Balances in Historical and International Context

The history of the U.S. current account balance in recent decades is presented in several different ways in Exhibit 11-2. Exhibit 11-2a shows the current account balance and the merchandise trade balance in nominal dollar terms—that is, in the dollar values that would have been announced in each year. Exhibit 11-2b shows the current account balance and merchandise account balance yet again, this time with the figures presented as a share of the GDP for that year. By dividing by the trade deficit in each year by GDP in that year, Exhibit 11-2b factors out both inflation and growth in the real economy.

By either measure, the general pattern of the U.S. balance of trade is clear. From the 1960s into the 1970s, the U.S. economy had mostly small trade surpluses—that is, the graphs of Exhibit 11-2 show positive numbers. However, starting in the 1980s, the trade deficit increased rapidly, and after a tiny trade surplus in 1991, the current account trade deficit got even larger in the late 1990s and into the mid-2000s. However, the trade deficit declines in 2009 after the recession has taken hold.

Exhibit 11-2   Current Account Balance and Merchandise Trade Balance, 1960–2009

(a) The current account and merchandise trade balance in nominal dollars.

(b) The current account and merchandise trade balance as a percentage of GDP.

	Exports of Goods and Services	Current Account Balance
United States	11.7%	−6.1%
Japan	16.1%	3.9%
Germany	45.1%	5.0%
United Kingdom	28.4%	−3.9%
Canada	36.3%	1.6%
Sweden	51.4%	8.5%
Korea	39.7%	0.6%
Mexico	28.1%	−0.2%
Brazil	14.4%	1.3%
China	40.0%	9.4%
India	22.2%	−1.1%
Nigeria	43.2%	−8.6%
World	—	0.0

Exhibit 11-3   Level and Balance of Trade in 2006 (figures as a percentage of GDP)

Exhibit 11-3 shows the U.S. trade picture in 2006 compared with some other economies from around the world. While the U.S. economy has consistently run trade deficits in recent years, Japan and many European nations, among them France and Italy have consistently run trade surpluses. Some of the other countries listed include Brazil, the largest economy in Latin America; Nigeria, the largest economy in Africa; and China, India, and Korea. The first column of the exhibit offers one measure of the globalization of an economy: specifically, exports of goods and services as a percentage of GDP. The second column shows the trade balance. Most of the time, most countries have trade surpluses or deficits that are less than 5% of GDP. But as the table shows, there are prominent of trade deficits larger than 5% of GDP, like the United States, and trade surpluses larger than 5% of GDP, like China.

All the trade deficits and trade surpluses of all the nations in the world must to sum to zero. Exports for one country are always imports for another country, and vice versa. In this sense, global trade by definition is always in perfect balance.

The Intimate Connection between Trade Balances and Flows of Financial Capital

The terminology of trade "deficits" and "surpluses" and "balance" can sometime be a barrier to understanding. Isn't "balance" a good thing? If not "balance," then isn't a "surplus" better than a "deficit"? In some settings, these quick judgments are true enough. But in the case of trade imbalances, these preconceptions must be stripped away. As economists see it, trade surpluses can be either good or bad, depending on circumstances, and trade deficits can be good or bad, too. The challenge is to avoid being hypnotized by the terminology, and instead understand the economic meaning of the trade balance and how international flows of goods and services are interconnected with international flows of financial capital. This section will illustrate the intimate connection between trade balances and flows of financial capital in two ways: a parable of trade between Robinson Crusoe and Friday and a circular flow diagram representing flows of trade and payments.

The Parable of Robinson Crusoe and Friday

To understand how economists view trade deficits and surpluses, consider a parable based on the story of Robinson Crusoe. Robinson, as you may remember from the classic novel by Daniel Defoe first published in 1719, was shipwrecked on a desert island. After living alone for some time, Robinson is joined by a second person, whom he names Friday. Think about the balance of trade in a two-person economy like that of Robinson and Friday.

Robinson and Friday trade goods and services with each other. Perhaps Robinson catches fish and trades them to Friday for coconuts. Or Friday weaves a hat out of tree fronds and trades it to Robinson for help in carrying water. For a period of time, each individual trade is self-contained and complete. Because each trade is voluntary, both Robinson and Friday must feel that they are receiving fair value for what they are giving. As a result, each person's exports are always equal to his imports, and trade is always in balance between the two men. Neither person experiences either a trade deficit or a trade surplus.

However, one day Robinson approaches Friday with a proposition. Robinson wants to dig ditches for an irrigation system for his garden, but he knows that if he starts this project, he won't have much time left to fish and gather coconuts to feed himself each day. He proposes that Friday supply him with a certain number of fish and coconuts for several months, and then after that time, he promises to repay Friday out of the extra produce that he will be able to grow in his irrigated garden. If Friday accepts this offer, then a trade imbalance comes into being. For several months, Friday will have a trade surplus: that is, he is exporting to Robinson more than he is importing. More precisely, he is giving Robinson fish and coconuts, and at least for the moment, he is receiving nothing in return. Conversely, Robinson will have a trade deficit, because he is importing more from Friday than he is exporting.

This parable raises several useful issues in thinking about what a trade deficit and a trade surplus really mean in economic terms.

The first issue raised by this story of Robinson and Friday is: Is it better to have a trade surplus or a trade deficit? The answer, as in any voluntary market interaction, is that if both parties agree to the transaction, then they may both be better off. Over time, if Robinson's irrigated garden is a success, it is certainly possible that both Robinson and Friday can benefit from this agreement.

A second issue raised by the parable is: What can go wrong? Robinson's proposal to Friday introduces an element of uncertainty. Friday is in effect making a loan of fish and coconuts to Robinson, and Friday's happiness with this arrangement will depend on whether that loan is repaid as planned, in full and on time. Perhaps Robinson spends several months loafing, and never builds the irrigation system. Or perhaps Robinson has been too optimistic about how much he will be able to grow with the new irrigation system, which instead turns out not to be very productive. Perhaps after building the irrigation system, Robinson decides that he doesn't want to repay Friday as much as previously agreed. Any of these developments will prompt a new round of negotiations between Friday and Robinson. Friday's attitude toward these renegotiations is likely to be shaped by why the repayment failed. If Robinson worked very hard and the irrigation system just didn't increase production as intended, Friday may have some sympathy. But if Robinson loafed, or if he just refuses to pay, Friday may become peeved. Whenever money is borrowed for an investment project and the project goes bad, a negotiation takes place between the borrower and the lender as to how much of the original loan will be repaid. Such negotiations are often full of accusations and anger.

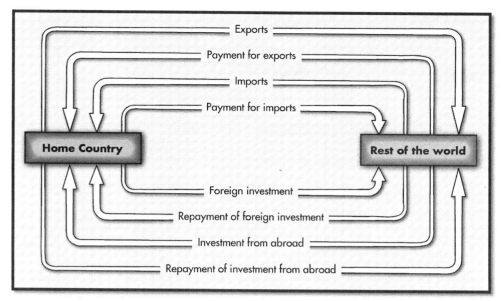

Exhibit 11-4   Flow of Investment Goods and Capital

Each element of the current account balance involves a flow of financial payments between countries. The top line shows exports of goods and services leaving the home country; the second line shows the flow of payments received by the home country for those exports. The third line shows imports received by the home country; the fourth line shows the payments sent abroad by the home country in exchange for these imports. The bottom four lines all show flows of financial capital, either financial investment received from abroad, or repayment of that investment.

A third issue raised by the parable of Robinson and Friday is that an intimate relationship exists between a trade deficit and international borrowing, and between a trade surplus and international lending. The size of Friday's trade surplus is exactly how much he is lending to Robinson. The size of Robinson's trade deficit is exactly how much he is borrowing from Friday. Indeed, to economists, a trade surplus literally means the same thing as an outflow of financial capital, and a trade deficit literally means the same thing as an inflow of financial capital. This last insight is worth exploring in greater detail.

The Balance of Trade as the Balance of Payments

The connection between trade balances and international flows of financial capital is so close that the balance of trade is sometimes described as the "balance of payments." Each category of the current account balance involves a corresponding flow of payments between a given country and the rest of the world economy.

Exhibit 11-4 shows with a circular flow diagram how flows of goods and services are counterbalanced by flows of payments back and forth between one country—the United States in this example—and the rest of the world. The top line shows U.S. exports of goods and services, with the second line showing that these exports involve financial payments flowing from purchasers in other countries back to the U.S. economy. The third line then shows imports of U.S. imports of goods, services, and investment capital, the fourth line showing a counterbalancing flow of payments leaving the home economy and headed to the rest of the world. The bottom four lines of Exhibit 11-4 show flows of financial investment running to and from the home country to the rest of the world, and then rates of return and repayments for these financial investments running in the other direction. Unilateral transfers aren't shown in this exhibit, but they shouldn't be forgotten.

If the current account balance is equal to zero, then the financial payments flowing in and out of the country will also be equal. Since inflows and outflows of international payments match in a country with a trade balance of zero, such a country is not an overall or a net investor in other countries.

A current account trade deficit means that, after taking all the flows of payments from goods, services, and income together, a larger flow of payments has left a nation's economy than has entered it. So a logical question arises—what happened to those extra payments? The answer is that a trade deficit represents an overall or net inflow of financial investment capital arriving from foreign investors. Indeed, a deficit in the current account balance is exactly equal to the overall or net inflow of foreign capital from abroad. Conversely, if the current account balance is positive, then the flow of payments out of a country must be larger than the flow of payments into a country. Just like the parable of Robinson and Friday, the lesson is that a trade surplus means an overall outflow of financial investment capital, as domestic investors put their funds abroad, while the deficit in the current account balance is exactly equal to the overall or net inflow of foreign investment capital from abroad.

It's important to recognize that an inflow and outflow of foreign capital does not necessarily refer to a debt that governments owe to other governments, although government debt may be part of the picture. Instead, these international flows of financial capital refer to all of the ways in which private investors in one country may invest in another country, by buying real estate, companies, and financial investments like stocks and bonds. The international flow of financial capital is not so much one large tide of payments as it is a million different rivers and streams all flowing in different directions.

The National Saving and Investment Identity

The close connection between trade balances and international flows of savings and investments leads to the macroeconomic way of thinking about trade balances. This approach views trade balances—and their associated flows of financial capital—in the context of the overall levels of savings and financial investment in the economy.

The National Saving and Investment Identity

An "identity" is a term lifted from mathematics that refers to a statement which is always true, by definition. For example, the statement that GDP = C + I + G + X – M is an identity, because it is true according to the definition of GDP. The **national saving and investment identity** provides a useful way to understand the determinants of the trade balance. In a nation's financial capital market, the quantity of financial capital supplied at any given time must equal the quantity of capital financial demanded for purposes of making investments.

There are two main sources for the supply of capital in the U.S. economy: saving by individuals and firms, called S, and the inflow of financial capital from foreign investors, which is equal to the trade deficit M – X, or imports minus exports. There are also two main sources of demand for financial capital in the U.S. economy: private sector investment, I, and government borrowing, where the government needs to borrow when government spending, G, is higher than the taxes collected, T. This national savings and investment identity can be expressed in algebraic terms:

national saving and investment identity: For any country, the quantity of financial capital supplied at any given time by savings must equal the quantity of financial capital demanded for purposes of making investments.

Supply of financial capital = Demand for financial capital

$$S + (M - X) = I + (G - T)$$

Again, in this equation, S is private savings, T is taxes, G is government spending, M is imports, X is exports, and I is investment. This relationship is true as a matter of definition, because for the macroeconomy, the quantity supplied of financial capital must be equal to the quantity demanded.

However, certain components of the national savings and investment identity can switch between the supply side and the demand side. Some countries, like the United States in most years since the 1970s, have budget deficits, which mean the amount that government is spending more than it collects in taxes, and so the government needs to borrow funds. In this case, the government term would be G–T, showing that spending is larger than taxes, and the government would be a demander of financial capital on the left-hand side of the equation (that is, a borrower), not a supplier of financial capital on the right-hand side. However, if the government runs a budget surplus so that the taxes exceed spending, as the U.S. government did from 1998 to 2001, then the government is in that year contributing to the supply of financial capital, and (T – G) would appear on the saving side of the national savings and investment identity.

Similarly, if a national economy runs a trade surplus, then instead of the trade sector providing an inflow and supply of financial capital, as it does for an economy with a trade deficit, the trade sector will involve an outflow of financial capital to other countries. A trade surplus means that the domestic financial capital is being demanded from within a country to be invested in other countries. When a trade surplus exists, X – M would move to "demand for financial capital" side of the national savings and investment identity.

Clearly, the national saving and investment identity must be thought through anew each time it is written out. The fundamental notion that total quantity of financial capital demanded equals total quantity of financial capital supplied must always remain true. Domestic savings will always appear as part of the supply of financial capital and domestic investment will always appear as part of the demand for financial capital. However, the government and trade balance elements of the equation can move back and forth as either suppliers or demanders of financial capital, depending on whether government budgets and the trade balance are in surplus or deficit.

Domestic Saving and Investment Determine the Trade Balance

One insight from the national saving and investment identity is that a nation's balance of trade is determined by that nation's own levels of domestic saving and domestic investment. To understand this point, rearrange the identity to put the balance of trade all by itself on one side of the equation. Consider first the situation with a trade deficit, and then the situation with a trade surplus.

In the case of a trade deficit, the national savings and investment identity can be rewritten as:

Trade deficit = Domestic investment – Private domestic savings – Government savings

$$(M - X) = I - S - (T - G)$$

In this case, domestic investment is higher than domestic savings, including both private and government savings. The only way that domestic investment can exceed domestic savings is if capital is flowing into a country from abroad. After all, that extra financial capital for investment has to come from someplace.

Now consider a trade *surplus* from the standpoint of the national savings and investment identity:

Trade surplus = Private domestic saving + Public saving – Domestic investment

$$X - M = S + (G - T) - I$$

In this case, the trade surplus is a situation where domestic savings (both private and public) is higher than domestic investment. That extra financial capital needs to go someplace, and if it is not being used in the domestic economy, then it must be flowing out to the rest of the world economy.

This connection from domestic savings and investment to the trade balance explains why economists view the balance of trade as a fundamentally macroeconomic phenomenon. As the national saving and investment identity shows, the trade balance isn't determined by the performance of certain sectors of an economy, like cars or steel. Nor is the trade balance determined by whether the nation's trade laws and regulations encourage free trade or protectionism.

Exploring Trade Balances One Factor at a Time

The national saving and investment identity also provides a framework for thinking about what will cause trade deficits to rise or fall. Begin with the version of the identity that has domestic savings and investment on the left and the trade deficit on the right:

Domestic investment – Private domestic savings – Public domestic savings = Trade deficit

$$I - S - (T - G) = (M - X)$$

Now consider the factors on the left-hand side of the equation one at a time, while holding the other factors constant.

As a first example, assume that the level of domestic investment in a country rises, while the level of private and public saving remains unchanged. The result is shown in the first row of Exhibit 11-5 under the equation. Since the equality of the national savings and investment identity must continue to hold—it is, after all, an identity that must be true by definition—the rise in domestic investment will mean a higher trade

Domestic Investment	–	Private Domestic Savings	–	Public Domestic Savings	=	Trade Deficit
I	–	S	–	(T – G)	=	(M – X)
Up		No change		No change		Then M – X must rise
No change		Down		No change		Then M – X must rise
No change		No change		Down		Then M – X must rise

Exhibit 11-5   Causes of a Changing Trade Balance

deficit. This situation occurred in the U.S. economy in the late 1990s. Because of the surge of new information and communications technologies that became available, business investment increased substantially. A fall in private savings during this time and a rise in government saving more-or-less offset each other. As a result, the financial capital to fund that business investment came from abroad, which is one reason for the very high U.S. trade deficits of the late 1990s and early 2000s.

As a second scenario, assume that the level of domestic savings rises, while the level of domestic investment and private saving remains unchanged. In this case, the trade deficit would decline. As domestic saving rises, there would be less need for foreign financial capital to meet investment needs. For this reason, a policy proposal often made for reducing the U.S. trade deficit is to increase private savings—although exactly how to increase the overall rate of savings has proven controversial.

As a third scenario, imagine that the government budget deficit increased dramatically, while domestic investment and private savings remained unchanged. This scenario occurred in the U.S. economy in the mid-1980s. The federal budget deficit increased from $79 billion in 1981 to $221 billion in 1986—an increase in the demand for financial capital of $142 billion. The current account balance collapsed from a surplus of $5 billion in 1981 to a deficit of $147 million in 1986—an increase in the supply of financial capital from abroad of $152 billion. The two numbers don't match exactly, since in the real world, private savings and investment didn't remain fixed. But the connection at that time is clear: a sharp increase in government borrowing increased the U.S. economy's demand for financial capital, and that increase was primarily supplied by foreign investors through the trade deficit.

How Short-Term Movements in the Business Cycle Can Affect the Trade Balance

In the short run, trade imbalances can be affected by whether an economy is in a recession or an upswing. A recession tends to make a trade deficit smaller, or a trade surplus larger, while a period of strong economic growth tends to make a trade deficit larger, or a trade surplus smaller.

As an example, notice that the U.S. trade deficit declined by almost half from 2006 to 2009. One primary reason for this change is that during the recession, as the U.S. economy slowed down, it purchased fewer of all goods, including fewer imports from abroad. However, buying power abroad was less by the U.S. recession, and so U.S. exports didn't fall by as much.

Conversely, in the mid-2000s, when the U.S. trade deficit became very large, a contributing short-term reason is that the U.S. economy was growing. As a result, there was lots of aggressive buying in the U.S. economy, including the buying of imports. Thus, a rapidly growing domestic economy is often accompanied by a trade deficit (or a much lower trade surplus), while a slowing or recessionary domestic economy is accompanied by a trade surplus (or a much lower trade deficit).

When the trade deficit rises, it necessarily means a greater net inflow of foreign financial capital. The national saving and investment identity teaches that the rest of the economy can absorb this inflow of foreign financial capital in several different ways. For example, the additional inflow of financial capital from abroad could be offset by reduced private savings, leaving domestic investment and public saving unchanged. Alternatively, the inflow of foreign financial capital could result in higher domestic investment, leaving private and public savings unchanged. Yet another possibility is that the inflow of foreign financial capital could be absorbed by greater government borrowing, leaving domestic saving and investment unchanged. The national saving and investment identity doesn't specify which of these scenarios, alone or in combination, will occur—only that one of them must occur.

When Are Trade Deficits and Surpluses Beneficial or Harmful?

Because flows of trade always involve flows of financial payments, flows of international trade are actually the same subject as flows of international financial capital. The question of whether trade deficits or surpluses are good or bad for an economy is, in economic terms, exactly the same question as whether it is a good idea for an economy to rely on net inflows of financial capital from abroad or to make net investments of financial capital abroad. Conventional wisdom often holds borrowing money is foolhardy, and that a prudent country, like a prudent person, should always rely on its own resources. But while it is certainly possible to borrow too much—as anyone with an overloaded credit card can testify—borrowing at certain times can also make sound economic sense. For both individuals and countries, there is no economic merit in a policy of abstaining from participation in financial capital markets.

It makes economic sense to borrow when you are buying something with a long-run payoff; that is, when you are making an investment. For this reason, it can make economic sense to borrow for a college education, because the education will typically allow you to earn higher wages, and so to repay the loan and still come out ahead. It can also make sense for a business to borrow to purchase a machine that will last 10 years, as long as the machine will increase output and profits by more than enough to repay the loan. Similarly, it can make economic sense for a national economy to borrow from abroad, as long as the money is wisely invested in ways that will tend to raise the nation's economic growth over time. Then, it will be possible for the national economy to repay the borrowed money over time and still end up better off than before.

One vivid example of a country that borrowed heavily from abroad, invested wisely, and did perfectly well is the United States during the nineteenth century. The United States ran a trade deficit in 40 of the 45 years from 1831 to 1875, which meant that it was importing capital from abroad over that time. However, that financial capital was by and large invested in projects like railroads that brought a substantial economic payoff. A more recent example along these lines is the experience of South Korea, which had trade deficits during much of the 1970s—and thus was an importer of capital over that time. However, South Korea also had high rates of investment in physical plant and equipment, and its economy grew rapidly. From the mid-1980s into the mid-1990s, South Korea often had trade surpluses—that is, it was repaying its past borrowing by sending capital abroad.

On the other side, some countries have run large trade deficits, borrowed heavily in global capital markets, and ended up in all kinds of trouble. Two sorts of trouble are worth examining.

First, a borrower nation can find itself in a bind if the incoming funds from abroad are not invested in a way that leads to increased productivity. Several of the large economies of Latin America, including Mexico and Brazil, ran large trade deficits and borrowed heavily from abroad in the 1970s, but the inflow of financial capital did not boost productivity sufficiently, which meant that these countries faced enormous

---

Are Trade Deficits Always Harmful?
The Case of Nineteenth-Century America

For most years of the nineteenth century, U.S. imports exceeded exports and the U.S. economy had a trade deficit. Yet the string of trade deficits didn't hold back the U.S. economy at all; instead, the trade deficits mildly contributed to the strong economic growth that gave the U.S. economy the highest per capita GDP in the world by around 1900.

The U.S. trade deficits meant that the U.S. economy was receiving a net inflow of foreign capital from abroad. Much of that foreign capital flowed into two areas of investment— railroads and public infrastructure like roads,

water systems, and schools—which were important to helping the growth of the U.S. economy.

The effect of foreign investment capital on assisting the U.S. economy shouldn't be overstated. In most years the foreign financial capital represented no more than 6–10% of the funds used for overall physical investment in the U.S. economy. Nonetheless, the U.S. trade deficit and the accompanying investment funds from abroad were clearly a help, not a hindrance, to the U.S. economy in the nineteenth century.

---

troubles in repaying when economic conditions shifted during the 1980s. Similarly, it appears that a number of African nations that borrowed foreign funds in the 1970s and 1980s did not invest in productive economic assets. As a result, several of those countries later faced large interest payments, with no economic growth to show for the borrowed funds.

A second problem is what happens if the foreign money flows in—and then suddenly flows out again. This scenario was raised at the start of this chapter. In the mid 1990s, a number of countries in East Asia—Thailand, Indonesia, Malaysia, and South Korea— ran large trade deficits and imported capital from abroad. However, in 1997 and 1998 many foreign investors became concerned about the health of these economies, and fled for the exits. The extremely rapid departure of that foreign capital staggered the banking systems and economies of these countries, plunging them into deep recession. We will investigate and discuss the links between international capital flows, banks, and recession in Chapter 17.

Nor is there any guarantee that running a trade surplus will bring robust economic health. For example, Germany and Japan ran substantial trade surpluses for most of the last three decades. But regardless of their persistent trade surpluses, both countries have nonetheless experienced occasional recessions and neither country has had especially robust annual growth in recent decades.

The sheer size and persistence of the U.S. trade deficits and inflows of foreign capital since the 1980s are a legitimate cause for concern. The huge U.S. economy will not be destabilized by an outflow of international capital as easily as say the comparatively tiny economies of Thailand and Indonesia were in 1997–1998. But even an economy that is not knocked down can still be shaken. American policymakers should certainly be paying attention to those cases where a pattern of extensive and sustained current account deficits and foreign borrowing has gone badly—if only as a precautionary measure.

The Difference between Level of Trade and the Trade Balance

A nation's *level* of trade may at first sound like much the same issue as the *balance* of trade, but these two issues are actually quite separate. It is perfectly possible for a country

Are Trade Surpluses Always Beneficial? Japan since the 1990s

Perhaps no economy around the world is better-known for its trade surpluses than Japan. Since 1990, the size of these surpluses has often been near $100 billion per year. When Japan's economy was growing vigorously in the 1960s and 1970s, its large trade surpluses were often described, especially by non-economists, as either a cause or a result of its robust economic health.

But from a standpoint of economic growth, Japan's economy has been teetering in and out of recession since 1990, with real GDP growth averaging only about 1% per year since the early 1990s, and an unemployment rate that has been creeping higher. Clearly, a whopping trade surplus is no guarantee of economic good health.

Instead, Japan's trade surplus reflects that Japan has a very high rate of domestic savings, more than the Japanese economy can invest domestically, and so the extra funds are invested abroad. In Japan's slow economy, the growth of consumption is relatively low, which also means that consumption of imports is relatively low. Thus, Japan's exports continually exceed its imports, leaving the trade surplus continually high.

to have a very high level of trade—say, measured by its exports of goods and services as a share of its GDP—while it also has a near-balance between exports and imports. It is also possible for a country's trade to be a relatively low share of GDP, relative to global averages, but for the imbalance between its exports and its imports to be quite large. This general theme was emphasized earlier in Exhibit 11-3, which offered some illustrative figures on trade levels and balances.

Three factors strongly influence a nation's level of trade: the size of its economy, its geographic location, and its history of trade. Large economies like the United States can do much of their trading internally, while small economies like Sweden have less ability to provide what they want internally and thus tend to have higher ratios of exports and imports to GDP. Nations that are geographically nearby tend to trade more, since costs of transportation and communication are lower. Moreover, some nations have long and established patterns of international trade, while others do not. Thus, a relatively small economy like Sweden, with many nearby trading partners across Europe and a long history of foreign trade, has a high level of trade. Brazil and India, which are fairly large economies that have often sought to inhibit trade in recent decades, have lower levels of trade. The United States and Japan are extremely large economies that have comparatively few nearby trading partners. Both countries actually have quite low levels of trade by world standards. The ratio of exports to GDP in either the United States or in Japan is about half of the world average.

The balance of trade is a separate issue from the level of trade. The United States has is a low level of trade, but had enormous trade deficits for most years from the mid 1980s into the 2000s. Japan has a low level of trade by world standards, but has typically shown large trade surpluses in recent decades. Nations like Germany and the United Kingdom have medium to high levels of trade by world standards, but Germany had a moderate trade surplus in 2008 while the United Kingdom had a moderate trade deficit. Their trade picture was roughly in balance in the late 1990s. Sweden had a high level of trade and a large trade surplus in 2007, while Mexico had a high level of trade and a moderate trade deficit that same year.

In short, it is quite possible for nations with a relatively low level of trade, expressed as a percentage of GDP, to have relatively large trade deficits. It is also quite possible for nations with a near balance between exports and imports to worry about the consequences of high levels of trade for the economy. There is no inconsistency in believing that a high level of trade is potentially beneficial to an economy, because of

> ## Are Trade Surpluses Always Beneficial? The Case of Colonial India
>
> India was formally under British rule from 1858 to 1947. During that time, India consistently had trade surpluses with Great Britain, typically equal to 1–2% of India's GDP per year. Anyone who believes that trade surpluses are a sign of economic strength and dominance while trade deficits are a sign of economic weakness must find this pattern odd, since it would mean that colonial India was successfully dominating and exploiting Great Britain for almost a century—which seems highly unlikely.
>
> Instead, India's trade surpluses with Great Britain meant that each year, there was an overall flow of financial capital from India to Great Britain. In India, this flow of financial capital was heavily criticized as the "drain," and eliminating the drain of financial capital was viewed as one of the many reasons why colonial India would benefit from achieving independence from Great Britain. Of course, if Britain's colonial rule over India had involved a net flow of financial capital from Britain to India, then India would have experienced a string of trade deficits.

the way it allow nations to play to their comparative advantages, but at the same time in being concerned about macroeconomic instability that might be caused by a long-term pattern of unwisely large trade deficits.

Final Thoughts about Trade Balances

Trade deficits can be a good or a bad sign for an economy, and trade surpluses can be a good or a bad sign. Even a trade balance of zero—which just means that a nation is neither a net borrower nor lender in the international economy—can be either a good or bad sign. The fundamental economic question is not whether a nation's economy is borrowing or lending at all, but whether the particular borrowing or lending in the particular economic conditions of that country makes sense.

It's interesting to reflect on how public attitudes toward trade deficits and surpluses might change if we could somehow change the labels that people and the news media affix to these occurrences. If a trade deficit was called "attracting foreign financial capital"—which accurately describes what a trade deficit means—then trade deficits might look more pleasant. Conversely, if a trade surplus were called "shipping financial capital abroad"—which accurately captures what a trade surplus does—then trade surpluses might look less attractive. Either way, the key to understanding trade balances is to understand the relationships between flows of trade and flows of international payments, and what these relationships imply about the causes, benefits and risks of different kinds of trade balances. The first step along this journey of understanding is to move beyond knee-jerk reactions to terms like "trade surplus," "trade balance," and "trade deficit."

Key Concepts and Summary

1. A nation has a **trade surplus** if **exports** exceed **imports,** and a **trade deficit** if imports exceed exports.

2. The **merchandise trade balance** measures only imports and exports of goods. The **current account balance** includes trade in goods, services, payments on foreign investments, and unilateral transfers.

3. The U.S. economy ran modest current account trade surpluses for most years from the 1950s to the 1970s. It developed large trade surpluses in the early 1980s, swung back to a tiny trade surplus in 1991, and then had even larger trade deficits in the late 1990s and early 2000s.

4. A trade deficit necessarily means a net inflow of financial capital from abroad, while a trade surplus necessarily means a net outflow of financial capital from an economy to other countries.

5. The **national saving and investment identity** is based on the relationship that the total quantity of financial capital supplied from all sources must equal the total quantity of financial capital demanded from all sources. If S is private saving, T is taxes, G is government spending, M is imports, X is exports, and I is investment, then for an economy with a current account deficit and a budget deficit:

$$\text{Supply of financial capital} = \text{Demand for financial capital}$$

$$S + (M - X) = I + (T - G)$$

6. A recession tends to increase the trade balance (meaning a higher trade surplus or lower trade deficit), while economic boom will tend to decrease the trade balance (meaning a lower trade surplus or a larger trade deficit).

7. Trade surpluses are no guarantee of economic health, and trade deficits are no guarantee of economic weakness. Either trade deficits or trade surpluses can work out well or poorly, depending on whether the corresponding flows of financial capital are wisely invested.

8. Small economies which have nearby trading partners and a history of international trade will tend to have higher levels of trade. Larger economies with few nearby trading partners and a limited history of international trade will tend to have lower levels of trade.

9. The level of trade, where trade is expressed as a share of GDP, is different from the trade balance. Nations with high levels of trade can have small trade imbalances, while nations with lower levels of trade can have larger trade imbalances.

Review Questions

1. If imports exceed exports, is it a trade deficit or a trade surplus? What about if exports exceed imports?

2. What is included in the current account balance?

3. In recent decades, has the U.S. trade balance usually been in deficit, surplus, or near balance?

4. Does a trade surplus mean an overall inflow of financial capital to an economy, or an overall outflow of financial capital? What about a trade deficit?

5. What are the two main sides of the national savings and investment identity?

6. What are the main components of the national savings and investment identity?

7. What determines whether the trade balance and the government budget will represent supply of financial capital or demand for financial capital?

8. Will the trade deficit tend to be higher or lower in a recession? What about during an economic upswing?

9. When is a trade deficit likely to work out well for an economy? When is it likely to work out poorly?

10. Does a trade surplus help to guarantee strong economic growth?

11. What three factors will determine whether a nation has a higher or lower share of trade relative to its GDP?

12. Will nations that are more involved in foreign trade tend to have higher trade imbalances, lower trade imbalances, or is the pattern unpredictable?

12

The Aggregate Supply–Aggregate Demand Model

Having goals is helpful when they provide a sense of direction. However, having four separate goals can cause confusion, if it is impossible to reach all of the goals at the same time. For example, it is impossible to accomplish simultaneously the four goals of being in Los Angeles, London, Beijing, and Rio de Janeiro. But if the four goals are to visit the Statue of Liberty, the Empire State Building, the New York Stock Exchange, and a Broadway show, then all four goals can be accomplished with a single trip to New York City. Are the four goals of macroeconomics—growth, low unemployment, low inflation, and a sustainable balance of trade—like trying to visit four different cities, in the sense that it is impossible to achieve all four at the same time? Or is it possible for an economy to attain (at least roughly) several or all of its macroeconomic goals at the same time?

U.S. economic experience during the last decade or so hints that some macroeconomic goals can be accomplished together, while others may involve trade-offs. The years from 1997 to 1999 were a golden time for economic growth, as annual increases in real GDP exceeded 4% per year. Then the economy sagged into recession for eight months in 2001, with real GDP growth for that year as a whole at only 0.8%, followed by sluggish growth of 1.6% in 2002. Real GDP growth then rebounded, rising at about 3% per year from 2004–2006. But real GDP growth then slowed starting in 2007, and was near-zero in 2008 and *negative* 2.4 % in 2009. The unemployment rate, which had been as high as 7.5% at the tail end of the recession in 1992, fell all the way to 4.0% by 2000. It rose to 6.0% by 2003, then sunk back to 4.6% by 2007, and climbed to 9.3% in 2009. Inflation as measured by the Consumer Price Index stayed low, although it edged up a little from 1.6% in 1998 to 3.4% in 2000. After the 2001 recession, inflation fell back to 1.6% in 2002. By 2005, inflation had again crept up to about 3% per year, where it stayed until 2008, before suddenly dropping to *negative* 0.4% in 2009. The current account deficit nearly tripled from

$140 billion in 1997 to $415 billion in 2000, and then almost doubled again to more than $800 billion in 2006, before falling to $420 billion in 2009.

Macroeconomic analysis inquires into the patterns of these macroeconomic goals and the connections between them. How is the rate of economic growth connected to rises and falls in the unemployment rate? Is there a reason why unemployment and inflation seem to move in opposite directions: lower unemployment and higher inflation from 1997 to 2000, higher unemployment and lower inflation in the early 2000s, lower unemployment and higher inflation in the mid 2000s, and then higher unemployment and lower inflation in 2009? Why did the current account deficit rise so high, but then decline in 2009?

To analyze questions like these, we must move beyond discussing the four macroeconomic goals one at a time, and begin building economic models that will capture the relationships and interconnections between them. The next three chapters take up this task. This chapter introduces the macroeconomic model of aggregate supply and aggregate demand, how they reach a macroeconomic equilibrium, and how shifts in aggregate demand or aggregate supply will affect that equilibrium. It also relates the model of aggregate supply and aggregate demand to the four goals of economic growth, low unemployment, low inflation, and a sustainable balance of trade, thus offering a framework for thinking about many of the connections and trade-offs between these goals. Chapter 13 will then discuss this model with an emphasis on the short run in which aggregate demand plays a crucial role, while Chapter 14 will discuss the model with an emphasis on the long run in which aggregate supply plays a crucial role.

Macroeconomic Perspectives on Demand and Supply

The gross domestic product (GDP), which is the sum of the values of all final goods and services produced in the economy, can be measured in several ways, as discussed in Chapter 7. One approach looked at what final goods and services were supplied in the economy, and divided them up into durable and nondurable goods, services, and construction (with an adjustment for inventories that build up or decline each year). An alternative method measured GDP through the five components of demand for these goods and services: consumption, investment, government, exports, and imports. The total amount demanded must equal the total amount supplied, because nothing can be sold unless something is being bought at the same time. However, macroeconomists over the last two centuries have often divided into two groups: those who argued that supply was the most important determinant of the size of the macroeconomy, while demand just tagged along, and those who argued that demand was the most important factor in the size of the macroeconomy, while supply just tagged along.

Say's Law and the Macroeconomics of Supply

Those economists who emphasize the role of supply in the macroeconomy often refer to the work of a famous French economist of the early nineteenth century named Jean-Baptiste Say (1767–1832). **Say's Law** is: "Supply creates its own demand." As a matter of historical accuracy, it seems clear that Say never actually wrote down this law and that the law oversimplifies his beliefs, but the law lives on as a useful shorthand for summarizing a point of view.

Say's Law: "Supply creates its own demand."

The intuition behind Say's Law is that each time a good or service is produced and sold, it represents income that is earned for someone: a worker, a manager, an owner, or those who are workers, managers, and owners at firms that supply inputs down the chain of production. The forces of supply and demand in individual markets will cause prices to rise and fall. But the bottom line remains that every sale represents income to someone, and so, Say's Law argues, a given value of supply must create an equivalent value of demand somewhere else in the economy. Because Jean-Baptiste Say, Adam Smith, and other economists writing around the turn of the nineteenth century who discussed this view were known as "classical" economists, modern economists who generally subscribe to the Say's law view on the importance of supply for determining the size of the macroeconomy are called **neoclassical economists.**

But if supply always creates exactly enough demand at the macroeconomic level, then (as Say himself recognized) it's hard to understand why periods of recession and high unemployment should ever occur. To be sure, even if total supply always creates an equal amount of total demand, the economy could still experience a situation of some firms earning profits while other firms suffer losses. Nevertheless, a recession is not a situation where all business failures are exactly counterbalanced by an offsetting number of successes. A recession is a situation in which the economy as a whole is shrinking in size, business failures outnumber the remaining success stories, and many firms end up suffering losses and laying off workers.

Say's law that supply creates its own demand does seem a good approximation for the long run of the economy. Over periods of some years or decades, as the productive power of an economy to supply goods and services increases, total demand in the economy grows as well at roughly the same pace. However, over shorter time horizons of a few months or even years, recessions or even depressions occur in which firms, as a group, seem to face a lack of demand for their products.

Keynes' Law and the Macroeconomics of Demand

The alternative to Say's Law, with its emphasis on supply, can be named **Keynes' Law:** "Demand creates its own supply." As a matter of historical accuracy, just as Jean-Baptiste Say never wrote down anything as simpleminded as Say's Law, John Maynard Keynes never wrote down Keynes' Law, but the law is a useful simplification that conveys a certain point of view.

When Keynes was writing his great work *The General Theory of Employment, Interest, and Money* during the Great Depression of the 1930s, he pointed out that during the Depression, the capacity of the economy to supply goods and services had not changed much. U.S. unemployment rates soared higher than 20% from 1933–35, but the number of possible workers had not increased or decreased much. Factories were closed and shuttered, but machinery and equipment had not disappeared. Technologies that had been invented in the 1920s were not disinvented and forgotten in the 1930s. Thus, Keynes argued that the Great Depression—and many ordinary recessions as well—were not caused by a drop in the ability of the economy to supply goods as measured by labor, physical capital, or technology. Keynes argued the economy often produced less than its full potential, not because it was technically impossible to produce more with the existing workers and machines, but because of a lack of demand for the economy as a whole led to inadequate incentives for firms to produce. In such cases, he argued the level of GDP in the economy was thus not primarily determined by the potential of what the economy could supply, but rather by the amount of total demand.

Keynes' Law seems to apply fairly well in the short run of a few months to a few years, when many firms experience either a drop in demand for their output during a recession or so much demand that they have trouble producing enough during an

neoclassical economists: Economists who generally emphasize the importance of aggregate supply in determining the size of the macroeconomy over the long run.

Keynes' Law: "Demand creates its own supply."

economic boom. However, demand cannot tell the whole macroeconomic story, either. After all, if demand was all that mattered at the macroeconomic level, then the government could make the economy as large as it wanted just by pumping up total demand through a large increase in the government spending (G) component or by legislating large tax cuts to push up the consumption (C) component. But economies do face genuine limits to how much they can produce, limits determined by the quantity of labor, physical capital, technology, and the institutional and market structures that bring these factors of production together. These constraints on what an economy can supply at the macroeconomic level do not disappear just because of an increase in demand.

Combining Supply and Demand in Macroeconomics

Two insights emerge from this overview of Say's Law with its emphasis on macroeconomic supply and Keynes' Law with its emphasis on macroeconomic demand. The first conclusion, which is not exactly a hot news flash, is that an economic approach that focuses only on the supply side or only on the demand side can only be a partial success. Both supply and demand need to be taken into account. The second conclusion is that since Keynes' law applies more accurately in the short run and Say's law applies more accurately in the long run, the trade-offs and connections between the four goals of macroeconomics may be different in the short run and the long run.

Building a Model of Aggregate Supply and Aggregate Demand

The discussion of macroeconomic supply and demand to this point has focused on them as quantities; for example, in using them to measure GDP. However, to build a useful macroeconomic model, we need to build a model that shows what determines total supply or total demand for the economy, and how total demand and total supply interact at the macroeconomic level. This model is called the aggregate supply-aggregate demand model. This section will explain aggregate supply, aggregate demand, and the equilibrium between them. The following sections will discuss the causes of shifts in aggregate supply and aggregate demand.

The Aggregate Supply Curve and Potential GDP

Firms make decisions about what quantity to supply based on the profits that they expect to earn. Profits, in turn, are also determined by the price of the outputs that the firm sells and by the price of the inputs like labor or supplies that the firm needs to buy. The **aggregate supply (AS)** curve shows the total quantity that firms choose to produce and sell at each different price level for output.

aggregate supply (AS): The relationship between the total quantity that firms choose to produce and sell and the price level for output, holding the price of inputs fixed.

Exhibit 12-1 shows an aggregate supply curve. Let us walk through the elements of the diagram one at a time: the horizontal and vertical axes, the aggregate supply curve itself, and the meaning of the potential GDP vertical line.

The horizontal axis of the diagram shows real GDP—that is, the level of GDP adjusted for inflation. The vertical axis shows the price level. Remember that the price *level* is different from the inflation rate. Visualize the price level as an index number, like that measured by the Consumer Price Index or the GDP deflator, while the inflation rate is the percentage change between price levels over time.

Exhibit 12-1   The Aggregate Supply Curve

Aggregate supply (AS) slopes up, because as the price level for outputs increases, with the price of inputs remaining fixed, firms have an incentive to produce more and to earn higher profits. The potential GDP line shows the maximum that the economy can produce with full employment of workers and physical capital.

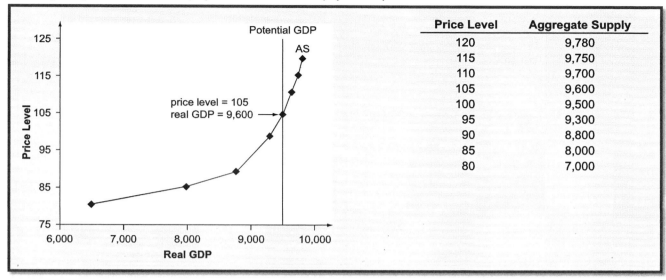

Price Level	Aggregate Supply
120	9,780
115	9,750
110	9,700
105	9,600
100	9,500
95	9,300
90	8,800
85	8,000
80	7,000

The accompanying table beside the exhibit gives an illustrative set of numbers that define the shape of an aggregate supply or AS curve. As the price level rises, the aggregate quantity of goods and services supplied rises as well. Why? The price level shown on the vertical axis represents prices for final goods or outputs bought in the economy—like the GDP deflator or the Consumer Price Index—not the price level for intermediate goods and services that are inputs to production. Thus, the AS curve describes how suppliers will react to a higher price level for final outputs of goods and services, *while holding the prices of inputs like labor and energy constant.* If firms across the economy face a situation where the price level of what they produce and sell is rising, but their costs of production are not rising, then the lure of higher profits will induce firms to expand production.

The slope of an AS curve changes from nearly flat at its far left to nearly vertical at its far right. At the far left of the aggregate supply curve, the level of output in the economy is far below **potential GDP,** which is defined as the maximum quantity that an economy can produce given its existing levels of labor, physical capital, and technology, in the context of its existing market and legal institutions. At these relatively low levels of output, levels of unemployment are high, and many factories are running only part-time, or have closed their doors. In this situation, a relatively small increase in the prices of the outputs that businesses sell—while making the ceteris paribus assumption of no rise in input prices—can encourage a considerable surge in the quantity of aggregate supply because so many workers and factories are ready to swing into production.

As the quantity produced increases, however, certain firms and industries will start running into limits: perhaps nearly all of the expert workers in a certain industry will have jobs, or factories in certain geographic areas or industries will be running at full speed. In the intermediate area of the AS curve, a higher price level for outputs continues to encourage a greater quantity—but as the increasingly steep upward slope

potential GDP: The maximum quantity that an economy can produce given its existing levels of labor, physical capital, technology, and institutions.

The aggregate supply curve is typically drawn to cross the potential GDP line. This shape may seem puzzling: How can an economy produce at an output level which is higher than its "potential" or "full employment" GDP? The economic intuition here is that if prices for outputs were high enough, producers would make fanatical efforts to produce: all workers would be on double-overtime, all machines would run 24 hours a day, seven days a week. Such hyper-intense production would go beyond using potential labor and physical capital resources fully, to using them in a way that is not sustainable in the long term. Thus, it is indeed possible for production to sprint above potential GDP, but only in the short run.

of the aggregate supply curve shows, the increase in quantity in response to a given rise in the price level won't be quite as large.

At the far right, the aggregate supply curve becomes nearly vertical. At this quantity, higher prices for outputs cannot encourage additional output, because even if firms desire to expand output, the inputs of labor and machinery in the economy are fully employed. In this example, the vertical line in the exhibit shows that potential GDP occurs at a total output of 9,500. When an economy is operating at its potential GDP, machines and factories are running at capacity, and the unemployment rate is relatively low at the natural rate of unemployment. For this reason, potential GDP is sometimes also called **full-employment GDP**.

The Aggregate Demand Curve

The total amount of demand in an economy is determined by a number of factors, but one of them is the price level of what is being purchased. The **aggregate demand (AD)** curve shows the total quantity of goods and services that will be demanded at each price level. The AD curve includes all five parts of demand: consumption, investment, government spending, exports, and imports.

Exhibit 12-2 presents an aggregate demand (AD) curve. Just like the aggregate supply curve, the horizontal axis shows real GDP and the vertical axis shows the price

full employment GDP:
Another name for potential GDP, when the economy is producing at its potential and unemployment is at the natural rate of unemployment.

aggregate demand (AD):
The relationship between the total quantity of goods and services and the price level for output.

Exhibit 12-2   The Aggregate Demand Curve

Aggregate demand (AD) slopes down, showing that as the price level rises, the quantity of aggregate demand declines.

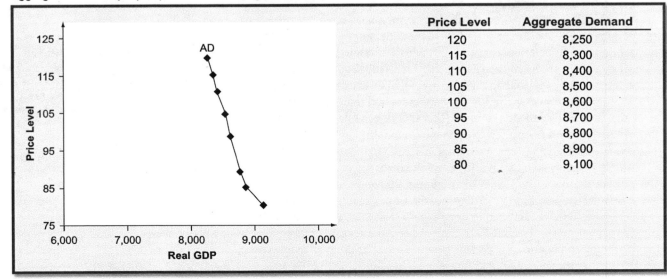

Price Level	Aggregate Demand
120	8,250
115	8,300
110	8,400
105	8,500
100	8,600
95	8,700
90	8,800
85	8,900
80	9,100

level. The AD curve slopes down, which means that increases in the price level of outputs lead to a lower quantity of aggregate demand. The reasons behind this shape are related to how changes in the price level affect the different components of aggregate demand: $C + I + G + X - M$.

The *wealth effect* holds that as the price level increases, the buying power of wealth that people have stored up in bank accounts and cash will diminish, eaten away to some extent by inflation. Because a rise in the price level reduces people's wealth, consumption will fall as the price level rises.

The *interest rate effect* is that as prices for outputs rise, it will be necessary for people making purchases to have more money or credit. This additional demand for money and credit will push interest rates higher. In turn, higher interest rates mean less borrowing by businesses for investment purposes and less borrowing by households for homes and cars—and thus a reduction in consumption and investment.

The *foreign price effect* points out that if prices rise in the United States while remaining fixed in other countries, then goods in the United States will be relatively more expensive compared to goods in the rest of the world. U.S. exports will be relatively more expensive, and the quantity of exports sold will fall. U.S. imports from abroad will be relatively cheaper, so the quantity of imports will rise. Thus, a higher domestic price level, relative to price levels in other countries, will be associated with a lower GDP.

Truth be told, all three of these effects are controversial among economists, in part because they do not seem to be very large. For this reason, the aggregate demand curve in Exhibit 12-2 slopes downward fairly steeply; the steep slope indicates that a higher price level for final outputs reduces aggregate demand for all three of these reasons, but that the change in the quantity of aggregate demand as a result of changes in price level is not very large.

Equilibrium in the Aggregate Supply-Aggregate Demand Model

The intersection of the aggregate supply and aggregate demand curves will determine equilibrium, which will involve with a combination of the real GDP and the price level in the economy. At a relatively low price level for output, firms have little incentive to produce, although consumers would be willing to demand a high quantity. As the price level for outputs rises, the quantity of aggregate supply rises and the quantity of aggregate demand falls until the equilibrium point is reached.

Exhibit 12-3 combines the AS curve from Exhibit 12-1 and the AD curve from Exhibit 12-2 and places them both on a single diagram. In this example, the equilibrium point occurs at point E, at a price level of 90 and an output level of 8,800. The equilibrium level can also be read off the table directly, even if there was no figure to look at; equilibrium is the price level where the real GDP of aggregate supply equals the real GDP of aggregate demand. In this example, the equilibrium point is below the level of potential GDP, which in this example is at an output of 9,600.

AS and AD Are Macro, not Micro

Confusion sometimes arises between the aggregate supply and aggregate demand model and the microeconomic analysis of demand and supply in particular markets for goods, services, labor, and capital. However, mixing up the macroeconomics of aggregate supply and aggregate demand with the microeconomics of individual markets leads only to confusion. These diagrams have a superficial resemblance, but they also have many underlying differences.

Exhibit 12-3   Aggregate Supply and Aggregate Demand

The equilibrium, where the quantity of aggregate supply (AS) and aggregate demand (AD) are equal, occurs at a price level of 90 and an output level of 8,800. In this example, the equilibrium occurs at a quantity of output that is below potential GDP.

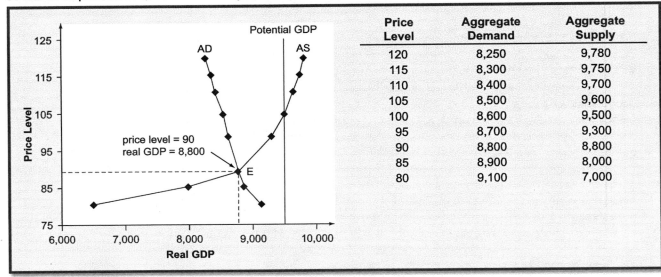

Price Level	Aggregate Demand	Aggregate Supply
120	8,250	9,780
115	8,300	9,750
110	8,400	9,700
105	8,500	9,600
100	8,600	9,500
95	8,700	9,300
90	8,800	8,800
85	8,900	8,000
80	9,100	7,000

For example, the vertical and horizontal axes have distinctly different meanings in macroeconomic and microeconomic diagrams. The vertical axis of a microeconomic demand and supply diagram expresses a price (or wage or rate of return) for an individual market. In contrast, the vertical axis of an aggregate supply and aggregate demand diagram expresses the level of a price index like the Consumer Price Index or the GDP deflator—combining a wide array of prices from across the economy. The horizontal axis of a microeconomic supply and demand curve measures the quantity of a particular good or service, or the quantity of labor or financial capital. In contrast, the horizontal axis of the aggregate demand and aggregate supply diagram measures GDP, which is the sum of all of the final goods and services produced in the economy, not the quantity in a specific market.

In addition, the economic reasons for the shapes of the curves in the macroeconomic model are different from the reasons behind the shapes of the curves in microeconomic models. Supply curves for markets for individual goods and services, for example, don't have any shape or level that represents full employment for an economy. Demand curves for individual goods or services slope down primarily because of the existence of substitute goods, not the wealth effects, interest rate, and foreign price effects associated with aggregate demand curves. The slopes of individual supply and demand curves can have a variety of different slopes, depending on the extent to which quantity demanded and quantity supplied react to price in that specific market, but the slopes of the AS and AD curves are much the same in every diagram (although as we shall see in later chapters, short-run and long-run perspectives will emphasize different parts of the AS curve).

In short, just because the AS-AD diagram has two lines that cross, do not assume that it is the same as every other diagram where two lines cross. The intuitions and meanings of the macro and micro diagrams are only distant cousins from different branches of the economics family tree.

Shifts in Aggregate Supply

The original equilibrium in the AS-AD diagram will shift to a new equilibrium if the AS or AD curve shifts. When the aggregate supply curve shifts to the right, then at every price level, a greater quantity is produced. When the AS curve shifts to the left, then at every price level, a lower quantity is produced. This section discusses two of the most important factors that can lead to shifts in the AS curve: productivity growth and input prices. The next section itemizes some factors that cause the AD curve to shift.

How Productivity Growth Shifts the AS Curve

In the long term, the most important factor shifting the AS curve is productivity growth. Historically, the real growth in per capita GDP in an advanced economy like the United States has averaged about 2–3% per year, but productivity growth has been faster during certain extended periods like the 1960s and the late 1990s and early 2000s, or slower during periods like the 1970s. A higher level of productivity shifts the AS curve to the right, because with improved productivity, firms can now produce a greater quantity at every given price level for output. Exhibit 12-4a shows an outward shift in productivity

Exhibit 12-4   Shifts in Aggregate Supply

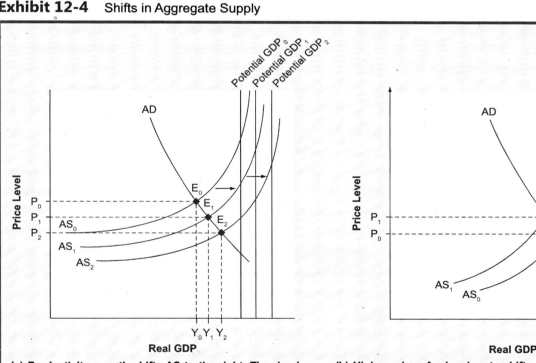

(a) Productivity growth shifts AS to the right. The rise in productivity causes the AS curve to shift to the right. The original equilibrium E_0 is at the intersection of AD and AS_0. When AS shifts right, then the new equilibrium E_1 is at the intersection of AD and AS_1, and then yet another equilibrium E_2 is at the intersection of AD and AS_2. Shifts in AS to the right lead to a greater level of output and to downward pressure on the price level.

(b) Higher prices for key inputs shifts AS to the left. A higher price for inputs means that at any given price level for outputs, a lower quantity will be produced so aggregate supply will shift to the left from AS_0 to AS_1. The new equilibrium E_1 has a reduced quantity of output and a higher price level than the original equilibrium E_0.

over two time periods. The AS curve shifts out from AS_0 to AS_1 to AS_2, reflecting the rise in potential GDP in this economy, and the equilibrium shifts from E_0 to E_1 to E_2.

A shift in the AS curve to the right will result in a greater quantity of macroeconomic output and downward pressure on the price level, if aggregate demand remains unchanged. However, if this shift in AS results from gains in productivity growth, which are typically measured in terms of a few percentage points per year, the effect will be relatively small over a few months or even a couple of years.

How Changes in Input Prices Shift the AS Curve

Higher prices for inputs that are widely used across the entire economy can have a macroeconomic impact on aggregate supply. Examples of such widely used inputs include wages and energy products. Increases in the price of such inputs will cause the AS curve shift to the left, which means that at each given price level for outputs, a higher price for inputs will discourage production because it will reduce the possibilities for earning profits. Exhibit 12-4*b* shows the aggregate supply curve shifting to the left from AS_0 to AS_1, causing the equilibrium to move from E_0 to E_1. The movement from the original equilibrium of E_0 to the new equilibrium of E_1 will bring a nasty set of effects: reduced GDP or recession, higher unemployment because the economy is now further away from potential GDP, and an inflationary higher price level as well. For example, the U.S. economy experienced recessions in 1974–75, 1980–82, and 1990–91, 2001, and 2007–2009 that were each preceded or accompanied by a rise in the key input of oil prices. In the 1970s, this pattern of a shift to the left in AS leading to a stagnant economy with high unemployment and inflation was nicknamed **stagflation.**

Conversely, a decline in the price of a key input like oil will shift the AS curve to the right, providing an incentive for more to be produced at every given price level for outputs. From 1985–86, for example, the average price of crude oil fell by almost half, from $24 a barrel to $12 a barrel. Similarly, from 1997–98, the price of a barrel of crude dropped from $17 per barrel to $11 per barrel. In both cases, the plummeting price of oil led to a situation like that presented earlier in Exhibit 12-4*a*, where the outward shift of AS to the right allowed the economy to expand, unemployment to fall, and inflation to decline.

Along with energy prices, two other key inputs that may shift the AS curve are the cost of labor, or wages, and the cost of imported goods that are used as inputs for other products. In these cases as well, the lesson is that lower prices for inputs cause AS to shift to the right, while higher prices cause it to shift back to the left.

stagflation: When an economy experiences stagnant growth and high inflation at the same time.

Shifts in Aggregate Demand

The components of aggregate demand spending are consumption (C), investment (I), government (G), and exports (X) minus imports (M). A shift of the AD curve to the right means that in at least one of these components of aggregate demand, a change occurred so that a greater quantity would be demanded at every price level. A shift of the AD curve to the left means that in at least one of these components of demand, a change occurred so that a lesser quantity would be demanded at every price level. The next chapter will discuss the components of aggregate demand and the factors that affect them one by one. Here, the discussion will sketch two broad categories that could cause AD curves to shift: changes in the behavior of consumers and firms, or changes in government tax and spending policy.

Oil Price Shocks and Recession

In the last three decades, the U.S. economy has experienced several recessions in which higher oil prices were one of the causes. In the 1973–75 recession, the members of the Organization of Petroleum Exporting Countries (OPEC), who produce much of the world's oil supply, acted together to reduce supply and raise the price of oil. The members of OPEC are Algeria, Libya, Nigeria, Indonesia, Iran, Iraq, Kuwait, Qatar, Saudi Arabia, United Arab Emirates, and Venezuela.

Just before the two back-to-back recessions from 1980–82, oil prices rose following hostilities between Iran and the United States, which significantly reduced the supply of oil.

In 1990, the supply of oil declined and prices rose after Iraq, under Saddam Hussein, invaded Kuwait, igniting a war, just before the recession of 1991–92.

In 1999, global demand for oil first plummeted and prices fell when economies in East Asia experienced a deep recession in 1997–98, and then demand for oil surged and prices increased when these economies recovered more quickly than expected, not too long before the recession of 2001.

In late 2007 and the first half of 2008, oil prices surged when world demand especially in China continued to increase rapidly, and several oil exporting countries suffered production setbacks, just as the recession that started in 2007 was gaining force.

In all five cases, the rise in the price of oil—a key imported economic input—contributed to a shift of the AS curve to the left. The table offers some illustrative data. Each recession is different, of course, and oil prices are only one of the factors at work. But the common pattern of higher oil prices, recession, higher unemployment, and (often but not always) higher inflation is unmistakable.

Date of Recessions	Change in Real Price of Crude Oil per Barrel	Unemployment Rate	Inflation Rate
November 1973 to March 1975	Up 62% from 1973–1974	4.9% in 1973; 8.5% in 1975	3.2% in 1973; 11% in 1974
January 1980 to July 1980 and July 1981 to November 1982	Up 173% from 1978–1981	5.9% in 1979; 9.7% in 1982	6.5% in 1977; 13.5% in 1980
July 1990 to March 1991	Up 48% from 1988–1990	5.3% in 1989; 7.5% in 1992	1.9% in 1986; 5.4% in 1990
March 2001 to November 2001	Up 137% from 1998–2000	4.0% in 2000; 5.8% in 2002	1.6% in 1998; 3.4% in 2000
December 2007 to June 2009	Up 125% from 2007–2008	4.6% in 2007; 9.3% in 2009	2.8% in 2007; −0.4% in 2009

How Changes by Consumers and Firms Can Affect AD

When consumers feel more confident about the future of the economy, they tend to consume more. If business confidence is high, then firms tend to invest more, believing that the future payoff to those investments will be substantial. Conversely, if consumer or business confidence drops, then consumption and investment decline.

The Conference Board, a business-funded research organization, carries out national surveys of consumers and executives to gauge their degree of optimism about the near-term future economy. The Conference Board asks a number of questions about how consumers and business executives perceive the economy and then combines the answers into an overall measure of confidence, rather like creating an index number to represent the price level from a variety of individual prices. For consumer confidence, the overall level of confidence in 1985 is used as a base year and set equal to 100, and confidence in every other year can be compared to that base year. Measured on this scale, for example, consumer confidence rose from 100 in August 2006 to 111 in February 2007, but had plummeted to 56 by early 2010. Business confidence is measured on a scale from 0 to 100, so that a score of 50 represents a neutral view, 100 would represent extreme confidence, and 0 would represent an extreme lack of confidence. Business confidence sunk from 57 in the first quarter of 2006 to 44 in the third quarter

Exhibit 12-5   Shifts in Aggregate Demand

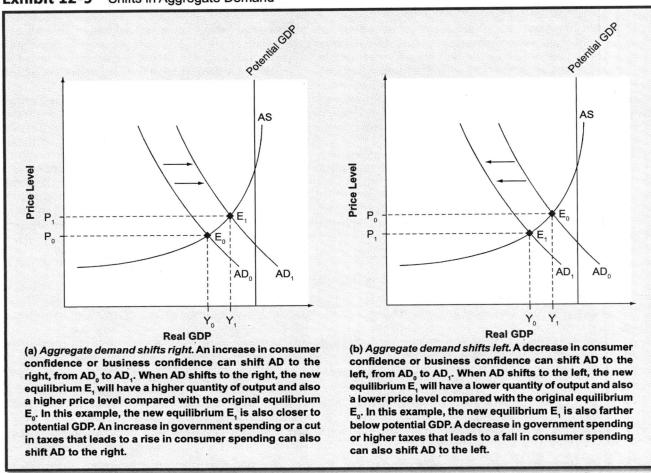

(a) *Aggregate demand shifts right.* An increase in consumer confidence or business confidence can shift AD to the right, from AD_0 to AD_1. When AD shifts to the right, the new equilibrium E_1 will have a higher quantity of output and also a higher price level compared with the original equilibrium E_0. In this example, the new equilibrium E_1 is also closer to potential GDP. An increase in government spending or a cut in taxes that leads to a rise in consumer spending can also shift AD to the right.

(b) *Aggregate demand shifts left.* A decrease in consumer confidence or business confidence can shift AD to the left, from AD_0 to AD_1. When AD shifts to the left, the new equilibrium E_1 will have a lower quantity of output and also a lower price level compared with the original equilibrium E_0. In this example, the new equilibrium E_1 is also farther below potential GDP. A decrease in government spending or higher taxes that leads to a fall in consumer spending can also shift AD to the left.

of 2006 before rebounding to 53 in the first quarter of 2007. It sunk as low as 35 in early 2009 before bouncing back to 58 by early 2010. Such survey measures are of course imprecise. But they can suggest when confidence is rising or falling, or relatively high or low compared to the past.

Because a rise in confidence is associated with higher consumption and investment demand, it will lead to an outward shift in the AD curve, and a move of the equilibrium from E_0 to E_1 to a higher quantity of output and a higher price level, as shown in Exhibit 12-5a. Consumer and business confidence often reflect macroeconomic realities; for example, confidence is usually high when the economy is growing briskly and low during a recession. However, economic confidence can sometimes rise or fall for reasons that do not have a close connection to the immediate economy, like a risk of war, election results, foreign policy events, or a pessimistic prediction about the future by a prominent public figure. U.S. presidents, for example, must be careful in their public pronouncements about the economy. If they offer economic pessimism, they risk provoking a decline in confidence that reduces consumption and investment and shifts AD to the left, and in a self-fulfilling prophecy, contributes to causing the recession that the president warned against in the first place. A shift of AD to the left, and the corresponding movement of the equilibrium from E_0 to E_1 to a lower quantity of output and a lower price level, is shown in Exhibit 12-5b.

Do Economists Favor Tax Cuts or Oppose Them?

One of the most fundamental divisions in American politics over the last few decades has been between those who believe that the government should cut taxes substantially and those who disagree. Ronald Reagan rode into the presidency in 1980 partly because of his promise, soon carried out, to enact a substantial tax cut. George Bush lost his bid for reelection against Bill Clinton in 1992 partly because he had promised in 1988: "Read my lips! No new taxes!" In the 2000 presidential election, both George W. Bush and Al Gore advocated substantial tax cuts and Bush succeeded in pushing a package of tax cuts through Congress early in 2001. Disputes over tax cuts often ignite at the state and local level as well.

What side are economists on? Do they support broad tax cuts or oppose them? The answer, unsatisfying to zealots on both sides, is that it depends.

One issue is whether the tax cuts are accompanied by equally large government spending cuts. Economists differ, as does any broad cross-section of the public, on how large government spending should be and what programs might be cut back.

A second issue, more relevant to the discussion in this chapter, concerns how close the economy is to the full employment level of output. In a recession, when the intersection of the AD and AS curves is far below the full employment level, tax cuts can make sense as a way of shifting AD to the right. However, when the economy is already doing extremely well, tax cuts may shift AD so far to the right that as to generate inflationary pressures, with little gain to GDP. With the AS-AD framework in mind, many economists have little difficulty believing that the Reagan tax cuts of 1981, which took effect just after two serious recessions, were beneficial economic policy. Similarly, the Bush tax cuts of 2001 and the Obama tax cuts of 2009 were enacted during recessions. However, some of the same economists who favor tax cuts in time of recession would be much more dubious about identical tax cuts at a time the economy is performing well and cyclical unemployment is low.

How Government Macroeconomic Policy Choices Can Shift AD

Government spending is one component of AD. Thus, higher government spending will cause AD to shift to the right, as in Exhibit 12-5a, while lower government spending will cause AD to shift to the left, as in Exhibit 12-5b. For example, U.S. government spending declined by 3.6% of GDP during the 1990s, from 22.2% of GDP in 1992 to 18.6% of GDP in 1999. However, from 2008 to 2009, U.S. government spending increased from 20.7% of GDP to 24.7% of GDP. If changes of a few percentage points of GDP seem small to you, remember that since GDP exceeded $14 trillion in 2009, a seemingly small change of 1.0% of GDP in annual spending is equal to more than $140 billion.

Tax policy can affect consumption and investment, too. Tax cuts for individuals will tend to increase consumption demand, while tax increases will tend to diminish it. Tax policy can also pump up investment demand by offering lower tax rates for corporations or tax reductions that benefit specific kinds of investment. Shifting C or I will shift in the AD curve as a whole.

During a recession, when unemployment is high and many businesses are suffering low profits or losses, the U.S. Congress often passes tax cuts. During the recession of 2001, for example, a tax cut was enacted into law. At such times, the political rhetoric often focuses on how people going through hard times need relief from taxes. But the aggregate supply and aggregate demand framework offers a complementary rationale, as illustrated in Exhibit 12-6. The original equilibrium during a recession is at point E0, relatively far from the full employment level of output. The tax cut, by increasing consumption, shifts the AD curve to the right. At the new equilibrium E1, real GDP rises and unemployment falls, and because in this diagram the economy has not yet reached its potential or full employment level of GDP, any rise in the price level remains muted.

The use of government spending and tax cuts can be a useful tool to affect aggregate demand, and it will be discussed in greater detail in Chapters 18 and 19. But other policy tools can shift the aggregate demand curve as well. For example, as will be discussed in Chapters 15–17, the government can affect interest rates and the availability of credit though the ways in which it affects interest rates. Higher interest rates will tend

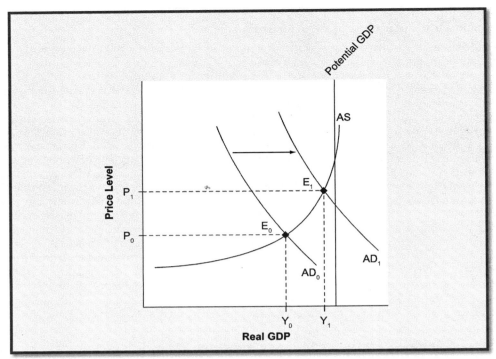

Exhibit 12-6
Recession and Full Employment in the AS-AD Model

Whether the economy is in a recession is illustrated in the AS-AD model by how close the equilibrium is to the potential GDP line. In this example, the level of output Y_0 at the equilibrium E_0 is relatively far from the potential GDP line, so it can represent an economy in recession, well below the full employment level of GDP. In contrast, the level of output Y_1 at the equilibrium E_1 is relatively close to potential GDP, and so it would represent an economy with a lower unemployment rate.

to discourage borrowing, and thus reduce both household consumption on big-ticket items like houses and cars, and investment by business. Conversely, lower interest rates will stimulate consumption and investment demand. Interest rates can also affect exchange rates, which in turn will have affects on the export and import components of aggregate demand.

But spelling out the details of these alternative policies and how they affect the components of aggregate demand can wait for later chapters. Here, the key lesson is that a shift of the aggregate demand curve to the right leads to a greater quantity of output and to upward pressure on the price level. Conversely, a shift of aggregate demand to the left leads to a lower quantity of output and a lower price level. However, whether these changes in output and price level are relatively large or relatively small, and how the change in equilibrium relates to potential GDP, depends on whether the shift in the AD curve is happening in the relatively flat or relatively steep portion of the AS curve.

How the AS-AD Model Combines Growth, Unemployment, Inflation, and the Balance of Trade

The AS-AD model can convey a number of interlocking relationships between the four macroeconomic goals of growth, unemployment, inflation, and trade balances. Moreover, the AS-AD framework is flexible enough to accommodate both the Keynes' Law approach that focuses on aggregate demand and the short run, while also including the Say's Law approach that focuses on aggregate supply and the long run. These advantages are considerable. But every model is a simplified version of the deeper reality, and in the context of the AS-AD model, the four macroeconomic goals arise in ways that are sometimes indirect or incomplete. Let's consider how the AS-AD model illustrates the four macroeconomic goals of growth, low unemployment, low inflation, and a sustainable balance of trade.

Growth and Recession in the AS-AD Diagram

In the AS-AD diagram, long-run economic growth due to productivity increases over time will be represented by a gradual shift to the right of aggregate supply. The dashed vertical line representing potential GDP (or the "full employment level of GDP") will gradually shift to the right over time as well. A pattern of economic growth over three years, with the AS curve shifting slightly out to the right each year, was shown earlier in Exhibit 12-4a. However, the factors that determine the speed of this long-term economic growth rate—like investment in physical and human capital, technology, and whether an economy can take advantage of catch-up growth—do not appear directly in the AS-AD diagram.

In the short run, GDP falls and rises in every economy, as the economy dips into recession or expands out of recession. Recessions are illustrated in the AS-AD diagram when the equilibrium level of real GDP is substantially below potential GDP, as occurred at the equilibrium point E_0 in Exhibit 12-6. On the other hand, in years of resurgent economic growth the equilibrium will typically be close to potential GDP, as shown at equilibrium point E_1 in that earlier exhibit.

Unemployment in the AS-AD Diagram

Two types of unemployment were described in Chapter 9. Cyclical unemployment bounces up and down according to the short-run movements of GDP. Over the long run in the United States, the unemployment rate typically hovers around 5% (give or take 1 percentage point or so), when the economy is healthy. In many of the national economies across Europe, the rate of unemployment in recent decades has only dropped to about 10% or a bit lower, even in a good economic year. This baseline level of unemployment that occurs year-in, year-out is determined by how well the structures of market and government institutions in the economy lead to a matching of workers and employers in the labor market; it is called the natural rate of unemployment. Potential GDP can imply different unemployment rates in different economies, depending on the natural rate of unemployment for that economy.

In the AS-AD diagram, cyclical unemployment is shown by how close the economy is to the potential or full employment level of GDP. Returning to Exhibit 12-6, relatively low cyclical unemployment for an economy occurs when the level of output is close to potential GDP, as in the equilibrium point E_1; conversely, high cyclical unemployment arises when the output is substantially to the left of potential GDP on the AS-AD diagram, as at the equilibrium point E_0. The factors that determine the natural rate of unemployment are not shown separately in the AS-AD model, although they are implicitly part of what determines potential GDP or full employment GDP in a given economy.

Inflationary Pressures in the AS-AD Diagram

Inflation fluctuates in the short run. Higher inflation rates have typically occurred either during or just after economic booms: for example, the biggest spurts of inflation in the U.S. economy during the twentieth century followed the wartime booms of World War I and World War II. Conversely, rates of inflation decline during recessions. As an extreme

Exhibit 12-7   Sources of Inflationary Pressure in the AD-AS Model

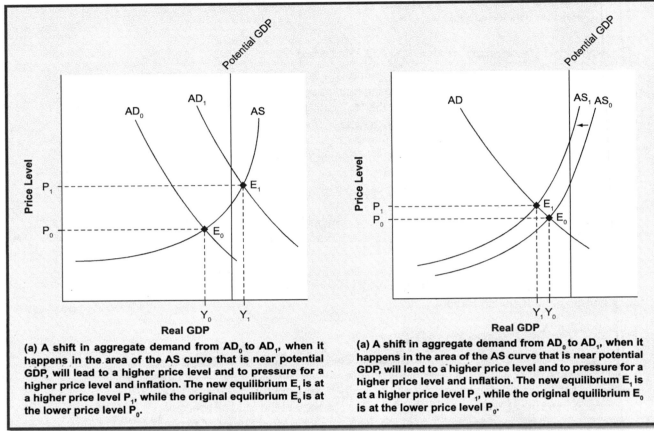

(a) A shift in aggregate demand from AD_0 to AD_1, when it happens in the area of the AS curve that is near potential GDP, will lead to a higher price level and to pressure for a higher price level and inflation. The new equilibrium E_1 is at a higher price level P_1, while the original equilibrium E_0 is at the lower price level P_0.

(a) A shift in aggregate demand from AD_0 to AD_1, when it happens in the area of the AS curve that is near potential GDP, will lead to a higher price level and to pressure for a higher price level and inflation. The new equilibrium E_1 is at a higher price level P_1, while the original equilibrium E_0 is at the lower price level P_0.

example, inflation actually became negative—a situation called "deflation"—during the Great Depression. Even during the relatively short recession of 1991–92, the rate of inflation declined from 5.4% in 1990 to 3.0% in 1992; during the relatively short recession of 2001, the rate of inflation declined from 3.4% in 2000 to 1.6% in 2002; during the deep recession of 2007-2009, the rate of inflation declined from 3.8% in 2008 to -0.4% in 2009. Some countries have experienced bouts of high inflation that lasted for years. But in the U.S. economy since the mid-1980s, inflation does not seem to have any long-term trend to be substantially higher or lower; instead, it has fluctuated in a range of 1–5%.

The AS-AD framework implies two ways that inflationary pressures may arise. One possible trigger is if aggregate demand continues to shift to the right when the economy is already at or near potential GDP and full employment, thus pushing the macroeconomic equilibrium into the steep portion of the AS curve. In Exhibit 12-7a, there is a shift of aggregate demand to the right; the new equilibrium E_1 is clearly at a higher price level than the original equilibrium E_0. In this situation, the aggregate demand in the economy has soared so high that firms in the economy are not capable of producing additional goods, because labor and physical capital are fully employed, and so additional increases in aggregate demand can only result in a rise in the price level.

An alternative source of inflationary pressures can occur due to a rise in input prices that affects many or most firms across the economy—perhaps an important input to production like oil or wages—causes the aggregate supply curve to shift back to the left.

In Exhibit 12-7*b*, the shift of the AS curve back to the left also increases the price level from P_0 at the original equilibrium E_0 to a higher price level of P_1 at the new equilibrium E_1. In effect, the rise in input prices ends up, after the final output is produced and sold, being passed along in the form of a higher price level for outputs.

The AS-AD diagram shows only a one-time shift in the price level. Thus, it does not address the question of what would cause inflation either to vanish after a year, or to sustain itself for several years. There are two explanations for why inflation may be persistent over time. One way that continual inflationary price increases can occur is if the government continually attempts to stimulate aggregate demand in a way that keeps pushing the AD curve when it is already in the steep portion of the AS curve. A second possibility is that if inflation has been occurring for several years, a certain level of inflation may come to be expected. For example, if consumers, workers, and businesses all expect prices and wages to rise by a certain amount, then these expected rises in the price level can become built into the annual increases of prices, wages, and interest rates of the economy. These two reasons are interrelated, because if a government fosters a macroeconomic environment with inflationary pressures, then people will grow to expect inflation. However, the AS-AD diagram does not show these patterns of ongoing or expected inflation in a direct way.

The Balance of Trade and the AS-AD Diagram

The balance of trade does not appear in the AS-AD diagram in a direct way. The current account balance is determined by the combination of exports, imports, savings, investment, and flows of financial capital between countries, as explained in Chapter 11.

In some cases, movements in the balance of trade will shift the aggregate demand or aggregate supply curves. As one example, if the economies of major U.S. trading partners like Germany and Canada grow relatively fast, then those economies are likely to purchase a larger quantity of U.S. exports, and thus raise aggregate demand for U.S. products. If the economies of U.S. trading partners grow relatively slowly, however, U.S. exports and aggregate demand are likely to diminish. Of course, a higher level of exports will tend to increase a trade surplus, or reduce a trade deficit. As another example, many imports are used as inputs to production of goods produced in the United States. When the price of imported oil increases sharply, the AS curve shifts to the left. In addition, the higher price of imports leads to a larger trade deficit, or a reduced trade surplus.

In other cases, movements in AD or AS that arise from other causes will also affect the balance of trade. For example, when a nation's economy is growing rapidly, more of everything tends to be bought—including imports. As a result, a rapidly growing economy often experiences a trade deficit or a reduced trade surplus. Conversely, when an economy is staggering in recession, less of everything is being purchased, including imports, which typically means a smaller trade deficit or a larger trade surplus. As another example, consider the situation where an economy experiences a boom in investment, shifting AD to the right, which is financed by an inflow of financial capital from abroad. The AD curve will shift to the right, as a result of the surge in the investment component of aggregate demand, and the current account balance will decline (or the current account deficit will fall further) as a result of the greater inflow of financial capital.

The graphical presentation of the AS-AD model contains no specific point or gap or line that shows the size or change in the trade balance. But exports, imports, and the impacts of international financial flows can either cause shifts in either the AD or AS curves, or can be the result of such shifts.

Aggregate Supply and Aggregate Demand

Macroeconomics takes an overall view of the economy, which means that it needs to juggle many different concepts. For example, start with the four macroeconomic goals of growth, low inflation, low unemployment, and a sustainable balance of trade. Aggregate demand has five elements: consumption, investment, government spending, exports and imports. Aggregate supply reveals how businesses throughout the economy will react to a higher price level for outputs. Finally, a wide array of economic events and policy decisions can affect aggregate demand and aggregate supply, including government tax and spending decisions; consumer and business confidence; changes in prices of key inputs like oil; and technology that brings higher levels of productivity.

The aggregate supply- aggregate demand model is one of the fundamental diagrams in this course (like the budget constraint diagram introduced in Chapter 2 and the supply and demand diagram introduced in Chapter 4) because it provides an overall framework for bringing these factors together in one diagram, shown here. Indeed, some version of the AS-AD model will appear in every chapter in the rest of this book. On an AS-AD diagram, the horizontal axis of the diagram measures real GDP. The vertical axis of the diagram measures the price level. The intersection of aggregate demand and aggregate supply determines the level of output and the price level in the economy. Movements of either AD or AS then lead to a new macroeconomic equilibrium with changes in the GDP and the price level.

In the model of aggregate demand and aggregate supply, the intersection of the AD and AS curves determines an equilibrium price level P_E and an equilibrium quantity level Y_E. Economic changes that alter consumption, investment, government spending, and exports or imports will move aggregate demand. Shifts in the productivity or the prices of key inputs to production will shift aggregate supply. Movements in AD or AS will lead to a new equilibrium quantity of output and also for inflationary pressures for change in the price level. In these ways, the AD-AS diagram serves as a fundamental diagram for organizing macroeconomic analysis.

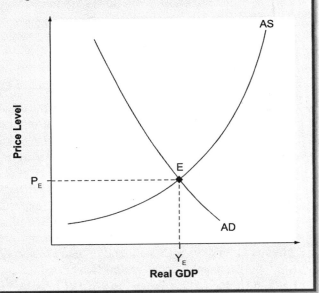

Keynes' Law and Say's Law in the AS-AD Model

The AS-AD model can be used to illustrate both Keynes' Law that demand creates its own supply and of Say's Law that supply creates its own demand. Consider the three zones of the AS curve as identified in Exhibit 12-8: the Keynesian zone, the neoclassical zone, and the intermediate zone.

Focus first on the *Keynesian zone*, that portion of the AS curve on the far left which is relatively flat. If the AD curve crosses this portion of the AS curve at an equilibrium point like E_K, then certain statements about the economic situation will follow. In the Keynesian zone, the equilibrium level of real GDP is far below potential GDP, the economy is in recession, and cyclical unemployment is high. If aggregate demand shifted to the right or left in the Keynesian zone, it will determine the resulting level of output (and thus unemployment). However, inflationary price pressure is not much of a worry in the Keynesian zone, since the price level does not vary much in this zone.

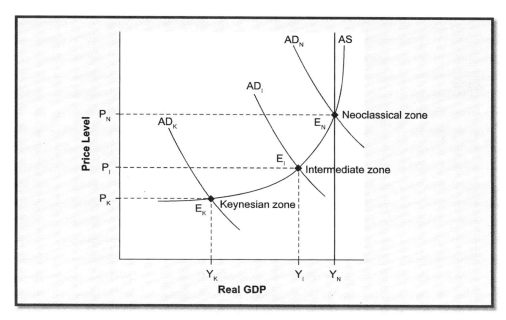

Exhibit 12-8   Keynes, Neoclassical, and Intermediate Zones in the Aggregate Supply Curve

Near the equilibrium E_K, in the Keynesian zone at the far left of the AS curve, small shifts in AD either to the right or the left will affect the output level Y_K, but will not much affect the price level. In the Keynesian zone, AD largely determines the quantity of output. Near the equilibrium E_N, in the neoclassical zone at the far right of the AS curve, small shifts in AD either to the right or the left will have relatively little effect on the output level Y_N, but instead will have a greater effect on the price level. In the neoclassical zone, the near-vertical AS curve close to the level of potential GDP largely determines the quantity of output. In the intermediate zone around equilibrium E_I, movement in AD to the right will increase both the output level and the price level, while a movement in AD to the left would decrease both the output level and the price level.

Now focus your attention on the *neoclassical zone* of the AS curve, which is the near-vertical portion on the right-hand side. If the AD curve crosses this portion of the AS curve at an equilibrium point like E_N where output is at or near potential GDP, then the size of potential GDP pretty much determines the level of output in the economy. Since the equilibrium is near potential GDP, cyclical unemployment is low in this economy, although structural unemployment may remain an issue. In the neoclassical zone, shifts of aggregate demand to the right or the left have little effect on the level of output or employment. The only way to increase the size of the real GDP in the neoclassical zone is for AS to shift to the right. However, shifts in AD in the neoclassical zone will create pressures to change the price level.

Finally, consider the intermediate portion of the AS curve in Exhibit 12-8. If the AD curve crosses this portion of the AS curve at an equilibrium point like E_I, then one might expect unemployment and inflation to move in opposing directions. For instance, a shift of AD to the right will move output closer to potential GDP and thus reduce unemployment, but will also lead to a higher price level and upward pressure on inflation. Conversely, a shift of AD to the left will move output further from potential GDP and raise unemployment, but will also lead to a lower price level and downward pressure on inflation.

This approach of dividing the AS curve into different zones works is a diagnostic test that can be applied to an economy, like a doctor checking a patient for symptoms. First figure out what zone the economy is in, and then the economic issues, trade-offs, and policy choices will be clarified. Some economists believe that the economy is strongly predisposed to be in one zone or another. Thus, hard-line Keynesian economists believe that the economies are in the Keynesian zone most of the time, and so they view the neoclassical zone as a theoretical abstraction. Conversely, hard-line neoclassical economists argue that economies are in the neoclassical zone most of the time and that the Keynesian zone is a distraction. The next two chapters should help to clarify the underpinnings and consequences of these contrasting views of the macroeconomy.

Key Concepts and Summary

1. **Neoclassical economists** emphasize **Say's Law,** which holds that supply creates its own demand. Keynesian economists emphasize **Keynes' Law,** which holds that demand creates its own supply. Many mainstream economists take a Keynesian perspective, emphasizing the importance of aggregate demand, for the short run and a neoclassical perspective, emphasizing the importance of aggregate supply, for the long run.

2. The upward-sloping **aggregate supply (AS)** curve shows the relationship between the price level for outputs and the level of output. Aggregate supply slopes up because when the price level for outputs increases, while the price level of inputs remains fixed, then the opportunity for additional profits encourages more production.

3. The aggregate supply curve is near-horizontal on the left and near-vertical on the right. This shape occurs because when the level of output is relatively low, there are a large number of available workers, machinery, and factories available, so a relatively small increase in the price level for outputs can easily encourage a large increase in output. However, when the level of output is relatively high, and the available workers and facilities are fully employed, then an increase in the price level for outputs cannot encourage much additional output.

4. A vertical line near the right-hand side of the AS curve shows the level of **potential GDP,** which is the maximum level of output that the economy can produce with its existing levels of workers, physical capital, technology, and economic institutions.

5. The downward-sloping **aggregate demand (AD)** curve shows the relationship between the price level for outputs and the quantity of aggregate demand in the economy. It slopes down because of: (a) the wealth effect, which means that a higher price level leads to lower real wealth, which reduces the level of consumption; (b) the interest rate effect, which holds that a higher price level will mean a greater demand for money, which will tend to drive up interest rates and reduce investment spending; and (c) the foreign price effect, which holds that a rise in the price level will make domestic goods relatively more expensive, discouraging exports and encouraging imports.

6. The aggregate supply-aggregate demand (AS-AD) diagram shows how AS and AD interact with each other. The intersection of the AD and AS curve shows the equilibrium output and price level in the economy. Movements of either AS or AD will result in a different equilibrium output and price level.

7. The aggregate supply curve will shift out to the right as productivity increases. It will shift back to the left as the price of key inputs rises, and will shift out to the right if the price of key inputs falls.

8. If the AS curve shifts back to the left, the combination of lower output, higher unemployment, and higher inflation called **stagflation** occurs. If AS shifts out to the right, a combination of lower inflation, higher output, and lower unemployment is possible.

9. The AD curve will shift out as the components of aggregate demand—C, I, G, and X – M—rise. It will shift back to the left as these components fall. These factors can change because of different personal choices, like those resulting from consumer or business confidence, or from policy choices like changes in government spending and taxes.

10. If the AD curve shifts to the right, then the equilibrium quantity of output and the price level will rise. If the AD curve shifts to the left, then the equilibrium quantity of output and the price level will fall. Whether equilibrium output changes relatively more than the price level or whether the price level changes relatively more than output is determined by where the AD curve intersects with the AS curve.

11. The AS-AD diagram superficially resembles the microeconomic supply and demand diagram on the surface, but in reality, what is on the horizontal and vertical axes and the underlying economic reasons for the shapes of the curves are very different.

12. Long-term economic growth is illustrated in the AS-AD framework by a gradual shift of the aggregate supply curve to the right. A recession is illustrated when the intersection of AD and AS is substantially below potential GDP, while an expanding economy is illustrated when the intersection of AS and AD is near potential GDP.

13. Cyclical unemployment is relatively large in the AS-AD framework when the equilibrium is substantially below potential GDP. Cyclical unemployment is small in the AS-AD framework when the equilibrium is near potential GDP. The natural rate of unemployment as determined by the labor market institutions of the economy is built into what is meant by potential GDP, but does not otherwise appear in an AS-AD diagram.

14. Pressures for inflation to rise or fall are shown in the AS-AD framework when the movement from one equilibrium to another causes the price level to rise or to fall.

15. The balance of trade does not appear directly in the AS-AD diagram, but it appears indirectly in several ways. Increases in exports or declines in imports can cause shifts in AD. Changes in the price of key imported inputs to production, like oil, can cause shifts in AS.

16. The AS curve can be divided into three zones. The Keynesian zone occurs at the left of the AS curve where it is fairly flat, so movements in AD will affect output, but have little effect on the price level. The neoclassical zone occurs at the right of the AS curve where it is fairly vertical, and so movements in AD will affect the price level, but have little impact on output. The intermediate zone in the middle of the AS curve is upward-sloping, so a rise in AD will cause higher output and price level, while a fall in AD will lead to a lower output and price level.

Review Questions

1. State Say's law.

2. State Keynes' law.

3. Do neoclassical economists believe in Keynes' law or Say's law?

4. Does Say's law apply more accurately in the long run or the short run? What about Keynes' law?

5. What is on the horizontal axis of the AS-AD diagram? What is on the vertical axis?

6. What is the economic reason why the AS curve slopes up?

7. What is the economic reason why the AD curve slopes down?

8. Briefly explain the reason for the near-horizontal shape of the AS curve on its far left.

9. Briefly explain the reason for the near-vertical shape of the AS curve on its far right.

10. What is potential GDP?

11. Name some factors that could cause the AS curve to shift, and say whether they would shift AS to the right or to the left.

12. Name some factors that could cause AD to shift, and say whether they would shift AS to the right or to the left.

13. Will the shift of AD to the right tend to make the equilibrium quantity and price level higher or lower? What about a shift of AD to the left?

14. Will the shift of AS to the right tend to make the equilibrium quantity and price level higher or lower? What about a shift of AS to the left?

15. What is stagflation?

16. How are the axes of an AS-AD diagram different from the axes for a microeconomic supply and demand diagram for a typical good?

17. How is the economic meaning behind an upward-sloping AS curve differ from that of an upward-sloping microeconomic supply curve for a good?

18. How does the economic meaning behind a downward-sloping AD curve differ from that of a downward-sloping microeconomic demand curve for a good?

19. How is long-term growth illustrated in an AS-AD model?

20. How is recession illustrated in an AS-AD model?

21. How is cyclical unemployment illustrated in an AS-AD model?

22. How is the natural rate of unemployment illustrated in an AS-AD model?

23. How is pressure inflationary price increases shown in an AS-AD model?

24. What are some of the ways in which exports and imports can affect the AS-AD model?

25. What is the Keynesian zone of the AS curve? How much is the price level likely to change in the Keynesian zone?

26. What is the neoclassical zone of the AS curve? How much is the output level likely to change in the neoclassical zone?

27. What is the intermediate zone of the AS curve? Will a rise in output be accompanied by a rise or a fall in the price level in this zone?

13

The Keynesian Perspective

An argument is sometimes made that an occasional recession should not cause too much concern, because it will soon be over, and in the meantime, tough economic times create a powerful incentive for firms to become more productive lest they be driven into bankruptcy. Perhaps the most compelling criticism of this argument that recessions should be viewed without overmuch concern came from the great economist John Maynard Keynes. Soon after the steep recession of 1920–1921, Keynes wrote:

> Now "in the long run" this [idea that recessions are part of a process of long-term economic growth] is probably true. . . . But this long run is a misleading guide to current affairs. *In the long run* we are all dead. Economists set themselves too easy, too useless a task if in tempestuous seasons they can only tell us that when the storm is long past the ocean is flat again.

The worst economic storm of the twentieth century was the Great Depression of the 1930s. Over several years, the U.S. GDP plummeted by 30%. Unemployment rocketed from 3.2% in 1929 to 24.9% in 1933, and even as late as 1939, unemployment still hovered above 17%. So few dollars were chasing so many goods that deflation resulted, with the price level falling by 24% from 1929 to 1933. (In a situation of deflation, if you have money to spend, every dollar *increases* substantially in purchasing power.) The human misery of the Depression was even worse than these grim statistics imply. Up to a million Americans were homeless. Hunger and malnutrition were widespread. In the early 1930s, comparatively few government social programs existed. Millions of people had literally no way to make a living—no way to feed or shelter themselves or their families.

Yet in the early years of the Great Depression, many well-known economists did not perceive anything fundamentally wrong with the economy. After all, the

247

1920s had seen several recessions: from January 1920 to July 1921, from May 1923 to July 1924, and from October 1926 to November 1927. But even including these recessions, real GDP had risen at a healthy annual average rate of 2.6% per year from 1919 to 1928. Thus, some economists argued that recessions every few years were part of the process of a growing economy. However, other economists, like Keynes, focused on the human costs of suffering through a recession every few years. More recently, the U.S. economy suffered a recession starting in December 2007, and the number of unemployed Americans rose from 6.8 million in May 2007 to 15.6 million in October 2009. It would not have been helpful to tell those additional 8.8 million unemployed workers that their joblessness is part of a process of long-term growth.

This chapter begins with a Keynesian diagnosis of causes of recession. The chapter then discusses the components of aggregate demand—consumption, investment, government spending, exports, and imports. The discussion will use the model of aggregate supply and aggregate demand to show how recessions occur and can be counteracted. This Keynesian model implies trade-offs between unemployment and inflation. The discussion then presents a macroeconomic model called the expenditure-output model. Finally, the chapter addresses the question of whether Keynesian economics should be viewed as opposing or complementary to a market-oriented economy.

The Building Blocks of Keynesian Analysis

Keynesian economics focuses on explaining why recessions and depressions occur and offering a policy prescription for minimizing their effects. Not all of what is now called "Keynesian economics" can be found in an exact form in the writings of John Maynard Keynes, because these ideas have evolved over time. However, the Keynesian view of recession is based on two key building blocks. First, aggregate demand is not always automatically high enough to provide firms with an incentive to hire enough workers to reach full employment. Second, the macroeconomy may adjust only slowly to shifts in aggregate demand because of stickiness of wages and prices. Let's consider these two claims in turn, and then see how they are represented in the model of aggregate supply and aggregate demand.

The Importance of Aggregate Demand in Recessions

A first element of the Keynesian diagnosis of recession is that a shift in aggregate demand is a more likely explanation of recession than a shift in aggregate supply. After all, even during the Great Depression, the physical capacity of the economy to supply goods did not alter much. No flood or earthquake or other natural disaster ruined factories in 1929 or 1930. No outbreak of disease decimated the ranks of workers. No key input price, like the price of oil, soared on world markets. The U.S. economy in 1933 had just about the same factories, workers, and state of technology as it had had four years earlier in 1929—and yet the economy shrunk dramatically. Indeed, most recessions are not accompanied by destruction of machinery and equipment on the supply side of the economy. It seems more plausible that they are caused by shifts of aggregate demand.

As Keynes recognized, the events of the Depression contradicted Say's law that "supply creates its own demand." Instead, Keynes argued, an economy has periods when its potential GDP changes little, but aggregate demand falls by a lot. One likely cause is that the demand for physical investment spending by firms can shift quickly. When firms are pessimistic or uncertain about the economic future, they postpone investment projects. When businesses become more optimistic, they may have a backlog of projects in mind that they can start up all at once. Thus, the investment component of aggregate demand is likely to surge and decline rapidly.

More recent analysis in a Keynesian spirit has also emphasized how a country's ailing financial system—especially if its banks are performing poorly—can drag down the economy. As the U.S. economy staggered into Depression during the early 1930s, many businesses and households were unable to repay their loans, and banks went bankrupt as a result. Of the 24,000 U.S. banks in operation in 1929, only 14,400 remained in 1933. When so many banks went out of business, the availability of loans diminished for firms seeking to invest and for households seeking to buy a home or car. Thus, the reduction in aggregate demand injured the banking system, making the reduction in aggregate demand even worse, creating a vicious cycle of worsening depression. The U.S. recession from 2007–2009 was also worsened by a weakened banking system.

Wage and Price Stickiness

A second major element of the Keynesian diagnosis of recession involves the stickiness of wages. If markets throughout the economy all had flexible and continually adjusting prices, then a shift in aggregate demand would result in changes in prices and wages, but not in any additional unemployment. To put it another way, if all prices and wages were flexible and continually adjusting, the economy would always head for its natural rate of unemployment, as discussed in Chapter 9.

Keynes emphasized one particular reason why wages were sticky: the *coordination argument*. The coordination argument points out that even if most people would be willing—at least hypothetically—to see a decline in their own wages in bad economic times *as long as everyone else also experienced such a decline,* a market-oriented economy has no obvious way to implement a plan of coordinated wage reductions. The discussion of unemployment in Chapter 9 proposed a number of reasons why wages might be sticky downwards, most of which come down to the argument that businesses avoid wage cuts, because they may in one way or another depress morale and hurt the productivity of the existing workers.

Some modern economists have argued in a Keynesian spirit that along with wages, other prices may be sticky, too. Many firms don't change their prices every day or even every month. For example, many companies publish sales catalogs every six months or every year, instead of announcing that the prices may change on any given day. When a firm considers changing prices, it must consider two sets of costs. First, changing prices uses company resources: managers must analyze the competition and market demand and decide what the new prices will be, sales materials must be updated, billing records will change, and product labels and price labels must be redone. Second, frequent price changes may leave customers confused or angry—especially if they find out that a product now costs more than expected. These costs of changing prices are called **menu costs**—like the costs of printing up a new set of menus with different prices in a restaurant. Prices do respond to forces of supply and demand, but from a macroeconomic perspective, the process of changing all prices throughout the economy takes time.

menu costs: The costs that firms face in changing prices.

To understand the effect of sticky wages and prices in the economy, consider Exhibit 13-1. Exhibit 13-1*a* illustrates the overall labor market, while Exhibit 13-1*b* illustrates a market for goods and services. The original equilibrium E_0 in each market occurs at the intersection of demand curve D_0 and supply curve S_0. When aggregate demand declines, the demand for labor shifts to the left to D_1 in Exhibit 13-1*a* and the

The Slow Speed of Price Adjustments

Probably few companies anywhere in the world know more about inflation and pricing strategies than the business magazine *Fortune*. But consider how the cover price of *Fortune* has changed over time. In May 1970, the cover price was raised $1.50 to $2.00. The price increases from 1970 to 2000 are shown in the first column of the table. The second column shows the Consumer Price Index for those years (using a base period where the average price level from 1982–84 was set equal to 100), and the third column converts the nominal cover price into real 2009 dollars.

Apparently, *Fortune* used to be a lot more expensive in 1970, measured in real dollars. During the high inflation of the 1970s, the magazine allowed its real price to fall. Since then, *Fortune*'s pricing strategy is apparently to wait until the price level has increased about 10–15%—and the real price of the magazine has been eroded by that amount—before it bumps

up the nominal price to about the same real level. However, by 2009 the real price had been allowed to fall even further.

	Cover Price	CPI	Real Price
May 1970	$2.00	38.8	$11.13
January 1980	$2.50	82.4	$6.55
May 1982	$3.00	96.5	$6.71
May 1985	$3.50	107.6	$7.02
April 1990	$3.95	130.7	$6.52
May 1994	$4.50	148.2	$6.56
October 1997	$4.95	160.5	$6.66
May 2001	$4.99	177.1	$6.08
December 2009	$4.99	215.9	$4.99

(a) Sticky wages in the labor market

(b) Sticky prices in the goods market

Exhibit 13-1   Sticky Prices and Falling Demand in the Labor and Goods Market

In both *a* and *b*, demand shifts left from D_0 to D_1. However, the wage in *a* and the price in *b* do not decline. In *a*, the quantity demanded of labor at the original wage w_0, but the new demand curve for labor D_1, will be q_1. In *b*, the quantity demanded of goods at the original price p_0 but the new demand curve D_1 will be q_1. An excess supply of labor will exist, called unemployment. An excess supply of goods will also exist, where the quantity demanded is substantially less than the quantity supplied. Thus, sticky wages and sticky prices combine with a drop in demand bring about unemployment and recession.

demand for goods shifts to the left to D_1 in Exhibit 13-1*b*. However, because of sticky wages and prices, the wage for a time remains at its original wage level w_0 and the price remains at its original level p_0. As a result, a situation of excess supply—where the quantity supplied exceeds the quantity demanded at the existing wage or price—exists in markets for both labor and goods, and q_1 is less than q_0 in both Exhibit 13-1*a* and Exhibit 13-1*b*. When many labor markets and many goods markets all across the economy find themselves in this position, the economy is in a recession: that is, firms cannot sell what they wish to produce at the existing market price and don't wish to hire all workers who are willing to work at the existing market wage.

The Two Keynesian Assumptions in the AS-AD Model

These two Keynesian assumptions—the importance of aggregate demand in causing recession and the stickiness of wages and prices—are illustrated by the AS-AD diagram in Exhibit 13-2. The original equilibrium of this economy occurs where the aggregate

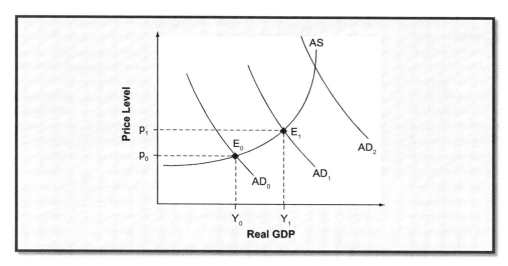

Exhibit 13-2
A Keynesian Perspective
on Recession

The equilibrium E_0 illustrates the two key assumptions behind Keynesian economics. The importance of aggregate demand is shown because this equilibrium is a recession which has occurred because aggregate demand is at AD_0 instead of AD_1. The importance of sticky wages and prices is shown because the economic logic of the AS curve is built on the assumption of fixed prices for inputs, like wages, and because the intersection E_0 occurs in the relatively flat portion of the AS curve where the price level for outputs doesn't change by much.

demand function AD_0 intersects with AS. Since this intersection occurs well below the full employment level, this economy is suffering a recession and high cyclical unemployment.

This description of the recession encompasses the two key building blocks of Keynesian economics. The importance of aggregate demand is illustrated because the output of the economy is being determined by the fact that AD_0 is far to the left of AD_1 and potential GDP. The importance of sticky wages and prices is illustrated because the aggregate supply curve is built on an assumption that the prices of inputs like wages are being held constant—so the AS curve assumes sticky wages. Because shifts of aggregate demand happens primarily in the flatter portion of the AS curve, to the left of the potential GDP level of output, they will have little impact on the price level—which fits well with the notion that prices are sticky and don't alter by much. Thus, the AS-AD model is well-designed to explain how the combination of a fall in demand and sticky wages and prices bring about a recession.

The Components of Aggregate Demand

What economic events or policies might cause aggregate demand to shift to the left, away from the potential GDP level of output? Conversely, what economic events or policies could cause AD to shift to the right? This section investigates the Keynesian approach by considering in turn each of the components of aggregate demand—consumption, investment, government, exports and imports.

What Causes Consumption to Shift?

Consumption is the largest component of aggregate demand. If consumption increases at every given price level, then the aggregate demand curve will shift to the right. If consumption declines, then the AD curve will shift to the left.

For most people, the single most powerful determinant of how much they consume is how much income they have in their take-home pay, after the government subtracts taxes. This insight suggests two factors that affect consumption: income and taxes. Higher incomes or tax cuts will tend to lead to more consumption and cause AD to shift out to the right. Lower incomes or tax increases will cause AD to shift to the left.

But in thinking about how much to consume in the present, people will also think about their *expectations about future incomes*. An economic theory known as the **permanent income hypothesis** points out that when individuals think about how much to consume, they won't look just at the current paycheck, but will look into the future, too, and calculate their expected "permanent income" over their lifetime. An implication of the permanent income hypothesis is that if people believe that their income is especially high this year, and is likely to be lower in the future, then they are likely to save more in the present. Conversely, if people think that their income is especially low this year, but will rise in the future, then they may not worry about saving much at all in the present. The permanent income hypothesis also implies that a temporary tax cut, which increases take-home income for only one year, will have a much smaller impact on current consumption than a permanent tax cut, which is expected to increase take-home income for many years.

> **permanent income hypothesis:** When individuals think about how much to consume, they look into the future and consider how much income they expect to earn in their lifetime.

Choices about whether to save or borrow in the present will also be influenced by the interest rate. For a borrower, the interest rate is the price that is paid for borrowing; for a saver, the interest rate is the price that is received for saving. Lower real interest rates will tend to encourage consumer borrowing for purchases of big-ticket items like cars or refrigerators and cause AD to shift to the right. Conversely, higher real interest rates will tend to discourage purchases on credit and thus shift AD to the left.

Finally, a variety of other factors combine to determine how much people save, including personal preferences and wealth. If household preferences about saving shift in a way that encourages consumption rather than saving, then AD would shift out to the right. When households experience a rise in wealth, then they may be willing to consume a higher share of their income and to save less. When the U.S. stock market rose dramatically in the late 1990s, for example, U.S. rates of saving declined, probably in part because people felt that their wealth had increased and there was less need to save. On the other side, when the U.S. stock market declined about 40% from March 2008 to March 2009, as the recession took hold and many people felt far greater uncertainty about their economic future, rates of saving increased while consumption declined.

What Causes Investment to Shift?

When a firm makes an investment in physical assets, like plants or equipment, or in intangible assets, like skills or a research and development project, it is spending in the present in the expectation (or perhaps the hope) that the future will bring a worthwhile rate of return. When a firm plans its investment demand, it calculates an expected rate of return—that is, the percentage return that the firm expects to receive over time, after all the costs of the investment are taken into account. If firms believe that they can make a high expected return, they will be more eager to invest.

The expected rate of return depends on several factors. One consideration is the range of investment opportunities open to the firm. The creation of new technologies, for example, may offer investment opportunities with a high expected rate of return. Another key factor is that if the economy appears likely to grow in the next few years, then businesses will perceive a growing market for their products, and their higher degree of business confidence will encourage investment. In the second half of the 1990s, the U.S. economy experienced both a wave of new information and communications technologies, like the Internet and vastly improved mobile phones, while also having a long period of sustained economic growth sometimes called the "dot-com boom." For both reasons, U.S. investment levels surged at this time from 18% of GDP in 1994 to 21% of GDP in 2000. However, a recession started in the U.S. economy in 2001, and many firms came to believe that the returns from investing in new computers was not as high as they had thought, so U.S. investment levels quickly sank back to 18% of GDP by 2002.

When considering the expected rate of gains from investment opportunities, firms need to take into account not only the direct costs of investments—like buying a new piece of machinery—but also an opportunity cost that involves the interest rate. When a firm borrows funds to make an investment in physical plant or equipment, this opportunity cost is readily apparent in the interest payments that the firm has to make. But even if a firm doesn't need to borrow money for a certain investment—perhaps because it is earning enough profits to finance its investment using its own internal funds—the firm could have chosen to invest those profits and receive interest payments. The interest payments that could have been received, but are not, because of the decision to invest profits in new plant and equipment, are also an opportunity cost of the investment decision. In either case, a higher real interest rate discourages a firm from investing in tangible or intangible capital by raising its cost.

Developments in the rest of the economy or in public policy can also affect the expected rate of return on investment. For example, if the price of energy declines, then investments that use energy as an input will have a higher expected rate of return. If government offers special incentives through the tax code for investment, then investment will look more attractive; conversely, if government removes special investment incentives from the tax code, or increases other business taxes, then investment will look less attractive.

Firms often have some flexibility about when to invest. It's easy to postpone or scale back physical investment decisions for a time if economic conditions are unfavorable, and it's often possible to accelerate or increase investments if economic conditions appear more favorable. Thus, investment often happens in waves, surging and then ebbing. A decline in investment would shift AD back and to the left, and unless it was offset by other portions of aggregate demand, it could bring on a recession.

What Causes Government Demand to Shift?

Governments make decisions for political reasons, which in turn can depend on the philosophy of those who are in power. Government presiding over an economy with a low level of GDP may decide that there is too little tax revenue to justify much government spending, or alternatively, it may decide that the economy is in desperate need of government programs and higher spending. Conversely, a government with a high level of GDP may decide that in a high-income country, people can afford a high level of government services, or it may decide that in a high-income country, most people should be responsible for purchasing their own goods and service and so the government services and government spending should be low. In any given year, a government can decide to run a budget surplus—that is, to collect more in taxes than it spends—or to run a budget deficit—that is, to spend more than it collects in taxes. Whatever its political justification, an increase in the government spending component of demand will cause AD to shift to the right, while a decline in government spending demand will cause AD to shift to the left.

What Causes Exports and Imports to Shift?

Two sets of factors can cause shifts in export and import demand: changes in relative growth rates between countries and changes in relative prices between countries. The level of demand for a nation's exports tends to be most heavily affected by what is happening in the economies of the other countries that would be purchasing those exports. For example, if major importers of American-made products like Canada, Japan, and Germany have recessions, exports of U.S. producers to those countries are likely to decline. Conversely, the quantity of a nation's imports is directly affected by the amount of income in the domestic economy: more income will cause a higher level of imports.

One implication of thinking about exports and imports in this way is that the trade deficit in an economy will tend to arise (or an existing trade surplus will shrink) when an economy is growing strongly, while a trade surplus will tend to arise (or an existing trade deficit will shrink) when an economy is stagnant or shrinking. A more rapidly growing domestic economy draws in more imports, but doesn't affect exports (which are determined by what happens in other countries), thus reducing the balance of trade. Conversely, a domestic recession will reduce imports, along with all other consumption, but will not much affect exports, thus increasing the balance of trade. For example, the U.S. economy ran very large trade deficits in the mid-2000s during a period of sustained growth, but the trade deficit fell by about half when the recession took full hold in 2009.

Exports and imports can also be affected by relative prices of goods in domestic and international markets. If U.S. goods are relatively cheaper compared with goods made in other places, perhaps because a group of U.S. producers has mastered certain productivity breakthroughs, then U.S. exports are likely to rise. But if U.S. goods become relatively more expensive, perhaps because a change in exchange rate between the U.S. dollar and other currencies has pushed up the price of inputs to production in the United States, then exports from U.S. producers are likely to decline. Chapter 17 will discuss exchange rates in more detail.

Exhibit 13-3 summarizes the reasons given in this section for why the aggregate demand curve might shift to the left, from AD_1 to AD_2, or alternatively to the right, from

Exhibit 13-3   Reasons for Shifts in the Components of Aggregate Demand

Reasons for a Shift of Aggregate Demand to the Left from AD_1 to AD_2

Consumption
- Rise in taxes
- Fall in income
- Rise in interest rates
- Desire to save more
- Decrease in wealth
- Fall in future expected income

Investment
- Fall in expected rate of return
- Rise in interest rates
- Drop in business confidence

Government
- Reduction in government spending

Export and Import
- Decrease in foreign demand
- Relative price increase of U.S. goods

Reasons for a Shift of Aggregate Demand to the Right from AD_2 to AD_1

Consumption
- Decrease in taxes
- Increase in income
- Fall in interest rates
- Desire to save less
- Rise in wealth
- Rise in future expected income

Investment
- Rise in expected rate of return
- Drop in interest rates
- Rise in business confidence

Government
- Increase in government spending

Export and Import
- Increase in foreign demand
- Relative price drop in U.S. goods

Exhibit 13-4   When Shifts in Aggregate Demand Increase the Price Level

A shift of aggregate demand to the right from AD_1 to AD_2 leads to a relatively small increase in the price level from P_1 to P_2, but a relatively large increase in real GDP from Y_1 to Y_2. When unemployment is relatively high, the inflationary increase in the price level is small. However, a similar shift of aggregate demand to the right from AD_3 to AD_4 leads to a relatively large increase in the price level from P_3 to P_4, and only a relatively small increase in real GDP from Y_3 to Y_4. When unemployment is relatively low, because the equilibrium is occurring in the near-vertical portion of the AS curve, close to potential GDP, then the pressure for inflationary price increases can be larger. This pattern suggests the trade-off that when unemployment is high, inflation may be low, and when unemployment is low, inflation may be high.

AD_2 to AD_1. Many of the reasons involve economic events, like changes in preference for saving, or the rate of growth in other economies that purchase exports. But some of the factors that shift aggregate demand can be affected by government policy.

The Phillips Curve

The Keynesian economic framework is based on an assumption that prices and wages are sticky and do not adjust rapidly. This assumption made some sense during the Great Depression, when Keynes was writing, and more generally during any recession when the intersection of AD and AS is below the potential GDP level of output. However, do prices still remain sticky when an economy is not in recession, but instead is near or even above its potential GDP?

The Discovery of the Phillips Curve

In the 1950s, a British economist named A.W. Phillips was studying the Keynesian analytical framework. He noticed that when the economy is in a recession, with real GDP well below potential GDP and high unemployment, the Keynesian theory implied that pressures for inflationary increases in the price level also tend to be low. However, when the level of output is at or even pushing beyond potential GDP, so that unemployment is low, Keynesian theory implied that the economy is at greater risk of inflationary pressures.

Exhibit 13-4 illustrates how during a recession, a move of aggregate demand from AD_1 to AD_2 barely shifts the equilibrium price level at all. However, if the economy is already near potential GDP at AD_3, then a move to AD_4 will increase the price level. When the level of output lies in the flatter part of the AS curve, far below potential GDP, then an increase in aggregate demand can easily encourage more firms to produce more. However, when an economy is already near potential GDP, it becomes increasingly difficult for an additional rise of aggregate demand to bring forth more supply—because the factories and workers in the economy are near full employment already. In this situation, the rise in aggregate demand begins to translate into a higher price level, rather than more output.

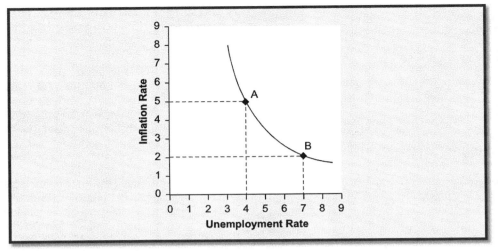

Exhibit 13-5
A Keynesian Phillips
Curve Trade-off between
Unemployment and
Inflation

A Phillips curve illustrates
a trade-off between the
unemployment rate and the
inflation rate; if one is higher,
the other must be lower. For
example, point A illustrates
an inflation rate of 5% and an
unemployment rate of 4%.
If the government attempts
to reduce inflation to 2%,
then it will experience a rise
in unemployment to 7%, as
shown at point B.

Phillips went searching in the historical data to see if these theoretical predictions held true: Is inflation high when unemployment is low, and vice versa? Phillips graphed annual British data over 60 years, with unemployment rates on the horizontal axis and the rise in wages (as a measure of inflation) on the vertical axis. He found that the British data over this period of time did indeed trace out a downward-sloping curve, which became known as a **Phillips curve.** Exhibit 13-5 shows a theoretical Phillips curve. In this example, society must choose between a point like A, with 4% unemployment and 5% inflation, and a point like B, with 7% unemployment and 2% inflation.

Phillips curve: The trade-off between unemployment and inflation.

The Instability of the Phillips Curve

American economists began graphing unemployment and inflation data to see if the Phillips curve relationship held in the U.S. economy as well. Exhibit 13-6*a* is based on U.S. unemployment and inflation data for the years 1960–69. Over this time, the U.S. economy seemed first to move down a Phillips curve, then back up toward the middle. With the image of the Phillips curve in mind, macroeconomists in the 1960s sought to identify the optimal point on the Phillips curve. The extremes of the Phillips curve—high unemployment or high inflation—were both undesirable. But in the middle ground, which point should be favored?

But by the 1970s, this debate became obsolete. Instead of a trade-off between unemployment and inflation, several deep recessions occurred in which unemployment and inflation rose *at the same time*. The U.S. economy experienced this pattern in the deep recession from 1973–75, and again in the back-to-back recessions from 1980–82. For example, the U.S. unemployment rate rose from 4.9% in 1973 to 8.5% by 1975, while inflation was rising from 3.2% in 1972 to 11% in 1974. The unemployment rate rose from 5.8% in 1979 to 9.7% in 1982, while inflation had risen from 7.6% in 1978 to 13.5% in 1980. Exhibit 13-6*b* graphs the data on U.S. unemployment and inflation from 1960–2009. It is clearly impossible to draw a single smooth curve through this forest of data points. Many nations around the world saw similar increases in unemployment and inflation. This pattern was known as **stagflation**—an unhealthy combination of a stagnating economy with high inflation.

stagflation: When an economy experiences stagnant growth and high inflation at the same time.

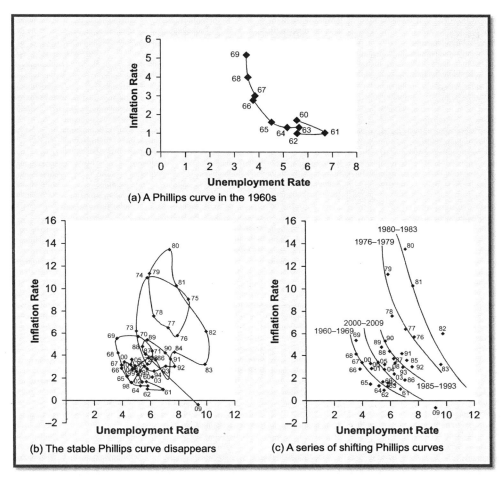

(a) A Phillips curve in the 1960s

(b) The stable Phillips curve disappears

(c) A series of shifting Phillips curves

Exhibit 13-6   The Evolution of the Keynesian Phillips Curve

(a) The points on this figure show the unemployment rate and the inflation rate for each year from 1960–69, with the last two digits of the year beside each point. The data for the 1960s traces out a relatively clear Phillips curve.

(b) The Phillips curve trade-off between unemployment and inflation looked fairly clear in the 1960s. But since the 1970s, that pattern has broken down. It seems crystal clear that it would be impossible to draw a single Phillips curve holds true over the recent decades of U.S. experience.

(c) Over the long term of several decades, it's difficult to see one single Phillips curve in the macroeconomic data. But when the data is separated into short-run periods, and a few years are removed from the diagram to simplify the figure, then several different Phillips curves can be traced out. For example, a Phillips curve for 1960–69 is at the lower left of the figure. A Phillips curve for 1980–83 is in the upper right. In between are Phillips curves for the 1986–93 period, for the 1976–79 period, and for the 2000–2009 period. A downward-sloping Phillips curve often does exist in the short run, but be aware that the relationship can and does shift in the long run.

Critics of a Phillips curve will sometimes point to a diagram like Exhibit 13-6*b* and argue that the Phillips curve doesn't exist, but that argument goes too far. Consider again the patterns of U.S. unemployment and inflation as portrayed in Exhibit 13-6*c*. The diagram shows five Phillips curves for the U.S. economy: one based on the years from 1960–1969; one based on the years from 1980–83; and three middle ones based on the years from 1976–79, 1986–93, 2000–2009. The diagram shows that a Phillips curve trade-off between unemployment and inflation does hold for periods of several years, but then the Phillips curve itself can shift.

This idea that a Phillips curve can shift over time is quite reasonable. After all, the original Phillips curve was based on a short-term Keynesian model, which looked at movements in aggregate demand in an economy where aggregate supply was not moving and prices did not adjust rapidly. Aggregate supply had been relatively stable in the 1960s, so the Phillips curve looked relatively stable. But then aggregate supply shifts to the left in 1974–75 and again in 1979–80, driven in part by higher prices for the key economic input of imported oil. These shifts in the AS curve led to shifts in the Phillips curve as shown in Exhibit 13-6*c*. Thus, a downward-sloping Phillips curve should be interpreted as valid for short-run periods of several years, but over longer periods when aggregate supply shifts, the downward-sloping Phillips curve can shift so that unemployment and inflation are both higher (as in the 1970s and early 1980s) or both lower (as in the early 1990s or first decade of the 2000s).

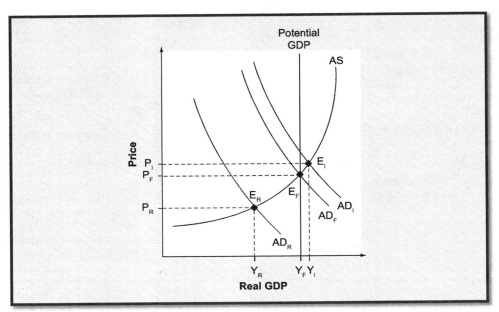

Exhibit 13-7   Fighting Recession and Inflation with Keynesian Policy

If an economy is in recession, with an equilibrium at E_R, then the Keynesian response would be to enact a policy to shift aggregate demand to the right from AD_R toward AD_F. If an economy is experiencing inflationary pressures with an equilibrium at E_I, then the Keynesian response would be to enact a policy response to shift aggregate demand to the left from AD_I toward AD_F.

Keynesian Policy for Fighting Unemployment and Inflation

Keynesian macroeconomics was born in the Great Depression, when the main concern was how to fight recession. Keynes argues that the solution to a recession would include policies to shift the aggregate demand curve to the right, like tax cuts for consumers and businesses to stimulate consumption and investment, or direct increases in government spending. For example, if aggregate demand was originally at AD_R in Exhibit 13-7, so that the economy was in recession, the appropriate policy would be for government to shift aggregate demand to the right from AD_R to AD_F, where the economy would be at potential GDP and full employment. Keynes noted that while it would be nice if government could spend additional money on housing, roads, and other amenities, he also argued that if the government couldn't agree on how to spend money in practical ways, then it could spend in impractical ways. For example, Keynes suggested building monuments, like a modern equivalent of the Egyptian pyramids. He proposed that the government could bury money underground, and let mining companies get started to dig the money up again. These suggestions were slightly tongue-in-cheek, but their purpose was to emphasize that a Great Depression is no time to quibble over the specifics of government spending programs and tax cuts when the goal should be to pump up aggregate demand by enough to lift the economy to potential GDP.

The other side of Keynesian policy occurs when the economy is operating at or even above potential GDP. In this situation, unemployment is low, but inflationary rises in the price level are a concern. The Keynesian response would be to use tax increases or government spending cuts to shift AD to the left. The result would be downward pressure on the price level, but very little reduction in output or very little rise in unemployment. If aggregate demand was originally at AD_I in Exhibit 13-7, so that the economy was experiencing inflationary rises in the price level, the appropriate policy would be for government to shift aggregate demand to the left from AD_I toward AD_F, which reduces the pressure for a higher price level while the economy remains at full employment.

In the Keynesian economic model, too little aggregate demand brings unemployment and too much brings inflation. Thus, you can think of Keynesian economics as pursuing a "Goldilocks" level of aggregate demand: not too much, not too little, but looking for what is just right.

The Expenditure-Output Model

The fundamental ideas of Keynesian economics were developed before the AS-AD model was popularized. From the 1930s up to the 1970s, Keynesian economics was often explained with a different model, known as the expenditure-output approach. (Some classes will choose to skip this discussion of the Keynesian cross model and move straight to the closing section of this chapter, which can be done without loss of continuity.) This approach is strongly rooted in the fundamental assumptions of Keynesian economics: it focuses on the total amount of expenditure or demand in the economy, with no explicit mention of aggregate supply or of the price level (although as you will see, it is possible to draw some inferences about aggregate supply and price levels based on the diagram). This laser-like focus on expenditures in the economy has a payoff. It allows a closer analysis of how shifts in demand or spending affect the rest of the economy; for example, it shows how a tax cut or spending increase of a certain amount, like $10 billion, can have more than $10 billion worth of impact on equilibrium GDP.

The Axes of the Expenditure-Output Diagram

The **expenditure-output model,** sometimes also called the "Keynesian cross diagram," determines the equilibrium level of real GDP by the point where the total or aggregate expenditures in the economy are equal to the amount produced in the economy. Thus, the axes of the Keynesian cross diagram as presented in Exhibit 13-8 show real GDP on the horizontal axis as a measure of output and aggregate expenditures on the vertical axis as a measure of spending.

> **expenditure-output model:** A macroeconomic model in which equilibrium output occurs where the total or aggregate expenditures in the economy are equal to the amount produced; also called the "Keynesian cross model."

Remember that GDP can be thought of in several equivalent ways: it measures both the value of spending on final goods and also the value of the production of final goods. All sales of the final goods and services that make up GDP will eventually end up as income for workers, for managers, and for investors and owners of firms. The sum of all the income received for contributing resources to GDP is called **national income** (Y). At some points in the discussion that follows, it will be useful to refer to real GDP as "national income." Both of these axes are measured in real (inflation-adjusted) terms.

> **national income (Y):** The sum of all income received for producing GDP.

The Potential GDP Line and the 45-degree Line

The Keynesian cross diagram contains two lines that serve as conceptual guideposts to orient the discussion. The first conceptual line is a vertical line shows the level of potential GDP. Potential GDP means the same thing here that it means in the AS-AD diagrams: it refers to the quantity of output that the economy can produce with full employment of its labor and physical capital.

The second conceptual line on the Keynesian cross diagram is the 45-degree line, which starts at the origin and reaches up and to the right. A line that stretches up at a 45-degree angle represents the set of points (1, 1), (2, 2), (3, 3) and so on, where the measurement on the vertical axis is equal to the measurement on the horizontal

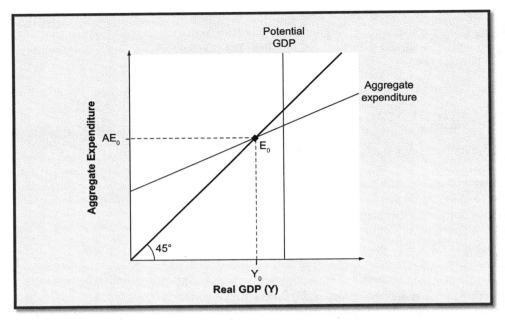

Exhibit 13-8 The Expenditure-Output Diagram

The aggregate expenditure-output model, sometimes called the Keynesian cross diagram, has aggregate expenditures on the vertical axis and real GDP as a measure of output on the horizontal axis. A vertical line shows potential GDP or full employment GDP. The 45° line shows all points where aggregate expenditures and output are equal. The aggregate expenditure schedule shows how total spending or aggregate expenditure increases as output or real GDP rises. The intersection of the aggregate expenditure schedule and the 45° line will be the equilibrium. Equilibrium occurs at E_0, where aggregate expenditure AE_0 is equal to the output level Y_0.

axis. In this diagram, the 45-degree line shows the set of points where the level of aggregate expenditure in the economy, measured on the vertical axis, is equal to the level of output or national income in the economy, measured by GDP on the horizontal axis. When the macroeconomy is in equilibrium, it must be true that the aggregate expenditures in the economy are equal to the real GDP—because by definition, GDP is the measure of what is spent on final sales of goods and services in the economy. Thus, the equilibrium calculated with a Keynesian cross diagram will always end up where aggregate expenditure and output are equal—which will only occur along the 45-degree line.

The Aggregate Expenditure Schedule

The final ingredient of the Keynesian cross or expenditure-output diagram is the aggregate expenditure schedule, which will show the total expenditures in the economy for each level of real GDP. The next section will explain the aggregate expenditure schedule in detail. But first, notice that the intersection of the aggregate expenditure line with the 45-degree line—at point E_0 in Exhibit 13-8—will show the equilibrium for the economy, because it is the point where aggregate expenditure is equal to output. After developing an understanding of what the aggregate expenditures schedule means in the next section, we'll return to this equilibrium and how to interpret it.

Building the Aggregate Expenditure Schedule

The aggregate expenditure schedule shows, either in the form of a table or on a graph, how aggregate expenditures in the economy rise as real GDP or national income rises. Thus, in thinking about the components of the aggregate expenditure line—consumption, investment, government spending, exports and imports—the key question is how expenditures in each category will adjust as national income rises.

Consumption as a Function of National Income

How do consumption expenditures increase as national income rises? People can do two things with their income: consume it or save it. (For the moment, let's ignore the need to pay taxes with some of it.) Each person who receives an additional dollar faces this choice. The **marginal propensity to consume,** or **MPC,** is the share of the additional dollar a person decides to consume. The **marginal propensity to save,** or **MPS,** is the share of the additional dollar a person decides to save. It must always hold true that

$$MPC + MPS = 1$$

For example, if the marginal propensity to consume out of the marginal amount of income earned is .9, then the marginal propensity to save is .1.

With this relationship in mind, consider the relationship among income, consumption and savings shown in Exhibit 13-9. An assumption commonly made in this model is that even if income were zero, people would have to consume *something*. In this example,

marginal propensity to consume (MPC): The share of an additional dollar of income that goes to consumption.

marginal propensity to save (MPS): The share of an additional dollar that goes to saving.

Exhibit 13-9 The Consumption Function

In the expenditure-output model, how does consumption increase with the level of national income? Output on the horizontal axis is conceptually the same as national income, since the value of all final output that is produced and sold must be income to someone, somewhere in the economy. At a national income level of zero, 600 is consumed. Then, each time income rises by 1,000, consumption rises by 800, because in this example, the marginal propensity to consume is .8. The pattern of consumption shown in the table is plotted on the diagram. To calculate consumption, multiply the income level by .8, for the marginal propensity to consume, and add 600, for the amount that would be consumed even if income was zero. Consumption plus savings must be equal to income.

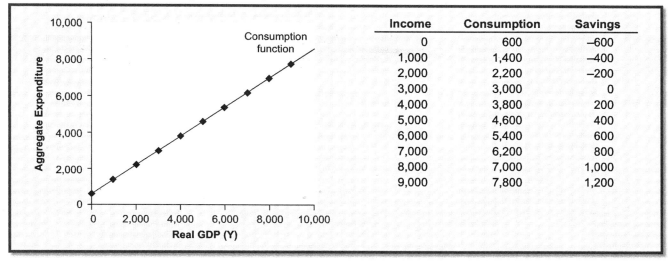

Income	Consumption	Savings
0	600	−600
1,000	1,400	−400
2,000	2,200	−200
3,000	3,000	0
4,000	3,800	200
5,000	4,600	400
6,000	5,400	600
7,000	6,200	800
8,000	7,000	1,000
9,000	7,800	1,200

consumption would be 600 even if income were zero. Then, the MPC is .8 and the MPS is .2 in this example. Thus, when income increases by 1,000, consumption rises by 800 and savings rises by 200. At an income of 4,000, for example, total consumption will be the 600 that would be consumed even without any income, plus 4,000 multiplied by the marginal propensity to consume of .8, or 3,200, for a total of 3,800. The total amount of consumption and saving must always add up to the total amount of income. (Exactly how a situation of zero income and negative savings would work in practice is not important, because even low-income societies are not literally at zero income, so the point is hypothetical.) This relationship between income and consumption, illustrated in the figure beside the table, is called the **consumption function.**

consumption function: The relationship between income and expenditures on consumption.

However, a number of factors other than income can also cause the entire consumption function to shift. These factors were summarized in the earlier discussion of consumption, and listed in Exhibit 13-3. When the consumption function moves, it can shift in two ways: either the entire consumption function can move up or down in a parallel manner, or the slope of the consumption function can shift so that it becomes steeper or flatter. For example, if a tax cut leads consumers to spend more, but doesn't affect their marginal propensity to consume, it would cause an upward shift to a new consumption function that is parallel to the original one. However, a change in household preferences for saving that reduced the marginal propensity to save would cause the slope of the consumption function to become steeper: that is, if the savings rate is lower, then every increase in income leads to a larger rise in consumption.

Investment as a Function of National Income

Investment decisions are forward-looking, based on expected rates of return. Precisely because investment decisions depend primarily on perceptions about future economic conditions, they do *not* depend primarily on the level of GDP in the current year. Thus, on a Keynesian cross diagram, the investment function can be drawn as a horizontal line, at a fixed level of expenditure. Exhibit 13-10 shows an investment function where the level of investment is, for the sake of concreteness, set at the specific level of 500. Just as a consumption function shows the relationship between consumption levels and real GDP (or national income), the investment function shows the relationship between investment levels and real GDP.

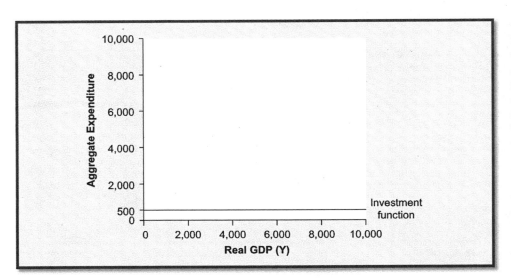

Exhibit 13-10 The Investment Function

The investment function is drawn as a flat line because investment is based on expectations about the future, and so it doesn't change with the level of current national income. In this example, investment expenditures are at a level of 500. However, changes in factors like technological opportunities, expectations about near-term economic growth, and real interest rates would all cause the investment function to shift up or down.

The appearance of the investment function as a horizontal line does *not* mean that the level of investment never moves. The horizontal line for investment means only that in the context of this two-dimensional diagram, the level of investment on the vertical aggregate expenditure axis does not vary according to the current level of real GDP on the horizontal axis. However, all the other factors that vary investment—new technological opportunities, expectations about near-term economic growth, real interest rates, the price of key inputs, and tax incentives for investment—can cause the horizontal investment function to shift up or down.

Government Spending and Taxes as a Function of National Income

In the Keynesian cross model, government spending appears as a horizontal line, as in Exhibit 13-11 where government spending is set at a level of 1,300. As in the case of investment spending, this horizontal line does not mean that government spending is unchanging. It means only that government spending changes for political reasons, rather than shifting in a predictable way with the current size of the real GDP shown on the horizontal axis.

The situation of taxes is different, because taxes often rise or fall with the size of the economy. For example, income taxes are based on the level of income earned and sales taxes are based on the amount of sales made, and both income and sales tend to be higher when the economy is growing and lower when the economy is in a recession. For the purposes of constructing the basic Keynesian cross model, it is helpful to view taxes as a proportionate share of GDP. (Specific taxes will be discussed in more detail in Chapter 18.) In the United States, for example, taking federal, state, and local taxes together, government typically collects about 30-35% of income as taxes.

Exhibit 13-12 revises the earlier table on the consumption function so that it takes taxes into account. The first column shows national income. The second column calculates taxes, which in this example are set at a rate of 30%, or .3. The third column shows after-tax income; that is, total income minus taxes. The fourth column then calculates consumption in the same manner as before; multiply after-tax income by .8, representing the marginal propensity to consume, and then add 600, for the amount that

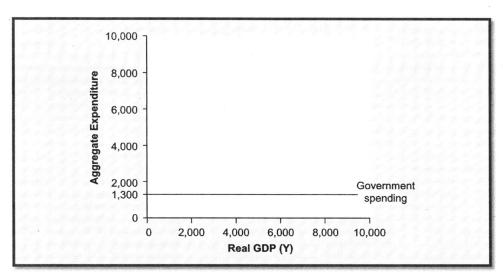

Exhibit 13-11 The Government Spending Function

The level of government spending is determined by political factors, not by the level of real GDP in a given year. Thus, government spending is drawn as a horizontal line. In this example, government spending is at a level of 1,300. Political decisions to increase government spending will cause this horizontal line to shift up, while political decisions to reduce spending would cause it to shift down.

would be consumed even if income was zero. When taxes are included, each additional dollar of income results in a smaller increase in consumption—because some of that income is now paid as taxes. For this reason, the consumption function with taxes included is flatter than the consumption function without taxes.

Exports and Imports as a Function of National Income

The export function, which shows how exports change with the level of a country's own real GDP, is drawn as a horizontal line, as in the example in Exhibit 13-13a where exports are drawn at a level of 840. Again, as in the case of investment spending and government spending, drawing the export function as horizontal does not imply that exports never change. It just means that they don't change because of what is on the horizontal axis—that is, a country's own level of domestic production—and instead are shaped by the level of aggregate demand in other countries. More demand for exports from other countries would cause the export function to shift up; less demand for exports from other countries would cause it to shift down.

Imports are drawn in the Keynesian cross diagram as a downward-sloping line, with the downward slope determined by the **marginal propensity to import, or MPI,** out of national income. In Exhibit 13-13b, the marginal propensity to import is .1. Thus, if real GDP is 5,000, imports are 500; if national income is 6,000, imports are 600, and so on. The import function is drawn as downward sloping and negative, because it represents a subtraction from the aggregate expenditures in the domestic economy. A change in the marginal propensity to import, perhaps as a result of changes in preferences or because of a change in relative prices of imported goods, would alter the slope of the import function.

marginal propensity to import (MPI): The share of an additional dollar of income that goes to imports.

Exhibit 13-12   The Consumption Function Before and After Taxes

The upper line repeats the consumption function from Exhibit 13-9. The lower line shows the consumption function if taxes must first be paid on income, and then consumption is based on after-tax income. The first column of the table shows income. The second column shows taxes, which in this example are 30% of income. The third column takes income and subtracts taxes to calculate after-tax income. The fourth column calculates consumption based on after-tax income, by multiplying after tax income by the MPC of .8 and adding 600. The final column calculates saving, given that consumption plus saving plus taxes must equal income. When taxes are included, each additional rise of income results in a smaller increase in consumption, which is why the consumption function with taxes included is flatter than when taxes are not included. In this example, taxes are .3 of income, MPC is .8 of after-tax income, and MPS is .2 of after-tax income.

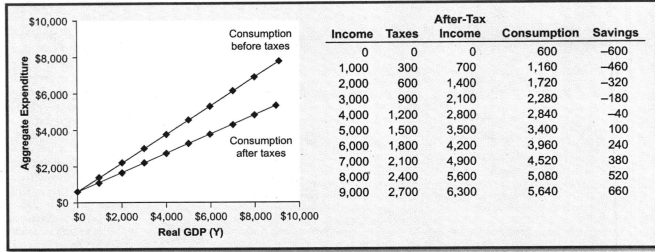

Income	Taxes	After-Tax Income	Consumption	Savings
0	0	0	600	−600
1,000	300	700	1,160	−460
2,000	600	1,400	1,720	−320
3,000	900	2,100	2,280	−180
4,000	1,200	2,800	2,840	−40
5,000	1,500	3,500	3,400	100
6,000	1,800	4,200	3,960	240
7,000	2,100	4,900	4,520	380
8,000	2,400	5,600	5,080	520
9,000	2,700	6,300	5,640	660

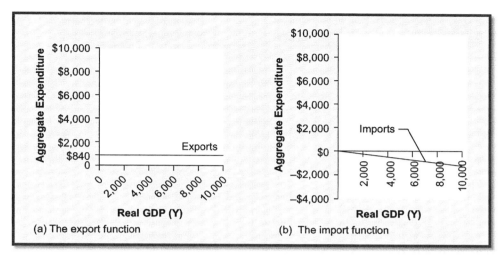

Exhibit 13-13   The Export and Import Functions

(a) The export function is drawn as a horizontal line because exports are determined by the buying power of other countries and thus do not change with the size of the domestic economy. In this example, exports are set at 840. However, exports can shift up or down, depending on buying patterns in other countries.

(b) The import function is drawn in negative territory because expenditures on imported products are a subtraction from expenditures in the domestic economy. In this example, the marginal propensity to import is .1, so imports are calculated by multiplying the level of income by –0.1.

Building the Combined Aggregate Expenditure Function

All the components of aggregate demand—consumption, investment, government spending, and the trade balance—are now in place to build the Keynesian cross diagram. Exhibit 13-14 builds up an aggregate expenditure function, based on the numerical illustrations of C, I, G, X, and M that have been used throughout this section. The first three columns under Exhibit 13-14 are lifted from the earlier Exhibit 13-12, which showed how to bring taxes into the consumption function. The first column is real GDP or national income, which is what appears on the horizontal axis of the income-expenditure diagram. The second column calculates after-tax income, based on the assumption in this case that 30% of real GDP is collected in taxes. The third column is based on an MPC of .8, so that as after-tax income rises by 700 from one row to the next, consumption rises by 560 (700 × .8) from one row to the next. Investment, government spending, and exports do not change with the level of current national income. In the previous discussion, investment was 500, government spending was 1,300, and exports were 840, for a total of 2,640. This total is shown in the fourth column. Imports are .1 of real GDP in this example, and the level of imports is calculated in the fifth column. The final column, aggregate expenditures, sums up C + I + G + X – M. This aggregate expenditure line is illustrated in Exhibit 13-14.

The aggregate expenditure function is conceptually formed by stacking on top of each other the consumption function (with taxes included), the investment function, the government spending function, the export function, and the import function. The point at which the aggregate expenditure function intersects the vertical axis will be determined by the levels of investment, government, and export expenditures—which do not vary with national income. The upward slope of the aggregate expenditure function will be determined by the marginal propensity to save, the tax rate, and the marginal propensity to import. A higher marginal propensity to save, a higher tax rate, and a higher marginal propensity to import will all make the slope of the aggregate expenditure function flatter—because out of any extra income, more is going to savings or taxes or imports and less to spending on domestic goods and services.

The equilibrium occurs where national income is equal to aggregate expenditure, which is shown on the graph as the point where the aggregate expenditure schedule crosses the 45° line. In this example, the equilibrium occurs at 6,000. This equilibrium

Exhibit 13-14   A Keynesian Cross Diagram

The table starts with national income on the left, and then shows after-tax consumption, government spending, investment, exports, and imports, which combine to form aggregate expenditure. On the graph, each combination of national income and aggregate expenditure is graphed. The equilibrium occurs where aggregate expenditure is equal to national income; on the graph, this occurs where the aggregate expenditure schedule crosses the 45° line, at a level of $6,000. Potential GDP in this example is $7,000, so the equilibrium is occurring at a level of output or real GDP below the potential GDP level.

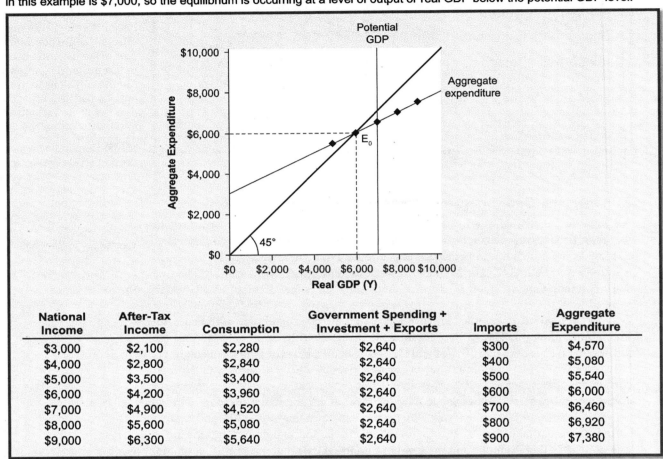

National Income	After-Tax Income	Consumption	Government Spending + Investment + Exports	Imports	Aggregate Expenditure
$3,000	$2,100	$2,280	$2,640	$300	$4,570
$4,000	$2,800	$2,840	$2,640	$400	$5,080
$5,000	$3,500	$3,400	$2,640	$500	$5,540
$6,000	$4,200	$3,960	$2,640	$600	$6,000
$7,000	$4,900	$4,520	$2,640	$700	$6,460
$8,000	$5,600	$5,080	$2,640	$800	$6,920
$9,000	$6,300	$5,640	$2,640	$900	$7,380

can also be read off the table under the figure; it's the level of national income where aggregate expenditure is equal to national income.

Equilibrium in the Keynesian Cross Model

With the aggregate expenditure line in place, the next step is to relate it to the two other elements of the Keynesian cross diagram. Thus, the first subsection interprets the intersection of the aggregate expenditure function and the 45° line, while the next subsection relates this point of intersection to the potential GDP line.

Where Equilibrium Occurs

The point where the aggregate expenditure line that is constructed from C + I + G + X − M crosses the 45-degree line will be the equilibrium for the economy. It is the only

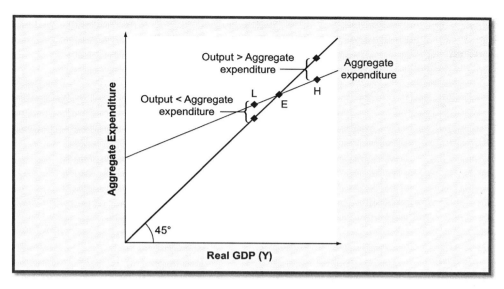

Output > Aggregate
expenditure

Aggregate
expenditure

Output < Aggregate
expenditure

L

E

H

Aggregate Expenditure

45°

Real GDP (Y)

Exhibit 13-15
Equilibrium in the
Keynesian Cross Diagram

If output was above the
equilibrium level, at H, then
the real output is greater than
the aggregate expenditure
in the economy. This pattern
cannot hold in the long term,
because it would mean that
goods are produced but
piling up unsold. If output was
below the equilibrium level at
L, then aggregate expenditure
would be greater than output.
This pattern cannot hold in
the long-run, either, because
it would mean that spending
exceeds the number of goods
being produced. Only point E
can be an equilibrium, where
output or national income
and aggregate expenditure
are equal. The equilibrium
E must lie on the 45° line,
which is the set of points
where national income and
aggregate expenditure are
equal to each other.

point on the aggregate expenditure line where the total amount being spent on aggregate demand is in balance with the total level of production. In Exhibit 13-14, this point of equilibrium E happens at 6,000, which can be read off the table or seen in the figure.

The meaning of "equilibrium" remains the same; that is, equilibrium is a point of balance where no incentive exists to shift away from that outcome. To understand why the point of intersection between the aggregate expenditure function and the 45-degree line is a macroeconomic equilibrium, consider what would happen if an economy found itself to the right of the equilibrium point E, say point H in Exhibit 13-15 where output is higher than the equilibrium. At point H, the level of aggregate expenditure is below the 45-degree line, so that the level of aggregate expenditure in the economy is less than the level of output. As a result, at point H output is piling up unsold—not a sustainable state of affairs in the long run.

Conversely, consider the situation where the level of output is at point L, where real output is lower than the equilibrium. In that case, the level of aggregate demand in the economy is above the 45-degree line, indicating that the level of aggregate expenditure in the economy is greater than the level of output. When the level of aggregate demand has emptied the store shelves, it cannot be sustained in the long run, either. Thus, the equilibrium must be the point where the amount produced and the amount spent are in balance, at the intersection of the aggregate expenditure function and the 45-degree line.

Recessionary and Inflationary Gaps

In the Keynesian cross diagram, if the aggregate expenditure line intersects the 45-degree line at the level of potential GDP, then the economy is in sound shape. There is no recession, and unemployment is low. But there's no guarantee that the equilibrium will occur at the potential GDP level of output. The equilibrium might be either higher or lower.

For example, Exhibit 13-16*a* illustrates a situation where the aggregate expenditure line intersects the 45-degree line at point E_0, which is a real GDP of 6,000, which is below the potential GDP of 7,000. In this situation, the level of aggregate expenditure is too low for GDP to reach its full employment level, and unemployment will occur. The distance between an output level like E_0 that is below potential GDP and the level

Exhibit 13-16   Addressing Recessionary and Inflationary Gaps

(a) If the equilibrium occurs at an output below potential GDP, then a recessionary gap exists. The policy solution to a recessionary gap is to shift the aggregate expenditure schedule up from AE_0 to AE_1, using policies like tax cuts or government spending increases. Then the new equilibrium E_1 occurs at potential GDP.

(b) If the equilibrium occurs at an output above potential GDP, then an inflationary gap exists. The policy solution to an inflationary gap is to shift the aggregate expenditure schedule down from AE_0 to AE_1, using policies like tax increases or spending cuts. Then, the new equilibrium E_1 occurs at potential GDP.

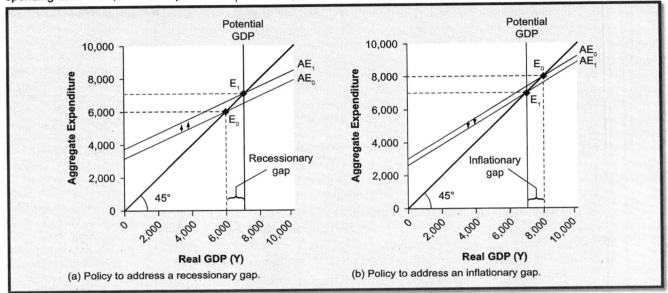

(a) Policy to address a recessionary gap.   (b) Policy to address an inflationary gap.

of potential GDP is called a **recessionary gap.** Because the equilibrium level of real GDP is so low, firms will not wish to hire the full employment number of workers.

Unemployment will be high. What might cause a recessionary gap? Anything that shifts the aggregate expenditure line down is a potential cause of recession, including a decline in consumption, a rise in savings, a fall in investment, a drop in government spending or a rise in taxes, or a fall in exports or a rise in imports. Moreover, an economy that is at equilibrium with a recessionary gap may just stay there and suffer high unemployment for a long time; remember, the meaning of equilibrium is that there is no particular adjustment of prices or quantities in the economy to chase the recession away.

The appropriate response to a recessionary gap is for the government to reduce taxes or increase spending so that the aggregate expenditure function shifts up from AE_0 to AE_1. When this shift occurs, the new equilibrium E_1 now occurs at potential GDP as shown in Exhibit 13-16*a*.

Conversely, Exhibit 13-16*b* shows a situation where the aggregate expenditure schedule AE_0 intersects the 45-degree line above potential GDP. The gap between the level of real GDP at the equilibrium E_0 and potential GDP is called an **inflationary gap.** The inflationary gap also requires a bit of interpreting. After all, a naïve reading of the Keynesian cross figure might suggest that if the aggregate expenditure function is just pushed up high enough, real GDP can be as large as desired—even doubling or tripling the potential GDP level of the economy! This implication is clearly wrong. An economy faces some supply-side limits on how much it can produce at a given time with its existing quantities of workers, physical and human capital, technology, and market institutions.

recessionary gap: The gap in output between an economy in recession and potential GDP.

inflationary gap: When an economy has output above potential GDP, the gap from that level of output to potential GDP.

The inflationary gap should be interpreted not as a literal prediction of how large real GDP will be, but as a statement of how much extra aggregate expenditure is in the economy beyond what is needed to reach potential GDP. An inflationary gap suggests that because the economy can't produce enough goods and services to absorb this level of aggregate expenditures, the spending will instead cause an inflationary increase in the price level. In this way, even though changes in the price level do not appear explicitly in the Keynesian cross equation, the notion of inflation is implicit in the concept of the inflationary gap.

The appropriate Keynesian response to an inflationary gap is shown in Exhibit 13-16b. The original intersection of aggregate expenditure line AE_0 and the 45-degree line occurs at 8,000, which is above the level of potential GDP at 7,000. If AE_0 shifts down to AE_1, so that the new equilibrium is at E_1, then the economy will be at potential GDP without pressures for inflationary price increases. The government can achieve a downward shift in aggregate expenditure by increasing taxes on consumers or firms, or by reducing government expenditures.

The Multiplier Effect

The Keynesian policy prescription has one final twist. Assume that for a certain economy, the intersection of the aggregate expenditure function and the 45-degree line is at a GDP of 700, while the level of potential GDP for this economy is 800. By how much does government spending need to be increased so that the economy reaches the full employment GDP? The obvious answer might seem to be 800−700 = 100, so raise government spending by 100. But that answer is incorrect. A change of say, 100 in government expenditures will have an effect of more than 100 on the equilibrium level of real GDP. The reason is that a change in aggregate expenditures circles through the economy: households buy from firms, firms pay workers and suppliers, workers and suppliers buy goods from other firms, those firms pay their workers and suppliers, and so on. In this way, the original change in aggregate expenditures is actually spent more than once.

How Does the Multiplier Work?

The process in which an original increase in aggregate expenditure cycles repeatedly through the economy and thus has a larger impact is called the **multiplier effect.** To understand how the multiplier effect works, return to the example in which the current equilibrium in the Keynesian cross diagram is a real GDP of 700 but the government, seeking to raise the equilibrium to a potential GDP of 800, increases government spending by 100. When the government first spends 100, it does indeed add 100 to aggregate expenditures—but this increase is only the first step. When the government increases spending by 100, someone in the economy receives that spending and can treat it as income. Assume that those who receive this income pay 30% in taxes, save 10% of after-tax income, spend 10% of total income on imports, and then spend the rest on domestically produced goods and services. As shown in the calculations in Exhibit 13-17, out of the original 100 in government spending in the first round, 53 is then cycled back into purchases of domestically produced goods and services in the spent second round. Moreover, a pattern begins. That 53 which was cycled back into additional expenditures is also income to someone, somewhere in the economy.

multiplier effect: How a given change in expenditure cycles repeatedly through the economy, and thus has a larger final impact than the initial change.

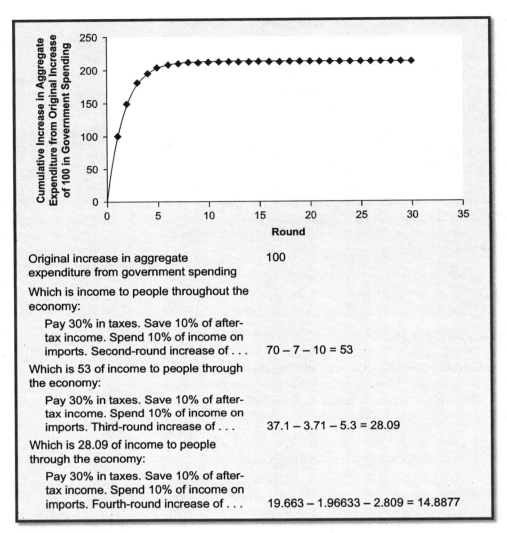

Original increase in aggregate
expenditure from government spending   100

Which is income to people throughout the
economy:

    Pay 30% in taxes. Save 10% of after-
    tax income. Spend 10% of income on
    imports. Second-round increase of . . .   70 − 7 − 10 = 53

Which is 53 of income to people through
the economy:

    Pay 30% in taxes. Save 10% of after-
    tax income. Spend 10% of income on
    imports. Third-round increase of . . .   37.1 − 3.71 − 5.3 = 28.09

Which is 28.09 of income to people
through the economy:

    Pay 30% in taxes. Save 10% of after-
    tax income. Spend 10% of income on
    imports. Fourth-round increase of . . .   19.663 − 1.96633 − 2.809 = 14.8877

Exhibit 13-17   The Multiplier Effect

An original increase of government spending of 100 causes a rise in aggregate expenditure of 100. But that 100 is income to others in the economy, and after they save, pay taxes, and buy imports, they spend 53 of that 100 in a second round. In turn, that 53 is income to others. Thus, the original government spending of 100 is multiplied by these cycles of spending, but the impact of each successive cycle gets smaller and smaller. Given the numbers in this example, the original government spending increase of 100 raises aggregate expenditure by 213; therefore, the multiplier in this example is 213/100 = 2.13.

Those who receive that income also pay 30% in taxes, save 10% of after-tax income, and spend 10% of total income on imports, as shown in Exhibit 13-18, so that an additional 28.09 (that is, 0.53 × 53) is spent in the third round. The people who receive that income then pay taxes, save, and buy imports, and the amount spent in the fourth round is 14.8877 (that is, .53 × 28.09).

    Thus, over the first four rounds of aggregate expenditures, the impact of the original increase in government spending of 100 creates a rise in aggregate expenditures of 100 + 53 + 28.09 + 14.8877 = 195.9777. Exhibit 13-17 shows these total aggregate expenditures after these first four rounds, and then the figure shows the total aggregate expenditures after 30 rounds. The additional boost to aggregate expenditures is shrinking in each round of consumption. After about 10 rounds, the additional increments are very small indeed—nearly invisible to the naked eye. After 30 rounds, the additional increments in each round are so small that they have no practical consequence. After 30 periods, the cumulative value of the initial boost in aggregate expenditure is approximately 213. Thus, the government spending increase of 100 eventually, after many cycles, produced an increase of 213 in aggregate expenditure and real GDP. The definition of the **multiplier** is:

$$\text{Multiplier} = \frac{\text{Total increase in aggregate expenditures}}{\text{Original increase in expenditures}}$$

multiplier: Total increase in aggregate expenditures divided by the original increase in expenditures.

In this example, the multiplier is $213/100 = 2.13$.

Calculating the Multiplier

Fortunately for everyone who isn't carrying around a computer with a spreadsheet program to project the impact of an original increase in expenditures over 20 or 50 or 100 cycles of spending, there is a formula for calculating the multiplier. The formula begins by calculating what fraction F of expenditures is recycled at each stage. To calculate this fraction, start off with a marginal dollar of income, and then adjust for how much money that flows into taxes, savings, and imports and thus doesn't become expenditures in the next round. In the example just presented,

Fraction of expenditures recycled = 1 – What goes into taxes – What goes into savings – What goes into imports

$$F = (1 - .3) - .1(1 - .3) - .1$$

$$F = .7 - .07 - .1 = .53$$

Deriving the Multiplier Formula

Say that the original change in aggregate expenditures is N. The fractional amount of how much expenditure is cycled back into the economy in the next stage—determined by tax rates, savings, and imports—is F. Then, the total aggregate expenditure T that is triggered by the original change N as it cycles through the economy will be

$$N + NF^1 + NF^2 + NF^3 + NF^4 + \ldots = T$$

If the N term is factored out, then the formula for the total expenditure T can be rewritten as

$$N(1 + F^1 + F^2 + F^3 + F^4 + \ldots) = T$$

The term in the parentheses is equal to the multiplier; it's the amount by which the original change in aggregate expenditures N is multiplied to get the change in equilibrium output T. Set the multiplier equal to M:

$$M = 1 + F^1 + F^2 + F^3 + F^4 + \ldots$$

This multiplier is an "infinite geometric series," a term you may have heard in a mathematics class. We want to express the multiplier in a simpler form that doesn't involve an infinite series. To accomplish this, we'll use a computational trick. Multiply both sides of the multiplier formula by F.

$$FM = F(1 + F^1 + F^2 + F^3 + F^4 + \ldots)$$
$$FM = F^1 + F^2 + F^3 + F^4 + \ldots$$

Then take the original equation for the multiplier and subtract the equation for the multiplier multiplied by F; that is, subtract the left-hand side of one equation from the other and the right-hand side of one equation from the other. In this calculation, the infinite series portion of one equation subtracts from the infinite series portion of the other equation and disappears, leaving only a value of 1 behind. Then manipulate the algebra so that the multiplier M is alone on the left-hand side.

$$M - FM = (1 + F^1 + F^2 + F^3 + F^4 + \ldots) - (F^1 + F^2 + F^3 + F^4 + \ldots) = 1$$
$$M - FM = 1$$
$$M(1 - F) = 1$$
$$M = 1/(1 - F)$$

This formula is the multiplier equation used in the text.

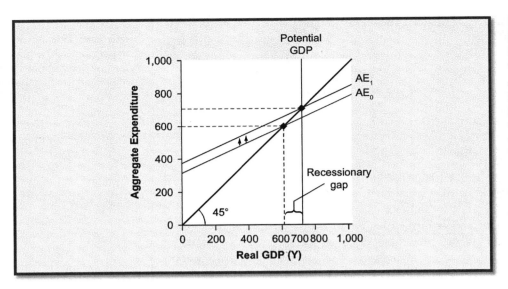

Exhibit 13-18 The Multiplier Effect in an Expenditure-Output Model

The power of the multiplier effect is that an increase in expenditure has a larger increase on the equilibrium output. The increase in expenditure is the vertical increase from AE_0 to AE_1. However, the increase in equilibrium output, shown on the horizontal axis, is clearly larger.

Given this fraction F, the equation for the multiplier (which is derived algebraically in the box) is:

$$\text{Multiplier} = \frac{1}{1 - F}$$

If F = .53, then the multiplier would be $1/(1 - .53) = 1/.47 = 2.13$. Thus, an original increase in expenditures of 100, when multiplied by 2.13, will lead to an increase in aggregate expenditure of 213. Not coincidentally, this result is exactly what was calculated in Exhibit 13-18 after many rounds of expenditures cycling through the economy.

The size of the multiplier is determined by what proportion of the marginal dollar of income goes into taxes, saving, and imports. These three factors are known as "leakages," because they determine how much demand "leaks out" in each round of the multiplier effect. If the leakages are relatively small, then each successive rounds of the multiplier effect will have larger amounts of demand, and the multiplier will be high. Conversely, if the leakages are relatively large, then any initial change in demand will diminish more quickly in the second, third, and later rounds, and the multiplier will be small. Changes in the size of the leakages—a change in the marginal propensity to save, the tax rate, or the marginal propensity to import—will change the size of the multiplier.

Calculating Keynesian Policy Interventions

Now return yet again to the original question of this section: What if the intersection of the aggregate expenditure function and the 45-degree line in a Keynesian cross diagram was happening at 700, but potential GDP were 800. How much should government spending be increased to produce a total increase in real GDP of 100? If the goal is to increase aggregate demand by 100, and the multiplier is 2.13, then the increase in government spending that would be necessary to achieve that goal would be 100/2.13 = 47. That is, an increase in government spending of approximately 47, when combined with a multiplier of 2.13 (which is, remember, based on the specific assumptions about tax, saving, and import rates), produces an overall increase in real GDP of 100.

Using the Multiplier to Analyze the Economic Impact of Professional Sports

What effect does a professional sports team have on a local economy? John Siegfried of Vanderbilt University and Andrew Zimbalist of Smith College used the multiplier to analyze this issue. Most professional athletes and owners of sports teams are rich enough to owe a lot of taxes, so let's say that 40% of any marginal income they earn is paid in taxes. Because athletes are often high earners with short careers, let's assume that they save one-third of their after-tax income. However, many professional athletes don't live year-round in the city in which they play, so let's say that one-half of the money that they do spend is spent outside the local area. One can think of spending outside a local economy, in this example, as the equivalent of imported goods for the national economy.

Now consider the impact of money spent at local entertainment venues other than professional sports. While the owners of these other businesses may be comfortably middle-income, few of them are in the economic stratosphere of professional athletes. Because their incomes are lower, so are their taxes; say that they pay only 35% of their marginal income in taxes. They don't have the same ability, or need, to save as much as professional athletes, so let's assume their MPC is just 0.8. Finally, because more of them live locally, they will spend a higher proportion of their income on local goods—say, 65%.

If these general assumptions hold true, then money spent on professional sports will have less local economic impact than money spent on other forms of entertainment. For professional athletes, out of a dollar earned, 40% goes to taxes, leaving 60 cents. Of that 60 cents, one-third is saved, leaving 40 cents, and half is spent outside the area, leaving 20 cents. Only 20 cents of each dollar is cycled into the local economy in the first round. For locally owned entertainment, out of a dollar earned, 35 cents goes to taxes, leaving 65 cents. Of the rest, .2 is saved, leaving 52 cents, and of that amount, 65% is spent in the local area, so that 33.8 cents of each dollar of income is recycled into the local economy.

Siegfried and Zimbalist make the plausible argument that within their household budgets, people have a fixed amount to spend on entertainment. If this assumption holds true, then money spent attending professional sports events is money that was not spent on other entertainment options in a given metropolitan area. Since the multiplier is lower for professional sports than for other local entertainment options, the arrival of professional sports to a city would reallocate entertainment spending in a way that causes the local economy to shrink, rather than to grow.

The multiplier does not just affect government spending, but applies to any change in the economy. Say that business confidence declines and investment falls off, or that the economy of a leading trading partner slows down so that export sales decline. These changes will reduce aggregate expenditures, and then will have an even larger effect on real GDP because of the multiplier effect.

The multiplier effect is also visible on the Keynesian cross diagram. Exhibit 13-18 shows the example we have been discussing: a recessionary gap with an equilibrium of 600, potential GDP of 700, the slope of the aggregate expenditure function AE_1 determined by the assumptions that taxes are .3 of income, savings are .1 of after-tax income, and imports are .1 of before-tax income. At AE_2, the aggregate expenditure function is moved up to reach potential GDP. Now compare the vertical shift upwards in the aggregate expenditure function, which is 47, with the horizontal shift outward in real GDP, which is 100 (as these numbers were calculated earlier). The rise in real GDP is more than double the rise in the aggregate expenditure function. (Similarly, if you look back at Exhibit 13-16, you will see that the vertical movements in the aggregate expenditure functions are smaller than the change in equilibrium output that is produced on the horizontal axis. Again, this is the multiplier effect at work.) In this way, the power of the multiplier is apparent in the income-expenditure graph, as well as in the arithmetic calculation.

Multiplier Trade-offs: Stability vs. the Power of Macroeconomic Policy

Is an economy healthier with a high multiplier or a low one? With a high multiplier, any change in aggregate demand will tend to be substantially magnified, and so the economy will be more unstable. With a low multiplier, by contrast, changes in aggregate demand will not be multiplied much, so the economy will tend to be more stable.

However, with a low multiplier, government policy changes in taxes or spending will tend to have less impact on the equilibrium level of real output. With a higher multiplier, government policies to raise or reduce aggregate expenditures will have a larger effect. Thus, a low multiplier means a more stable economy, but also weaker government macroeconomic policy, while a high multiplier means a more volatile economy, but also an economy in which government macroeconomic policy is more powerful.

Is Keynesian Economics Pro-Market or Anti-Market?

Ever since the birth of Keynesian economics in the 1930s, controversy has simmered over the extent to which government should play an active role in managing the economy. In the aftermath of the human devastation and misery of the Great Depression, many people—including many economists—lost their confidence in a market-oriented economic system. Some supporters of Keynesian economics advocated a high degree of government planning in all parts of the economy.

However, John Maynard Keynes himself was careful to separate the issue of aggregate demand from the issue of how well individual markets worked. He argued that individual markets for goods and services were appropriate and useful, but that sometimes that level of aggregate demand was just too low. For example, Keynes argued that when 10 million people are willing and able to work, but one million of them are unemployed, individual markets may be doing a perfectly good job of allocating the efforts of the 9 million workers—the problem is that insufficient aggregate demand exists to support jobs for all 10 million. Thus, Keynes believed that while government should assure that overall level of aggregate demand is sufficient for an economy to reach full employment, this task did not imply that the government should attempt to set prices and wages throughout the economy, nor to take over and manage large corporations or entire industries directly.

Even if one accepts the Keynesian economic theory, a number of practical questions remain. In the real world, can government economists identify potential GDP accurately? Is a desired increase in aggregate demand better accomplished by a tax cut or by an increase in government spending? Given the inevitable delays and uncertainties as policies are enacted into law, is it reasonable to expect that the government can implement Keynesian economics? Can fixing a recession really be just as simple as pumping up aggregate demand? Chapters 18–19 on government tax and spending policy will probe these issues. The Keynesian approach, with its focus on aggregate demand and sticky prices, has proved useful in understanding how the economy fluctuates in the short run and why recessions and cyclical unemployment occur. In the next chapter, we'll consider some of the shortcomings of the Keynesian approach and why it is not especially well-suited for long-run macroeconomic analysis.

Key Concepts and Summary

1. Keynesian economics is based on two main ideas: a) aggregate demand is more likely than aggregate supply to be the primary cause of a short-run economic event like a recession, because aggregate supply usually moves slowly; b) wages and prices can be sticky, and so in an economic downturn unemployment can result.

2. **Menu costs** are the costs of changing prices. They include internal costs a business faces in changing prices in terms of labeling, record keeping, and accounting, and also the costs of communicating the price change to (possibly unhappy) customers.

3. The aggregate demand curve will shift based on movements in consumption, investment, government spending or taxes, exports, and imports. Consumption will change for a number of reasons, including movements in income, taxes, expectations about future incomes, and changes in wealth levels. Investment will change in response to its expected rate of return, which in turn is shaped by the real interest rate, the creation of new technologies, expectations about future economic growth, the price of key inputs, and tax incentives for investment. Government spending and taxes are determined by political considerations. Exports and imports change according to relative growth rates and prices between two economies.

4. A **Phillips curve** shows the trade-off between unemployment and inflation in an economy. From a Keynesian viewpoint, the Phillips curve should slope down so that higher unemployment means lower inflation, and vice versa. However, a downward-sloping Phillips curve is a short-term relationship that may shift after a few years.

5. Keynesian macroeconomic policy suggests that aggregate demand should be increased (shifted to the right) when the economy is in recession, and decreased (shifted to the left) when the economy faces a situation of high inflation.

6. The **expenditure-output model** or "Keynesian cross diagram" shows how the level of aggregate expenditure (on the vertical axis) varies with the level of economic output (shown on the horizontal axis). Since the value of all macroeconomic output also represents income to someone somewhere else in the economy, the horizontal axis can also be interpreted as **national income (Y).** The equilibrium in the diagram will occur where the aggregate expenditure line crosses the 45-degree line, which represents the set of points where aggregate expenditure in the economy is equal to output (or national income). Equilibrium in a Keynesian cross diagram can happen at potential GDP, or below or above that level.

7. The **consumption function** shows the upward-sloping relationship between national income and consumption. The **marginal propensity to consume (MPC)** is the amount consumed out of an additional dollar of income. A higher marginal propensity to consume means a steeper consumption function; a lower marginal propensity to consume means a flatter consumption function. The **marginal propensity to save (MPS)** is the amount saved out of an additional dollar of income. It is necessarily true that MPC + MPS = 1.

8. The investment function is drawn as a flat line, showing that investment in the current year doesn't change with regard to the current level of national income. However, the investment function will move up and down based on the expected rate of return in the future.

9. Government spending is drawn as a horizontal line in the Keynesian cross diagram, because its level is determined by political considerations, not by the current level of income in the economy. Taxes in the basic Keynesian cross model are taken into account by adjusting the consumption function.

10. The export function is drawn as a horizontal line in the Keynesian cross diagram, because exports don't change as a result of changes in domestic income, but they move as a result of changes in foreign income, as well as changes in exchange rates. The import function is drawn as a downward-sloping line, because imports rise with national income, but imports are a subtraction from aggregate demand. Thus, a higher level of imports means a lower level of expenditure on domestic goods. The **marginal propensity to import (MPI)** can be changed by movements in exchange rates.

11. In a Keynesian cross diagram, the equilibrium may be at a level below potential GDP, which is called a **recessionary gap,** or at a level above potential GDP, which is called an **inflationary gap.**

12. The **multiplier effect** describes how the impact of an original change in aggregate demand is multiplied as it cycles repeatedly through the economy. The size of the **multiplier** is determined by three leakages: spending on savings, taxes, and imports. The multiplier is defined as:

$$\text{Multiplier} = \frac{\text{Total increase in aggregate expenditures}}{\text{Original increase in expenditures}}$$

13. An economy with a lower multiplier is more stable—it is less affected either by economic events or by government policy than an economy with a higher multiplier.

14. The Keynesian macroeconomic prescription for adjusting aggregate demand higher or lower, as needed, need not imply that the government should be passing laws or regulations that set prices and quantities in microeconomic markets.

Review Questions

1. From a Keynesian point of view, which is more likely to cause a recession: aggregate demand or aggregate supply?

2. Why do sticky wages and prices increase the impact of an economic downturn on unemployment and recession?

3. What do economists mean by "menu costs"?

4. Name some economic events, not related to government policy, which could cause aggregate demand to shift.

5. Name some government policies that could cause aggregate demand to shift.

6. What trade-off is shown by a Phillips curve?

7. Would you expect to see long-run data trace out a stable downward-sloping Phillips curve?

8. What is the Keynesian prescription for recession? For inflation?

9. What is on the axes of an expenditure-output diagram?

10. What does the 45-degree line show?

11. What determines the slope of a consumption function?

12. What is the marginal propensity to consume, and how is it related to the marginal propensity to import?

13. Why are the investment function, the government spending function, and the export function all drawn as flat lines?

14. Why does the import function slope down? What is the marginal propensity to import?

15. What are the components on which the aggregate expenditure function is based?

16. Is the equilibrium in a Keynesian cross diagram usually expected to be at or near potential GDP?

17. What is an inflationary gap? A recessionary gap?

18. What is the multiplier effect?

19. Why are savings, taxes, and imports referred to as "leakages" in calculating the multiplier effect?

20. Will an economy with a high multiplier be more stable or less stable than an economy with a low multiplier in response to changes in the economy or in government policy?

14

The Neoclassical Perspective

In Chicago, Illinois, the highest recorded temperature was 105° in July 1995, while the lowest recorded temperature was 27° below zero in January 1958. Understanding why these extreme weather patterns occurred would be interesting. But if you wanted to understand the typical weather pattern in Chicago, instead of focusing on one-time extremes, you need to look at the entire pattern of data over time.

A similar lesson applies to the study of macroeconomics. It's interesting to study extreme situations, like the Great Depression of the 1930s or what many have called the Great Recession of 2007–2009. But if you want to understand the typical patterns, you need to look at the long-term. Consider the unemployment rate. Since 1955, the highest annual unemployment rate was 9.7% in 1982 and the lowest was 3.5% in 1969. (The annual unemployment rate in 2009 was 9.3%.) But even as the U.S. unemployment rate rose during recessions and declined during periods of sustained growth, it kept returning to the general neighborhood of 5.0–5.5%. For example, in 1960, the unemployment rate was 5.5%. In 1972, the unemployment rate was 5.6%. In 1979, the unemployment rate was 5.8%. In 1988, the unemployment rate was 5.5%. In 1996, the unemployment rate was 5.6%. In 2004, the unemployment rate was 5.5%. When the nonpartisan Congressional Budget Office carried out its long-range economic forecasts in 2010, it assumed that from 2015–2020, after this recession is safely in the past, the unemployment rate would be 5.0%. From a long-run perspective, the economy seems to keep adjusting back to a roughly similar level of unemployment.

The neoclassical perspective on macroeconomics emphasizes that in the long run, the economy seems to rebound back to its potential GDP and its natural rate of unemployment. This chapter begins with two building blocks of neoclassical economics: in the long run, the size of the economy is determined by potential GDP, and wages and prices will adjust in a flexible manner. A neoclassical version of the aggregate supply and aggregate demand model can illustrate these building blocks. If the neoclassical assumptions hold true—and some controversy exists over the extent to which they hold true—several policy implications follow. For example, the government should focus more on long-term growth and on controlling inflation than on worrying about recession or cyclical unemployment. The overall theme is not that Keynesian economics is "wrong" while neoclassical economics is "right," nor vice versa, but rather that the two approaches complement each other, with Keynesian economics more useful for analyzing the macroeconomic short run and neoclassical economics more useful for the long run.

The Building Blocks of Neoclassical Analysis

Neoclassical economics argues that over time, the economy adjusts back to its potential GDP level of output. The neoclassical approach is based on two key building blocks. First, over the long term the expansion of potential GDP due to economic growth will determine the size of the economy. Second, even if the Keynesian assumption of price and wage stickiness is reasonable in the short run, over the longer run levels of prices and wages will adjust in a flexible manner. Let's consider these two claims in turn, and how they can be embodied in the aggregate supply-aggregate demand model.

The Importance of Potential GDP in the Long Run

Over the long run, the level of potential GDP determines the size of real GDP. For example, the U.S. GDP was approximately 25 times larger in 2000 than it was in 1900.

The reasons for this phenomenal change are based in how the productive power of labor, physical capital, and technological capabilities have expanded. The U.S. population rose by a factor of 3.6 in the twentieth century, from 76 million in 1900 to 275 million by 2000. The human capital of modern workers was far higher, too, because the education and skills of workers have risen dramatically. In 1900 only about one-eighth of the U.S. population had completed high school and just one person in 40 had completed a four-year college degree. By 2000, more than four-fifths of Americans had a high school degree and one out of four had a four-year college degree as well. The average amount of physical capital per worker has grown dramatically, but even more important, the technology available to modern workers is extraordinarily better than a century ago: cars, airplanes, electrical machinery, telephones, computers, chemical and biological advances, materials science, health care—the list of technological advances could run on and on. Horse-drawn plows were effective tools for farmers back in 1900, but a plow made of high-strength, low-weight materials mounted on the front of a powerful tractor, and combined with modern seeds, fertilizer, irrigation, and computerized knowledge of soils types, crop possibilities, and weather, is a truly remarkable combination of technologies. The number of bushels of corn that a U.S. farmer could grow on an acre of land was roughly six times higher in 2000 than it was in 1900.

Put these factors together—more workers, higher skill levels, larger amounts of physical capital per worker, and amazingly better technology—and potential GDP for the U.S. economy has clearly increased a great deal since 1900. Sure, in certain years the economy may fall below its potential GDP, perhaps because of a Keynesian lack of

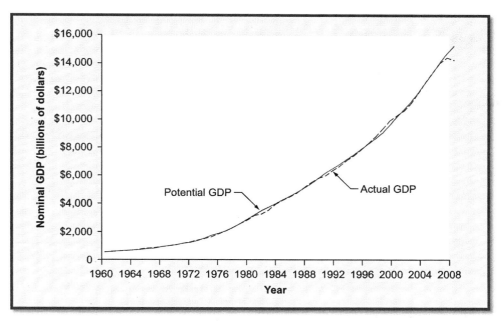

Exhibit 14-1   Potential and Actual GDP (in nominal dollars)

Actual GDP falls below potential GDP during and after recessions, like the recessions of 1980 and 1981–82, 1990–91, 2001, and 2007–2009. In other cases, actual GDP can be above potential GDP for a time, as in the late 1990s.

aggregate demand. From 2007 to 2009, the U.S. economy tumbled into recession. At other times, like in the late 1990s, the economy runs at potential GDP—or even slightly ahead—for a time. One line in Exhibit 14-1 shows the actual data for the increase in nominal GDP since 1960. The slightly smoother line shows the potential GDP since 1960 as estimated by the nonpartisan Congressional Budget Office. During periods of recession, like 1980–82, 1990–91, and 2007–2009, actual GDP is below its potential. In the red-hot economy of the late 1990s, however, actual GDP was above its potential for a time. Most economic recessions and upswings are times when the economy is 1–3% below or above potential GDP. Clearly, short-run fluctuations around potential GDP do exist, but over the long run, the upward trend of potential GDP determines the size of the economy.

In the neoclassical version of the model of aggregate supply and aggregate demand, potential GDP is shown as a vertical line. Neoclassical economists who focus on potential GDP as the primary determinant of real GDP argue that the aggregate supply curve should look the same as potential GDP—that is, the aggregate supply curve is a vertical line drawn at the level of potential GDP, as shown in Exhibit 14-2. A vertical AS curve means that the level of aggregate supply (or potential GDP) will determine the real GDP of the economy, regardless of the level of aggregate demand. Over time, economic growth shifts potential GDP and the vertical AS curve gradually to the right.

The Role of Flexible Prices

How does the macroeconomy adjust back to its level of potential GDP in the long run? What if aggregate demand increases or decreases? The neoclassical view of how the macroeconomy adjusts is based on the insight that even if wages and prices are sticky in the short run, they can be flexible over time. To understand the neoclassical view of how the macroeconomy works, let's follow the connections from the short-run to the long-run situation.

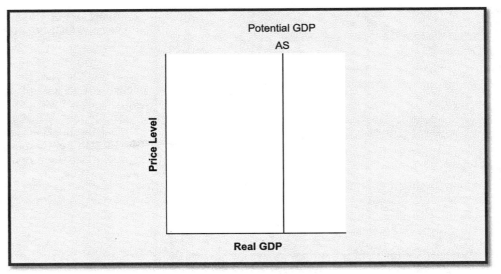

Exhibit 14-2   A Vertical AS Curve

In the neoclassical model, the aggregate supply curve is drawn as a vertical line at the level of potential GDP. If AS is vertical, then it determines the level of real output, no matter where the aggregate demand curve is drawn. Over time, the AS curve shifts to the right as productivity increases and potential GDP expands.

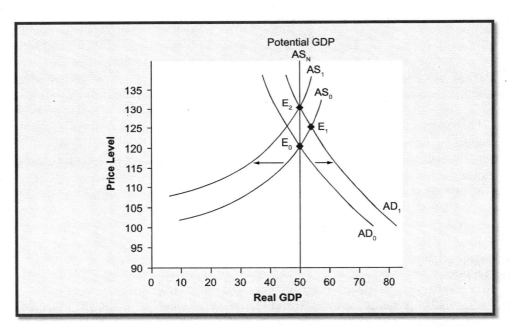

Exhibit 14-3   The Rebound to Potential GDP after AD Increases

The original equilibrium E_0, at an output level of 50 and a price level of 120, happens at the intersection of the aggregate demand curve AD_0 and the short-run aggregate supply curve AS_0. The output at E_0 is equal to potential GDP. Aggregate demand shifts right from AD_0 to AD_1. The new equilibrium is E_1, with a higher output level of 55 and an inflationary increase in the price level to 125. With unemployment rates unsustainably low, wages are bid up by eager employers. Higher wages are an economy-wide increase in the price of a key input, which shifts short-run aggregate supply to the left from AS_0 to AS_1. The new equilibrium E_2 is at the same original level of output, 50, but at a higher price level of 130. Thus, the long-run aggregate supply curve AS_N, which is vertical at the level of potential GDP, determines the level of real GDP in this economy in the long run.

The aggregate demand and aggregate supply diagram shown in Exhibit 14-3 shows two aggregate supply curves. The original aggregate supply curve AS_0 is a short-run or Keynesian AS curve. The vertical aggregate supply curve AS_N is the long-run or neoclassical AS curve, which is located at potential GDP. The original aggregate demand curve, labeled AD_0, is drawn so that the original equilibrium occurs at point E_0, at which point the economy is producing at its potential GDP.

Now imagine that some economic event boosts aggregate demand: perhaps a surge of export sales or a rise in business confidence that leads to more investment, or perhaps a policy decision like higher government spending or a tax cut that leads to additional aggregate demand. The short-run Keynesian analysis is that the rise in aggregate demand will shift the aggregate demand curve out to the right from AD_0 to AD_1, leading to a

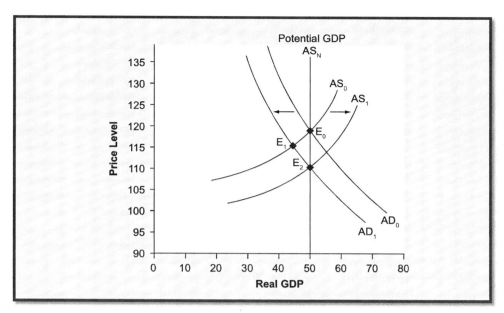

Exhibit 14-4
A Rebound Back to Potential GDP from a Shift to the Left in Aggregate Demand

The original equilibrium E_0, at an output level of 50 and a price level of 120, happens at the intersection of the aggregate demand curve AD_0 and the short-run aggregate supply curve AS_0. The output at E_0 is equal to potential GDP. Aggregate demand shifts left from AD_0 to AD_1. The new equilibrium is E_1, with a higher output level of 45 and downward pressure on the price level of 115. But with high unemployment rates, wages are held down. Lower wages are an economy-wide decrease in the price of a key input, which shifts short-run aggregate supply to the right from AS_0 to AS_1. The new equilibrium E_2 is at the same original level of output, 50, but at a lower price level of 110. Thus, the long-run aggregate supply curve AS_N, which is vertical at the level of potential GDP, ultimately determines the real GDP of this economy.

new equilibrium at point E_1 with higher output, lower unemployment, and pressure for an inflationary rise in the price level.

But in the long-run neoclassical analysis, the chain of economic consequences is just beginning. As economic output rises above potential GDP, the level of unemployment falls. Eager employers are trying to bid workers away from other companies and to encourage their current workers to exert more effort and to put in longer hours. This high demand for labor will drive up wages. Most workers have their salaries reviewed only once or twice a year, and so it will take time before the higher wages filter through the economy. But as wages do rise, it will mean a leftward shift in the short-run Keynesian aggregate supply curve back to AS_1, because the price of a major input to production has increased. The economy moves to a new equilibrium E_2. The new equilibrium has the same level of real GDP as did the original equilibrium E_0. However, an inflationary increase in the price level has occurred.

This description of the short-run shift from E_0 to E_1 and the long-run shift from E_1 to E_2 is a step-by-step way of making a simple point: the economy can't sustain production above its potential GDP in the long run. An economy may produce above its level of potential GDP in the short run, under pressure from a surge in aggregate demand. But over the long run, that surge in aggregate demand ends up as an increase in the price level, not as a rise in output.

The rebound of the economy back to potential GDP also works in response to a shift to the left in aggregate demand. Exhibit 14-4 again starts with two aggregate supply curves, with AS_0 showing the original short-run Keynesian AS curve and AS_N showing the vertical long-run neoclassical aggregate supply curve. A decrease in aggregate demand—say, because of a decline in consumer confidence that leads to less consumption and more saving—causes the original aggregate demand curve AD_0 to shift back to AD_1. The shift from the original equilibrium E_0 to the new equilibrium E_1 results in a decline in output. As output falls below potential GDP, unemployment rises.

Again, from the neoclassical perspective, this short-run scenario is only the beginning of the chain of events. The higher level of unemployment means more workers looking for jobs. As a result, employers can hold down on pay increases—or perhaps even replace some of their higher-paid workers with unemployed people willing to accept a lower wage. As wages stagnate or fall, this decline in the price of a key input means that the short-run Keynesian aggregate supply curve shifts to the right from its original AS_0 to AS_1. The overall impact in the long run, as the macroeconomic equilibrium shifts from E_0 to E_1 to E_2, is that the level of output returns to potential GDP, where it started. But there is downward pressure on the price level—or at least pressure for a lower level of inflation.

Thus, in the neoclassical view, changes in aggregate demand can have a short-run impact on output and on unemployment, but only a short-run impact. In the long run, when wages and prices are flexible, potential GDP and aggregate supply determine the size of real GDP.

How Fast Is the Speed of Macroeconomic Adjustment?

How long does it take for wage and prices to adjust, and for the economy to rebound back to its potential GDP? This subject has been highly contentious. Keynesian economists argue that if the adjustment from recession to potential GDP takes a very long time, then neoclassical theory may be more hypothetical than practical. In the immortal words of John Maynard Keynes quoted in the previous chapter, "In the long run we are all dead." Neoclassical economists respond that even if the adjustment takes as long as, say, ten years—and it may happen in five years or less—then it becomes of central importance in understanding the economy.

One subset of neoclassical economists holds that the adjustment of wages and prices in the macroeconomy might be quite rapid indeed. The theory of **rational expectations** holds that people form the most accurate possible expectations about the future that they can using all information available to them. In an economy where most people have rational expectations, economic adjustments may happen very quickly.

rational expectations:
The theory that people form the most accurate possible expectations about the future that they can using all information available to them.

To understand how rational expectations may affect the speed of price adjustments, think about a situation in the real estate market. Imagine that several events are announced that seem likely to push up the value of homes in the neighborhood. For example, perhaps a local employer announces that it is going to hire many more people or the city announces that it is going to build a local park or a library in that neighborhood. The theory of rational expectations points out that even though none of the changes will happen immediately, home prices in the neighborhood will rise immediately, because the expectation that homes will be worth more in the future will lead buyers to be willing to pay more for homes in the present. The amount of the immediate increase in home prices will depend on how likely it seems that the announcements about the future will actually happen and on how distant the local jobs and neighborhood improvements are in the future. The key point is that because of rational expectations, prices do not wait on events, but adjust immediately.

At a macroeconomic level, the theory of rational expectations points out that if the aggregate supply curve is vertical over time, then people should rationally expect this pattern. When a shift in aggregate demand occurs, people and businesses with rational expectations will know that its impact on output and employment will only be temporary, while its impact on the price level will be permanent. If firms and workers perceive the outcome of the process in advance, and if all firms and workers know that everyone else is perceiving the process in the same way, then they have no incentive to go through an extended series of short-run scenarios, like a firm first hiring more people when aggregate demand shifts out and then firing those same people when aggregate supply shifts back.

Do You, and Everyone around You, Have Rational Expectations?

Here's a social experiment to reveal both your rationality and your expectations about the rationality of others. You and everyone else in a group of people are asked to choose a number between 0 and 100. The winner is whoever makes a guess that is closest to one-half of the average of all the numbers chosen. What number should you pick? Think about it for a moment.

You might begin by reasoning that if the guesses of the other parties are distributed randomly over the interval from 0 to 100, then the average of the other guesses will be 50, and therefore you should guess 25. But if everyone reasons in this way, then everyone will guess 25, and so you should guess 12 or 13. But if everyone follows the logic of this choice, then every else will guess 12 or 13 as well, so you should guess 6. But if everyone else follows the logic

of this choice, then everyone will guess 6 and you should guess 3. You can see where this train of logic is headed. If everyone is fully rational, and everyone expects everyone else to be fully rational, then everyone should guess zero. A group of economists who call themselves "experimental economists" organize games like this and see how people respond. When the game is first played, guesses of about 25 are common. As the game is then repeated, the guesses sink lower and lower. But very few people ever guess zero.

These results suggest several conclusions. People are not fully rational in their expectations, and they do not expect others to be fully rational, either. However, when people repeat a situation several times, they do learn and adapt their behavior in the direction of greater rationality.

Instead, everyone will recognize where this process is heading—toward a change in the price level—and then will act on that expectation. In this scenario, the expected long-run change in the price level may happen very quickly, without a drawn-out zigzag of output and employment first moving one way and then the other.

The theory that people and firms have rational expectations can be a useful simplification, but as a statement about how people and businesses actually behave, the assumption seems too strong. After all, many people and firms are not especially well informed either about what is happening in the economy or about how the economy works. It is probably more realistic to believe that people and firms act with **adaptive expectations:** they look at past experience and gradually adapt their beliefs and behavior as circumstances change, but are not perfect synthesizers of information and accurate predictors of the future in the sense of rational expectations theory. If most people and businesses have some form of adaptive expectations, then the adjustment from the short-run and long-run will be traced out in incremental steps that occur over time.

adaptive expectations: The theory that people look at past experience and gradually adapt their beliefs and behavior as circumstances change.

The empirical evidence on the speed of macroeconomic adjustment of prices and wages is not clear-cut. Indeed, the speed of macroeconomic adjustment probably varies among different countries and time periods. But a reasonable guess is that the initial short-run effect of a shift in aggregate demand might last two to five years, before the adjustments in wages and prices cause the economy to adjust back to potential GDP. Thus, one might think of the short run for applying Keynesian analysis as time periods less than 2–5 years, and the long run for applying neoclassical analysis as longer than five years. For practical purposes, this guideline is frustratingly imprecise, but when analyzing a complex social mechanism like an economy as it evolves over time, some imprecision seems unavoidable.

Policy Implications of the Neoclassical Perspective

The neoclassical school of macroeconomics argues that the economy has a self-correcting tendency to move back to potential GDP. If one accepts this theory, then it has implications for how to view the main problems of the macroeconomy. For example,

Data on Inflation Expectations

Expectations about inflation may seem like a highly theoretical concept, but in fact, data do exist on this subject.

Joseph Livingston, a financial journalist for the *Philadelphia Inquirer,* started a twice-a-year survey of economists about their expectations of inflation in 1946. After Livingston's death in 1969, the survey was continued by the Federal Reserve Bank of Philadelphia. The Institute of Survey Research at the University of Michigan started carrying out a survey of inflation expectations of 500 random households in 1948. Finally, the American Statistical Association together with a private organization called the National Bureau of Economic Research started carrying out a survey of professional economic forecasters that included expectations about inflation in 1968.

Economic research can then compare these expectations to the actual inflation that occurred, but the results are mixed. Expectations do not seem to be purely adaptive and based on past experience of inflation; instead, people are clearly looking ahead. In fact, the average forecast of households is roughly as accurate as the average forecasts of the professionals. However, expectations do not seem to be perfectly rational forecasts of the future, either, because people often repeat past errors. For example, all parties have a tendency to overestimate future inflation when inflation is currently low and to underestimate future inflation when inflation is currently high. However, the forecasts of economists have become notably more accurate in the last few decades. Economists are actively researching how expectations of inflation and other economic variables are formed and changed.

fighting recession seems relatively less important, while encouraging long-term growth seems more important. For similar reasons, fighting unemployment seems relatively less important, while fighting inflation seems more important. Let's consider these choices in turn, along with their implications for the shape of the Phillips curve trade-off between unemployment and inflation.

Fighting Recession or Encouraging Long-Term Growth?

Late in 2007, the U.S. economy entered a severe recession. Real GDP declined through the middle of 2009. Most Keynesian economists would probably focus on the immediate recession. But neoclassical economists might well argue that the economy will rebound out of the recession in a year or two. From the neoclassical point of view, perhaps a more important question is the growth rate of long-term productivity, which determined the rate at which potential GDP expands. As measured by growth in output per hour in the business sector, productivity growth was very strong from 1998 to 2003, growing at an annual rate of 3.4%. However, productivity growth then sagged to less than 2% per year in 2006 and 2007. The year 2009 actually saw high productivity growth at a rate of 3.8%. However, it was a peculiar year for the economy, with a deep recession seeming to come to an end in mid-year, but no one being quite certain that the worst was over. As a result, firms expanded output in the second half of 2009 without doing much hiring. More output with about the same labor input looks good for productivity, but it is unlikely to continue for the long-run. From a neoclassical perspective, the key question of the next few years is whether productivity growth returns to the high levels of the late 1990s and early 2000s, or whether it ends up at the slower rates of 2006 and 2007.

Neoclassical economists are often skeptical of the government's ability to manipulate aggregate demand skillfully and in a timely manner, as Keynesian economics recommends. Instead, neoclassical economists are likely to focus their attention on the underpinnings of long-run productivity growth: namely, an economy's investments in human capital, physical capital, and technology, operating together in a market-oriented environment that rewards innovation.

Fighting Unemployment or Inflation?

In the neoclassical model, the level of real GDP is determined by potential GDP, which is illustrated with a vertical aggregate supply curve. Unemployment can be divided into two categories, as explained in Chapter 9: cyclical unemployment and the natural rate of unemployment. Cyclical unemployment is created when the economy is producing below potential GDP, giving potential employers less incentive to hire. When the economy is producing at potential GDP, cyclical unemployment will be zero. Historical evidence shows that the unemployment rate never falls to 0%, not even when the economy is producing at or even slightly above potential GDP. The unemployment rate that is created by the forces of supply and demand in the labor market, even when the economy is at potential GDP, is called the natural rate of unemployment.

The neoclassical view of unemployment tends to focus attention away from the problem of cyclical unemployment—that is, unemployment caused by recession—while putting more attention on the issue of the rates of unemployment that prevail even when the economy is operating at potential GDP. To put it another way, the neoclassical view of unemployment tends to focus on how public policy might be adjusted to reduce the natural rate of unemployment. Such policy changes might involve redesigning unemployment and welfare programs so that they still support those in need, but also offer greater encouragement for job-hunting. It might involve redesigning business rules with an eye to whether they are unintentionally discouraging businesses from taking on new employees. It might involve building institutions to improve the flow of information about jobs and the mobility of workers, to help bring together workers and employers more quickly.

Neoclassical economists will not tend to see aggregate demand as a useful tool for reducing unemployment; after all, if economic output is determined by a vertical aggregate supply curve, then aggregate demand has no effect on unemployment. Instead, neoclassical economists believe that aggregate demand should be allowed to expand only to match the gradual shifts of aggregate supply to the right—keeping the price level much the same and inflationary pressures low.

If aggregate demand rises rapidly in the neoclassical model, it leads only to inflationary pressures. Exhibit 14-5 shows a vertical long-run AS curve and three different levels of aggregate demand, rising from AD_0 to AD_1 to AD_2. As the macroeconomic equilibrium rises from E_0 to E_1 and E_2, the price level rises. But real GDP does not budge. Nor does the rate of unemployment, which adjusts to its natural rate. Conversely, reducing inflation has no long-term costs, either. Think about Exhibit 14-5 in reverse, as the aggregate demand curve shifts from AD_2 to AD_1 to AD_0, and the equilibrium moves from E_2 to E_1 to E_0. During this process, the price level falls, but neither real GDP nor the natural rate of unemployment is changed.

A shift to the left in aggregate supply can also push up the price level. Exhibit 14-6 shows a shift to the left of a vertical aggregate supply, which might result from an increase in prices of key inputs, like oil or wages. It can also result from a breakdown of key market institutions, like banks, which could prevent the economy from operating as smoothly as it had before. A shift back to the left of AS means that potential GDP has fallen, and perhaps conditions of the labor market have shifted in such a way such that the natural rate of unemployment is higher as well. But at the new AS curve, it remains true that aggregate supply determines the level of output, while changes in aggregate demand will determine the price level.

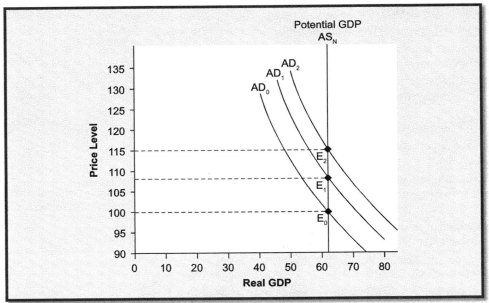

Exhibit 14-5   How Aggregate Demand Determines the Price Level in the Long Run

As aggregate demand shifts to the right from AD_0 to AD_1 to AD_2, real GDP in this economy and the level of unemployment do not change. However, there is inflationary pressure for a higher price level as the equilibrium changes from E_0 to E_1 to E_2.

The Neoclassical Phillips Curve Trade-Off

A neoclassical long-run aggregate supply curve will imply a vertical shape for the Phillips curve trade-off between inflation and unemployment. Exhibit 14-7a shows the vertical AS curve, with three different levels of aggregate demand resulting in three different equilibria at three different price levels. At every point along that vertical AS curve, potential GDP and the rate of unemployment remains the same. Assume that in this economy, the natural rate of unemployment when the economy is producing at potential GDP is 5%. As a result, the long-run Phillips curve relationship shown in Exhibit 14-7b is a vertical line, rising up from 5% unemployment, at any level of inflation.

The unemployment rate on the long-run Phillips curve will be the natural rate of unemployment. A small inflationary increase in the price level from AD_0 to AD_1 will have the same natural rate of unemployment as a larger inflationary increase in the price level from AD_0 to AD_2. The macroeconomic equilibrium along the vertical aggregate supply curve can occur at a variety of different price levels, and the natural rate of unemployment can be consistent with all different rates of inflation. The great economist Milton Friedman (1912–2006) summed up the neoclassical view of the long-term Phillips curve trade-off in a 1967 speech: "[T]here is always a temporary trade-off between inflation and unemployment; there is no permanent trade-off."

In the Keynesian perspective, the primary focus is on getting the level of aggregate demand right in relationship to an upward-sloping aggregate supply curve; that is, AD should be adjusted so that the economy produces at its potential GDP, not so low that cyclical unemployment results and not so high that inflation results. In the neoclassical perspective, aggregate supply will determine output at potential GDP, unemployment is determined by the natural rate of unemployment churned out by the forces of supply and demand in the labor market, and shifts in aggregate demand are the primary determinant of changes in the price level.

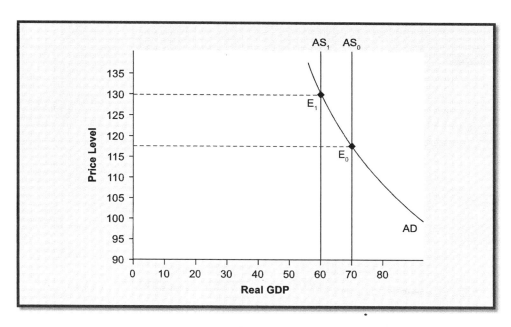

Exhibit 14-6   How a Shift to the Left in AS Can Push Up the Price Level

A shift in aggregate supply to the left from AS_0 to AS_1 causes inflationary pressure for a higher price level as the equilibrium shifts from E_0 to E_1.

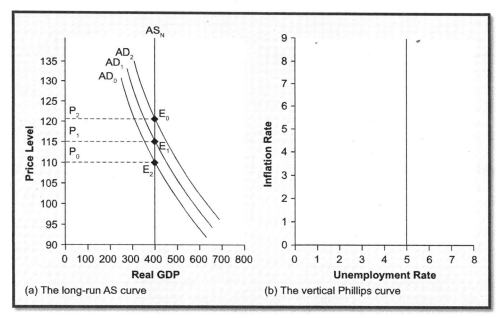

(a) The long-run AS curve   (b) The vertical Phillips curve

Exhibit 14-7   From a Long-Run AS Curve to a Long-Run Phillips Curve

(a) With a vertical AS curve, shifts in aggregate demand do not alter the level of output but do lead to inflationary changes in the price level. Because output is unchanged between the equilibria E_0, E_1 and E_2, all unemployment in this economy will be due to the natural rate of unemployment.

(b) If the natural rate of unemployment is 5%, then the Phillips curve will be vertical. That is, regardless of inflationary changes in the price level, the unemployment rate remains at 5%.

Macroeconomists Riding Two Horses

When a circus performer stands up on two horses, with a foot on each one, much of the excitement for the viewer resides in contemplating the gap between the two. As modern macroeconomists ride into the future with one foot on the short-term Keynesian perspective and another foot on the long-term neoclassical perspective, the balancing act may appear to be an uncomfortable one, but there doesn't seem to be any way to avoid it. Each approach, Keynesian and neoclassical, has its strengths and weaknesses.

The short-term Keynesian model, built on the importance of aggregate demand as a cause of business cycles and a degree of wage and price rigidity, does a sound job of explaining many recessions and why cyclical unemployment rises and falls. However, Keynesian economics does a less good job of capturing the reality that the economy does usually seem to revert to a natural rate of unemployment over time. By focusing on the short run adjustments of aggregate demand, Keynesian economics creates some danger of overlooking the long-term causes of economic growth or the natural rate of unemployment that exists even when the economy is producing at potential GDP.

The neoclassical model, with its emphasis on aggregate supply, focuses on the underlying determinants of output and employment in markets, and thus tends to put more emphasis on economic growth and how labor markets work. However, the neoclassical view is not especially helpful in explaining why unemployment moves up and down over short time horizons of a few years. Nor is the neoclassical model especially helpful when the economy is mired in an especially deep and long-lasting recession, like the Depression. Keynesian economics tends to view inflation as a price that might sometimes be paid for lower unemployment; neoclassical economics tends to view inflation as a cost that offers no offsetting gains in terms of lower unemployment.

The Keynesian and neoclassical approaches differ in their views of government macroeconomic policy, too. Keynesian macroeconomic policy requires some optimism about the ability of the government to recognize a situation of too little or too much aggregate demand, and to adjust aggregate demand accordingly with the right level of changes in taxes or spending, all enacted in a timely fashion. Conversely, even when neoclassical economists admit that a Keynesian increase in aggregate demand might in theory help to avoid a recession, they often argue it is unlikely to work well in practice. After all, neoclassical economists argue, it takes government statisticians months to produce even preliminary estimates of GDP so that politicians know whether a recession is occurring—and those preliminary estimates may be revised substantially later. Moreover, the political process can take more months to enact a tax cut or a spending increase; the amount of those tax or spending changes will be determined as much by political considerations as economic ones; and then the economy will take still more months to put changes in aggregate demand into effect through spending and production.

But macroeconomics cannot be summed up as an argument between one group of economists who are pure Keynesians and another group who are pure neoclassicals. Instead, many economists believe that all of these statements are true—it's just that the Keynesian statements are more relevant in the short run and the neoclassical statements in the long run. Robert Solow, the Nobel laureate in economics in 1987, described the dual approach in this way: "At short time scales, I think, something sort of 'Keynesian' is a good approximation, and surely better than anything straight 'neoclassical.' At very long time scales, the interesting questions are best studied in a neoclassical framework, and attention to the Keynesian side of things would be a minor distraction. At the five-to-ten-year time scale, we have to piece things together as best we can, and look for a hybrid model that will do the job."

Many modern macroeconomists spend considerable time and energy trying to construct models that blend the most attractive aspects of the Keynesian and neoclassical approaches. It's possible to construct a somewhat complex mathematical model where aggregate demand and sticky wages and prices matter in the short run, but wages, prices and aggregate supply adjust in the long run. However, creating an overall model that encompasses both short-term Keynesian and long-term neoclassical models is not easy. Even if one of these hybrid models eventually becomes well accepted in the economics profession, it will probably still feel like riding two separate horses, but now with a double-saddle arrangement linking them together more closely, so that the rider is not quite so precarious.

Key Comments and Summary

1. Neoclassical economics argues that in the long run, the economy will adjust back to its potential GDP level of output through flexible price levels.

2. In the neoclassical view, potential GDP and the natural rate of unemployment are determined in the long run by market forces. Thus, the neoclassical perspective views the long-run AS curve as vertical.

3. A **rational expectations** perspective argues that people have excellent information about economic events and how the economy works, and that as a result, price and other economic adjustments will happen very quickly. **Adaptive expectations** is a milder theory in which people have limited information about economic information and how the economy works, and so price and other economic adjustments can be slow.

4. Neoclassical economists tend to put relatively more emphasis on long-term growth than on fighting recession, because they believe that recessions will fade in a few years and long-term growth will ultimately determine the standard of living.

5. Neoclassical economists tend to focus more on reducing the natural rate of unemployment caused by economic institutions and government policies than the cyclical rate of unemployment caused by recession.

6. Neoclassical economists see no social benefit to inflation. With an upward-sloping Keynesian AS curve, inflation can arise because an economy is approaching full employment. But with a vertical long-run neoclassical AS curve, inflation does not accompany any rise in output.

7. If aggregate supply is vertical, then aggregate demand does not affect the quantity of output. Instead, aggregate demand can only cause inflationary changes in the price level.

8. A vertical aggregate supply curve, where the quantity of output is consistent with many different price levels, also implies a vertical Phillips curve.

9. Many mainstream economists take a Keynesian perspective, assuming sticky wages and prices and emphasizing the power of aggregate demand, for purposes of short-run analysis and a neoclassical perspective, assuming adjustment of wages and prices and emphasizing the power of long-run supply, for purposes of long-run analysis.

Review Questions

1. Does neoclassical economics focus on the long term or the short term?

2. Does neoclassical economics view prices and wages as sticky or flexible?

3. What shape is the long-run aggregate supply curve?

4. What is the difference between rational expectations and adaptive expectations?

5. Do neoclassical economists tend to focus more on economic growth or on recessions? Explain briefly.

6. Do neoclassical economists tend to focus more on cyclical unemployment or on inflation? Explain briefly.

7. Do neoclassical economists see a value in tolerating a little more inflation if it brings additional economic output?

8. If aggregate supply is vertical, what role does aggregate demand play in determining output? In determining the price level?

9. What is the shape of the neoclassical long-run Phillips curve?

15

Money and Banks

Money is not an end in itself. You can't eat dollar bills or wear your bank account. Ultimately, the usefulness of money rests in exchanging it for goods or services. As the American writer and humorist Ambrose Bierce (1842–1914) wrote in 1911, money is a "blessing that is of no advantage to us excepting when we part with it."

Here's a trivia question: In the history of the world, what item was used for money over the broadest geographic area and the longest period of time? The answer isn't gold or silver, or any precious metal. It's the cowrie, a mollusk shell found mainly off the Maldive Islands in the Indian Ocean. Cowries served as money as early as 700 B.C. in China. By the 1500s, they were in widespread use across India and Africa. For several centuries after that, cowries were used in markets including southern Europe, western Africa, India and China for a wide range of purchases: everything from buying lunch or a ferry ride to paying for a shipload of silk or rice. Cowries were still acceptable as a way of paying taxes in certain African nations in the early twentieth century.

What made cowries work so well as money? First, they are extremely durable and last a century or more. As one writer put it, they can be "poured, sacked, shoveled, hoarded in heaps" while remaining "clean, dainty, stainless, polished, and milk-white." Second, parties could use cowries either by counting shells of a certain size, or—for large purchases—by measuring the weight or volume of the total shells to be exchanged. Third, it was impossible to counterfeit a cowrie shell, but gold or silver coins could be counterfeited by making copies with cheaper metals. Finally, in the heyday of cowrie money from the 1500s into the 1800s, the collection of cowries was tightly controlled, first by the Portuguese and later by the Dutch and the English. As a result, the supply of cowries was allowed to grow quickly enough to serve the needs of commerce, but not so quickly that they were no longer scarce.

The discussion of money and banking in this chapter begins a new main section in the study of macroeconomics. At this point, you should have firmly in mind the four main goals of macroeconomics: economic growth, low unemployment, low inflation, and a sustainable balance of trade. You should also understand Keynesian and neoclassical frameworks for macroeconomic analysis and how these frameworks can be embodied in the aggregate demand-aggregate supply (AD-AS) model. With the goals and frameworks for macroeconomic analysis in mind, the final step is to discuss the two main categories of macroeconomic policy: monetary policy, which focuses on money, banking and interest rates; and fiscal policy, which focuses on government spending, taxes, and borrowing. This chapter discusses what economists mean by money, and how money is closely interrelated with the banking system. Chapter 16 discusses how central banks, such as the U.S. Federal Reserve, can affect the money supply in the economy. Chapter 17 discusses the international dimensions of money, including the economic and policy factors that determine exchange rates between the money from different countries.

Defining Money by Its Functions

Money is what people in a society regularly use when purchasing or selling goods and services, and thus money must be widely accepted by both buyers and sellers. This concept of money is intentionally flexible, because money has taken a wide variety of forms in different cultures. Money has been made of gold, silver, and paper. Native Americans and early American settlers used strings of beads called wampum as money. In the islands of Fiji in the southern Pacific Ocean, islanders once exchanged the teeth of the sperm whale as money. People have used cattle as money over the centuries; in certain areas of what was then Russia, horses were the main form of money well into the twentieth century, with sheep and lambskins used for small change. Metal forms of money have included not only coins, but metal anklets and bracelets have been used as a type of wearable money, especially in western Africa. In prisons and prisoner-of-war camps in the twentieth century, cigarettes have sometimes served as money. Modern examples of money include U.S. dollars, European euros, the Chinese yuan, India's rupee, Japanese yen, Nigerian naira, Brazilian reals, Polish zlotys, and the coins and bills of every country.

Barter and the Double Coincidence of Wants

To understand the usefulness of money, consider the inconvenience of exchange without money. **Barter**—literally trading one good or service for another—is a completely inadequate mechanism for trying to coordinate the trades in a modern advanced economy. In an economy without money, an exchange between two people would involve a **double coincidence of wants,** a situation in which both of two people each wants some good or service that the other person can provide. For example, if an accountant wants a pair of shoes, this accountant must find someone who has a pair of shoes in the correct size and who is willing to exchange the shoes for some hours of accounting services. Such a trade is likely to be difficult to arrange. Think about the complexity of such trades in a modern economy, with its extensive division of labor that involves thousands upon thousands of different jobs and goods.

barter: Literally, trading one good or service for another, without using money.

double coincidence of wants: A situation in which both of two people each wants some good or service that the other person can provide.

Mademoiselle Zelie's Problems with Barter

In 1875, famous British economist William Stanley Jevons (1835–1882) wrote a book called *Money and the Mechanics of Exchange,* in which he illustrated the problems of barter with the following example:

> Some years since, Mademoiselle Zelie, a singer of the Theatre Lyrique at Paris, made a professional tour around the world, and gave a concert in the Society Islands. In exchange for an air from *Norma* and a few other songs, she was to receive a third part of the receipts. When counted, her share was found to consist of three pigs, twenty-three turkeys, forty-four chickens, five thousand cocoa-nuts, besides considerable quantities of bananas, lemons, and oranges. At the Halle in Paris, as the prima donna remarks in her lively letter, printed by M. Wolowski, this amount of live stock and vegetables might have brought four thousand francs, which would have been good remuneration for five songs. In the Society Islands, however, pieces of money were very scarce; and as Mademoiselle could not consume any considerable portion of the receipts herself, it became necessary in the mean time to feed the pigs and poultry with the fruit. . . .

> In modern civilized society the inconveniences of the primitive method of exchange are wholly unknown, and might almost seem to be imaginary. Accustomed as we are to the use of money, we are unconscious of the inestimable benefits which it confers upon us; and only when we recur to altogether different states of society can we realize the difficulties which arise in its absence.

Money greases the social machinery of exchange. In an economy with money, an accountant doesn't need to seek out people who sell shoes and find out if they want to exchange them for a few hours of accounting services. Instead, the accountant works for a company and receives money wages, which can then be used to purchase shoes or other goods. Employers don't need to pay their workers in apartments, food, or clothing; instead, employers pay money. People don't need to save for their retirement by piling up canned food in their basements; they save money in the bank instead. Money is a marvelous invention that makes the division of labor and other complex economic activities possible.

Three Functions for Money

Economists have identified three specific functions of money. First, money serves as a **medium of exchange,** which means that money must be very widely accepted as a method of payment in the markets for goods, labor, and financial capital. U.S. paper money, for example, carries the statement: "THIS NOTE IS LEGAL TENDER FOR ALL DEBTS, PUBLIC AND PRIVATE." In other words, if you owe a debt, then legally speaking, you can pay that debt with currency.

medium of exchange: Whatever is widely accepted as a method of payment.

Second, money serves as a **unit of account,** which means that it is the ruler by which other values are measured. Without money, you would have to carry around list of all the possible opportunity costs in your head: for example, a loaf of bread will have an opportunity cost of 10 minutes of work or a rental movie. Money acts as a common denominator, an accounting method that simplifies thinking about trade-offs. At a supermarket, the unit of account function of money allows the cashier to add the values of many individual items into a single value. A common unit of account allows government statisticians to add up the value of cars, haircuts, Internet service providers and all other goods and services into a single money value to calculate GDP.

unit of account: The common way in which market values are measured in an economy.

Third, money serves as a **store of value;** that is, when you receive money, you know that you don't need to spend it immediately because it will still hold its value the next day, or the next year. Holding money is a much easier and less wasteful way of storing

store of value: Something that serves as a way of preserving economic value that can be spent or consumed in the future.

value than trying to purchase physical goods, such as apples or refrigerators, storing those goods, and then trying to exchange them in the future. This function of money does not require that money is a *perfect* store of value. In an economy with inflation, money loses some buying power each year, but it remains money.

Money needs to serve all three of these functions—medium of exchange, unit of account, and store of value. Serving only one of these functions is not enough. For example, a house may serve as a store of value, in the sense that it can be sold later. But houses do not serve as mediums of exchange or units of account, and so they are not money.

Measuring Money: Currency, M1, and M2

Cash in your pocket certainly serves as a medium of exchange, unit of account, and a store of value. But what about checks or credit cards? Are they money, too? Rather than trying to state a single way of measuring money, economists offer a series of ever-broader definitions of money.

Money certainly includes **currency,** the coins and bills that circulate in an economy. Closely related to currency are two items that you can use, in most circumstances, almost as easily as cash. One of them is *traveler's checks*, which you purchase from a bank or financial company, sign, and then redeem with an additional signature when you want to spend them. Traveler's checks have the advantage of being accepted almost as widely as currency, and, if they are lost or stolen, the company that issued them will replace them. Cash offers no such protection. The other item closely related to currency is personal checks, also known to economists as **demand deposits,** because they are deposits in banks that are available by making a cash withdrawal or writing a check. These three items together—currency, traveler's checks, and checking accounts in banks—make up the definition of money known as **M1.**

A broader definition of money, known as **M2,** includes everything in M1, but also adds the bank accounts on which money can be withdrawn fairly easily, but not as easily as with personal checks. For example, M2 includes **savings deposits** in banks, which are bank accounts on which you can't write a check directly, but you can easily withdraw the money at an automatic teller machine or bank. Many banks and other financial institutions offer a chance to invest in **money market funds,** where the deposits of many individual investors are pooled together and invested in a safe way like short-term government bonds. Another ingredient of M2 are the relatively small (that is, less than about $100,000) **certificates of deposit** or **time deposits,** which are accounts that the depositor has committed to leaving in the bank for a certain period of time, ranging from a few months to a few years, in exchange for a higher interest rate. In short, these ingredients of M2 are money that you can withdraw and spend, but with a greater effort than the items in M1.

Exhibit 15-1 should help in visualizing the relationship between M1 and M2. Note that M1 is nested in M2. In 2009, M1 was $1,693 billion, while M2 was $8,524 billion. For comparison, the size of the U.S. GDP in 2009 was $14.2 trillion.

The lines between separating M1 and M2 can become a little blurry. Sometimes elements of M1 are not treated alike; for example, some businesses won't accept personal checks for large amounts, but will accept traveler's checks or cash. Changes in banking practices and technology have made the savings accounts in M2 more similar to the checking accounts in M1. For example, some savings accounts will allow depositors

money: Whatever serves society in three functions: medium of exchange, unit of account, and store of value.

currency: Coins and paper bills.

demand deposits: Deposits in banks that are available by making a cash withdrawal or writing a check.

M1: A narrow definition of the money supply that includes currency, traveler's checks, and checking accounts in banks.

M2: A definition of the money supply that includes everything in M1, but also adds savings deposits, money market funds, and certificates of deposit.

savings deposits: Bank accounts where you can't withdraw money by writing a check, but can withdraw the money at a bank—or can transfer it easily to a checking account.

money market funds: Where the deposits of many investors are pooled together and invested in a safe way like short-term government bonds.

certificate of deposit (CD): A mechanism for a saver to deposit funds at a bank and promise to leave them at the bank for a time, in exchange for a higher rate of interest.

time deposits: Accounts that the depositor has committed to leaving in the bank for a certain period of time, in exchange for a higher rate of interest; also called certificates of deposit.

The Case of the Missing Currency

Here is a puzzle. The Federal Reserve reported that about $862 billion in currency—that is, paper money and coins—was in circulation in 2009. Dividing the total currency by roughly 220 million U.S. adults 20 or older works out to an average of approximately $3,900 in currency for every man and woman.

This average seems ridiculously high. Survey results suggest that the average holdings of currency for each adult are more like $350—and that number takes into account well-off people who hold large amounts of cash in safes and safety deposit boxes. If 220 million adults are each holding $350, then total holdings of U.S. currency by individuals is about $77 billion. Businesses traditionally hold about 3% of all currency, or about $26 billion. After all, most businesses try not to hold currency, but instead quickly get money to the bank where it can earn some interest.

So if households and firms together hold about $103 billion in currency, where is the other $759 billion? No one is quite sure. There are three possible answers: it may be held by children; as part of the unmeasured "underground" economy; or by foreigners. Even if one believes that

teenage buying power is important to certain sectors of the economy, and that underground, unreported businesses are everywhere, it is very hard to believe that these two components are larger than the uses of money by adults and legal businesses. As a result, it seems likely that hundreds of billions of dollars of U.S. currency is circulating in the hands of foreigners.

When a country's own currency is plagued with uncertainty, perhaps because of a high inflation rate, people in that country may start carrying out transactions and saving money by using U.S. dollars. But this explanation is not completely satisfactory either. In high-income economies like those of the European nations, Japan, and Canada, people have relatively little need to use U.S. currency for transactions or saving. People may invest in the United States, but they can do so with electronic money; they don't need actual currency in the form of paper and coins. In the middle and low-income countries of the world, the average families are too poor to account for hundreds of billions of dollars of U.S. currency.

The case of the missing currency remains unsolved.

Exhibit 15-1   Defining Money with M1 and M2

The money stock has several definitions, ranging from narrow to broad. M1 is mainly currency and checking accounts. M2 is everything in M1, plus savings accounts, small time deposits, and money market funds.

Currency	$862 billion
Traveler's checks	$5 billion
Demand deposits and other checking accounts	$826 billion
Total M1	**$1,693 billion**
Savings accounts	$4,849 billion
Small time deposits	$1,168 billion
Individual money market mutual fund balances	$814 billion
Total M2	**$8,524 billion**

M2 ($8,524 billion) M1 ($1,693 billion)

to write checks, use automatic teller machines, and pay bills over the Internet, which has made it easier to access savings accounts. As with many other economic terms and statistics, the important point is to know the strengths and limitations of the various definitions of money, not to believe that such definitions are as clear-cut to economists as, say, the definition of nitrogen is to chemists.

Where does "plastic money" like credit cards fit into this picture? When you make a purchase with a credit card, the credit card company immediately transfers money from its checking account to the seller, and at the end of the month, the credit card company sends you a bill for what you have charged that month. Until you pay the credit card bill, you have effectively borrowed money from the credit card company, although typically no interest is charged on the loan if you pay your credit card bill on time. When you make a purchase with a *debit card*, another kind of plastic money, the funds are transferred directly and immediately from your bank account to the seller. With a *smart card*, you can store a certain value of money on the card and then use the card to make purchases. Some "smart cards" used for specific purposes, like long-distance phone calls or making purchases at a campus bookstore and cafeteria, aren't really all that smart, because they can only be used for certain purchases or in certain places. However, in the Netherlands, millions of smart cards that are good for small purchases in many stores have been in circulation since the late 1990s. In short, credit cards, debit cards, and smart cards are different ways to move money when a purchase is made. But having more credit cards or debit cards doesn't change the quantity of money in the economy, any more than having more checks printed increases the amount of money in your checking account.

One key message underlying this discussion of M1 and M2 is that money in a modern economy is not just paper bills and coins; instead, money is closely linked to bank accounts. Indeed, the macroeconomic policies concerning money are largely conducted through the banking system. The next section explains how banks function and how a nation's banking system has the power to create money.

How Banks Work

An old-time bank robber named Willie Sutton (1901–1980) was once asked why he robbed banks. He answered: "That's where the money is." From the perspective of modern economists, Sutton is both right and wrong. He is wrong because the overwhelming majority of money in the economy is not in the form of currency sitting in vaults or drawers at banks, waiting for a robber to appear. Most money is in the form of bank accounts, which exist only as electronic records on computers. From a broader perspective, however, the bank robber was more right than he may have known. Banking is intimately tied up with money and consequently, with the broader economy.

Banks make it far easier for a complex economy to carry out the extraordinary range of transactions that occur in goods, labor, and financial capital markets. Imagine for a moment what the economy would be like if all payments had to be made in cash. When shopping for a large purchase or going on vacation you might need to carry hundreds of dollars in a pocket or purse. Even small businesses would need stockpiles of cash to pay workers and to purchase supplies. In a world where large quantities of cash are common, burglars and pickpockets would be rampant. But along with making transactions much safer and easier, banks play a key role in the saving and borrowing that takes place in financial capital markets.

Banks as Financial Intermediaries

An "intermediary" is one who stands between two other parties; for example, a person who arranges a blind date between two friends is one kind of intermediary. Banks are a **financial intermediary**—that is, an institution that operates between a saver who deposits money in a bank and a borrower who receives a loan from that bank. But when a bank serves as a financial intermediary, unlike the situation with a couple on a blind date, the saver and the borrower never meet. All the funds deposited are mingled in

financial intermediary:
An institution that operates between a saver with financial assets to invest and an entity who will receive those assets and pay a rate of return.

Banks, Savings and Loans, and Credit Unions

Banks have a couple of close cousins: *savings institutions* and *credit unions*. Banks, as explained in the text, receive deposits from individuals and businesses and make loans with the money.

Savings institutions are also sometimes called "savings and loans" or "thrifts." They also take loans and make deposits. However, from the 1930s until the 1980s, federal law limited how much interest savings institutions were allowed to pay to depositors. They were also required to make most of their loans in the form of housing-related loans, either to homebuyers or to real-estate developers and builders.

A *credit union* is a nonprofit financial institution that its members own and run. Members of each credit union decide who is eligible to be a member. Usually, potential members would be everyone in a certain community, or groups of employees, or members of a certain organization. The credit union accepts deposits from members and focuses on making loans back to its members. While there are more credit unions than banks and more banks than savings and loans, the total assets of credit unions are relatively small.

In 2008, the U.S. economy had 7,085 banks, 1,220 thrifts, and 7,806 credit unions. The banks and savings and loans tend to be roughly the same size. In 2008, on average, these institutions held $1.6 billion in assets each. Credit unions are much smaller. In 2009, they averaged about $100 million in assets each.

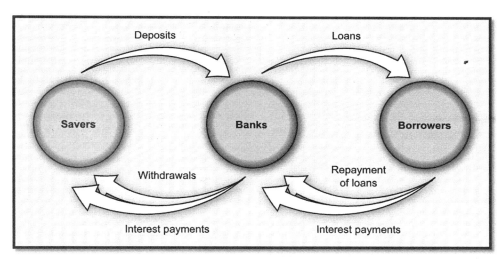

Exhibit 15-2   Banks as Financial Intermediaries

Banks act as financial intermediaries because they stand between savers and borrowers. Savers place deposits with banks, and then receive interest payments and withdraw money. Borrowers receive loans from banks, and repay the loans with interest. In turn, banks return money to savers in the form of withdrawals, which also include interest payments from banks to savers.

one big pool, which is then loaned out. Exhibit 15-2 illustrates the position of banks as financial intermediaries, with deposits flowing into a bank and loans flowing out. Of course, when banks make loans to firms, the banks will try to funnel financial capital to healthy businesses that have good prospects for repaying the loans, not to firms that are suffering losses and may be unable to repay.

A bank receives revenue from two sources: interest payments to the bank from those who have received bank loans, and other fees and charges imposed by the bank. Conversely, banks have four main categories of expenses: interest payments to depositors; loans that are not repaid; operating costs of employees, office space and equipment; and taxes. Exhibit 15-3 shows the combined statistics for revenues and expenses for the roughly 8,000 U.S. banks and savings institutions. The U.S. banking industry as a whole earned $20 billion in accounting profits in 2008. Of course, just because the overall banking industry earned a profit doesn't mean that every individual bank did so; in fact, during the recession of 2007–2009, many banks experienced high costs of loans that were not repaid as expected, and lost money as a result.

Total Revenues		Total Costs	
Interest income	$603 billion	Interest payments	$246 billion
Other income (fees and charges)	$208 billion	Cost of loans that are not repaid	$174 billion
		Operating expenses (salaries, office space, equipment)	$365 billion
		Taxes	$6 billion
Total revenues	$811 billion	Total costs	$791 billion
Accounting profits = Total revenues − Total costs = $20 billion			

Exhibit 15-3
Revenues, Expenses, and Profits for the U.S. Banking Industry in 2008

Assets		Liabilities	
Loans	$5 million	Deposits	$10 million
Bonds	$4 million		
Reserves	$2 million		

Net worth = Assets − Liabilities
$1 million = $11 million − $10 million

Exhibit 15-4
A Balance Sheet for the Safe and Secure Bank

The "T" in a T-account separates the assets of a firm on the left from its liabilities on the right. All firms use (much more complex) T-accounts. But for a bank, the assets are the financial instruments that either the bank is holding—its reserves—or those instruments where other parties owe money to the bank—like loans made by the bank and bonds purchased by the bank. Liabilities are what the bank owes to others: specifically, the bank owes any deposits made in the bank to those who have made them. The net worth of the bank is the total assets minus total liabilities. For a healthy business, net worth will be positive. For a bankrupt firm, net worth will be negative.

A Bank's Balance Sheet

Banks calculate their profits at the end of each quarter or year. But banks also evaluate their financial condition by comparing their **assets,** which are defined as items of value owned by the firm, with their **liabilities,** which are any amounts or debts owed by the firm. A **balance sheet** is an accounting tool that lists assets and liabilities. Exhibit 15-4 illustrates a hypothetical balance sheet for the Safe and Secure Bank. Because of the two-column format of the balance sheet, with the T-shape formed by the vertical line down the middle and the horizontal line under "Assets" and "Liabilities," it is sometimes called a **T-account.**

When bank customers deposit money into a checking account, savings account, or a certificate of deposit, the bank views these deposits as liabilities. After all, the bank owes these deposits to its customers, when the customers wish to withdraw their money. The Safe and Secure Bank holds $10 million in deposits.

Loans are the first category of bank assets shown in Exhibit 15-4. Say that a family takes out a 30-year mortgage loan to purchase a house, which means that the borrower will repay the loan over the next 30 years. This loan is clearly an asset from the bank's perspective, because the borrower has a legal obligation to make payments to the bank over time. But in practical terms, how can the value of the mortgage loan that is being paid over 30 years be measured in the present? One way of measuring the value of something—whether a loan or anything else—is by estimating what another party in the market is willing to pay for it. Many banks issue home loans, and charge various handling and processing fees for doing so, but then sell the loans to other banks or financial institutions who collect the loan payments. The market where loans are made to borrowers is called the *primary loan market*, while the market in which these loans are bought and sold by financial institutions is the *secondary loan market*.

One key factor that affects what financial institutions are willing to pay for a loan, when they buy it in the secondary loan market, is the perceived riskiness of the loan:

assets: Items of value owned by a firm or an individual.

liabilities: Any amounts or debts owed by a firm or an individual.

balance sheet: An accounting tool that lists assets and liabilities.

T-account: A balance sheet with two-column format, with the T-shape formed by the vertical line down the middle and the horizontal line under the column headings for "Assets" and "Liabilities."

that is, given the characteristics of the borrower like income level and whether the local economy is performing strongly, what proportion of loans of this type will be repaid? The greater the risk that a loan will not be repaid, the less that any financial institution will pay to acquire the loan. Another key factor is to compare the interest rate charged on the original loan with the current interest rate in the economy. If the original loan made at some point in the past requires the borrower to pay a low interest rate, but current interest rates are relatively high, then a financial institution will pay less to acquire the loan. In contrast, if the original loan requires the borrower to pay a high rate, while current interest rates are relatively low, then a financial institution will pay more to acquire the loan. For the Safe and Secure Bank in this example, the total value of its loans if they were sold to other financial institutions in the secondary market is $5 million.

The second category of bank asset is **bonds,** which are a contract that works this way: when someone buys a bond, the party that issued the bond receives money in the present and promises to repay with interest in the future. Bonds are a common mechanism for borrowing, used not only by the federal government but also by state governments, private companies, and nonprofit organizations. A bank takes some of the money it has received in deposits and uses the money to buy bonds—typically bonds issued by the government. Government bonds are low-risk because the government is virtually certain to pay off the bond, albeit at a low rate of interest. These bonds are an asset for banks in the same way that loans are an asset; that is, the bank will receive a stream of payments in the future. The Safe and Secure Banks holds bonds with a total value of $4 million.

The final entry under assets is **reserves,** which is money that the bank keeps on hand, and that is not loaned out or invested in bonds—and thus does not lead to interest payments. The Safe and Secure Bank is holding $2 million in reserves. Government regulators typically set minimum reserve levels that banks must hold. The next chapter will explain how the level of these required reserves are one policy tool that governments have to influence bank behavior.

The **net worth** of a bank is defined as its total assets minus its total liabilities. For the Safe and Secure Bank shown in Exhibit 15-4, net worth is equal to $1 million; that is, $11 million in assets minus $10 million in liabilities. For a financially healthy bank, the net worth will be positive. If a bank has negative net worth, and depositors tried to withdraw their money, the bank would not be able to give all depositors their money.

bond: A financial contract through which a borrower like a corporation, a city or state, or the federal government agrees to repay the amount that was borrowed and also a rate of interest over a period of time in the future.

reserves: Funds that a bank keeps on hand and that are not loaned out or invested in bonds.

net worth: Total assets minus total liabilities.

How Banks Go Bankrupt

A bank that is bankrupt will have a negative net worth; that is, its assets will be worth less than its liabilities. How can this happen? The balance sheet helps to explain.

A well-run bank will assume that a small percentage of borrowers do not repay their loans on time, or at all, and factor these missing payments into its planning. Remember, the calculations of the expenses of banks every year includes a factor for loans that are not repaid, and the value of a bank's loans on its balance sheet assumes a certain level

Securitized Subprime Loans and the Financial Crisis of 2007–2009

Many banks make mortgage loans so that people can buy a home, but then don't keep the loans on their books as an asset. Instead, the bank sells the loan. These loans are commonly "securitized," which means that they are bundled together into a financial security, which is sold to investors. Investors in these mortgage-backed securities receive a rate of return based on level of payments that people make on all the mortgages that stand behind the security.

Securitization offers certain advantages. If a bank makes most of its loans in a local area, then the bank may be financially vulnerable if the local economy declines, so that many people are unable to make their payments. But if a bank sells its local loans, and then buys a mortgage-backed security based on home loans in many parts of the country, it can avoid being exposed to local financial risks. (In the simple example in the text, banks just own "bonds." In reality, banks can own a number of financial instruments, as long as these financial investments are safe enough to satisfy the government bank regulators.) From the standpoint of a local homebuyer, securitization offers the benefit that a local bank doesn't need to have lots of extra funds to make a loan, because the bank is only planning to hold that loan for a short time, before selling the loan so that it can be pooled into a financial security.

But securitization also offers one potentially large disadvantage. If a bank is going to hold a mortgage loan as an asset, the bank has an incentive to scrutinize the borrower carefully to ensure that the loan is likely to be repaid. However, a bank that is going to sell the loan may be less careful in making the loan in the first place. The bank will be more willing to make what are called "subprime loans," which are loans which have characteristics like low or zero down-payment, little scrutiny of whether the borrower has a reliable income, and sometimes low payments for the next year or two that will be followed by much higher payments after that. Some subprime loans made in the mid-2000s were later dubbed NINJA loans: that is, loans made even though the borrower had demonstrated No Income, No Job, or Assets.

These subprime loans were typically sold and turned into financial securities—but with a twist. The idea was that if losses occurred on these mortgage-backed securities, certain investors would agree to take the first, say, 5% of such losses. Other investors would agree to take, say, the next 5% of losses. By this approach, still other investors would not need to take any losses unless these mortgage-backed financial securities lost 25% or 30% or more of their total value. These complex securities, along with other economic factors, encourages a large expansion of subprime loans in the mid-2000s.

The economic stage was now set for a banking crisis. Banks thought they were buying only ultra-safe securities, because even though the securities were ultimately backed by risky subprime mortgages, the banks only invested in the part of those securities where they were protected from small or moderate levels of losses. But as housing prices fell after 2007, and the deepening recession made it harder for many people to make their mortgage payments, many banks found that their mortgage-backed financial assets could end up being worth much less than they had expected—and so the banks were staring bankruptcy in the face.

of riskiness because some loans will not be repaid. But even if a bank expects a certain number of loan defaults, it will suffer if the number of loan defaults is much greater than expected, as can happen during a recession. For example, if the Safe and Secure Bank in Exhibit 15-4 experienced a wave of unexpected defaults, so that its loans declined in value from $5 million to $3 million, then the assets of the Safe and Secure Bank would decline so that the bank had negative net worth.

The risk of an unexpectedly high level of loan defaults can be especially difficult for banks because of a bank's liabilities, namely the deposits of its customers, can be withdrawn quickly, but many of the bank's assets like loans and bonds will only be repaid over years or even decades. This **asset-liability time mismatch**—a bank's liabilities can be withdrawn in the short term while its assets are repaid in the long term—can cause severe problems for a bank. For example, imagine a bank that has loaned a substantial amount of money at a certain interest rate, but then sees interest rates rise substantially. The bank can find itself in a precarious situation. If it doesn't raise the interest rate it pays to depositors, then deposits will flow to other institutions that offer the higher interest rates that are now prevailing. However, if the bank raises the interest rates that it pays to depositors, it may end up in a situation where it is paying a higher interest rate to depositors than it is collecting from those past loans that were made at lower interest

asset-liability time mismatch: A bank's liabilities can be withdrawn in the short term while its assets are repaid in the long term.

rates. Clearly, the bank can't survive in the long term if it is paying out more in interest to depositors than it is receiving from borrowers.

How can banks protect themselves against an unexpectedly high rate of loan defaults and against the risk of an asset-liability time mismatch? One strategy is for a bank to **diversify** its loans, which means lending to a variety of customers. For example, suppose a bank specialized in lending to a niche market—say, making a high proportion of its loans to construction companies that build offices in one downtown area. If that one area suffers an unexpected economic downturn, the bank will suffer large losses. However, if a bank loans both to consumers who are buying homes and cars and also to a wide range of firms in many industries and geographic areas, the bank is less exposed to risk. When a bank diversifies its loans, those categories of borrowers who have an unexpectedly large number of defaults will tend to be balanced out, according to random chance, by other borrowers who have an unexpectedly low number of defaults. Thus, diversification of loans can help banks to keep a positive net worth. However, if a widespread recession occurs that touches many industries and geographic areas, diversification won't help.

Along with diversifying their loans, banks have several other strategies to reduce the risk of an unexpectedly large number of loan defaults. For example, banks can sell some of the loans they make in the secondary loan market, as described earlier, and instead hold a greater share of assets in the form of government bonds or reserves. Nevertheless, in a lengthy recession, most banks will see their net worth decline because a higher share of loans will not be repaid in tough economic times.

diversify: Making loans or investments with a variety of firms, to reduce the risk of being adversely affected by events at one or a few firms.

How Banks Create Money

Banks and money are intertwined. It's not just that most money is in the form of bank accounts. In addition, the banking system can literally create money through the process of making loans. This section describes how banks create money.

The Story of System Bank

Let's start with a hypothetical example. The people in an economy have $10 million in money, and they all deposit all of their money in a single bank, called System Bank. System Bank starts off with a simple business plan: It keeps the depositor's money safe by holding all money in the form of reserves. The T-account balance sheet for System Bank with 100% reserves is shown in Exhibit 15-5. Obviously, System Bank can't afford to pay interest to depositors, because it isn't earning any interest by making loans. In this form, System Bank is basically just a big piggy bank for keeping money safe.

However, the owners of System Bank notice that from month to month, the inflows of deposits from some people are pretty much counterbalanced by the withdrawals of others. Thus, in some months the deposits and reserves of System Bank grow a little higher than $10 million, and sometimes they fall a little below $10 million, but there is

Assets		Liabilities	
Reserves	$10 million	Deposits	$10 million

Exhibit 15-5 System Bank's Balance Sheet, 100% Reserves

A bank with 100% reserves would hold all of its deposits as reserves, and not make any loans.

Assets		Liabilities	
Loans	$9 million	Deposits	$19 million
Reserves	$10 million		

Exhibit 15-6   System Bank's Balance Sheet: 10% Reserves, One Round of Loans

Imagine that System Bank starts with the situation in Exhibit 15-5, but then decides to hold only 10% of its original $10 million in deposits as reserves and to loan out the remaining $9 million. However, since System Bank is the only bank in this economy, the $9 million that is loaned out also ends up being deposited in the bank by the recipients of the loan. Thus, bank deposits rise from the original $10 million to $19 million. With deposits of $19 million and loans of $9 million, the remaining reserves are still $10 million.

always at least $9.5 million in the bank. So the owners of System Bank come up with a new business plan. They will hold reserves of only 10%, rather than 100%, and they will loan out the remaining $9 million. By loaning out the $9 million and charging interest, they reason, they will be able to make interest payments to depositors. Instead of becoming just a storage place for deposits, System Bank can become a financial intermediary between savers and borrowers.

This change in business plan alters System Bank's balance sheet, as shown in Exhibit 15-6. In this economy, remember, people either deposit all of their money in System Bank, or they buy something from a firm that deposits the money in the firm's account at System Bank. So the total deposits in this economy—that is, the liabilities for System Bank—now total $19 million; that is, the original $10 million in deposits plus the additional $9 million in deposits resulting from the loans. The assets of System Bank also total $19 million. Although the bank loaned out $9 million, thus reducing its original reserves from $10 million to $1 million, the bank also received $9 million in additional deposits to put back into reserves, raising its reserves back to the original $10 million. In addition, System Bank now has $9 million in loan assets.

Before discussing further the situation of System Bank, pause for a moment and notice a remarkable fact: when System Bank decided to stop holding all money in reserves and instead to hold only a portion in reserves and loan out the rest, the quantity of money in the economy expanded. By making loans, System Bank created money.

Of course, the assumption that an economy has only one bank is a gross oversimplification, but the banking system as a whole will work to create money, just like in the example of System Bank. When banks start making loans, and people and firms start redepositing the loans in other bank accounts, money is created in the economy. System Bank uses the metaphor of a single bank for the entire economy to describe the process of money creation for the banking system as a whole.

The Money Multiplier

The owners of System Bank now notice another intriguing fact. They had originally decided that holding reserves equal to 10% of deposits was a sufficient margin for safety, to assure that System Bank would have enough cash on hand for those who are withdrawing money. But after making one round of loans, System Bank has $19 million in deposits. If the bank wishes to hold 10% of that amount in reserves, it need hold only $1.9 million in reserves. But if System Bank has $10 million in reserves, and wishes to hold only $1.9 million in reserves, then the bank can make a second round of loans, this time of $8.1 million.

Again, those people who receive the loans either deposit the money in System Bank themselves, or spend the money with a business that deposits the money in System Bank. The new balance sheet of System Bank appears in Exhibit 15-7. The liabilities of System Bank—that is, its deposits—now total $27.1 million, which is the previous $19 million in deposits plus $8.1 million. The total loans of the bank are now $17.1 million; that is, the $9 million in loans from the first round plus $8.1 million in loans from the second

Assets		Liabilities	
Loans	$17.1 million	Deposits	$27.1 million
Reserves	$10 million		

Exhibit 15-7   System Bank's Balance Sheet: 10% Reserves, Second Round of Loans

Imagine that System Bank starts off with the situation in Exhibit 15-6, but still wishes to hold only 10% of its deposits as reserves. Thus, starting with $19 million in deposits, it wishes to hold $1.9 million in reserves. Since the bank currently has $10 million in reserves, it can loan out $8.1 million. Total loans increase from $9 million to $17.1 million. However, since System Bank is the only bank in this economy, the $8.1 million that is loaned out also ends up being deposited in the bank by the recipients of the loan. Thus, bank deposits rise from $19 million to $27.1 million. With deposits of $27.1 million and loans of $17.1 million, the remaining reserves are still at $10 million.

round. Finally, the reserves of the bank remain at $10 million. System Bank loaned out $8.1 million of its reserves, but it also received deposits of $8.1 million, which it is holding in its reserves.

But now System Bank is holding $27.1 million in deposits, and for a 10% margin of safety, it wishes to hold only $2.71 million in reserves. Since the bank is holding $10 million in reserves, it can now make a third round of loans, this time of $10 million – $2.71 million = $7.29 million. A pattern is forming here. System Bank is making cycle after cycle of loans, but each cycle is less than the previous one.

Exactly how much money will exist in this economy as System Bank (or the banking system) makes all of these successive rounds of loans? The original quantity of money in this economy was $10 million. In the first round of lending, System Bank kept 10% of that $10 million in reserves and loaned out the remaining $9 million, which then came back to the bank in the form of deposits. In the second round of lending, System Bank kept 10% of that additional $9 million in reserve, and loaned out the remaining $8.1 million. In a third round, System Bank would keep 10% of that $8.1 million in reserve, and loan out the remaining $7.29 million. These rounds of lending will continue through a fourth, fifth, sixth, and indeed an infinite number of rounds. Each round of lending will create additional money, but the marginal additions become smaller and smaller.

Fortunately, a formula exists for calculating the total of these many rounds of lending in a banking system. If the **reserve ratio** is the proportion of deposits that the bank wished to hold in reserves, then the formula is:

$$\text{Total quantity of money} = \text{Original quantity of reserves} \times \frac{1}{\text{Reserve ratio}}$$

reserve ratio: The proportion of deposits that the bank holds in the form of reserves.

$$= \$10 \text{ million} \times \frac{1}{0.1}$$

$$= \$10 \text{ million} \times 10 = \$100 \text{ million}$$

Thus, in this example, the total quantity of money generated in this economy after all rounds of lending are completed will be $100 million. The **money multiplier** is equal to the total money in the economy divided by the original quantity of money. The formula to calculate the money multiplier is 1/reserve ratio. In this example, the reserve ratio is 10% or 0.1, and the money multiplier is 10. The money multiplier also shows how much the total supply of money in the economy would be altered if the original quantity of reserves was increased or decreased by $1.

money multiplier: Total money in the economy divided by the original quantity of money, or change in the total money in the economy divided by a change in the original quantity of money.

Cautions about the Money Multiplier

The money multiplier will depend on the proportion of reserves that banks choose to hold. System Bank chose to hold reserves equal to 10% of deposits, leading to a money multiplier of 10. But if System Bank had chosen to hold reserves of 20% of deposits, then the money multiplier would fall to 5. Banks may decide to vary how much they hold in reserves for two reasons: macroeconomic conditions and government rules. When an economy is in recession, banks are likely to hold a higher proportion of reserves because they fear that loans are less likely to be repaid when the economy is slow. The government may also raise or lower the required reserves held by banks as a policy move to affect the quantity of money in an economy, as the next chapter will discuss.

The process of how banks create money shows how the quantity of money in an economy is closely linked to the quantity of lending or credit in the economy. Indeed, all of the money in the economy, except for the original reserves, is a result of bank loans that are redeposited and loaned out, again and again.

The additional creation of money in this economy isn't making anyone rich. Sure, the total quantity of bank deposits gets larger as the money multiplier operates, but so does the total quantity of loans. If you borrow $5,000 and put the money in your bank account, you haven't made yourself any richer, because the money in your bank account is exactly equal to the money you owe. The money multiplier reflects an increase in lending and borrowing in the economy, but lending and borrowing by themselves don't mean that real goods and services have been produced.

Finally, the money multiplier depends on people redepositing the money that they receive in the banking system. If people instead store their cash in safe-deposit boxes or in shoeboxes hidden in their closets, then banks cannot recirculate the money in the form of loans. Indeed, governments have an incentive to assure that bank deposits are safe because if people worry that they may lose their bank deposits, they may start holding more money in cash, instead of depositing it in banks, and the quantity of loans in an economy will decline. In low-income countries, economists sometimes refer to "mattress savings," by which they mean money that people are hiding in their homes, because they don't trust banks. When mattress savings in an economy are substantial, then banks cannot lend out those funds and the money multiplier cannot operate as effectively, the overall quantity of money and loans in such an economy will therefore be reduced.

Conclusion

Money and banks are marvelous social inventions that help a modern economy to function. Compared with the alternative of barter, money makes market exchanges vastly easier in goods, labor, and financial markets. Banking makes money still more effective in facilitating exchanges in goods and labor markets. Moreover, the process of banks making loans in financial capital markets is intimately tied to the creation of money.

But the extraordinary economic gains that are possible through money and banking also suggest some possible corresponding dangers. If banks aren't working well, it sets off a decline in convenience and safety of transactions throughout the economy. If the banks are under financial stress, because of a widespread decline in the value of their assets, loans may become far less available, which can deal a crushing blow to sectors of the economy that depend on borrowed money like business investment, home construction, and car manufacturing. The recession of 2007–2009 illustrated this pattern. Given the macroeconomic dangers of a malfunctioning banking system, the next chapter will discuss government policies for controlling the money supply and for keeping the banking system safe.

Key Concepts and Summary

1. **Money** is what people in a society regularly use when purchasing or selling goods and services.

2. If money were not available, people would need to **barter** with each other, meaning that each person would need to identify others with whom they have a **double coincidence of wants**—that is, each party has a specific good or service that the other desires.

3. Money serves three functions: a **medium of exchange,** a **unit of account** and as a **store of value.**

4. Money is measured with several definitions: **M1** includes **currency,** traveler's checks, and money in checking accounts **(demand deposits). M2** includes all of M1, plus **savings deposits,** small **time deposits** like **certificates of deposit,** and **money market funds.**

5. Banks facilitate the use of money for transactions in the economy, since people and firms can use bank accounts when selling or buying goods and services, when paying a worker or being paid, and when saving money or receiving a loan. In the financial capital market, banks are **financial intermediaries;** that is, they operate between savers who supply financial capital and borrowers who demand loans.

6. A **balance sheet** (sometimes called a **T-account**) is an accounting tool which lists **assets** in one column and **liabilities** in another column. The liabilities of a bank are its deposits. The assets of a bank include its loans, its ownership of **bonds,** and its **reserves** (which are not loaned out). The **net worth** of a bank is calculated by subtracting the bank's liabilities from its assets.

7. Banks run a risk of negative net worth if the value of their assets declines. The value of assets can decline because of an unexpectedly high number of defaults on loans, or if interest rates rise and the bank suffers an **asset-liability time mismatch** in which the bank is receiving a low rate of interest on its long-term loans but must pay the currently higher market rate of interest to attract depositors. Banks can protect themselves against these risks by choosing to **diversify** their loans or to hold a greater proportion of their assets in bonds and reserves.

8. If banks hold only a fraction of their deposits as reserves, then the process of banks lending money, those loans being redeposited in banks, and the banks making additional loans will create money in the economy.

9. The **money multiplier** is defined as the quantity of money that the banking system can generate from each $1 of bank reserves. The formula for calculating the multiplier is 1/reserve ratio, where the **reserve ratio** is the fraction of deposits that the bank wishes to hold as reserves.

10. The quantity of money in an economy and the quantity of credit for loans are inextricably intertwined. Much of the money in an economy is created by the network of banks making loans, people making deposits, and banks making more loans.

Review Questions

1. What are the three functions served by money?

2. How does the existence of money simplify the process of buying and selling?

3. What is the double-coincidence of wants?

4. Define M1 and M2.

5. Why is a bank called a financial intermediary?

6. How do banks help money to work better as a medium of exchange?

7. What does a balance sheet show?

8. What are the assets of a bank? What are its liabilities?

9. How do you calculate the net worth of a bank?

10. How can a bank end up with negative net worth?

11. What is the asset-liability time mismatch that all banks face?

12. What is the risk if a bank does not diversify its loans?

13. How do banks create money?

14. What is the formula for the money multiplier?

16

Monetary Policy and Bank Regulation

M oney, loans, and banks are all tied together. Money is held in bank accounts. A banking system creates money when loans made by one bank are deposited and thus counted as money in other banks. When interlocking system of money, loans, and banks works well, economic transactions are made smoothly in goods and labor markets and savers are connected with borrowers. But if the money and banking system doesn't operate smoothly, the economy can tumble into recession.

The government of every country has public policies that attempt to assure that the system of money, loans, and banking functions well. But these policies don't always work perfectly, and the result can either be recession or a prolonged inflation. This chapter begins by discussing the policies that can affect the quantity of money in the economy. These monetary policy decisions are made by an institution called a central bank. In the United States, the central bank is called the Federal Reserve. In making decisions about the money supply, a central bank decides to raise or lower interest rates, and in this way, to affect some goals of macroeconomic policy like low unemployment and inflation. Another set of policies related to the money and banking system involves reinforcing the stability of a nation's banking system with a combination of protections for bank depositors and regular government inspections of the balance sheets of banks. In the U.S. economy, these policies to assure stability of the banking system involve both the Federal Reserve and several other regulatory institutions within the U.S. Department of the Treasury.

Monetary Policy and the Central Bank

Monetary policy involves altering the quantity of money (and the quantity of loans) in the economy. The **central bank** is the institution designed to control the quantity of money in the economy and also to oversee the safety and stability of the banking system. This section introduces the U.S. Federal Reserve and some other examples of central banks, while the next section discusses how central banks conduct monetary policy.

The Federal Reserve

The most important task of a central bank is to determine the quantity of money in the economy. Article I, Section 8 of the U.S. Constitution gives Congress the power "to coin money" and "to regulate the value thereof." As part of the 1913 legislation that created the Federal Reserve, Congress delegated these powers to the Fed.

The Federal Reserve is a peculiar organization, because it mixes government appointees with representation from private-sector banks. The Federal Reserve at the national level is run by a Board of Governors, which consists of seven members who the President of the United States appoints and the U.S. Senate must confirm. Board of Governor appointments are for 14-year terms and they are arranged so that one term expires January 31 of every even-numbered year. A person may serve only one full term on the Board of Governors. However, the 14-year terms are so long that board members often leave before their term is completed. If a person is appointed to fill out the remainder of someone else's term, that person can still be appointed to a full 14-year term of their own. One member of the Board of Governors is designated as the Chairman. For example, from 1987 until the early 2006, the Fed Chairman was Alan Greenspan. Greenspan was appointed in 1987 to fill out someone else's term, but then he was appointed to his own 14-year term in 1992. Since 2006, the Federal Reserve chairman has been Ben Bernanke.

The Federal Reserve System is set up in 12 districts, which are headquartered in the cities shown in Exhibit 16-1. The commercial banks in each district elect a Board of Directors for each regional Fed bank, and that board chooses a president for each regional Federal Reserve district. In turn, on certain key policy-making committees, as explained below, members of the politically appointed Board of Governors are combined with presidents of the regional Fed banks.

Other Tasks and Funding of Central Banks

Along with its glamorous task of managing the money supply, the Federal Reserve has a number of everyday responsibilities. For example, a central bank must ensure that enough currency and coins are circulating through the financial system to meet public demands. Thus, each year the Federal Reserve increases the amount of currency available in banks around the Christmas shopping season and reduces it again in January.

The Federal Reserve is also responsible for assuring that banks are in compliance with a wide variety of consumer protection laws. For example, banks are forbidden from discriminating on the basis of age, race, sex, or marital status. Banks are also required to disclose publicly information about the loans they make for buying houses and how those loans are distributed geographically, as well as by sex and race of the loan applicants. Banks are required to disclose certain information to customers about interest rates and fees, but also required to protect the privacy of bank customers unless government authorities follow specific procedures. Most banks are examined on these

monetary policy: Policy that involves altering the quantity of money and thus affecting the level of interest rates and the extent of borrowing.

central bank: An institution to conduct monetary policy and regulate the banking system.

Exhibit 16-1   The Twelve Federal Reserve Districts

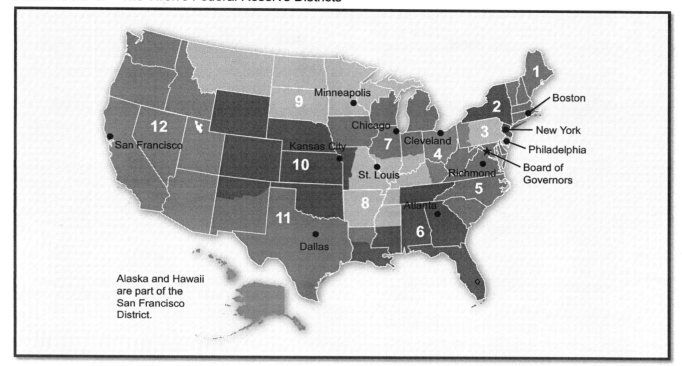

matters about every 18 months, although those with a poor record of past performance are examined more frequently.

The Fed is also responsible for check processing. When you write a check, say, to buy a pizza, the pizza restaurant deposits the check in its bank. Then, the physical check (or an image of that actual check) needs to be returned to your bank. The Fed contracts out a substantial amount of this work of collecting, sorting, and transmitting checks to private firms. In addition, money needs to be transferred from your bank account to the account of the pizza restaurant. The Fed acts as a bank for the banks and transfers funds as needed between banks to reflect the flows of checks.

The Federal Reserve is financially self-supporting. The Fed holds reserves from member banks, and uses that money to purchase government bonds, which then pay interest to the Fed. The Fed also makes some money from charging banks about 2 cents per check for helping to send checks back from the bank that receives the check to the bank on which the check was written. If the Fed has any extra money left over after paying its expenses, it goes to the U.S. Treasury. Typically, about 90% of the total money received by the Federal Reserve—most of it in the form of interest payments on U.S. government bonds—is returned to the U.S. government. Thus, even though the Federal Reserve is self-supporting, it is only allowed to keep enough money to cover its own funding needs.

Each currency is managed by a different central bank. These central banks share the common task of determining the money supply for their currencies. Thus, a European Central Bank determines the quantity of euros, the Bank of Japan determines the quantity of the Japanese yen, and the Bank of England determines the quantity of the British pound. In some nations, almost all of the bank supervision and regulation happens through the central bank. In other nations, like the United States, bank supervision and regulation are shared with other government agencies.

Money at the Millennium

As January 1, 2000, approached, fears abounded of a great computer crash. One fear was that certain computer software might not be able to handle the change from 1999 to 2000. Another concern was that a hidden computer virus that had already spread secretly to many computers might be triggered by the change in date. No one knew quite how seriously to take the threat; after all, the financial and accounting systems of the world hadn't been running on computers in 1900. But U.S. firms spent roughly $150 billion to protect themselves against Y2K, as the change to the year 2000 was called.

With regard to the nation's banking system, the fear was that people might make especially large cash withdrawals in the days leading up to January 1. If credit card networks and check-clearing systems failed to function after Y2K, then people might flock to banks for even larger cash withdrawals. At worst, a financial panic could set in. Thus, by October 1, 1999, the Fed announced that it had stockpiled $200 billion in cash in Federal Reserve banks and commercial banks all around the country.

After New Year's Day in the year 2000, a number of minor computer mishaps occurred. For example, the U.S. government lost touch with a set of spy satellites for four days. A number of airports experienced short-term glitches in the computers that run their air traffic control systems. Seven nuclear power plants experienced problems with their computer systems. About 4,000 small businesses found that their systems for processing credit cards didn't work.

In the banking system, people's demand for currency did surge right around January 1, 2000, but the increase was only about $20 billion—far less than the Fed had on hand. By the end of January, that extra $20 billion in cash had been deposited back into the banking system. By having cash readily on hand, and by letting everyone know that cash would be readily available, the Federal Reserve fulfilled its function of helping to assure the stability in the nation's financial system.

In the end, January 1, 2000, brought only some minor computer hitches. But for the Fed, having extra currency on hand, just in case, was a relatively cheap form of insurance against the risk that something might have gone badly wrong.

How a Central Bank Affects the Money Supply

A central bank has three traditional tools to affect the quantity of money in the economy: open market operations, reserve requirements, and the discount rate. In discussing how these three tools work, it's useful to think of the central bank as a "bank for banks"—that is, each private-sector bank has its own account at the central bank. Let's discuss these monetary policy tools in turn. In the recession of 2007–2009, these three traditional tools proved too weak, and so the Federal Reserve turned to an innovative set of monetary policies that are often summarized as "quantitative easing."

Open Market Operations

Open market operations involve the central bank buying or selling U.S. Treasury bonds in such a way as to influence the quantity of money and the level of interest rates. To understand how open market operations affect the money supply, consider the balance sheet of Happy Bank shown in Exhibit 16-2. Exhibit 16-2a shows that Happy Bank starts with $460 million in assets, divided among reserves, bonds and loans, and $400 million in liabilities in the form of deposits, with a net worth of $60 million. Now the central bank purchases $20 million in bonds from Happy Bank, so that the bond holdings of Happy Bank fall by $20 million and the bank's reserves rise by $20 million, as shown in Exhibit 16-2b. However, Happy Bank only wants to hold $40 million in reserves (the quantity of reserves that it started with in Exhibit 16-2a), so the bank now decides to loan out the extra $20 million in reserves, and its loans rise by $20 million as shown in Exhibit 16-2c. The open market operation by the central bank causes Happy Bank to make loans instead of holding its assets in the form of government bonds, which expands the money supply. As the new loans are deposited in banks throughout the

open market operations: The central bank buying or selling bonds to influence the quantity of money and the level of interest rates.

Assets		Liabilities	
Loans	300	Deposits	400
Reserves	40		
Bonds	120		

Net worth is 60

(a) The original balance sheet

Assets		Liabilities	
Loans	300	Deposits	400
Reserves	40 + 20 = 60		
Bonds	120 – 20 = 100		

Net worth is 60

(b) The central bank buys bonds

Assets		Liabilities	
Loans	300 + 20 = 320	Deposits	400
Reserves	60 – 20 = 40		
Bonds	100		

Net worth is 60

(c) The bank makes additional loans

Exhibit 16-2   Tracing an Open Market Operation through the Happy Bank's Balance Sheets

(a) Original balance sheet of Happy Bank.

(b) The central bank buys 20 in bonds from Happy Bank; Happy Bank receives money, and the central bank gets bonds.

(c) Happy Bank now has more reserves than it wants, so will lend out extra assets. Notice that total assets, total liabilities, and net worth of the bank don't change. All that changes is that because of the open market operation, the bank now holds its assets in a different form.

economy, these banks will in turn loan out some of the deposits they receive, triggering the money multiplier discussed in the previous chapter.

Where did the Federal Reserve get the $20 million that it used to purchase the bonds? A central bank has the power to create money. In practical terms, the Federal Reserve would write a check to Happy Bank, so that Happy Bank can have that money credited to its bank account at the Federal Reserve. To be blunt about it, the Federal Reserve created the money to purchase the bonds out of thin air—or with a few clicks on some computer keys.

Open market operations can also reduce the quantity of money and loans in an economy. Exhibit 16-3a shows the balance sheet of Happy Bank before the central bank sells bonds in the open market. When Happy Bank purchases $30 million in bonds, Happy Bank sends $30 million of its reserves to the central bank, but now holds an additional $30 million in bonds, as shown in Exhibit 16-3b. However, Happy Bank wants to hold $40 million in reserves, as in Exhibit 16-3a, so it will adjust down the quantity of its loans by $30 million, to bring its reserves back to the desired level, as shown in Exhibit 16-3c. In practical terms, a bank can easily reduce its quantity of loans. At any given time, a bank is receiving payments on loans that it made previously and also making new loans. If the bank just slows down or briefly halts making new loans, and instead adds those funds to its reserves, then its overall quantity of loans will decrease. A decrease in the quantity of loans also means fewer deposits in other banks, and other banks reducing their lending as well, as the money multiplier discussed in the previous chapter takes effect.

Within the Federal Reserve, the 12-member Federal Open Market Committee (FOMC) is responsible for making decisions about when to buy U.S. government bonds and increase the quantity of money and loans in the economy, or to sell government

Clearing It Up

Does Selling or Buying Bonds Increase the Money Supply?

Should a central bank buy bonds or sell bonds to increase the money supply? To avoid confusion, keep track of whether money is flowing in or out of the central bank. When a central bank buys bonds, money is flowing out of the central bank to individual banks in the economy, and thus increasing the money supply. When a central bank sells bonds, then money from individual banks in the economy is flowing into the central bank—reducing the quantity of money in the economy.

Assets		Liabilities	
Loans	300	Deposits	400
Reserves	40		
Bonds	120		

Net worth is 60
(a) The original balance sheet

Assets		Liabilities	
Loans	300	Deposits	400
Reserves	40 – 30 = 10		
Bonds	120 + 30 = 150		

Net worth is 60
(b) The central bank sells bonds to the bank

Assets		Liabilities	
Loans	300 – 30 = 270	Deposits	400
Reserves	10 + 30 = 40		
Bonds	150		

Net worth is 60
(c) The bank makes fewer loans

Exhibit 16-3   An Open Market Operation to Contract the Money Supply

(a) Balance sheet of Happy Bank at start.

(b) The central bank sells 30 in bonds to Happy Bank. Happy Bank receives the bonds, and the central bank gets money from the reserves of Happy Bank.

(c) Happy Bank now has less reserves than it wants, so it will build up its reserves by making fewer loans, which decreases the money supply. Because of the open market operation, Happy Bank now holds its assets in a different form—that is, more bonds and fewer loans—which decreases the money supply.

bonds and decrease the quantity of money and loans in the economy. The FOMC includes the seven members of the Fed's Board of Governors who are appointed by the president. It also includes five voting members who are drawn from the 12 regional Federal Reserve Banks—although all of the regional bank presidents typically attend the meetings and participate in the discussions of the FOMC. Thus, while the Board of Governors members hold a majority on the FOMC, the representatives of banks from different regions participate in the decision, too. The FOMC typically meets every six weeks. The FOMC tries to act by consensus; however, the chairman of the Fed has traditionally played a very powerful role in defining and shaping that consensus. For the Federal Reserve, and for most central banks, open market operations have over the last few decades been the most commonly used tool of monetary policy. For example, the Federal Reserve announced 78 separate open market operations from 1990 to 2009.

Reserve Requirements

A second method of conducting monetary policy is for the central bank to raise or lower the **reserve requirement,** which is the proportion of its deposits that a bank is

reserve requirement: The proportion of its deposits that a bank is legally required to deposit with the central bank.

legally required to deposit with the central bank. If banks are required to hold a greater amount in reserves, they have less money available to lend out. If banks are allowed to hold a smaller amount in reserves, they will have a greater amount of money available to lend out.

At the end of 2009, the Federal Reserve required banks to hold reserves equal to 0% of the first $10.7 million in deposits, then to hold reserves equal to 3% of the deposits up to $55.2 million in checking and savings accounts, and 10% of any amount above $55.2 million. Small changes in the reserve requirements are made almost every year: for example, the $55.2 million dividing line is sometimes bumped up or down by a few million dollars or rulings are issued to clarify definitions of certain financial accounts. But changes in reserve requirements that have a large effect on bank reserves are rare. One exception was during the recession of 1990–91 when the Federal Reserve used changes in reserve requirements in a more dramatic way. In December 1990, the reserves that banks needed to hold on deposits that could not be immediately accessed, like certificates of deposit, were reduced to zero, which decreased the reserves that banks needed to hold by $13.2 billion. In April 1992, the reserve requirements on larger amounts of deposits was cut from 12% to their current level of 10%, which decreased the reserves that banks needed to hold by another $8.9 billion.

The Discount Rate

A third traditional method for conducting monetary policy is to raise or lower the **discount rate,** which is the interest rate charged by the central bank when it makes loans to commercial banks. If a bank finds that it is not holding enough in reserves to meet the reserve requirements, it needs to borrow at least for the short term from the central bank. If the central bank raises the discount rate, then banks will hold a higher level of reserves to reduce the chance of needing to borrow at that higher interest rate. When banks hold these higher reserves, it reduces the money supply in the economy as a whole. If the central bank lowers the discount rate it charges to banks, then banks will be less concerned about the prospect of needing a short-term loan to fill out their reserves. In turn, the bank will be more willing to lend aggressively, which will increase the money supply.

discount rate: The interest rate charged by the central bank when it makes loans to commercial banks.

As it turns out, the Federal Reserve has traditionally loaned relatively little money at the discount rate. Before a bank borrows from the Federal Reserve to fill out its needed reserves, the bank is expected to first borrow from other available sources, like other banks. When banks ended up turning to the Federal Reserve for a discount rate loan, it was often taken as a sign that the bank was in financial trouble, and no other bank was willing to lend to it. Given that most banks borrowed little at the discount rate, changing the discount rate up or down has little impact on their behavior. Consequently, altering the discount rate is a relatively weak tool of monetary policy.

Quantitative Easing

The most powerful and commonly used of the three traditional tools of monetary policy—open market operations—works by expanding or contracting the money supply in a way that influences the interest rate. But in late 2008, as the U.S. economy struggled with recession, the Federal Reserve had already reduced the interest rate to near-zero. With the recession still ongoing, the Fed decided to take innovative and nontraditional steps to expand the quantity of money and credit.

One method of quantitative easing was that the Federal Reserve began to make discount rate loans broadly available to many financial firms like those who buy and sell financial securities or even insurance companies, not just to banks. In addition, the Fed figured out a way so that firms which wanted to receive these loans could bid to receive the loans anonymously, so that firms didn't need to worry about whether receiving a loan from the Fed was a signal of being weak financially. Another method was that in the recessionary period from 2007–2009, the Federal Reserve bought some financial securities directly, including several hundred billion dollars of bonds issued by the U.S. Treasury and also more than a trillion dollars worth of private sector financial securities that were backed by mortgage loans. In these cases, the Fed expanded the supply of money and credit in the economy simply by creating the money and credit outright.

The quantitative easing policies adopted by the Federal Reserve (and by other central banks around the world) are usually thought of as temporary emergency measures. But if these steps are indeed to be temporary, then the Federal Reserve will need to stop making these additional loans and sell off the financial securities it has accumulated—and the process of quantitative easing may prove more difficult to reverse than it was to enact.

A central bank that desires to increase the quantity of money in the economy can buy bonds in an open market operation, reduce the reserve requirement, lower the discount rate, or engage in quantitative easing. Conversely, a central bank that desires to reduce the quantity of money in the economy can sell bonds in an open market operation, raise the reserve requirement, raise the discount rate, or reverse its past practices of quantitative easing.

Monetary Policy and Economic Outcomes

A monetary policy that expands the quantity of money and loans is known as an **expansionary monetary policy** or a "loose" monetary policy. Conversely, a monetary policy which reduces the amount of money and loans in the economy is a **contractionary monetary policy** or a "tight" monetary policy. This section will discuss how expansionary and contractionary monetary policies affect interest rates and aggregate demand, and thus how such policies will affect macroeconomic goals like unemployment and inflation.

expansionary monetary policy: A monetary policy that increases the supply of money and the quantity of loans; also called a "loose" monetary policy.

contractionary monetary policy: A monetary policy that reduces the supply of money and loans; also called a "tight" monetary policy.

The Effect of Monetary Policy on Interest Rates

Consider the market for loanable bank funds, shown in Exhibit 16-4. The original equilibrium E_0 occurs at an interest rate of 8% and a quantity of funds loaned and borrowed of $10 billion. An expansionary monetary policy will shift the supply of loanable funds to the right from the original supply curve S_0 to S_1, leading to an equilibrium E_1 with a lower interest rate of 6% and a quantity of funds loaned of $14 billion. Conversely, a contractionary monetary policy will shift the supply of loanable funds to the left from the original supply curve S_0 to S_2, leading to an equilibrium E_2 with a higher interest rate of 10% and a quantity of funds loaned of $8 billion.

When describing the monetary policy actions taken by a central bank, it's common to hear that the central bank "raised interest rates" or "lowered interest rates." Such statements are potentially misleading if they are taken to imply that the central bank is a dictator that can force banks to charge a certain interest rate. Instead, the central bank alters the quantity of money in a way which affects the supply curve in the market for loanable funds, and in that way can move the interest rate higher or lower.

Since 1995, when the Federal Reserve carries out open market operations, it has announced in advance what effect it wishes to have on one particular interest rate—the

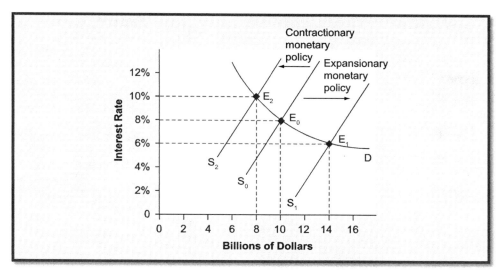

Exhibit 16-4
Monetary Policy and
Interest Rates

The original equilibrium occurs at E_0. A expansionary monetary policy will shift the supply of loanable funds to the right from the original supply curve S_0 to the new supply curve S_1 and to a new equilibrium of E_1, reducing the interest rate from 8% to 6%. A contractionary monetary policy will shift the supply of loanable funds to the left from the original supply curve S_0 to the new supply S_2, and raise the interest rate from 8% to 10%.

federal funds rate, which is the interest rate at which one bank lends funds to another bank overnight.

For example, an overnight loan might occur when a bank needs money to meet its legal reserve requirement, and so it borrows the money from another bank. By selling and buying U.S. government bonds through open market operations, the Federal Reserve can move the federal funds interest rate that banks charge each other higher or lower.

Of course, financial capital markets display a wide range of interest rates, representing borrowers with different risk premiums and loans that are to be repaid over different periods of time. In general, when the federal funds rate drops substantially, other interest rates drop, too, and when the federal funds rate rises, other interest rates rise. But a fall or rise of 1 percentage point in the federal funds rate—which remember is for borrowing overnight!—will typically have an effect of less than 1 percentage point on a 30-year loan to purchase a house or a three-year loan to purchase a car. Monetary policy can push the entire spectrum of interest rates higher or lower, but the specific interest rates are set by the forces of supply and demand in those specific markets for lending and borrowing.

federal funds rate: The interest rate at which one bank lends funds to another bank overnight.

The Effect of Monetary Policy on Aggregate Demand

Monetary policy affects interest rates and the available quantity of loanable funds, which in turn affects several components of aggregate demand. Tight or contractionary monetary policy that leads to higher interest rates and a reduced quantity of loanable funds will reduce two components of aggregate demand. Business investment will decline because it is less attractive for firms to borrow money, and even firms that have money will notice that with higher interest rates, it is relatively more attractive to put those funds in a financial investment than to make an investment in physical capital. In addition, higher interest rates will discourage consumer borrowing for big-ticket items like houses and cars. Conversely, loose or expansionary monetary policy that leads to lower interest rates and a higher quantity of loanable funds will tend to increase business investment and consumer borrowing for big-ticket items.

If the economy is suffering a recession and high unemployment, with output below potential GDP, loose monetary policy can help the economy return to potential GDP. Exhibit 16-5*a* illustrates this situation. This example uses a short-run upward-sloping

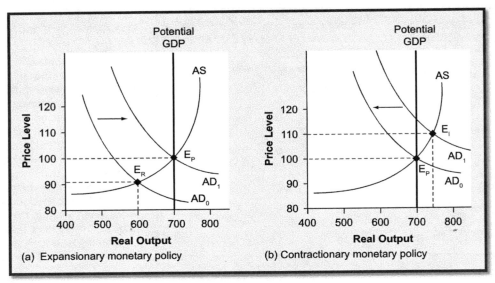

(a) Expansionary monetary policy

(b) Contractionary monetary policy

Exhibit 16-5

Expansionary or Contractionary Monetary Policy

(a) The economy is originally in a recession with the equilibrium output and price level shown at E_R. Expansionary monetary policy will reduce interest rates and shift aggregate demand to the right from AD_0 to AD_1, leading to the new equilibrium E_P at the potential GDP level of output with a relatively small rise in the price level.

(b) The economy is originally producing above the potential GDP level of output at the equilibrium E_I and is experiencing pressures for an inflationary rise in the price level. Contractionary monetary policy will shift aggregate demand to the left from AD_0 to AD_1, thus leading to a new equilibrium E_P at the potential GDP level of output.

Keynesian aggregate supply curve AS. The original equilibrium during a recession of E_R occurs at an output level of 600. An expansionary monetary policy will reduce interest rates and stimulate investment and consumption spending, causing the original aggregate demand curve AD_0 to shift right to AD_1, so that the new equilibrium E_P occurs at the potential GDP level of 700.

Conversely, if an economy is producing at a quantity of output above its potential GDP, a tight or contractionary monetary policy can reduce the inflationary pressures for a rising price level. In Exhibit 16-5b, the original equilibrium E_I occurs at an output of 750, which is above potential GDP. A contractionary monetary policy will raise interest rates, discourage borrowing for investment and consumption spending, and cause the original demand curve AD_0 to shift left to AD_1, so that the new equilibrium E_P occurs at the potential GDP level of 700.

These examples suggest that monetary policy should be **countercyclical;** that is, it should act to counterbalance the business cycles of economic downturns and upswings. Monetary policy should be loosened when a recession has caused unemployment to increase and tightened when inflation threatens. Of course, countercylical policy does pose a danger of overreaction. If loose monetary policy seeking to end a recession goes too far, it may push aggregate demand so far to the right that it triggers inflation. If tight monetary policy seeking to reduce inflation goes too far, it may push aggregate demand so far to the left that a recession begins. Exhibit 16-6 summarizes the chain of effects that connect loose and tight monetary policy to changes in output and the price level.

countercyclical: Moving in the opposite direction of the business cycle of economic downturns and upswings.

What the Federal Reserve Has Done

For the period from the mid-1970s up through the end of 2007, Federal Reserve monetary policy can largely be summed up by looking at how it targeted the federal funds interest rate using open market operations. But in the Great Recession of 2007–2009, Fed policy began to use creative policies of quantitative easing.

Of course, telling the story of the U.S. economy since 1975 in terms of Federal Reserve actions leaves out many other macroeconomic factors that were influencing unemployment, recession, economic growth, and inflation over this time. But the

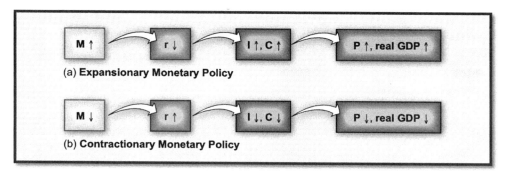

(a) Expansionary Monetary Policy

(b) Contractionary Monetary Policy

Exhibit 16-6
The Pathways of Monetary Policy

(a) The story of expansionary monetary policy is that the central bank causes the supply of money and loanable funds in the economy to increase, which causes the interest rate to fall. The lower interest rate stimulates additional borrowing for investment and consumption, causing AD to shift right. The result is both a higher price level and, at least in the short run, higher real GDP.

(b) The story of contractionary monetary policy is that the central bank causes the supply of money and credit in the economy to decrease, which causes the interest rate to rise. The higher interest rate discourages borrowing for investment and consumption, causing AD to shift to the left. The result is a lower price level and, at least in the short run, lower real GDP.

nine episodes quickly sketched here also demonstrate that when telling the story of a macroeconomy, the central bank must be treated as one of the leading characters. Indeed, the single person with the greatest power to influence the U.S. economy is probably the chairman of the Federal Reserve, who has considerable power over the monetary policies of the Fed, rather than the President of the United States, who can only act through laws that must first be passed by Congress.

Exhibit 16-7 shows how the Federal Reserve has carried out monetary policy by targeting the federal funds interest rate in the last few decades. The graph shows the federal funds interest rate (remember, this interest rate is set through open market operations), the unemployment rate, and the inflation rate since 1975. Different episodes of monetary policy during this period are indicated on the exhibit.

Consider *Episode 1* in the late 1970s. The rate of inflation was very high, exceeding 10% in 1979 and 1980, so the Fed used a tight monetary policy to raise interest rates, with the federal funds rate rising from 5.5% in 1977 to 16.4% in 1981. By 1983, inflation was down to 3.2%, but aggregate demand contracted sharply enough that back-to-back recessions occurred in 1980 and in 1981–82, and the unemployment rate rose from 5.8% in 1979 to 9.7% in 1982.

In *Episode 2,* when the Federal Reserve was persuaded in the early 1980s that inflation was declining, the Fed began slashing interest rates to reduce unemployment. The federal funds interest rate fell from 16.4% in 1981 to 6.8% in 1986. By 1986 or so, inflation had fallen to about 2% and the unemployment rate had come down to 7%, and was still falling.

However, in *Episode 3* in the late 1980s, inflation appeared to be creeping up again, rising from 2% in 1986 up toward 5% by 1989. In response, the Fed used contractionary monetary policy to raise the federal funds rates from 6.6% in 1987 to 9.2% in 1989. The tighter monetary policy stopped inflation, which fell from above 5% in 1990 to under 3% in 1992, but it also helped to cause the recession of 1990–91, and the unemployment rate rose from 5.3% in 1989 to 7.5% by 1992.

In *Episode 4* in the early 1990s, when the Fed was confident that inflation was back under control, it then reduced interest rates, with the federal funds interest rate falling from 8.1% in 1990 to 3.5% in 1992. As the economy expanded, the unemployment rated declined from 7.5% in 1992 to less than 5% by 1997.

In *Episode 5,* the Fed perceived a risk of inflation in 1994 and raised the federal funds rate from 3% in 1993 to 5.8% in 1995. Inflation didn't rise, and the period of economic growth during the 1990s continued. The federal funds rate changed little for several years.

In *Episode 6,* in 1999 and 2000, the Fed was concerned that inflation seemed to be creeping up from 1.6% in 1998 to 3.4% by 2000, and so it raised the federal funds

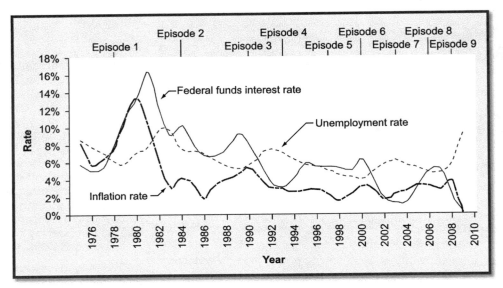

Exhibit 16-7
Monetary Policy,
Unemployment, and
Inflation

Through the episodes shown here, the Federal Reserve typically reacted to higher inflation with a contractionary monetary policy and a higher interest rate, and reacted to higher unemployment with an expansionary monetary policy and a lower interest rate.

interest rate from 4.6% in December 1998 to 6.5% in June 2000. By early 2001, inflation was declining again, headed for a rate of just 1.6% in 2002, but a recession occurred in 2001 and the unemployment rate rose from 4.0% in 2000 to 5.8% in 2002.

In *Episode 7,* the Federal Reserve conducted a loose monetary policy and slashed the federal funds rate from 6.2% in 2000 to just 1.7% in 2002. The recession ended, but just as it had taken some years for unemployment rates to decline after the recessions of the early 1980s and the early 1990s, unemployment rates were slow to decline in the early 2000s.

In *Episode 8,* the federal funds interest rate bottomed out at about 1% in late 2003 and early 2004. The unemployment rate had stayed low and declining, but inflation had perked up just a bit, and so the Federal Reserve began to raise the federal funds rate until it reached 5% by 2007.

In *Episode 9,* as the Great Recession took hold in 2008, the Federal Reserve was quick to slash interest rates, taking them down to 2% in 2008 and to nearly 0% in 2009. But when the Fed had taken interest rates down to near-zero by December 2008, the economy was still deep in recession. Open market operations could not make the interest rate turn negative! Thus, the Federal Reserve turned to the alternative policies of quantitative easing, greatly expanding the direct loans that it made and also creating money to purchase some financial securities directly.

Pitfalls for Monetary Policy

Monetary policy may seem straightforward. If the economy is in a recession, substantially below potential GDP, then the central bank should raise the supply of money and credit, first by reducing interest rates, and then by considering the use of "quantitative easing" and direct loans. If the economy is producing in overdrive above potential GDP, experiencing high inflation, then the central bank should raise interest rates by holding down growth of the money supply. However, in the real world, matters are more complicated than they may at first appear.

Long and Variable Time Lags

Monetary policy affects the economy only after a time lag that is typically long and of variable length. Remember, monetary policy involves a chain of events: the central bank must perceive a situation in the economy, hold a meeting, and make a decision to react by tightening or loosening monetary policy. The change in monetary policy must percolate through the banking system, changing the quantity of loans and affecting interest rates. When interest rates changes, businesses must change their investment levels and consumers must change their borrowing patterns when purchasing homes or cars. Then it takes time for these changes to filter through the rest of the economy.

As a result of this chain of events, monetary policy has little effect in the immediate future; instead, its primary effects are felt perhaps 1–3 years in the future. Monetary policy is like steering a car down a twisting, turning road, where you can see the road behind you, but you have to turn the steering wheel to match the curves you cannot yet see that are ahead. For example, when a central bank decides to loosen monetary policy, it must consider the possibility that by the time the policy actually takes effect in 1–3 years, it will wish it had actually decided to tighten or to take no action at all. The reality of long and variable time lags doesn't mean that a central bank should refuse to make decisions—after all, refusing to make a decision is, in itself, a decision. But it does mean that central banks should be humble about taking action, because of the risk that their actions can create as much or more economic instability as they resolve.

Excess Reserves

Banks are legally required to hold a minimum level of reserves, but no rule prohibits them from holding additional **excess reserves** above the legally mandated limit. For example, during a recession banks may be hesitant to lend, because they fear that when the economy is contracting, a high proportion of loan applicants become less likely to repay their loans.

excess reserves: Reserves that banks hold above the legally mandated limit.

When many banks are choosing to hold excess reserves, expansionary monetary policy may not work well. For example, consider an economy in the throes of a recession, with output substantially below potential GDP. The central bank diagnoses the situation and decides to use an open market operation to conduct an expansionary monetary policy. The hope and intention of the open market operation is that when the central bank buys bonds from banks, the banks will find themselves holding more money and will choose to make additional loans. But there's an old proverb that says, "You can lead a horse to water, but you can't make him drink." Similarly, a central bank can buy bonds from individual banks, but if the banks prefer to hold excess reserves above the legally required level, the central bank can't force individual banks to make loans. Similarly, sensible businesses and consumers may be reluctant to borrow substantial amounts of money in a recession, because they recognize that firms' sales and employees' jobs are more insecure in a recession, and they don't want to face the unrelenting need to make interest payments. The result is that during an especially deep recession, an expansionary monetary policy may have little effect on either the price level or the real GDP.

Japan experienced this situation in the 1990s and early 2000s. Japan's economy entered a period of very slow growth, dipping in and out of recession, in the early 1990s. By February 1999, the Bank of Japan had lowered the equivalent of its federal funds rate to 0% and kept it there most of the time through 2003. Moreover, in the two years from March 2001 to March 2003, the Bank of Japan also expanded the money supply of the country by about 50%—an enormous increase. But even this highly expansionary

Should Monetary Policy Decisions Be Made More Democratically?

Should monetary policy be conducted by a nation's Congress or legislature made up of elected representatives? Or should it be conducted by a politically appointed central bank that is more independent of voters? Here are some of the arguments made by each side.

The Case for Greater Democratic Control of Monetary Policy

Elected representatives conduct fiscal policy by passing tax and spending bills. They could handle monetary policy in the same way. Sure, they will sometimes make mistakes, but in a democracy, it's better to have mistakes made by elected officials accountable to voters than by political appointees. After all, the people appointed to the top governing positions at the Federal Reserve—and to most central banks around the world—are typically bankers and economists. They aren't representatives of borrowers like small businesses or farmers, or representatives of labor unions. Central banks might not be so quick to raise interest rates if they had to pay more attention to firms and people in the real economy.

The Case for an Independent Central Bank

America's judicial system is governed by judges who are presidential appointees. These judges interpret the laws made by elected officials. Few people believe that the legislature should vote on legal cases, and many of the same arguments apply to the central bank. Because the central bank has some insulation from day-to-day politics, its members can take a nonpartisan look at specific economic situations and make tough, immediate decisions when necessary. The idea of giving a legislature the ability to create money and hand out loans is likely to end up badly, sooner or later. Also, a central bank, acting according to the laws passed by elected officials, can respond far more quickly than a legislature. For example, the U.S. budget takes months to debate, pass, and be signed into law, but monetary policy decisions can be made much more rapidly. Day-to-day democratic control of monetary policy is impractical and seems likely to lead to an overly expansionary monetary policy and higher inflation.

Who Wins This Debate?

This debate isn't going away. Nevertheless, the trend in the 2000s has been that countries around the world are moving toward writing specific rules for the central bank to follow—like targeting a certain rate of inflation—and then leaving it up to the central bank to achieve that goal, rather than moving toward greater day-to-day democratic control of the central bank.

monetary policy had no substantial effect on stimulating aggregate demand. Japan's economy continued to experience extremely slow growth into the mid 2000s.

The problem of excess reserves does not affect contractionary policy. Central bankers have an old saying that monetary policy can be like pulling and pushing on a string: when the central bank pulls on the string and uses contractionary monetary policy, it can definitely raise interest rates and reduce aggregate demand. However, when the central bank tries to push on the string of expansionary monetary policy, the string may sometimes just fold up limp and have little effect, because banks decide not to loan out their excess reserves. This analogy shouldn't be taken too literally—expansionary monetary policy usually does have real effects, after that inconveniently long and variable lag. But there are also times, like Japan's economy in the late 1990s and early 2000s, when expansionary monetary policy has been insufficient to lift a recession-prone economy.

Unpredictable Movements of Velocity

Velocity is a term that economists use to describe how quickly money circulates through the economy. The velocity of money in a year is defined as:

$$\text{Velocity} = \frac{\text{nominal GDP}}{\text{money supply}}.$$

velocity: The speed with which money circulates through the economy, calculated as the nominal GDP divided by the money supply.

In 2009, for example, M1 was $1.7 trillion and nominal GDP was $14.3 trillion, so the velocity of M1 was $14.3 trillion/$1.7 trillion = 8.4. A higher velocity of money means that the average dollar circulates more times in a year; a lower velocity means that the average dollar circulates fewer times in a year. Velocity can also be measured using other definitions of the money supply, like M2.

Episodes of Deflation

Deflation occurs when the rate of inflation is negative; that is, instead of money having less purchasing power over time, as occurs with inflation, money is worth more. Having money be worth more may not sound so bad! But when deflation interacts with interest rates, it can cause recessions that are difficult for monetary policy to address.

Remember that the real interest rate is the nominal interest rate minus the rate of inflation. If the nominal interest rate is 7% and the rate of inflation is 3%, then the borrower is effectively paying a 4% real interest rate. But if the nominal interest rate is 7% and there is *deflation* of 2%, then the real interest rate is actually 9%. In this way, an unexpected deflation raises the real interest payments for borrowers. It can lead to a situation where an unexpectedly high number of loans are not repaid and banks find that their net worth is decreasing or negative. When banks are suffering losses, they become less able and eager to make new loans. Aggregate demand declines, which can lead to recession.

Then comes the double-whammy: After causing a recession, deflation can make it difficult for monetary policy to work. Say that the central bank uses expansionary monetary policy to reduce the nominal interest rate all the way to zero—but the economy has 5% deflation. As a result, the real interest rate is 5%, and because a central bank can't make the nominal interest rate negative, expansionary policy can't reduce the real interest rate further.

In the U.S. economy during the early 1930s, deflation was 6.7% per year from 1930–33, which caused many borrowers to default on their loans and many banks to end up bankrupt, which in turn contributed substantially to the Great Depression. But not all episodes of deflation end in Depression. Japan experienced deflation of slightly less than 1% per year from 1999–2002, and while Japan's economy was mired in slow growth, it did grow by about 0.9% per year over this period. Indeed, there is at least one historical example of deflation coexisting with rapid growth. The U.S. economy experienced deflation of about 1.1% per year over the quarter-century from 1876–1900, but real GDP also expanded at a rapid clip of 4% per year over this time, despite some occasional severe recessions.

The central bank should be on guard against deflation, and if necessary use expansionary monetary policy to prevent any long-lasting or extreme deflation from occurring. But except in severe cases like the Great Depression, deflation does not guarantee economic disaster.

Changes in velocity can cause problems for monetary policy. To understand why, rewrite the definition of velocity so that the money supply is on the left-hand side of the equation. That is,

$$\text{Money supply} \times \text{Velocity} = \text{Nominal GDP}$$

This equation is sometimes called the **basic quantity equation of money,** but as you can see, it's just the definition of velocity written in a different form. This equation must hold true, by definition.

basic quantity equation of money: Money supply × Velocity = Nominal GDP.

If velocity is constant over time, then a certain percentage rise in the money supply on the left-hand side of the basic quantity equation of money will inevitably lead to the same percentage rise in nominal GDP—although this change could happen through an increase in inflation, or an increase in real GDP, or some combination of the two. If velocity is changing over time but in a constant and predictable way, then changes in the money supply will continue to have a predictable effect on nominal GDP. But if velocity changes unpredictably over time, then the affect of changes in the money supply on nominal GDP becomes unpredictable.

The actual velocity of money in the U.S. economy as measured by using M1, the most common definition of the money supply, is illustrated in Exhibit 16-8. From 1960 up to about 1980, velocity appears fairly predictable; that is, it is increasing at a fairly constant rate. In the early 1980s, however, velocity as calculated with M1 becomes more variable. The reasons for these sharp changes in velocity remain a puzzle. Economists suspect that the changes in velocity are related to innovations in banking and finance which have changed how money is used in making economic transactions: for example, the growth of electronic payments; a rise in personal borrowing and credit card usage;

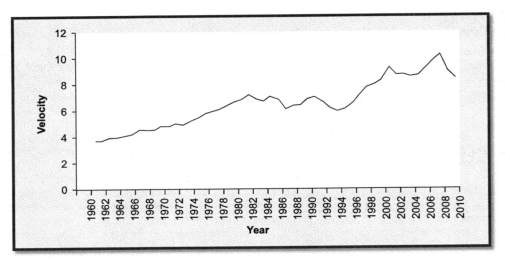

Exhibit 16-8   Velocity

Velocity is the nominal GDP divided by the money supply for a given year. Different measures of velocity can be calculated by using different measures of the money supply. Velocity as calculated by using M1 has lacked a steady trend since the 1980s, instead bouncing up and down.

and accounts that make it easier for people to hold money in savings accounts, where it is counted as M2, right up to the moment that they want to write a check on the money and transfer it to M1. But at least so far, it has proven difficult to draw clear links between these kinds of factors and the specific up-and-down fluctuations in M1.

In the 1970s, when velocity as measured by M1 seemed predictable, a number of economists, led by Nobel laureate Milton Friedman (1912–2006), argued that the best monetary policy was for the central bank to increase the money supply slowly and steadily over time. These economists argued that with the long and variable lags of monetary policy, and the political pressures on central bankers, central bank monetary policies were as likely to have undesirable as to have desirable effects. Thus, these economists believed that the monetary policy should seek steady growth in the money supply of 3% per year. They argued that a steady rate of monetary growth would be correct over longer time periods, since it would roughly match the growth of the real economy. In addition, they argued that giving the central bank less discretion to conduct monetary policy would prevent an overly activist central bank from becoming a source of economic instability and uncertainty. In this spirit, Friedman wrote in 1967: "The first and most important lesson that history teaches about what monetary policy can do—and it is a lesson of the most profound importance—is that monetary policy can prevent money itself from being a major source of economic disturbance."

But as the velocity of M1 began to fluctuate in the 1980s, having the money supply grow at a predetermined and unchanging rate seemed less desirable, because as the quantity theory of money shows, the combination of constant growth in the money supply and fluctuating velocity would cause nominal GDP to rise and fall in unpredictable ways. The jumpiness of velocity in the 1980s caused many central banks to focus less on the rate at which the quantity of money in the economy was increasing, and instead to set monetary policy by reacting to whether the economy was experiencing or in danger of higher inflation or unemployment.

Is Unemployment or Inflation More Important?

If you were to survey central bankers around the world and ask them what they believe should be the primary task of monetary policy, the most popular answer by far would be fighting inflation. Most central bankers believe that the neoclassical model of economics accurately represents the economy over the medium and long term. Remember that in the neoclassical model of the economy, the aggregate supply curve is drawn as a vertical line at the level of potential GDP, as shown in Exhibit 16-9. In the neoclassical model, the level of potential GDP (and the natural rate of unemployment that exists when the economy is producing at potential GDP) is determined by real economic factors. If the original level of aggregate demand is AD_0, then an expansionary monetary policy that shifts aggregate demand to AD_1 only creates an inflationary increase in the price level, but it does not alter GDP or unemployment. From this perspective, all that monetary policy can do is to lead to low inflation or high inflation—and low inflation provides a better climate for a healthy and growing economy. After all, low inflation means that businesses making investments can focus on real economic issues, not on figuring out ways to protecting themselves from the costs and risks of inflation. In this way, a consistent pattern of low inflation can contribute to long-term growth.

This vision of focusing monetary policy on a low rate of inflation is so attractive that many countries have rewritten their central banking laws since in the 1990s to have their bank practice **inflation-targeting,** which means that the central bank is legally required to focus only on keeping inflation low. By 2010, central banks in 26 countries from all over the world faced a legal requirement to target the inflation rate, including Austria, Brazil, Canada, Israel, Korea, Mexico, New Zealand, Spain, Sweden, Thailand, and the United Kingdom. The legislation establishing the European Central Bank, which controls the quantity of euros, sets "price stability" as its primary goal, which it defines as an inflation rate of 2% per year or less. However, the Federal Reserve in the United States does not practice inflation-targeting. Instead, the law governing the Federal Reserve requires it to take both unemployment and inflation into account.

inflation-targeting:
A rule that the central bank is required to focus only on keeping inflation low.

Economists have no final consensus on whether a central bank should be required to focus only on inflation or should have greater discretion. For those who subscribe to the inflation-targeting philosophy, the fear is that when politicians who are worried about slow economic growth and unemployment will constantly pressure the central bank to conduct a loose monetary policy—even if the economy is already producing at potential GDP. In some countries, the central bank may lack the political power to resist such pressures, with the result of higher inflation but no long-term reduction in unemployment. The U.S. Federal Reserve has a tradition of independence, but central banks in other countries may be under greater political pressure. Or in another scenario, central bankers may be tempted to tinker continually with the interest rate, pushing it up and down from month to month in a way that creates uncertainty and risk in the economy. However, inflation-targeting has its risks, too. A central bank that focuses only on inflation will not use expansionary monetary policy to fight a recession. In the early 2000s, for example, unemployment rates rose in many European countries, but the European Central Bank focused only on keeping inflation rates low, not on whether it might have been wise to run a more expansionary monetary policy.

For all of these reasons—long and variable lags, excess reserves, unstable velocity, and controversy over economic goals—monetary policy in the real world is often difficult. But the basic message remains that central banks can affect aggregate demand through the conduct of monetary policy, and in that way influence macroeconomic outcomes.

Should the Central Bank Tackle Asset Bubbles and Leverage Cycles?

One long-standing concern about having the central bank focus on inflation and unemployment is that it may be overlooking certain other economic problems that are coming in the future. For example, in the late 1990s during what was known as

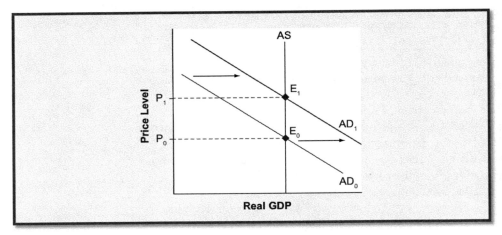

Exhibit 16-9
Monetary Policy in a
Neoclassical Model

In a neoclassical view,
monetary policy affects only
the price level, not the level
of output in the economy. For
example, an expansionary
monetary policy causes
aggregate demand to shift
from the original AD_0 to AD_1.
However, the adjustment of
the economy from the original
equilibrium E_0 to the new
equilibrium E_1 represents
an inflationary increase in
the price level from P_0 to
P_1, but has no effect in the
long run on output or the
unemployment rate. In fact,
no shift in AD will affect the
equilibrium quantity of output
in this model.

the "dot-com" boom, the U.S. stock market as measured by the Dow Jones Industrial Index, which includes 30 very large companies from across the U.S. economy, nearly tripled in value from 1994 to 2000. The Nasdaq index, which includes many smaller technology companies, increased in value by a multiple of five from 1994 to 2000. These rates of increase were clearly not sustainable. Indeed, stock values as measured by the Dow Jones were almost 20% lower in 2009 than they had been in 2000. Stock values in the Nasdaq index were 50% lower in 2009 than they had been in 2000. The drop-off in stock market values contributed to the recession of 2001 and the higher unemployment that followed.

A similar story can be told about housing prices in the mid-2000s. During the 1970s, 1980s, and 1990s, housing prices increased at about 6% per year on average. But during what came to be known as the "housing bubble" from 2003 to 2005, housing prices increased at almost double this annual rate. These rates of increase were clearly not sustainable. When the price of housing fell in 2007 and 2008, many banks and households found that their assets were worth less than they expected, which contributed to the recession that started in 2007.

At a broader level, some economists worry about a "leverage cycle," where "leverage" is a term used by financial economists to mean "borrowing." When economic times are good, banks and the financial sector are eager to lend, and people and firms are eager to borrow. Remember that the amount of money and credit in an economy is determined by a money multiplier—a process of loans being made, money being deposited, and more loans being made. In good economic times, this surge of lending exaggerates the episode of economic growth. It can even be part of what lead prices of certain assets—like stock prices or housing prices—to rise at unsustainably high annual rates. At some point, when economic times turn bad, then banks and the financial sector become much less willing to lend, and credit becomes expensive or unavailable to many potential borrowers. The sharp reduction in credit, perhaps combined with the deflating prices a dot-com stock price bubble or a housing bubble, makes the economic downturn worse than it would otherwise be.

Thus, some economists have suggested that the central bank should not just look at economic growth, inflation, and unemployment rates, but should also keep an eye on asset prices and leverage cycles. Such proposals are quite controversial. If a central bank had announced in 1997 that stock prices were rising "too fast" or in 2004 that housing prices were rising "too fast," and then taken action to hold down price increases, many people and their elected political representatives would have been outraged. Neither the Federal Reserve nor any other central banks want to the responsibility of deciding when stock prices and housing prices are too high, too low, or just right. But as further research explores how asset price bubbles and leverage cycles can affect an economy, central banks may need to think about whether they should conduct monetary policy in a way that would seek to moderate these effects.

Bank Regulation

The safety and stability of a nation's banking system is a matter of macroeconomic concern. If banks falter at their tasks of collecting deposits and making loans, the effect can be similar to a contractionary monetary policy enacted by the central bank: that is, a lower quantity of loans, a reduction in aggregate demand, and a recession. This section begins by discussing two scenarios in which weaknesses in the banking system have caused macroeconomic harm: (1) when households lose confidence in banks and rush to withdraw their money; and (2) when a large proportion of the banks in an economy have extremely low or negative net worth and decide not to make many loans. The discussion then turns to three government policies for assuring safe and stable banking systems: (1) the provision of deposit insurance to reassure households that their bank deposits are safe; (2) examining the financial records of banks to ensure that they have positive net worth; and (3) making emergency short-term loans to banks in times of financial chaos.

Bank Runs

Back in the nineteenth century and during the first few decades of the twentieth century, putting your money in a bank could be nerve-wracking. Imagine that the net worth of your bank became negative, so that the bank's assets weren't enough to cover its liabilities. In this situation, whoever withdrew their deposits first received all of their money, and those who didn't rush to the bank quickly enough lost their money. This scenario, in which depositors raced to the bank to withdraw their deposits for fear that otherwise they would be lost, is called a **bank run.** The drama of bank runs has even entered the plot of some well-known movies. In *Mary Poppins,* the little boy Michael wants his tuppence back, and when someone overhears that the bank director played by Dick Van Dyke won't give back his money, a comic bank run results. In *It's a Wonderful Life,* the bank manager played by Jimmy Stewart faces a mob of worried bank depositors who want to withdraw their money, but manages to allay their fears by allowing some of them to withdraw a portion of their deposits—using the money from his own pocket that was supposed to pay for his honeymoon.

bank run: When depositors race to the bank to withdraw their deposits for fear that otherwise they would be lost.

   The risk of bank runs created instability in the banking system. Even a rumor that a bank might experience negative net worth could trigger a bank run, and in a bank run, even healthy banks could be destroyed. Because a bank loans out most of the money it receives, and because it keeps only limited reserves on hand, a bank run of any size would quickly drain any of the bank's available cash. When the bank had no cash remaining, it only intensified the fears of remaining depositors that they could lose their money. Moreover, a bank run at one bank often triggered a chain reaction of runs on other banks. In the late nineteenth and early twentieth century, bank runs were typically not the original cause of a recession—but bank runs could make a recession much worse.

A Weakened Banking Sector

In a nation with many banks, the failure of any one bank probably won't affect the macroeconomy much. But if many banks are simultaneously close to failing, and as a result the bank system substantially reduces the quantity of loans, the result can be slow growth or recession.

Japan's economy offers a vivid connection from insolvent banks to a weak economy over the last decade or so. Japanese banks (unlike U.S. banks) are allowed to hold some of their assets in the form of real estate and company stock. But from late 1989 to late 1992, real estate and stock prices in Japan fell, on average, by about 60%. Many Japanese banks suffered a dramatic decline in the value of their assets and faced negative net worth. As a result, Japan's banks became extremely reluctant to make loans. This is one reason why Japan's economy was sleepwalking from the early 1990s to the early 2000s, dipping in and out of recession with an average real growth rate of less than 1% per year.

The U.S. economy during the Great Recession of 2007–2009 also experienced the link from a weakened financial sector to an economic slowdown. Over 160 U.S. banks failed in 2008 and 2009; many others were on the verge of failing. Again, a cycle can begin in which a weakened economy means that fewer people repay their loans, thus weakening many banks; then banks that are financially weak become reluctant to lend, which makes the economy weaker.

Given the macroeconomic dangers from an unstable banking system, government laws and regulations have sought to reassure households that their bank deposits are safe and also to supervise banks to make sure that their balance sheets show positive net worth and a moderate level of risk. The following sections describe the government policies to address these goals.

Deposit Insurance

Deposit insurance is an insurance system that makes sure depositors in a bank do not lose their money, even if the bank goes bankrupt. About 70 countries around the world, including all of the major economies, have deposit insurance programs. In the United States, the Federal Deposit Insurance Corporation (FDIC) is responsible for deposit insurance. Banks pay an insurance premium to the FDIC. The insurance premium is based on the bank's level of deposits, and then adjusted according to the riskiness of a bank's financial situation. In 2009, for example, a fairly safe bank with a high net worth might have paid 10–20 cents in insurance premiums for every $100 in bank deposits, while a risky bank with very low net worth might have paid 50–60 cents for every $100 in bank deposits. Bank examiners from the FDIC evaluate the balance sheets of banks, looking at the value of assets and liabilities, to determine the level of riskiness. The FDIC provides deposit insurance for about 8,200 banks. Even if a bank has negative net worth and the executives of the bank lose their jobs, the government guarantees that depositors will receive their money up to $250,000, which is enough for almost all individuals, although not for some businesses.

Since the United States enacted deposit insurance in the 1930s, no one has lost any of their insured deposits. Bank runs no longer happen at insured banks. But the costs to government of providing deposit insurance can be substantial. One study found that from 1976–1996, 59 banking crises occurred in low- and middle-income countries around the world. The average cost of these bank crises to the government because of deposit insurance was a whopping 9% of one year's GDP.

deposit insurance: An insurance system that makes sure depositors in a bank do not lose their money, even if the bank goes bankrupt.

Bank Supervision

Several government agencies also check the balance sheets of banks to make sure they have positive net worth and are not taking too high a level of risk. Within the U.S. Department of the Treasury, the Office of the Comptroller of the Currency has a national staff of bank examiners who conduct on-site reviews of the 1,500 or so largest national banks. The bank examiners also review any foreign banks that have branches in the United States. Also within the Treasury, the Office of Thrift Supervision monitors and regulates about 800 savings and loan institutions. The National Credit Union Administration (NCUA) supervises credit unions, which are nonprofit banks owned and run by their members. There are over 10,000 credit unions in the U.S. economy, but the typical credit union is small compared to most banks. The Federal Reserve also has some responsibility for supervising financial institutions. For example, there are firms that own banks and other businesses called "bank holding companies." While other regulators like the Office of the Comptroller of the Currency supervises the banks, the Federal Reserve supervises the holding companies.

When the supervision of banks (and bank-like institutions such as savings and loans and credit unions) works well, most banks will remain financially healthy most of the time. If the bank supervisors find that a bank has low or negative net worth, or is making too high a proportion of risky loans, they can require that the bank change its behavior—or in extreme cases even force the bank to be closed or sold to a financially healthy bank.

But bank supervision can run into both practical and political questions. The practical question is that measuring the value of a bank's assets is not always straightforward. As discussed in the previous chapter, a bank's assets are its loans, and the value of these assets depends on estimates about the risk that these loans will not be repaid. These issues can become even more complex when a bank makes loans to banks or firms in other countries, or arranges financial deals that are much more complex than a basic loan. The political question arises because the decision by a bank supervisor to require a bank to close or to change its financial investments is often controversial, and the bank supervisor often comes under political pressure from the owners of the bank and the local politicians where the bank is located to shut up and back off. For example, many observers have pointed out that Japan's banks were in deep financial trouble through most of the 1990s; however, nothing substantial had been done about it by the early 2000s. A similar unwillingness to confront problems with struggling banks is visible across the rest of the world, in East Asia, Latin America, eastern Europe and Russia and elsewhere.

In the United States, laws were passed in the 1990s requiring that bank supervisors make their findings open and public, and that they act as soon as a problem is identified. But as many U.S. banks were staggered by the recession of 2007–2009, critics of the bank regulators asked pointed questions about why the regulators hadn't foreseen the financial shakiness of the banks earlier, before such large losses had a chance to accumulate.

Lender of Last Resort

When a panic spreads in financial markets, a situation can arise in which a financial institution needs a short-term emergency loan. In the old days of bank runs, for example, a healthy bank could have positive net worth, but not enough cash on hand so that a flock of depositors could withdraw their money. In such cases, the central bank can step in as a **lender of last resort,** which involves providing short-term emergency loans when a financial crisis occurs. For banks, the central bank acting

lender of last resort: An institution that provides short-term emergency loans in conditions of financial crisis.

The Emancipation of U.S. Banks

During the Great Depression of the 1930s, the banking system crashed along with the economy. Politicians at that time believed the solution was to pass the Glass-Steagall Act of 1933, which restricted the types of business in which banks could become involved. For example, the Glass-Steagall Act restricted banks to making loans only to businesses and individuals. Banks were not allowed to own companies, own stock in companies, sell stock, or offer other financial products such as insurance. A few years earlier, the McFadden Act of 1927 had placed geographic limits on banks, prohibiting such institutions from establishing branches across state lines. Many state laws also restricted the number of branches that a bank could have per state.

The idea behind these restrictions was that if banks were limited in what they could do, they were less likely to get into financial trouble. But as economists pointed out, such legislation limited banks' ability to diversify their risks, and in that way made it *more* likely that they would be financially shaky, rather than less likely. Banks in other high-income countries around the world did not face these kinds of restrictions.

In the 1990s, banking laws began to change. In 1994, the Riegle-Neal Act allowed banks to set up as many branches as they wished, both within states and across state lines. In 1999, the Gramm-Leach-Bliley Act allowed banks to set up overall companies ("financial holding companies") that contained banks within them, as well as insurance companies and companies that sell stocks and bonds. However, unlike the situation in any other high-income economies, except for Japan, U.S. banks are still prohibited from owning commercial businesses, and commercial businesses are prohibited from owning banks. Some in the banking industry would like to eliminate these restrictions, too.

But in the aftermath of the 2007–2009 recession, there was a widespread sense that many U.S. banks had borrowed and loaned unwisely. Perhaps returning to the laws of the 1930s was not the correct response, but banks seemed likely to face new restrictions and limitations on their risk-taking.

as a lender of last resort helps to reinforce the effect of deposit insurance and thus to reassure bank customers that they won't lose their money. But the lender of last resort task can come up in other financial crises. During the panic of the stock market crash in 1987, when the value of U.S. stocks fell by 25% in a single day, the Federal Reserve made a number of short-term emergency loans so that the financial system could keep functioning. When fears were expressed late in 1999 that bank computers might malfunction on January 1, 2000, the Federal Reserve loudly announced that if any problems occurred, it was standing by to act as a lender of last resort until the problems were sorted out. During the recession of 2007–2009, the "quantitative easing" policies of the Federal Reserve can be interpreted as a willingness to make short-term credit available as needed in a time when the banking and financial system was under stress.

Summary

Overall, bank regulation in the United States is coordinated by the Federal Financial Institutions Examination Council (FFIEC), which in turn draws its membership from the agencies mentioned in this section: the Federal Deposit Insurance Corporation (FDIC), the National Credit Union Administration (NCUA), the Office of the Comptroller of the Currency (OCC), and the Office of Thrift Supervision (OTS), and the Federal Reserve. The task of the FFIEC is to assure that this alphabet soup of bank regulators all communicate with each other and use similar standards when evaluating the riskiness of banks.

The failure of a single bank can be treated like any other business failure. Yet if many banks fail, it can reduce aggregate demand in a way that can bring on or deepen a recession. The combination of deposit insurance, bank supervision, and lender of last resort policies help to prevent weaknesses in the banking system from causing recessions.

Conclusion

Through expansionary monetary policy, a central bank can reduce interest rates and increase the quantity of loans, increase aggregate demand to the right, and help a recession-stricken economy return to potential GDP. Through contractionary monetary policy, a central bank can raise interest rates and decrease the quantity of loans, shift aggregate demand to the left, and reduce inflation. The appropriate timing and direction of monetary policy isn't always clear, because of issues like long and variable lags, banks that hold excess reserves, movements in velocity, and disagreements over whether reducing inflation or unemployment should take higher priority. Moreover, in the long run the neoclassical model shows that economic output and unemployment are determined by real factors in markets, while monetary policy determines only the inflation rate. But during the ups and downs of the business cycle, when recessions and inflations occur, monetary policy can play some role in stabilizing the swings of the economy.

The discussion in this chapter has focused on domestic monetary policy; that is, the view of monetary policy within an economy. The next chapter explores the international dimension of monetary policy, and how monetary policy becomes involved with exchange rates and international flows of financial capital.

Key Concepts and Summary

1. The most prominent task of a **central bank** is to conduct **monetary policy,** which involves controlling the quantity of money (and loans) in the economy. Some prominent central banks around the world include the U.S. Federal Reserve, the European Central Bank, the Bank of Japan, and the Bank of England.

2. A central bank has three traditional tools to conduct monetary policy: **open market operations,** which involves buying and selling government bonds with banks; **reserve requirements,** which determine what level of reserves a bank is legally required to hold; and **discount rates,** which is the interest rate at which a central bank makes loans to individual banks. The most commonly used tool is open market operations. During the 2007–2009 recession, central banks around the world also used quantitative easing to expand the supply of money and credit.

3. A loose or **expansionary monetary policy** raises the quantity of money and credit above what it otherwise would have been and reduces interest rates.

4. A **contractionary monetary policy,** also called a tight monetary policy, reduces the quantity of money and credit below what it otherwise would have been and raises interest rates, seeking to hold down inflation. An expansionary monetary policy, also called a loose monetary policy, seeks to boost aggregate demand, and thus to counter recession.

5. Monetary policy is inevitably imprecise, for a number of reasons: (a) the effects occur only after **long and variable lags;** (b) if banks decide to hold **excess reserves,** monetary policy cannot force them to lend; and (c) **velocity** may shift in unpredictable ways.

6. The **basic quantity equation of money** is MV = PQ, where M is the money supply, V is the velocity of money, P is the price level, and Q is the real output of the economy.

7. Some central banks like the European Central Bank practice **inflation-targeting,** which means that the only goal of the central bank is to keep inflation within a low target range. Other central banks like the U.S. Federal Reserve are free to focus on either reducing inflation or stimulating an economy that is in recession, whichever goal seems most important at the time.

8. A **bank run** occurs when there are rumors (possibly true, possibly false) that a bank is at financial risk of having negative net worth. As a result, depositors rush to the bank to withdraw their money and put it someplace safer. Even false rumors, if they cause a bank run, can force a healthy bank to lose its deposits and be forced to close.

9. **Deposit insurance** guarantees bank depositors that even if the bank has negative net worth, their deposits will be protected. In the United States, the Federal Deposit Insurance Corporation (FDIC) collects deposit insurance premiums from banks and guarantees bank deposits up to $100,000.

10. Bank supervision involves inspecting the balance sheets of banks to make sure that they have positive net worth and that their assets are not too risky. In the United States, the Office of the Comptroller of the Currency (OCC) is responsible for supervising banks, the Office of Thrift Supervision (OTS) is responsible for inspecting savings and loans, and the National Credit Union Administration (NCUA) is responsible for inspecting credit unions. The FDIC and the Federal Reserve also play a role in bank supervision. These agencies coordinate their efforts through the Federal Financial Institutions Examination Council (FFIEC).

11. When a central bank acts as a **lender of last resort,** it makes short-term loans available in situations of sever financial panic or stress.

Review Questions

1. How is a central bank different from a typical commercial bank?

2. List the three traditional tools that a central bank has for controlling the money supply.

3. Explain how to use an open market operation to expand the money supply.

4. Explain how to use the reserve requirement to expand the money supply.

5. Explain how to use the discount rate to expand the money supply.

6. Explain how to use quantitative easing to expand the money supply.

7. How do the following types of monetary policy affect the quantity of money: expansionary or contractionary?

8. How do the following types of monetary policy affect interest rates: tight or loose?

9. How do the following types of monetary policy affect aggregate demand: expansionary, tight, contractionary, and loose?

10. Which kind of monetary policy would you expect in response to high inflation: expansionary or contractionary? Why?

11. Which kind of monetary policy would you expect in response to recession: expansionary or contractionary? Why?

12. How might each of the following factors complicate the implementation of monetary policy: long and variable lags, excess reserves, and movements in velocity?

13. Define the velocity of the money supply.

14. What is the basic quantity equation of money?

15. How does a monetary policy of inflation targeting work?

16. How is bank regulation linked to the conduct of monetary policy?

17. What is a bank run?

18. In a program of deposit insurance as it is operated in the United States, what is being insured and who pays the insurance premiums?

19. In government programs of bank supervision, what is being supervised?

20. What is the lender of last resort?

21. Name and briefly describe the responsibilities of each of the following agencies: FFIEC, FDIC, NCUA, OCC, and OTS.

Exchange Rates and International Capital Flows

The world has over 150 different currencies, from the Afghanistan afghani and the Albanian lek all the way through the alphabet to the Zambian kwacha and the Zimbabwean dollar. For international economic transactions, households or firms will wish to exchange one currency for another. Perhaps the need for exchanging currencies will come from a German firm that exports products to Russia, but then wishes to exchange the Russian rubles it has earned for euros, so that the firm can pay its workers and suppliers in Germany. Perhaps it will be a South African firm that wishes to purchase a mining operation in Angola, but to make the purchase so it must convert South African rand to Angolan kwanza. Perhaps it will be an American tourist visiting China, who wishes to convert U.S. dollars to Chinese yuan to pay the hotel bill.

Exchange rate can sometimes move very swiftly. For example, in the United Kingdom the pound was worth $2 in U.S. currency in spring 2008, but was worth only $1.40 in U.S. currency six months later. For firms engaged in international buying, selling, lending, and borrowing, these swings in exchange rates can have an enormous effect on profits.

This chapter discusses the international dimension of money, which involves conversions from one currency to another at an exchange rate. Exchange rates are nothing more than a price—that is, the price of one currency in terms of another currency—and so they can be analyzed with the tools of demand and supply. The first main section of this chapter begins with an overview of foreign exchange markets: their size, their main participants, and the vocabulary for discussing movements of exchange rates. The next section uses demand and supply graphs to analyze some main factors that cause shifts in exchange rates. A final section then brings the central bank and monetary policy back into the picture. Each country must decide whether to allow its exchange rate to be determined in the market, or whether the central bank should intervene in the exchange rate market. All of the choices for exchange rate policy involve distinctive trade-offs and risks.

How the Foreign Exchange Market Works

Most countries have different currencies, but not all. Sometimes small economies use the currency of an economically larger neighbor. For example, Ecuador, El Salvador, and Panama have decided to **dollarize**—that is, to use the U.S. dollar as their currency. Sometimes nations share a common currency. A large-scale example of a common currency is the decision by 16 European nations—including some very large economies such as France, Germany, and Italy—to replace their former currencies with the euro. However, with these exceptions duly noted, most of the international economy takes place in a situation of multiple national currencies, and people and firms need to convert from one currency to another when selling, buying, hiring, borrowing, traveling, or investing across national borders. The market in which people or firms use one currency to purchase another currency is called the **foreign exchange market.**

dollarize: When a country that is not the United States uses the U.S. dollar as its currency.

You have encountered the basic concept of exchange rates in earlier chapters. Chapter 7, for example, discussed how exchange rates are used to compare GDP statistics from countries where GDP is measured in different currencies. But these earlier examples took the actual exchange rate as given, as if it were a fact of nature. In reality, the exchange rate is a price—the price of one currency expressed in terms of units of another currency. The key framework for analyzing prices, whether in this course, any other economics course, or in public policy and business examples, or on any planet in the solar system, or in any galaxy in the universe, is the operation of supply and demand in markets.

foreign exchange market: The market in which people buy one currency while using another currency.

The Extraordinary Size of the Foreign Exchange Markets

The quantities traded in foreign exchange markets are breathtaking. A survey done in 2007 by the Bank of International Settlements, an international organization for banks and the financial industry, found that $3.2 trillion *per day* was traded on foreign exchange markets, which makes the foreign exchange market the largest market in the world economy.

Exhibit 17-1 shows the currencies most commonly traded on foreign exchange markets. The foreign exchange market is dominated by the U.S. dollar, the currencies used by nations in western Europe (the euro, the British pound, and the Swiss franc), and the Japanese yen.

Demanders and Suppliers of Currency in Foreign Exchange Markets

In foreign exchange markets, demand and supply become closely interrelated, because a person or firm who demands one currency must at the same time supply another currency—and vice versa. To get an intuitive sense of how demand and supply operate in foreign exchange markets, it's useful to consider four groups of people or firms who participate in the market: (1) firms that are involved in international trade of goods and services; (2) tourists visiting other countries; (3) international investors buying ownership (or part-ownership) of a foreign firm; (4) international investors making financial investment that don't involve ownership. Let's consider these categories in turn.

Currency	Share of Foreign Exchange Market Transactions
U.S. dollar	41.4%
Euro	30.3%
Japanese yen	5.8%
British pound	6.3%
Swiss franc	4.7%
Canadian dollar	1.2%
Australian dollar	1.5%
Swedish krona	1.0%
All other	7.4%

Exhibit 17-1
Currencies Traded Most on Foreign Exchange Markets in 2007

Firms that buy and sell on international markets find that their costs for workers, suppliers and investors are measured in the currency of the nation where their production occurs, but their revenues from sales are measured in the currency of the different nation where their sales happened. Thus, a Chinese firm exporting abroad will earn some other currency—say, U.S. dollars—but will need Chinese yuan to pay the workers, suppliers, and investors who are based in China. In the foreign exchange markets, this firm will be a supplier of U.S. dollars and a demander of Chinese yuan.

International tourists will supply their home currency to receive the currency of the country they are visiting. For example, an American tourist who is visiting China will both supply U.S. dollars into the foreign exchange market and demand Chinese yuan.

Financial investments that cross international boundaries, and thus require exchanging currency, are often divided into two categories. **Foreign direct investment** refers to purchases of firms in another country that involve taking a management responsibility; for example, in 2008 the Belgian beer-brewing company InBev bought the U.S. beer-maker Anheuser-Busch for $52 billion. To make this purchase of a U.S. firm, InBev would have to supply euros (the currency of Belgium) to the foreign exchange market and demand U.S. dollars.

foreign direct investment: Purchases of firms in another country that involve taking a management responsibility.

The other kind of international financial investment, **portfolio investment,** involves a purely financial investment that doesn't involve any management responsibility. An example would be a U.S. financial investor who purchased bonds issued by the government of the United Kingdom, or deposited money in a British bank. To make such investments, the American investor would supply U.S. dollars in the foreign exchange market and demand British pounds.

portfolio investment: An investment in another country that is purely financial and doesn't involve any management responsibility.

Portfolio investment is often linked to expectations about how exchange rates will shift. For example, consider a U.S. financial investor who is considering purchasing bonds issued in the United Kingdom. For simplicity, ignore any interest paid by the bond (which will be small in the short run anyway) and focus on exchange rates. Say that a British pound is currently worth $1.50 in U.S. currency. However, the investor believes that in a month, the British pound will be worth $1.60 in U.S. currency. Thus, as Exhibit 17-2*a* shows, this investor would change $24,000 for 16,000 British pounds. In a month, if the pound is indeed worth $1.60, then the portfolio investor can trade back to U.S. dollars at the new exchange rate, and have $25,600—a nice profit. A portfolio investor who believes that the foreign exchange rate for the pound will work in the opposite direction can also invest accordingly. Say that an investor expects that the pound, now worth $1.50 in U.S. currency, will decline to $1.40. Then, as shown in Exhibit 17-2*b,* that investor could start off with 20,000 pounds (borrowing the money

Exhibit 17-2   A Portfolio Investor Trying to Benefit from Exchange Rate Movements

if necessary), convert it to $30,000 in U.S. currency, wait a month, and then convert back to approximately 21,428 British pounds—again making a nice profit. Of course, this kind of investing comes without guarantees, and an investor will suffer losses if the exchange rates do not move as predicted.

Many portfolio investment decisions are not as simple as betting that the value of the currency will change in one direction or the other. Instead, they involve firms trying to protect themselves from movements in exchange rates. Imagine that you are running a U.S. firm that is exporting to France. You have signed a contract to deliver certain products and will receive 1 million euros a year from now. But you don't know how much this contract will be worth in U.S. dollars, because the dollar/euro exchange rate can fluctuate in the next year. Let's say you want to know for sure what the contract will be worth, and not take a risk that the euro will be worth less in U.S. dollars than it currently is. You can **hedge**, which means using a financial transaction to protect yourself against risk. Specifically, you can sign a financial contract and pay a fee that guarantees you a certain exchange rate one year from now—regardless of what the market exchange rate is at that time. Now, it's possible that the euro will be worth more in dollars a year from now, your hedging contract will be unnecessary, and you will have paid a fee for nothing. But if the value of the euro in dollars declines, then you are protected by the hedge. Financial contracts like hedging, where parties wish to be protected against exchange rate movements, also commonly lead to a series of portfolio investments by the firm that is receiving a fee to provide the hedge.

hedge: Using a financial transaction as protection against risk.

Both foreign direct investment and portfolio investment involve an investor who supplies domestic currency and demands a foreign currency. However, purely financial portfolio investment often has a short-run focus, while foreign direct investment usually involves at least partial ownership and managerial responsibility, and thus tends to have a more long-run focus. As a practical matter, portfolio investments can be withdrawn from a country much more quickly than foreign direct investments. A U.S. portfolio investor who wants to buy or sell bonds issued by the government of the United Kingdom can do so with a phone call or a few clicks of a computer key. However, a U.S. firm

Exhibit 17-3 The Demand and Supply Line-Ups in Foreign Exchange Markets

Demand for the U.S. Dollar Comes from . . .	Supply of the U.S. Dollar Comes from . . .
A U.S. exporting firm that earned foreign currency and is trying to pay U.S.-based expenses	A foreign firm that has sold imported goods in the United States, earned U.S. dollars, and is trying to pay expenses incurred in its home country
Foreign tourists visiting the United States	U.S. tourists leaving to visit other countries
Foreign investors who wish to make direct investments in the U.S. economy	U.S. investors who want to make foreign direct investments in other countries
Foreign investors who wish to make portfolio investments in the U.S. economy	U.S. investors who want to make portfolio investments in other countries

that wants to buy or sell a company that manufactures automobile parts in the United Kingdom will find that planning and carrying out the transaction takes at least a few weeks, and perhaps even many months. Portfolio investments are often made based on beliefs about how exchange rates or rates of return are likely to move in the near future; in contrast, foreign direct investments, like ownership of a foreign firm, is usually made with a longer-term horizon in mind. Exhibit 17-3 summarizes the main categories of demanders and suppliers of currency.

Participants in the Exchange Rate Market

The foreign exchange market does not involve the ultimate suppliers and demanders of foreign exchange literally seeking each other out. If Martina decides to leave her home in Venezuela and take a trip in the United States, she doesn't need to find a U.S. citizen who is planning to take a vacation in Venezuela and arrange a person-to-person currency trade. Instead, the foreign exchange market works through financial institutions, and it operates on several levels.

Most people and firms who are exchanging a substantial quantity of currency go to a bank, and most banks provide foreign exchange as a service to customers. However, behind the scenes these banks then turn to a smaller number of financial firms known as "dealers," who are actively involved in large quantities of foreign exchange trading. Most foreign exchange dealers are banks, so this behind-the-scenes market is sometimes called the "interbank market," although a few insurance companies and other kinds of financial firms are involved. Trades between foreign exchange dealers can be very large, involving hundreds of millions of dollars. In the world economy, roughly 2,000 firms are foreign exchange dealers. The U.S. economy has less than 100 total foreign exchange dealers, but largest 12 or so dealers carried out more than half of the total transactions. The foreign exchange market has no central location, although the major dealers keep a close watch on each other at all times.

The foreign exchange market is huge not because of the demands of tourists, firms, or even foreign direct investment, but instead because of portfolio investment and the actions of interlocking foreign exchange dealers. International tourism is a very large industry, involving about $950 billion per year in spending in 2008. Global exports are about 25% of global GDP; say, about $15 trillion per year. Foreign direct investment totaled about $1 trillion in 2009. But these quantities are dwarfed by the $3.2 trillion *per day* being traded in foreign exchange markets. Most transactions in the foreign exchange market are for portfolio investment—relatively short-term movements of financial capital between currencies—and by the actions of the large foreign exchange dealers as they constantly buy and sell with each other.

Strengthening and Weakening Currency

When the prices of most goods and services change, the price is said to "rise" or "fall." For exchange rates, the terminology is different. When the exchange rate for a currency rises, so that the currency exchanges for more of other currencies, it is referred to as **appreciating** or "strengthening." When the exchange rate for a currency falls, so that a currency trades for less of other currencies, it is referred to as **depreciating** or "weakening."

appreciating: When a currency is worth more in terms of other currencies; also called "strengthening."

To illustrate the use of these terms, consider the exchange rate between the U.S. dollar and the Canadian dollar since 1980 shown in Exhibit 17-4. The vertical axis in Exhibit 17-4a shows the price of $1 in U.S. currency, measured in terms of Canadian currency. Clearly, exchange rates can move up and down substantially. A U.S. dollar traded for $1.17 Canadian in 1980. The U.S. dollar appreciated or strengthened to $1.39 Canadian in 1986, depreciated or weakened to $1.15 Canadian in 1991, and then appreciated or strengthened to $1.60 Canadian by early in 2002, fell to roughly $1.20 Canadian in 2009, and then had a sharp spike up and decline in 2009 and 2010. The units in which exchange rates are measured can be confusing, because the exchange rate of the U.S. dollar is being measured using a different currency—the Canadian dollar. But exchange rates always measure the price of one unit of currency by using a different currency.

depreciating: When a currency is worth less in terms of other currencies; also called "weakening."

In looking at the exchange rate between two currencies, the appreciation or strengthening of one currency must mean the depreciation or weakening of the other. Exhibit 17-4b shows the exchange rate for the Canadian dollar, measured in terms of U.S. dollars. The exchange rate of the U.S. dollar measured in Canadian dollars shown in Exhibit 17-4a is a perfect mirror image with the exchange rate of the Canadian dollar measured in U.S. dollars shown in Exhibit 17-4b. A fall in the Canada $/U.S. $ ratio means a rise in the U.S. $/Canada $ ratio, and vice versa.

With the price of a typical good or service, it's clear that higher prices benefit sellers and hurt buyers, while lower prices benefit buyers and hurt sellers. In the case of exchange rates, where the buyers and sellers are not always intuitively obvious, it's useful to trace through how different participants in the market will be affected by a stronger or weaker currency. Consider, for example, the impact of a stronger U.S. dollar on six different groups of economic actors as shown in Exhibit 17-5: (1) U.S. exporters selling abroad; (2) foreign exporters (that is, firms selling imports in the U.S. economy); (3) U.S. tourists abroad; (4) foreign tourists visiting the United States; (5) U.S. investors (either foreign direct investment or portfolio investment) considering opportunities in other countries; (6) and foreign investors considering opportunities in the U.S. economy.

For a U.S. firm selling abroad, a stronger U.S. dollar is a curse. A strong U.S. dollar means that foreign currencies are correspondingly weak. When this exporting firm earns foreign currencies through its export sales, and then converts them back to U.S. dollars to pay workers, suppliers, and investors, the stronger dollar means that the foreign currency buys fewer U.S. dollars than would have been expected if the currency had not strengthened, and that the firm's profits (as measured in dollars) fall. As a result, the firm may choose to reduce its exports, or it may raise its selling price, which will also tend to reduce its exports. In this way, a stronger currency reduces a country's exports.

Conversely, for a foreign firm selling in the U.S. economy, a stronger dollar is a blessing. Each dollar earned through export sales, when traded back into the

(a) U.S. dollar exchange rate in Canadian dollars

(b) Canadian dollar exchange rate in U.S. dollars

Exhibit 17-4
Strengthen or Appreciate
vs. Weaken or Depreciate

Exchange rates move up
and down substantially, even
between close neighbors
like the United States and
Canada. Exhibit 17-4*a* is a
mirror image of Exhibit 17-4*b*:
that is, any appreciation of
one currency must mean
depreciation of the other
currency, and vice versa.

home currency of the exporting firm, will now buy more of the home currency than expected before the dollar had strengthened. As a result, the stronger dollar means that the importing firm will earn higher profits than expected before the dollar had strengthened. The firm will seek to expand its sales in the U.S. economy, or it may reduce prices, which will also lead to expanded sales. In this way, a stronger U.S. dollar means that consumers will purchase more from foreign producers, expanding the country's level of imports.

For a U.S. tourist abroad, who is exchanging U.S. dollars for foreign currency as necessary, a stronger U.S. dollar is a benefit. The tourist receives more foreign currency for each U.S. dollar, and consequently the cost of the trip in U.S. dollars is lower. When a country's currency is strong, it's a good time for citizens of that country to tour abroad. For example, imagine a U.S. tourist who has saved up $5,000 for a trip to South Africa. In January 2008, $1 bought 7 South Africa rand, so the tourist had 35,000 rand to spend. In January 2009, $1 bought 10 rand, so the tourist had 50,000 rand to spend. By January 2010, $1 bought 7.5 rand. Clearly, 2009 was the year for U.S. tourists to visit South Africa! For foreign visitors to the United States, the opposite pattern holds true. A relatively stronger U.S. dollar means that their own currencies are relatively

Exhibit 17-5   How Do Exchange Rate Movements Affect Each Group?

weaker, so that as they shift from their own currency to U.S. dollars, they have fewer U.S. dollars than previously. When a country's currency is strong, it's not an especially good time for foreign tourists to visit.

A stronger dollar injures the prospects of a U.S. financial investor who has already invested money in another country. A U.S. financial investor abroad must first convert U.S. dollars to a foreign currency, invest in a foreign country, and then later convert that foreign currency back to U.S. dollars. If in the meantime the U.S. dollar becomes stronger and the foreign currency becomes weaker, then when the investor converts back to U.S. dollars, the rate of return on that investment will be less than originally expected at the time it was made.

However, a stronger U.S. dollar boosts the returns of a foreign investor putting money into a U.S. investment. That foreign investor converts from their home currency to U.S. dollars and seeks a U.S. investment, while later planning to switch back to their home currency. If, in the meantime, the dollar grows stronger, then when the time comes to convert from U.S. dollars back to the foreign currency, the investor will receive more foreign currency than expected at the time the original investment as made.

The preceding paragraphs all focus on the case where the U.S. dollar becomes stronger. The corresponding happy or unhappy economic reactions are illustrated in the first column of Exhibit 17-5. As an exercise, describe in your own words the reasons for the reactions to a weaker dollar, illustrated by the reactions in the second column of the exhibit. Think through these connections for another currency, like how American firms, consumers, and investors might feel if the Mexican peso rose or fell.

At this point, you should have a good sense of who many of the players are in the foreign exchange market: firms involved in international trade, tourists, international financial investors, banks, and foreign exchange dealers. The next section shows how the tools of demand and supply can be used in foreign exchange markets to explain the underlying causes of stronger and weaker currencies.

Demand and Supply Shifts in Foreign Exchange Markets

The foreign exchange market involves firms, households and investors who demand and supply currencies coming together through their banks and the key foreign exchange dealers. Exhibit 17-6*a* offers an example for the exchange rate between the U.S. dollar and the Mexican peso. The vertical axis shows the exchange rate for U.S. dollars, which in this case is measured in pesos. The horizontal axis shows the quantity of U.S. dollars being traded in the foreign exchange market each day. The demand curve D for U.S. dollars intersects with the supply curve S of U.S. dollars at the equilibrium point E, which is an exchange rate of 10 pesos per dollar and a total volume of $8.5 billion.

Exhibit 17-6*b* presents the same demand and supply information from the perspective of the Mexican peso. The vertical axis shows the exchange rate for Mexican pesos, which is measured in U.S. dollars. The horizontal axis shows the quantity of Mexican pesos traded in the foreign exchange market. The demand curve D for Mexican pesos intersects with the supply curve S of Mexican pesos at the equilibrium point E, which is an exchange rate of 10 cents in U.S. currency for each Mexican peso and a total volume of 85 billion pesos. In the actual foreign exchange market, almost all of the trading for Mexican pesos is done for U.S. dollars. What factors would cause the demand or supply to shift, thus leading to a change in the equilibrium exchange rate?

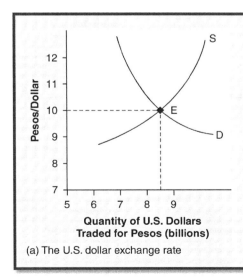

(a) The U.S. dollar exchange rate

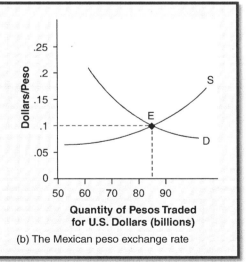

(b) The Mexican peso exchange rate

Exhibit 17-6   Demand and Supply for the U.S. Dollar and Mexican Peso Exchange Rate

(a) The quantity measured on the horizontal axis is in U.S. dollars, and the exchange rate on the vertical axis is the price of U.S. dollars measured in Mexican pesos.

(b) The quantity measured on the horizontal axis is in Mexican pesos, while the price on the vertical axis is the price of pesos measured in U.S. dollars. In both graphs, the equilibrium exchange rate occurs at point E, at the intersection of the demand curve D and the supply curve S.

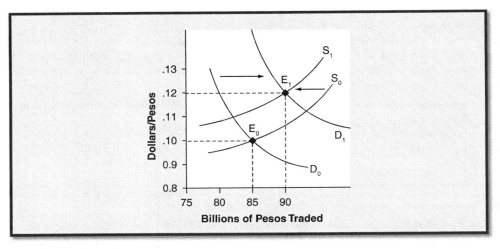

Exhibit 17-7
Exchange Rate Market for
Mexican Peso Reacts to
Expectations about Future
Exchange Rates

An announcement that
the peso exchange rate is
likely to strengthen in the
future will lead to greater
demand for the peso in the
present from investors who
wish to benefit from the
appreciation. Similarly, it will
make investors less likely to
supply pesos to the foreign
exchange market. Both the
shift of demand to the right
and the shift of supply to
the left cause an immediate
appreciation in the exchange
rate.

Expectations about Future Exchange Rates

One reason to demand a currency on the foreign exchange market is the belief that the value of the currency is about to increase. One reason to supply a currency—that is, sell it on the foreign exchange market—is the expectation that the value of the currency is about to decline. For example, imagine that a leading business newspaper, like the *Wall Street Journal* or the *Financial Times*, runs an article predicting that the Mexican peso will appreciate in value. The likely effects of such an article are illustrated in Exhibit 17-7. Demand for the Mexican peso shifts to the right from D_0 to D_1, as investors become eager to purchase pesos. Conversely, the supply of pesos shifts to the left from S_0 to S_1, because investors will be less willing to give them up. The result is that the equilibrium exchange rate rises from 10 cents/peso to 12 cents/peso and the equilibrium exchange rate rises from 85 billion to 90 billion pesos as the equilibrium moves from E_0 to E_1.

Exhibit 17-7 also illustrates some peculiar traits of supply and demand diagrams in the foreign exchange market. In contrast to all the other cases of supply and demand you have considered, in the foreign exchange market, supply and demand typically both move at the same time. Groups of participants in the foreign exchange market like firms and investors include some who are buyers and some who are sellers. An expectation of a future shift in the exchange rate affects both buyers and sellers—that is, it affects both demand and supply for a currency. The shifts in demand and supply curves both cause the exchange rate to shift in the same direction; in this example, they both make the peso exchange rate stronger. However, the shifts in demand and supply work in opposing directions on the quantity traded. In this example, the rising demand for pesos is causing the quantity to rise while the falling supply of pesos is causing quantity to fall. In this specific example, the result is a higher quantity. But in other cases, the result could be that quantity remains unchanged or declines.

This example also helps to explain why exchange rates often move quite substantially in a short period of a few weeks or months. When investors expect a country's currency to strengthen in the future, they buy the currency and cause it to appreciate immediately. The appreciation of the currency can lead other investors to believe that future appreciation is likely—and thus lead to even further appreciation. Similarly, a fear that a currency *might* weaken quickly leads to an *actual* weakening of the currency, which often reinforces the belief that the currency is going to weaken further. Thus, beliefs about the future path of exchange rates can be self-reinforcing, at least for a time, and a large share of

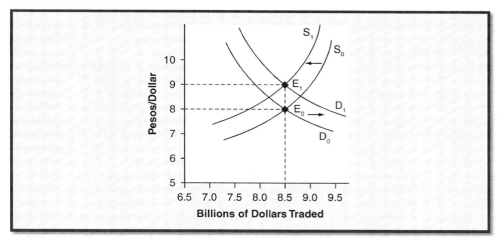

Exhibit 17-8
Exchange Rate Market for U.S. Dollars Reacts to Higher Interest Rates

A higher rate of return for U.S. dollar makes holding dollars more attractive. Thus, the demand for dollars in the foreign exchange market shifts to the right from D_0 to D_1, while the supply of dollars shifts to the left from S_0 to S_1. The new equilibrium E_1 has a stronger exchange rate than the original equilibrium E_0, but in this example, the equilibrium quantity traded does not change.

the trading in foreign exchange markets involves dealers trying to outguess each other on what direction exchange rates will move next.

Differences across Countries in Rates of Return

The motivation for investment, whether domestic or foreign, is to earn a return. If rates of return in a country look relatively high, then that country will tend to attract funds from abroad. Conversely, if rates of return in a country look relatively low, then funds will tend to flee to other economies. Changes in the expected rate of return will shift demand and supply for a currency. For example, imagine that interest rates rise in the United States as compared with Mexico. Thus, financial investments in the United States promise a higher return than they previously did. As a result, more investors will demand U.S. dollars so that they can buy interest bearing assets and more will be willing to supply U.S. dollars to foreign exchange markets. Demand for the U.S. dollar will shift to the right from D_0 to D_1 and supply will shift to the left from S_0 to S_1, as shown in Exhibit 17-8. The new equilibrium E_1, will occur at an exchange rate of 9 pesos/dollar and the same quantity of $8.5 billion. Thus, a higher interest rate or rate of return relative to other countries leads a nation's currency to appreciate or strengthen, and a lower interest rate relative to other countries leads a nation's currency to depreciate or weaken. Since a nation's central bank can use monetary policy to affect its interest rates, a central bank can also cause changes in exchange rates—a connection that will be discussed in more detail later in this chapter.

Relative Inflation

If a country experiences a relatively high inflation rate compared with other economies, then the buying power of its currency is eroding, which will tend to discourage anyone from wanting to acquire or to hold the currency. Exhibit 17-9 shows an example based on an episode for the Mexican peso. Back in 1986–87, Mexico experienced an inflation rate of over 200%. Not surprisingly, as inflation dramatically decreased the purchasing power of the peso in Mexico, the exchange rate value of the peso declined as well. As shown in Exhibit 17-9, demand for the peso on foreign exchange markets decreased from D_0 to D_1, while supply of the peso increased from S_0 to S_1. The equilibrium exchange rate fell from $2.50 per peso at the original equilibrium E_0 to $0.50 per peso at the

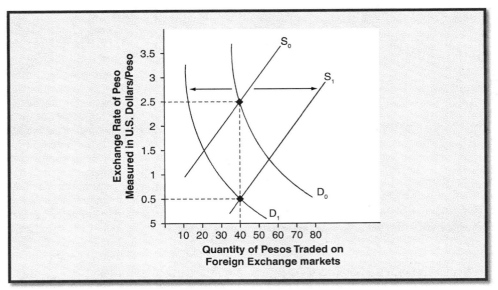

Exhibit 17-9
Exchange Rate Markets
React to Higher Inflation

If a currency is experiencing
relatively high inflation,
then its buying power is
decreasing and international
investors will be less eager
to hold it. Thus, a rise in
inflation in the Mexican peso
would lead demand to shift
from D_0 to D_1, and supply
to increase from S_0 to S_1.
Both movements in demand
and supply would cause
the currency to depreciate.
The effect on the quantity
trades is drawn here as a
decrease, but in truth it could
be an increase or no change,
depending on the actual
movements of demand and
supply.

new equilibrium E_1. In this example, the quantity of pesos traded on foreign exchange markets remained the same, even as the exchange rate shifted.

Purchasing Power Parity

Over the long term, exchange rates must bear some relationship to the buying power of the currency in terms of goods that are internationally traded. If at a certain exchange rate it was much cheaper to buy internationally traded goods—such as oil, steel, computers, and cars—in one country than in another country, businesses would start buying in the cheap country, selling in other countries, and pocketing the profits. For example, if a U.S. dollar is worth $1.60 in Canadian currency, then a car that sells for $20,000 in the United States should sell for $32,000 in Canada. If the price of cars in Canada was much lower than $32,000, then at least some U.S. car-buyers would convert their U.S. dollars to Canadian dollars and buy their cars in Canada. If the price of cars was much higher than $32,000 in this example, then at least some Canadian buyers would convert their Canadian dollars to U.S. dollars and come south of the border to purchase their cars. This process of buying and selling goods across international borders may occur slowly, but over time, it will force prices and exchange rates to align so that the price of internationally traded goods is similar in all countries.

The exchange rate that equalizes the prices of internationally traded goods across countries is called the **purchasing power parity** or **PPP** exchange rate. A group of economists at the International Comparison Program, run by the World Bank, have calculate the PPP exchange rate for all countries, based on detailed studies of the prices and qualities of internationally tradable goods.

purchasing power parity (PPP): The exchange rate that equalizes the prices of internationally traded goods across countries.

The purchasing power parity exchange rate serves two main functions. First, PPP exchange rates can be useful for making comparisons between countries. Imagine that you are preparing a table showing the size of GDP in many countries in several recent years, and for ease of comparison, you are converting all the values into U.S. dollars. When you insert the value for Japan, you need to use a yen/dollar exchange rate. But should you use the market exchange rate or the PPP exchange rate? Market exchange rates bounce around. In summer 2008, the exchange rate was 108 yen/dollar, but in late 2009 the U.S. dollar exchange rate versus the yen was to 90 yen/dollar. For simplicity, say that Japan's GDP was 500 trillion yen in both 2008 and 2008. But if you use the market exchange rates, then Japan's GDP will be $4.6 trillion in 2000 (that is, 500 trillion yen/(108 yen/dollar)) and $5.5 trillion in 2009 (that is, 500 trillion yen/(90 yen/dollar)). Of course, it's not true that Japan's economy increased enormously in 2009—in fact, Japan had a recession like much of the rest of the world. The misleading appearance of a booming Japanese economy occurs only because of using the market exchange rate, which often has short-run rises and falls. However, PPP exchange rates stay fairly constant from day to day or week to week, and change only modestly, if at all, from year to year. Thus, PPP exchange rates are often used for international comparisons of GDP and other economic statistics.

Second, over a period of years, exchange rates do tend to move in the general direction of the PPP exchange rate. It's true that in the short run and medium run, as exchange rates adjust to relative inflation rates, rates of return, and to expectations about how interest rates and inflation will shift, the exchange rates will often move away from the PPP exchange rate for a time. But there is some value in knowing in which direction the exchange rate is more likely to shift over the long run.

Macroeconomic Effects of Exchange Rates

A central bank will be concerned about the exchange rate for three reasons: (1) Movements in the exchange rate will affect the quantity of aggregate demand in an economy; (2) Frequent substantial fluctuations in the exchange rate can disrupt international trade and cause problems in a nation's banking system; (3) The exchange rate may contribute to an unsustainable balance of trade and large inflows of international financial capital, which can set the economy up for a deep recession if international investors decide to move their money to another country. Let's discuss these scenarios in turn. Then, the next section will consider a range of exchange rate policies.

Exchange Rates, Aggregate Demand, and Aggregate Supply

Foreign trade in good and services typically involves incurring the costs of production in one currency while receiving revenues from sales in another currency. As a result, movements in exchange rates can have a powerful effect on incentives to export and import, and thus on aggregate demand in the economy as a whole.

For example, in 1999 when the euro first became a currency, its value measured in U.S. currency was $1.06/euro. By the middle of 2001, the euro had fallen (and the U.S. dollar had correspondingly strengthened) to 87 cents/euro. Consider the situation of a French firm that each year incurs 10 million euros in costs, and sold its products in the United States for $10 million. In 1999, when this firm converted $10 million back to euros at the exchange rate of $1.06/euro (that is, $10 million × [1 euro/$1.06]), it had 9.4 million euros, and suffered a loss. In 2001, when this same firm converted $10 million back to euros at the exchange rate of 87 cents/euro (that is, $10 million × 1 euro/[87 cents]), it had 11.5 million euros and a substantial profit. This example shows how a weaker euro encourages exports by the French firm, because it makes the costs of production in the domestic currency lower relative to the sales revenues earned in another country. From the point of view of the U.S. economy, the example also shows how a stronger U.S. dollar encouraged imports.

From a macroeconomic point of view, increases in exports are an addition to aggregate demand, while increases in imports are a subtraction from aggregate demand.

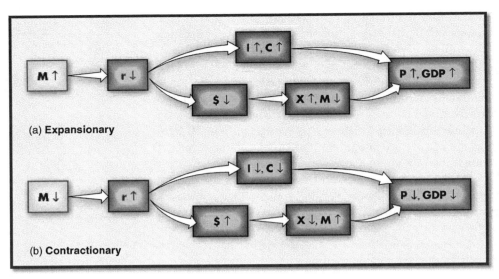

Exhibit 17-10
Monetary Policy with Exchange Rate Effects

(a) Exchange rates add another channel through which monetary policy can operate. When expansionary monetary policy reduces interest rates, it will depreciate the exchange rate, which in turn leads to higher exports and lower imports. These exchange rate effects will boost aggregate demand, and thus work with the higher levels of investment and consumption. The ultimate result is still a higher price level and higher GDP.

(b) When contractionary monetary policy raises interest rates, it will cause the exchange rate to appreciate, which in turn leads to lower exports and higher imports. These exchange rate effects will reduce aggregate demand, and thus work with the lower levels of investment and consumption. The ultimate result is still a lower price level and lower GDP.

Thus, a weaker currency should stimulate aggregate demand. In fact, bringing exchange rates into the picture provides another economic pathway to explain how monetary policy works (see Exhibit 17-10a). Expansionary monetary policy lowers interest rates, and increases demand for investment and consumer borrowing, which shifts aggregate demand to the right. However, the lower interest rates will also weaken the exchange rate, which makes exports more attractive and imports less attractive. These factors will cause aggregate demand to rise as well. Exhibit 17-10b shows how exchange rates can also reinforce the effects of contractionary monetary policy in reducing aggregate demand. A tight monetary policy raises interest rates, which reduces investment, consumption, and aggregate demand in the domestic economy. In addition, the higher interest rates also strengthen the exchange rate, which decreases aggregate demand further by stimulating exports and reducing imports. Thus, exchange rate adjustments make monetary policy more powerful in affecting aggregate demand.

However, while monetary policy can help an economy that is suffering a recession to move toward the potential output level of GDP, it does not increase the level of potential GDP. This lesson continues to apply when exchange rates are added to the picture. In the aggregate demand-aggregate supply diagram in Exhibit 17-11, the original equilibrium of the aggregate demand curve AD_0 and the short-run aggregate supply curve AS_0 occurs at equilibrium E_0, with an output of 700 and a price level of 95. The central bank uses expansionary monetary policy to increase the supply of money and loans, reduce interest rates, and shift aggregate demand from AD_0 to AD_1. With a short-run upward-sloping AS_0 curve, the equilibrium shifts from E_0 to E_1, as output rises to 740 and the price level rises to 100. This shift includes both the effect of expansionary monetary policy on domestic investment and also the effect through exchange rates on exports and imports.

However, let's say that the potential GDP level of output for this economy is 720. A long-run neoclassical AS curve would thus be a vertical line at this quantity of output. When a country has a weaker exchange rate, all imported inputs to production become relatively more expensive (which is why the quantity of imports decreases). A higher cost for a wide range of inputs shifts the short-run aggregate supply curve to the left from AS_0 to AS_1, for the same reasons that a hike in the price of imported oil shifts an AS curve to the left. At the resulting equilibrium, E_2, the price level has risen to 105, while the equilibrium quantity has fallen 720.

Exhibit 17-11 How a Weaker Exchange Rate Affects Inflation and Output

Why can't a nation expand its economy by depreciating its currency? After all, a weaker currency will stimulate exports and reduce imports, and thus cause aggregate demand to shift to the right from AD_0 to AD_1, and from the original equilibrium E_0 to E_1. But a weaker currency also affects aggregate supply. When the currency depreciates, then all inputs to production imported from other countries become more expensive (which is why imports fall, after all). The increase in costs of goods and services causes the original aggregate supply curve AS_0 to shift to the left to AS_1. The resulting equilibrium E_2 at the intersection of AD_1 and AS_1 will definitely have a higher price level than the original equilibrium E_0. However, the change in GDP is unlikely to be very large; it may be a little larger or a little smaller, but the effects of AS and AD on the quantity of output are shifting in opposite directions, and in the long term the economy ends up producing at potential GDP.

Upon reflection, the idea that a weaker currency leads to higher inflation, both from the effects of aggregate demand shifting to the right and aggregate supply shifting to the left, should make intuitive sense. After all, a weaker exchange rate means that a nation's currency has less buying power in other nations with different currencies—and inflation also means that a currency has less buying power. Thus, exchange rates can help monetary policy to be more powerful in affecting aggregate demand in the short run, but cannot avoid the reality that national output is determined by potential GDP in the long run.

Fluctuations in Exchange Rates

Exchange rates can fluctuate a great deal in the short run. As yet one more example, the Indian rupee moved from 39 rupees/dollar in February 2008 to 51 rupees/dollar in March 2009, a decline of more than one-fourth in the value of the rupee on foreign exchange markets. Exhibit 17-4 earlier showed that even two well-developed neighboring economies like the United States and Canada can see significant movements in exchange rates over a few years. For firms that depend on export sales, or firms that rely on imported inputs to production, or even purely domestic firms that compete with firms tied into international trade—which in many countries adds up to half or more of a nation's GDP—sharp movements in exchange rates can lead to dramatic changes in profits and losses. Thus, a central bank may desire to keep exchange rates from moving too much as part of providing a stable business climate, where firms can focus on productivity and innovation, not on reacting to exchange rate fluctuations.

One of the most economically destructive effects of exchange rate fluctuations can happen through the banking system. Most international loans are measured in a few large currencies, like U.S. dollars, European euros, and Japanese yen. In countries that do not use these currencies, banks often borrow funds in the currencies of other countries, like U.S. dollars, but then lend in their own domestic currency. The left-hand chain of events in Exhibit 17-12 shows how this pattern of international borrowing can work. A bank in Thailand borrows $1 million in U.S. dollars. Then the bank converts the dollars to its domestic currency—in the case of Thailand, the currency is the baht—at a rate of 40 baht/dollar. The bank then lends the baht to a firm in Thailand. The business repays the loan in baht, and the bank converts it back to U.S. dollars to pay off its original U.S. dollar loan.

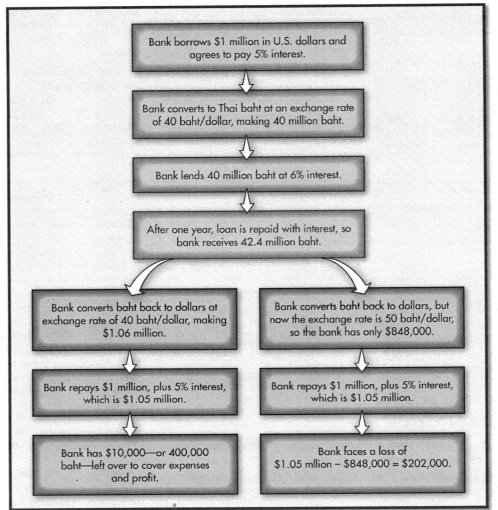

This process of borrowing in a foreign currency and lending in a domestic currency can work just fine, as long as the exchange rate doesn't shift. But if the dollar strengthens and the baht weakens, a problem arises. The right-hand chain of events in Exhibit 17-12 illustrates what happens when the baht unexpectedly weakens from 40 baht/dollar to 50 baht/dollar. The Thai firm still repays the loan in full to the bank. But because of the shift in the exchange rate, the bank cannot repay its loan in U.S. dollars. (Of course, if the exchange rate had changed in the other direction, making the Thai currency stronger, the bank could have realized an unexpectedly large profit.)

In 1997–98, countries across eastern Asia like Thailand, Korea, Malaysia, and Indonesia experienced a sharp depreciation of their currencies, often 50% or more. These countries had been experiencing substantial inflows of foreign investment capital, with bank lending increasing 20–30% per year through the mid-1990s. When their exchange rates depreciated, the banking systems in these countries were bankrupt. As noted at the start of this chapter, Argentina experienced a similar chain of events in 2002. When the Argentine peso depreciated, Argentina's banks found themselves unable to pay back what they had borrowed in U.S. dollars. Banks play a vital role in any economy in facilitating transactions and in making loans to firms and consumers. When most of a country's largest banks become bankrupt simultaneously, a sharp decline in aggregate demand and a deep recession results. Since the main responsibilities of a central bank are to control the money supply and to assure that the banking system is stable, a central bank must be concerned about whether a large and unexpected exchange rate depreciation will drive most of the country's existing banks into bankruptcy.

Exchange Rates, Trade Balances, and International Capital Flows

An economy with a trade deficit experiences a net inflow of international financial capital, while an economy with a trade surplus always experiences a net outflow of international capital. This connection was explained in Chapter 11. The exchange rate can help to explain these linkages further—and also explain why movements in exchange rates, trade balances, and international flows of capital sometimes lead to macroeconomic disaster.

In the foreign exchange market, the quantity demanded of a currency in equilibrium must equal the quantity supplied of that currency. In the foreign exchange market for U.S. dollars, U.S. dollars are supplied by foreign firms who have sold imported goods and services to the U.S. economy and by U.S. investors who wish to make financial investments in other countries. Conversely, U.S. dollars are demanded by U.S. firms that have earned foreign currencies and now wish to trade back to U.S. dollars, and by foreign investors who wish to make financial investments in the U.S. economy. (For simplicity, let's include the tourism industry here as part of exports and imports.) Thus, the following relationships must hold:

$$\begin{array}{cc} \text{Quantity supplied of U.S. dollars} \\ \text{in the foreign exchange market} \end{array} = \begin{array}{cc} \text{Quantity demanded of U.S. dollars} \\ \text{in the foreign exchange market} \end{array}$$

$$\text{Imports} + \begin{array}{c} \text{U.S. investors who wish} \\ \text{to make financial investments} \\ \text{in other countries} \end{array} = \text{Exports} + \begin{array}{c} \text{Foreign investors who wish} \\ \text{to make financial investments} \\ \text{in the U.S. economy} \end{array}$$

When a trade deficit exists, then imports exceed exports. If the quantity demanded is to equal the quantity supplied in foreign exchange markets, then it must also be true that international financial investment entering the U.S. economy is larger than international financial investment leaving the U.S. economy. Thus, a trade deficit always and inevitably means a net inflow of international financial capital. When a trade surplus exists, and exports exceed imports, then it must also be true that international financial investment entering the U.S. economy is smaller than international financial investment leaving the U.S. economy. A trade surplus always and inevitably means a net outflow of international financial capital. When the balance of trade in goods and services is zero, then the inflows and outflows of international financial capital must be equal. Exhibit 17-13 summarizes the three scenarios of trade deficit, trade balance, and trade surplus, and how they are connected to net flows of international financial capital.

There is no reason that each national economy should have a trade balance of zero. In fact, any time there is a net inflow or outflow of financial capital across international border, that economy will also have an imbalance of trade. If low-income countries around the world succeed in their goal of attracting net investment from high-income economies, they will also necessarily experience trade deficits.

Exhibit 17-13   Trade Balances and International Financial Flows

Scenario 1	Scenario 2	Scenario 3
Trade Deficit	**Trade Balance**	**Trade Surplus**
Imports greater than exports	Imports equal to exports	Exports greater than imports
The value of U.S. dollars earned by foreign producers who sell goods and services in the United States is greater than the value of foreign currencies earned by U.S. producers selling abroad.	The value of U.S. dollars earned by foreign producers who sell goods and services in the United States is equal to the value of foreign currencies earned by U.S. producers selling abroad.	The value of U.S. dollars earned by foreign producers who sell goods and services in the U.S. economy is less than the value of foreign currencies earned by U.S. producers selling abroad.
Inflow of international financial capital greater than outflow of financial capital	Inflow of financial capital equal to outflow of financial capital	Outflow of financial capital to other economies greater than inflow of financial capital

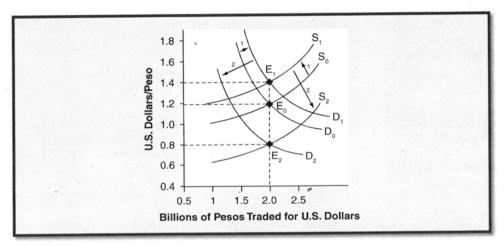

Billions of Pesos Traded for U.S. Dollars

Exhibit 17-14   From Appreciation to Depreciation

The exchange rate starts at E_0. The local economy grows and attracts an inflow of international financial capital. Demand for the currency on foreign exchange markets increases from D_0 to D_1, supply falls from S_0 to S_1, and the currency appreciates from $1.20/peso at E_0 to $1.40/peso at E_1. But at some point, the enthusiasm of foreign investors for this economy diminishes. As international financial investors move funds to other countries, and as the depreciation causes even more disenchantment with this currency, the supply of this currency on foreign exchange markets shifts to the right from S_1 to S_2, and demand for the currency shifts to the left from D_1 to D_2. Eventually, the exchange rate has fallen from $1.40 at E_1 to $0.80 at E_2. This sharp decline in exchange rates can stagger firms involved in international trade, the banking system, and the macroeconomy.

A stronger or appreciating currency is associated with a larger trade deficit. To understand why, imagine that the economy of Argentina starts with balanced trade in goods and services. Say that the exchange rate at the equilibrium E_0 is $1.20 U.S. dollar per peso and the equilibrium quantity is $2 billion per day, as shown in Exhibit 17-14. Now imagine that Argentina's economy appears to be growing in a healthy way, so that U.S. and other international investors want to make financial investments in Argentina. The demand for the pesos in the foreign exchange market increases from D_0 to D_1, and the supply of U.S. dollars decreases from S_0 to S_1. At the new equilibrium E_1, the equilibrium quantity in the market remains the same but the exchange rate has risen to $1.40/peso. This higher exchange rate will discourage exports from Argentina and encourage imports. Thus, the exchange rate provides a connection through which an economy that experiences a rise in net capital inflows will also have a trade deficit.

But a dangerous macroeconomic scenario has repeated itself a number of times in recent years: a nation's economy appears to have good prospects for future growth, and so it attracts inflows of international financial capital leading to a stronger currency. Indeed, many low-income and middle-income countries hope to experience a steady inflow of foreign financial investment, which not only brings funds for physical capital investment, but is often accompanied by management expertise, international business contacts, and improved training for local workers. However, at some point, the economic growth of the country suffered an inevitable hiccup, from one cause or another. The hiccup need not be large, but only large enough to make international investors fear that the country's exchange rate is likely to weaken. This fear causes some international investors to withdraw their short-term portfolio investments in the country. But as foreign investors sell their financial investments in the country, they increase the supply of currency that country's currency on foreign exchange markets and reduce their demand for the currency, thus causing the currency to fall. A self-fulfilling prophecy had occurred: expectations that the currency would fall led to an immediate decline. The falling currency led to expectations of a further decline, which led to more financial investment fleeing the country and more downward pressure on the currency. By the time this avalanche has ended, the supply of currency in Exhibit 17-14 increases from S_0 to S_1 and the demand for that currency falls from D_0 to D_1. The new equilibrium E_2 has the same quantity, but now the exchange rate is only 80 cents per peso.

A sharp decline in the exchange rate will reduce the trade deficit (or increase a trade surplus) by benefiting exporters and making imports more expensive. But severe problems can arise in the banking system. At various times in the late 1990s and early 2000s, banks in Mexico and Thailand and Russia and Argentina had borrowed extensively in U.S. dollars and loaned in their local currencies. When the local currencies depreciated, the banks could not repay their international loans. As entire banking systems went bankrupt, the national economies plummeted. GDP fell by 10%, 20%, and more within a year or two. The risk of these extremely severe recessions mean that central banks must be concerned that an inflow of financial capital will turn into an outflow, leading to a sharp decline in exchange rates that cripples the financial sector of the economy and leads to deep recession.

The U.S. economy has experienced large trade deficits in the 2000s: for example, in 2008 the current account trade balance for the U.S. economy was a deficit of $840 billion, which was 4.9% of GDP. Nonetheless, the U.S. economy is clearly less vulnerable to a sharp downturn in the exchange rate of its currency than many other countries. One protection is that the U.S. dollar is so widely held—as shown in Exhibit 17-1 earlier, it makes up almost half of all exchange rate trading. It's possible for international markets to flee small currencies like those of Argentina or Thailand, but it's harder to flee the U.S. dollar. Also, U.S. banks typically have both liabilities and assets in U.S. dollars, so they would not be crippled by a fall in the dollar exchange rate like the banks in Argentina or Thailand. Still, a sharp decline in the value of the U.S. dollar would increase aggregate demand by raising exports and reducing imports. It would also shift aggregate supply to the left by raising the price of imported goods and services throughout the U.S. economy. If the Federal Reserve attempted to fight the resulting inflationary pressures with a contractionary monetary policy, a recession might result. Even the mighty U.S. economy is not invulnerable to pressures from the globalized economy.

Summing Up Public Policy and Exchange Rates

Every nation would prefer a stable exchange rate to facilitate international trade and reduce the degree of risk and uncertainty in the economy. However, a nation may sometimes want a weaker exchange rate to stimulate aggregate demand and reduce a recession, or a stronger exchange rate to fight inflation. The country must also be concerned that rapid movements from a weak to a strong exchange rate may cripple its export industries, while rapid movements from a strong to a weak exchange rate can cripple its banking sector. In short, every choice of an exchange rate—whether it should be stronger or weaker, or

Exhibit 17-15
A Spectrum of Exchange
Rate Policies

fixed or changing—represents potential trade-offs. The next section discusses the range of policy choices that a country can make about its exchange rate.

Exchange Rate Policies

Exchange rate policies come in a range of different forms listed in Exhibit 17-15: let the foreign exchange market determine the exchange rate; let the market set the value of the exchange rate most of the time, but have the central bank sometimes intervene to prevent fluctuations that seem too large; have the central bank guarantee a specific exchange rate; or share a currency with other countries. Let's discuss each type of exchange rate policy and its trade-offs in turn.

Floating Exchange Rates

A policy which allows the foreign exchange market to set exchange rates is referred to as a **floating exchange rate.** The U.S. dollar is a floating exchange rate, as are currencies of about 40% of the countries in the world economy. The major concern with this policy is that exchange rates can move a great deal in a short time.

floating exchange rate:
When a country lets the value of its currency be determined in the exchange rate market.

Consider the U.S. exchange rate expressed in terms of another fairly stable currency, the Japanese yen, as shown in Exhibit 17-16. On January 1, 2002, the exchange rate was 133 yen/dollar. On January 1, 2005, it was 103 yen/dollar. On June 1, 2007, it was 122 yen/dollar, and on January 1, 2009, it was 90 yen/dollar. As investor sentiment swings back and forth, driving exchange rates up and down, exporters, importers, and banks involved in international lending are all affected. At worst, large movements in exchange rates can drive companies into bankruptcy or trigger a nationwide banking collapse. But even in the moderate case of the yen/dollar exchange rate, these movements of roughly 30 percent back and forth impose stress on both economies as firms must alter their export and import plans to take the new exchange rates into account. Especially in smaller economies where international trade is a relatively large share of GDP, exchange rate movements can rattle their economies.

However, movements of floating exchange rates have advantages, too. After all, prices of goods and services rise and fall throughout a market economy, as demand and supply shift. If an economy experiences strong inflows or outflows of international financial capital, or has relatively high inflation, or if it experiences strong productivity growth so that purchasing power changes relative to other economies, then it makes economic sense for the exchange rate to shift as well.

Floating exchange rate advocates often argue that if government policies were more predictable and stable, then inflation rates and interest rates would be more predictable

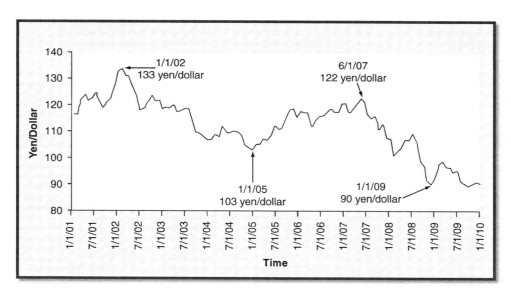

Exhibit 17-16 U.S. Dollar Exchange Rate in Japanese Yen

Even relatively stable exchange rates can vary a fair amount. The exchange rate for the U.S. dollar, measured in Japanese yen, fell about 30% from the start of 2002 to the start of 2005, rose back by mid-2007, and then dropped again by early 2009.

and stable; exchange rates would bounce around less, too. The great economist Milton Friedman (1912–2006), for example, wrote a defense of floating exchange rates in 1961 in his book *Capitalism and Freedom:*

> Being in favor of floating exchange rates does not mean being in favor of unstable exchange rates. When we support a free price system [for goods and services] at home, this does not imply that we favor a system in which prices fluctuate wildly up and down. What we want is a system in which prices are free to fluctuate but in which the forces determining them are sufficiently stable so that in fact prices move within moderate ranges. This is equally true in a system of floating exchange rates. The ultimate objective is a world in which exchange rates, while free to vary, are, in fact, highly stable because basic economic policies and conditions are stable.

Thus, advocates of floating exchange rates admit that, yes, exchange rates may sometimes fluctuate. But they point out that if a central bank focuses on preventing either high inflation or deep recession, with low and reasonably steady interest rates, then exchange rates will have less reason to vary.

Using Soft Pegs and Hard Pegs

When a government intervenes in the foreign exchange market so that the exchange rate of its currency is different from what the market would have produced, it is said to have established a "peg" for its currency. A **soft peg** is the name for an exchange rate policy where the government usually allows the exchange rate to be set by the market, but in some cases, especially if the exchange rate seems to be moving rapidly in one direction, the central bank will intervene in the market. With a **hard peg** exchange rate policy, the central bank sets a fixed and unchanging value for the exchange rate. This section explains how a central bank can implement soft peg and hard peg policies, while the next section discusses the trade-offs and costs of these policies.

Suppose that the market exchange rate for the Brazilian currency, the real, would be 35 cents/real with a daily quantity of 15 billion real traded in the market, as shown at the equilibrium E_0 in Exhibit 17-17a and Exhibit 17-17b. However, the government of Brazil decides that the exchange rate should be 30 cents/real, as shown in Exhibit 17-17a.

soft peg: An exchange rate policy where the government usually allows the exchange rate to be set by the market, but in some cases, especially if the exchange rate seems to be moving rapidly in one direction, the central bank will intervene.

hard peg: An exchange rate policy in which the central bank sets a fixed and unchanging value for the exchange rate.

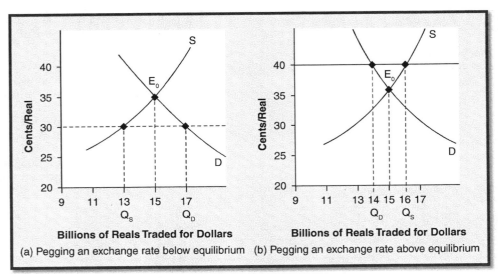

(a) Pegging an exchange rate below equilibrium   (b) Pegging an exchange rate above equilibrium

Exhibit 17-17
Pegging an Exchange Rate

(a) If an exchange rate is pegged below what would otherwise be the equilibrium, then the quantity demanded of the currency will exceed the quantity supplied. The central bank can fill this gap in two ways. One approach would be an expansionary monetary policy to reduce interest rates, which will reduce demand for the currency in foreign exchange markets and increase supply. Alternatively, the central bank could create money and supply it directly in the foreign exchange market.

(b) If an exchange rate is pegged above what would otherwise be the equilibrium, then the quantity supplied of the currency exceeds the quantity demanded. The central bank can create this situation with a contractionary monetary policy to raise interest rates, and thus to increase demand for its currency and reduce supply of its currency in foreign exchange markets. Alternatively, the central bank can use its reserves of foreign currency to purchase its own currency on foreign exchange markets and thus to increase demand directly.

Perhaps Brazil sets this lower exchange rate to benefit its export industries; perhaps it is an attempt to stimulate aggregate demand by stimulating exports; perhaps Brazil believes that the current market exchange rate is higher than the long-term purchasing power parity value of the real, so it is minimizing fluctuations in the real by keeping it at this lower rate; perhaps the target exchange rate was set sometime in the past, and is now being maintained for the sake of stability. Whatever the reason, if Brazil's central bank wishes to keep the exchange rate below the market level, it must face the reality that at this weaker exchange rate of 30 cents/real, the quantity demanded of its currency at 17 billion reals is greater than the quantity supplied of 13 billion reals in the foreign exchange market.

The Brazilian central bank could weaken its exchange rate in two ways. One approach is to use an expansionary monetary policy that leads to lower interest rates. In foreign exchange markets, the lower interest rates will reduce demand and increase supply of the real and lead to depreciation. Alternatively, Brazil's central bank could trade directly in the foreign exchange market. The central bank can expand the money supply by creating reals, use the reals to purchase foreign currencies, and avoid selling any of its own currency. In this way, it can fill the gap between quantity demanded and quantity supplied of its currency.

Exhibit 17-17*b* shows the opposite situation. Here, the Brazilian government desires a stronger exchange rate of 40 cents/real than the market rate of 35 cents/real. Perhaps Brazil desires the stronger currency to reduce aggregate demand and to fight inflation, or perhaps Brazil believes that that current market exchange rate is temporarily lower than the long-term rate. But whatever the reason, at the higher desired exchange rate, the quantity supplied of 16 billion reals exceeds the quantity demanded of 14 billion reals.

Brazil's central bank can use a contractionary monetary policy to raise interest rates, which will increase demand and reduce supply of the currency on foreign exchange markets, and lead to an appreciation. Alternatively, Brazil's central bank can trade directly in the foreign exchange market. In this case, with an excess supply of its own currency in foreign exchange markets, the central bank must use reserves of foreign currency, like U.S. dollars, to demand its own currency and thus cause an appreciation of its exchange rate.

Both a soft peg and a hard peg policy require that the central bank intervene in the foreign exchange market. However, a hard peg policy attempts to preserve a fixed exchange rate at all times. A soft peg policy typically allows the exchange rate to move up and down by relatively small amounts in the short run of several months or a year, and to move by larger amounts over time, but seeks to avoid extreme short-term fluctuations.

Trade-offs of Soft Pegs and Hard Pegs

When a country decides to alter the market exchange rate, it faces a number of trade-offs. If it uses monetary policy to alter the exchange rate, it then cannot at the same time use monetary policy to address issues of inflation or recession. If it uses direct purchases and sales of foreign currencies in exchange rates, then it must face the issue of how it will handle its reserves of foreign currency. Finally, a pegged exchange rate can even create additional movements of the exchange rate; for example, even the possibility of government intervention in exchange rate markets will lead to rumors about whether and when the government will intervene, and dealers in the foreign exchange market will react to those rumors. Let's consider these issues in turn.

A first concern with pegged exchange rate policies is that they imply that a country's monetary policy is no longer focused on controlling inflation or shortening recessions, but now must also take the exchange rate into account. For example, when a country pegs its exchange rate, it will sometimes face economic situations where it would like to have an expansionary monetary policy to fight recession—but it cannot do so because that policy would depreciate its exchange rate and break its hard peg. With a soft peg exchange rate policy, the central bank can sometimes ignore the exchange rate and focus on domestic inflation or recession—but in other cases the central bank may ignore inflation or recession and instead focus on its soft peg exchange rate. With a hard peg policy, domestic monetary policy is effectively no longer determined by domestic inflation or unemployment, but only by what monetary policy is needed to keep the exchange rate at the hard peg.

A second issue arises when a central bank intervenes directly in the exchange rate market. If a central bank ends up in a situation where it is perpetually creating and selling its own currency on foreign exchange markets, it will be buying the currency of other countries, like U.S. dollars or euros, to hold as reserves. Holding large reserves of other currencies has an opportunity cost, and central banks will not wish to boost such reserves without limit. Also, a central bank that causes a large increase in the supply of money is also risking an inflationary surge in aggregate demand. Conversely, when a central bank wishes to buy its own currency, it can do so by using its reserves of international currency like the U.S. dollar or the euro. But if the central bank runs out of such reserves, it can no longer use this method to strengthen its currency. Thus, buying foreign currencies in exchange rate markets can be expensive and inflationary, while selling foreign currencies can only work until a central bank runs out of reserves.

A third issue is that when a government pegs its exchange rate, it may unintentionally create another reason for additional fluctuation. With a soft peg policy, foreign exchange dealers and international investors react to every rumor about how or when the central bank is likely to intervene to influence the exchange rate, and as they react to rumors the exchange rate will shift up and down. Thus, even though the goal of a soft peg policy is to reduce short-term fluctuations of the exchange rate, the existence of the policy—when anticipated in the foreign exchange market—may sometimes increase short-term fluctuations of the exchange rate as international investors try to anticipate how and when the central bank will act.

Capital Controls and Tobin Taxes

Some countries like Chile and Malaysia have sought to reduce movements in exchange rates by limiting inflows and outflows of international financial capital. This policy can be enacted either through targeted taxes or by regulations.

Taxes on international capital flows are sometimes known as "Tobin taxes," named after James Tobin, the 1981 Nobel laureate in economics who proposed such a tax in a 1972 lecture. For example, a government might tax all foreign exchange transactions, or attempt to tax short-term portfolio investment while exempting long-term foreign direct investment. Countries can also use regulation either to forbid certain kinds of foreign investment in the first place or to make it difficult for international financial investors to withdraw their funds from a country.

The goal of such policies is to reduce international capital flows, especially short-term portfolio flows, in the hope that doing so will reduce the chance of large movements in exchange rates that can bring macroeconomic disaster.

But proposals to limit international financial flows have severe practical difficulties. Taxes are imposed by national governments, not international ones. If one government imposes a Tobin tax on exchange rate transactions carried out within its territory, the exchange rate market might easily be operated by a firm based someplace like the Grand Caymans, an island nation in the Caribbean well-known for allowing some financial wheeling and dealing. In an interconnected global economy, if goods and services are allowed to flow across national borders, then payments need to flow across borders, too. It is very difficult—close to impossible—for a nation to allow only the flows of payments that relate to goods and services, while clamping down or taxing other flows of financial capital. If a nation participates in international trade, it must also participate in international capital movements.

Finally, countries all over the world, especially low-income countries, are crying out for foreign investment to help develop their economies. Policies that discourage international financial investment may prevent some possible harms, but they rule out potentially substantial economic benefits as well.

A hard peg exchange rate policy will not allow short-term fluctuations in the exchange rate. But if the government first announces a hard peg but later changes its mind—for example, perhaps the government becomes unwilling to keep interest rates high or to hold high levels of foreign exchange reserves—then the result of abandoning a hard peg could be a dramatic shift in the exchange rate.

In the mid-2000s, about one-third of the countries in the world used a soft peg approach and about one-quarter used a hard peg approach. The general trend in the 1990s was been to shift away from a soft peg approach in favor of either floating rates or a hard peg. The concern is that a successful soft peg policy may for a time lead to very little variation in exchange rates, so that firms and banks in the economy begin to act as if a hard peg exists. When the exchange rate does move, the effects are especially painful because firms and banks haven't planned and hedged against a possible change. Thus, the argument went, it is better either to be clear that the exchange rate is always flexible, or that it is fixed, but choosing an in-between soft peg option may end up being worst of all.

A Single Currency

A final approach to exchange rate policy is for a nation to choose a common currency shared with one or more nations. A single currency approach eliminates foreign exchange risk altogether. Just as no one worries about exchange rate movements when buying and selling between New York and California, Europeans know that the value of the euro will be the same in Germany and France and other European nations that have adopted the euro.

However, a single currency also poses problems. Like a hard peg, a single currency means that a nation has given up altogether on domestic monetary policy,

Exhibit 17-18   Trade-offs of Exchange Rate Policies

	Floating Exchange Rates	Soft Peg	Hard Peg	Merging Currencies
Large short-run fluctuations in exchange rates?	Often a lot in the short term	Maybe less in the short run, but still large changes over time	None, unless a change in the fixed rate	None
Large long-term fluctuations in exchange rates?	Can often happen	Can often happen	Can't happen unless hard peg changes	Can't happen
Power of central bank to conduct countercyclical monetary policy	Flexible exchange rates make monetary policy stronger	Some power, although conflicts may arise between exchange rate policy and countercyclical policy	Very little; central bank must keep exchange rate fixed	None; nation doesn't have its own currency
Costs of holding foreign exchange reserves	Don't need to hold reserves	Hold moderate reserves that rise and fall over time	Hold large reserves	No need to hold reserves
Risk of being stuck with an exchange rate that causes a large trade imbalance and very high inflows or outflows of financial capital	A floating rate adjusts often	A soft peg will adjust over the medium term, if not the short term	A hard peg may become stuck over time either far above or below the market level	A merged currency cannot adjust

and instead has put its interest rate policies in other hands. When Ecuador uses the U.S. dollar as its currency, it has no voice in whether the Federal Reserve raises or lowers interest rates. The European Central Bank that determines monetary policy for the euro has representatives from all the euro nations. However, from the standpoint of, say, Portugal, there will be times when the decisions of the European Central Bank about monetary policy do not match the decisions that would have been made by a Portuguese central bank.

The lines between these four different exchange rate policies can blend into each other. For example, a soft peg exchange rate policy in which the government almost never acts to intervene in the exchange rate market will look a great deal like a floating exchange rate. Conversely, a soft peg policy in which the government intervenes often to keep the exchange rate near a specific level will look a lot like a hard peg. A decision to merge currencies with another country is, in effect, a decision to have a permanently fixed exchange rate with those countries, which is like a very hard exchange rate peg. The range of exchange rates policy choices, with their advantages and disadvantages, are summarized in Exhibit 17-18.

Conclusion

Global macroeconomics would be easier if the whole world had one currency and one central bank. The exchange rates between more than different currencies complicate the picture. If exchange rates are set solely by financial markets, they fluctuate substantially as short-term portfolio investors try to anticipate tomorrow's news. If the government attempts to intervene in exchange rate markets through soft pegs or hard pegs, it gives up at least some of the power to use monetary policy to focus on domestic inflations and recessions, and it risks causing even greater fluctuations in foreign exchange markets. There is no consensus among economists about which exchange rate policies are best: floating, soft peg, hard peg, or merged currencies. The choice depends both on how well a nation's central bank can implement a specific exchange rate policy and on how well a nation's firms and banks can adapt to different exchange rate policies. A national economy that does a fairly good job at achieving the four main economic goals of growth, low inflation, low unemployment, and a sustainable balance of trade will probably do just fine the vast majority of the time with any exchange rate policy; conversely, no exchange rate policy is likely to save an economy that consistently fails at achieving these goals.

Key Concepts and Summary

1. The **foreign exchange market** is the market in which people and firms exchange one currency to purchase another currency.

2. On the demand side of the foreign exchange market for the trading of U.S. dollars are U.S. export firms seeking to convert their earnings in foreign currency back into U.S. dollars; foreign tourists in the United States; and foreign investors seeking to make financial investments in the U.S. economy. On the supply side of the foreign exchange market for the trading of U.S. dollars are foreign firms that have sold imports in the U.S. economy and are seeking to convert their earnings back to their home currency; U.S. tourists abroad; and U.S. investors seeking to make financial investments in foreign economies.

3. When currency A can buy more of currency B, then currency A has strengthened or **appreciated** relative to B. When currency A can buy less of currency B, then currency A has weakened or **depreciated** relative to B. If currency A strengthens or appreciates relative to currency B, then currency B must necessarily weaken or depreciate with regard to currency A. A stronger currency benefits those who are buying with that currency and injures those who are selling. A weaker currency injures those, like importers, who are buying with that currency and benefits those who are selling with it, like exporters.

4. In the extreme short run, ranging from a few minutes to a few weeks, exchange rates are influenced by speculators who are trying to invest in currencies that will grow stronger, and to sell currencies that will grow weaker. Such speculation can create a self-fulfilling prophecy, at least for a time, where an expected appreciation leads to a stronger currency and vice versa.

5. In the relatively short run, exchange rate markets are influenced by differences in rates of return. Countries with relatively high real rates of return (for example, high interest rates) will tend to experience stronger currencies as they attract money from abroad, while countries with relatively low rates of return will tend to experience weaker exchange rates as investors convert to other currencies.

6. In the medium run of a few months or a few years, exchange rate markets are influenced by inflation rates. Countries with relatively high inflation will tend to experience less demand for their currency than countries with lower inflation, and thus currency depreciation.

7. Over long periods of many years, exchange rates tend to adjust toward the **purchasing power parity (PPP)** rate, which is the exchange rate such that the prices of internationally tradable goods in different countries, when converted at the PPP exchange rate to a common currency, are similar in all economies.

8. A central bank will be concerned about the exchange rate for several reasons. Exchange rates will affect imports and exports, and thus affect aggregate demand in the economy. Fluctuations in exchange rates may cause difficulties for many firms, but especially banks. The exchange rate may accompany unsustainable flows of international financial capital.

9. In a **floating exchange rate** policy, a country's exchange rate is determined in the foreign exchange market. In a **soft peg** exchange rate policy, a country's exchange rate is usually determined in the foreign exchange market, but the government sometimes intervenes to strengthen or weaken the exchange rate. In a **hard peg** exchange rate policy, the government chooses an exchange rate.

10. A central bank can intervene in exchange markets in two ways. It can raise or lower interest rates to make the currency stronger or weaker. Or it can directly purchase or sell its currency in foreign exchange markets.

11. All exchange rates policies face trade-offs. A hard peg exchange rate policy will reduce exchange rate fluctuations, but means that a country must focus its monetary policy on the exchange rate, not on fighting recession or controlling inflation. When a nation merges its currency with another nation, it give up on nationally-oriented monetary policy altogether. A soft peg exchange rate may create additional volatility as exchange rate markets try to anticipate when and how the government will intervene. A flexible exchange rate policy allows monetary policy to focus on inflation and unemployment, and allows the exchange rate to change with inflation and rates of return, but also raises a risk that exchange rates may sometimes make large and abrupt movements.

12. The spectrum of exchange rate policies includes: (a) a floating exchange rate, (b) exchange rate zones, (c) a pegged exchange rate, and (d) a single currency.

13. Monetary policy can focus on a variety of goals: (a) focus on inflation; (b) focus on inflation or unemployment, depending on which is the most dangerous obstacle; and (c) focus on the money supply or a long-term rule.

Review Questions

1. What is the foreign exchange market?

2. Describe some buyers and some sellers in the market for U.S. dollars.

3. What's the difference between foreign direct investment and portfolio investment?

4. What does it mean to hedge a financial transaction?

5. What does it mean to say that a currency appreciates? Depreciates? Becomes stronger? Becomes weaker?

6. Does an expectation of a stronger exchange rate in the future affect the exchange rate in the present? If so, how?

7. Does a higher rate of return in a nation's economy, other things being equal, affect the exchange rate of its currency? If so, how?

8. Does a higher inflation rate in an economy, other things being equal, affect the exchange rate of its currency? If so, how?

9. What is the purchasing power parity exchange rate?

10. What are some of the reasons a central bank is likely to care, at least to some extent, about the exchange rate?

11. How can an unexpected fall in exchange rates injure the financial health of a nation's banks?

12. What's the difference between a floating exchange rate, a soft peg, a hard peg, and dollarization?

13. List some advantages and disadvantages of the different exchange rate policies.

18

Government Budgets and Fiscal Policy

All levels of government—federal, state and local—have budgets that show how much money the government expects to have available to spend and how the government plans to spend it. However, budgets can shift dramatically within a few years, as policy decisions and unexpected events shake up earlier tax and spending plans.

For example, during Barack Obama's first year as President of the United States in 2009, the U.S. government experienced its largest budget deficit ever in nominal terms, as the federal government spent $1.4 trillion more than it collected in taxes. This deficit was about 10% of the size of the U.S. GDP in 2009, making it by far the largest budget deficit relative to GDP since the mammoth borrowing used to finance the fighting of World War II. Did this humongous budget deficits mainly results from the recession the U.S. economy experienced starting in late 2007, before Obama's term of office began? Or was this deficit caused by tax cuts and spending increases seeking to stimulate consumption and thus shorten the length of the recession? How will the effects of a short-term deficit during a recession differ from the effects of long-term and sustained deficits?

The previous three chapters discussed monetary policy, while this chapter and the next will discuss the other main channel of macroeconomic policy— government fiscal policies of taxes and spending. The discussion will focus on the macroeconomics of government budgets, not the microeconomics; for example, this chapter will focus on how government taxes and spending taken as a whole affect aggregate demand for the economy as a whole, not on the merits of specific taxes or spending programs. This chapter begins with an overview of U.S. government spending and taxes. It then discusses fiscal policy from a short-run perspective; that is, how government might use tax and spending policies to address issues of recession, unemployment and inflation; how periods of recession and growth affect government budgets; and the merits of proposals that the government should seek a perfect balance between taxes and spending—a balanced budget—each and every year.

An Overview of Government Spending

The "fisc," an old-fashioned word that appears in dictionaries but seldom in print anymore, is defined as a nation's treasury, the department that handles the inflow of taxes and the outflow of spending. **Fiscal policies** are the set of policies relating to government spending, taxation, and borrowing. Both words, fisc and fiscal, stem from the Latin word *fiscus,* which can mean "treasury" or, more descriptively, "basket," as in an imaginary basket in which inflows of money are gathered and from which outflows are distributed. This section presents an overview of government spending in the United States; the next section provides an overview of government taxes; and the following section discusses budget deficits and debt.

fiscal policy: Economic policies that involve government spending and taxes.

Total U.S. Government Spending

Federal spending in nominal dollars has grown by a multiple of more than 38 over in the last four decades, from $92 billion in 1960 to $3.5 trillion in 2009. But comparing nominal dollars between two years can be highly deceiving, because it doesn't take into account either inflation or how the real economy has grown. A more useful comparison is to examine government spending as a percent of GDP.

The top line in Exhibit 18-1 shows the level of federal spending since 1960, expressed as a share of GDP. Despite a widespread sense among many Americans that the federal government has been growing steadily larger, the graph shows that this perception is incorrect. Federal spending has hovered in a range from 18–22% of GDP during most of the time since 1960, although in 2009 it was above that range. The other lines in Exhibit 18-1 show some major categories of federal spending: national defense, Social Security, health programs, and interest payments. National defense spending as a

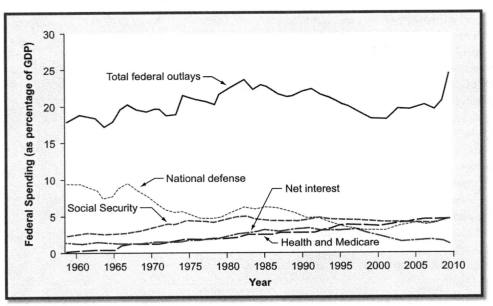

Exhibit 18-1   Federal Spending, 1960–2009

Since 1960, total federal spending has ranged from about 18–22% of GDP, although it climbed above that level in 2009. The share being spent on national defense has generally declined, while the share spent on Social Security and on health care expenses (mainly Medicare and Medicaid) has increased.

share of GDP has generally declined since the 1960s, although there were some upward bumps in the 1980s build-up under President Ronald Reagan and in the aftermath of the terrorist attacks on September 11, 2001. In 2009, defense spending was more than 5% of GDP, representing about one-fifth of all federal spending.

Although defense spending as a share of GDP has sagged over time, spending in other areas has risen. Spending on Social Security payments for the elderly has grown substantially during the last few decades. Government spending on health care has also increased. The two main federal health care programs are Medicare, which pays for health care to the elderly, and Medicaid, in which the federal government pays some of the bill for health care to those with low incomes (part of the Medicaid program is also funded by state governments).

Interest payments are a final main category of government spending shown in Exhibit 18-1. When the government receives more in taxes than it spends in a year, it runs a **budget surplus.** Conversely, when the federal government spends more than it collects in taxes in a given year, it runs a **budget deficit.** If government spending and taxes are equal, it is said to have a **balanced budget.** The government borrows funds to cover its budget deficits by issuing Treasury bonds, thus borrowing from the public and promising to repay with interest in the future. The U.S. government ran budget deficits, and thus borrowed money, every year but one from 1961 to 1997, had budget surpluses from 1998 to 2001, and then returned to budget deficits. The interest payments on past federal government borrowing were typically 1–2% of GDP in the 1960s and 1970s but then climbed above 3% of GDP in the 1980s and stayed there until the late 1990s. However, the government was able to repay some of its past borrowing by running surpluses from 1998–2001, and with help from low interest rates, interest payments had fallen to 1.3% of GDP by 2009. We'll investigate the patterns of government borrowing and debt in more detail later in this chapter.

These four categories—national defense, Social Security, health care, and interest payments—account for roughly 70% of all federal spending, as Exhibit 18-2 shows. The remaining 30% wedge of the pie chart covers all other categories of federal government spending: international affairs; science and technology; natural resources and the environment; transportation; housing; education; income support for the poor; community and regional development; law enforcement and the judicial system; and the administrative costs of running the government.

budget surplus: When the government receives more in taxes than it spends in a year.

budget deficit: When the federal government spends more than it collects in taxes in a given year.

balanced budget: When government spending and taxes are equal.

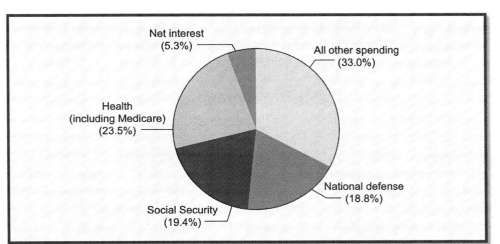

Exhibit 18-2   Slices of Federal Spending, 2009

About 70% of government spending goes to four major areas: national defense, Social Security, health care, and interest payments on past borrowing. This leaves about 30% of federal spending for all other functions of the U.S. government.

U.S. Government Spending in the Twentieth Century

Although the spending levels of the U.S. federal government haven't changed much in the last 50 years, they rose quite a bit earlier in the twentieth century. In 1900, the federal government spent only about 2–3% of GDP each year. But federal spending spiked upward sharply during World War I and World War II, because during the wars the U.S. government purchased large quantities of supplies and weapons and paid large numbers of soldiers, and also became very active in organizing industry to promote the war efforts. Although federal spending declined substantially after each war, it never quite returned to the pre-war levels. Instead, Americans seemed to become more comfortable after each war with their government collecting higher levels of taxes and providing a more extensive array of programs.

U.S. Government Spending since 1900

Federal government spending was only 2–3% of GDP in the early 1900s. However, it spiked sharply upward during World War I and World War II, and in both cases, government spending was substantially higher a few years after the war had finished than before it had begun. Since about 1960, federal government spending has had little upward trend, but instead has fluctuated in the range of 18–22% of GDP.

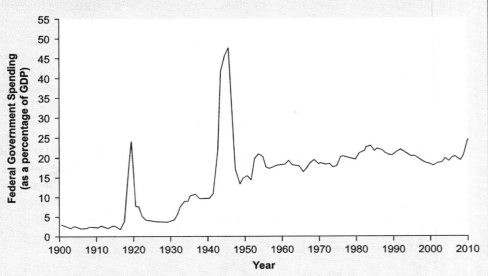

Keeping Federal Budget Numbers in Perspective

When you're listening to some of the perennial arguments over specific federal spending programs, it's useful to keep the overall size of the federal budget in mind. For example, there has been controversy for many years concerning the National Endowment for the Arts (NEA). Supporters argue that the government has an important role to play in supporting the arts. Detractors insist that much of what is supported is "art" only in a loose sense of the word, and that even if state and local governments want to support the arts for their local residents, the federal government has little reason to do so. Whatever side one takes in this dispute, it's worth remembering that the total NEA budget in 2009 was around $150 million. Maybe the NEA is a good idea; maybe it's a waste of money. Either way, in the overall federal budget, $150 million is less than one one-hundredth of 1% of total federal spending.

Similarly, many people believe that foreign aid accounts for a large portion of federal spending; according to one poll a few years ago, the average U.S. citizen thinks that foreign aid accounts for about 24% of the federal budget. However, the foreign aid budget in the first decade of the 2000s has been roughly 1% of federal spending. Again, foreign aid may be a good idea or a bad idea, and 1% of the federal budget is certainly worth more attention than the $150 million for the NEA. But in the context of the $3.5 trillion in federal spending in 2009, either eliminating foreign aid or doubling it wouldn't make a huge difference to the overall picture. Moreover, a certain amount

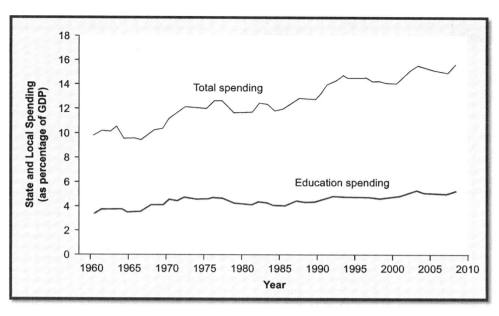

Exhibit 18-3   State and Local Spending, 1960–2007

Spending by state and local government increased from about 10% of GDP in the early 1960s to the range of 14–16% of GDP by the mid-1970s. It has mostly remained at roughly that level since then. The single biggest spending item of state and local government is education spending, including both K–12 spending and support for public colleges and universities, which has been about 5–6 percent of GDP in recent decades.

of that foreign aid has more to do with foreign policy—like encouraging peace and stability in the Middle East—than with financial aid to poor countries.

State and Local Government Spending

Although federal government spending often gets most of the media attention, the spending of state and local government is substantial, too, at about $2.2 trillion in 2007. Exhibit 18-3 shows that state and local government spending as a share of GDP has increased during the last four decades from about 10% of GDP to above 16% of GDP. The single biggest item on the tab of state and local spending is education, which accounts for about one-third of the total. The rest covers programs like highways, libraries, hospitals and health care, parks, and police and fire protection.

U.S. presidential candidates often run for office pledging to improve the public schools or to get tough on crime. But in the U.S. system of government, these tasks are primarily the responsibilities of state and local governments, not the federal government. Indeed, in 2006–2007, state and local government spent about $776 billion per year on education, including K–12 education and college and university education—a total that exceeds either the federal defense budget or federal spending on Social Security. A politician who earnestly wants hands-on responsibility for reforming education or reducing crime might do better to run for mayor of a large city or for state governor rather than for president of the United States.

An Overview of Taxation

Just as many Americans think that federal spending has grown considerably, many also believe that taxes have increased substantially. The top line of Exhibit 18-4 shows total federal taxes as a share of GDP since 1960. Although the line rises and falls, it typically remains within the range of 17–20% of GDP. In 2009, however, taxes fell substantially below this common level.

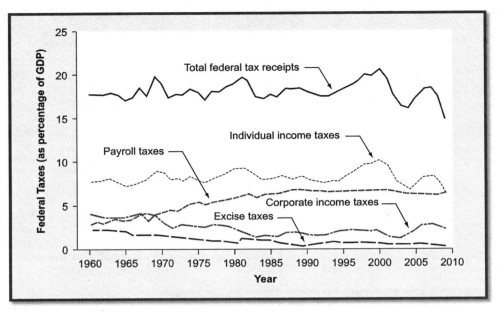

Exhibit 18-4   Federal Taxes, 1960–2009

Federal taxes have been about 17–20% of GDP during most periods in recent decades. The primary sources of federal taxes are individual income taxes and the payroll taxes that finance Social Security and Medicare. Corporation income taxes, excise taxes, and other taxes provide smaller shares of revenue.

Exhibit 18-4 also shows the patterns of taxation for the main categories of taxes levied by the federal government: personal income taxes, payroll taxes, corporate income taxes, and excise taxes. When most people think of taxes levied by the federal government, the first tax that comes to mind is the **individual income tax** that is due on April 15 (or the first business day after). The personal income tax is the largest single source of federal government revenue, but it still represents less than half of federal tax money. The personal income tax collects 8–10% of GDP in most years—although it was well below this level in 2009. The second largest source of federal revenue is the **payroll tax,** which provides funds for Social Security and Medicare. Payroll taxes have increased steadily over time. Together, the personal income tax and the payroll tax accounted for about 85% of federal tax revenues in 2009.

Although the personal income tax accounts for more total revenue than the payroll tax, over half the households in the country pay more in payroll taxes than in income taxes. The reason is that income tax is a **progressive tax**, which means that it collects a greater share of income from those with high incomes than from those with lower incomes. The income tax works this way: The first dollars of income earned are not subject to the income tax. This amount that is exempt from taxation is determined by the size of the family and is adjusted each year. For example, A single person in 2009 paid no taxes on the first $9,350 in income earned. However, this person then paid 10% on next $8,350 of income earned; 15% of any additional amount between $8,350 and $33,950; 20% of any additional amount from $33,950 to $82,250; 28% from $82,250 to $171,550; 33% of any additional income from $171,550 to $372,950; and 35% of any income above that level. Of course, income taxes are much more complex than this simple example. Taxes vary with marital status, family size, and many other features. But the key lesson here is that the federal income tax is designed so that high-income citizens pay a larger share of income in taxes. In 2006, for example, the top 20% of taxpayers paid 86.3% of total income taxes collected, while the bottom 60% of taxpayers paid only 0.8% of income taxes collected.

The payroll taxes that support Social Security and Medicare are designed in a different way. The payroll taxes for Social Security are currently imposed at a rate

individual income tax: A tax based on the income of all forms received by individuals.

payroll tax: A tax based on the pay received from employers; the taxes provide funds for Social Security and Medicare.

progressive tax: A tax that collects a greater share of income from those with high incomes than from those with lower incomes.

The Complexity of Individual Income Taxes

The basic income tax calculation is straightforward. Figure out how much income you received, remembering to include all wage or salary income, as well as income from any other source like interest payments. Figure out whether you're married and count up your children. Then look in a table how much you owe in taxes. But some tax calculations can get far more complex. As two economists noted a few years ago: "Although length is not necessarily synonymous with complexity, the U.S. income tax code now has more than 700 times as many words as the U.S. Constitution." The complications arise in several main areas.

Deductions

A deduction is an amount that you are allowed to subtract ("deduct") from your income before figuring out how much you owe in taxes. The trick here is to compare the *standard deduction*, which was $11,400 for a married couple filing a joint tax return in 2009, with specific deductions allowed by Congress. Everyone can take the standard deduction automatically. If the deductions allowed by Congress are higher than the standard deduction, then it makes sense to list, or "itemize," the other deductions. Some common deductions in the tax code include interest paid on a home mortgage, charitable contributions, state and local taxes, and costly medical procedures, and certain other expenses. About 30% of taxpayers itemize deductions on their returns, while the rest take the standard deduction.

Tax Credits

A tax credit is an amount you are allowed to subtract directly from the amount of taxes owed (unlike a deduction, which is subtracted from the income on which you owe taxes). Certain tax credits for the working poor are designed so that even if people do not owe income taxes (because their income is so low), the amount of the tax credit will still be paid to people as a tax "refund."

Establishing When Taxpayers Become Employers

If you hire a nanny to look after children, or any employee who works for you regularly and earns more than $750 per quarter, then you become an employer and are treated as a business by the state and national governments. You are now an employer, and must fill out a whole new set of forms. If you are self-employed, then your taxes must show both revenues and business-related costs. Your tax will be based on the income left over.

Simplification Is Difficult

It's easy to plead for a simpler tax code, but difficult to achieve it. Many parts of the tax code have some justification—it's just that when they are all combined together, the result is exceedingly complex. Tax lawyers and accountants are always trying to find loopholes in the tax code that can reduce the taxes owed. Legislators are always tinkering with the tax code, closing up some loopholes, but opening others for favored groups. Everyone is willing to eliminate deductions or tax credits used by others, but unwilling to eliminate the ones they use themselves. Substantial simplification of the tax code is politically quite difficult.

---

of 14.4% up to a certain earnings limit, set at $106,800 in 2010. This limit rises in step with the average increase in wages across the economy. The payroll taxes that support the part of Medicare that pays for hospitalization for the elderly is imposed at a rate of 2.9% of all income earned, with no upper ceiling. In both cases, the taxes are technically collected half from employee paychecks and half from employers. However, as economists are quick to point out, the employer's half of the taxes is probably passed along to the employees in the form of lower wages. The Medicare payroll tax is a **proportional tax;** that is, a flat percentage of all income earned. The Social Security payroll tax is proportional up to the earnings limit, but above that level of income it becomes a **regressive tax**, meaning that people with higher incomes pay a smaller share of their income in tax. As a result, income taxes are paid mainly by the relatively small number of those with incomes of six-figures and higher, while payroll taxes are paid mainly by the larger number of five-figure earners.

The third-largest source of federal tax revenue shown in Exhibit 18-4 is the **corporate income tax**—and the common name for corporate income is "profits." Over time, corporate income tax receipts have declined as a share of GDP, from about 4% of GDP in the 1960s to 1–2% of GDP in the first decade of the 2000s. The federal government has a few other, smaller sources of revenue. The federal government imposes **excise taxes**—that is, taxes on a particular good—on gasoline, tobacco, and alcohol.

proportional tax: A tax that is a flat percentage of income earned, regardless of level of income.

regressive tax: A tax in which people with higher incomes pay a smaller share of their income in tax.

corporate income tax: A tax imposed on corporate profits.

excise taxes: A tax on a specific good—on gasoline, tobacco, and alcohol.

The Size of U.S. Government in International Perspective

In round numbers, the U.S. GDP is about one-fourth of the world economy, and the U.S. federal budget is about one-fifth of the U.S. GDP. Multiply those two proportions, and the United States' federal budget, all by itself, makes up about one-twentieth of *world* GDP.

When comparing the size of U.S. government to the governments of other high-income countries, it's conventional to look at all levels of government combined; in the case of the United States, that means combining federal, state, and local government. The reason is that some countries have a larger role for the national government, while others have a larger role for regional, provincial, state, city, or local governments. Rather than trying to adjust for these differences, it is easier to compare overall levels of total government spending. The bar chart shows United States

has a substantially smaller sector for government spending than do most European countries and Canada—although a similar proportion to Australia and Japan.

Why is the level of U.S. government spending relatively low? One reason is that most other countries have government-run health care sectors, while in the United States, a large share of health care spending happens in the private sector—although about half of all U.S. health care spending, like the Medicare and Medicaid spending mentioned earlier, is in the government sector. Ultimately, the reason for the difference is that people in other high-income countries, acting through their own democratic institutions, prefer to see a greater share of society's resources allocated by political decisions rather than by market forces.

Government Expenditures as a Percentage of GDP, 2008

Compared to other high-income countries around the world, U.S. government spending (combining federal, state, and local levels) is a relatively low share of the U.S. economy.

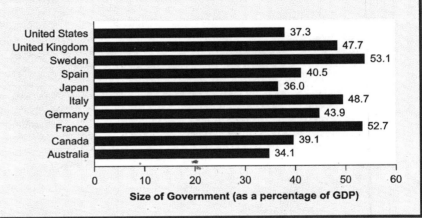

Country	Size of Government (as a percentage of GDP)
United States	37.3
United Kingdom	47.7
Sweden	53.1
Spain	40.5
Japan	36.0
Italy	48.7
Germany	43.9
France	52.7
Canada	39.1
Australia	34.1

As a share of GDP, the amount collected by these taxes has also declined over time, from about 2% of GDP in the 1960s to roughly .5% of GDP by 2010. The government also imposes an **estate and gift tax** on people who pass large amounts of assets to the next generation—either after death or during life in the form of gifts. These estate and gift taxes collected about .2% of GDP in the first decade of the 2000s. By a quirk of legislation, the estate and gift tax was repealed just in 2010, but is scheduled to be reinstated in 2011. Other federal taxes, which are also relatively small in magnitude, include tariffs collected on imported goods, and charges for inspections of goods entering the country.

estate and gift tax: A tax on people who pass assets to the next generation—either after death or during life in the form of gifts.

State and Local Taxes

At the state and local level, taxes have been rising as a share of GDP over the last few decades to match the gradual rise in spending, as Exhibit 18-5 illustrates. The main revenue sources for state and local governments are sales taxes, property taxes, and revenue passed along from the federal government, but many state and local governments also levy personal and corporate income taxes, as well as imposing a wide variety of fees and charges. The specific sources of tax revenue vary widely

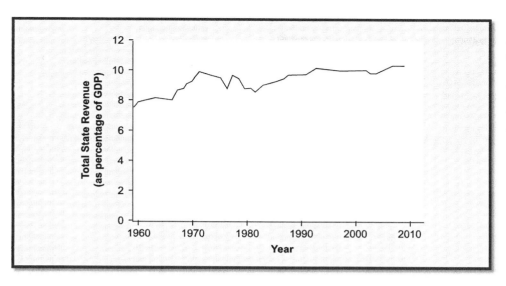

Exhibit 18-5   State and Local Tax Revenue as a Share of GDP, 1960–2007

State and local tax revenues have increased to match the rise in state and local spending.

across state and local governments. Some states rely more on property taxes, some on sales taxes, some on income taxes, and some more on revenues from the federal government.

Federal Deficits and Debt

The federal budget picture turned a somersault in the 1990s and first decade of the 2000s, from large deficits in the early 1990s to surpluses in the late 1990s and back to deficits for the first decade of the 2000s. Exhibit 18-6 shows the pattern of annual federal budget deficits and surpluses all the way back to 1930 as a share of GDP. When the line is above the horizontal axis in positive territory, the budget is in surplus; when the line is below the horizontal axis in negative territory, a budget deficit occurred. Clearly, the biggest deficits as a share of GDP during this time were incurred to finance the fighting

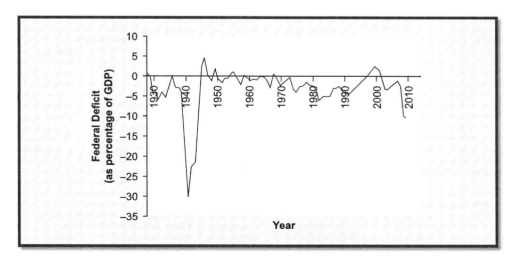

Exhibit 18-6   Pattern of Federal Budget Deficits and Surpluses, 1930–2009

The federal government had huge budget deficits during World War II. Budget deficits were also relatively large during the Great Depression of the 1930s and during the 1980s and early 1990s. The budget was briefly in surplus in the late 1990s, before heading into deficit again in the first decade of the 2000s—and especially deep deficits in the recession of 2007–2009.

> The difference between the deficit and the debt lies in the time frame. The government deficit (or surplus) refers to what happens each year. The government debt is accumulated over time; it is the sum of all past deficits and surpluses. Similarly, if you borrow $10,000 per year for each of four years of college, you might say that your annual deficit was $10,000, but your accumulated debt over the four years is $40,000.

Clearing It Up

The Deficit Is Not the Debt

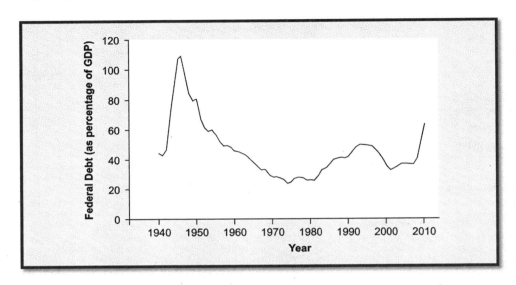

Exhibit 18-7   Federal Debt as a Percentage of GDP, 1940–2010

Federal debt is the sum of annual budget deficits and surpluses. Debt increases when deficits are large, like during World Wars I and II and during the 1980s and early 1990s. However, annual deficits do not always mean that the debt/GDP ratio is rising. During the 1960s and 1970s, the government often ran small deficits, but since the debt was growing more slowly than the economy, the debt/GDP ratio was declining over this time. In the 2007–2009 recession, the debt/GDP ratio rose sharply.

of World War II. Deficits were also large during the 1980s and early 1990s, and most recently during the recession of 2007–2009.

Debt/GDP Ratio

Another useful way to view the budget deficit is through the prism of accumulated debt rather than annual deficits. **Government debt** refers to the total amount that the government has borrowed over time; in contrast, the budget deficit or the budget surplus refers to how much has been borrowed in one particular year. Exhibit 18-7 shows the ratio of debt/GDP since 1940. Until the 1970s, the debt/GDP ratio revealed a fairly clear pattern of federal borrowing. The government ran up large deficits and raised the debt/GDP ratio in World War II, but from the 1950s to the 1970s the government ran either surpluses or relatively small deficits, and so the debt/GDP ratio drifted down. Large deficits in the 1980s and early 1990s caused the debt/GDP ratio to rise sharply. When budget surpluses arrived from 1998 to 2001, the debt/GDP ratio declined substantially. The budget deficits starting in 2002 then tugged the debt/GDP ratio higher—with a big jump when the recession took hold in 2008.

government debt: The total accumulated amount that the government has borrowed and not yet paid back over time.

The Path from Deficits to Surpluses to Deficits

Why did the budget deficits suddenly turn to surpluses from 1998 to 2001? And why did the surpluses return to deficits in 2002? Why did the deficit become so large in 2009? Exhibit 18-8 suggests some answers. The exhibit combines the earlier information on total federal spending and taxes in a single graph, but focuses on the federal budget since 1990.

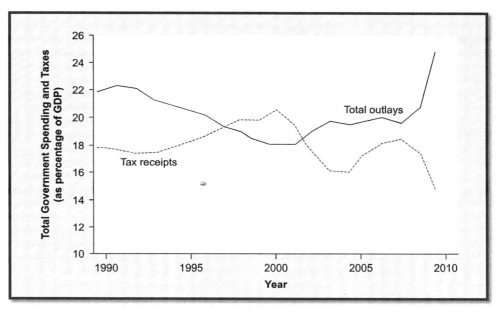

Exhibit 18-8   Total Government Spending and Taxes as a Share of GDP, 1990–2009

When government spending exceeds taxes, the gap is the budget deficit. When taxes exceed spending, the gap is a budget surplus. Thus, the 1990s saw a decline in government spending and a rise in tax receipts that led to a budget surplus from 1998–2001, and then a fall in tax receipts and a rise in spending that caused a return to budget deficits starting in 2002. The recessionary period starting in late 2007 saw higher spending and lower taxes, combining to create a large deficit in 2009.

Government spending as a share of GDP declined steadily through the 1990s. The biggest single reason was that defense spending declined from 5.2% of GDP in 1990 to 3.0% of GDP in 2000, but interest payments by the federal government also fell by about 1.0% of GDP.

However, federal taxes increased substantially in the later 1990s, jumping from 18.1% of GDP in 1994 to 20.8% of GDP in 2000. Powerful economic growth in the late 1990s fueled the boom in taxes. Personal income taxes rise as income goes up; payroll taxes rise as jobs and payrolls go up; corporate income taxes rise as profits go up. This sharp increase in tax revenues was largely unexpected even by experienced budget analysts, and so budget surpluses came as a surprise.

But in the early 2000s, many of these factors started running in reverse. Tax revenues sagged. One reason is that just as economic growth in the late 1990s pumped up tax revenues, the recession that started in March 2001 pulled down revenues. Another reason is a series of tax cuts enacted by Congress and signed into law by President George W. Bush starting in 2001. In addition, government spending increased because of a combination of spending increases on defense, health care, education, Social Security, and providing support to people who were suffering economically during the recession and the slow growth that followed. Deficits returned. When the severe recession hit in late 2007, spending climbed and taxes fell to historically unusual levels, resulting in enormous deficits.

Longer-term forecasts of the U.S. budget, a decade or more into the future, predict enormous deficits. The primary reason is the "baby boom"—the exceptionally high birthrates that began in 1946, right after World War II, and lasted for about two decades. Starting in 2010, the front edge of the baby boom generation will begin to reach age 65, and in the following two decades, the proportion of Americans over the age of 65 will increase substantially. The current level of the payroll taxes that support Social Security and Medicare will fall well short of the projected expenses of these programs; thus, the forecast is for large budget deficits. A decision either to collect more revenue to support these programs or to decrease their benefit levels would alter this long-term forecast.

The Aging of America and the Long-Term Budget Outlook

In 1946, just one American in 13 was over age 65. By 2000, it was one in eight. By 2030, one American in five will be over age 65. Two enormous U.S. federal programs focus on the elderly—Social Security and Medicare. The growing numbers of elderly Americans will increase spending on these programs. The current payroll tax levied on workers, which support all of Social Security and the hospitalization insurance part of Medicare, won't be enough to cover the expected costs.

None of the possible reactions to the expected growth of these programs for the elderly is very attractive. Spending on these programs could be cut. Taxes could be raised to fund these programs. Other programs could be cut instead. Or the government could run very large budget deficits and borrow the money to finance these programs. Some proposals also suggest moving Social Security and Medicare from systems in which workers pay for retirees toward programs that set up accounts where workers save money over their lifetime and then draw it out after retirement. Whatever the merits of such plans, they don't solve the problem that Social Security and Medicare are not sustainable as currently constructed.

Long-term projections from the Congressional Budget Office in 2009 are that Medicare and Social Security spending combined will rise from 8.3% of GDP in 2009 to 12.9% of GDP by 2035 and 19.6% of GDP in 2080. If this rise in spending occurs, then some mix of three changes must occur: 1) taxes will need to be increased dramatically to finance it; 2) other spending will need to be cut dramatically; or 3) the U.S. government will need to run extremely large budget deficits for decades. None of these options is especially attractive.

The United States is not alone in this problem. Indeed, the problems of providing the promised level of retirement and health benefits to a growing proportion of elderly with a falling proportion of workers is even more severe in many European nations and in Japan. Addressing the question of how to pay promised levels of benefits to the elderly will be a difficult public policy challenge for many high-income nations in the twenty-first century.

With the broad shape of fiscal policy in mind, let's shift attention to how fiscal policy might be used to affect business cycle fluctuations that lead to unemployment or inflation? Conversely, how will business cycle fluctuations like recession affect budget deficits? How do economists evaluate proposed policies that would require a balanced budget—that is, for government spending and taxes to be equal each year? Chapter 19 will then look at how fiscal policy and government borrowing will affect national saving—and thus affect economic growth and trade imbalances.

Using Fiscal Policy to Affect Recession, Unemployment and Inflation

A healthy economy follows a long-term trend of economic growth, but also experiences occasional recessions. Exhibit 18-9 illustrates the process by using an aggregate demand/aggregate supply diagram. The original equilibrium occurs at E_0, the intersection of aggregate demand curve AD_0 and aggregate supply curve AS_0, at an output level of 200 and a price level of 90. One year later, aggregate supply has shifted to the right to AS_1 in the process of long-term economic growth, and aggregate demand has also shifted to the right to AD_1, keeping the economy operating at the new level of potential GDP. The new equilibrium E_1 is an output level of 206 and a price level of 92. One more year later, aggregate supply has again shifted to the right, now to AS_2, and aggregate demand shifts right as well to AD_2. Now the equilibrium is E_2, with an output level of 212 and a price level of 94. In short, the figure shows an economy that is growing steadily year to year, producing at its potential GDP each year, with only small inflationary increases in the price level.

But aggregate demand and aggregate supply do not always dance neatly together. Aggregate demand may fail to increase smoothly along with aggregate supply, or aggregate demand may even shift left, for a number of possible causes: households

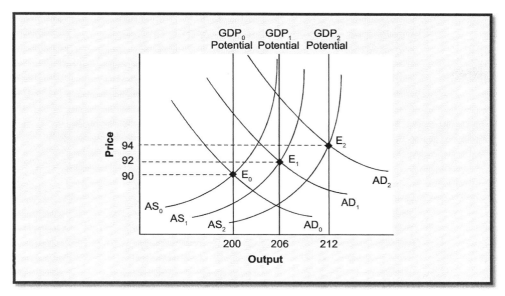

Exhibit 18-9
A Healthy, Growing Economy

In this well-functioning economy, each year aggregate supply and aggregate demand shift to the right so that the economy proceeds from equilibrium E_0 to E_1 to E_2. Each year, the economy produces at potential GDP with only a small inflationary increase in the price level. But if aggregate demand does not smoothly shift to the right and match increases in aggregate supply, either recession or inflation can develop.

become hesitant about consuming; firms decide against investing as much; or perhaps the demand from other countries for exports diminishes. For example, investment by private firms in physical capital in the U.S. economy boomed during the late 1990s, rising from 14.1% of GDP in 1993 to 17.2% of GDP in 2000, before falling back to 15.2% of GDP by 2002. Conversely, if shifts in aggregate demand run ahead of increases in aggregate supply, then the inflationary increases in the price level will result. When aggregate demand and aggregate supply fall out of step, the business cycles of economic recessions and upswings are the result.

The previous discussion of monetary policy taught that a central bank can use its powers over the banking system to engage in countercyclical—or "against the business cycle"—policy. If recession threatens, the central bank uses an expansionary monetary policy to increase the quantity of loans, reduce interest rates, and shift aggregate demand to the right. If inflation threatens, the central bank uses contractionary monetary policy to reduce the quantity of loans, raise interest rates, and shift aggregate demand to the left. Fiscal policy is another macroeconomic policy tool for adjusting aggregate demand by using either government spending or taxation policy.

Expansionary Fiscal Policy

Expansionary fiscal policy increases the level of aggregate demand, through either increases in government spending or reductions in taxes. **Contractionary fiscal policy** decreases the level of aggregate demand, either through cuts in government spending or increases in taxes. The aggregate demand/aggregate supply model is useful in judging whether expansionary or contractionary fiscal policy is appropriate.

Consider first the situation in Exhibit 18-10, which is similar to the U.S. economy during the recession in 2009. The intersection of aggregate demand AD_0 and aggregate supply AS_0 is occurring below the level of potential GDP. At the equilibrium E_0, a recession occurs and unemployment rises. (The figure uses the upward-sloping AS curve associated with a Keynesian economic approach, rather than the vertical AS curve associated with a neoclassical approach; this is because our focus here is on macroeconomic policy over the short-run business cycle rather than over the long run.) In this case, expansionary fiscal policy can shift aggregate

expansionary monetary policy: A monetary policy that increases the supply of money and the quantity of loans; also called a "loose" monetary policy.

contractionary fiscal policy: When fiscal policy decreases the level of aggregate demand, either through cuts in government spending or increases in taxes.

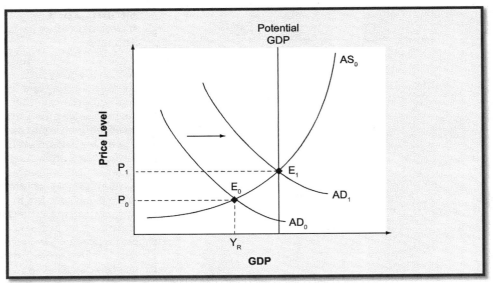

Exhibit 18-10
Expansionary Fiscal Policy

The original equilibrium E_0 represents a recession, occurring at a quantity of output Y_R below potential GDP. However, a shift of aggregate demand from AD_0 to AD_1, enacted through an expansionary fiscal policy that combines some mixture of spending increases and tax cuts, can move the economy to a new equilibrium output of E_1 at the level of potential GDP. Since the economy was originally producing below potential GDP, any inflationary increase in the price level from P_0 to P_1 that results form this expansionary fiscal policy should be relatively small.

demand to AD_1, closer to the full-employment level of output. There is relatively little danger that this increase in aggregate demand will increase inflation—although there if the AD curve were pushed too far to the right, pressures for a higher rate of inflation could arise.

Should the government use tax cuts or spending increases, or a mix of the two, to carry out its expansionary fiscal policy? After the recession of 2007–2009, U.S. government spending rose from 19.6% of GDP in 2007 to 24.6% of GDP in 2009, while taxes declined from 18.5% of GDP in 2007 to 14.8% of GDP in 2009. The choice between whether to use tax or spending tools often has a political tinge. As a general statement, conservatives and Republicans prefer to see expansionary fiscal policy carried out by tax cuts, while liberals and Democrats prefer that expansionary fiscal policy be implemented through spending increases. This ambiguity over which policy tool to use can be frustrating to those who want to categorize economics as "liberal" or "conservative," or who want to use economic models to argue against their political opponents. But the AD-AS model can be readily used both by advocates of smaller government, who seek to reduce taxes and government spending, and also by advocates of bigger government, who seek to raise taxes and government spending. Economic studies of specific taxing and spending programs can help to inform decisions about whether taxes or spending should be changed, and in what ways. Ultimately, decisions about whether to use tax or spending mechanisms to implement macroeconomic policy is in part a political decision, rather than a purely economic one.

Contractionary Fiscal Policy

Fiscal policy can also contribute to pushing aggregate demand beyond potential GDP in a way that leads to inflation. For example, in the terribly mismanaged economy of Zimbabwe, the government budget deficit was 40% of GDP in 2010, after a long string of similarly enormous deficits. Not coincidentally, inflation in Zimbabwe was immeasurably high, in millions of percent per year: for a period in early 2009, the value of the Zimbabwe dollar was falling by half against the U.S. dollar *every two days*. As shown in Exhibit 18-11, a very large budget deficit was pushing up aggregate demand, so that the intersection of aggregate demand AD_0 and aggregate supply AS_0

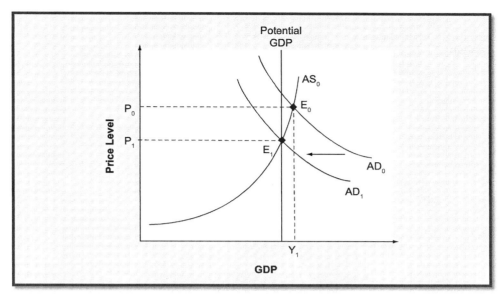

Exhibit 18-11
A Contractionary Fiscal Policy

The economy starts at the equilibrium quantity of output E_0, which is above potential GDP and thus cannot be sustained in the long run. Instead, the extremely high level of aggregate demand will generate inflationary increases in the price level. A contractionary fiscal policy can shift aggregate demand from AD_0 to AD_1, thus leading to a new equilibrium output E_1, which occurs at potential GDP.

occurs at equilibrium E_0, which is a level output above potential GDP. In this situation, contractionary fiscal policy involving spending cuts or tax increases can help to reduce the upward pressure on the price level by shifting aggregate demand to the left to AD_1 and causing the new equilibrium E_1 to be at potential GDP.

Again, the AD/AS model does not dictate how this contractionary fiscal policy is to be carried out. Some may prefer spending cuts; others may prefer tax increases; still others may say that it depends on the specific situation. The model only argues that aggregate demand needs to be reduced in this situation.

Automatic Stabilizers

The quantities of government spending and taxes can change for two broad sets of reasons. The first type of decision, called **discretionary fiscal policy,** occurs when the government passes a new law that explicitly changes tax or spending levels. A second type of taxing and spending changes happens because of laws that are already in place. For example, an economy that grows more rapidly will increase household incomes and firm profits, and thus lead to higher tax revenues, even if the existing tax laws don't change at all. These changes in tax and spending levels that happen without any specific change in law are called **automatic stabilizers,** because without the government passing any new laws, they have the effect of stimulating aggregate demand in a recession and holding down aggregate demand in a potentially inflationary boom.

discretionary fiscal policy: When the government passes a new law that explicitly changes overall tax or spending levels.

automatic stabilizers: Tax and spending rules that have the effect of increasing aggregate demand when the economy slows down and restraining aggregate demand when the economy speeds up, without any additional change in legislation.

Counterbalancing Recession and Boom

Consider first the situation where aggregate demand has risen sharply, and during this economic boom the equilibrium is occurring at a level of output above potential GDP so that inflationary increases in the price level are occurring. The policy prescription in this setting would be a dose of contractionary fiscal policy, implemented through either higher taxes or lower spending. To some extent, *both* of these changes happen automatically. On the tax side, a rise in aggregate demand means that workers and firms throughout the economy earn more income. Because taxes are based on personal income and corporate profits, a rise in aggregate demand automatically increases tax payments. On the spending side, stronger aggregate demand typically means lower unemployment and fewer layoffs, and so there is less need for government spending on unemployment benefits, welfare, Medicaid, and other programs in the social safety net.

The process works in reverse, too. If aggregate demand were to fall sharply so that a recession occurs, then the prescription would be for expansionary fiscal policy—some mix of tax cuts and spending increases. The lower level of aggregate demand and higher unemployment will tend to pull down personal incomes and corporate profits, an effect that will reduce the amount of taxes owed automatically. Higher unemployment and a weaker economy should lead to increased government spending on unemployment benefits, welfare, and other similar domestic programs. Thus, the automatic stabilizers react to a weakening of aggregate demand with expansionary fiscal policy and react to a strengthening of aggregate demand with contractionary fiscal policy, just as the AS-AD analysis suggests.

The very large budget deficit of 2009 was produced by a combination of automatic stabilizers and discretionary fiscal policy. The severe U.S. recession starting in late 2007 meant less tax-generating economic activity, which triggered the automatic stabilizers that reduce taxes. Also, both President Bush in 2008 and President Obama in 2009 signed additional tax cuts into law. On the spending side, President Obama with bipartisan support signed a fiscal stimulus package of spending increases into effect early in 2009. Most economists, even those who are concerned about a possible pattern of persistently large budget deficits, are much less concerned or even quite supportive of larger budget deficits in the short-run of a few years during and immediately after a recession.

A glance back at economic history provides a second illustration of the power of automatic stabilizers. Remember that the length of economic upswings between recessions has become longer in the U.S. economy in recent decades (as discussed in Chapter 7). The three longest economic booms of the twentieth century happened in the 1960s, the 1980s, and the 1991–2001. One reason why the economy has tipped into recession less frequently in recent decades is that the size of government spending and taxes has increased in the second half of the twentieth century. Thus, the automatic stabilizing effects from spending and taxes are now larger than they were in the first half of the twentieth century. Around 1900, for example, federal spending was only about 2% of GDP. In 1929, just before the Great Depression hit, government spending was still just 4% of GDP. In those earlier times, the smaller size of government made automatic stabilizers far less powerful than in the last few decades, when government spending often hovers at 20% of GDP or more.

The Standardized Employment Deficit or Surplus

Each year, the nonpartisan Congressional Budget Office (CBO) calculates the **standardized employment budget**—that is, what the budget deficit or surplus would be if the economy was producing at potential GDP. In effect, the standardized employment deficit eliminates the impact of the automatic stabilizers. Exhibit 18-12 compares the actual budget deficits of recent decades with the CBO's standardized deficit.

Notice that in recession years, like the early 1990s or around 2001 or in 2009, the standardized employment deficit is smaller than the actual deficit. During recessions, the automatic stabilizers tend to increase the budget deficit, so if the economy was instead at full employment, the deficit would be reduced. However, in the late 1990s the

standardized employment budget: The budget deficit or surplus in any given year adjusted for what it would have been if the economy was producing at potential GDP.

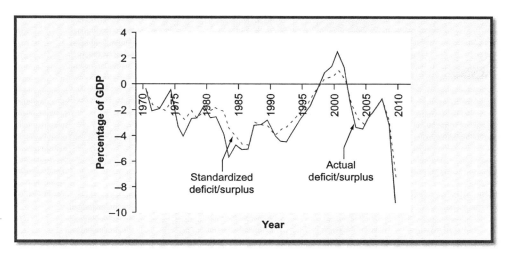

Exhibit 18-12
Comparison of Actual Budget Deficits with the Standardized Employment Deficit

When the economy is suffering a recession, like in the early 1990s, the standardized employment budget deficit is less than the actual budget deficit because the economy is below potential GDP, so the automatic stabilizers are reducing taxes and increasing spending. When the economy is performing extremely well, like in the late 1960s or the late 1990s, the standardized employment deficit (or surplus) is higher than the actual budget deficit (or surplus) because the economy is producing about potential GDP, so the automatic stabilizers are increasing taxes and reducing the need for government spending.

standardized employment budget surplus is lower than the actual budget surplus. The Congressional Budget Office believed (along with many other mainstream economics forecasters) that the rate of unemployment in the late 1990s was unsustainably low, and that the economy was operating above its potential GDP level. As a result, the automatic stabilizers were having a contractionary fiscal impact, trying to slow the economy, and if the impact of the automatic stabilizers were set aside, the budget surpluses would have been smaller. The gap between the standardized budget deficit or surplus and the actual budget deficit or surplus shows the impact of the automatic stabilizers. More generally, the standardized budget figures allow you to see what the budget deficit would look like with the economy held constant—at its potential GDP level of output.

Automatic stabilizers are implemented quickly. Lower income means that a lower quantity of taxes is withheld from paychecks right away. Higher unemployment or poverty means that government spending in those areas rises as quickly as people apply for benefits. However, while the automatic stabilizers offset part of the shifts in aggregate demand, they do not offset all or even most of it. As an historical pattern, the automatic stabilizers on the tax and spending side offset about 10% of any initial movement in the level of output. This offset may not seem enormous, but it is still useful. Automatic stabilizers, like shock absorbers in a car, can be useful if they reduce the impact of the worst bumps, even if they don't eliminate the bumps altogether.

Practical Problems with Discretionary Fiscal Policy

In the early 1960s, when the Keynesian economic framework had been developed and was fairly well understood by many economists, the economics profession had a few years of extreme (and unaccustomed) cheerfulness. Many leading economists believed that the problem of the business cycle, and the swings between cyclical unemployment and inflation, were a thing of the past. On the cover of its December 31, 1965, issue, *Time* magazine ran a picture of John Maynard Keynes, and the story inside identified Keynesian theories as "the prime influence on the world's economies." Policymakers have "used Keynesian principles not only to avoid the violent [business] cycles of prewar days but to produce phenomenal economic growth and to achieve remarkably stable prices," reported the article.

But this happy consensus didn't last. The U.S. economy suffered one recession from December 1969 to November 1970, a deeper recession from November 1973 to March 1975, and then double-dip recessions from January to June 1980 and from July 1981 to November 1982. At various times, inflation and unemployment both soared. Clearly, the problems of macroeconomic policy had not been completely solved! As economists began to consider what had gone wrong, they identified a number of issues that make discretionary fiscal policy more difficult than it had seemed in the rosy optimism of the mid-1960s.

Fiscal Policy and Interest Rates

Because fiscal policy affects the quantity that the government borrows in financial capital markets, it doesn't only affect aggregate demand—it also affects interest rates. In Exhibit 18-13, the original equilibrium E_0 in the financial capital market occurs at a quantity of $800 billion and an interest rate of 6%. However, an increase in government budget deficits shifts the demand for financial capital from D_0 to D_1. The new equilibrium E_1 occurs at a quantity of $900 billion and an interest rate of 7%. (If the federal government is running surpluses, then it is acting as a supplier in financial capital markets. A lower budget surplus will shift the supply of financial capital to the left, also leading to a higher interest rate.) A consensus estimate based on a number of studies is that an increase in budget deficits (or a fall in budget surplus) by 1% of GDP will cause an increase of 0.5–1.0% in the long-term interest rate.

A problem arises here. An expansionary fiscal policy, with tax cuts or spending increases, is intended to increase aggregate demand. But if an expansionary fiscal policy also causes higher interest rates, then firms and households are discouraged from borrowing and spending (as occurs with tight monetary policy), thus reducing aggregate demand. Even if the direct effect of expansionary fiscal policy on increasing demand is not totally offset by lower aggregate demand from higher interest rates, fiscal policy can end up being less powerful than was originally expected.

The broader lesson is that fiscal and monetary policy must be coordinated. If expansionary fiscal policy is to work well, then the central bank needs to prevent interest rates from rising. Conversely, monetary policy can also help to ensure that contractionary fiscal policy doesn't lead to a recession.

Long and Variable Time Lags

Monetary policy can be changed several times each year, but fiscal policy is much slower to be enacted. Imagine that the economy starts to slow down. It often takes some months before the economic statistics signal clearly that a downturn has started, and a few months more to confirm that it is truly a recession and not just a one- or two-month blip. Policymakers become aware of the problem and propose fiscal policy bills. The bills go into various congressional committees for hearings, negotiations, votes, and then, if passed, eventually for the president's signature. Many fiscal policy bills about spending or taxes propose changes that would start in the next budget year or would be phased in gradually over time.

Moreover, the exact level of fiscal policy to be implemented is never completely clear. Should the budget deficit be increased by 0.5% of GDP? By 1% of GDP? By 2% of GDP? In an AS-AD diagram, it's straightforward to sketch an aggregate demand curve shifting to the potential GDP level of output. But in the real world, the actual level of potential output is known only roughly, not precisely, and exactly how a spending cut or tax increase will affect aggregate demand is always somewhat controversial.

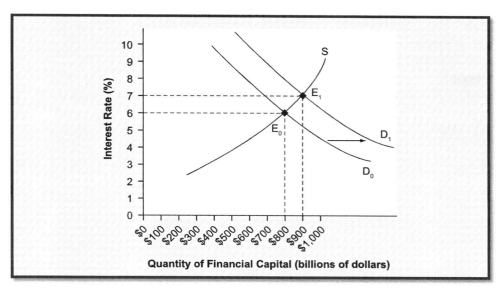

Quantity of Financial Capital (billions of dollars)

Exhibit 18-13   Fiscal Policy and Interest Rates

When a government borrows money in the financial capital market, it causes a shift in the demand for financial capital from D_0 to D_1. As the equilibrium moves from E_0 to E_1, the equilibrium interest rate rises from 6% to 7% in this example. In this way, an expansionary fiscal policy that is intended to shift aggregate demand to the right can also lead to a higher interest rate, which has the effect of shifting aggregate demand to the left. The impact of the higher interest rate can be reduced if fiscal and monetary policy work together.

Thus, it can take many months or even more than a year to begin an expansionary fiscal policy after a recession started—and even then, uncertainty will remain over exactly how much to expand or contract taxes and spending. When politicians attempt to use countercyclical fiscal policy to fight recession or inflation, they run the risk of responding to the macroeconomic situation of two or three years ago, in a way that may be exactly wrong for the economy at that time. George P. Schultz, a professor of economics who also had an illustrious political career as Secretary of Labor and also Director of the Office of Management and Budget during the Nixon administration, and as Secretary of State during the Reagan administration, once wrote: "While the economist is accustomed to the concept of lags, the politician likes instant results. The tension comes because, as I have seen on many occasions, the economist's lag is the politician's nightmare."

Temporary and Permanent Fiscal Policy

A temporary tax cut or spending increase will explicitly last only for a year or two, and then revert back to its original level. A permanent tax cut or spending increase is expected to stay in place for the foreseeable future. The effect of temporary and permanent fiscal policies on aggregate demand can be very different. Consider how you would react if the government announced a tax cut that would last one year, and then be repealed, in comparison with how you would react if the government announced a permanent tax cut. Most people and firms will react more strongly to a permanent policy change than a temporary one.

This fact creates an unavoidable difficulty for countercyclical fiscal policy. The appropriate policy may be to have an expansionary fiscal policy with large budget deficits during a recession, and then a contractionary fiscal policy with budget surpluses when the economy is growing well. But if both of these policies are explicitly temporary ones, they will have a less powerful effect than a permanent policy.

Structural Economic Change Takes Time

When an economy recovers from a recession, it does not usually revert back to its exact earlier shape. Instead, the internal structure of the economy evolves and changes, and this process can take time. For example, much of the economic growth of the mid-2000s was involved in the sectors of construction (especially of housing) and finance. However, when housing prices started falling in 2007 and the resulting financial crunch led into recession (as discussed in Chapter 16), both of these sectors contracted. The manufacturing sector of the U.S. economy has been losing jobs in recent years as well, under pressure from technological change and foreign competition. Many of the people thrown out of work from these sectors in the recession of 2007–2009 will never return to the same jobs in the same sectors of the economy; instead, the economy will need to grow in new and different directions. Fiscal policy can increase overall demand, but the process of structural economic change—the expansion of a new set of industries and the movement of workers to those industries—inevitably takes time.

The Limitations of Potential GDP and the Natural Rate of Unemployment

Fiscal policy can help an economy that is producing below its potential GDP to expand aggregate demand so that it produces closer to potential GDP. But fiscal policy cannot help an economy produce at an output level above potential GDP. Similarly, expansionary fiscal policy can help in reducing the cyclical unemployment that is associated with recession. But it cannot help in reducing the natural rate of unemployment that exists as a result of the incentives for hiring and working in the economy.

Educating Politicians

A final problem for discretionary fiscal policy arises out of the difficulties of explaining to politicians how countercyclical fiscal policy that runs against the tide of the business cycle should work. Politicians often have a gut-level belief that when the economy and tax revenues slow down, it's time to hunker down, pinch pennies, and trim expenses. Countercyclical policy, however, says that when the economy has slowed down, it's time for the government to go on a spree, raising spending and cutting taxes. Conversely, when economic times are good and tax revenues are rolling in, politicians often feel that it's prime time for tax cuts and new spending. But countercyclical policy says that this economic boom should be an appropriate time for keeping taxes high and restraining spending.

Politicians tend to prefer expansionary fiscal policy over contractionary policy. There is rarely a shortage of proposals for tax cuts and spending increases, especially during recessions. However, politicians are less willing to hear the message that in good economic times, they should propose tax increases and spending limits. In the economic upswing of the late 1990s and early 2000s, for example, the U.S. GDP grew rapidly. Estimates from respected government economic forecasters like the nonpartisan Congressional Budget Office and the Office of Management and Budget (which is run by the White House) stated that the GDP was above potential GDP, and that unemployment rates were unsustainably low. However, no mainstream politician took the lead in saying that the booming economic times might be an appropriate time for spending cuts or tax increases.

Summing Up Discretionary Fiscal Policy

Expansionary fiscal policy can help to end recessions, and contractionary fiscal policy can help to reduce inflation. But given the uncertainties over interest rate effects, time lags, temporary and permanent policies, and the uncertainties of political behavior, many economists and knowledgeable policymakers had concluded by the mid-1990s that discretionary fiscal policy was a blunt instrument, more like a club than a scalpel. It might still make sense to use it in extreme economic situations like an especially deep or long recession. But for milder situations, it was often preferable to let fiscal policy work through the automatic stabilizers and then focus on monetary policy to steer short-term countercyclical policy.

Requiring a Balanced Budget?

For many decades, going back to the 1930s, proposals have been put forward to require that the U.S. government balance its budget every year. In 1995, a proposed constitutional amendment that would require a balanced budget passed the U.S. House of Representatives by a wide margin, and failed in the U.S. Senate by only a single vote.

Most economists view the proposals for a perpetually balanced budget with bemusement. After all, in the short term, economists would expect the budget deficits and surpluses to fluctuate up and down with the economy and the automatic stabilizers. Economic recessions should automatically lead to larger budget deficits or smaller budget surpluses, while economic booms lead to smaller deficits or larger surpluses. A requirement that the budget be balanced each and every year would prevent these automatic stabilizers from working and thus would worsen the severity of economic fluctuations.

Some supporters of the balanced budget amendment like to argue that since households must balance their own budgets, the government should, too. But this analogy between household and government behavior is badly flawed. Most households do not balance their budgets every year. Some years households borrow money to buy houses or cars or to pay for medical expenses or college tuition. Other years they repay loans and save money in retirement accounts. After retirement they withdraw and spend those savings. Also, the government is not a household for many reasons, one of which is that the government has macroeconomic responsibilities. The argument of Keynesian macroeconomic policy is that the government needs to lean against the wind, spending when times are hard and saving when times are good for the sake of the overall economy.

There is also no particular reason to expect a government budget to be balanced in the medium term of a few years. For example, a government may decide that by running large budget deficits, it can make crucial long-term investments in human capital and physical infrastructure that will build the long-term productivity of a country. These decisions may work out well or poorly, but they are not inevitably irrational. Such policies of ongoing government budget deficits may persist for decades. As the U.S. experience from the end of World War II up to about 1980 shows, it is perfectly possible to run budget deficits almost every year for decades, but as long as the percentage increases in debt are smaller than the percentage growth of GDP, then debt/GDP ratio will decline at the same time.

Nothing in this argument should be taken as a claim that budget deficits are always a wise policy. In the short-run, government that runs extremely large budget deficits can shift aggregate demand to the right so violently that it causes severe inflation.

Governments may borrow for foolish or impractical reasons. The next chapter will discuss how large budget deficits, by reducing national saving, can in certain cases reduce economic growth and even contribute to international financial crises. But a requirement that the budget be balanced in each calendar year is a misguided overreaction to the fear that in some cases, budget deficits can become too large.

Conclusion

The relationship between government fiscal policy and the macroeconomy goes in both directions. The sheer size of government spending and taxes mean that they play an important role in a nation's macroeconomy. Fiscal policy affects aggregate demand in a number of ways: for example, through government spending and through the impact of taxes on consumption and investment. Conversely, automatic stabilizers exist because the levels of government spending and taxes are affected by a country's macroeconomic performance. This chapter has focused on fiscal policy in the context of recession, cyclical unemployment, inflation and short-run business cycles. The next chapter focuses on how government spending and taxes affect national savings and thus have an impact on long-run economic growth as well as the trade balance and international flows of financial capital.

Key Concepts and Summary

1. **Fiscal policy** is the set of policies that relate to government spending, taxation, and borrowing.

2. In recent decades, the level of federal government spending and taxes, expressed as a share of GDP, has not changed much, typically fluctuating between about 18 to 22% of GDP. However, the level of state spending and taxes, as a share of GDP, has risen by more than 40% over the last four decades.

3. The four main areas of federal spending are national defense, Social Security, health care, and interest payments, which together account for about 70% of all federal spending.

4. When a government spends more than it collects in taxes, it is said to have a **budget deficit.** When a government collects more in taxes than it spends, it is said to have a **budget surplus.** If government spending and taxes are equal, it is said to have a **balanced budget.**

5. The two main federal taxes are **individual income taxes** and **payroll taxes** that provide funds for Social Security and Medicare. These taxes together account for more than 80% of federal revenues. Other federal taxes include the **corporate income tax, excise taxes** on alcohol, gasoline and tobacco, and the **estate and gift tax.**

6. A **progressive tax** is one, like the federal income tax, where those with higher incomes pay a higher share of income in taxes than those with lower incomes. A **proportional tax** is one, like the payroll tax for Medicare, where everyone pays the same share of income in taxes regardless of income level, like the payroll tax for Medicare. A **regressive tax** is one, like the payroll tax that supports Social Security where those with high income pay a lower share of income in taxes than those with lower incomes.

7. For most of the twentieth century, the U.S. government took on debt during wartime and then paid down that debt slowly in peacetime. However, the U.S. government took on quite substantial debts in peacetime in the 1980 and early 1990s, before a brief period of budget surpluses from 1998 to 2001, followed by a return to annual budget deficits since 2002, with very large deficits in the recession of 2008 and 2009.

8. A budget deficit or budget surplus is measured annually. Total **government debt** is the sum of budget deficits and budget surpluses over time.

9. **Expansionary fiscal policy** increases the level of aggregate demand, either through increases in government spending or through reductions in taxes. Expansionary fiscal policy is most appropriate when an economy is in recession and producing below its potential GDP. **Contractionary fiscal policy** decreases the level of aggregate demand, either through cuts in government spending or increases in taxes. Contractionary fiscal policy is most appropriate when an economy is producing above its potential GDP.

10. Fiscal policy is conducted both through **discretionary fiscal policy,** which occurs when the government enacts taxation or spending changes in response to economic events, or through **automatic stabilizers,** which are taxing and spending mechanisms that by their design shift in response to economic events without any further legislation.

11. The **standardized employment budget** is the calculation of what the budget deficit or budget surplus would have been in a given year if the economy had been producing at its potential GDP in that year.

12. Discretionary fiscal policy faces some practical difficulties: (a) expansionary fiscal policy can raise interest rates, which tends to reduce the expansionary impact of the policy; (b) there are long and variable time lags in enacting fiscal policy and waiting for it to have an effect; (c) the impact of temporary fiscal policy is smaller than the impact of permanent fiscal policy; (d) fiscal policy cannot push economic output above the potential GDP level of output; (e) it may be hard to persuade politicians of the merits of countercyclical fiscal policy.

13. Laws requiring a balanced budget every year would inhibit both automatic stabilizers and discretionary fiscal policy, as well as long-term uses of fiscal policy to increase national saving or to invest in a nation's future.

Review Questions

1. What is fiscal policy?

2. Has spending and taxes of the U.S. federal government generally have an upward or a downward trend in the last few decades?

3. What are the main categories of U.S. federal government spending?

4. What's the difference between a budget deficit, a balanced budget, and a budget surplus?

5. Has spending and taxes by state and local governments in the United States had a generally upward or downward trend in the last few decades?

6. What are the main categories of U.S. federal government taxes?

7. What's the difference between a progressive tax, a proportional tax, and a regressive tax?

8. What has been the general pattern of U.S. budget deficits in recent decades?

9. What's the difference between a budget deficit and the government debt?

10. What's the difference between expansionary fiscal policy and contractionary fiscal policy?

11. Under what general macroeconomic circumstances might a government use expansionary fiscal policy? Contractionary fiscal policy?

12. What's the difference between discretionary fiscal policy and automatic stabilizers?

13. Why do automatic stabilizers function "automatically"?

14. What is the standardized employment budget?

15. What are some practical weaknesses of discretionary fiscal policy?

16. What are some of the arguments for and against a requirement that the federal government budget be balanced every year?

19

Government Borrowing and National Savings

W hen a government spends more than it collects in taxes and runs a budget deficit, it needs to borrow. When government borrowing becomes especially large and sustained, it can substantially reduce the financial capital available to private-sector firms, as well as leading to trade imbalances and even financial crises.

The previous chapter introduced the concepts of deficits and debt, and how a government could use fiscal policy during the short-run of the business cycle to address recession or inflation. This chapter begins by building upon the national savings and investment identity, first introduced in Chapter 11, to show how government borrowing affects physical capital investment levels of firms and trade balances. A prolonged period of budget deficits may lead to lower economic growth, in part because the funds borrowed by the government to fund its budget deficits are typically no longer available for investment. Moreover, a sustained pattern of large budget deficits can lead to disruptive economic patterns of high inflation, substantial inflows of financial capital from abroad, plummeting exchange rates, and heavy strains on a country's banking and financial system.

How Government Borrowing Affects Investment and the Trade Balance

When governments are borrowers in financial capital markets, there are three possible sources for the funds from a macroeconomic point of view: (1) households might save more; (2) private firms might borrow less; and (3) the funds might come outside the country, from foreign financial investors. Let's begin with a review of why one of these three options must occur, and then explore how interest rates and exchange rates can help to explain these connections.

The National Saving and Investment Identity

The national saving and investment identity, first introduced in Chapter 11, provides a framework for showing the relationships between the sources of demand and supply in financial capital markets. The identity begins with a statement that must always hold true: the quantity of financial capital supplied in the market must equal the quantity of financial capital demanded. The U.S. economy has two main sources for financial capital: private savings S from households and firms inside the U.S. economy; and the inflow of foreign financial investment from abroad. The inflow of savings from abroad is by definition equal to the trade deficit, as explained in Chapter 11, so this inflow of foreign investment capital can be written as imports M minus exports X. There are also two main sources of demand for financial capital: private sector investment I and government borrowing. Government borrowing in any given year is equal to the budget deficit, and thus can be written as the difference between government spending G and taxes T. Thus, in algebraic terms, the national savings and investment identity can be written like this:

Quantity supplied of financial capital = Quantity demanded of financial capital

$$\text{Private savings} + \text{Inflow of foreign savings} = \text{Private investment} + \text{Government budget deficit}$$

$$S + (M - X) = I + (G - T)$$

A change in any part of the national saving and investment identity *must* be accompanied by offsetting changes in at least one other part of the equation, because the equality of quantity supplied and quantity demanded will continue to hold true. Thus, if the government budget deficit changes, then either private saving or investment or the trade balance or some combination of the three *must* change as well. Exhibit 19-1 lists the possible effects.

What about Budget Surpluses and Trade Surpluses?

The national saving and investment identity must always hold true, because the quantity supplied and quantity demanded in the financial capital market must always be equal by definition. However, the formula will look somewhat different if the government budget is in deficit rather than surplus or if the balance of trade is in surplus rather than deficit. For example, from 1998 to 2001, the U.S. government had budget surpluses, although the economy was still experiencing trade deficits. When the government was running budget surpluses, it was acting as a saver rather than a borrower, and supplying financial capital rather than demanding it. As a result, the national saving and investment identity during this time would be more properly written:

Quantity supplied of financial capital = Quantity demanded of financial capital

Private savings + Trade deficit + Government surplus = Private investment

$$S + (M - X) + (T - G) = I$$

Exhibit 19-1   Effects of Change in Budget Surplus or Deficit

Notice that this expression is mathematically the same as the earlier version of the national saving and investment identity, except that (T – G) has been added to each side. Instead of a government deficit appearing in the equation as part of the quantity demanded of financial capital, now the budget surplus appears as part of the quantity supplied of financial capital.

During the 1960s, the U.S. government was often running a budget deficit but the economy was typically running trade surpluses. Since a trade surplus means that an economy is experiencing a net outflow of financial capital, the national saving and investment identity would be written:

Quantity supplied of financial capital = Quantity demanded of financial capital demand

Private savings = Private investment + Government budget deficit + Trade surplus

$$S = I + (G - T) + (X - M)$$

Instead of the balance of trade representing part of the supply of financial capital, which occurs with a trade deficit, a trade surplus represents an outflow of financial capital leaving the domestic economy and being invested elsewhere in the world.

The moral to this parade of equations is that the national saving and investment identity is always true, but when you write these relationships it is important to engage your brain and think about what is on the supply side and the demand side of the financial capital market before your pencil moves into gear. In the circumstances of the U.S. government as it begins the second decade of the 2000s, a rise in the budget deficit must cause one of three possible effects: a fall in domestic investment, a rise in private savings, or a rise in the trade deficit. The following sections discuss each of these possible effects in more detail.

Fiscal Policy, Investment, and Economic Growth

The underpinnings of economic growth are investments in physical capital, human capital, and technology, all set in an economic environment where firms and individuals can react to the incentives provided by well-functioning markets and flexible prices. Government borrowing can reduce the financial capital available for private firms to invest in physical capital. But government spending can also encourage certain elements of long-term growth. Examples include government spending on publicly owned physical capital like roads or water systems, on education that creates human capital, or on research and development that creates new technology.

Crowding Out Physical Capital Investment

A larger budget deficit will increase demand for financial capital. If private saving and the trade balance remain the same, then less financial capital will be available for private investment in physical capital. When government borrowing soaks up available financial capital and leaves less for private investment in physical capital, the result is known as **crowding out.**

crowding out: When government borrowing soaks up available financial capital and leaves less for private investment in physical capital.

To understand the potential impact of crowding out, consider the situation of the U.S. economy before the exceptional circumstances of the recession that started in late 2007. In 2005, for example, the budget deficit was roughly 4% of GDP. Private investment by firms in the U.S. economy has hovered in the range of 14–18% of GDP in recent decades. However, in any given year, roughly half of U.S. investment in physical capital just replaces machinery and equipment that has worn out or become technologically obsolete. Thus, only about half of total investment in physical capital represents an increase for the total quantity of physical capital in the economy. With this adjustment in mind, investment in new physical capital in any year is about 7–9% of GDP. In this situation, even U.S. budget deficits in the range of 4% of GDP can potentially crowd out a substantial share of the new investment spending in the U.S. economy. Conversely, a smaller budget deficit (or an increased budget surplus) would increase the pool of financial capital available for private investment.

The patterns of U.S. budget deficits and private investment since 1980 are shown in Exhibit 19-2. If greater government deficits lead to less private investment in physical capital, while reduced government deficits or budget surpluses lead to more investment in physical capital, then these two lines should move up and down at the same time. This pattern occurred in the U.S. economy in the late 1990s and early 2000s. The U.S. federal budget went from a deficit of 2.2% of GDP in 1995 to a budget surplus of 2.4% of GDP in 2000—a swing of 4.6% of GDP. From 1995 to 2000, private investment in physical capital rose from 15% of to 18% of GDP—a rise of 3% of GDP. Then, when the U.S. government again started running budget deficits in the early 2000s, less financial capital became available for private investment, and the U.S. rate of private investment fell back to about 15% of GDP by 2003.

This argument does not claim that a government's budget deficits will exactly shadow its national rate of private investment: after all, as the national saving and income identity shows, private saving and inflows of foreign financial investment must also be taken into account. In the mid-1980s, for example, government budget deficits increase substantially without a corresponding drop-off in private investment. In 2009, investment drops off primarily because during the recession, firms lack both the funds and the incentive to invest—not because budget deficits increased. However, government borrowing can clearly have an effect in crowding out private investment in physical capital, while a reduction in government borrowing can offer private investment a chance to expand.

The Interest Rate Connection

A government which is borrowing substantial amounts will have an effect on financial capital markets. In Exhibit 19-3, the original equilibrium E_0 where the demand curve D_0 for financial capital intersects with the supply curve S_0 occurs at an interest rate of 5%

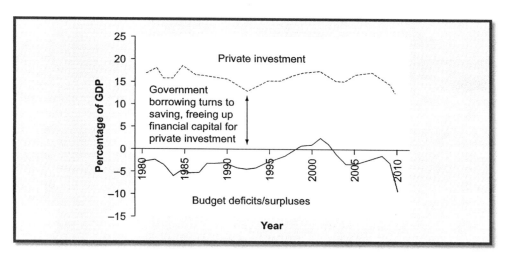

The connection from government borrowing to private investment in physical capital is not a precise one. After all, private savings and flows of international capital also play a role. But government borrowing and private investment sometimes rise and fall together. For example, the 1990s show a pattern in which reduced government borrowing helped to reduce crowding out so that more funds were available for private investment.

and an equilibrium quantity equal to 20% of GDP. However, the government budget deficit increases and the demand curve for financial capital shifts from D_0 to D_1. The new equilibrium E_1 occurs at an interest rate of 6% and an equilibrium quantity of 21% of GDP.

A survey of economic studies on the connection between government borrowing and interest rates in the U.S. economy suggests that an increase of 1% in the budget deficit will lead to a rise in interest rates of between 0.5 and 1.0%, other factors held equal. In turn, a higher interest rate tends to discourage firms from making physical capital investments. Thus, one reason that government budget deficits crowd out private investment is because of the increase in interest rates.

At this point, you may wonder about the Federal Reserve. After all, can't the Federal Reserve use expansionary monetary policy to reduce interest rates, or in this case, to prevent interest rates from rising? This useful question emphasizes the importance of considering how fiscal and monetary policies work in relation to each other. Imagine a central bank faced with a government that is running large budget deficits, thus causing an increase in interest rates and crowding out private investment. If the budget deficits are increasing aggregate demand when the economy is already producing near potential GDP such that that an inflationary increase in price level is threatened, then

Exhibit 19-3 Budget Deficits and Interest Rates

In the financial capital market, an increase in government borrowing can shift the demand curve for financial capital to the right from D_0 to D_1. As the equilibrium interest rate shifts from E_0 to E_1, the interest rate rises from 5% to 6% in this example. The higher interest rate is one economic mechanism by which government borrowing can crowd out private investment.

Crowding Out Private Investment in Russia

Budget deficits in Russia averaged 8.1% of GDP from 1993 to 1998. During this time, Russia was making a transition from a command economy, where the government made most of the economic decisions, and toward a more market-oriented economy. Government spending rose as a share of GDP, since many people in the country were under great economic stress. But taxes sagged, in part because it took time to create a new tax system.

One effect of these large budget deficits was to crowd out investment. Investment in Russia's economy sunk from 25% of GDP in 1995 to 16% of GDP. In addition, by overstimulating aggregate demand, the large budget deficit contributed to high levels of inflation, which was as high as 131% in 1995 and 84% in 1998, but also as low as 11% in 1997.

Russia's large budget deficits were not financed by an inflow of financial capital from abroad. Instead, Russia had current account trade surpluses for most years in the 1990s, which means that Russia's economy was experiencing a net outflow of financial investment to other countries.

Of course, budget deficits are only one of many factors affecting Russia's macroeconomic performance. But it is no coincidence that as Russia's budget came under control, ending its pattern of budget deficits and even moving to budget surpluses from 2000–2002, Russia's economy also began a pattern of sustained growth, with real GDP rising 5% or more per year from 1999–2002.

the central bank may react with a contractionary monetary policy. In this situation, the higher interest rates from the government borrowing would be made even higher by contractionary monetary policy, and the government borrowing might crowd out a great deal of private investment. On the other hand, if the budget deficits are increasing aggregate demand when the economy is producing substantially less than potential GDP, then an inflationary increase in the price level is not much of a danger and the central bank might react with expansionary monetary policy. In this situation, any higher interest rates from government borrowing would be largely offset by the lower interest rates from expansionary monetary policy, and little crowding out of private investment would occur.

However, even a central bank cannot erase the overall message of the national savings and investment identity. If government borrowing rises, then private investment must fall, or private saving must rise, or the trade deficit must fall. By reacting with contractionary or expansionary monetary policy, the central bank can only help to determine which of these outcomes is likely to occur.

Public Investment in Physical Capital

Government can invest in physical capital directly: roads and bridges; water supply and sewers; seaports and airports; schools and hospitals; plants that generate electricity like hydroelectric dams, nuclear power or windmills; telecommunications facilities; and weapons used by the military. In 2007, the U.S. federal government spent $38 billion on highways and state and local governments spent roughly another $145 billion. Exhibit 19-4 shows the total value of the physical capital that was owned by federal, state, and local governments in the United States in 2005. Physical capital related to the military or to residences where people live is left out of this table, because the focus here is on public investments that have a direct effect on raising output in the private sector. Still, the tally reaches an astonishing total of more than $6 trillion in publicly-owned physical capital. About 90% of the physical capital in the table is owned by state and local governments, not by the federal government.

Public physical capital investment of this sort can increase the output and productivity of the economy. After all, an economy with reliable roads and electricity will be able to produce more. But it is hard to draw a general lesson about how

Type of Public Physical Capital	Value in 2005
Highways and streets	$2,077 billion
Water supply and sewer systems	$782 billion
Schools, hospitals, police, and fire	$1,745 billion
Conservation and development structures	$232 billion
Transportation and power	$633 billion
Equipment and software	$814 billion
Total	*$6,283 billion*

Exhibit 19-4
Nonmilitary, Nonresidential Public Physical Capital in 2005

much government investment in physical capital will benefit the economy, because government responds to political incentives as well as to economic incentives. When a firm makes an investment in physical capital it is subject to the discipline of the market: if the firm doesn't receive a positive return on its investment, the firm may lose money or even go out of business. However, legislatures don't have to worry much about going broke. In some cases, lawmakers might make investments in physical capital as a way of spending money in the districts of key politicians. Unnecessary roads or office buildings may be built. Even if a project is useful and necessary, it might be done in a way that is excessively large and costly, because local contractors who make campaign contributions to politicians appreciate the extra business. Managing public investment so that it is done in a cost-effective way can be difficult, because the discipline imposed by political decisions is different than the discipline imposed by market competition.

If a government decides to finance an investment in public physical capital with higher taxes or lower government spending in other areas, it need not worry that it is crowding out private investment. However, if a government decides to finance an investment in public physical capital by borrowing, it may end up increasing the quantity of public physical capital at the cost of crowding out investment in private physical capital.

Public Investment in Human Capital

In most countries, the government plays a large role in society's investment in human capital through the education system. In 2006, in the high-income countries of the world, public spending on education is 5.2% of GDP; in the middle-income countries, it is 4.2% of GDP; in the low-income countries, it is 3.5% of GDP. A highly educated and skilled workforce contributes to a higher rate of economic growth, and especially for the low-income nations of the world, an additional investment in human capital seems likely to increase productivity and growth.

But for United States, tough questions have been raised about how much increases in government spending on education will improve the actual level of education achieved. Among economists, discussions of education reform often begin with some uncomfortable facts. As shown in Exhibit 19-5, spending per student for kindergarten through grade 12 (K–12) has increased substantially in real dollars; for example, real (that is, adjusted for inflation) education spending per student more than doubled from about $5,600 per student in 1970 to more than $12,000 per student by the late 2000s. However, as measured by standardized tests like the SAT, the level of student academic achievement has barely budged in recent decades. Indeed, on international tests, the U.S. students lag behind students from many other countries. (Of course, test scores are

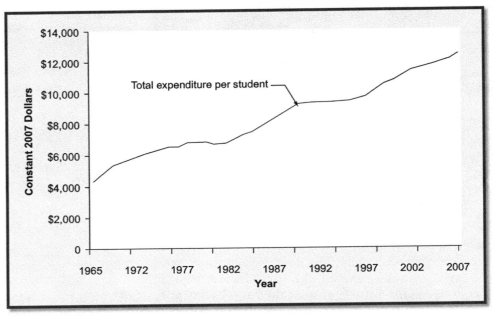

Exhibit 19-5   Higher Education Spending per Student

Despite higher spending per student, educational achievement as measured by test scores has been largely stagnant since 1970.

an imperfect measure of education for a variety of reasons. But it would be difficult to argue that all the problems of the U.S. education system are due to mismeasurement!)

The fact that increased financial resources per student has not brought greater measurable gains in student performance has led some education experts to question whether the problems of education may be due to the incentive structure of education, not just the resources spent on education. U.S. states have implemented many different proposals: rewarding schools financially when students make exceptional gains, and threatening to close schools where students are not making sufficient gains; requiring testing of students at various grades, including tests as a requirement for high school graduation; requiring additional teacher training; allowing students a greater degree of choice between public schools, to put pressure on weak schools to perform better; and allowing teachers and parents to start new schools, sometimes called charter schools, to compete with existing schools. The most controversial proposals have called for giving students a voucher that they could use at any state-accredited school, public or private, and to let families choose where their children attend. All these proposals have their supporters and detractors, but relatively little firm evidence has accumulated for or against any of them.

In 2001, Congress passed and President George W. Bush signed into law the No Child Left Behind Act. The act requires all states to test children in grades 3–8, to publish the results, to intervene in schools where inadequate progress is occurring, and to assure that a growing share of teachers are highly qualified in the specific subjects they are teaching. As states react to this new law in different ways, additional data should become available about what methods for improving education work best.

Other government programs seek to increase human capital either before or after the K–12 education system. Programs for early childhood education, like the federal Head Start program, are directed at families where the parents may have limited educational and financial resources. Early preschool education does not seem to increase scores on standardized tests, but it can make students more attached to school, more motivated to persevere and avoid dropping out of school, and thus ultimately more likely to get better jobs later in life.

Government also offers substantial support for universities and colleges. One of the great strengths of the U.S. education system is the relatively high proportion of students who go on to additional education after the high school level. For example, in the United States about three-quarters of students take at least a few college or university classes beyond the high school level. In Germany and Japan, only about half of all students take classes beyond the comparable high school level. In the countries of Latin America, only about one student in four takes classes beyond the high school level, and in the nations of sub-Saharan Africa, only about one student in 20 takes classes beyond the high school level. Of course, American colleges and universities could teach more effectively if high school graduates were better prepared to take full advantage of a college-level education.

Not all spending on educational human capital needs to happen through the government: for example, many college students in the United States pay a substantial share of the cost of their education. But if low-income countries of the world are going to experience a widespread increase in their education levels for grade-school children, government spending seems likely to play a substantial role. For the U.S. economy, and for other high-income countries, the primary focus at this time is more on how to get a bigger return from existing spending on education and how to improve the performance of the average high school graduate, rather than on advocating dramatic increases in education spending.

How Fiscal Policy Can Improve Technology

Research and development (R&D) efforts are the lifeblood of new technology. But U.S. levels of R&D spending have been between 2.1% and 2.8% of GDP since the 1960s, and has shown no particular increases in recent decades. For comparison, U.S. R&D in 2008, at 2.8% of GDP, was a bit ahead of Germany's R&D effort of 2.5% of GDP but behind Japan's R&D spending of 3.7% of GDP. Also, about one-fifth of U.S. R&D spending goes to defense and space-oriented research, a much greater share than in Japan and Germany. Although this defense-oriented R&D spending may sometimes eventually produce consumer-oriented spin-offs, R&D which is aimed at producing new weapons is less likely to benefit the civilian economy than direct civilian R&D spending.

Fiscal policy can encourage R&D using either direct spending or tax policy. Government could spend more on the R&D that is carried out in government laboratories, as well as expanding federal R&D grants to universities and colleges, nonprofit organizations, and the private sector. In the mid-1960s, the U.S. federal government paid for about two-thirds of the nation's R&D. By 2008, however, the federal share of R&D spending had fallen to only about one-fourth—that is, $104 billion from the federal government out of total R&D spending of $397 billion. Fiscal policy can also support R&D through tax incentives, which allow firms to reduce their tax bill as they increase spending on research and development.

Summary of Fiscal Policy, Investment, and Economic Growth

Investment in physical capital, human capital and new technology is essential for long-term economic growth. In a market-oriented economy, private firms will undertake most of the investment in physical capital, and fiscal policy should seek to avoid a long series of outsized budget deficits that might crowd out such investment. Governments can invest directly in publicly-owned physical capital and in educational human capital, and can encourage R&D both by direct spending and by incentives for the private sector. A high rate of investment is not enough to guarantee the process of economic growth, which also benefits from a non-recessionary, low-inflation, market-oriented economy with an innovative and flexible business sector. Moreover, the effects of many growth-oriented policies will only be seen very gradually over time, as students are better educated, physical capital investments are made, and new technologies are invented and implemented. But with these limitations duly noted, greater investment will typically produce a higher rate of economic growth.

Will Private Saving Offset Government Borrowing?

A change in government budgets may affect private saving. Imagine that people carefully watch government budgets and adjust their savings accordingly. For example, whenever the government runs a budget deficit, people might reason: "Well, a higher budget deficit means that I'm just going to owe more taxes in the future to pay off all that government borrowing, so I'll start saving now." If the government runs budget surpluses, people might reason: "With these budget surpluses (or lower budget deficits), interest rates are falling, so that saving is less attractive. Moreover, with a budget surplus the country will be able to afford a tax cut sometime in the future. I won't bother saving as much now."

    The theory that rational private households might shift their saving to offset government saving or borrowing is known as **Ricardian equivalence** because the idea has intellectual roots in the writings of the early-nineteenth-century economist David Ricardo (1772–1823). If Ricardian equivalence holds completely true, then in the national saving and investment identity, any change in budget deficits or budget surpluses would be completely offset by a corresponding change in private saving. As a result, changes in government borrowing would have no effect at all on either physical capital investment or trade balances.

    In practice, the private sector only sometimes and partially adjusts its savings behavior to offset government budget deficits and surpluses. Exhibit 19-6 shows the patterns of U.S. government budget deficits and surpluses and the rate of private saving—

Ricardian equivalence:
The theory that rational private households might shift their saving to offset government saving or borrowing.

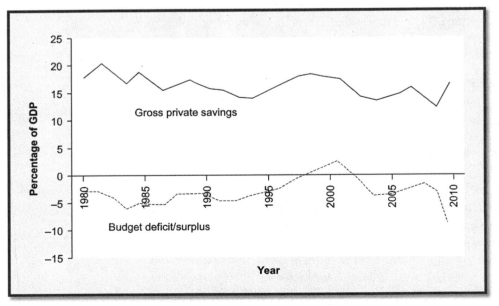

Exhibit 19-6   U.S. Budget Deficits and Private Savings

The theory of Ricardian neutrality suggests that any increase in government borrowing will be offset by additional private saving, while any decrease in government borrowing will be offset by reduced private saving. At some times, this theory holds true; for example, in the 1990s, the reduction in government borrowing was accompanied by a fall in private savings, and in 2008–2009, a rise in government borrowing was accompanied by a rise in private saving. However, such offsets are often only partial, and sometimes do not occur at all.

which includes saving by both households and firms—since 1980. The connection between the two is not at all obvious. In the mid-1980s, for example, government budget deficits were quite large, but there is no corresponding surge of private saving. However, when budget deficits turn to surpluses in the late 1990s, there is a simultaneous decline in private saving. When budget deficits get very large in 2008 and 2009, on the other hand, there is some sign of a rise in saving. A variety of statistical studies based on the U.S. experience suggests that when government borrowing increases by $1, private saving rises by about 30 cents. A World Bank study done in the late 1990s, looking at government budgets and private saving behavior in countries around the world, found a similar result.

Thus, private saving does increase to some extent when governments run large budget deficits, and private saving falls when governments reduce deficits or run large budget surpluses. However, the offsetting effects of private saving compared to government borrowing are much less than one-to-one. In addition, this effect can vary a great deal from country to country, from time to time, and over the short run and the long run.

Fiscal Policy and the Trade Balance

Government budget balances can affect the trade balance. When government borrowing increases, one possible source of funding is an inflow of foreign financial investment. As Chapter 11 discussed, a net inflow of foreign financial investment always accompanies a trade deficit, while a net outflow of financial investment always accompanies a trade surplus. One way to understand the connection from budget deficits to trade deficits is that when government creates a budget deficit with some combination of tax cuts or spending increases, it will increase aggregate demand in the economy, and some of that increase in aggregate demand will result in a higher level of imports. A higher level of imports, with exports remaining fixed, will cause a larger trade deficit.

Twin Deficits?

In the mid-1980s, it was common to hear economists and even newspaper articles refer to the "twin deficits," as the budget deficit and trade deficit both grew substantially. Exhibit 19-7 shows the pattern. The federal budget deficit went from 2.6% of GDP in 1981 to 5.1% of GDP in 1985—a drop of 2.5% of GDP. Over that time, the trade deficit moved from 0.5% in 1981 to 2.9% in 1985—a drop of 2.4% of GDP. In the mid-1980s, the considerable increase in government borrowing was filled with an inflow of foreign investment capital, so the government budget deficit and the trade deficit moved together.

Of course, no one should expect the budget deficit and trade deficit to move in lockstep, because the other parts of the national saving and investment identity—investment and private savings—will often change as well. In the late 1990s, for example, the government budget balance turned from deficit to surplus, but the trade deficit remained large and growing. During this time, the inflow of foreign financial investment was supporting a surge of physical capital investment by U.S. firms. In the first half of the 2000s, the budget and trade deficits again increased together, but in 2009, the budget deficit increased while the trade deficit declined. The budget deficit and the trade deficits are related to each other, but they are more like cousins than twins.

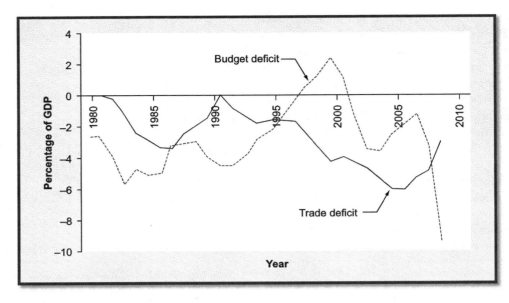

Exhibit 19-7 U.S. Budget Deficits and Trade Deficits

In the 1980s, the budget deficit and the trade deficit both declined at the same time, leading to much discussion of the "twin deficits." However, since then, the deficits have stopped being twins. The trade deficit grew smaller in the early 1990s as the budget deficit increased, and then the trade deficit grew larger in the late 1990s as the budget deficit turned into a surplus. In the first half of the 2000s, both budget and trade deficits increased. But in 2009, the trade deficit declined as the budget deficit increased.

Fiscal Policy and Exchange Rates

Exchange rates can also help to explain why budget deficits are linked to trade deficits. Exhibit 19-8 shows a situation using the exchange rate for the U.S. dollar, measured in euros. At the original equilibrium E_0, where the demand for U.S. dollars D_0 intersects with the supply of U.S. dollars S_0 on the foreign exchange market, the exchange rate is .9 euros per U.S. dollar and the equilibrium quantity traded in the market is $200 billion per day (which was roughly the quantity of dollar-euro trading in exchange rate markets in the mid-2000s). But then the U.S. budget deficit rises, and foreign financial investment provides the source of funds for that budget deficit. International financial investors as a group will demand more U.S. dollars on foreign exchange markets to purchase the U.S. government bonds, and they will supply fewer of the U.S. dollars that they already hold in these markets. Demand for U.S. dollars on the foreign exchange market shifts from D_0 to D_1 and the supply of U.S. dollars falls from S_0 to S_1. At the new equilibrium E_1, the exchange rate has appreciated to 1.05 euros per dollar, while in this example the quantity traded remains the same.

A stronger exchange rate, of course, makes it more difficult for exporters to sell their goods abroad while making imports cheaper, so a trade deficit (or a reduced trade surplus) results. Thus, a budget deficit can easily result in an inflow of foreign financial capital, a stronger exchange rate, and a trade deficit.

You can also imagine this appreciation of the exchange rate as being driven by interest rates. As explained earlier in Exhibit 19-3, a budget deficit increases demand in markets for domestic financial capital, raising the domestic interest rate. A higher interest rate will attract an inflow of foreign financial capital, appreciate the exchange rate, and lead to a larger trade deficit (or reduced trade surplus). The connections between inflows of foreign investment capital, interest rates and exchange rates are all just different ways of drawing the same economic connections: A larger budget deficit can result in a larger trade deficit, although the connection should not be expected to be one to one.

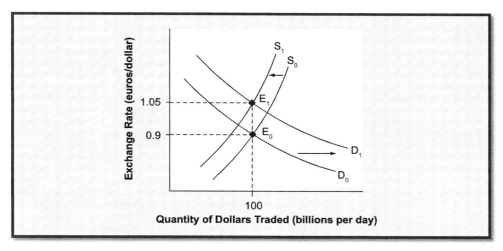

Exhibit 19-8   Budget Deficits and Exchange Rates

Imagine that the U.S. government increases its borrowing and the funds come from European financial investors. To purchase U.S. government bonds, those European investors will need to demand more U.S. dollars on foreign exchange markets, causing the demand for U.S. dollars to shift to the right from D_0 to D_1. European financial investors as a group will also be less likely to supply U.S. dollars to the foreign exchange markets, causing supply of U.S. dollars to shift from S_0 to S_1. The equilibrium exchange rate strengthens from 0.9 euro/dollar at E_0 to 1.05 euros/dollar at E_1.

From Budget Deficits to International Economic Crisis

The economic story of how an outflow of international financial capital can cause a deep recession was laid out step-by-step in Chapter 17. When international financial investors decide to withdraw their funds from a country like Turkey, they increase the supply of the Turkish lira and reduce the demand for lira, depreciating the lira exchange rate. But when firms and the government in a country like Turkey borrow money in international financial markets, they typically do so in stages. First, banks in Turkey borrow in a widely used currency like U.S. dollars or euros, then convert those U.S. dollars to lira, and then lend the money to borrowers in Turkey. If the value of the lira exchange rate depreciates, then Turkey's banks will find it impossible to repay the international loans that are in U.S. dollars or euros. The combination of less foreign investment capital and banks that are bankrupt can sharply reduce aggregate demand which causes a deep recession. Many countries around the world have experienced this kind of recession in recent years: along with Turkey in 2002, this general pattern was followed by Mexico in 1995, Thailand and countries across East Asia in 1997–98, Russia in 1998, and Argentina in 2002.

In many of these countries, large government budget deficits played a role in setting the stage for the financial crisis. A moderate increase in a budget deficit that leads to a moderate increase in a trade deficit and a moderate appreciation of the exchange rate is not necessarily a cause for concern. But beyond some point that is hard to define in advance, a series of large budget deficits can become a cause for concern among international investors.

One reason for concern is that extremely large budget deficits mean that aggregate demand may shift so far to the right as to cause high inflation. The example of Turkey at the beginning of this chapter is a situation where very large budget deficits brought inflation rates well into double digits. In addition, very large budget deficits at some point begin to raise a fear that the borrowing will not be repaid. In the last 175 years, the government of Turkey has been unable to pay its debts and defaulted on its loans six times. Brazil's government has been unable to pay its debts and defaulted on its loans seven times; Venezuela, nine times; Argentina, five times. The risk of high inflation or a default on repaying international loans will worry international financial investors, since both factors imply that the rate of return on their investments in that country may end up lower than expected. If international financial investors start withdrawing the

The Risks of Chronic Large Deficits

If a government runs large budget deficits for a sustained period of time, what can go wrong? Eventually, the ratio of government debt/GDP grows high enough that both domestic and foreign lenders become concerned that the government will not be able to repay. At that point, some combination of the following effects is likely to happen.

The interest rate that the government must pay in order to continue its borrowing will start to increase to offset the additional risk perceived by investors, so that the cost of financing debt rises as well.

As the costs of borrowing rise, the government will face enormous financial pressure to take dramatic steps to reduce its budget deficits through spending cuts and tax increases. These steps will be politically painful, and they will also have a contractionary effect on aggregate demand in the economy.

Government debt often expands in response to a private-sector financial crisis, which means that private firms, banks and households are all having trouble repaying their borrowing from earlier years. Thus, at the same time that the government is running contractionary fiscal policy, the private sector is also trying to reduce its debts by cutting back on spending and physical capital investment.

The government will be strongly tempted to allow a surge of inflation. After all, if the government has borrowed at a fixed interest rate of, say, 5%, and it lets inflation rise above that 5%, then it will effectively be able to repay its debt at a negative real interest rate.

What is the danger-level of debt where these sorts of changes take effect? Kenneth Rogoff of Harvard University and Carmen Reinhart have for the last few years been compiling and studying an international database of financial crises and episodes of high government borrowing over recent decades—and in some cases reaching back over the last two centuries. They find that a country's government debt/GDP ratio has relatively little effect until it reaches 90%. However, countries where the government debt/GDP ratio rises above 90% experience substantially slower economic growth for some years.

Of course, a 90% debt/GDP ratio is not an irrevocable law of nature—the situation of every country is different—but it offers a guidepost for how much to worry. For example, the government of Greece experienced substantial difficulties with its borrowing early in 2010, roughly when its debt/GDP ratio exceeded 100% of GDP. In the U.S. economy, the non-partisan Congressional Budget Office was projecting early in 2010 that the U.S. government debt/GDP ratio would exceed 90% in the year 2020.

funds from a country rapidly, the scenario of less investment, a depreciated exchange rate, widespread bank failure, and deep recession can occur.

Using Fiscal Policy to Address Trade Imbalances

If a nation is experiencing the inflow of foreign investment capital associated with a trade deficit because foreign investors are making long-term direct investments in firms, there may be no substantial reason for concern. After all, many low-income nations around the world would welcome direct investment by multinational firms that ties them more closely into the global networks of production and distribution of goods and services. In this case, the inflows of foreign investment capital and the trade deficit are attracted by the opportunities for a good rate of return on private sector investment in an economy.

However, governments should beware a sustained pattern of high budget deficits and high trade deficits. The danger arises in particular when the inflow of foreign investment capital is not funding long-term physical capital investment by firms, but instead is short-term portfolio investment in government bonds. When inflows of foreign financial investment reach high levels, foreign financial investors will be on the alert for any reason to fear that the country's exchange rate may decline or the government may be unable to repay what it has borrowed on time. Just as a few falling rocks can trigger an avalanche, a relatively small piece of bad news about an economy can trigger an enormous outflow of short-term financial capital. Reducing a nation's budget deficit will not always be a successful method of reducing its trade deficit, because other elements of the national saving and investment identity like private saving or investment may change instead. But in those cases when the budget deficit is the main cause of the trade deficit, governments should take steps to reduce their budget deficits, lest they make their economy vulnerable to a rapid outflow of international financial capital that could bring a deep recession.

Conclusion

Nothing in this chapter should be taken to suggest that government budgets should be balanced or in surplus every year, regardless of whether an economy is in recession. A government need not fear annual budget deficits, or even a sustained pattern of budget deficits, as long as its overall debt/GDP ratio is not continually increasing. After all, just as firms borrow to make investments in physical capital, governments might reasonably borrow to make investments in publicly owned physical capital, in the education system that builds human capital, and in the research and development that creates the technologies of the future.

But although a wise government may sometimes run budget deficits, it will also take care that its borrowing does not grow ever-larger for a sustained period of time. Government budget deficits involve borrowing in financial capital markets, and when deficits are large for a sustained period of time, high levels of government borrowing can cause severe economic problems. The previous chapter discussed the danger that if high levels of government spending or tax cuts cause large budget deficits, the resulting increase in aggregate demand can cause inflationary increases in the price level. Within the domestic economy, high levels of government borrowing can drive up interest rates and crowd out financial capital that would otherwise have been available to private firms. If government borrowing is being financed mainly with an inflow of foreign investment capital, the economy can become vulnerable to exchange rate depreciation and a deep recession if those foreign investors decide to stop providing financial capital. The economic costs of a sustained pattern of overly large budget deficits can be very high.

Key Concepts and Summary

1. A change in any part of the national saving and investment identity points out that if the government budget deficit changes, then either saving, private investment in physical capital or the trade balance—or some combination of the three—*must* change as well.

2. Economic growth comes from a combination of investment in physical capital, human capital and technology. Government borrowing can **crowd out** private sector investment in physical capital, but fiscal policy can also increase investment in publicly owned physical capital, human capital (education) and research and development.

3. Possible methods for improving education and society's investment in human capital include spending more money on teachers and other educational resources and reorganizing the education system to provide greater incentives for success.

4. Methods for increasing research and development spending to generate new technology include direct government spending on R&D and tax incentives for business to conduct additional R&D.

5. The theory of **Ricardian equivalence** holds that changes in government borrowing or saving will be offset by changes in private saving. Thus, higher budget deficits will be offset by greater private saving, while larger budget surpluses would be offset by greater private borrowing. If the theory holds true, then changes in government borrowing or saving would have no effect on private investment in physical capital or on the trade balance. However, empirical evidence suggests that the theory holds true only partially.

6. If the funding for a larger budget deficit comes from international financial investors, then a budget deficit may be accompanied by a trade deficit. In some countries, this pattern of "twin deficits" has set the stage for international financial investors first to send their funds to a country and cause an appreciation of its exchange rate and then to pull their funds out and cause a depreciation of the exchange rate and a financial crisis as well.

7. The government need not balance its budget every year. However, a sustained pattern of large budget deficits over time risks causing several negative macroeconomic outcomes: a shift to the right in aggregate demand that causes an inflationary increase in the price level; crowding out private investment in physical capital in a way that slows down economic growth; and creating a dependence on inflows of international portfolio investment which can sometimes turn into outflows of foreign financial investment that can be injurious to a macroeconomy.

Review Questions

1. Based on the national saving and investment identity, what are the three ways the macroeconomy might react to greater government budget deficits?

2. How would you expect larger budget deficits to affect private-sector investment in physical capital? Why?

3. What are some of the ways that fiscal policy might encourage economic growth?

4. What are some fiscal policies for improving society's level of human capital?

5. What are some fiscal policies of improving the technologies that the economy will have to draw upon in the future?

6. What is the theory of Ricardian equivalence?

7. Under what conditions will a larger budget deficit cause a trade deficit?

Macroeconomic Policy around the World

Given the extraordinary differences across the economies of all the countries of the world, can the same macroeconomic analysis possibly apply to all of them? For example, China has a population of 1.3 billion people in 2010, a per capita GDP of about $6,500, and a fast-growing economy over the last several decades. The U.S. economy has a population about 300 million, less than one-fourth that of China, but had a per capita GDP over $46,000 in 2010. Although inflation in the U.S. economy has been quite low in recent years, the U.S. economy in the mid-2000s had several years in which its budget deficit and trade deficit exceeded 4% of GDP. Venezuela has a population of 28 million, less than one-tenth of the U.S. population. Its per capita GDP has declined by more than 1% per year through the 1990s and the first decade of the 2000s, while inflation in Venezuela hit 31% in 2009.

Despite the obvious and enormous differences across the more than 200 countries of the world, the general structure of macroeconomic analysis can be applied in China, the United States, Venezuela, and other countries as well. Of course, every economy has its own distinctive characteristics, and thus may well require macroeconomic policies aimed at its own specific issues. Nevertheless, the four goals of macroeconomic policy—growth in standard of living, low unemployment, low inflation, and a sustainable balance of trade—are universal. The macroeconomic frameworks of analysis, including a short-run Keynesian perspective that focuses on fluctuations in aggregate demand and a long-term neoclassical perspective that focuses on economic growth and gradual increases in potential GDP, are useful in the analysis of any economy. The macroeconomic toolkit of monetary policy and fiscal policy is available to every country. This chapter begins with a discussion of the diversity of the economies in the world. It then discusses how countries around the world can seek to address the four macroeconomic goals, using the Keynesian and neoclassical frameworks for analysis and the tools of monetary and fiscal policy.

The Diversity of Countries and Economies across the World

The national economies that make up the global economy are remarkably diverse. The GDP of Spain, for example, with its population of approximately 45 million, is approximately 50% larger than the total GDP of all the nations of sub-Saharan Africa, which have a combined population of over 818 million.

Exhibit 20-1 presents a snapshot view of the world GDP and population in 2008, in which the world is divided into seven regions. The differences across these regions are remarkable. For example, per capita GDP for the 565 million people living in Latin America and the Caribbean region is approximately four or five times larger than the per capita GDP of the 2.3 billion people living in South Asia and sub-Saharan Africa. In turn, the people in the high-income nations of the world, including the United States, western Europe and Japan, have a per capita GDP that is more than triple that of the people of Latin America. The high-income economies of the world have 16% of the world's population, but they produce and consume over 70% of the world's GDP.

Such comparisons between regions of the world are admittedly rough. After all, per capita GDP does not capture the standard of living in a precise way. Many other factors have a large impact, like health, education, human rights, crime and personal safety, cleanliness of environment, and others. Exhibit 20-2 shows some selected measures of health and education: malnourishment, the death rate for children under age five, life expectancy, and illiteracy rates. These measures also reveal very wide differences in the standard of living across the regions of the world.

Yet the differences in economic statistics and other measures of well-being, substantial though they are, do not fully capture the enormous differences among countries that also shape their economic situation. Countries have geographic differences: some have extensive coastlines, some are landlocked; some have large rivers that have been a path of commerce for centuries, others have mountains that have been a barrier to trade; some have deserts, some have rain forests. Countries have considerable differences in the age distribution of the population. Many high-income nations are approaching a situation by 2020 or so in which the elderly will form a much larger share of the population; most low-income countries still have a higher proportion of youth and young adults, but by about 2050, the elderly populations in these low-income countries

	GDP (in billions of dollars)	Population (in millions)	Per Capita GDP
East Asia and the Pacific	$5,658	1,931	$5,399
Eastern Europe and Central Asia	$3,861	441	$12,220
Latin America and the Caribbean	$4,247	565	$10,309
Middle East and North Africa	$1,117	325	$7,308
South Asia	$1,531	1,543	$2,733
Sub-Saharan Africa	$987	818	$1,991
High income	$43,190	1,069	$37,141

Exhibit 20-1   Global Comparisons of GDP and Population in 2008

Exhibit 20-2   Other Measures of Standard of Living in 2008

	Percentage of Children under Age 5 Who Are Malnourished	Death Rate for under Age 5 Population	Life Expectancy at Birth in Years	Adult Literacy Rate
East Asia and the Pacific	12%	29	72	93%
Eastern Europe and Central Asia	*	22	70	98%
Latin America and the Caribbean	4%	23	73	92%
Middle East and North Africa	12%	34	70	73%
South Asia	41%	76	64	61%
Sub-Saharan Africa	25%	144	52	66%
High income	*	7	80	99%

*The rate is very low, and thus data are not available.

are expected to boom as well. Countries have differences in industry structure. In the high-income economies of the world, only about 2% of GDP comes from agriculture; the average for the rest of the world is 12%. Countries have strong differences in degree of urbanization: in the high income countries of the world, along with the regions of Latin America and eastern Europe/Central Asia, about 65–75% of people live in urban areas. In East Asia, sub-Saharan Africa, and South Asia, only about 30–40% of the population lives in urban areas. Countries have strong differences in economic institutions: some nations have economies that are extremely market-oriented, while other nations have command economies. Some nations are open to international trade, while others use tariffs and import quotas to limit the impact of trade. Some nations are torn by long-standing armed conflicts; other nations are largely at peace. There are differences in political institutions, religious, and social institutions as well.

No nation intentionally aims for a low standard of living, high rates of unemployment and inflation, or an unsustainable trade imbalance. However, nations will differ in their priorities and in the situations in which they find themselves, and so their policy choices can reasonably vary, too. The next sections will discuss how nations around the world, from high-income to low-income, approach the four macroeconomic goals of economic growth, low unemployment, low inflation, and a sustainable balance of trade.

Economic Growth

Economic growth is built on a foundation of productivity improvements. In turn, productivity improvements are the result of improvements in human capital, physical capital, and technology, interacting in a market-driven economy. But in the pursuit of economic growth, some countries and regions are starting from a higher level than others, as illustrated by the differences in per capita GDP presented earlier in Exhibit 20-1. In thinking about how nations around the world should pursue the goal of raising their standard of living, it's useful to divide the nations of the world into three groups: (1) technology leaders, which includes high-income countries like the United States,

Canada, Japan, and western Europe; (2) converging countries, which have shown some ability, even if not always sustained, to catch up to the technology leaders; and (3) the technologically disconnected, a group representing perhaps a third of the world's population, which has lagged behind economically.

Growth Policies for the Technological Leaders

For the high-income countries, the problem of economic growth is to push continually for a more educated workforce that can create, invest in and apply new technologies. In effect, the goal of their growth-oriented public policy is to shift their aggregate supply curves to the right. Their main public policies targeted at achieving this goal are fiscal policies focused on investment, including investment in human capital, in technology, and in physical plant and equipment. These countries also recognize that economic growth works best in a stable and market-oriented economic climate, and they thus use monetary policy to keep inflation low and stable, to minimize the risk of exchange rate fluctuations, while also encouraging domestic and international competition.

However, early in the second decade of the 2000s, many high-income countries find themselves more focused on the short-term than on the long-term. The United States, western Europe, Japan, have all experienced a combination of financial crisis and deep recession, and the after-effects of the recession—like high unemployment rates—seem likely to linger for several years. Most of these governments took aggressive and in some cases controversial steps to cushion the pain of the recession and to attempt to jump-start their economies. But having run very large budget deficits as part of an expansionary fiscal policy to fight recession, they now find themselves needing to chart a politically unpleasant but economically necessary course toward some combination of lower spending and higher taxes in the future. Similarly, many central banks ran highly expansionary monetary policies, with both near-zero interest rates and with unconventional monetary policies that involved having central banks make an array of loans and investments. The process of raising interest rates back to more normal levels and withdrawing these extraordinary loans and investments will also be sticky, but it needs to be done.

As earlier chapters have discussed, macroeconomics needs to have both a short-run and a long-run focus. The challenge for many high-income countries in the next few years will be to extricate themselves from the 2007–2009 recession, along with the policies adopted in fighting that recession, while not neglecting their foundation for future long-term growth. After all, for the high income countries of the world, the combination of new technology, education, and physical capital investment has now been generating long-run economic growth since the Industrial Revolution of the early 1800s.

Growth Policies for the Converging Economies

The converging countries include China, India, many countries in the regions of East Asia and the Pacific, Latin America and the Caribbean, and eastern Europe. Firms and workers in these economies can often build upon or copy technologies and industries developed by the technology leaders. They can also find niches that they are well-suited to fill in the global networks of economic production.

The world's great economic success stories in the last few decades started back in the 1970s with that group of nations sometimes known as the east Asian "tigers": South Korea, Thailand, Malaysia, Indonesia, and Singapore. (The list of east Asian tigers also sometimes includes Hong Kong and Taiwan, although these are often treated under international law as part of China, rather than as separate countries.) The economic growth of these east Asian tigers has been phenomenal, typically averaging 5.5% real per capita growth for several decades. In the 1980s, the economy of China began growing rapidly, often at annual rates of 8–10% per year. In the 1990s, the economy of India began growing rapidly, first at rates of about 5% per year, but then increasing in the first decade of the 2000s.

It's worth pausing a moment to marvel at these growth rates. If per capita GDP grows at, say, 6% per year, then applying the formula for compound growth rates—that is $(1 + .06)^{30}$—a nation's level of per capita GDP will rise by a multiple of almost 6 over 30 years. In a technological leader, chugging along with per capita growth rates of about 2% per year, multiplying per capita GDP by a factor of five would take about 80 years. But in these fast-growing, the average standard of living in these countries rose by a factor of five in a time period less than an adult's working life—for instance, as a person ages from 25 to 55.

The underlying causes of these rapid growth rates are fairly clear. China and the east Asian tigers, in particular, have been among the highest savers in the world, often saving one-third or more of GDP, as compared to the roughly 20% of GDP which would be a more typical saving rate in Latin America and Africa. These countries invested heavily in human capital, first building up primary-level education and then expanding secondary-level education, with a particular focus on encouraging the math and science skills that are useful in engineering and business. They made a concerted effort to seek out applicable technology, both by sending students and government commissions abroad to look at the most efficient industrial operations elsewhere and by opening up to foreign companies that wished to build plants in their countries. China and India in particular also allowed greater far freedom for market forces, both within their own domestic economies and also in encouraging their firms to participate in world markets. This combination of technology, human capital, and physical capital, combined with the incentives of a market-oriented economic context, proved an extremely powerful stimulant to growth.

Some of the economic policies of the governments of east Asia, China, India, and others fast-growing countries around the world have gone beyond providing a generally fertile climate for free markets and practiced more interventionist economic policies. Many of these converging countries have a legacy of government economic controls—for example, China, in India, and in the countries of eastern Europe that used to be part of the Soviet Union—that for political reasons can be dismantled only slowly over time. In many of these countries, the banking and financial sector is heavily regulated. The governments of these countries have also sometimes selected certain industries to receive low-interest loans or government subsidies. Such policies often raise the eyebrows of market-oriented economists, but economic policies should be evaluated on their actual effects, which can be positive or negative, not on the basis of the promises of their supporters or the theories of economists. The appropriate mixture between markets and government will not look the same for every country. But while government will play a different role across countries, all the converging economies have found that an increased dose of market-oriented incentives for firms and workers has been a critical ingredient in the recipe for faster growth.

Growth Policies for the Technologically Disconnected

Many of the technologically excluded areas of the world are in Africa, but pockets of disconnection are found in other areas as well: southern Mexico and certain tropical areas of central America and Brazil; interior portions of China far from the coastal

Exhibit 20-3   Transportation and Communications in 2008 (except where shown)

	Fixed Line and Mobile Subscriptions per 100 People	Internet Users per 100 People	Percentage of Roads That Are Paved
East Asia and the Pacific	75	19	34% (2000)
Eastern Europe and Central Asia	136	29	66% (1999)
Latin America and the Caribbean	99	29	24% (2000)
Middle East and North Africa	74	19	76% (2007)
South Asia	36	5	57% (2007)
Sub-Saharan Africa	35	7	12% (2000)
High income	153	69	87% (2007)

trading areas; some of the central Asian nations that used to be part of the Soviet Union, like Mongolia. The level of poverty and human deprivation in these areas can be heartrending. The only short answer to the question of what many people of these countries need is "almost everything." Thus, they need to invest in human capital, first by improving basic levels of education and health, and then building toward additional education and health services. They need banks and financial intermediaries to help mobilize domestic investment. They need economic and legal stability, along with market-oriented institutions, both to provide a fertile climate for domestic economic growth and to attract foreign investment. They need to find ways to participate in global trade and investment.

But even this vast agenda has something missing. After all, these countries are not just lagging behind, but they have shown little evidence of catching up, or even of being much connected to the rest of the world economy. Along with the general growth-oriented agenda, these countries need an improved infrastructure of communication and transportation, along with research into technology focused on their particular economic realities.

Connecting the economy of a region or country used to require transportation of goods: roads for wagons and trucks and ports for barges and ships. It still takes these kinds of transportation links, but in the modern economy, communications have become at least as important. If a company in Europe is thinking about relying on a supplier based in Africa, it must have the ability to communicate with that African firm to place orders, to check on delivery dates, to send engineering plans of what product is desired, to deal with billing, and all the other day-to-day issues of a modern firm. If communication isn't reliable, then the supplier is not viewed as reliable either—regardless of how hardworking the employees are or what high-quality goods or services they produce. In a growing number of industries, communications can provide a way of delivering the services themselves. For example, customer service calls can be answered and records updated from far-distant locations. Exhibit 20-3 compares the major regions of the world economy in some measures of transportation and communication: roads, telephones, and computers. Given that these disconnected areas have found it difficult or impossible to generate these sorts of investments for themselves, or to find foreign investors willing to put up the money, perhaps foreign aid will need to play in funding these sorts of projects.

A second main set of policies for the technologically disconnected is to recognize that these countries often face local technology issues. For example, in much of Africa, annual rainfall is low and the soil is composed of a particular type of rock ("Basement Complex") which is low in what agriculture specialists call "micronutrients." As a result, many of the high-yield plants and specific fertilizers developed for use in the United States or western Europe, or even for climates like India and Latin America, don't grow as well in Africa. Research and development focused on African agriculture might find ways for remarkable gains in output, but research applicable to U.S. and European farmers often won't do much for African farmers.

Another important technology area for these countries involves health and medical research. For example, approximately 500 million cases of malaria occur each year, resulting in one million or more deaths a year. Almost all of these deaths are in low-income tropical areas of the world. If a fraction of the pharmaceutical research currently devoted to finding ways to reduce hair loss or increase sexual performance for middle-aged men in high-income economies could be directed to anti-malarial drugs, the gain to global human welfare could be very large. One economy study found that countries with intensive malaria had rates of economic growth that averaged 1.3% per year less than comparable countries without intensive malaria and that a 10% reduction in malaria, all by itself, could increase a country's economic growth rate by 0.3%. If the poorest people in the world could spend less time sick and more time learning and working, their economies could benefit considerably.

Although all countries desire economic growth, the focus of their policies is somewhat different. High-income technology leaders must find ways to generate and apply new technologies. Converging economies must improve their educational systems and seek out their niches in the global economy. The technologically disconnected need a full economic growth agenda: investment in private and public physical capital, education, applying existing technology and finding new technologies that apply specifically to their situation.

Lower Unemployment

The causes of unemployment in high-income countries of the world can be categorized in two ways: either cyclical unemployment caused by the economy being in a recession, or the natural rate of unemployment caused by factors in labor markets like government regulations about conditions of hiring and starting businesses, which have discouraged employment.

Unemployment from a Recession

For unemployment caused by a recession, the Keynesian economic model points out that both monetary and fiscal policy tools are available. The monetary policy prescription for dealing with recession is straightforward: run an expansionary monetary policy to increase the quantity of money and loans, drive down interest rates, and increase aggregate demand. In a recession, there is usually relatively little danger of inflation taking off, and so even a central bank which has fighting inflation as its top priority can usually justify some reduction in interest rates in a recession. With regard to fiscal policy, the automatic stabilizers embodied in fiscal policy should be allowed to work, even if this means larger budget deficits in time of recession. There is less agreement over whether, in addition to automatic stabilizers, governments in a recession should try to adopt discretionary fiscal policy of additional tax cuts or spending increases. In the case of the Great Recession from 2007–2009, the case for this kind of extra-aggressive

The Debate over Foreign Aid

About $90 billion per year in foreign aid flows from the high-income countries of the world to the low-income ones. Relative to the size of their populations or economies, this is not a large amount for either donors or recipients. For low-income countries of the world, aid averages about 1.3% of their GDP, although the amount is larger in some countries and smaller in others. But even this relatively small amount has been highly controversial.

Supporters of additional foreign aid point to the extraordinary human suffering in the low- and middle-income countries of the world. They see opportunities all across Africa, Asia, and Latin America to set up health clinics and schools. The want to help with the task of building economic infrastructure: clean water, plumbing, electricity, and roads. Some also suggest helping start businesses to provide jobs and income in poor areas, by supporting all kinds of businesses from small farming and handcraft operations to factories that would make clothing or steel.

Opponents of increased aid don't quarrel with the goal of reducing human suffering, but they suggest that foreign aid has often proven a poor tool for advancing that goal. For example, what if a foreign aid donor gives money for a health program, and then the government of the recipient country cuts back its own spending on health care and instead spends that money on weapons used for attacking another country or persecuting a disfavored group in its own country? What if the aid donor tries to provide technology for helping farmers be more productive, but the government reacts to political pressure by urban food consumers by imposing price ceilings on farm products, so the farmers can't make a living anyway? Even worse, foreign aid has sometimes financed projects that turned out to be environmentally destructive and economically questionable, like dams across large rivers which required enormous forced resettlement of poor people, to produce electricity that the local economy couldn't use and most individuals couldn't afford.

Finally, if the government of a country creates a reasonably stable and market-oriented macroeconomic climate, then foreign investors will be likely to provide funds for many profitable activities. Conversely, if the government creates an unstable economic environment, foreign aid can't fix the problem. As a result, foreign aid is either redundant or ineffective.

Policymakers are now sadder and wiser about the limitations of foreign aid than they were a few decades ago. But wisdom need not mean cynicism. In targeted and specific cases, foreign aid can have a modest role to play in reducing the extreme levels of deprivation experienced by hundreds of millions of people around the world.

expansionary fiscal policy is stronger, but for a smaller recession, given the time lags of implementing fiscal policy, discretionary fiscal policy should be used with caution.

However, the aftermath of the 2007–2009 recession emphasizes that expansionary fiscal and monetary policy do not turn off a recession like flipping a switch turns off a lamp. Even after a recession is officially over, and positive growth has returned, it can takes some months—or even a couple of years—before private-sector firms believe fully that the economic climate is healthy enough so that they can expand their workforce.

The Natural Rate of Unemployment

Unemployment rates in the nations of Europe have typically been higher than in the United States. For example, in 2006 before the start of the 2007–2009 recession, the U.S. unemployment rate was 4.6%, compared with 9% in France, 10.4% in Germany, and 7.1% in Sweden. The pattern of generally higher unemployment rates in Europe, which dates back to the 1970s, is typically attributed to the fact that European economies have a higher natural rate of unemployment because they have passed a greater number of rules and restrictions that have discourage firms from hiring and unemployed workers from taking jobs.

Addressing the natural rate of unemployment is straightforward in theory, but difficult in practice. Government can play a useful role in providing unemployment and welfare payments, passing rules about where and when businesses can operate, assuring that the workplace is safe, and so on. But these well-intended laws can in some cases become so intrusive that businesses decide to place limits on their hiring. For example, a law that imposes large costs on a business that tries to fire or lay off workers will mean that businesses try to avoid hiring in the first place. Laws that require employers to offer generous benefits to workers, like health insurance, child care, and vacation time, will make it more expensive to hire workers. Laws that offer generous and lengthy unemployment benefits or family leave will reduce the incentives of workers to find new jobs.

In recent decades, the world champion in restrictive labor laws in the last few decades was probably India. The government of India has gone through a number of economic reforms in the last decade or so to ease these laws. But looking back to the late 1990s, India had about 50 major labor laws. They required that employers did everything from providing pensions and health insurance, which isn't all that unusual, to running health clinics and subsidizing lunchrooms, which is less common. There were rules that any employer with more than 100 employees must notify the government of any change in job content or employee status, and in some industries, employees must agree before any changes were made. If a firm had more than 25 workers, it had to fill all job vacancies from a state list. If a firm had more than 100 workers, it needed government permission before firing anyone. It was also forbidden for a firm in India to react to these laws by declaring bankruptcy. Public sector jobs in India offered not only lifetime employment, but sometimes even a guarantee of a job after death, since an employee's job could be inherited by a relative. Little wonder, when faced with this blizzard of laws, that only about 3% of India's "official" economy was officially in private firms of more than 10 employees, since small firms are not affected by these laws. The attempts to get around these restrictions create weird categories, like people who are "working nonemployees," and then in turn create more laws to deal with these categories. India has made some attempts to scale back on these laws, but in 2007, over 90% of the workers in India still worked in the "informal" sector. Given these kinds of laws, it is little wonder that firms in India are reluctant to hire anyone who might legally be treated as an official employee.

The challenge in addressing the natural rate of unemployment is to be both softhearted and hardheaded. Yes, workers deserve certain protections. But if those protections are implemented in a way that leads to a high natural rate of unemployment, then they need to be redesigned.

Undeveloped Labor Markets

The low-income and middle-income countries of this world face an employment issue that goes beyond unemployment as it is understood in the high-income economies of the world. A substantial number of workers in these economies provide many of their own needs by farming, fishing, or hunting. They barter and trade with others and may take a succession of short-term or one-day jobs, sometimes being paid with food or shelter, sometimes with money. They are not "unemployed" in the sense that term is used in the United States and Europe, but neither do they have an activity which utilizes their energies and talents appropriately, nor a regular wage-paying job.

The starting point of economic activity, as discussed back in Chapter 1, is the division of labor, in which workers specialize in certain tasks and trade the fruits of their labor with others. Workers who are not connected to a labor market are often unable to specialize very much. Because these workers are not "officially" employed, they are often not eligible for social benefits like unemployment insurance or old-age payments—if such payments are even available in their low-income economy. Helping these workers to become more connected to the labor market and the economy is an important policy goal. Indeed, recent research by development economists suggests that one of the key factors in raising people in low-income countries out of the worst kind of poverty is whether they can make a connection to a somewhat regular wage-paying job.

Policies for Lower Inflation

Here's a bold prediction of the sort that economists almost always live to regret making: among the high-income economies of the world, inflation isn't likely to be a severe problem in the foreseeable future. Yes, mild spurts of inflation may occur now and then. In the aftermath of the recession of 2007–2009, when governments around the world made aggressive use of expansionary fiscal and monetary policy, it's possible that inflation will eventually rise by a few percentage points for a few years. At some point in the future, aggregate demand may suddenly jump ahead of potential GDP, perhaps fueled by overoptimistic lending by banks or a surge of export sales or a wave of government spending when the economy is already near full employment. At some times, the short-term aggregate supply curve will shifts back to the left, creating inflationary pressures. One common cause is a sudden rise in input prices, perhaps from higher oil prices or because a nation's exchange rate suddenly weakens, driving up the price of all imported inputs to production at once.

But while inflationary pressures will sometimes arise in the short run, policymakers of the high-income economies appear to have learned some lessons about fighting inflation. First, whatever happens with aggregate supply and aggregate demand in the short run, monetary policy can be used to prevent inflation from becoming entrenched in the economy in the medium and long term. Second, there is no long-run gain to letting inflation become established. As the neoclassical model points out, in the long run the potential output of the economy and its growth rate, along with its natural rate of unemployment, are determined by the underlying economic factors like levels of investment in human capital, physical capital, and technology, and by the incentives provided in markets. In fact, allowing inflation to become lasting and persistent poses undesirable risks and trade-offs. When inflation is high, businesses and individuals need to spend time and effort worrying about protecting themselves against inflation, rather than seeking out better ways to serve customers.

In short, the high-income economies appear to have both a political consensus to hold inflation low and the economic tools to do so. To be sure, disputes will continue over whether the central bank should use contractionary monetary policy to raise interest rates if the inflation rate, is, say, 5% rather than 2% per year. But people who live in countries that have experienced hyperinflation at rates of 50% *per month* and more would laugh at the idea that inflation at rates of less than 5% a year is a devastating economic problem.

In a number of middle- and low-income economies around the world, inflation is far from a solved problem. In the early 2000s, Turkey experienced inflation of more than 50% per year for several years. Belarus had inflation of about 100% per year from 2000–2001. From 2008–2010, Venezuela and Myanmar had inflation rates of 20–30% per year. Indonesia, Iran, Nigeria, the Russian Federation, and Ukraine all had double-digit inflation for most of the years from 2000–2010. Zimbabwe had hyperinflation, with inflation rates that went from more than 100% per year in the mid-2000s to a rate of several million percent in 2008.

In these countries, the problem of very high inflation generally arises from undisciplined macroeconomic policy. For example, a government may run an expansionary policy of huge and sustained budget deficits, which shift aggregate demand to the right so that output is beyond the potential GDP level, leading to inflationary increases in the price level. In some countries, the central bank is viewed as a mechanism for making loans to politically favored firms, without much regard to the effect on aggregate demand. Such policies can clearly lead to a sustained inflation.

But even when a small economy runs sensible fiscal and monetary policies, it can be vulnerable to inflation. One set of risks comes from global economic factors. For example, imagine a small economy that relies heavily on a few exported products, like coffee or copper. If the price of these goods should rise sharply on world markets, it will cause a flood of buying power for the local economy. Or imagine a small economy which becomes this year's popular destination for tourism, or for foreign investment. An amount of aggregate demand which is relatively small by the standards of the American or European economy can be a relatively large increase in consumer and investment spending in a small middle- or low-income economy. Yet another set of inflationary risks for a converging economy follow from the patterns of growth in that economy. If the GDP is growing quite briskly, at an annual rate of 6%, 8%, or even 10% per year, if aggregate demand jumps out ahead of aggregate supply, it may do so in a fairly dramatic fashion—much more dramatic than if the economy was only growing at the technological leader rate of 2% or so per year.

No country benefits from extremely high levels of inflation. However, a number of countries have managed to sustain solid levels of economic growth for sustained periods of time with levels of inflation that would sound high by recent U.S. standards, like 10–30% per year. In such economies, most contracts, wage levels, and interest rates are either indexed to inflation, or take place using the currency of another country, like the U.S. dollar or Europe's euro, to sidestep the problem of inflation. It is clearly possible—and perhaps sometimes necessary—for a converging economy to live with a degree of uncertainty over inflation that would be politically unacceptable in the high-income economies.

Policies for a Sustainable Balance of Trade

In the 1950s and 1960s, and even into the 1970s, openness to global flows of goods, services, and financial capital was often viewed in a negative light by low- and middle-income countries of the world. These countries feared that foreign trade would mean both economic losses as their economy was "exploited" by high-income trading partners and a loss of domestic political control to powerful business interests and multinational corporations.

These negative feelings about international trade have evolved. After all, the great economic success stories of recent years like Japan, the east Asian tiger economies, and China, and India, all took advantage of opportunities to sell in global markets. The economies of Europe thrive with high levels of trade. In the North American Free Trade Agreement, the United States, Canada, and Mexico pledged themselves to reduce trade barriers. Many countries have clearly learned that reducing barriers to trade is at least *potentially* beneficial to their economy. Indeed, many smaller economies of the world have learned an even tougher lesson: if they don't participate actively in world trade, they are unlikely to join the success stories among the converging economies. There are no examples in world history of small economies that remained apart from the global economy but still attained a high standard of living.

But although almost every country now claims that its goal is to participate in global trade, the possible negative consequences of trade have remained highly controversial in recent years. It is useful to divide up these possible negative consequences into issues involving trade of goods and services and issues involving flows of international capital. These issues are related, but not the same. An economy may have a high level of trade in goods and services relative to GDP, but if exports and imports are balanced, the net flow of foreign investment in and out of the economy will be zero. Conversely, an economy may have only a moderate level of trade relative to GDP, but find that it has a substantial current account trade imbalance. Thus, it is useful to consider the concerns over international trade of goods and services and international flows of financial capital separately.

Concerns over International Trade in Goods and Services

There is a long list of worries about foreign trade in goods and services: fear of job loss, environmental dangers, unfair labor practices, and many other concerns. These arguments were discussed at some length in Chapter 6, and there's no need to review the details here. But in this final chapter, it's useful to remember the overall response of many economists to these issues about free trade in goods and services. There's an old saying: "Don't throw out the baby with the bathwater." In other words, when you're discarding stuff you don't want, be careful not to throw out something precious, too. Sure, international trade raises many public policy issues—in fact, many of the issues raised by the competitive forces of international trade are the same issues raised by competitive market forces in the domestic economy as well, as one state or region or company within a national economy competes against others. Fortunately, in every policy concern involving trade, there are policy steps to take that don't involve substantial restrictions on trade.

Of all of the arguments for limitations on trade, perhaps the most controversial one among economists is the infant industry argument; that is, subsidizing or protecting new industries for a time until they become established. Such policies have been used with some success at certain points in time, but in the world as a whole, support for key industries is far more often directed at long-established industries with substantial political power that are suffering losses and laying off workers, rather than potentially vibrant new industries that have yet to be established. If government is going to favor certain industries, it needs to do so in a way that is temporary and that orients them toward a future of market competition, rather than a future of unending government subsidies and trade protection.

Concerns over International Flows of Capital

The expected pattern of trade imbalances in the world economy is that high-income economies will run trade surpluses, which means they will experience an net outflow of capital to foreign destinations, while low- and middle-income economies will run trade deficits, which means that they will experience a net inflow of foreign capital. This pattern of international investing can benefit all sides. Investors in the high-income countries benefit because they can receive high returns on their investments, and also because they can diversify their investments so that they are at less risk of a downturn in their own domestic economy. The low-income economies that receive an inflow of capital presumably have potential for rapid catch-up economic growth, and they can use the inflow of international financial capital to help spur their physical capital investment. In addition, inflows of financial capital often come with management, technological expertise, and training.

How Much Economic Growth Is Enough?

In 1930, with the world economy slipping down into the Depression, the great economist John Maynard Keynes wrote a famous essay called "Economic Possibilities for Our Grandchildren," in which he fearlessly prophesied that with sustained economic growth, the "economic problem" of humanity would be solved in about 100 years, because people will have pretty much all the goods and services that they want. Keynes wrote:

> If capital increases, say, 2 percent per annum, the capital equipment of the world will have increased by a half in 20 years, and seven and a half times in 100 years. Think of this in terms of material things—houses, transport, and the like. . . . I would predict that the standard of life in progressive countries one hundred years hence will be between four to eight times as high as it is to-day. There would be nothing surprising about this even in the light of our present

knowledge. It would not be foolish to contemplate the possibility of a far greater progress still. . . . I draw the conclusion that, assuming no important wars and no important increase in population, the *economic problem* may be solved, or be at least within sight of solution, within a hundred years. . . . Thus for the first time since his creation man will be faced with his real, his permanent problem—how to use his freedom from pressing economic cares, how to occupy the leisure, which science and compound interest will have won for him, to live wisely and agreeably and well.

Keynes's prediction of economic growth rates of about 2% per year has (roughly) come true. Do you agree with his conclusion that by 2030, the economic problem will have been overcome, at least in certain parts of the world? Or will people's expectations and demands continue to rise over time?

But for the last couple of decades, this cheerful scenario faces two dark clouds. The first cloud is the very large current account deficits in the U.S. economy. Instead of offering net financial investment abroad, the U.S. economy is soaking up financial investment from all over the world. These substantial U.S. trade deficits cannot grow forever. The question is whether they will be reduced gradually or with a bang. In the gradual scenario, U.S. exports could grow more rapidly than imports over a period of years, aided by a depreciation of the U.S. dollar. But the U.S. trade deficit could also be reduced with a bang. Here's one scenario: if foreign investors became less willing to hold U.S. dollar assets, the dollar exchange rate could weaken. As speculators see this process happening, they might rush to unload their dollar assets, which would drive the dollar down still further. A lower U.S. dollar would stimulate aggregate demand by making exports cheaper and imports more expensive. It would mean higher prices for imported inputs throughout the economy, shifting the short-term aggregate supply curve to the left. The result could be a burst of inflation, and if the Federal Reserve were to run a tight monetary policy to reduce the inflation, it could also lead to recession. People sometimes talk as if the U.S. economy, with its great size, is invulnerable to this sort of pressure from international markets. But while it's tough to rock the $14 trillion U.S. economy, it's not impossible.

The second major issue is how the smaller economies of the world should deal with the possibility of sudden inflows and outflows of foreign financial capital. Perhaps the most vivid recent example of the potentially destructive forces of international capital movements occurred in the economies of the East Asian tigers in 1997–98. Thanks to their excellent growth performance over the last few decades, these economies had attracted considerable interest from foreign investors. But in the mid-1990s, foreign investment into these countries surged even further. Much of this money was funneled through banks which borrowed in U.S. dollars and loaned in their national currencies. Bank lending surged at rates of 20% per year or more. This inflow of foreign capital meant that investment in these economies exceeded the level of domestic savings, so that current account deficits in these countries jumped into the range of 5–10% of GDP.

But the surge in bank lending meant that many banks in these east Asian countries did not do an especially good job of screening out safe and unsafe borrowers. Many of the loans—as high as 10–15% of all loans in some of these countries—started to turn bad. Fearing losses, foreign investors started pulling their money out. As the foreign money left, the exchange rates of these countries crashed, often falling by 50% or more in a few months. The banks were stuck with a mismatch: even if the rest of their domestic loans were repaid, they could never pay back the U.S. dollars that they owed. The banking sector as a whole went bankrupt. The lack of credit and lending in the economy collapsed aggregate demand, bringing on a deep recession.

If the flow and ebb of international capital markets can flip even the economies of the East Asian tigers, with their stellar growth records, into a recession, then it is no wonder that other middle- and low-income countries around the world are concerned. Moreover, similar episodes of an inflow and then an outflow of foreign financial capital have rocked a number of economies around the world: for example, in the last few years economies like Ireland, Iceland and Greece have all experienced severe shocks when foreign lenders decided to stop extending funds. Thus, many nations are taking steps to reduce the risk that their economy will be injured if foreign financial capital takes flight, including having their central banks hold large reserves of foreign exchange and stepping up their regulation of domestic banks to avoid a wave of imprudent lending. The most controversial steps in this area involve countries should try to take steps to control or reduce the flows of foreign capital. If a country could discourage some of the inflow of speculative short-term capital, and instead only encourage investment capital that was committed for the medium term and the long term, then it could be at least somewhat less susceptible to swings in the sentiments of global investors.

If economies participate in the global trade of goods and services, they will also need to participate in international flows of financial payments and investments. These linkages can offer great benefits to an economy. But any nation that is experiencing a substantial and sustained pattern of trade deficits, along with the corresponding net inflow of international financial capital, has some reason for concern.

Final Thoughts on Economics and Market Institutions

The standard of living has increased dramatically for billions of people around the world in the last half century. Such increases have occurred not only in the technological leaders like the United States, Canada, the nations of Europe and Japan, but also in the east Asian tigers and in many nations of Latin America and eastern Europe.

In more recent years, some of the world's strongest growth rates have occurred where they are most needed, among some of the poorest people in the world. China has a population of 1.3 billion; India has a population of 1.1 billion. Together, these two countries have more than one-third of the world's population. Many of their citizens have been among the poorest people in the world. Starting in the late 1970s, although China remained officially a government-controlled command economy, the government began to allow a greater degree of economic freedom. For example, once Chinese farmers had grown the amount that they were required to grow under law, they were allowed to sell any extra they could produce at the market price. A variety of small manufacturing plants, many owned by townships and villages, were allowed to start.

These modest steps toward a more market-oriented economy triggered an extraordinary wave of economic growth.

India took a different path. For some decades after its independence in 1948, India's GDP seemed to grow in a solid but unexciting way, at about 3% per year. By the late 1980s, however, this rate of growth began to look less acceptable. Since it was very similar to the growth rates of high-income countries like the United States and Western Europe, India's 3% rate of growth was not helping its economy to catch up. Moreover, the experience of China, along with nations in East Asia like South Korea and Thailand, seemed to demonstrate a potential for considerably faster rates of growth. India had long had a heavily regulated economy, with detailed rules and regulations about hiring, starting businesses, selling, and every other detail of a market transaction. In the early 1990s, India began to eliminate and relax some of these rules and to allow additional freedom in the market. These moderate steps that have been taken encouraged India's GDP to increase by 5–8% per year since the early 1990s.

The average person in China and India remains poor, but the growth has been remarkable. In 1980, China had a per capital GDP of about $500 and India had a per capita GDP around $900. By 2010, China's per capita GDP exceeded $6,000 and India's exceeded $3,000. In both countries, market-oriented economic reforms have brought economic gains to hundreds of millions of the poorest people in the world.

Other than the issue of economic growth, the other three main goals of macroeconomic policy—that is, low unemployment, low inflation, and a sustainable balance of trade—all involve situations in which, for some reason, the economy fails to coordinate the forces of supply and demand. In the case of cyclical unemployment, for example, aggregate demand falls behind aggregate supply. In the case of the natural rate of unemployment, government regulations create a situation where otherwise-willing employers become unwilling to hire otherwise-willing workers. Inflation is a situation in which aggregate demand outstrips aggregate supply, at least for a time, so that too much buying power is chasing too few goods. A trade imbalance is a situation where, because of a net inflow or outflow of foreign capital, domestic savings are not aligned with domestic investment. Each of these situations can create a range of easier or harder policy choices. But none of these macroeconomic problems are unanswerable or insoluble.

The importance of market economies and market institutions does not mean a one-size-fits-all economic policy. Economies come in a wide range of flavors. A U.S.-style market economy gives a comparatively free rein to business, with a relatively small government sector. A western European-style market economy has more rules and regulations for business, a larger government sector, a stronger labor union movement, and more efforts by government to impose higher taxes on the wealthy and offer higher benefits to the unemployed and poor. Countries like Canada and Australia fall in between the U.S. and European models. Japan is a market-oriented economy with a relatively small government as measured by the size of GDP taken in taxes, but a relatively dense network of business and social connections that can limit the incentives for economic change. In some countries, fiscal policy involves more than half of GDP; in the United States and Japan, government taxes and spending are more like one-third of GDP. Some countries have a central bank that focuses on inflation; others on a mix of inflation and unemployment; still others on exchange rates.

Reasonable people can differ in the flavor of economic policy that they prefer. Economic wisdom is not limited to Republicans or Democrats in the United States, nor to business or union leaders, nor to the policies that are popular in Sweden or the United Kingdom or Japan. But among the high-income countries of the world, these differences of opinion all begin by agreeing that market forces will play a primary role in economic production, and the economic policy discussion that follows is about the appropriate set of laws and institutions to accompany the market.

Economists are sometimes accused of being joyless creatures who see every glass as half empty, every choice as nothing but a trade-off. Economists are certainly no friends of public policy schemes that focus only on good intentions, while ignoring trade-offs and incentives. But from a different perspective, economists may be among the greatest optimists of all. Economists believe that it is possible for the division of labor, operating through the interconnected web of market transactions, to raise the standard of living for everyone in the world. Economists have a shared vision that as people come together in a market-oriented economy, acting as consumers, workers, managers, savers and investors, they have the possibility to make everyone who participates better off than they could otherwise be on their own. To be sure, a market-oriented economy must be watched with a wary eye. Economic growth doesn't just happen. Macroeconomic flows can become imbalanced, resulting in unemployment, inflation and trade imbalances. But even with these issues noted, the coordinating power of the economy should also be watched with a marveling eye. The economy allows people acting as individuals to pool together their skills and desires in a decentralized way that is far beyond the planning or organizational capacity of any government or company or supercomputer, to create a vast system of social interaction that holds forth a great promise of improving the human condition.

Key Concepts and Summary

1. There are wide differences in standards of living in regions around the world, whether one measures by economic measures like per capita GDP or by education and health statistics.

2. The fundamentals of growth are the same in every country: that is, improvements in human capital, physical capital, and technology interacting in the context of a market-oriented economy. But countries that are high-income technology leaders will tend to focus more on developing and using new technology. Countries that are converging economies will focus more on increasing human capital and becoming more interconnected to the technology and markets in the global economy. Low-income, technologically disconnected countries have many needs, but they also face the challenge of becoming reliably connected to the rest of the global economy and finding the technologies that work best for them.

3. Cyclical unemployment can be addressed by expansionary fiscal and monetary policy. The natural rate of unemployment can be harder to deal with, because it involves thinking carefully about the trade-offs involved in laws that affect employment and hiring.

4. Most high-income economies have learned that their central banks can control inflation in the medium- and the long-term. In addition, they have learned that inflation has no long-term benefits but potentially substantial long-term costs if it distracts businesses from focusing on real productivity gains. However, smaller economies around the world may face more volatile inflation because their smaller economies can be unsettled by international movements of capital and goods.

5. There are many legitimate concerns over possible negative consequences of free trade. Perhaps the single strongest response to these concerns is that there are good ways to address the concerns without restricting trade and thus losing its benefits.

6. There are two major issues involving trade imbalances. One is what will happen with the large U.S. trade deficits, and whether they will come down gradually or with a rush. The other is whether smaller countries around the world should take some steps to limit flows of international capital, in the hope that they will not be quite so susceptible to economic whiplash from international financial capital flowing in and out of their economies.

Review Questions

1. What are some of the ways of comparing the standard of living in countries around the world?

2. What's the difference between a country that is a technology leader, a country that is a converging economy, and a country that is technologically disconnected?

3. What are the different policy tools for dealing with cyclical unemployment or the natural rate of unemployment?

4. In low-income countries, does it make sense to argue that most of the people without long-term jobs that pay regular wages are unemployed?

5. Is inflation likely to be a severe problem for at least some high-income economies in the near future?

6. Is inflation likely to be a problem for at least some low- and middle-income economies in the near future?

7. What are the major issues with regard to trade imbalances for the U.S. economy? For low- and middle-income countries?

Interpreting Graphs

Numerical data can be presented in two ways: digital or analogue. Digital presentation uses numbers. For example, a digital clock might report the time as 3:46:11 P.M.—that is, as 46 minutes and 11 seconds after three o'clock in the afternoon. An analogue presentation uses a physical image to convey the information. An analogue clock, with an hour hand, a minute hand, and a second hand, would report the time of 3:46:11 P.M. by showing the hour hand a little before the four on the clock face, the minute hand just past the nine, and the second hand just past the two. Which presentation is best, digital or analogue? It depends on the purpose. If you are timing a runner who is training for a five-mile cross-country race, then a digital clock that clearly displays seconds is most useful. If you are on your way to 4:00 doctor's appointment and you want to know if you will make it on time, a glance at an analogue clock tells you everything you need to know.

Graphs are an analogue method of presenting numerical patterns. They condense detailed numerical information into a visual form in which relationships and numerical patterns can be perceived more easily. For example, which countries have larger or smaller populations? A careful reader could examine a long list of numbers representing the populations of many countries, but with over 200 nations in the world, searching through such a list would take concentration and time. Putting these same numbers on a graph can quickly reveal population patterns. Economists use graphs both for a compact and readable presentation of groups of numbers and for building an intuitive grasp of relationships and connections.

This appendix discusses the three graphs used in this book: pie *graphs, bar graphs, and line graphs.* It also provides warnings about how graphs can be manipulated to alter viewers' perceptions of the relationships in the data.

Pie Graphs

Pie graphs (sometimes called pie charts) are used to show how an overall total is divided into parts. A circle represents a group as a whole. The slices of this circular "pie" show the relative sizes of subgroups.

Exhibit 1-A1 shows how the U.S. population is divided among children, working-age adults, and the elderly in 1970, 2000, and projected for 2030. The information is first conveyed with numbers in a table, and then in three pie charts. The first column of the table shows the total U.S. population for each of the three years. Columns 2–4 categorize the total in terms of age groups—from birth to 18 years, from 19 to 64 years, and 65 years and above. In columns 2–4, the top number shows the actual number of people in each age category, while the percentage underneath, in parentheses, shows the percentage of the total population comprised by that age group.

In a pie graph, each slice of the pie represents a share of the total, or a percentage. For example, 50% would be half of the pie and 20% would be one-fifth of the pie. The three pie graphs in Exhibit 1-A1 show that the share of the U.S. population 65 and over is growing. The pie graphs allow you to get a feel for the relative size of the different age groups from 1970 to 2000 to 2030, without requiring you to slog through the specific

Year	Total Population	Divided into Age Groups		
		19 and Under	*20–64 years*	*Over 65*
1970	205.0	77.2 (37.6%)	107.7 (52.5%)	20.1 (9.8%)
2000	275.4	78.4 (28.5%)	162.2 (58.9%)	34.8 (12.6%)
2030	351.1	92.6 (26.4%)	188.2 (53.6%)	70.3 (20.0%)

20.1 Million (9.8%)
77.2 Million (37.6%)
107.7 Million (52.5%)
(a) U.S. Age distribution in 1970

34.8 Million (12.6%)
78.4 Million (28.5%)
162.2 Million (58.9%)
(b) U.S. age distribution in 2000

70.3 Million (20%)
92.6 Million (26.4%)
188.2 Million (53.6%)
(c) U.S. age distribution in 2030

■ 19 and under
■ 20–64 years
■ Over 65

Exhibit 1-A1   Pie Graphs of the U.S. Age Distribution (numbers in millions)

The first column shows the total U.S. population in 1970, 2000, and projected for 2030. The next three columns divide up that total into three age groups. The three pie graphs illustrate the division of total population into these three age groups for the three years.

numbers and percentages in the table. Some common examples of how pie graphs are used include dividing the population into groups by age, income level, ethnicity, religion, occupation; dividing different firms into categories by size, industry, number of employees; and dividing up government spending or taxes into its main categories.

Bar Graphs

A *bar graph* uses the height of different bars to compare quantities. Exhibit 1-A2 provides a bar graph of the 12 most populous countries in the world. The height of the bars corresponds to the population of each country. In 2009, the world population was about 6.4 billion (that is, 6,400 million) people. Although it is widely known that China and India are the most populous countries in the world, seeing how the bars on the graph tower over the other countries helps illustrate the magnitude of the difference between the sizes of national populations.

Bar graphs can be subdivided in a way that reveals information similar to pie charts. Exhibit 1-A3 offers three bar graphs based on the information from Exhibit 1-A1 about the U.S. age distribution in 1970, 2000, and 2030. Exhibit 1-A3*a* shows three bars for each year, representing the total number of persons in each age bracket for each year. Exhibit 1-A3*b* shows just one bar for each year, but the different age groups are now shaded inside the bar. In Exhibit 1-A3*c*, still based on the same data, the vertical axis measures percentages rather than the number of persons. In this case, all three bar graphs are the same height, representing 100% of the population, with each bar divided according to the percentage of population in each age group. It is sometimes easier for the eyes of the reader to run across several bar graphs, comparing the shaded areas, rather than trying to compare several pie graphs.

Exhibit 1-A2   Leading Countries of the World by Population, 2009 (in millions)

The table shows the 12 countries of the world with the largest population. The height of the bars in the bar graph shows the size of the population for each country.

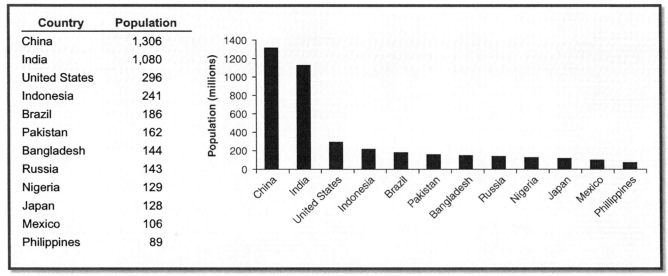

Country	Population
China	1,306
India	1,080
United States	296
Indonesia	241
Brazil	186
Pakistan	162
Bangladesh	144
Russia	143
Nigeria	129
Japan	128
Mexico	106
Philippines	89

Exhibit 1-A3   U.S. Population with Bar Graphs

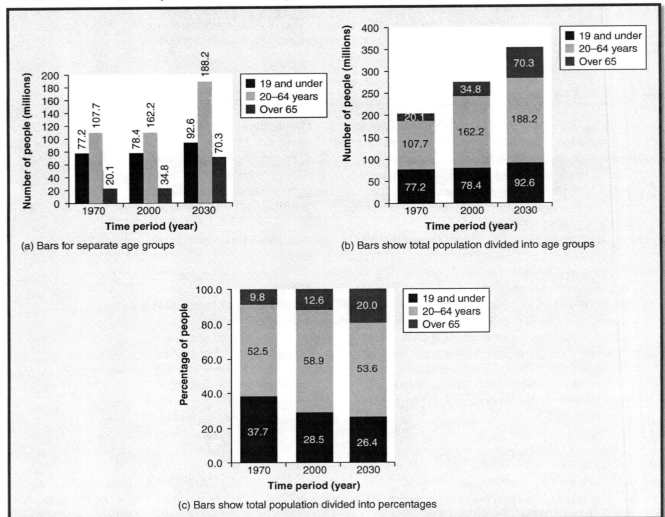

(a) Bars for separate age groups

(b) Bars show total population divided into age groups

(c) Bars show total population divided into percentages

Exhibits 1-A2 and 1-A3 show how the bars can represent countries or years, and how the vertical axis can represent a numerical or a percentage value. Bar graphs can also compare size, quantity, rates, distances, and other quantitative categories.

Line Graphs

To a mathematician or an economist, a "variable" is the name given to a quantity that may assume a range of values. Line graphs show a relationship between two variables: one measured on the horizontal axis and the other measured on the vertical axis.

Line Graphs with Two Variables

Exhibit 1-A4 shows the relationship between two variables: length and median weight for American baby boys and girls during the first three years of their life. (The "median" means that half of all babies weigh more than this and half weigh less.) The line graph measures length in inches on the horizontal axis and weight in pounds on the vertical axis. For example, point A on the figure shows that a boy who is 28 inches long will have a median weight of about 19 pounds. One line on the graph shows the length-weight relationship for boys and the other line shows the relationship for girls. This kind of graph is widely used by health care providers to check whether a child's physical development is roughly on track.

Exhibit 1-A5 presents another example of a line graph. In this case, the line graph shows how thin the air becomes when you climb a mountain. The horizontal axis of the figure shows altitude, measured in meters above sea level. The vertical axis measures the density of the air at each altitude. Air density is measured by the weight of the air in a cubic meter of space (that is, a box measuring one meter in height, width, and depth). As the graph shows, air pressure is heaviest at ground level and becomes lighter as you climb. Exhibit 1-A5 shows that a cubic meter of air at an altitude of 500 meters weighs approximately 1 kilogram (about 2.2 pounds). However, as the altitude increases, air density decreases. A cubic meter of air at the top of Mount Everest, at about 8,828 meters, would weigh only .023 kilograms. The thin air at high altitudes explains why many mountain climbers need to breathe oxygen from tanks as they reach the top of a mountain.

The length-weight relationship and the altitude-air density relationships in these two exhibits represent averages. If you were to collect actual data on air pressure at different altitudes, the same altitude in different geographic locations will have slightly different air density, depending on factors like how far you are from the equator, the local weather conditions, and the humidity in the air. Similarly, in measuring the height and weight of children for the previous line graph, children of a particular height would have a range of different weights, some above average and some below. In the real world, this sort of

Exhibit 1-A4   The Length-Weight Relationship for American Boys and Girls

The line graph shows the relationship between height and weight for boys and girls from birth to 36 months. Point A, for example, shows that a boy of 28 inches in height (measured on the horizontal axis) is typically 19 pounds in weight (measured on the vertical axis). These data apply only to children in the first three years of life.

Boys from Birth to 36 Months		Girls from Birth to 36 Months	
Height (inches)	Weight (pounds)	Height (inches)	Weight (pounds)
20.0	8.0	20.0	7.9
22.0	10.5	22.0	10.5
24.0	13.5	24.0	13.2
26.0	16.4	26.0	16.0
28.0	19.0	28.0	18.8
30.0	21.8	30.0	21.2
32.0	24.3	32.0	24.0
34.0	27.0	34.0	26.2
36.0	29.3	36.0	28.9
38.0	32.0	38.0	31.3

Exhibit 1-A5   Altitude-Air Density Relationship

This line graph shows the relationship between altitude, measured in meters above sea level, and air density, measured in kilograms of air per cubic meter. As altitude rises, air density declines. The point at the top of Mount Everest, shown in the diagram, has an altitude of approximately 8,828 meters above sea level (the horizontal axis) and air density of 0.23 kilograms per cubic meter (the vertical axis).

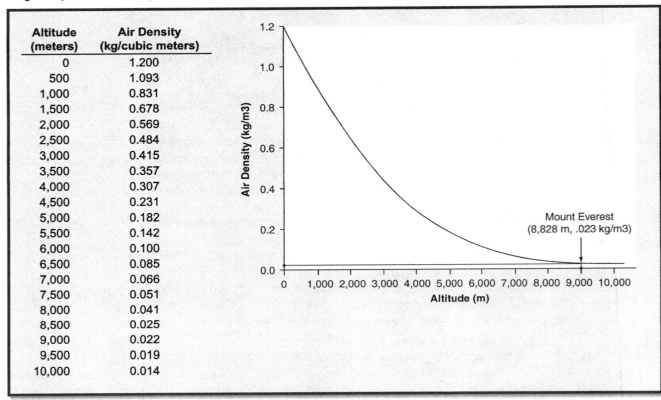

Altitude (meters)	Air Density (kg/cubic meters)
0	1.200
500	1.093
1,000	0.831
1,500	0.678
2,000	0.569
2,500	0.484
3,000	0.415
3,500	0.357
4,000	0.307
4,500	0.231
5,000	0.182
5,500	0.142
6,000	0.100
6,500	0.085
7,000	0.066
7,500	0.051
8,000	0.041
8,500	0.025
9,000	0.022
9,500	0.019
10,000	0.014

variation in data is common. The task of a researcher is to organize that data in a way that helps to understand typical patterns. The study of statistics, especially when combined with computer statistics and spreadsheet programs, is a great help in organizing this kind of data, plotting line graphs, and looking for typical underlying relationships. For most economics and social science majors, a statistics course will be required at some point.

Time Series

One common line graph is called a **time series**, in which the horizontal axis shows time and the vertical axis displays another variable. Thus, a time series graph shows how a variable changes over time. Exhibit 1-A6 shows the unemployment rate in the United States since 1975, where unemployment is defined as the percentage of adults who want jobs and are looking for a job, but cannot find one. The points for the unemployment rate in each year are plotted on the graph, and a line then connects the points, showing how the unemployment rate has moved up and down since 1975. The line graph makes it easy to see, for example, that the highest unemployment rate during this time period was slightly less than 10% in the early 1980s, while the unemployment rate declined from the early 1990s to the end of the 1990s, before rising and then falling back in the early 2000s, and then rising sharply during the recession from 2007-2009.

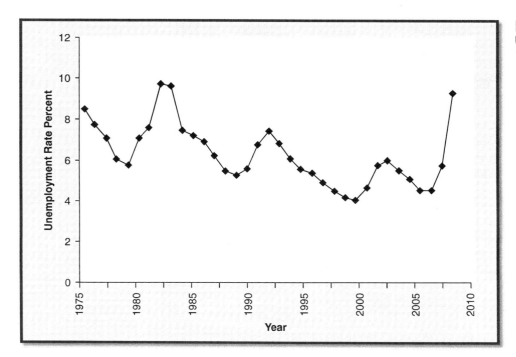

Exhibit 1-A6   U.S. Unemployment Rate, 1975–2009

Slope

In discussing the shape of line graphs, the concept of slope is often helpful. Slope is defined as "rise over run." More specifically, if y is the variable on the vertical axis, x is the variable on the horizontal axis, and the Greek letter delta Δ means "the change in," then the definitions of slope is:

$$\text{Slope} = \frac{\Delta y \ (\text{rise})}{\Delta x \ (\text{run})}$$

A *positive slope* means that as a line on the line graph moves from left to right, the line rises. The length-weight relationship in Exhibit 1-A4 has a positive slope. A negative slope means that as the line on the line graph moves from left to right, the line falls. The altitude-air density relationship in Exhibit 1-A5 has a *negative slope*. A slope of zero means that the line is flat; that is, zero rise over the run. Exhibit 1-A6 of the unemployment rate illustrates a common pattern of many line graphs: some segments where the slope is positive, other segments where the slope is negative, and still other segments where the slope is close to zero.

The slope of a straight line between two points can be calculated in numerical terms. To calculate slope, begin by designating one point as the "starting point" and the other point as the "end point" and then calculating the rise over run between these two points. As an example, consider the slope of the air density graph between the points representing an altitude of 4,000 meters and an altitude of 6,000 meters:

Rise: Change in variable on vertical axis (end point minus original point)
$$= .100 - .307 = -.207$$

Run: Change in variable on horizontal axis (end point minus original point)
$$= 6,000 - 4,000 = 2,000$$

Thus, the slope of a straight line between these two points would be that from the altitude of 4,000 meters up to 6,000 meters, the density of the air decreases by approximately .1 kilograms/cubic meter for each of the next 1,000 meters.

Many graphs of data are not perfectly straight lines, at least not in all places, so that trying to draw a single straight line will not accurately capture the relationship between the two variables. For example, the true relationship between altitude and air density in Exhibit 1-A5 is a curve, not a straight line. However, you can draw a close approximation of a curved line by using a series of many short straight lines with different slopes. Thus, it is common to calculate the slope of a part of a curved line by choosing a starting point and an ending point that are quite close together, in which case the slope of the straight line between those two close points will offer a good approximation of the slope of the curved line between those two points. A straight line will have the same slope, regardless of what starting point and end point you choose; in contrast, a curved line will have different slopes depending on what starting point and end point you choose.

A higher positive slope means a steeper upward tilt to the line, while a smaller positive slope means a flatter upward tilt to the line. A negative slope that is larger in absolute value (that is, more negative) means a steeper downward tilt to the line. A slope of zero is a horizontal flat line. A vertical line has an infinite slope.

Slope of Straight Lines in Algebraic Terms

Straight lines can also be expressed as an algebraic formula, and when they are, the slope is easily visible in the formula. The algebraic equation for a straight line is

$$y = a + bx$$

where x and y are the variables, with x on the horizontal axis and y on the vertical axis, and a and b representing factors that determine the shape of the line. To see how this equation works, consider a numerical example:

$$y = 9 + 3x$$

In this equation for a specific line, the a term has been set equal to 9 and the b term has been set equal to 3. Exhibit 1-A7 shows this equation with a table and a graph. To

x	y
0	9
1	12
2	15
3	18
4	21
5	24
6	27

Exhibit 1-A7 Slope and the Algebra of Straight Lines

This line graph has x on the horizontal axis and y on the vertical axis. The y-intercept—that is, the point where the line intersects the y-axis—is 9. The slope of the line is 3; that is, there is a rise of 3 on the vertical axis for every increase of 1 on the horizontal axis. The slope is the same all along a straight line.

construct the table, just plug in a series of different values for *x*, and then calculate what value of *y* results. In the figure, these points are plotted and a line is drawn through them.

This example illustrates how the *a* and *b* terms in an equation for a straight line determine the shape of the line. The *a* term is called the *y-intercept*. The reason for this name is that if *x* = 0, then the *a* term will reveal where the line intercepts, or crosses, the vertical or *y*-axis. In this example, the line hits the vertical axis at 9. The *b* term in the equation for the line is the slope. Remember that slope is defined as rise over run; more specifically, the change in the vertical axis divided by the change in the horizontal axis. In this example, each time the *x* term increases by 1 (the run), the *y* term rises by 3. Thus, the slope of this line is 3. Specifying a y-intercept and a slope—that is, specifying *a* and *b* in the equation for a line—will identify a specific line. Although it is rare for real-world data points to arrange themselves as an exact straight line, it often turns out that a straight line can offer a reasonable approximation of actual data.

Comparing Line Graphs with Pie Charts and Bar Graphs

Now that you are familiar with pie graphs, bar graphs, and line graphs, how do you know which graph to use for your data? Pie graphs are often better than line graphs at showing how an overall group is divided. However, if a pie graph has too many slices, it can become difficult to interpret.

Bar graphs are especially useful when comparing quantities. For example, if you are studying the populations of different countries, as in Exhibit 1-A2, bar graphs can show the relationships between the population sizes of multiple countries. Not only can it show these relationships, but it can also show breakdowns of different groups within the population.

A line graph is often the most effective format for illustrating a relationship between two variables that are both changing. For example, time series graphs can show patterns as time changes, like the unemployment rate over time. Line graphs are widely used in economics to present continuous data about prices, wages, quantities bought and sold, the size of the economy, and other economic variables.

How Graphs Can Be Misleading

Graphs not only reveal patterns; they can also alter how patterns are perceived. To see some of the ways this can be done, consider the line graphs of Exhibit 1-A8. These graphs all illustrate the unemployment rate—but from different perspectives.

Imagine that you wanted a graph which gives an impression that the rise in unemployment in 2009 wasn't all that large, or all that extraordinary by historical standards. You might choose to present your data as in Exhibit 1-A8*a*. Exhibit 1-A8*a* shows the exact data presented earlier in Exhibit 1-A6, but stretches the horizontal axis out longer relative to the vertical axis. By spreading the graph wide and flat, the visual appearance is that the rise in unemployment isn't so large, and similar to some past rises in unemployment. Now imagine you wanted to emphasize how unemployment spiked substantially higher in 2009. In this case, using the same data, you can stretch the vertical axis out relative to the horizontal axis, as in Exhibit 1-A8*b*, which makes all rises and falls in unemployment appear larger.

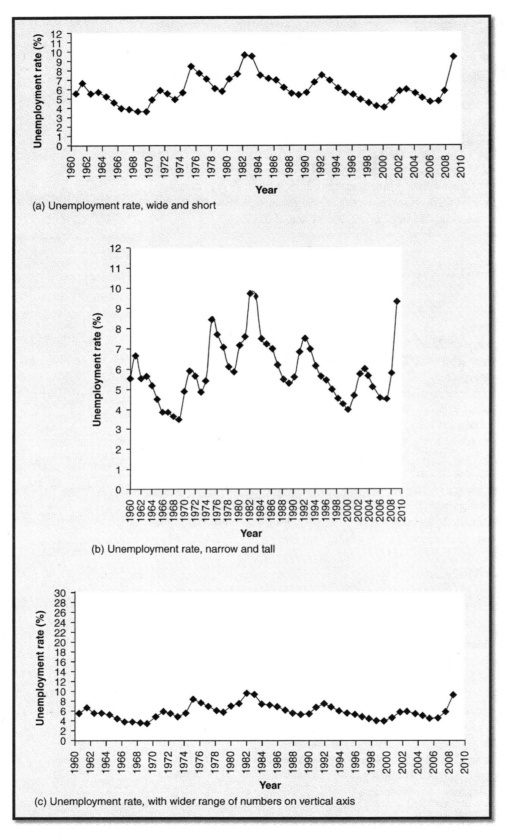

Exhibit 1-A8
Presenting Unemployment Rates in Different Ways, All of Them Accurate

(a) Unemployment rate, wide and short

(b) Unemployment rate, narrow and tall

(c) Unemployment rate, with wider range of numbers on vertical axis

Exhibit 1-A8   *Continued*

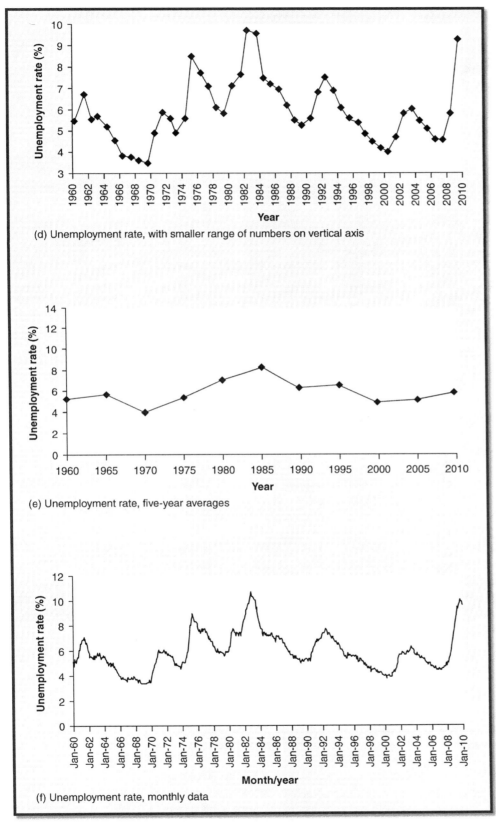

(d) Unemployment rate, with smaller range of numbers on vertical axis

(e) Unemployment rate, five-year averages

(f) Unemployment rate, monthly data

Exhibit 1-A8   *Continued*

(g) Unemployment rates, since 1975 only

A similar effect can be accomplished without changing the length of the axes, but by changing the scale on the vertical axis. In Exhibit 1-A8*c*, the scale on the vertical axis runs from 0% to 30%, while in Exhibit 1-A8*d*, the vertical axis runs from 3% to 10%. Compared to Exhibit 1-A6, where the vertical scale runs from 0% to 12%, Exhibit 1-A8*c* makes the fluctuation in unemployment look smaller while Exhibit 1-A8*d* makes it look larger.

Another way to alter the perception of the graph is to reduce the amount of variation by changing the number of points plotted on the graph. Exhibit 1-A8*e* shows the unemployment rate according to five-year averages. By averaging out some of the year-to-year changes the line appear smoother and with fewer highs and lows. In reality, the unemployment rate is reported monthly, and Exhibit 1-A8*f* shows the monthly figures since 1960, which fluctuate more than the five-year average. Exhibit 1-A8*f* is also a vivid illustration of how graphs can compress lots of data. The graph includes monthly data since 1960, which over almost 50 years works out to nearly 600 data points. Reading that list of 600 data points in numerical form would be hypnotic. But you can get a good intuitive sense of these 600 data points very quickly from the graph.

A final trick in manipulating the perception of graphical information is that, by choosing the starting and ending points carefully, you can influence the perception of whether the variable is rising or falling. The original data shows a general pattern with unemployment low in the 1960s, but spiking up in the mid-1970s, early 1980s, early 1990s, early 2000s, and late 2000s. But Exhibit 1-A8*g* shows a graph that goes back only to 1975, which gives an impression that unemployment was more-or-less gradually falling over time until the 2009 recession pushed it back up to its "original" level—which is a plausible interpretation if one starts at the high point around 1975.

These kinds of tricks—or shall we just call them "choices about presentation"?—are not limited to line graphs. In a pie chart with many small slices and one large slice, someone must decided what categories should be used to produce these slices in the first place, thus making some slices appear bigger than others. If you are making a bar graph, you can make the vertical axis either taller or shorter, which will tend to make variations in the height of the bars appear more or less.

Being able to read graphs is an essential skill, both in economics and in life. But a graph is just one perspective or point of view, shaped by choices such as those discussed in this section. Don't always believe the first quick impression from a graph. View with caution.

Summary and Key Concepts

1. Graphs allow you to illustrate data graphically. They can illustrate patterns, comparisons, trends, and apportionment by condensing the numerical data and providing an intuitive sense of relationships in the data.

2. A *pie graph* shows how something is allotted, such as a sum of money or a group of people. The size of each slice of the pie is drawn to represent the corresponding percentage of the whole.

3. A *bar graph* uses the height of bars to show a relationship, where each bar represents a certain entity, like a country or a group of people. The bars on a bar graph can also be divided into segments to show subgroups.

4. A *line graph* shows the relationship between two variables: one is shown on the horizontal axis and one on the vertical axis.

5. Slope means "rise over run." The slope of the line on a line graph can be positive (upward-sloping), negative (downward-sloping), zero (flat), or infinite (vertical). The slope of a line on a graph may vary: for example, it may be positive in some segments, zero in other segments, and negative in other segments.

6. The algebraic equation for a line is $y = a + bx$, where x is the variable on the horizontal axis and y is the variable on the vertical axis, the a term is the *y-intercept* and the b term is the slope. The slope of a line is the same at any point on the line.

7. Any graph is a single visual perspective on a subject. The impression it leaves will be based on many choices like what data or time frame is included, how data or groups are divided up, the relative size of vertical and horizontal axes, whether the scale used on a vertical starts at zero, and others. Thus, any graph should be regarded somewhat skeptically, remembering that the underlying relationship can be open to different interpretations.

Appendix Review Questions

1. Name three kinds of graphs and briefly state when is most appropriate to use each type of graph.

2. What do the slices of a pie chart represent?

3. Why is a bar chart the best way to illustrate comparisons?

4. What is slope on a line graph?

5. How does the appearance of positive slope differ from negative slope and from zero slope?

An Algebraic Approach to the Expenditure-Output Model

In the expenditure-output or Keynesian cross model, the equilibrium occurs where the aggregate expenditure line AE line crosses the 45-degree line. Given algebraic equations for two lines, the point where they cross can be readily calculated. Imagine an economy with the following characteristics.

$$Y = \text{Real GDP or national income}$$

$$T = \text{Taxes} = .3Y$$

$$C = \text{Consumption} = 140 + .9(Y - T)$$

$$I = \text{Investment} = 400$$

$$G = \text{Government spending} = 800$$

$$X = \text{Exports} = 600$$

$$M = \text{Imports} = .15Y$$

The aggregate expenditure function in this case is:

$$AE = C + I + G + X - M$$

$$AE = 140 + .9(Y - T) + 400 + 800 + 600 - .15Y$$

The equation for the 45° line is the set of points where GDP or national income on the horizontal axis is equal to aggregate expenditure on the vertical axis. Thus, the equation for the 45-degree line is:

$$AE = Y.$$

The next step is to solve these two equations for Y (or AE, since they will be equal to each other).

$$Y = AE \quad AE = 140 + .9(Y - T) + 400 + 800 + 600 - .15Y$$

Substituting Y from the first equation into the AE in the second equation, and inserting the term .3Y for the tax rate T, produces a equation with only one variable, Y. The next step is to work through the algebra and solve for Y.

$$Y = 140 + .9(Y - .3Y) + 400 + 800 + 600 - .15Y.$$

$$Y - .63Y + .15Y = 1,940$$

$$.52Y = 1,940$$

$$Y = 3,730$$

This algebraic framework is flexible and useful in predicting how economic events and policy actions will affect real GDP. Say, for example, that because of changes in the relative prices of domestic and foreign goods, the marginal propensity to import falls to .1 Or say that because of a surge of business confidence, investment rises to 500. Simply plug the new numbers into the algebra, and you should be able to confirm that in the first case, the equilibrium output rises to 4,127 and in the second case rises to 3,923. Here's the calculation, when the marginal propensity to import has changed to .1.

$$Y = AE = 140 + .9(Y - .3Y) + 400 + 800 + 600 - .1Y.$$

$$Y - .63Y + .1Y = 1940$$

$$.47Y = 1940$$

$$Y = 4127$$

For investment rising to 500

$$Y = AE = 140 + .9(Y - .3Y) + 500 + 800 + 600 - .15Y.$$

Solving for Y means working through the algebra:

$$Y - .63Y + .15Y = 2,040$$

$$.52Y = 2,040$$

$$Y = 3,923$$

Chapter 13 Appendix   An Algebraic Approach to the Expenditure-Output Model

437

For issues of policy, the key questions would be how to adjust government spending levels or tax rates so that the equilibrium level of output is the full employment level. In this case, let the economic parameters be:

$$Y = \text{National income}$$

$$T = \text{Taxes} = .3Y$$

$$C = \text{Consumption} = 200 + .9(Y - T)$$

$$I = \text{Investment} = 600$$

$$G = \text{Government spending} = 1,000$$

$$X = \text{Exports} = 600$$

$$Y = \text{Imports} = .1(Y - T)$$

The equilibrium for this economy is:

$$Y = AE = 200 + .9(Y - .3Y) + 600 + 1000 + 600 - .1(Y - .3Y)$$

$$Y - .63Y + .07Y = 2,400$$

$$.44Y = 2,400$$

$$Y = 5,454$$

Let's assume that the full employment level of output is 6,000. What level of government spending would be necessary to reach that level? To answer this question, plug in 6,000 as equal to Y, but leave G as a variable, and solve for G. Thus:

$$6,000 = 200 + .9(6,000 - .3(6,000)) + 600 + G + 600 - .1(6,000 - .3(6,000))$$

Solving this problem is just arithmetic: G = 1,240. In other words, increasing government spending by 240, from its original level of 1,000 to 1,240, would raise output to the full employment level of GDP.

Indeed, the question of how much to increase government spending so that equilibrium output will rise from 5,454 to 6,000 can be answered without working through the algebra, just by using the multiplier formula. The multiplier equation in this case is $1/(1 - .56) = 2.27$. Thus, to raise output by 546 would require an increase in government spending of $546/2.27 = 240$, which is the same as the answer derived from the algebraic calculation.

This algebraic framework is highly flexible. For example, taxes can be treated as a total set by political considerations (like government spending) and not dependent on national income. Imports might be based on before-tax income, not after-tax income. For certain purposes, it may be helpful to analyze the economy without exports and imports. A more complicated approach could divide up consumption, investment, government, exports and imports into smaller categories, or to build in some variability in the rates of taxes, savings, and imports. A wise economist will shape the model to fit the specific question under investigation.

Question

1. An economy has the following characteristics:

$$Y = \text{National income}$$

$$\text{Taxes} = T = .25Y$$

$$C = \text{Consumption} = 400 + .85(Y - T)$$

$$I = 300$$

$$G = 200$$

$$X = 500$$

$$M = .1(Y - T)$$

Find the equilibrium for this economy. If potential GDP is 3,500, then what change in government spending is needed to achieve this level? Do this problem two ways. First, plug 3,500 into the equations and solve for G. Second, calculate the multiplier and figure it out that way.

Answer

1. Set up the calculation:

$$AE = 400 + .85(Y - T) + 300 + 200 + 500 - .1(Y - T)$$

$$AE = Y$$

$$Y = 400 + .85(Y - .25Y) + 300 + 200 + 500 - .1(Y - .25Y)$$

$$Y = 1{,}400 + .6375Y - .075Y$$

$$.4375Y = 1{,}400$$

$$Y = 3{,}200$$

If full employment is 3,500, then one approach is to plug in 3,500 for Y throughout the equation, but to leave G as a separate variable.

$$Y = 400 + .85(Y - .25Y) + 300 + G + 500 + .1(Y - .25Y)$$

$$3500 = 400 + .85(3{,}500 - .25(3{,}500)) + 300 + G + 500 - .1(3{,}500 - .25(3{,}500))$$

$$3,500 - 400 - 2,231.25 - 300 - 500 + 262.5 = G$$

G = 331.25, which is an increase of 131.25 from its original level of 200

Alternatively, the multiplier is that out of every dollar spent, .25 goes to taxes, leaving .75, and out of after-tax income, .15 goes to savings and .1 to imports. Because (.75)(.15) = .1125 and (.75)(.1) = .075, this means that out of every dollar spent, 1 −.25 −.1125 −.075 = .5625.

Thus, using the formula, the multiplier is 1/(1 −.5625) = 2.2837.

To increase equilibrium GDP by 300, it will take a boost of 300/2.2837, which again works out to 131.25.

Glossary

absolute advantage: When one nation can produce a product at lower cost relative to another nation.

adaptive expectations: The theory that people look at past experience and gradually adapt their beliefs and behavior as circumstances change.

adjustable rate mortgage (ARM): A loan used to purchase a home in which the interest rate varies with the rate of inflation.

aggregate demand (AD): The relationship between the total quantity of goods and services and the price level for output.

aggregate production function: The process of an economy as a whole turning economic inputs like labor, machinery, and raw materials into outputs like goods and services used by consumers.

aggregate supply (AS): The relationship between the total quantity that firms choose to produce and sell and the price level for output, holding the price of inputs fixed.

allocative efficiency: When the mix of goods being produced represents the allocation that society most desires.

anti-dumping laws: Laws that block imports sold below the cost of production and impose tariffs that would increase the price of these imports to reflect their cost of production.

appreciating: When a currency is worth more in terms of other currencies; also called "strengthening."

asset-liability time mismatch: A bank's liabilities can be withdrawn in the short term while its assets are repaid in the long term.

assets: Items of value owned by a firm or an individual.

automatic stabilizers: Tax and spending rules that have the effect of increasing aggregate demand when the economy slows down and restraining aggregate demand when the economy speeds up, without any additional change in legislation.

balance of trade: The gap, if any, between a nation's exports and imports.

balance sheet: An accounting tool that lists assets and liabilities.

balanced budget: When government spending and taxes are equal.

bank run: When depositors race to the bank to withdraw their deposits for fear that otherwise they would be lost.

barter: Literally, trading one good or service for another, without using money.

basic quantity equation of money: Money supply × Velocity = Nominal GDP.

basket of goods and services: A hypothetical group of different items, with specified quantities of each one, used as a basis for calculating how the price level changes over time.

black market: An illegal market that breaks government rules on prices or sales.

bonds: A financial instrument through which corporations and governments borrow money from financial investors and promise to repay with interest.

budget constraint: A diagram which shows what choices are possible, given the prices.

budget deficit: When the federal government spends more than it collects in taxes in a given year.

business cycle: The relatively short-term movement of the economy in and out of recession.

capital deepening: When an economy has a higher average level of physical and/or human capital per person.

central bank: An institution to conduct monetary policy and regulate the banking system.

certificates of deposit (CD): Accounts that the depositor has committed to leaving in the bank for a certain period of time, in exchange for a higher rate of interest; also called time deposits.

ceteris paribus: Other things being equal.

circular flow diagram: A diagram that views the economy as consisting of households and firms that interact in a goods and services market, a labor market, and a financial capital market.

command economy: An economy in which government either makes or strongly influences how most economic decisions are made.

comparative advantage: The goods in which a nation has its greatest productivity advantage or its smallest productivity disadvantage; also, the goods that a nation can produce at a lower cost when measured in terms of opportunity cost.

complements: Goods that are often used together, so that consumption of one good tends to increase consumption of the other.

compound interest: When interest payments accumulate, so that in later time periods, the interest rate is paid on the interest that has been earned and reinvested in previous years.

Consumer Price Index (CPI): A measure of inflation calculated by U.S. government statisticians based on the price level from a basket of goods and services that represents the purchases of the average consumer.

consumer surplus: The benefit consumers receive from buying a good or service, measured by what the individuals would have been willing to pay minus the amount that they actually paid.

consumption function: The relationship between income and expenditures on consumption.

contractionary fiscal policy: When fiscal policy decreases the level of aggregate demand, either through cuts in government spending or increases in taxes.

contractionary monetary policy: A monetary policy that reduces the supply of money and loans; also called a "tight" monetary policy.

convergence: When economies with low per capita incomes are growing faster than economies with high per capita incomes.

corporate income tax: A tax imposed on corporate profits.

cost-of-living adjustments (COLAs): A contractual provision that wage increases will keep up with inflation.

countercyclical: Moving in the opposite direction of the business cycle of economic downturns and upswings.

crowding out: When government borrowing soaks up available financial capital and leaves less for private investment in physical capital.

currency: Coins and paper bills.

current account balance: A broad measure of the balance of trade that includes trade in goods and services, as well as international flows of income and foreign aid.

cyclical unemployment: Unemployment closely tied to the business cycle, like higher unemployment during a recession.

deadweight loss: The loss in social surplus that occurs when a market produces an inefficient quantity.

deflation: Negative inflation.

demand: A relationship between price and the quantity demanded of a certain good or service.

demand curve: A line that shows the relationship between price and quantity demanded of a certain good or service on a graph, with quantity on the horizontal axis and the price on the vertical axis.

demand deposits: Deposits in banks that are available by making a cash withdrawal or writing a check.

demand schedule: A table that shows a range of prices for a certain good or service and the quantity demanded at each price.

deposit insurance: An insurance system that makes sure depositors in a bank do not lose their money, even if the bank goes bankrupt.

depreciating: When a currency is worth less in terms of other currencies; also called "weakening."

depression: An especially lengthy and deep decline in output.

discount rate: The interest rate charged by the central bank when it makes loans to commercial banks.

discretionary fiscal policy: When the government passes a new law that explicitly changes overall tax or spending levels.

diversify: Making loans or investments with a variety of firms, to reduce the risk of being adversely affected by events at one or a few firms.

division of labor: The way in which the work required to produce a good or service is divided into tasks performed by different workers.

dollarize: When a country that is not the United States uses the U.S. dollar as its currency.

double coincidence of wants: A situation in which both of two people each wants some good or service that the other person can provide.

double counting: A potential mistake to be avoided in measuring GDP, in which output is counted two or more times as it travels through the stages of production.

dumping: Selling internationally traded goods below their cost of production.

durable goods: Long-lasting goods like cars and refrigerators.

economics: The study of the production, distribution and consumption of goods and services.

economies of scale: When the average cost of producing each individual unit declines as total output increases.

economy: The social arrangements that determine what is produced, how it is produced, and for whom it is produced.

efficiency: When it is impossible to get more of something without experiencing a trade-off of less of something else.

efficiency wage theory: The theory that the productivity of workers, either individually or as a group, will increase if they are paid more.

Employment Cost Index: A measure of inflation based on wage paid in the labor market.

equilibrium: The combination of price and quantity where there is no economic pressure from surpluses or shortages that would cause price or quantity to shift.

equilibrium price: The price where quantity demanded is equal to quantity supplied.

equilibrium quantity: The quantity at which quantity demanded and quantity supplied are equal at a certain price.

estate and gift tax: A tax on people who pass assets to the next generation—either after death or during life in the form of gifts.

excess demand: At the existing price, the quantity demanded exceeds the quantity supplied, also called "shortage."

excess reserves: Reserves that banks hold above the legally mandated limit.

excess supply: When at the existing price, quantity supplied exceeds the quantity demanded; also called a "surplus."

exchange rate: The rate at which one currency exchanges for another.

excise taxes: A tax on a specific good—on gasoline, tobacco, and alcohol.

expansionary monetary policy: A monetary policy that increases the supply of money and the quantity of loans; also called a "loose" monetary policy.

expenditure-output model: A macroeconomic model in which equilibrium output occurs where the total or aggregate expenditures in the economy are equal to the amount produced; also called the "Keynesian cross model."

exports: Goods and services that are produced domestically and sold in another country.

federal funds rate: The interest rate at which one bank lends funds to another bank overnight.

final goods and services: Output used directly for consumption, investment, government, and trade purposes; contrast with "intermediate goods."

financial capital market: The market in which those who save money provide financial capital and receive a rate of return from those who wish to raise money and pay a rate of return.

financial intermediary: An institution, like a bank, that receives money from savers and provides funds to borrowers.

fiscal policy: Economic policies that involve government spending and taxes.

floating exchange rate: When a country lets the value of its currency be determined in the exchange rate market.

foreign direct investment: Purchases of firms in another country that involve taking a management responsibility.

foreign exchange market: The market in which people buy one currency while using another currency.

frictional unemployment: Unemployment that occurs as workers move between jobs.

full employment GDP: Another name for potential GDP, when the economy is producing at its potential and unemployment is at the natural rate of unemployment.

GDP deflator: A measure of inflation based on all the components of GDP.

globalization: The trend in which buying and selling in markets have increasingly crossed national borders.

goods and services market: A market in which firms are sellers of what they produce and households are buyers.

government debt: The total accumulated amount that the government has borrowed and not yet paid back over time.

gross domestic product (GDP): The value of the output of all goods and services produced within a country.

hard peg: An exchange rate policy in which the central bank sets a fixed and unchanging value for the exchange rate.

hedge: Using a financial transaction as protection against risk.

human capital: The skills and education of workers.

hyperinflation: Extremely high rates of inflation.

implicit contract: An unwritten agreement in the labor market that the employer will try to keep wages from falling when the economy is weak or the business is having trouble, and the employee will not expect huge salary increases when the economy or the business is strong.

import quotas: Numerical limitations on the quantity of products that can be imported.

imports: Goods and services produced abroad and then sold domestically.

index number: When one arbitrary year is chosen to equal 100, and then values in all other years are set proportionately equal to that base year.

indexed: When a price, wage, or interest rate is adjusted automatically for inflation.

individual income tax: A tax based on the income of all forms received by individuals.

Industrial Revolution: The widespread use of power-driven machinery and the economic and social changes that occurred in the first half of the 1800s.

infant industry argument: An argument to block imports for a short time, to give the infant industry time to mature, before eventually it starts competing on equal terms in the global economy.

inferior goods: Goods where the quantity demanded falls as income rises.

inflation: A general and ongoing rise in the level of prices in an economy.

inflationary gap: When an economy has output above potential GDP, the gap from that level of output to potential GDP.

inflation-targeting: A rule that the central bank is required to focus only on keeping inflation low.

insider-outsider model: A model which divides workers into "insiders" already working for the firm who know the procedures and "outsiders" who are recent or prospective hires.

interest rate: A payment calculated as a percentage of the original amount saved or borrowed, and paid by the borrower to the saver.

intermediate goods and services: Output provided to other businesses at an intermediate stage of production, not for final users; contrast with "final goods and services."

International Price Index: A measure of inflation based on the prices of merchandise that is exported or imported.

intra-industry trade: International trade of goods within the same industry.

inventories: Goods that have been produced, but not yet been sold.

Keynes' Law: "Demand creates its own supply."

labor market: The market in which households sell their labor as workers to business firms or other employers.

law of demand: The common relationship that a higher price leads to a lower quantity demanded of a certain good or service.

law of diminishing marginal utility: As a person receives more of a good, the marginal utility from each additional unit of the good is smaller than from the previous unit.

law of supply: The common relationship that a higher price is associated with a greater quantity supplied.

lender of last resort: An institution that provides short-term emergency loans in conditions of financial crisis.

liabilities: Any amounts or debts owed by a firm or an individual.

loss: When total cost exceeds total revenue for a firm.

M1: A narrow definition of the money supply that includes currency, traveler's checks, and checking accounts in banks.

M2: A definition of the money supply that includes everything in M1, but also adds savings deposits, money market funds, and certificates of deposit.

macroeconomics: The branch of economies that focuses on the economy as a whole, including issues like growth, unemployment, inflation, and the balance of trade.

marginal analysis: Comparing the benefits and costs of choosing a little more or a little less of a good.

marginal propensity to consume (MPC): The share of an additional dollar of income that goes to consumption.

marginal propensity to import (MPI): The share of an additional dollar of income that goes to imports.

marginal propensity to save (MPS): The share of an additional dollar that goes to saving.

market: An institution that brings together buyers and sellers of goods or services.

market-oriented economy: An economy in which most economic decisions are made by buyers and sellers, who may be individuals or firms.

medium of exchange: Whatever is widely accepted as a method of payment.

menu costs: The costs that firms face in changing prices.

merchandise trade balance: The balance of trade looking only at goods.

microeconomics: The branch of economics that focuses on actions of particular actors within the economy, like households, workers, and business firms.

minimum wage: A price floor that makes it illegal for an employer to pay employees less than a certain hourly rate.

model: A simplified representation of an object or situation that includes enough of the key features to be useful.

monetary policy: Policy that involves altering the quantity of money and thus affecting the level of interest rates and the extent of borrowing.

money: Whatever serves society in three functions: medium of exchange, unit of account, and store of value.

money market funds: Where the deposits of many investors are pooled together and invested in a safe way like short-term government bonds.

money multiplier: Total money in the economy divided by the original quantity of money, or change in the total money in the economy divided by a change in the original quantity of money.

multiplier: Total increase in aggregate expenditures divided by the original increase in expenditures.

multiplier effect: How a given change in expenditure cycles repeatedly through the economy, and thus has a larger final impact than the initial change.

national income (Y): The sum of all income received for producing GDP.

national saving and investment identity: For any country, the quantity of financial capital supplied at any given time by savings must equal the quantity of financial capital demanded for purposes of making investments.

natural rate of unemployment: The unemployment rate that would exist in a growing and healthy economy from the combination of economic, social and political factors that exist at a time.

neoclassical economists: Economists who generally emphasize the importance of aggregate supply in determining the size of the macroeconomy over the long run.

net worth: Total assets minus total liabilities.

nominal value: The economic statistic actually announced at that time, not adjusted for inflation; contrast with real value.

nondurable goods: Short-lived goods like food and clothing.

nontariff barriers: All the other ways a nation can draw up rules, regulations, inspections, and paperwork to make it more costly or difficult to import products.

normal good: A good where the quantity demanded rises when income rises.

normative statements: Statements which describe how the world should be.

open market operations: The central bank buying or selling bonds to influence the quantity of money and the level of interest rates.

opportunity cost: Whatever must be given up to obtain something that is desired.

opportunity set: Another name for the budget constraint.

out of the labor force: Those who are not working and not looking for work.

payroll tax: A tax based on the pay received from employers; the taxes provide funds for Social Security and Medicare.

peak: During the business cycle, the highest point of output before a recession begins.

per capita GDP: GDP divided by the population.

permanent income hypothesis: When individuals think about how much to consume, they look into the future and consider how much income they expect to earn in their lifetime.

Phillips curve: The trade-off between unemployment and inflation.

physical capital: The plant and equipment used by firms in production.

portfolio investment: An investment in another country that is purely financial and doesn't involve any management responsibility.

positive statements: Statements which describe the world as it is.

potential GDP: The maximum quantity that an economy can produce given its existing levels of labor, physical capital, technology, and institutions.

price ceiling: A law that prevents a price from rising above a certain level.

price controls: Government laws to regulate prices.

price floor: A law that prevents a price from falling below a certain level.

principal: The amount of an original financial investment, before any rate of return is paid.

Producer Price Index: A measure of inflation based on prices paid for supplies and inputs by producers of goods and services.

producer surplus: The benefit producers receive from selling a good or service, measured by the price the producer actually received minus the price the producer would have been willing to accept.

production function: The process of a firm turning economic inputs like labor, machinery, and raw materials into outputs like goods and services used by consumers.

production possibilities frontier: A diagram that shows the combinations of output that are possible for an economy to produce.

productive efficiency: When it is impossible to produce more of one good without decreasing the quantity produced of another good.

productivity: What is produced per worker, or per hour worked.

profit: Total revenues minus total costs for a firm.

progressive tax: A tax that collects a greater share of income from those with high incomes than from those with lower incomes.

proportional tax: A tax that is a flat percentage of income earned, regardless of level of income.

protectionism: Government policies to reduce or block imports.

purchasing power parity (PPP): The exchange rate that equalizes the prices of internationally traded goods across countries.

quality/new goods bias: Inflation calculated using a fixed basket of goods over time tends to overstate the true rise in cost of living, because it doesn't take into account improvements in the quality of existing goods or the invention of new goods.

quantity demanded: The total number of units of a good or service purchased at a certain price.

quantity supplied: The total number of units of a good or service sold at a certain price.

race to the bottom: When production locates in countries with the lowest environmental (or other) standards, putting pressure on all countries to reduce their environmental standards.

rate of return: The payment from those who have received financial capital to those who provided it.

rational expectations: The theory that people form the most accurate possible expectations about the future that they can using all information available to them.

real interest rate: The rate of interest with inflation subtracted.

real value: An economic statistic after it has been adjusted for inflation; contrast with nominal value.

recession: A significant decline in national output.

recessionary gap: The gap in output between an economy in recession and potential GDP.

redistribution: Taking income from those with higher incomes and providing income to those with lower incomes.

regressive tax: A tax in which people with higher incomes pay a smaller share of their income in tax.

reserve ratio: The proportion of deposits that the bank holds in the form of reserves.

reserve requirement: The proportion of its deposits that a bank is legally required to deposit with the central bank.

reserves: Funds that a bank keeps on hand and that are not loaned out or invested in bonds.

Ricardian equivalence: The theory that rational private households might shift their saving to offset government saving or borrowing.

risk premium: A payment to make up for the risk of not being repaid in full.

savings deposits: Bank accounts where you can't withdraw money by writing a check, but can withdraw the money at a bank—or can transfer it easily to a checking account.

Say's Law: "Supply creates its own demand."

shift in demand: When a change in some economic factor related to demand causes a different quantity to be demanded at every price.

shift in supply: When a change in some economic factor related to supply causes a quantity to be supplied at every price.

shortage: At the existing price, the quantity demanded exceeds the quantity supplied, also called "excess demand."

social surplus: The sum of consumer surplus and producer surplus.

soft peg: An exchange rate policy where the government usually allows the exchange rate to be set by the market, but in some cases, especially if the exchange rate seems to be moving rapidly in one direction, the central bank will intervene.

specialization: When workers or firms focus on particular tasks in the overall production process for which they are well-suited.

splitting up the value chain: When many of the different stages of producing a good happen in different geographic locations.

stagflation: When an economy experiences stagnant growth and high inflation at the same time.

standardized employment budget: The budget deficit or surplus in any given year adjusted for what it would have been if the economy was producing at potential GDP.

store of value: Something that serves as a way of preserving economic value that can be spent or consumed in the future.

substitutes: Goods that can replace each other to some extent, so that greater consumption of one good can mean less of the other.

substitution bias: An inflation rate calculated using a fixed basket of goods over time tends to overstate the true rise in the cost of living, because it doesn't take into account that the person can substitute away from goods whose prices rise by a lot.

sunk cost: Costs that were incurred in the past and cannot be recovered, and thus should not affect current decisions.

supply: A relationship between price and the quantity supplied of a certain good or service.

supply curve: A line that shows the relationship between price and quantity supplied on a graph, with quantity supplied on the horizontal axis and price on the vertical axis.

supply schedule: A table that shows a range of prices for a good or service and the quantity supplied at each price.

surplus: When at the existing price, quantity supplied exceeds the quantity demanded; also called "excess supply."

T-account: A balance sheet with two-column format, with the T-shape formed by the vertical line down the middle and the horizontal line under the column headings for "Assets" and "Liabilities."

tariffs: Taxes imposed on imported products.

technology: All the ways in which existing machines produce more or higher quality, as well as producing different and altogether new products.

time deposits: Accounts that the depositor has committed to leaving in the bank for a certain period of time, in exchange for a higher rate of interest; also called certificates of deposit.

time value of money: The cost of having to wait for repayment.

total cost: All the costs that a firm must incur in the process of production.

total revenue: The quantity of goods and services sold by the firm multiplied by the selling price of these goods and services.

trade balance: Gap between exports and imports.

trade deficit: When imports exceed exports.

trade surplus: When exports exceed imports.

trough: During the business cycle, the lowest point of output in a recession, before a recovery begins.

unemployment rate: The percentage of adults who are in the labor force and thus seeking jobs, but who do not have jobs.

unit of account: The common way in which market values are measured in an economy.

usury laws: Laws that impose an upper limit on the interest rate that lenders can charge.

utility: The level of satisfaction or pleasure that people receive from their choices.

velocity: The speed with which money circulates through the economy, calculated as the nominal GDP divided by the money supply.

Index

Note: Page numbers in *italics* refer to exhibits.